A Thousand Plateaus

A THOUSAND PLATEAUS
Capitalism and Schizophrenia

Gilles Deleuze
Félix Guattari

Translation and Foreword by Brian Massumi

University of Minnesota Press, Minneapolis

The University of Minnesota Press gratefully acknowledges translation assistance provided for this book by the French Ministry of Culture and by the National Endowment for the Humanities, an independent federal agency.

Published by the University of Minnesota Press
2037 University Avenue Southeast, Minneapolis MN 55414.
Published simultaneously in Canada
by Fitzhenry & Whiteside Limited, Markham.
Printed in the United States of America.

Library of Congress Cataloging-in-Publication Data
Deleuze, Gilles.
[Mille plateaux. English]
A thousand plateaus: capitalism and schizophrenia/Gilles Deleuze, Félix Guattari; translation and foreword by Brian Massumi.
p. cm.
Translation of: Mille plateaux, v. 2 of Capitalisme et schizophrénie.
A companion volume to Anti-Oedipus: capitalism and schizophrenia.
Bibliography: p.
Includes index.
ISBN 0-8166-1401-6
ISBN 0-8166-1402-4 (pbk.)
1. Philosophy. I. Guattari, Félix. II. Title
B77.D413 1987
194—dc19 87-18623
CIP

Originally published as *Mille Plateaux*, volume 2 of *Capitalisme et Schizophrénie* © 1980 by Les Editions de Minuit, Paris.

Contents

Translator's Foreword: Pleasures of Philosophy

Brian Massumi

This is a book that speaks of many things, of ticks and quilts and fuzzy subsets and noology and political economy. It is difficult to know how to approach it. What do you do with a book that dedicates an entire chapter to music and animal behavior—and then claims that it isn't a chapter? That presents itself as a network of "plateaus" that are precisely dated, but can be read in any order? That deploys a complex technical vocabulary drawn from a wide range of disciplines in the sciences, mathematics, and the humanities, but whose authors recommend that you read it as you would listen to a record?[1]

"Philosophy, nothing but philosophy."[2] Of a bastard line.

The annals of official philosophy are populated by "bureaucrats of pure reason" who speak in "the shadow of the despot" and are in historical complicity with the State.[3] They invent "a properly spiritual . . . absolute State that . . . effectively functions in the mind." Theirs is the discourse of sovereign judgment, of stable subjectivity legislated by "good" sense, of rocklike identity, "universal" truth, and (white male) justice. "Thus the exercise of their thought is in conformity with the aims of the real State, with the dominant significations, and with the requirements of the established order."[4]

Gilles Deleuze was schooled in that philosophy. The titles of his earliest books read like a Who's Who of philosophical giants. "What got me by during that period was conceiving of the history of philosophy as a kind of ass-fuck, or, what amounts to the same thing, an immaculate conception. I imagined myself approaching an author from behind and giving him a child that would indeed be his but would nonetheless be monstrous."[5] Hegel is absent, being too despicable to merit even a mutant offspring.[6] To Kant he dedicated an affectionate study of "an enemy." Yet much of positive value came of Deleuze's flirtation with the greats. He discovered an orphan line of thinkers who were tied by no direct descendance but were united in their opposition to the State philosophy that would nevertheless accord them minor positions in its canon. Between Lucretius, Hume, Spinoza, Nietzsche, and Bergson there exists a "secret link constituted by the critique of negativity, the cultivation of joy, the hatred of interiority, the exteriority of forces and relations, the denunciation of power."[7] Deleuze's first major statements written in his own voice, *Différence et répétition* (1968) and *Logique du sens* (1969), cross-fertilized that line of "nomad" thought with contemporary theory. The ferment of the student-worker revolt of May 1968 and the reassessment it prompted of the role of the intellectual in society[8] led him to disclaim the "ponderous academic apparatus"[9] still in evidence in those works. However, many elements of the "philosophy of difference" they elaborated were transfused into a continuing collaboration, of which *A Thousand Plateaus* is the most recent product.

Félix Guattari is a practicing psychoanalyst and lifelong political activist. He has worked since the mid-1950s at La Borde, an experimental psychiatric clinic founded by Lacanian analyst Jean Oury. Guattari himself was among Lacan's earliest trainees, and although he never severed his ties with Lacan's Freudian School the group therapy practiced at La Borde took him in a very different direction. The aim at La Borde was to abolish the hierarchy between doctor and patient in favor of an interactive group dynamic that would bring the experiences of both to full expression in such a way as to produce a collective critique of the power relations in society as a whole. "The central perspective is . . . to promote human relations that do not automatically fall into roles or stereotypes but open onto fundamental relations of a metaphysical kind that *bring out* the most radical and basic alienations of madness or neurosis"[10] and channel them into revolutionary practice. Guattari collaborated beginning in 1960 on group projects dedicated to developing this radical "institutional psychotherapy,"[11] and later entered an uneasy alliance with the international antipsychiatry movement spearheaded by R.D. Laing in England and Franco Basaglia in Italy.[12] As Lacanian schools of psychoanalysis gained ground against psychiatry, the contractual Oedipal relationship between the analyst and the transference-bound analysand became as much of a target for Guattari as the legal bondage of the institutionalized patient in the conventional State hospital. He came to occupy the same position in relation to psychoanalysis as he had all along in relation to the parties of the left: an ultra-opposition within the opposition. His antihierarchical leanings made him a precursor to the events of May 1968 and an early partisan of the social movements that grew from them, including feminism and the gay rights movement.[13] *Anti-Oedipus* (1972),[14] his first book with Deleuze, gave philosophical weight to his convictions and created one of the intellectual sensations of postwar France with its spirited polemics against State-happy or pro-party versions of Marxism and school-building strains of psychoanalysis, which separately and in various combinations represented the dominant intellectual currents of the time (in spite of the fundamentally anarchist nature of the spontaneous popular uprisings that had shaken the world in 1968). "The most tangible result of *Anti-Oedipus* was that it short-circuited the connection between psychoanalysis and the far left parties," in which he and Deleuze saw the potential for a powerful new bureaucracy of analytic reason.[15]

For many French intellectuals, the hyperactivism of post-May gave way to a mid-seventies slump, then a return to religion (*Tel Quel*) or political conservatism (the Nouveaux Philosophes) in a foreshadowing of the Reagan eighties. Deleuze and Guattari never recanted. Nor did they simply revive the polemics. *A Thousand Plateaus* (1980), written over a seven-year period, was billed as a sequel to *Anti-Oedipus* and shares its subtitle, *Capitalism and Schizophrenia*. But it constitutes a very different project. It is less a critique than a positive exercise in the affirmative "nomad" thought called for in *Anti-Oedipus*.

"State philosophy" is another word for the representational thinking that has characterized Western metaphysics since Plato, but has suffered an at least momentary setback during the last quarter century at the hands of Jacques Derrida, Michel Foucault, and poststructuralist theory generally. As described by Deleuze,[16] it reposes on a double identity: of the thinking subject, and of the concepts it creates and to which it lends its own presumed attributes of sameness and constancy. The subject, its concepts, and also the objects in the world to which the concepts are applied have a shared, internal essence: the self-resemblance at the basis of identity. Representational thought is analogical; its concern is to establish a correspondence between these symmetrically structured domains. The faculty of judgment is the policeman of analogy, assuring that each of the three terms is honestly itself, and that the proper correspondences obtain. In thought its end is truth, in action justice. The weapons it wields in their pursuit are limitative distribution (the determination of the exclusive set of properties possessed by each term in contradistinction to the others: *logos*, law) and hierarchical ranking (the measurement of the degree of perfection of a term's self-resemblance in relation to a supreme standard, man, god, or gold: value, morality). The modus operandi is negation: $x = x = \text{not } y$. Identity, resemblance, truth, justice, and negation. The rational foundation for order. The established order, of course: philosophers have traditionally been employees of the State. The collusion between philosophy and the State was most explicitly enacted in the first decade of the nineteenth century with the foundation of the University of Berlin, which was to become the model for higher learning throughout Europe and in the United States. The goal laid out for it by Wilhelm von Humboldt (based on proposals by Fichte and Schleiermacher) was the "spiritual and moral training of the nation," to be achieved by "deriving everything from an original principle" (truth), by "relating everything to an ideal" (justice), and by "unifying this principle and this ideal in a single Idea" (the State). The end product would be "a fully legitimated subject of knowledge and society"[17]—each mind an analogously organized mini-State morally unified in the supermind of the State. Prussian mind-meld.[18] More insidious than the well-known practical cooperation between university and government (the burgeoning military funding of research) is its philosophical role in the propagation of the form of representational thinking itself, that "properly spiritual absolute State" endlessly reproduced and disseminated at every level of the social fabric. Deconstruction-influenced feminists such as Hélène Cixous and Luce Irigaray have attacked it under the name "phallogocentrism" (what the most privileged model of rocklike identity is goes without saying). In the introduction to *A Thousand Plateaus*, Deleuze and Guattari describe it as the "arborescent model" of thought (the proudly erect tree under whose spreading boughs latter-day Platos conduct their class).

"Nomad thought" does not immure itself in the edifice of an ordered interiority; it moves freely in an element of exteriority. It does not repose on identity; it rides difference. It does not respect the artificial division between the three domains of representation, subject, concept, and being; it replaces restrictive analogy with a conductivity that knows no bounds. The concepts it creates do not merely reflect the eternal form of a legislating subject, but are defined by a communicable force in relation to which their subject, to the extent that they can be said to have one, is only secondary. They do not reflect upon the world but are immersed in a changing state of things. A concept is a brick. It can be used to build the courthouse of reason. Or it can be thrown through the window. What is the subject of the brick? The arm that throws it? The body connected to the arm? The brain encased in the body? The situation that brought brain and body to such a juncture? All and none of the above. What is its object? The window? The edifice? The laws the edifice shelters? The class and other power relations encrusted in the laws? All and none of the above. "What interests us are the circumstances."[19] Because the concept in its unrestrained usage *is* a set of circumstances, at a volatile juncture. It is a vector: the point of application of a force moving through a space at a given velocity in a given direction. The concept has no subject or object other than itself. It is an act. Nomad thought replaces the closed equation of representation, $x = x = \text{not } y$ (I = I = not you) with an open equation: . . . + y + z + a + . . . (. . . + arm + brick + window + . . .). Rather than analyzing the world into discrete components, reducing their manyness to the One of identity, and ordering them by rank, it sums up a set of disparate circumstances in a shattering blow. It synthesizes a multiplicity of elements without effacing their heterogeneity or hindering their potential for future rearranging (to the contrary). The modus operandi of nomad thought is affirmation, even when its apparent object is negative. Force is not to be confused with power. Force arrives from outside to break constraints and open new vistas. Power builds walls.

The space of nomad thought is qualitatively different from State space. Air against earth. State space is "striated," or gridded. Movement in it is confined as by gravity to a horizontal plane, and limited by the order of that plane to preset paths between fixed and identifiable points. Nomad space is "smooth," or open-ended. One can rise up at any point and move to any other. Its mode of distribution is the *nomos:* arraying oneself in an open space (hold the street), as opposed to the *logos* of entrenching oneself in a closed space (hold the fort).

A Thousand Plateaus is an effort to construct a smooth space of thought. It is not the first such attempt. Like State philosophy, nomad thought goes by many names. Spinoza called it "ethics." Nietzsche called it the "gay science." Artaud called it "crowned anarchy." To Maurice Blanchot, it is the "space of literature." To Foucault, "outside thought."[20] In this book, Deleuze and Guattari employ the terms "pragmatics" and "schizoanalysis," and in the introduction describe a rhizome network strangling the roots of the infamous tree. One of the points of the book is that nomad thought is not confined to philosophy. Or that the kind of philosophy it is comes in many forms. Filmmakers and painters are philosophical thinkers to the extent that they explore the potentials of their respective mediums and break away from the beaten paths.[21] On a strictly formal level, it is mathematics and music that create the smoothest of the smooth spaces.[22] In fact, Deleuze and Guattari would probably be more inclined to call philosophy music with content than music a rarefied form of philosophy.

Which returns to our opening question. How should *A Thousand Plateaus* be played? When you buy a record there are always cuts that leave you cold. You skip them. You don't approach a record as a closed book that you have to take or leave. Other cuts you may listen to over and over again. They follow you. You find yourself humming them under your breath as you go about your daily business.

A Thousand Plateaus is conceived as an open system.[23] It does not pretend to have the final word. The authors' hope, however, is that elements of it will stay with a certain number of its readers and will weave into the melody of their everyday lives.

Each "plateau" is an orchestration of crashing bricks extracted from a variety of disciplinary edifices. They carry traces of their former emplacement, which give them a spin defining the arc of their vector. The vectors are meant to converge at a volatile juncture, but one that is sustained, as an open equilibrium of moving parts each with its own trajectory. The word "plateau" comes from an essay by Gregory Bateson on Balinese culture, in which he found a libidinal economy quite different from the West's orgasmic orientation.[24] In Deleuze and Guattari, a plateau is reached when circumstances combine to bring an activity to a pitch of intensity that is not automatically dissipated in a climax. The heightening of energies is sustained long enough to leave a kind of afterimage of its dynamism that can be reactivated or injected into other activities, creating a fabric of intensive states between which any number of connecting routes could exist. Each section of *A Thousand Plateaus* tries to combine conceptual bricks in such a way as to construct this kind of intensive state in thought. The way the combination is made is an example of what Deleuze and Guattari call consistency—not in the sense of a homogeneity, but as a holding together of disparate elements (also known as a "style").[25] A style in this sense, as a dynamic holding together or mode of composition, is not something limited to writing. Filmmakers, painters, and musicians have their styles, mathematicians have theirs, rocks have style, and so do tools, and technologies, and historical periods, even—especially—punctual events. Each section is dated, because each tries to reconstitute a dynamism that has existed in other mediums at other times. The date corresponds to the point at which that particular dynamism found its purest incarnation in matter, the point at which it was freest from interference from other modes and rose to its highest degree of intensity. That never lasts more than a flash, because the world rarely leaves room for uncommon intensity, being in large measure an entropic trashbin of outworn modes that refuse to die. Section 12, for example, the "Treatise on Nomadology," is dated 1227 A.D. because that is when the nomad war machine existed for a moment in its pure form on the vacant smooth spaces of the steppes of Inner Asia.

The reader is invited to follow each section to the plateau that rises from the smooth space of its composition, and to move from one plateau to the next at pleasure. But it is just as good to ignore the heights. You can take a concept that is particularly to your liking and jump with it to its next appearance. They tend to cycle back. Some might call that repetitious. Deleuze and Guattari call it a refrain.

Most of all, the reader is invited to lift a dynamism out of the book entirely, and incarnate it in a foreign medium, whether it be painting or politics. The authors steal from other disciplines with glee, but they are more than happy to return the favor. Deleuze's own image for a concept is not a brick, but a "tool box."[26] He calls his kind of philosophy "pragmatics" because its goal is the invention of concepts that do not add up to a system of belief or an architecture of propositions that you either enter or you don't, but instead pack a potential in the way a crowbar in a willing hand envelops an energy of prying.

The best way of all to approach the book is to read it as a challenge: to pry open the vacant spaces that would enable you to build your life and those of the people around you into a plateau of intensity that would leave afterimages of its dynamism that could be reinjected into still other lives, creating a fabric of heightened states between which any number, the greatest number, of connecting routes would exist. Some might call that promiscuous. Deleuze and Guattari call it revolution.

The question is not: is it true? But: does it work? What new thoughts does it make it possible to think? What new emotions does it make it possible to feel? What new sensations and perceptions does it open in the body?

The answer for some readers, perhaps most, will be "none." If that happens, it's not your tune. No problem. But you would have been better off buying a record.

Notes on the Translation and Acknowledgments

AFFECT/AFFECTION. Neither word denotes a personal feeling (*sentiment* in Deleuze and Guattari). *L'affect* (Spinoza's *affectus*) is an ability to affect and be affected. It is a prepersonal intensity corresponding to the passage from one experiential state of the body to another and implying an augmentation or diminution in that body's capacity to act. *L'affection* (Spinoza's *affectio*) is each such state considered as an encounter between the affected body and a second, affecting, body (with body taken in its broadest possible sense to include "mental" or ideal bodies).

DRAW. In *A Thousand Plateaus*, to draw is an act of creation. What is drawn (the Body without Organs, the plane of consistency, a line of flight) does not preexist the act of drawing. The French word *tracer* captures this better: It has all the graphic connotations of "to draw" in English, but can also mean to blaze a trail or open a road. "To trace" (*décalquer*), on the other hand, is to copy something from a model.

FLIGHT/ESCAPE. Both words translate *fuite*, which has a different range of meanings than either of the English terms. *Fuite* covers not only the act of fleeing or eluding but also flowing, leaking, and disappearing into the distance (the vanishing point in a painting is a *point de fuite*). It has no relation to flying.

MILIEU. In French, *milieu* means "surroundings," "medium" (as in chemistry), and "middle." In the philosophy of Deleuze and Guattari, "milieu" should be read as a technical term combining all three meanings.

PLANE. The word *plan* designates both a "plane" in the geometrical sense and a "plan." The authors use it primarily in the first sense. Where both meanings seem to be present (as in discussions of the *plan d'organisaton*) "plan(e)" has been used in the translation.

POWER. Two words for "power" exist in French, *puissance* and *pouvoir.* In Deleuze and Guattari, they are associated with very different concepts (although the terminological distinction is not consistently observed). *Puissance* refers to a range of potential. It has been defined by Deleuze as a "capacity for existence," "a capacity to affect or be affected," a capacity to multiply connections that may be realized by a given "body" to varying degrees in different situations. It may be thought of as a scale of intensity or fullness of existence (or a degree on such a scale), analogous to the capacity of a number to be raised to a higher "power." It is used in the French translation of Nietzsche's term "will to power." Like its English counterpart, it has an additional mathematical usage, designating the number of elements in a finite or infinite set. Here, *puissance* pertains to the virtual (the plane of consistency), *pouvoir* to the actual (the plane of organization). The authors use *pouvoir* in a sense very close to Foucault's, as an instituted and reproducible relation of force, a selective concretization of potential. Both *puissance* and *pouvoir* have been translated here as "power," since the distinction between the concepts is usually clear from the context. The French terms have been added in parentheses where confusion might arise, and in occasional passages where *puissance* is rendered as "potential."

PROCESS/PROCEEDING. The authors employ two words normally translated as "process." *Processus* in their usage is the more general of the two, covering both the stratified and destratified dimensions of an occurrence. *Procès* pertains only to the stratification. In standard French, *procès* also means "trial" (as in the title of the Kafka novel). Deleuze and Guattari exploit this polysemy as a way of emphasizing the role of organizations of social power and regimes of signs in operations constitutive of the subject, or *procès de subjectivation*. *Procès* is usually (once again, there is slippage in their usage) translated as "proceeding," despite the occasional awkwardness this produces in English, in an attempt to preserve both associations: a process, or way of proceeding, and a legal proceeding, or trial. *Processus* is always "process."

SELF. Both *Moi* and *Soi* have usually been translated as "Self," with the French in brackets. *Soi* is the self in its broadest sense, but as a neuter third-person pronoun implies an impersonality at the basis of the self. *Moi* is a more restricted concept: the "me" as subject of enunciation for the "I" (*je*) as subject of the statement. It is also the French term for the Freudian ego.

SIGNIFIANCE/INTERPRETANCE. I have followed the increasingly common practice of importing *signifiance* and *interprétance* into English without modification. In Deleuze and Guattari these terms refer respectively to the syntagmatic and paradigmatic processes of language as a "signifying regime of signs." They are borrowed from Benveniste ("signifying capacity" and "interpretative capacity" are the English translations used in Benveniste's work).

STATEMENT. *Enoncé* (often "utterance") has been translated here as "statement," in keeping with the choice of the English translators of Foucault, to whose conception Deleuze and Guattari's is closest. "Enunciation" is used for *énonciation*.

TRAIT. The word *trait* has a range of meanings not covered by any single word in English. Literally, it refers to a graphic drawing, and to the act of drawing a line. Abstractly, it is the purely graphic element. Figuratively, it is an identifying mark (a feature, or trait in the English sense), or any act constituting a mark or sign. In linguistics, "distinctive features" (*traits distinctifs* or *traits pertinents*) are the elementary units of language that combine to form a phoneme. *Trait* also refers to a projectile, especially an arrow, and to the act of throwing a projectile. Here, "trait" has been retained in all but narrowly linguistic contexts.

GENDER-BIASED USAGE has been largely eliminated through pluralization or the use of male and female pronouns. However, where Deleuze and Guattari seem deliberately to be using "man" to designate a socially constructed, patriarchal standard of human behavior applied to both men and women, the masculine generic has been retained.

* * *

ACKNOWLEDGMENTS. I would like to express my gratitude to the National Endowment for the Humanities and the French Ministry of Culture for their generous assistance, without which this translation would not have been possible, and to the authors for their patience in answering my questions. Winnie Berman, Ken Dean, Nannie Doyle, Shoshana Felman, Jim Fleming, Robert Hurley, Fredric Jameson, Sylvère Lotringer, Susan McClary, Giorgio Passerone, Paul Patton, Dana Polan, Mary Quaintance, Michael Ryan, Lianne Sullivan, Susan Yazijian, and Caveh Zahedi provided much-appreciated aid and advice. Glenn Hendler likes to see his name in print.

I consulted the following translations: "Rhizome" (first version), trans. Paul Foss and Paul Patton, *Ideology and Consciousness*, no. 8 (Spring 1981, pp. 49-71); "Rhizome" (final version), trans. John Johnston in Deleuze and Guattari, *On the Line* (New York: Semiotext[e], 1983); "One or Several Wolves?" (first version), trans. Mark Seem, *Semiotext(e)*, vol. 2, no. 3, pp. 137-147 (1977); "How to Make Yourself a Body without Organs" (first version, abridged), trans. Suzanne Guerlac, *Semiotext(e)* vol. 4, no. 1 (1981), pp. 265-270.

Portions of this translation have appeared previously. "Treatise on Nomadology" was published as a separate book entitled *Nomad Machine* (New York: Semiotext(e), 1986). Extracts from "Becoming-Intense . . ." appeared under the title "Becoming-Woman" in *Subjects/Objects*, no. 3 (Spring 1985), pp. 24-32, and from "The Smooth and the Striated" under the title "Nomad Art" in *Art and Text*, no. 19 (Oct.-Nov. 1985), pp. 16-23.

Authors' Note

This book is the companion volume to *Anti-Oedipus* (paperback ed., University of Minnesota Press, 1983). Together they make up *Capitalism and Schizophrenia*.

It is composed not of chapters but of "plateaus." We will try to explain why later on (and also why the texts are dated). To a certain extent, these plateaus may be read independently of one another, except the conclusion, which should be read at the end.

A Thousand Plateaus

1. Introduction: Rhizome

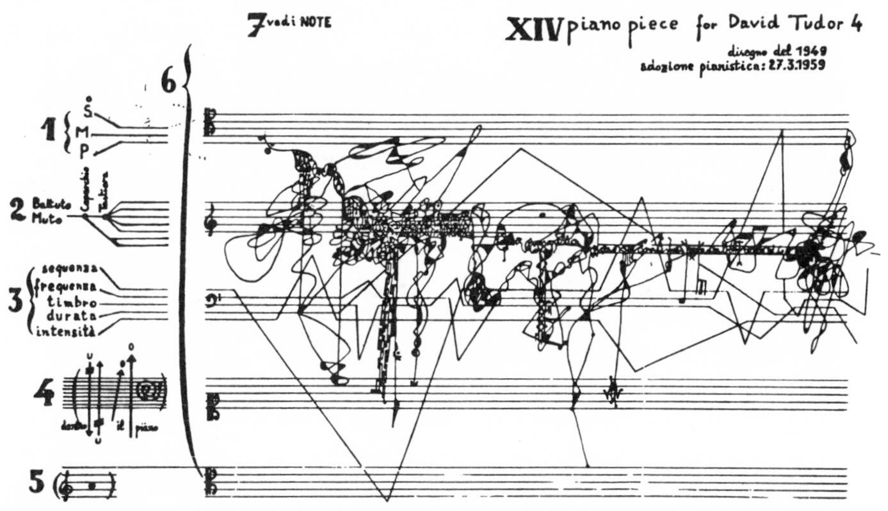

SYLVANO BUSSOTI

The two of us wrote *Anti-Oedipus* together. Since each of us was several, there was already quite a crowd. Here we have made use of everything that came within range, what was closest as well as farthest away. We have assigned clever pseudonyms to prevent recognition. Why have we kept our own names? Out of habit, purely out of habit. To make ourselves unrecognizable in turn. To render imperceptible, not ourselves, but what makes us act, feel, and think. Also because it's nice to talk like everybody else, to say the sun rises, when everybody knows it's only a manner of speaking. To reach, not the point where one no longer says I, but the point where it is no longer of any importance whether one says I. We are no longer ourselves. Each will know his own. We have been aided, inspired, multiplied.

A book has neither object nor subject; it is made of variously formed matters, and very different dates and speeds. To attribute the book to a subject is to overlook this working of matters, and the exteriority of their relations. It is to fabricate a beneficent God to explain geological movements. In a book, as in all things, there are lines of articulation or segmentarity, strata and territories; but also lines of flight, movements of deterritorialization and destratification. Comparative rates of flow on these lines produce phenomena of relative slowness and viscosity, or, on the contrary, of acceleration and rupture. All this, lines and measurable speeds, constitutes an *assemblage*. A book is an assemblage of this kind, and as such is unattributable. It is a multiplicity—but we don't know yet what the multiple entails when it is no longer attributed, that is, after it has been elevated to the status of a substantive. One side of a machinic assemblage faces the strata, which doubtless make it a kind of organism, or signifying totality, or determination attributable to a subject; it also has a side facing a *body without organs*, which is continually dismantling the organism, causing asignifying particles or pure intensities to pass or circulate, and attributing to itself subjects that it leaves with nothing more than a name as the trace of an intensity. What is the body without organs of a book? There are several, depending on the nature of the lines considered, their particular grade or density, and the possibility of their converging on a "plane of consistency" assuring their selection. Here, as elsewhere, the units of measure are what is essential: *quantify writing*. There is no difference between what a book talks about and how it is made. Therefore a book also has no object. As an assemblage, a book has only itself, in connection with other assemblages and in relation to other bodies without organs. We will never ask what a book means, as signified or signifier; we will not look for anything to understand in it. We will ask what it functions with, in connection with what other things it does or does not transmit intensities, in which other multiplicities its own are inserted and metamorphosed, and with what bodies without organs it makes its own converge. A book exists only through the outside and on the outside. A book itself is a little machine; what is the relation (also measurable) of this literary machine to a war machine, love machine, revolutionary machine, etc.—and an *abstract machine* that sweeps them along? We have been criticized for overquoting literary authors. But when one writes, the only question is which other machine the literary machine can be plugged into, must be plugged into in order to work. Kleist and a mad war machine, Kafka and a most extraordinary bureaucratic machine . . . (What if one became animal or plant *through* literature, which certainly does not mean literarily? Is it not first through the voice that one becomes animal?) Literature is an assemblage. It has nothing to do with ideology. There is no ideology and never has been.

All we talk about are multiplicities, lines, strata and segmentarities, lines of flight and intensities, machinic assemblages and their various types, bodies without organs and their construction and selection, the plane of consistency, and in each case the units of measure. *Stratometers, deleometers, BwO units of density, BwO units of convergence*: Not only do these constitute a quantification of writing, but they define writing as always the measure of something else. Writing has nothing to do with signifying. It has to do with surveying, mapping, even realms that are yet to come.

A first type of book is the root-book. The tree is already the image of the world, or the root the image of the world-tree. This is the classical book, as noble, signifying, and subjective organic interiority (the strata of the book). The book imitates the world, as art imitates nature: by procedures specific to it that accomplish what nature cannot or can no longer do. The law of the book is the law of reflection, the One that becomes two. How could the law of the book reside in nature, when it is what presides over the very division between world and book, nature and art? One becomes two: whenever we encounter this formula, even stated strategically by Mao or understood in the most "dialectical" way possible, what we have before us is the most classical and well reflected, oldest, and weariest kind of thought. Nature doesn't work that way: in nature, roots are taproots with a more multiple, lateral, and circular system of ramification, rather than a dichotomous one. Thought lags behind nature. Even the book as a natural reality is a taproot, with its pivotal spine and surrounding leaves. But the book as a spiritual reality, the Tree or Root as an image, endlessly develops the law of the One that becomes two, then of the two that become four . . . Binary logic is the spiritual reality of the root-tree. Even a discipline as "advanced" as linguistics retains the root-tree as its fundamental image, and thus remains wedded to classical reflection (for example, Chomsky and his grammatical trees, which begin at a point S and proceed by dichotomy). This is as much as to say that this system of thought has never reached an understanding of multiplicity: in order to arrive at two following a spiritual method it must assume a strong principal unity. On the side of the object, it is no doubt possible, following the natural method, to go directly from One to three, four, or five, but only if there is a strong principal unity available, that of the pivotal taproot supporting the secondary roots. That doesn't get us very far. The binary logic of dichotomy has simply been replaced by biunivocal relationships between successive circles. The pivotal taproot provides no better understanding of multiplicity than the dichotomous root. One operates in the object, the other in the subject. Binary logic and biunivocal relationships still dominate psychoanalysis (the tree of delusion in the Freudian interpretation of Schreber's case), linguistics, structuralism, and even information science.

The radicle-system, or fascicular root, is the second figure of the book, to which our modernity pays willing allegiance. This time, the principal root has aborted, or its tip has been destroyed; an immediate, indefinite multiplicity of secondary roots grafts onto it and undergoes a flourishing development. This time, natural reality is what aborts the principal root, but the root's unity subsists, as past or yet to come, as possible. We must ask if reflexive, spiritual reality does not compensate for this state of things by demanding an even more comprehensive secret unity, or a more extensive totality. Take William Burroughs's cut-up method: the folding of one text onto another, which constitutes multiple and even adventitious roots (like a cutting), implies a supplementary dimension to that of the texts under consideration. In this supplementary dimension of folding, unity continues its spiritual labor. That is why the most resolutely fragmented work can also be presented as the Total Work or Magnum Opus. Most modern methods for making series proliferate or a multiplicity grow are perfectly valid in one direction, for example, a linear direction, whereas a unity of totalization asserts itself even more firmly in another, circular or cyclic, dimension. Whenever a multiplicity is taken up in a structure, its growth is offset by a reduction in its laws of combination. The abortionists of unity are indeed angel makers, *doctores angelici*, because they affirm a properly angelic and superior unity. Joyce's words, accurately described as having "multiple roots," shatter the linear unity of the word, even of language, only to posit a cyclic unity of the sentence, text, or knowledge. Nietzsche's aphorisms shatter the linear unity of knowledge, only to invoke the cyclic unity of the eternal return, present as the nonknown in thought. This is as much as to say that the fascicular system does not really break with dualism, with the complementarity between a subject and an object, a natural reality and a spiritual reality: unity is consistently thwarted and obstructed in the object, while a new type of unity triumphs in the subject. The world has lost its pivot; the subject can no longer even dichotomize, but accedes to a higher unity, of ambivalence or overdetermination, in an always supplementary dimension to that of its object. The world has become chaos, but the book remains the image of the world: radicle-chaosmos rather than root-cosmos. A strange mystification: a book all the more total for being fragmented. At any rate, what a vapid idea, the book as the image of the world. In truth, it is not enough to say, "Long live the multiple," difficult as it is to raise that cry. No typographical, lexical, or even syntactical cleverness is enough to make it heard. The multiple *must be made*, not by always adding a higher dimension, but rather in the simplest of ways, by dint of sobriety, with the number of dimensions one already has available—always $n - 1$ (the only way the one belongs to the multiple: always subtracted). Subtract the unique from the multiplicity to be constituted; write at $n - 1$ dimensions. A system of this kind could be called a rhizome. A rhizome as subterranean stem is absolutely different from roots and radicles. Bulbs and tubers are rhizomes. Plants with roots or radicles may be rhizomorphic in other respects altogether: the question is whether plant life in its specificity is not entirely rhizomatic. Even some animals are, in their pack form. Rats are rhizomes. Burrows are too, in all of their functions of shelter, supply, movement, evasion, and breakout. The rhizome itself assumes very diverse forms, from ramified surface extension in all directions to concretion into bulbs and tubers. When rats swarm over each other. The rhizome includes the best and the worst: potato and couchgrass, or the weed. Animal and plant, couchgrass is crabgrass. We get the distinct feeling that we will convince no one unless we enumerate certain approximate characteristics of the rhizome.

1 and 2. Principles of connection and heterogeneity: any point of a rhizome can be connected to anything other, and must be. This is very different from the tree or root, which plots a point, fixes an order. The linguistic tree on the Chomsky model still begins at a point S and proceeds by dichotomy. On the contrary, not every trait in a rhizome is necessarily linked to a linguistic feature: semiotic chains of every nature are connected to very diverse modes of coding (biological, political, economic, etc.) that bring into play not only different regimes of signs but also states of things of differing status. *Collective assemblages of enunciation* function directly within *machinic assemblages*; it is not impossible to make a radical break between regimes of signs and their objects. Even when linguistics claims to confine itself to what is explicit and to make no presuppositions about language, it is still in the sphere of a discourse implying particular modes of assemblage and types of social power. Chomsky's grammaticality, the categorical S symbol that dominates every sentence, is more fundamentally a marker of power than a syntactic marker: you will construct grammatically correct sentences, you will divide each statement into a noun phrase and a verb phrase (first dichotomy . . .). Our criticism of these linguistic models is not that they are too abstract but, on the contrary, that they are not abstract enough, that they do not reach the *abstract machine* that connects a language to the semantic and pragmatic contents of statements, to collective assemblages of enunciation, to a whole micropolitics of the social field. A rhizome ceaselessly establishes connections between semiotic chains, organizations of power, and circumstances relative to the arts, sciences, and social struggles. A semiotic chain is like a tuber agglomerating very diverse acts, not only linguistic, but also perceptive, mimetic, gestural, and cognitive: there is no language in itself, nor are there any linguistic universals, only a throng of dialects, patois, slangs, and specialized languages. There is no ideal speaker-listener, any more than there is a homogeneous linguistic community. Language is, in Weinreich's words, "an essentially heterogeneous reality."[1] There is no mother tongue, only a power takeover by a dominant language within a political multiplicity. Language stabilizes around a parish, a bishopric, a capital. It forms a bulb. It evolves by subterranean stems and flows, along river valleys or train tracks; it spreads like a patch of oil.[2] It is always possible to break a language

down into internal structural elements, an undertaking not fundamentally different from a search for roots. There is always something genealogical about a tree. It is not a method for the people. A method of the rhizome type, on the contrary, can analyze language only by decentering it onto other dimensions and other registers. A language is never closed upon itself, except as a function of impotence.

3. Principle of multiplicity: it is only when the multiple is effectively treated as a substantive, "multiplicity," that it ceases to have any relation to the One as subject or object, natural or spiritual reality, image and world. Multiplicities are rhizomatic, and expose arborescent pseudomultiplicities for what they are. There is no unity to serve as a pivot in the object, or to divide in the subject. There is not even the unity to abort in the object or "return" in the subject. A multiplicity has neither subject nor object, only determinations, magnitudes, and dimensions that cannot increase in number without the multiplicity changing in nature (the laws of combination therefore increase in number as the multiplicity grows). Puppet strings, as a rhizome or multiplicity, are tied not to the supposed will of an artist or puppeteer but to a multiplicity of nerve fibers, which form another puppet in other dimensions connected to the first: "Call the strings or rods that move the puppet the weave. It might be objected that *its multiplicity* resides in the person of the actor, who projects it into the text. Granted; but the actor's nerve fibers in turn form a weave. And they fall through the gray matter, the grid, into the undifferentiated. . . . The interplay approximates the pure activity of weavers attributed in myth to the Fates or Norns."[3] An assemblage is precisely this increase in the dimensions of a multiplicity that necessarily changes in nature as it expands its connections. There are no points or positions in a rhizome, such as those found in a structure, tree, or root. There are only lines. When Glenn Gould speeds up the performance of a piece, he is not just displaying virtuosity, he is transforming the musical points into lines, he is making the whole piece proliferate. The number is no longer a universal concept measuring elements according to their emplacement in a given dimension, but has itself become a multiplicity that varies according to the dimensions considered (the primacy of the domain over a complex of numbers attached to that domain). We do not have units (*unités*) of measure, only multiplicities or varieties of measurement. The notion of unity (*unité*) appears only when there is a power takeover in the multiplicity by the signifier or a corresponding subjectification proceeding: This is the case for a pivot-unity forming the basis for a set of biunivocal relationships between objective

elements or points, or for the One that divides following the law of a binary logic of differentiation in the subject. Unity always operates in an empty dimension supplementary to that of the system considered (overcoding).

The point is that a rhizome or multiplicity never allows itself to be overcoded, never has available a supplementary dimension over and above its number of lines, that is, over and above the multiplicity of numbers attached to those lines. All multiplicities are flat, in the sense that they fill or occupy all of their dimensions: we will therefore speak of a *plane of consistency* of multiplicities, even though the dimensions of this "plane" increase with the number of connections that are made on it. Multiplicities are defined by the outside: by the abstract line, the line of flight or deterritorialization according to which they change in nature and connect with other multiplicities. The plane of consistency (grid) is the outside of all multiplicities. The line of flight marks: the reality of a finite number of dimensions that the multiplicity effectively fills; the impossibility of a supplementary dimension, unless the multiplicity is transformed by the line of flight; the possibility and necessity of flattening all of the multiplicities on a single plane of consistency or exteriority, regardless of their number of dimensions. The ideal for a book would be to lay everything out on a plane of exteriority of this kind, on a single page, the same sheet: lived events, historical determinations, concepts, individuals, groups, social formations. Kleist invented a writing of this type, a broken chain of affects and variable speeds, with accelerations and transformations, always in a relation with the outside. Open rings. His texts, therefore, are opposed in every way to the classical or romantic book constituted by the interiority of a substance or subject. The war machine-book against the State apparatus-book. *Flat multiplicities of n dimensions* are asignifying and asubjective. They are designated by indefinite articles, or rather by partitives (*some* couchgrass, *some* of a rhizome . . .).

4. Principle of asignifying rupture: against the oversignifying breaks separating structures or cutting across a single structure. A rhizome may be broken, shattered at a given spot, but it will start up again on one of its old lines, or on new lines. You can never get rid of ants because they form an animal rhizome that can rebound time and again after most of it has been destroyed. Every rhizome contains lines of segmentarity according to which it is stratified, territorialized, organized, signified, attributed, etc., as well as lines of deterritorialization down which it constantly flees. There is a rupture in the rhizome whenever segmentary lines explode into a line of flight, but the line of flight is part of the rhizome. These lines always tie back to one another. That is why one can never posit a dualism or a dichotomy, even in the rudimentary form of the good and the bad. You may make a rupture, draw a line of flight, yet there is still a danger that you will reencounter organizations that restratify everything, formations that restore power to a signifier, attributions that reconstitute a subject—anything you like, from Oedipal resurgences to fascist concretions. Groups

and individuals contain microfascisms just waiting to crystallize. Yes, couchgrass is also a rhizome. Good and bad are only the products of an active and temporary selection, which must be renewed.

How could movements of deterritorialization and processes of reterritorialization not be relative, always connected, caught up in one another? The orchid deterritorializes by forming an image, a tracing of a wasp; but the wasp reterritorializes on that image. The wasp is nevertheless deterritorialized, becoming a piece in the orchid's reproductive apparatus. But it reterritorializes the orchid by transporting its pollen. Wasp and orchid, as heterogeneous elements, form a rhizome. It could be said that the orchid imitates the wasp, reproducing its image in a signifying fashion (mimesis, mimicry, lure, etc.). But this is true only on the level of the strata—a parallelism between two strata such that a plant organization on one imitates an animal organization on the other. At the same time, something else entirely is going on: not imitation at all but a capture of code, surplus value of code, an increase in valence, a veritable becoming, a becoming-wasp of the orchid and a becoming-orchid of the wasp. Each of these becomings brings about the deterritorialization of one term and the reterritorialization of the other; the two becomings interlink and form relays in a circulation of intensities pushing the deterritorialization ever further. There is neither imitation nor resemblance, only an exploding of two heterogeneous series on the line of flight composed by a common rhizome that can no longer be attributed to or subjugated by anything signifying. Rémy Chauvin expresses it well: "the *aparallel evolution* of two beings that have absolutely nothing to do with each other."[4] More generally, evolutionary schemas may be forced to abandon the old model of the tree and descent. Under certain conditions, a virus can connect to germ cells and transmit itself as the cellular gene of a complex species; moreover, it can take flight, move into the cells of an entirely different species, but not without bringing with it "genetic information" from the first host (for example, Benveniste and Todaro's current research on a type C virus, with its double connection to baboon DNA and the DNA of certain kinds of domestic cats). Evolutionary schemas would no longer follow models of arborescent descent going from the least to the most differentiated, but instead a rhizome operating immediately in the heterogeneous and jumping from one already differentiated line to another.[5] Once again, there is *aparallel evolution*, of the baboon and the cat; it is obvious that they are not models or copies of each other (a becoming-baboon in the cat does not mean that the cat "plays" baboon). We form a rhizome with our viruses, or rather our viruses cause us to form a rhizome with other animals. As François Jacob says, transfers of genetic material by viruses or through other procedures, fusions of cells originating in different species, have results analogous to those of "the abominable couplings dear to antiquity and the Middle Ages."[6] Transversal communications between different lines scramble the genealogical trees. Always look for the molecular, or even submolecular, particle with which we are allied. We evolve and die more from our polymorphous and rhizomatic flus than from hereditary diseases, or diseases that have their own line of descent. The rhizome is an antigenealogy.

The same applies to the book and the world: contrary to a deeply rooted belief, the book is not an image of the world. It forms a rhizome with the world, there is an aparallel evolution of the book and the world; the book assures the deterritorialization of the world, but the world effects a reterritorialization of the book, which in turn deterritorializes itself in the world (if it is capable, if it can). Mimicry is a very bad concept, since it relies on binary logic to describe phenomena of an entirely different nature. The crocodile does not reproduce a tree trunk, any more than the chameleon reproduces the colors of its surroundings. The Pink Panther imitates nothing, it reproduces nothing, it paints the world its color, pink on pink; this is its becoming-world, carried out in such a way that it becomes imperceptible itself, asignifying, makes its rupture, its own line of flight, follows its "aparallel evolution" through to the end. The wisdom of the plants: even when they have roots, there is always an outside where they form a rhizome with something else—with the wind, an animal, human beings (and there is also an aspect under which animals themselves form rhizomes, as do people, etc.). "Drunkenness as a triumphant irruption of the plant in us." Always follow the rhizome by rupture; lengthen, prolong, and relay the line of flight; make it vary, until you have produced the most abstract and tortuous of lines of *n* dimensions and broken directions. Conjugate deterritorialized flows. Follow the plants: you start by delimiting a first line consisting of circles of convergence around successive singularities; then you see whether inside that line new circles of convergence establish themselves, with new points located outside the limits and in other directions. Write, form a rhizome, increase your territory by deterritorialization, extend the line of flight to the point where it becomes an abstract machine covering the entire plane of consistency. "Go first to your old plant and watch carefully the watercourse made by the rain. By now the rain must have carried the seeds far away. Watch the crevices made by the runoff, and from them determine the direction of the flow. Then find the plant that is growing at the farthest point from your plant. All the devil's weed plants that are growing in between are yours. Later . . . you can extend the size of your territory by following the watercourse from each point along the way."[7] Music has always sent out lines of flight, like so many "transformational multiplicities," even overturning the very codes that structure or arborify it; that is why musical form, right down to its ruptures and proliferations, is comparable to a weed, a rhizome.[8]

5 and 6. Principle of cartography and decalcomania: a rhizome is not amenable to any structural or generative model. It is a stranger to any idea of genetic axis or deep structure. A genetic axis is like an objective pivotal unity upon which successive stages are organized; a deep structure is more like a base sequence that can be broken down into immediate constituents, while the unity of the product passes into another, transformational and subjective, dimension. This does not constitute a departure from the representative model of the tree, or root—pivotal taproot or fascicles (for example, Chomsky's "tree" is associated with a base sequence and represents the process of its own generation in terms of binary logic). A variation on the oldest form of thought. It is our view that genetic axis and profound structure are above all infinitely reproducible principles of *tracing*. All of tree logic is a logic of tracing and reproduction. In linguistics as in psychoanalysis, its object is an unconscious that is itself representative, crystallized into codified complexes, laid out along a genetic axis and distributed within a syntagmatic structure. Its goal is to describe a de facto state, to maintain balance in intersubjective relations, or to explore an unconscious that is already there from the start, lurking in the dark recesses of memory and language. It consists of tracing, on the basis of an overcoding structure or supporting axis, something that comes ready-made. The tree articulates and hierarchizes tracings; tracings are like the leaves of a tree.

The rhizome is altogether different, a *map and not a tracing*. Make a map, not a tracing. The orchid does not reproduce the tracing of the wasp; it forms a map with the wasp, in a rhizome. What distinguishes the map from the tracing is that it is entirely oriented toward an experimentation in contact with the real. The map does not reproduce an unconscious closed in upon itself; it constructs the unconscious. It fosters connections between fields, the removal of blockages on bodies without organs, the maximum opening of bodies without organs onto a plane of consistency. It is itself a part of the rhizome. The map is open and connectable in all of its dimensions; it is detachable, reversible, susceptible to constant modification. It can be torn, reversed, adapted to any kind of mounting, reworked by an individual, group, or social formation. It can be drawn on a wall, conceived of as a work of art, constructed as a political action or as a meditation. Perhaps one of the most important characteristics of the rhizome is that it always has multiple entryways; in this sense, the burrow is an animal rhizome, and sometimes maintains a clear distinction between the line of flight as passageway and storage or living strata (cf. the muskrat). A map has multiple entryways, as opposed to the tracing, which always comes back "to the same." The map has to do with performance, whereas the tracing always involves an alleged "competence." Unlike psychoanalysis, psychoanalytic competence (which confines every desire and statement to a genetic axis or overcoding structure, and makes infinite, monotonous tracings of the stages on that axis or the constituents of that structure), schizoanalysis rejects any idea of pretraced destiny, whatever name is given to it—divine, anagogic, historical, economic, structural, hereditary, or syntagmatic. (It is obvious that Melanie Klein has no understanding of the cartography of one of her child patients, Little Richard, and is content to make ready-made tracings—Oedipus, the good daddy and the bad daddy, the bad mommy and the good mommy—while the child makes a desperate attempt to carry out a performance that the psychoanalyst totally misconstrues.)[9] Drives and part-objects are neither stages on a genetic axis nor positions in a deep structure; they are political options for problems, they are entryways and exits, impasses the child lives out politically, in other words, with all the force of his or her desire.

Have we not, however, reverted to a simple dualism by contrasting maps to tracings, as good and bad sides? Is it not of the essence of the map to be traceable? Is it not of the essence of the rhizome to intersect roots and sometimes merge with them? Does not a map contain phenomena of redundancy that are already like tracings of its own? Does not a multiplicity have strata upon which unifications and totalizations, massifications, mimetic mechanisms, signifying power takeovers, and subjective attributions take root? Do not even lines of flight, due to their eventual divergence, reproduce the very formations their function it was to dismantle or outflank? But the opposite is also true. It is a question of method: *the tracing should always be put back on the map*. This operation and the previous one are not at all symmetrical. For it is inaccurate to say that a tracing reproduces the map. It is instead like a photograph or X ray that begins by selecting or isolating, by artificial means such as colorations or other restrictive procedures, what it intends to reproduce. The imitator always creates the model, and attracts it. The tracing has already translated the map into an image; it has already transformed the rhizome into roots and radicles. It has organized, stabilized, neutralized the multiplicities according to the axes of signifiance and subjectification belonging to it. It has generated, structuralized the rhizome, and when it thinks it is reproducing something else it is in fact only reproducing itself. That is why the tracing is so dangerous. It injects redundancies and propagates them. What the tracing reproduces of the map or rhizome are only the impasses, blockages, incipient taproots, or points of structuration. Take a look at psychoanalysis and linguistics: all the former has ever made are tracings or photos of the unconscious, and the latter of language, with all the betrayals that implies (it's not surprising that psychoanalysis tied its fate to that of linguistics).

Look at what happened to Little Hans already, an example of child psychoanalysis at its purest: they kept on BREAKING HIS RHIZOME and BLOTCHING HIS MAP, setting it straight for him, blocking his every way out, until he began to desire his own shame and guilt, until they had rooted shame and guilt in him, PHOBIA (they barred him from the rhizome of the building, then from the rhizome of the street, they rooted him in his parents' bed, they radicled him to his own body, they fixated him on Professor Freud). Freud explicitly takes Little Hans's cartography into account, but always and only in order to project it back onto the family photo. And look what Melanie Klein did to Little Richard's geopolitical maps: she developed photos from them, made tracings of them. Strike the pose or follow the axis, genetic stage or structural destiny—one way or the other, your rhizome will be broken. You will be allowed to live and speak, but only after every outlet has been obstructed. Once a rhizome has been obstructed, arborified, it's all over, no desire stirs; for it is always by rhizome that desire moves and produces. Whenever desire climbs a tree, internal repercussions trip it up and it falls to its death; the rhizome, on the other hand, acts on desire by external, productive outgrowths.

That is why it is so important to try the other, reverse but nonsymmetrical, operation. Plug the tracings back into the map, connect the roots or trees back up with a rhizome. In the case of Little Hans, studying the unconscious would be to show how he tries to build a rhizome, with the family house but also with the line of flight of the building, the street, etc.; how these lines are blocked, how the child is made to take root in the family, be photographed under the father, be traced onto the mother's bed; then how Professor Freud's intervention assures a power takeover by the signifier, a subjectification of affects; how the only escape route left to the child is a becoming-animal perceived as shameful and guilty (the becoming-horse of Little Hans, a truly political option). But these impasses must always be resituated on the map, thereby opening them up to possible lines of flight. The same applies to the group map: show at what point in the rhizome there form phenomena of massification, bureaucracy, leadership, fascization, etc., which lines nevertheless survive, if only underground, continuing to make rhizome in the shadows. Deligny's method: map the gestures and movements of an autistic child, combine several maps for the same child, for several different children.[10] If it is true that it is of the essence of the map or rhizome to have multiple entryways, then it is plausible that one could even enter them through tracings or the root-tree, assuming the necessary precautions are taken (once again, one must avoid any Manichaean dualism). For example, one will often be forced to take dead ends, to work with signifying powers and subjective affections, to find a foothold in formations that are Oedipal or paranoid or even worse, rigidified territorialities that open the way for other transformational operations. It is even possible for psychoanalysis to serve as a foothold, in spite of itself. In other cases, on the contrary, one will bolster oneself directly on a line of flight enabling one to blow apart strata, cut roots, and make new connections. Thus, there are very diverse map-tracing, rhizome-root assemblages, with variable coefficients of deterritorialization. There exist tree or root structures in rhizomes; conversely, a tree branch or root division may begin to burgeon into a rhizome. The coordinates are determined not by theoretical analyses implying universals but by a pragmatics composing multiplicities or aggregates of intensities. A new rhizome may form in the heart of a tree, the hollow of a root, the crook of a branch. Or else it is a microscopic element of the root-tree, a radicle, that gets rhizome production going. Accounting and bureaucracy proceed by tracings: they can begin to burgeon nonetheless, throwing out rhizome stems, as in a Kafka novel. An intensive trait starts working for itself, a hallucinatory perception, synesthesia, perverse mutation, or play of images shakes loose, challenging the hegemony of the signifier. In the case of the child, gestural, mimetic, ludic, and other semiotic systems regain their freedom and extricate themselves from the "tracing," that is, from the dominant competence of the teacher's language—a microscopic event upsets the local balance of power. Similarly, generative trees constructed according to Chomsky's syntagmatic model can open up in all directions, and in turn form a rhizome.[11] To be rhizomorphous is to produce stems and filaments that seem to be roots, or better yet connect with them by penetrating the trunk, but put them to strange new uses. We're tired of trees. We should stop believing in trees, roots, and radicles. They've made us suffer too much. All of arborescent culture is founded on them, from biology to linguistics. Nothing is beautiful or loving or political aside from underground stems and aerial roots, adventitious growths and rhizomes. Amsterdam, a city entirely without roots, a rhizome-city with its stem-canals, where utility connects with the greatest folly in relation to a commercial war machine.

Thought is not arborescent, and the brain is not a rooted or ramified matter. What are wrongly called "dendrites" do not assure the connection of neurons in a continuous fabric. The discontinuity between cells, the role of the axons, the functioning of the synapses, the existence of synaptic microfissures, the leap each message makes across these fissures, make the brain a multiplicity immersed in its plane of consistency or neuroglia, a whole uncertain, probabilistic system ("the uncertain nervous system"). Many people have a tree growing in their heads, but the brain itself is much more a grass than a tree. "The axon and the dendrite twist around each other like bindweed around brambles, with synapses at each of the thorns."[12] The same goes for memory. Neurologists and psychophysiologists distinguish between long-term memory and short-term memory (on the order of a minute). The difference between them is not simply quantitative: short-term memory is of the rhizome or diagram type, and long-term memory is arborescent and centralized (imprint, engram, tracing, or photograph). Short-term memory is in no way subject to a law of contiguity or immediacy to its object; it can act at a distance, come or return a long time after, but always under conditions of discontinuity, rupture, and multiplicity. Furthermore, the difference between the two kinds of memory is not that of two temporal modes of apprehending the same thing; they do not grasp the same thing, memory, or idea. The splendor of the short-term Idea: one writes using short-term memory, and thus short-term ideas, even if one reads or rereads using long-term memory of long-term concepts. Short-term memory includes forgetting as a process; it merges not with the instant but instead with the nervous, temporal, and collective rhizome. Long-term memory (family, race, society, or civilization) traces and translates, but what it translates continues to act in it, from a distance, off beat, in an "untimely" way, not instantaneously.

The tree and root inspire a sad image of thought that is forever imitating the multiple on the basis of a centered or segmented higher unity. If we consider the set, branches-roots, the trunk plays the role of *opposed segment* for one of the subsets running from bottom to top: this kind of segment is a "link dipole," in contrast to the "unit dipoles" formed by spokes radiating from a single center.[13] Even if the links themselves proliferate, as in the radicle system, one can never get beyond the One-Two, and fake multiplicities. Regenerations, reproductions, returns, hydras, and medusas do not get us any further. Arborescent systems are hierarchical systems with centers of signifiance and subjectification, central automata like organized memories. In the corresponding models, an element only receives information from a higher unit, and only receives a subjective affection along preestablished paths. This is evident in current problems in information science and computer science, which still cling to the oldest modes of thought in that they grant all power to a memory or central organ. Pierre Rosenstiehl and Jean Petitot, in a fine article denouncing "the imagery of command trees" (centered systems or hierarchical structures), note that "accepting the primacy of hierarchical structures amounts to giving arborescent structures privileged status. . . . The arborescent form admits of topological explanation. . . . In a hierarchical system, an individual has only one active neighbor, his or her hierarchical superior. . . . The channels of transmission are preestablished: the arborescent system preexists the individual, who is integrated into it at an allotted place" (signifiance and subjectification). The authors point out that even when one thinks one has reached a multiplicity, it may be a false one—of what we call the radicle

type—because its ostensibly nonhierarchical presentation or statement in fact only admits of a totally hierarchical solution. An example is the famous *friendship theorem*: "If any two given individuals in a society have precisely one mutual friend, then there exists an individual who is the friend of all the others." (Rosenstiehl and Petitot ask who that mutual friend is. Who is "the universal friend in this society of couples: the master, the confessor, the doctor? These ideas are curiously far removed from the initial axioms." Who is this friend of humankind? Is it the *philo*-sopher as he appears in classical thought, even if he is an aborted unity that makes itself felt only through its absence or subjectivity, saying all the while, I know nothing, I am nothing?) Thus the authors speak of dictatorship theorems. Such is indeed the principle of roots-trees, or their outcome: the radicle solution, the structure of Power.[14]

To these centered systems, the authors contrast acentered systems, finite networks of automata in which communication runs from any neighbor to any other, the stems or channels do not preexist, and all individuals are interchangeable, defined only by their *state* at a given moment—such that the local operations are coordinated and the final, global result synchronized without a central agency. Transduction of intensive states replaces topology, and "the graph regulating the circulation of information is in a way the opposite of the hierarchical graph. . . . There is no reason for the graph to be a tree" (we have been calling this kind of graph a map). The problem of the war machine, or the firing squad: is a general necessary for n individuals to manage to fire in unison? The solution without a General is to be found in an acentered multiplicity possessing a finite number of states with signals to indicate corresponding speeds, from a war rhizome or guerrilla logic point of view, without any tracing, without any copying of a central order. The authors even demonstrate that this kind of machinic multiplicity, assemblage, or society rejects any centralizing or unifying automaton as an "asocial intrusion."[15] Under these conditions, n is in fact always $n - 1$. Rosenstiehl and Petitot emphasize that the opposition, centered-acentered, is valid less as a designation for things than as a mode of calculation applied to things. Trees may correspond to the rhizome, or they may burgeon into a rhizome. It is true that the same thing is generally susceptible to both modes of calculation or both types of regulation, but not without undergoing a change in state. Take psychoanalysis as an example again: it subjects the unconscious to arborescent structures, hierarchical graphs, recapitulatory memories, central organs, the phallus, the phallus-tree—not only in its theory but also in its practice of calculation and treatment. Psychoanalysis cannot change its method in this regard: it bases its own dictatorial power upon a dictatorial conception of the unconscious. Psychoanalysis's margin of maneuverability is therefore very limited. In both psychoanalysis and its object, there is always a general, always a leader (General Freud). Schizoanalysis, on the other hand, treats the unconscious as an acentered system, in other words, as a machinic network of finite automata (a rhizome), and thus arrives at an entirely different state of the unconscious. These same remarks apply to linguistics; Rosenstiehl and Petitot are right to bring up the possibility of an "acentered organization of a society of words." For both statements and desires, the issue is never to reduce the unconscious or to interpret it or to make it signify according to a tree model. The issue is to *produce the unconscious*, and with it new statements, different desires: the rhizome is precisely this production of the unconscious.

It is odd how the tree has dominated Western reality and all of Western thought, from botany to biology and anatomy, but also gnosiology, theology, ontology, all of philosophy . . . : the root-foundation, *Grund*, *racine*, *fondement*. The West has a special relation to the forest, and deforestation; the fields carved from the forest are populated with seed plants produced by cultivation based on species lineages of the arborescent type; animal raising, carried out on fallow fields, selects lineages forming an entire animal arborescence. The East presents a different figure: a relation to the steppe and the garden (or in some cases, the desert and the oasis), rather than forest and field; cultivation of tubers by fragmentation of the individual; a casting aside or bracketing of animal raising, which is confined to closed spaces or pushed out onto the steppes of the nomads. The West: agriculture based on a chosen lineage containing a large number of variable individuals. The East: horticulture based on a small number of individuals derived from a wide range of "clones." Does not the East, Oceania in particular, offer something like a rhizomatic model opposed in every respect to the Western model of the tree? André Haudricourt even sees this as the basis for the opposition between the moralities or philosophies of transcendence dear to the West and the immanent ones of the East: the God who sows and reaps, as opposed to the God who replants and unearths (replanting of offshoots versus sowing of seeds).[16] Transcendence: a specifically European disease. Neither is music the same, the music of the earth is different, as is sexuality: seed plants, even those with two sexes in the same plant, subjugate sexuality to the reproductive model; the rhizome, on the other hand, is a liberation of sexuality not only from reproduction but also from genitality. Here in the West, the tree has implanted itself in our bodies, rigidifying and stratifying even the sexes. We have lost the rhizome, or the grass. Henry Miller: "China is the weed in the human cabbage patch. . . . The weed is the Nemesis of human endeavor. . . . Of all the imaginary existences we attribute to plant, beast and star the weed leads the most satisfactory life of all. True, the weed produces no lilies, no battleships, no Sermons on the Mount. . . . Eventually the weed gets the upper hand. Eventually things fall back into a state of China. This condition is usually referred to by historians as the Dark Age. Grass is the only way out. . . . The weed exists only to fill the waste spaces left by cultivated areas. *It grows between*, among other things. The lily is beautiful, the cabbage is provender, the poppy is maddening—but the weed is rank growth . . . : it points a moral."[17] Which China is Miller talking about? The old China, the new, an imaginary one, or yet another located on a shifting map?

America is a special case. Of course it is not immune from domination by trees or the search for roots. This is evident even in the literature, in the quest for a national identity and even for a European ancestry or genealogy (Kerouac going off in search of his ancestors). Nevertheless, everything important that has happened or is happening takes the route of the American rhizome: the beatniks, the underground, bands and gangs, successive lateral offshoots in immediate connection with an outside. American books are different from European books, even when the American sets off in pursuit of trees. The conception of the book is different. *Leaves of Grass*. And directions in America are different: the search for arborescence and the return to the Old World occur in the East. But there is the rhizomatic West, with its Indians without ancestry, its ever-receding limit, its shifting and displaced frontiers. There is a whole American "map" in the West, where even the trees form rhizomes. America reversed the directions: it put its Orient in the West, as if it were precisely in America that the earth came full circle; its West is the edge of the East.[18] (India is not the intermediary between the Occident and the Orient, as Haudricourt believed: America is the pivot point and mechanism of reversal.) The American singer Patti Smith sings the bible of the American dentist: Don't go for the root, follow the canal . . .

Are there not also two kinds of bureaucracy, or even three (or still more)? Western bureaucracy: its agrarian, cadastral origins; roots and fields; trees and their role as frontiers; the great census of William the Conqueror; feudalism; the policies of the kings of France; making property the basis of the State; negotiating land through warfare, litigation, and marriages. The kings of France chose the lily because it is a plant with deep roots that clings to slopes. Is bureaucracy the same in the Orient? Of course it is all too easy to depict an Orient of rhizomes and immanence; yet it is true that in the Orient the State does not act following a schema of arborescence corresponding to preestablished, arborified, and rooted classes; its bureaucracy is one of channels, for example, the much-discussed case of hydraulic power with "weak property," in which the State engenders channeled and channelizing classes (cf. the aspects of Wittfogel's work that have not been refuted).[19] The despot acts as a river, not as a fountainhead, which is still a point, a tree-point or root; he flows with the current rather than sitting under a tree; Buddha's tree itself becomes a rhizome; Mao's river and Louis's tree. Has not America acted as an intermediary here as well? For it proceeds both by internal exterminations and liquidations (not only the Indians but also the farmers, etc.), and by successive waves of immigration from the outside. The flow of capital produces an immense channel, a quantification of power with immediate "quanta," where each person profits from the passage of the money flow in his or her own way (hence the reality-myth of the poor man who strikes it rich and then falls into poverty again): in America everything comes together, tree and channel, root and rhizome. There is no universal capitalism, there is no capitalism in itself; capitalism is at the crossroads of all kinds of formations, it is neocapitalism by nature. It invents its eastern face and western face, and reshapes them both—all for the worst.

At the same time, we are on the wrong track with all these geographical distributions. An impasse. So much the better. If it is a question of showing that rhizomes also have their own, even more rigid, despotism and hierarchy, then fine and good: for there is no dualism, no ontological dualism between here and there, no axiological dualism between good and bad, no blend or American synthesis. There are knots of arborescence in rhizomes, and rhizomatic offshoots in roots. Moreover, there are despotic formations of immanence and channelization specific to rhizomes, just as there are anarchic deformations in the transcendent system of trees, aerial roots, and subterranean stems. The important point is that the root-tree and canal-rhizome are not two opposed models: the first operates as a transcendent model and tracing, even if it engenders its own escapes; the second operates as an immanent process that overturns the model and outlines a map, even if it constitutes its own hierarchies, even if it gives rise to a despotic channel. It is not a question of this or that place on earth, or of a given moment in history, still less of this or that category of thought. It is a question of a model that is perpetually in construction or collapsing, and of a process that is perpetually prolonging itself, breaking off and starting up again. No, this is not a new or different dualism. The problem of writing: in order to designate something exactly, anexact expressions are utterly unavoidable. Not at all because it is a necessary step, or because one can only advance by approximations: anexactitude is in no way an approximation; on the contrary, it is the exact passage of that which is under way. We invoke one dualism only in order to challenge another. We employ a dualism of models only in order to arrive at a process that challenges all models. Each time, mental correctives are necessary to undo the dualisms we had no wish to construct but through which we pass. Arrive at the magic formula we all seek—PLURALISM = MONISM—via all the dualisms that are the enemy, an entirely necessary enemy, the furniture we are forever rearranging.

Let us summarize the principal characteristics of a rhizome: unlike trees or their roots, the rhizome connects any point to any other point, and its traits are not necessarily linked to traits of the same nature; it brings into play very different regimes of signs, and even nonsign states. The rhizome is reducible neither to the One nor the multiple. It is not the One that becomes Two or even directly three, four, five, etc. It is not a multiple derived from the One, or to which One is added $(n + 1)$. It is composed not of units but of dimensions, or rather directions in motion. It has neither beginning nor end, but always a middle (*milieu*) from which it grows and which it overspills. It constitutes linear multiplicities with n dimensions having neither subject nor object, which can be laid out on a plane of consistency, and from which the One is always subtracted $(n - 1)$. When a multiplicity of this kind changes dimension, it necessarily changes in nature as well, undergoes a metamorphosis. Unlike a structure, which is defined by a set of points and positions, with binary relations between the points and biunivocal relationships between the positions, the rhizome is made only of lines: lines of segmentarity and stratification as its dimensions, and the line of flight or deterritorialization as the maximum dimension after which the multiplicity undergoes metamorphosis, changes in nature. These lines, or lineaments, should not be confused with lineages of the arborescent type, which are merely localizable linkages between points and positions. Unlike the tree, the rhizome is not the object of reproduction: neither external reproduction as image-tree nor internal reproduction as tree-structure. The rhizome is an antigenealogy. It is a short-term memory, or antimemory. The rhizome operates by variation, expansion, conquest, capture, offshoots. Unlike the graphic arts, drawing, or photography, unlike tracings, the rhizome pertains to a map that must be produced, constructed, a map that is always detachable, connectable, reversible, modifiable, and has multiple entryways and exits and its own lines of flight. It is tracings that must be put on the map, not the opposite. In contrast to centered (even polycentric) systems with hierarchical modes of communication and preestablished paths, the rhizome is an acentered, nonhierarchical, nonsignifying system without a General and without an organizing memory or central automaton, defined solely by a circulation of states. What is at question in the rhizome is a relation to sexuality—but also to the animal, the vegetal, the world, politics, the book, things natural and artificial—that is totally different from the arborescent relation: all manner of "becomings."

A plateau is always in the middle, not at the beginning or the end. A rhizome is made of plateaus. Gregory Bateson uses the word "plateau" to designate something very special: a continuous, self-vibrating region of intensities whose development avoids any orientation toward a culmination point or external end. Bateson cites Balinese culture as an example: mother-child sexual games, and even quarrels among men, undergo this bizarre intensive stabilization. "Some sort of continuing plateau of intensity is substituted for [sexual] climax," war, or a culmination point. It is a regrettable characteristic of the Western mind to relate expressions and actions to exterior or transcendent ends, instead of evaluating them on a plane of consistency on the basis of their intrinsic value.[20] For example, a book composed of chapters has culmination and termination points. What takes place in a book composed instead of plateaus that communicate with one another across microfissures, as in a brain? We call a "plateau" any multiplicity connected to other multiplicities by superficial underground stems in such a way as to form or extend a rhizome. We are writing this book as a rhizome. It is composed of plateaus. We have given it a circular form, but only for laughs. Each morning we would wake up, and each of us would ask himself what plateau he was going to tackle, writing five lines here, ten there. We had hallucinatory experiences, we watched lines leave one plateau and proceed to another like columns of tiny ants. We made circles of convergence. Each plateau can be read starting anywhere and can be related to any other plateau. To attain the multiple, one must have a method that effectively constructs it; no typographical cleverness, no lexical agility, no blending or creation of words, no syntactical boldness, can substitute for it. In fact, these are more often than not merely mimetic procedures used to disseminate or disperse a unity that is retained in a different dimension for an image-book. Technonarcissism. Typographical, lexical, or syntactic creations are necessary only when they no longer belong to the form of expression of a hidden unity, becoming themselves dimensions of the multiplicity under consideration; we only know of rare successes in this.[21] We ourselves were unable to do it. We just used words that in turn function for us as plateaus. RHIZOMATICS = SCHIZOANALYSIS = STRATOANALYSIS = PRAGMATICS = MICROPOLITICS. These words are concepts, but concepts are lines, which is to say, number systems attached to a particular dimension of the multiplicities (strata, molecular chains, lines of flight or rupture, circles of convergence, etc.). Nowhere do we claim for our concepts the title of a science. We are no more familiar with scientificity than we are with ideology; all we know are assemblages. And the only assemblages are machinic assemblages of desire and collective assemblages of enunciation. No signifiance, no subjectification: writing to the *n*th power (all individuated enunciation remains trapped within the dominant significations, all signifying desire is associated with dominated subjects). An assemblage, in its multiplicity, necessarily acts on semiotic flows, material flows, and social flows simultaneously (independently of any recapitulation that may be made of it in a scientific or theoretical corpus). There is no longer a tripartite division between a field of reality (the world) and a field of representation (the book) and a field of subjectivity (the author). Rather, an assemblage establishes connections between certain multiplicities drawn from each of these orders, so that a book has no sequel nor the world as its object nor one or several authors as its subject. In short, we think that one cannot write sufficiently in the name of an outside. The outside has no image, no signification, no subjectivity. The book as assemblage with the outside, against the book as image of the world. A rhizome-book, not a dichotomous, pivotal, or fascicular book. Never send down roots, or plant them, however difficult it may be to avoid reverting to the old procedures. "Those things which occur to me, occur to me not from the root up but rather only from somewhere about their middle. Let someone then attempt to seize them, let someone attempt to seize a blade of grass and hold fast to it when it begins to grow only from the middle."[22] Why is this so difficult? The question is directly one of perceptual semiotics. It's not easy to see things in the middle, rather than looking down on them from above or up at them from below, or from left to right or right to left: try it, you'll see that everything changes. It's not easy to see the grass in things and in words (similarly, Nietzsche said that an aphorism had to be "ruminated"; never is a plateau separable from the cows that populate it, which are also the clouds in the sky).

History is always written from the sedentary point of view and in the name of a unitary State apparatus, at least a possible one, even when the topic is nomads. What is lacking is a Nomadology, the opposite of a history. There are rare successes in this also, for example, on the subject of the Children's Crusades: Marcel Schwob's book multiplies narratives like so many plateaus with variable numbers of dimensions. Then there is Andrzejewski's book, *Les portes du paradis* (The gates of paradise), composed of a single uninterrupted sentence; a flow of children; a flow of walking with pauses, straggling, and forward rushes; the semiotic flow of the confessions of all the children who go up to the old monk at the head of the procession to make their declarations; a flow of desire and sexuality, each child having left out of love and more or less directly led by the dark posthumous pederastic desire of the count of Vendôme; all this with circles of convergence. What is important is not whether the flows are "One or multiple"—we're past that point: there is a collective assemblage of enunciation, a machinic assemblage of desire, one inside the other and both plugged into an immense outside that is a multiplicity in any case. A more recent example is Armand Farrachi's book on the Fourth Crusade, *La dislocation*, in which the sentences space themselves out and disperse, or else jostle together and coexist, and in which the letters, the typography begin to dance as the crusade grows more delirious.[23] These are models of nomadic and rhizomatic writing. Writing weds a war machine and lines of flight, abandoning the strata, segmentarities, sedentarity, the State apparatus. But why is a model still necessary? Aren't these books still "images" of the Crusades? Don't they still retain a unity, in Schwob's case a pivotal unity, in Farrachi's an aborted unity, and in the most beautiful example, *Les portes du paradis*, the unity of the funereal count? Is there a need for a more profound nomadism than that of the Crusades, a nomadism of true nomads, or of those who no longer even move or imitate anything? The nomadism of those who only assemble (*agencent*). How can the book find an adequate outside with which to assemble in heterogeneity, rather than a world to reproduce? The cultural book is necessarily a tracing: already a tracing of itself, a tracing of the previous book by the same author, a tracing of other books however different they may be, an endless tracing of established concepts and words, a tracing of the world present, past, and future. Even the anticultural book may still be burdened by too heavy a cultural load: but it will use it actively, for forgetting instead of remembering, for underdevelopment instead of progress toward development, in nomadism rather than sedentarity, to make a map instead of a tracing. RHIZOMATICS = POP ANALYSIS, even if the people have other things to do besides read it, even if the blocks of academic culture or pseudoscientificity in it are still too painful or ponderous. For science would go completely mad if left to its own devices. Look at mathematics: it's not a science, it's a monster slang, it's nomadic. Even in the realm of theory, especially in the realm of theory, any precarious and pragmatic framework is better than tracing concepts, with their breaks and progress changing nothing. Imperceptible rupture, not signifying break. The nomads invented a war machine in opposition to the State apparatus. History has never comprehended nomadism, the book has never comprehended the outside. The State as the model for the book and for thought has a long history: logos, the philosopher-king, the transcendence of the Idea, the interiority of the concept, the republic of minds, the court of reason, the functionaries of thought, man as legislator and subject. The State's pretension to be a world order, and to root man. The war machine's relation to an outside is not another "model"; it is an assemblage that makes thought itself nomadic, and the book a working part in every mobile machine, a stem for a rhizome (Kleist and Kafka against Goethe).

Write to the *n*th power, the $n - 1$ power, write with slogans: Make rhizomes, not roots, never plant! Don't sow, grow offshoots! Don't be one or multiple, be multiplicities! Run lines, never plot a point! Speed turns the point into a line![24] Be quick, even when standing still! Line of chance, line of hips, line of flight. Don't bring out the General in you! Don't have just ideas, just have an idea (Godard). Have short-term ideas. Make maps, not photos or drawings. Be the Pink Panther and your loves will be like the wasp and the orchid, the cat and the baboon. As they say about old man river:

> He don't plant 'tatos
> Don't plant cotton
> Them that plants them is soon forgotten
> But old man river he just keeps rollin' along

A rhizome has no beginning or end; it is always in the middle, between things, interbeing, *intermezzo.* The tree is filiation, but the rhizome is alliance, uniquely alliance. The tree imposes the verb "to be," but the fabric of the rhizome is the conjunction, "and . . . and . . . and . . ." This conjunction carries enough force to shake and uproot the verb "to be." Where are you going? Where are you coming from? What are you heading for? These are totally useless questions. Making a clean slate, starting or beginning again from ground zero, seeking a beginning or a foundation—all imply a false conception of voyage and movement (a conception that is methodical, pedagogical, initiatory, symbolic. . .). But Kleist, Lenz, and Büchner have another way of traveling and moving: proceeding from the middle, through the middle, coming and going rather than starting and finishing.[25] American literature, and already English literature, manifest this rhizomatic direction to an even greater extent; they know how to move between things, establish a logic of the AND, overthrow ontology, do away with foundations, nullify endings and beginnings. They know how to practice pragmatics. The middle is by no means an average; on the contrary, it is where things pick up speed. *Between* things does not designate a localizable relation going from one thing to the other and back again, but a perpendicular direction, a transversal movement that sweeps one *and* the other away, a stream without beginning or end that undermines its banks and picks up speed in the middle.

2. 1914: One or Several Wolves?

Field of Tracks, or Wolf Line

That day, the Wolf-Man rose from the couch particularly tired. He knew that Freud had a genius for brushing up against the truth and passing it by, then filling the void with associations. He knew that Freud knew nothing about wolves, or anuses for that matter. The only thing Freud understood was what a dog is, and a dog's tail. It wasn't enough. It wouldn't be enough. The Wolf-Man knew that Freud would soon declare him cured, but that it was not at all the case and his treatment would continue for all eternity under Brunswick, Lacan, Leclaire. Finally, he knew that he was in the process of acquiring a veritable proper name, the Wolf-Man, a name more properly his than his own, since it attained the highest degree of singularity in the instantaneous apprehension of a generic multiplicity: wolves. He knew that this new and true proper name would be disfigured and misspelled, retranscribed as a patronymic.

Freud, for his part, would go on to write some extraordinary pages. Entirely practical pages: his article of 1915 on "The Unconscious," which deals with the difference between neurosis and psychosis. Freud says that hysterics or obsessives are people capable of making a global comparison between a sock and a vagina, a scar and castration, etc. Doubtless, it is at one and the same time that they apprehend the object globally and perceive it as lost. Yet it would never occur to a neurotic to grasp the skin erotically as a multiplicity of pores, little spots, little scars or black holes, or to grasp the sock erotically as a multiplicity of stitches. The psychotic can: "we should expect the multiplicity of these little cavities to prevent him from using them as substitutes for the female genital."[1] Comparing a sock to a vagina is OK, it's done all the time, but you'd have to be insane to compare a pure aggregate of stitches to a field of vaginas: that's what Freud says. This represents an important clinical discovery: a whole difference in style between neurosis and psychosis. For example, Salvador Dali, in attempting to reproduce his delusions, may go on at length about THE rhinoceros horn; he has not for all of that left neurotic discourse behind. But when he starts comparing goosebumps to a field of tiny rhinoceros horns, we get the feeling that the atmosphere has changed and that we are now in the presence of madness. Is it still a question of a comparison at all? It is, rather, a pure multiplicity that changes elements, or *becomes.* On the micrological level, the little bumps "become" horns, and the horns, little penises.

No sooner does Freud discover the greatest art of the unconscious, this art of molecular multiplicities, than we find him tirelessly at work bringing back molar unities, reverting to his familiar themes of *the* father, *the* penis, *the* vagina, Castration with a capital *C* . . . (On the verge of discovering a rhizome, Freud always returns to mere roots.) The reductive procedure of the 1915 article is quite interesting: he says that the comparisons and identifications of the neurotic are guided by representations of things, whereas all the psychotic has left are representations of words (for example, the word "hole"). "What has dictated the substitution is not the resemblance between the things denoted but the sameness of the words used to express them" (p. 201). Thus, when there is no unity in the thing, there is at least unity and identity in the word. It will be noted that names are taken in their *extensive* usage, in other words, function as common nouns ensuring the unification of an aggregate they subsume. The proper name can be nothing more than an extreme case of the common noun, containing its already domesticated multiplicity within itself and linking it to a being or object posited as unique. This jeopardizes, on the side of words and things both, the relation of the proper name as an *intensity* to the multiplicity it instantaneously apprehends. For Freud, when the thing splinters and loses its identity, the word is still there to restore that identity or invent a new one. Freud counted on the word to reestablish a unity no longer found in things. Are we not witnessing the first stirrings of a subsequent adventure, that of *the* Signifier, the devious despotic agency that substitutes itself for asignifying proper names and replaces multiplicities with the dismal unity of an object declared lost?

We're not far from wolves. For the Wolf-Man, in his second so-called psychotic episode, kept constant watch over the variations or changing path of the little holes or scars on the skin of his nose. During the first episode, which Freud declares neurotic, he recounted a dream he had about six or seven wolves in a tree, and drew five. Who is ignorant of the fact that wolves travel in packs? Only Freud. Every child knows it. Not Freud. With false scruples he asks, How are we to explain the fact that there are five, six, or seven wolves in this dream? He has decided that this is neurosis, so he uses the other reductive procedure: free association on the level of the representation of things, rather than verbal subsumption on the level of the representation of words. The result is the same, since it is always a question of bringing back the unity or identity of the person or allegedly lost object. The wolves will have to be purged of their multiplicity. This operation is accomplished by associating the dream with the tale, "The Wolf and the Seven Kid-Goats" (only six of which get eaten). We witness Freud's reductive glee; we literally see multiplicity leave the wolves to take the shape of goats that have absolutely nothing to do with the story. Seven wolves that are only kid-goats. Six wolves: the seventh goat (the Wolf-Man himself) is hiding in the clock. Five wolves: he may have seen his parents make love at five o'clock, and the roman numeral V is associated with the erotic spreading of a woman's legs. Three wolves: the parents may have made love three times. Two wolves: the first coupling the child may have seen was the two parents *more ferarum*, or perhaps even two dogs. One wolf: the wolf is the father, as we all knew from the start. Zero wolves: he lost his tail, he is not just a castrater but also castrated. Who is Freud trying to fool? The wolves never had a chance to get away and save their pack: it was already decided from the very beginning that animals could serve only to represent coitus between parents, or, conversely, be represented by coitus between parents. Freud obviously knows nothing about the fascination exerted by wolves and the meaning of their silent call, the call to become-wolf. Wolves watch, intently watch, the dreaming child; it is so much more reassuring to tell oneself that the dream produced a reversal and that it is really the child who sees dogs or parents in the act of making love. Freud only knows the

Oedipalized wolf or dog, the castrated-castrating daddy-wolf, the dog in the kennel, the analyst's bow-wow.

Franny is listening to a program on wolves. I say to her, Would you like to be a wolf? She answers haughtily, How stupid, you can't be one wolf, you're always eight or nine, six or seven. Not six or seven wolves all by yourself all at once, but one wolf among others, with five or six others. In becoming-wolf, the important thing is the position of the mass, and above all the position of the subject itself in relation to the pack or wolf-multiplicity: how the subject joins or does not join the pack, how far away it stays, how it does or does not hold to the multiplicity. To soften the harshness of her response, Franny recounts a dream: "There is a desert. Again, it wouldn't make any sense to say that I am *in* the desert. It's a panoramic vision of the desert, and it's not a tragic or uninhabited desert. It's only a desert because of its ocher color and its blazing, shadowless sun. There is a teeming crowd in it, a swarm of bees, a rumble of soccer players, or a group of Tuareg. *I am on the edge of the crowd, at the periphery; but I belong to it, I am attached to it by one of my extremities, a hand or foot.* I know that the periphery is the only place I can be, that I would die if I let myself be drawn into the center of the fray, but just as certainly if I let go of the crowd. This is not an easy position to stay in, it is even very difficult to hold, for these beings are in constant motion and their movements are unpredictable and follow no rhythm. They swirl, go north, then suddenly east; none of the individuals in the crowd remains in the same place in relation to the others. So I too am in perpetual motion; all this demands a high level of tension, but it gives me a feeling of violent, almost vertiginous, happiness." A very good schizo dream. To be fully a part of the crowd and at the same time completely outside it, removed from it: to be on the edge, to take a walk like Virginia Woolf (never again will I say, "*I am this, I am that*").[2]

Problems of peopling in the unconscious: all that passes through the pores of the schizo, the veins of the drug addict, swarming, teeming, ferment, intensities, races and tribes. This tale of white skin prickling with bumps and pustules, and of dwarfish black heads emerging from pores grimacing and abominable, needing to be shaved off every morning—is it a tale by Jean Ray, who knew how to bring terror to phenomena of micromultiplicity? And how about the "Lilliputian hallucinations" on ether? One schizo, two schizos, three: "There are babies growing in my every pore"—"With me, it's not in the pores, it's in my veins, little iron rods growing in my veins"—"I don't want them to give me any shots, except with camphorated alcohol. Otherwise breasts grow in my every pore." Freud tried to approach crowd phenomena from the point of view of the unconscious, but he did not see clearly, he did not see that the unconscious itself was fundamentally a crowd. He was myopic and hard of hearing; he mistook crowds for a single person. Schizos, on the other hand, have sharp eyes and ears. They don't mistake the buzz and shove of the crowd for daddy's voice. Once Jung had a dream about bones and skulls. A bone or a skull is never alone. Bones are a multiplicity. But Freud wants the dream to signify the death of *someone*. "Jung was surprised and pointed out that there were several skulls, not just one. Yet Freud still . . ."[3]

A multiplicity of pores, or blackheads, of little scars or stitches. Breasts, babies, and rods. A multiplicity of bees, soccer players, or Tuareg. A multiplicity of wolves or jackals . . . All of these things are irreducible but bring us to a certain status of the formations of the unconscious. Let us try to define the factors involved: first, something plays the role of the full body—the body without organs. In the preceding dream it was the desert. In the Wolf-Man's dream it is the denuded tree upon which the wolves are perched. It is also the skin as envelope or ring, and the sock as reversible surface. It can be a house or part of a house, any number of things, anything. Whenever someone makes love, really makes love, that person constitutes a body without organs, alone and with the other person or people. A body without organs is not an empty body stripped of organs, but a body upon which that which serves as organs (wolves, wolf eyes, wolf jaws?) is distributed according to crowd phenomena, in Brownian motion, in the form of molecular multiplicities. The desert is populous. Thus the body without organs is opposed less to organs as such than to the organization of the organs insofar as it composes an organism. The body without organs is not a dead body but a living body all the more alive and teeming once it has blown apart the organism and its organization. Lice hopping on the beach. Skin colonies. The full body without organs is a body populated by multiplicities. The problem of the unconscious has most certainly nothing to do with generation but rather peopling, population. It is an affair of worldwide population on the full body of the earth, not organic familial generation. "I love to invent peoples, tribes, racial origins . . . I return from my tribes. As of today, I am the adoptive son of fifteen tribes, no more, no less. And they in turn are my adopted tribes, for I love each of them more than if I had been born into it." People say, After all, schizophrenics have a mother and a father, don't they? Sorry, no, none as such. They only have a desert with tribes inhabiting it, a full body clinging with multiplicities.

This brings us to the second factor, the nature of these multiplicities and their elements. RHIZOME. One of the essential characteristics of the dream of multiplicity is that each element ceaselessly varies and alters its distance in relation to the others. On the Wolf-Man's nose, the elements, determined as pores in the skin, little scars in the pores, little ruts in the scar tissue, ceaselessly dance, grow, and diminish. These variable distances are not extensive quantities divisible by each other; rather, each is indivisible, or "relatively indivisible," in other words, they are not divisible below or above a certain threshold, they cannot increase or diminish *without their elements changing in nature.* A swarm of bees: here they come as a rumble of soccer players in striped jerseys, or a band of Tuareg. Or: the wolf clan doubles up with a swarm of bees against the gang of Deulhs, under the direction of Mowgli, who runs on the edge (yes, Kipling understood the call of the wolves, their libidinal meaning, better than Freud; and in the Wolf-Man's case the story about wolves is followed by one about wasps and butterflies, we go from wolves to wasps). What is the significance of these indivisible distances that are ceaselessly transformed, and cannot be divided or transformed without their elements changing in nature each time? Is it not the intensive character of this kind of multiplicity's elements and the relations between them? Exactly like a speed or a temperature, which is not composed of other speeds and temperatures but rather is enveloped in or envelops others, each of which marks a change in nature. The metrical principle of these multiplicities is not to be found in a homogeneous milieu but resides elsewhere, in forces at work within them, in physical phenomena inhabiting them, precisely in the libido, which constitutes them from within, and in constituting them necessarily divides into distinct qualitative and variable flows. Freud himself recognizes the multiplicity of libidinal "currents" that coexist in the Wolf-Man. That makes it all the more surprising that he treats the multiplicities of the unconscious the way he does. For him, there will always be a reduction to the One: the little scars, the little holes, become subdivisions of the great scar or supreme hole named castration; the wolves become substitutes for a single Father who turns up everywhere, or wherever they put him. (As Ruth Mack Brunswick says, Let's go all the way, the wolves are "*all* the fathers and doctors" in the world; but the Wolf-Man thinks, "You trying to tell me my ass isn't a wolf?")

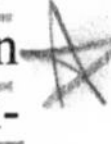

What should have been done is the opposite, all of this should be understood in intensity: the Wolf is the pack, in other words, the multiplicity instantaneously apprehended as such insofar as it approaches or moves away from zero, each distance being nondecomposable. Zero is the body without organs of the Wolf-Man. If the unconscious knows nothing of negation, it is because there is nothing negative in the unconscious, only indefinite moves toward and away from zero, which does not at all express lack but rather the positivity of the full body as support and prop ("for an afflux is necessary simply to signify the absence of intensity"). The wolves designate an intensity, a band of intensity, a threshold of intensity on the Wolf-Man's body without organs. A dentist told the Wolf-Man that he "would soon lose all his teeth because of the violence of his bite"—and that his gums were pocked with pustules and little holes.[4] Jaw as high intensity, teeth as low intensity, and pustular gums as approach to zero. The wolf, as the instantaneous apprehension of a multiplicity in a given region, is not a representative, a substitute, but an *I feel*. I feel myself becoming a wolf, one wolf among others, on the edge of the pack. A cry of anguish, the only one Freud hears: Help me not become wolf (or the opposite, Help me not fail in this becoming). It is not a question of representation: don't think for a minute that it has to do with believing oneself a wolf, representing oneself as a wolf. The wolf, wolves, are intensities, speeds, temperatures, nondecomposable variable distances. A swarming, a wolfing. Who could ever believe that the anal machine bears no relation to the wolf machine, or that the two are only linked by an Oedipal apparatus, by the all-too-human figure of the Father? For in the end the anus also expresses an intensity, in this case the approach to zero of a distance that cannot be decomposed without its elements changing in nature. *A field of anuses, just like a pack of wolves*. Does not the child, on the periphery, hold onto the wolves by his anus? The jaw descends to the anus. Hold onto those wolves by your jaw and your anus. The jaw is not a wolf jaw, it's not that simple; jaw and wolf form a multiplicity that is transformed into eye and wolf, anus and wolf, as a function of other distances, at other speeds, with other multiplicities, between thresholds. Lines of flight or of deterritorialization, becoming-wolf, becoming-inhuman, deterritorialized intensities: that is what multiplicity is. To become wolf or to become hole is to deterritorialize oneself following distinct but entangled lines. A hole is no more negative than a wolf. Castration, lack, substitution: a tale told by an overconscious idiot who has no understanding of multiplicities as formations of the unconscious. A wolf is a hole, they are both particles of the unconscious, nothing but particles, productions of particles, particulate paths, as elements of molecular multiplicities. It is not even sufficient to say that intense and moving particles pass through holes; a hole is just as much a particle as what passes through it. Physicists say that holes are not the absence of particles but particles traveling faster than the speed of light. Flying anuses, speeding vaginas, there is no castration.

Let us return to the story of *multiplicity*, for the creation of this substantive marks a very important moment. It was created precisely in order to escape the abstract opposition between the multiple and the one, to escape dialectics, to succeed in conceiving the multiple in the pure state, to cease treating it as a numerical fragment of a lost Unity or Totality or as the organic element of a Unity or Totality yet to come, and instead distinguish between different types of multiplicity. Thus we find in the work of the mathematician and physicist Riemann a distinction between discreet multiplicities and continuous multiplicities (the metrical principle of the second kind of multiplicity resides solely in forces at work within them). Then in Meinong and Russell we find a distinction between multiplicities of magnitude or divisibility, which are extensive, and multiplicities of distance, which are closer to the intensive. And in Bergson there is a distinction between numerical or extended multiplicities and qualitative or durational multiplicities. We are doing approximately the same thing when we distinguish between arborescent multiplicities and rhizomatic multiplicities. Between macro- and micromultiplicities. On the one hand, multiplicities that are extensive, divisible, and molar; unifiable, totalizable, organizable; conscious or preconscious—and on the other hand, libidinal, unconscious, molecular, intensive multiplicities composed of particles that do not divide without changing in nature, and distances that do not vary without entering another multiplicity and that constantly construct and dismantle themselves in the course of their communications, as they cross over into each other at, beyond, or before a certain threshold. The elements of this second kind of multiplicity are particles; their relations are distances; their movements are Brownian; their quantities are intensities, differences in intensity.

This only provides the logical foundation. Elias Canetti distinguishes between two types of multiplicity that are sometimes opposed but at other times interpenetrate: mass ("crowd") multiplicities and pack multiplicities. Among the characteristics of a mass, in Canetti's sense, we should note large quantity, divisibility and equality of the members, concentration, sociability of the aggregate as a whole, one-way hierarchy, organization of territoriality or territorialization, and emission of signs. Among the characteristics of a pack are small or restricted numbers, dispersion, nondecomposable variable distances, qualitative metamorphoses, inequalities as remainders or crossings, impossibility of a fixed totalization or hierarchization, a Brownian variability in directions, lines of deterritorialization, and projection of particles.[5] Doubtless, there is no more equality or any less hierarchy in packs than in masses, but they are of a different kind. The leader of the pack or the band plays move by move, must wager everything every hand, whereas the group or mass leader consolidates or capitalizes on past gains. The pack, even on its own turf, is constituted by a line of flight or of deterritorialization that is a component part of it, and to which it accredits a high positive value, whereas masses only integrate these lines in order to segment them, obstruct them, ascribe them a negative sign. Canetti notes that in a pack each member is alone even in the company of others (for example, wolves on the hunt); each takes care of himself at the same time as participating in the band. "In the changing constellation of the pack, in its dances and expeditions, he will again and again find himself at its edge. He may be in the center, and then, immediately afterwards, at the edge again; at the edge and then back in the center. When the pack forms a ring around the fire, each man will have neighbors to the right and left, but no one behind him; his back is naked and exposed to the wilderness."[6] We recognize this as the schizo position, being on the periphery, holding on by a hand or a foot . . . As opposed to the paranoid position of the mass subject, with all the identifications of the individual with the group, the group with the leader, and the leader with the group; be securely embedded in the mass, get close to the center, never be at the edge except in the line of duty. Why assume (as does Konrad Lorenz, for example) that bands and their type of companionship represent a more rudimentary evolutionary state than group societies or societies of conjugality? Not only do there exist bands of humans, but there are particularly refined examples: "high-society life" differs from "sociality" in that it is closer to the pack. Social persons have a certain envious and erroneous image of the high-society person because they are ignorant of high-society positions and hierarchies, the relations of force, the very particular ambitions and projects. High-society relations are never coextensive with social relations, they do not coincide. Even "mannerisms" (all bands have them) are specific to micromultiplicities and distinct from social manners or customs.

There is no question, however, of establishing a dualist opposition between the two types of multiplicities, molecular machines and molar machines; that would be no better than the dualism between the One and the multiple. There are only multiplicities of multiplicities forming a single *assemblage*, operating in the same *assemblage*: packs in masses and masses in packs. Trees have rhizome lines, and the rhizome points of arborescence. How could mad particles be produced with anything but a gigantic cyclotron? How could lines of deterritorialization be assignable outside of circuits of territoriality? Where else but in wide expanses, and in major upheavals in those expanses, could a tiny rivulet of new intensity suddenly start to flow? What do you not have to do in order to produce a new sound? Becoming-animal, becoming-molecular, becoming-inhuman, each involves a molar extension, a human hyperconcentration, or prepares the way for them. In Kafka, it is impossible to separate the erection of a great paranoid bureaucratic machine from the installation of little schizo machines of becoming-dog or becoming-beetle. In the case of the Wolf-Man, it is impossible to separate the becoming-wolf of his dream from the military and religious organization of his obsessions. A military man does a wolf; a military man does a dog. There are not two multiplicities or two machines; one and the same machinic assemblage produces and distributes the whole, in other words, the set of statements corresponding to the "complex." What does psychoanalysis have to say about all of this? Oedipus, nothing but Oedipus, because it hears nothing and listens to nobody. It flattens everything, masses and packs, molecular and molar machines, multiplicities of every variety. Take the Wolf-Man's second dream during his so-called psychotic episode: in the street, a wall with a closed door, to the left an empty dresser; in front of the dresser, the patient, and a big woman with a little scar who seems to want to skirt around the wall; behind the wall, wolves, rushing for the door. Even Brunswick can't go wrong: although she recognizes herself in the big woman, she does see that this time the wolves are Bolsheviks, the revolutionary mass that had emptied the dresser and confiscated the Wolf-Man's fortune. *The wolves, in a metastable state, have gone over to a large-scale social machine*. But psychoanalysis has nothing to say about all of these points—except what Freud already said: it all leads back to daddy (what do you know, he was one of the leaders of the liberal party in Russia, but that's hardly important; all that needs to be said is that the revolution "assuaged the patient's feelings of guilt"). You'd think that the investments and counterinvestments of the libido had nothing to do with mass disturbances, pack movements, collective signs, and particles of desire.

Thus it does not suffice to attribute molar multiplicities and mass machines to the preconscious, reserving another kind of machine or multiplicity for the unconscious. For it is the assemblage of both of these that is the province of the unconscious, the way in which the former condition the latter, and the latter prepare the way for the former, or elude them or return to them: the libido suffuses everything. Keep everything in sight at the same time—that a social machine or an organized mass has a molecular unconscious that marks not only its tendency to decompose but also the current components of its very operation and organization; that any individual caught up in a mass has his/her own pack unconscious, which does not necessarily resemble the packs of the mass to which that individual belongs; that an individual or mass will live out in its unconscious the masses and packs of another mass or another individual. What does it mean to love somebody? It is always to seize that person in a mass, extract him or her from a group, however small, in which he or she participates, whether it be through the family only or through something else; then to find that person's own packs, the multiplicities he or she encloses within himself or herself which may be of an entirely different nature. To join them to mine, to make them penetrate mine, and for me to penetrate the other person's. Heavenly nuptials, multiplicities of multiplicities. Every love is an exercise in depersonalization on a body without organs yet to be formed, and it is at the highest point of this depersonalization that someone can be *named*, receives his or her family name or first name, acquires the most intense discernibility in the instantaneous apprehension of the multiplicities belonging to him or her, and to which he or she belongs. A pack of freckles on a face, a pack of boys speaking through the voice of a woman, a clutch of girls in Charlus's voice, a horde of wolves in somebody's throat, a multiplicity of anuses in the anus, mouth, or eye one is intent upon. We each go through so many bodies in each other. Albertine is slowly extracted from a group of girls with its own number, organization, code, and hierarchy; and not only is this group or restricted mass suffused by an unconscious, but Albertine has her own multiplicities that the narrator, once he has isolated her, discovers on her body and in her lies—until the end of their love returns her to the indiscernible.

Above all, it should not be thought that it suffices to distinguish the masses and exterior groups someone belongs to or participates in from the internal aggregates that person envelops in himself or herself. The distinction to be made is not at all between exterior and interior, which are always relative, changing, and reversible, but between different types of multiplicities that coexist, interpenetrate, and change places—machines, cogs, motors, and elements that are set in motion at a given moment, forming an assemblage productive of statements: "I love you" (or whatever). For Kafka, Felice is inseparable from a certain social machine, and, as a representative of the firm that manufactures them, from parlograph machines; how could she not belong to that organization in the eyes of Kafka, a man fascinated by commerce and bureaucracy? But at the same time, Felice's teeth, her big carnivorous teeth, send her racing down other lines, into the molecular multiplicities of a becoming-dog, a becoming-jackal . . . Felice is inseparable from the sign of the modern social machines belonging to her, from those belonging to Kafka (not the same ones), and from the particles, the little molecular machines, the whole strange becoming or journey Kafka will make and have her make through his perverse writing apparatus.

There are no individual statements, only statement-producing machinic assemblages. We say that the assemblage is fundamentally libidinal and unconscious. It is the unconscious in person. For the moment, we will note that assemblages have elements (or multiplicities) of several kinds: human, social, and technical machines, organized molar machines; molecular machines with their particles of becoming-inhuman; Oedipal apparatuses (*yes, of course there are Oedipal statements, many of them*); and counter-Oedipal apparatuses, variable in aspect and functioning. We will go into it later. We can no longer even speak of distinct machines, only of types of interpenetrating multiplicities that at any given moment form a single machinic assemblage, the faceless figure of the libido. Each of us is caught up in an assemblage of this kind, and we reproduce its statements when we think we are speaking in our own name; or rather we speak in our own name when we produce its statement. And what bizarre statements they are; truly, the talk of lunatics. We mentioned Kafka, but we could just

as well have said the Wolf-Man: a religious-military machine that Freud attributes to obsessional neurosis; an anal pack machine, an anal becoming-wolf or -wasp or -butterfly machine, which Freud attributes to the hysteric character; an Oedipal apparatus, which Freud considers the sole motor, the immobile motor that must be found everywhere; and a counter-Oedipal apparatus—incest with the sister, schizo-incest, or love with "people of inferior station"; and anality, homosexuality?—all that Freud sees only as Oedipal substitutes, regressions, and derivatives. In truth, Freud sees nothing and understands nothing. He has no idea what a libidinal assemblage is, with all the machineries it brings into play, all the multiple loves.

Of course, there are Oedipal statements. For example, Kafka's story, "Jackals and Arabs," is easy to read in that way: you can always do it, you can't lose, it works every time, even if you understand nothing. The Arabs are clearly associated with the father and the jackals with the mother; between the two, there is a whole story of castration represented by the rusty scissors. But it so happens that the Arabs are an extensive, armed, organized mass stretching across the entire desert; and the jackals are an intense pack forever launching into the desert following lines of flight or deterritorialization ("they are madmen, veritable madmen"); between the two, at the edge, the Man of the North, the jackal-man. And aren't those big scissors the Arab sign that guides or releases jackal-particles, both to accelerate their mad race by detaching them from the mass and to bring them back to the mass, to tame them and whip them, to bring them around? Dead camel: Oedipal food apparatus. Counter-Oedipal carrion apparatus: kill animals to eat, or eat to clean up carrion. The jackals formulate the problem well: it is not that of castration but of "cleanliness" (*propreté*, also "ownness"), the test of desert-desire. Which will prevail, mass territoriality or pack deterritorialization? The libido suffuses the entire desert, the body without organs on which the drama is played out.

There are no individual statements, there never are. Every statement is the product of a machinic assemblage, in other words, of collective agents of enunciation (take "collective agents" to mean not peoples or societies but multiplicities). The proper name (*nom propre*) does not designate an individual: it is on the contrary when the individual opens up to the multiplicities pervading him or her, at the outcome of the most severe operation of depersonalization, that he or she acquires his or her true proper name. The proper name is the instantaneous apprehension of a multiplicity. The proper name is the subject of a pure infinitive comprehended as such in a field of intensity. What Proust said about the first name: when I said Gilberte's name, I had the impression that I was holding her entire body naked in my mouth. The Wolf-Man, a true proper name, an intimate first name linked to the becomings, infinitives, and intensities of a multiplied and depersonalized individual. What does psychoanalysis know about multiplication? The desert hour when the dromedary becomes a thousand dromedaries snickering in the sky. The evening hour when a thousand holes appear on the surface of the earth. Castration! Castration! cries the psychoanalytic scarecrow, who never saw more than a hole, a father or a dog where wolves are, a domesticated individual where there are wild multiplicities. We are not just criticizing psychoanalysis for having selected Oedipal statements exclusively. For such statements are to a certain extent part of a machinic assemblage, for which they could serve as correctional indexes, as in a calculation of errors. We are criticizing psychoanalysis for having used Oedipal enunciation to make patients believe they would produce individual, personal statements, and would finally speak in their own name. The trap was set from the start: never will the Wolf-Man speak. Talk as he might about wolves, howl as he might like a wolf, Freud does not even listen; he glances at his dog and answers, "It's daddy." For as long as that lasts, Freud calls it neurosis; when it cracks, it's psychosis. The Wolf-Man will receive the psychoanalytic medal of honor for services rendered to the cause, and even disabled veterans' benefits. He could have spoken in his own name only if the machinic assemblage that was producing particular statements in him had been brought to light. But there is no question of that in psychoanalysis: at the very moment the subject is persuaded that he or she will be uttering the most individual of statements, he or she is deprived of all basis for enunciation. Silence people, prevent them from speaking, and above all, when they do speak, pretend they haven't said a thing: the famous psychoanalytic neutrality. The Wolf-Man keeps howling: Six wolves! Seven wolves! Freud says, How's that? Goats, you say? How interesting. Take away the goats and all you have left is a wolf, so it's your father . . . That is why the Wolf-Man feels so fatigued: he's left lying there with all his wolves in his throat, all those little holes on his nose, and all those libidinal values on his body without organs. The war will come, the wolves will become Bolsheviks, and the Wolf-Man will remain suffocated by all he had to say. All we will be told is that he became well behaved, polite, and resigned again, "honest and scrupulous." In short, cured. He gets back by pointing out that psychoanalysis lacks a truly zoological vision: "Nothing can be more valuable for a young person than the love of nature and a comprehension of the natural sciences, in particular zoology."[7]

3. 10,000 B.C.: The Geology of Morals (Who Does the Earth Think It Is?)

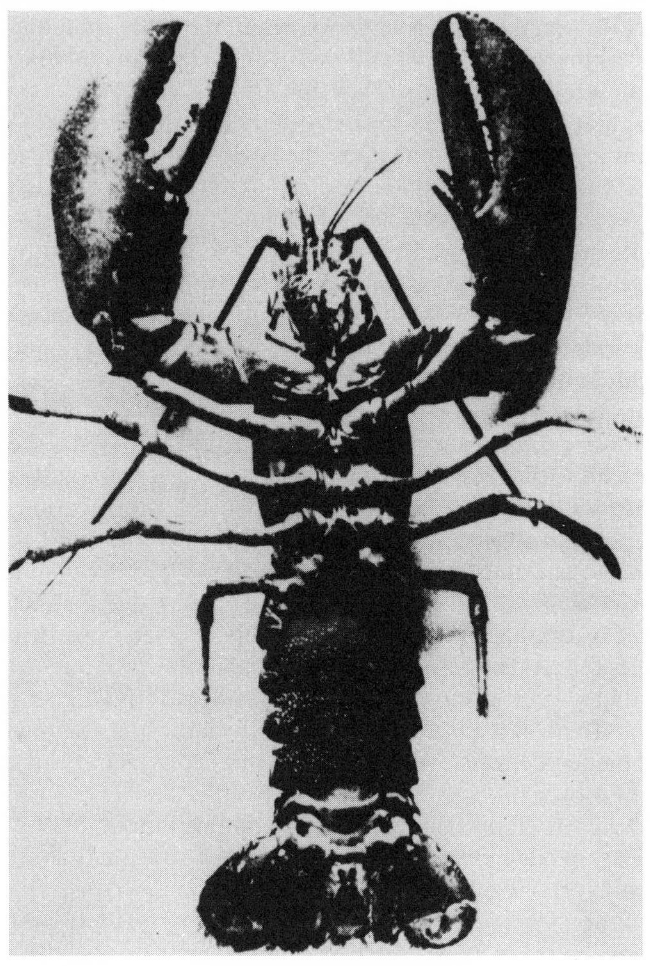

Double Articulation

The same Professor Challenger who made the Earth scream with his pain machine, as described by Arthur Conan Doyle, gave a lecture after mixing several textbooks on geology and biology in a fashion befitting his simian disposition. He explained that the Earth—the Deterritorialized, the Glacial, the giant Molecule—is a body without organs. This body without organs is permeated by unformed, unstable matters, by flows in all directions, by free intensities or nomadic singularities, by mad or transitory particles. That, however, was not the question at hand. For there simultaneously occurs upon the earth a very important, inevitable phenomenon that is beneficial in many respects and unfortunate in many others: stratification. Strata are Layers, Belts. They consist of giving form to matters, of imprisoning intensities or locking singularities into systems of resonance and redundancy, of producing upon the body of the earth molecules large and small and organizing them into molar aggregates. Strata are acts of capture, they are like "black holes" or occlusions striving to seize whatever comes within their reach.[1] They operate by coding and territorialization upon the earth; they proceed simultaneously by code and by territoriality. The strata are judgments of God; stratification in general is the entire system of the judgment of God (but the earth, or the body without organs, constantly eludes that judgment, flees and becomes destratified, decoded, deterritorialized).

Challenger quoted a sentence he said he came across in a geology textbook. He said we needed to learn it by heart because we would only be in a position to understand it later on: "A surface of stratification is a more compact plane of consistency lying between two layers." The layers are the strata. They come at least in pairs, one serving as *substratum* for the other. The surface of stratification is a machinic assemblage distinct from the strata. The assemblage is between two layers, between two strata; on one side it faces the strata (in this direction, the assemblage is an *interstratum*), but the other side faces something else, the body without organs or plane of consistency (here, it is a *metastratum*). In effect, the body without organs is itself the plane of consistency, which becomes compact or thickens at the level of the strata.

God is a Lobster, or a double pincer, a double bind. Not only do strata come at least in pairs, but in a different way each stratum is double (it itself has several layers). Each stratum exhibits phenomena constitutive of *double articulation*. Articulate twice, B-A, BA. This is not at all to say that the strata speak or are language based. Double articulation is so extremely variable that we cannot begin with a general model, only a relatively simple case. The first articulation chooses or deducts, from unstable particle-flows, metastable molecular or quasi-molecular units (*substances*) upon which it imposes a statistical order of connections and successions (*forms*).

The second articulation establishes functional, compact, stable structures (*forms*), and constructs the molar compounds in which these structures are simultaneously actualized (*substances*). In a geological stratum, for example, the first articulation is the process of "sedimentation," which deposits units of cyclic sediment according to a statistical order: flysch, with its succession of sandstone and schist. The second articulation is the "folding" that sets up a stable functional structure and effects the passage from sediment to sedimentary rock.

It is clear that the distinction between the two articulations is not between substances and forms. Substances are nothing other than formed matters. Forms imply a code, modes of coding and decoding. Substances as formed matters refer to territorialities and degrees of territorialization and deterritorialization. But each articulation has a code *and* a territoriality; therefore each possesses both form and substance. For now, all we can say is that each articulation has a corresponding type of segmentarity or multiplicity: one type is supple, more molecular, and merely ordered; the other is more rigid, molar, and organized. Although the first articulation is not lacking in systematic interactions, it is in the second articulation in particular that phenomena constituting an overcoding are produced, phenomena of centering, unification, totalization, integration, hierarchization, and finalization. Both articulations establish binary relations between their respective segments. But between the segments of one articulation and the segments of the other there are biunivocal relationships obeying far more complex laws. The word "structure" may be used to designate the sum of these relations and relationships, but it is an illusion to believe that structure is the earth's last word. Moreover, it cannot be taken for granted that the distinction between the two articulations is always that of the molecular and the molar.

He skipped over the immense diversity of the energetic, physicochemical, and geological strata. He went straight to the organic strata, or the existence of a great organic stratification. The problem of the organism—*how to "make" the body an organism*—is once again a problem of articulation, of the articulatory relation. The Dogons, well known to the professor, formulate the problem as follows: an organism befalls the body of the smith, by virtue of a machine or machinic assemblage that stratifies it. "The shock of the hammer and the anvil broke his arms and legs at the elbows and knees, which until that moment he had not possessed. In this way, he received the articulations specific to the new human form that was to spread across the earth, a form dedicated to work. . . . His arm became folded with a view to work."[2] It is obviously only a manner of speaking to limit the articulatory relation to the bones. The entire organism must be considered in relation to a double articulation, and on different levels.

First, on the level of morphogenesis: on the one hand, realities of the molecular type with aleatory relations are caught up in crowd phenomena or statistical aggregates determining an order (the protein fiber and its sequence or segmentarity); on the other hand, these aggregates themselves are taken up into stable structures that "elect" stereoscopic compounds, form organs, functions, and regulations, organize molar mechanisms, and even distribute centers capable of overflying crowds, overseeing mechanisms, utilizing and repairing tools, "overcoding" the aggregate (the folding back on itself of the fiber to form a compact structure; a second kind of segmentarity).[3] Sedimentation and folding, fiber and infolding.

On a different level, the cellular chemistry presiding over the constitution of proteins also operates by double articulation. This double articulation is internal to the molecular, it is the articulation between small and large molecules, a segmentarity by successive modifications and polymerization. "First, the elements taken from the medium are combined through a series of transformations. . . . All this activity involves hundreds of chemical reactions. But ultimately, it produces a limited number of small compounds, a few dozen at most. In the second stage of cellular chemistry, the small molecules are assembled to produce larger ones. It is the polymerization of units linked end-to-end that forms the characteristic chains of macromolecules. . . . The two stages of cellular chemistry, therefore, differ in their function, products and nature. The first carves out chemical motifs; the second assembles them. The first forms compounds that exist only temporarily, for they are intermediaries on the path of biosynthesis; the second constructs stable products. The first operates by a series of different reactions; the second by repeating the same reaction."[4] There is, moreover, a third level, upon which cellular chemistry itself depends. It is the genetic code, which is in turn inseparable from a double segmentarity or a double articulation, this time between two types of independent molecules: the sequence of protein units and the sequence of nucleic units, with binary relations between units of the same type and biunivocal relationships between units of different types. Thus there are always two articulations, two segmentarities, two kinds of multiplicity, each of which brings into play both forms and substances. But the distribution of these two articulations is not constant, even within the same stratum.

The audience rather sulkily denounced the numerous misunderstandings, misinterpretations, and even misappropriations in the professor's presentation, despite the authorities he had appealed to, calling them his "friends." Even the Dogons . . . And things would presently get worse. The professor cynically congratulated himself on taking his pleasure from behind, but the offspring always turned out to be runts and wens, bits and pieces, if not stupid vulgarizations. Besides, the professor was not a geologist or a biologist, he was not even a linguist, ethnologist, or psychoanalyst; what his specialty had been was long since forgotten. In fact, Professor Challenger was double, articulated twice, and that did not make things any easier; people never knew which of him was present. He (?) claimed to have invented a discipline he referred to by various names: rhizomatics, stratoanalysis, schizoanalysis, nomadology, micropolitics, pragmatics, the science of multiplicities. Yet no one clearly understood what the goals, method, or principles of this discipline were. Young Professor Alasca, Challenger's pet student, tried hypocritically to defend him by explaining that on a given stratum the passage from one articulation to the other was easily verified because it was always accompanied by a loss of water, in genetics as in geology, and even in linguistics, where the importance of the "lost saliva" phenomenon is measured. Challenger took offense, preferring to cite his friend, as he called him, the Danish Spinozist geologist, Hjelmslev, that dark prince descended from Hamlet who also made language his concern, precisely in order to analyze its "stratification." Hjelmslev was able to weave a net out of the notions of *matter, content* and *expression, form* and *substance*. These were the strata, said Hjelmslev. Now this net had the advantage of breaking with the form-content duality, since there was a form of content no less than a form of expression. Hjelmslev's enemies saw this merely as a way of rebaptizing the discredited notions of the signified and signifier, but something quite different was actually going on. Despite what Hjelmslev himself may have said, the net is not linguistic in scope or origin (the same must be said of double articulation: if language has a specificity of its own, as it most certainly does, that specificity consists neither in double articulation nor in Hjelmslev's net, which are general characteristics of strata).

He used the term *matter* for the plane of consistency or Body without Organs, in other words, the unformed, unorganized, nonstratified, or destratified body and all its flows: subatomic and submolecular particles, pure intensities, prevital and prephysical free singularities. He used the term *content* for formed matters, which would now have to be considered from two points of view: substance, insofar as these matters are "chosen," and form, insofar as they are chosen in a certain order (*substance and form of content*). He used the term *expression* for functional structures, which would also have to be considered from two points of view: the organization of their own specific form, and substances insofar as they form compounds (*form and content of expression*). A stratum always has a dimension of the expressible or of expression serving as the basis for a relative invariance; for example, nucleic sequences are inseparable from a relatively invariant expression by means of which they determine the compounds, organs, and functions of the organism.[5] To express is always to sing the glory of God.

Every stratum is a judgment of God; not only do plants and animals, orchids and wasps, sing or express themselves, but so do rocks and even rivers, every stratified thing on earth. *The first articulation concerns content, the second expression.* The distinction between the two articulations is not between forms and substances but between content and expression, expression having just as much substance as content and content just as much form as expression. The double articulation sometimes coincides with the molecular and the molar, and sometimes not; this is because content and expression are sometimes divided along those lines and sometimes along different lines. There is never correspondence or conformity between content and expression, only isomorphism with reciprocal presupposition. The distinction between content and expression is *always real,* in various ways, but it cannot be said that the terms preexist their double articulation. It is the double articulation that distributes them according to the line it draws in each stratum; it is what constitutes their real distinction. (On the other hand, there is no real distinction between form and substance, only a mental or modal distinction: since substances are nothing other than formed matters, formless substances are inconceivable, although it is possible in certain instances to conceive of substanceless forms.)

Even though there is a real distinction between them, content and expression are relative terms ("first" and "second" articulation should also be understood in an entirely relative fashion). Even though it is capable of invariance, expression is just as much a variable as content. Content and expression are two variables of a function of stratification. They not only vary from one stratum to another, but intermingle, and within the same stratum multiply and divide ad infinitum. Since every articulation is double, there is not an articulation of content *and* an articulation of expression—the articulation of content is double in its own right and constitutes a relative expression within content; the articulation of expression is also double and constitutes a relative content within expression. For this reason, there exist *intermediate states* between content and expression, expression and content: the levels, equilibriums, and exchanges through which a stratified system passes. In short, we find forms and substances of content that play the role of expression in relation to other forms and substances, and conversely for expression. These new distinctions do not, therefore, coincide with the distinction between forms and substances within each articulation; instead, they show that each articulation is already, or still, double. This can be seen on the organic stratum: proteins of content have two forms, one of which (the infolded fiber) plays the role of functional expression in relation to the other. The same goes for the nucleic acids of expression: double articulations cause certain formal and substantial elements to play the role of content in relation to others; not only does the half of the chain that is reproduced become a content, but the reconstituted chain itself becomes a content in relation to the "messenger." There are double pincers everywhere on a stratum; everywhere and in all directions there are double binds and lobsters, a multiplicity of double articulations affecting both expression and content. Through all of this, Hjelmslev's warning should not be forgotten: "The terms expression plane and content plane . . . are chosen in conformity with established notions and are quite arbitrary. Their functional definition provides no justification for calling one, and not the other, of these entities *expression*, or one, and not the other, *content*. They are defined only by their mutual solidarity, and neither of them can be identified otherwise. They are defined only oppositively and relatively, as mutually opposed functives of one and the same function."[6] We must combine all the resources of real distinction, reciprocal presupposition, and general relativism.

The question we must ask is what on a given stratum varies and what does not. What accounts for the unity and diversity of a stratum? Matter, the pure matter of the plane of consistency (or inconsistency) lies outside the strata. The molecular materials borrowed from the substrata may be the same throughout a stratum, but that does not mean that the molecules will be the same. The substantial elements may be the same throughout the stratum without the substances being the same. The formal relations or bonds may be the same without the forms being the same. In biochemistry, there is a *unity of composition* of the organic stratum defined at the level of materials and energy, substantial elements or radicals, bonds and reactions. But there is a variety of different molecules, substances, and forms.

Should we not sing the praise of Geoffroy Saint-Hilaire? For in the nineteenth century he developed a grandiose conception of stratification. He said that matter, considered from the standpoint of its greatest divisibility, consists in particles of decreasing size, flows or elastic fluids that "deploy themselves" by radiating through space. Combustion is the process of this escape or infinite division on the plane of consistency. Electrification is the opposite process, constitutive of strata; it is the process whereby similar particles group together to form atoms and molecules, similar molecules to form bigger molecules, and the biggest molecules to form molar aggregates: "the attraction of like by like," as in a double pincer or double articulation. Thus there is no vital matter specific to the organic stratum, matter is the same on all the strata. But the organic stratum does have a specific unity of composition, a single abstract Animal, a single machine embedded in the stratum, and presents everywhere the same molecular materials, the same elements or anatomical components of organs, the same formal connections. Organic forms are nevertheless different from one another, as are organs, compound substances, and molecules. It is of little or no importance that Geoffroy chose anatomical elements as the substantial units rather than protein and nucleic acid radicals. At any rate, he already invoked a whole interplay of molecules. The important thing is the principle of the simultaneous unity and variety of the stratum: isomorphism of forms but no correspondence; identity of elements or components but no identity of compound substances.

This is where the dialogue, or rather violent debate, with Cuvier came in. To keep the last of the audience from leaving, Challenger imagined a particularly epistemological dialogue of the dead, in puppet theater style. Geoffroy called forth Monsters, Cuvier laid out all the Fossils in order, Baer flourished flasks filled with embryos, Vialleton put on a tetrapod's belt, Perrier mimed the dramatic battle between the Mouth and the Brain, and so on. *Geoffroy*: The proof that there is isomorphism is that you can always get from one form on the organic stratum to another, however different they may be, by means of "folding." To go from the Vertebrate to the Cephalopod, bring the two sides of the Vertebrate's backbone together, bend its head down to its feet and its pelvis up to the nape of its neck . . . *Cuvier* (angrily): That's just not true! You go from an Elephant to a Medusa; I know, I tried. There are irreducible axes, types, branches. There are resemblances between organs and analogies between forms, nothing more. You're a falsifier, a metaphysician. *Vialleton* (a disciple of Cuvier and Baer): Even if folding gave good results, who could endure it? It's not by chance that Geoffroy only considers anatomical elements. No muscle or ligament would survive it. *Geoffroy*: I said that there was isomorphism but not correspondence. You have to bring "degrees of development or perfection" into the picture. It is not everywhere on a stratum that materials reach the degree at which they form a given aggregate. Anatomical elements may be arrested or inhibited in certain places by molecular clashes, the influence of the milieu, or pressure from neighbors to such an extent that they compose different organs. The same formal relations or connections are then effectuated in entirely different forms and arrangements. It is still the same abstract Animal that is realized throughout the stratum, only to varying degrees, in varying modes. Each time, it is as perfect as its surroundings or milieu allows it to be (it is obviously not yet a question of evolution: neither folding nor degrees imply descent or derivation, only autonomous realizations of the same abstract relations). This is where Geoffroy invoked Monsters: human monsters are embryos that were retarded at a certain degree of development, the human in them is only a straitjacket for inhuman forms and substances. Yes, the Heteradelph is a crustacean. *Baer* (an ally of Cuvier and contemporary of Darwin, about whom he had reservations, in addition to being an enemy of Geoffroy): That's not true, you can't confuse degrees of development with types of forms. A single type has several degrees, a single degree is found in several types, but never will you make types out of degrees. An embryo of one type cannot display another type; at most, it can be of the same degree as an embryo of the second type. *Vialleton* (a disciple of Baer's who took both Darwin and Geoffroy one further): And then there are things that only an embryo can do or endure. It can do or endure these things precisely because of its type, not because it can go from one type to another according to degrees of development. Admire the Tortoise. Its neck requires that a certain number of protovertebrae change position, and its front limbs must slide 180 degrees in relation to that of a bird. You can never draw conclusions about phylogenesis on the basis of embryogenesis. Folding does not make it possible to go from one type to another; quite the contrary, the types testify to the irreducibility of the forms of folding . . . (Thus Vialleton presented two kinds of interconnected arguments in the service of the same cause, saying first that there are things no animal can do by reason of its substance, and then that there are things that only an embryo can do by reason of its form. Two strong arguments.)[7]

We're a little lost now. There is so much going on in these retorts. So many endlessly proliferating distinctions. So much getting even, for epistemology is not innocent. The sweet and subtle Geoffroy and the violent and serious Cuvier do battle around Napoleon. Cuvier, the rigid specialist, is pitted against Geoffroy, always ready to switch specialities. Cuvier hates Geoffroy, he can't stomach Geoffroy's lighthearted formulas, his humor (yes, Hens do indeed have teeth, the Lobster has skin on its bones, etc.). Cuvier is a man of Power and Terrain, and he won't let Geoffroy forget it; Geoffroy, on the other hand, prefigures the nomadic man of speed. Cuvier reflects a Euclidean space, whereas Geoffroy thinks topologically. Today let us invoke the folds of the cortex with all their paradoxes. Strata are topological, and Geoffroy is a great artist of the fold, a formidable artist; as such, he already has a presentiment of a certain kind of animal rhizome with aberrant paths of communication—Monsters. Cuvier reacts in terms of discontinuous photographs, and casts of fossils. But we're a little lost, because distinctions have proliferated in all directions.

We have not even taken Darwin, evolutionism, or neoevolutionism into account yet. This, however, is where a decisive phenomenon occurs: our puppet theater becomes more and more nebulous, in other words, collective and differential. Earlier, we invoked two factors, and their uncertain relations, in order to explain the diversity within a stratum—degrees of development or perfection and types of forms. They now undergo a profound transformation. There is a double tendency for types of forms to be understood increasingly in terms of populations, packs and colonies, collectivities or multiplicities; and degrees of development in terms of speeds, rates, coefficients, and differential relations. A double deepening. This, Darwinism's fundamental contribution, implies a new coupling of individuals and milieus on the stratum.[8]

First, if we assume the presence of an elementary or even molecular population in a given milieu, the forms do not preexist the population, they are more like statistical results. The more a population assumes divergent forms, the more its multiplicity divides into multiplicities of different nature, the more its elements form distinct compounds or matters—the more efficiently it distributes itself in the milieu, or divides up the milieu. Thus the relationship between embryogenesis and phylogenesis is reversed: the embryo does not testify to an absolute form preestablished in a closed milieu; rather, the phylogenesis of populations has at its disposal, in an open milieu, an entire range of relative forms to choose from, none of which is preestablished. In embryogenesis, "It is possible to tell from the parents, anticipating the outcome of the process, whether a pigeon or a wolf is developing. . . . But here the points of reference themselves are in motion: there are only fixed points for convenience of expression. At the level of universal evolution, it is impossible to discern that kind of reference point. . . . Life on earth appears as a sum of relatively independent species of flora and fauna with sometimes shifting or porous boundaries between them. Geographical areas can only harbor a sort of chaos, or, at best, extrinsic harmonies of an ecological order, temporary equilibriums between populations."[9]

Second, simultaneously and under the same conditions, the degrees are not degrees of preexistent development or perfection but are instead global and relative equilibriums: they enter into play as a function of the advantage they give particular elements, then a particular multiplicity in the milieu, and as a function of a particular variation in the milieu. Degrees are no longer measured in terms of increasing perfection or a differentiation and increase in the complexity of the parts, but in terms of differential relations and coefficients such as selective pressure, catalytic action, speed of propagation, rate of growth, evolution, mutation, etc. Relative progress, then, can occur by formal and quantitative simplification rather than by complication, by a loss of components and syntheses rather than by acquisition (it is a question of speed, and speed is a differential). It is through populations that one is formed, assumes forms, and through loss that one progresses and picks up speed. Darwinism's two fundamental contributions move in the direction of a science of multiplicities: the substitution of populations for types, and the substitution of rates or differential relations for degrees.[10] These are nomadic contributions with shifting boundaries determined by populations or variations of multiplicities, and with differential coefficients or variations of relations. Contemporary biochemistry, or "molecular Darwinism" as Monod calls it, confirms, on the level of a single statistical and global individual, or a simple sample, the decisive importance of molecular populations and microbiological rates (for example, the endlessness of the sequence composing a chain, and the chance variation of a single segment in the sequence).

Challenger admitted having digressed at length but added that there was no possible way to distinguish between the digressive and the nondigressive. The point was to arrive at several conclusions concerning the unity and diversity of a single stratum, in this case the organic stratum.

To begin with, a stratum does indeed have a unity of composition, which is what allows it to be called *a* stratum: molecular materials, substantial elements, and formal relations or traits. Materials are not the same as the unformed matter of the plane of consistency; they are already stratified, and come from "substrata." But of course substrata should not be thought of only as substrata: in particular, their organization is no less complex than, nor is it inferior to, that of the strata; we should be on our guard against any kind of ridiculous cosmic evolutionism. The materials furnished by a substratum are no doubt simpler than the compounds of a stratum, but their level of organization in the substratum is no lower than that of the stratum itself. The difference between materials and substantial elements is one of organization; there is a change in organization, not an augmentation. The materials furnished by the substratum constitute an *exterior milieu* for the elements and compounds of the stratum under consideration, but they are not exterior *to* the stratum. The elements and compounds constitute an interior of the stratum, just as the materials constitute an exterior *of* the stratum; both belong to the stratum, the latter because they are materials that have been furnished to the stratum and selected for it, the former because they are formed from the materials. Once again, this exterior and interior are relative; they exist only through their exchanges and therefore only by virtue of the stratum responsible for the relation between them. For example, on a crystalline stratum, the amorphous milieu, or medium, is exterior to the seed before the crystal has formed; the crystal forms by interiorizing and incorporating masses of amorphous material. Conversely, the interiority of the seed of the crystal must move out to the system's exterior, where the amorphous medium can crystallize (the aptitude to switch over to the other form of organization). To the point that the seed itself comes from the outside. In short, both exterior and interior are interior to the stratum. The same applies to the organic stratum: the materials furnished by the substrata are an exterior medium constituting the famous prebiotic soup, and catalysts play the role of seed in the formation of interior substantial elements or even compounds. These elements and compounds both appropriate materials and exteriorize themselves through replication, even in the conditions of the primordial soup itself. Once again, interior and exterior exchange places, and both are interior to the organic stratum. The limit between them is the membrane that regulates the exchanges and transformation in organization (in other words, the distributions interior to the stratum) and that defines all of the stratum's formal relations or traits (even though the situation and role of the limit vary widely depending on the stratum, for example, the limit of the crystal as compared to the cellular membrane). We may therefore use the term central layer, or central ring, for the following aggregate comprising the unity of composition of a stratum: exterior molecular materials, interior substantial elements, and the limit or membrane conveying the formal relations. There is a single *abstract machine* that is enveloped by the stratum and constitutes its unity. This is the Ecumenon, as opposed to the Planomenon of the plane of consistency.

It would be a mistake to believe that it is possible to isolate this unitary, central layer of the stratum, or to grasp it in itself, by regression. In the first place, a stratum necessarily goes from layer to layer, and from the very beginning. It already has several layers. It goes from a center to a periphery, at the same time as the periphery reacts back upon the center to form a new center in relation to a new periphery. Flows constantly radiate outward, then turn back. There is an outgrowth and multiplication of intermediate states, and this process is one of the local conditions of the central ring (different concentrations, variations that are tolerated below a certain threshold of identity). These intermediate states present new figures of milieus or materials, as well as of elements and compounds. They are intermediaries between the exterior milieu and the interior element, substantial elements and their compounds, compounds and substances, and between the different formed substances (substances of content and substances of expression). We will use the term *epistrata* for these intermediaries and superpositions, these outgrowths, these levels. Returning to our two examples, on the crystalline stratum there are many intermediaries between the exterior milieu or material and the interior seed: a multiplicity of perfectly discontinuous states of metastability constituting so many hierarchical degrees. Neither is the organic stratum separable from so-called interior milieus that are interior elements in relation to exterior materials but also exterior elements in relation to interior substances.[11] These internal organic milieus are known to regulate the degree of complexity or differentiation of the parts of an organism. A stratum, considered from the standpoint of its unity of composition, therefore exists only in its substantial epistrata, which shatter its continuity, fragment its ring, and break it down into gradations. The central ring does not exist independently of a periphery that forms a new center, reacts back upon the first center, and in turn gives forth discontinuous epistrata.

That is not all. In addition to this new or second-degree relativity of interior and exterior, there is a whole history on the level of the membrane or limit. To the extent that elements and compounds incorporate or appropriate materials, the corresponding organisms are forced to turn to other "more foreign and less convenient" materials that they take from still intact masses or other organisms. The milieu assumes a third figure here: it is no longer an interior or exterior milieu, even a relative one, nor an intermediate milieu, but instead an *annexed or associated milieu.* Associated milieus imply sources of energy different from alimentary materials. Before these sources are obtained, the organism can be said to nourish itself but not to breathe: it is in a state of suffocation.[12] Obtaining an energy source permits an increase in the number of materials that can be transformed into elements and compounds. The associated milieu is thus defined by the capture of energy sources (respiration in the most general sense), by the discernment of materials, the sensing of their presence or absence (perception), and by the fabrication or nonfabrication of the corresponding compounds (response, reaction). That there are molecular perceptions no less than molecular reactions can be seen in the economy of the cell and the property of regulatory agents to "recognize" only one or two kinds of chemicals in a very diverse milieu of exteriority. The development of the associated milieus culminates in the animal worlds described by von Uexküll, with all their active, perceptive, and energetic characteristics. The unforgettable associated world of the Tick, defined by its gravitational energy of falling, its olfactory characteristic of perceiving sweat, and its active characteristic of latching on: the tick climbs a branch and drops onto a passing mammal it has recognized by smell, then latches onto its skin (an associated world composed of three factors, and no more). Active and perceptive characteristics are themselves something of a double pincer, a double articulation.[13]

Here, the associated milieus are closely related to organic forms. An organic form is not a simple structure but a structuration, the constitution of an associated milieu. An animal milieu, such as the spider web, is no less "morphogenetic" than the form of the organism. One certainly cannot say that the milieu determines the form; but to complicate things, this does not make the relation between form and milieu any less decisive. Since the form depends on an autonomous code, it can only be constituted in an associated milieu that interlaces active, perceptive, and energetic characteristics in a complex fashion, in conformity with the code's requirements; and the form can develop only through intermediary milieus that regulate the speeds and rates of its substances; and it can experience itself only in a milieu of exteriority that measures the comparative advantages of the associated milieus and the differential relations of the intermediary milieus. Milieus always act, through selection, on entire organisms, the forms of which depend on codes those milieus sanction indirectly. Associated milieus divide a single milieu of exteriority among themselves as a function of different forms, just as intermediate milieus divide a milieu of exteriority among themselves as a function of the rates or degrees of a single form. But the dividing is done differently in the two cases. In relation to the central belt of the stratum, the intermediate strata or milieus constitute "epistrata" piled one atop the other, and form new centers for the new peripheries. We will apply the term "parastrata" to the second way in which the central belt fragments into sides and "besides," and the irreducible forms and milieus associated with them. This time, it is at the level of the limit or membrane of the central belt that the formal relations or traits common to all of the strata necessarily assume entirely different forms or types of forms corresponding to the parastrata. A stratum exists only in its epistrata and parastrata, so that in the final analysis these must be considered strata in their own right. The ideally continuous belt or ring of the stratum—the Ecumenon defined by the identity of molecular materials, substantial elements, and formal relations—exists only as shattered, fragmented into epistrata and parastrata that imply concrete machines and their respective indexes, and constitute different molecules, specific substances, and irreducible forms.[14]

We may now return to the two fundamental contributions of Darwinism and answer the question of why forms or types of forms in the parastrata must be understood in relation to populations, and degrees of development in the epistrata as rates or differential relations. First, parastrata envelop the very codes upon which the forms depend, and these codes necessarily apply to populations. There must already be an entire molecular population to be coded, and the effects of the code, or a change in the code, are evaluated in relation to a more or less molar population, depending on the code's ability to propagate in the milieu or create for itself a new associated milieu within which the modification will be popularizable. Yes, we must always think in terms of packs and multiplicities: a code does or does not take hold because the coded individual belongs to a certain population, "the population inhabiting test tubes, a flask full of water, or a mammal's intestine." What does it mean to say that new forms and associated milieus potentially result from a change in the code, a modification of the code, or a variation in the parastratum? The change is obviously not due to a passage from one preestablished form to another, in other words, a translation from one code to another. As long as the problem was formulated in that fashion, it remained insoluble, and one would have to agree with Cuvier and Baer that established types of forms are irreducible and therefore do not admit of translation or transformation. But as soon as it is recognized that a code is inseparable from a process of decoding that is inherent to it, the problem receives a new formulation. There is no genetics without "genetic drift." The modern theory of mutations has clearly demonstrated that a code, which necessarily relates to a population, has an essential margin of decoding: not only does every code have supplements capable of free variation, but a single segment may be copied twice, the second copy left free for variation. In addition, fragments of code may be transferred from the cells of one species to those of another, Man and Mouse, Monkey and Cat, by viruses or through other procedures. This involves not translation between codes (viruses are not translators) but a singular phenomenon we call surplus value of code, or side-communication.[15] We will have occasion to discuss this further, for it is essential to all becomings-animal. Every code is affected by a margin of decoding due to these supplements and surplus values—supplements in the order of a multiplicity, surplus values in the order of a rhizome. Forms in the parastrata, the parastrata themselves, far from lying immobile and frozen upon the strata, are part of a machinic interlock: they relate to populations, populations imply codes, and codes fundamentally include phenomena of relative decoding that are all the more usable, composable, and addable by virtue of being relative, always "beside."

Forms relate to codes and processes of coding and decoding in the parastrata; substances, being formed matters, relate to territorialities and movements of deterritorialization and reterritorialization on the epistrata. In truth, the epistrata are just as inseparable from the movements that constitute them as the parastrata are from their processes. Nomadic waves or flows of deterritorialization go from the central layer to the periphery, then from the new center to the new periphery, falling back to the old center and launching forth to the new.[16] The organization of the epistrata moves in the direction of increasing deterritorialization. Physical particles and chemical substances cross thresholds of deterritorialization on their own stratum and between strata; these thresholds correspond to more or less stable intermediate states, to more or less transitory valences and existences, to engagements with this or that other body, to densities of proximity, to more or less localizable connections. Not only are physical particles characterized by speeds of deterritorialization—Joycean tachyons, particles-holes, and quarks recalling the fundamental idea of the "soup"—but a single chemical substance (sulfur or carbon, for example) has a number of more and less deterritorialized states. The more interior milieus an organism has on its own stratum, assuring its autonomy and bringing it into a set of aleatory relations with the exterior, the more deterritorialized it is. That is why degrees of development must be understood relatively, and as a function of differential speeds, relations, and rates. Deterritorialization must be thought of as a perfectly positive power that has degrees and thresholds (epistrata), is always relative, and has reterritorialization as its flipside or complement. An organism that is deterritorialized in relation to the exterior necessarily reterritorializes on its interior milieus. A given presumed fragment of embryo is deterritorialized when it changes thresholds or gradients, but is assigned a new role by the new surroundings. Local movements are alterations. Cellular migration, stretching, invagination, folding are examples of this. Every voyage is intensive, and occurs in relation to thresholds of intensity between which it evolves or that it crosses. One travels by intensity; displacements and spatial figures depend on intensive thresholds of nomadic deterritorialization (and thus on differential relations) that simultaneously define complementary, sedentary reterritorializations. Every stratum operates this way: by grasping in its pincers a maximum number of intensities or intensive particles over which it spreads its forms and substances, constituting determinate gradients and thresholds of resonance (deterritorialization on a stratum always occurs in relation to a complementary reterritorialization).[17]

As long as preestablished forms were compared to predetermined degrees, all one could do was affirm their irreducibility, and there was no way of judging possible communication between the two factors. But we see now that forms depend on codes in the parastrata and plunge into processes of decoding or drift and that degrees themselves are caught up in movements of intensive territorialization and reterritorialization. There is no simple correspondence between codes and territorialities on the one hand and decodings and deterritorialization on the other: on the contrary, a code may be a deterritorialization and a reterritorialization a decoding. Wide gaps separate code and territoriality. The two factors nevertheless have the same "subject" in a stratum: it is populations that are deterritorialized and reterritorialized, and also coded and decoded. In addition, these factors communicate or interlace in the milieus.

On the one hand, modifications of a code have an aleatory cause in the milieu of exteriority, and it is their effects on the interior milieus, their compatibility with them, that decide whether they will be popularized. Deterritorializations and reterritorializations do not bring about the modifications; they do, however, strictly determine their selection. On the other hand, every modification has an associated milieu that in turn entails a certain deterritorialization in relation to the milieu of exteriority and a certain reterritorialization on intermediate or interior milieus. Perceptions and actions in an associated milieu, even those on a molecular level, construct or produce *territorial signs* (indexes). This is especially true of an animal world, which is constituted, marked off by signs that divide it into zones (of shelter, hunting, neutrality, etc.), mobilize special organs, and correspond to fragments of code; this is so even at the margin of decoding inherent in the code. Even the domain of learning is defined by the code, or prescribed by it. But indexes or territorial signs are inseparable from a double movement. Since the associated milieu always confronts a milieu of exteriority with which the animal is engaged and in which it takes necessary risks, a *line of flight* must be preserved to enable the animal to regain its associated milieu when danger appears (for example, the bull's line of flight in the arena, which it uses to regain the turf it has chosen).[18] A second kind of line of flight arises when the associated milieu is rocked by blows from the exterior, forcing the animal to abandon it and strike up an association with new portions of exteriority, this time leaning on its interior milieus like fragile crutches. When the seas dried, the primitive Fish left its associated milieu to explore land, forced to "stand on its own legs," now carrying water only on the inside, in the amniotic membranes protecting the embryo. In one way or the other, the animal is more a fleer than a fighter, but its flights are also conquests, creations. Territorialities, then, are shot through with lines of flight testifying to the presence within them of movements of deterritorialization and reterritorialization. In a certain sense, they are secondary. They would be nothing without these movements that deposit them. In short, the epistrata and parastrata are continually moving, sliding, shifting, and changing on the Ecumenon or unity of composition of a stratum; some are swept away by lines of flight and movements of deterritorialization, others by processes of decoding or drift, but they all communicate at the intersection of the milieus. The strata are continually being shaken by phenomena of cracking and rupture, either at the level of the substrata that furnish the materials (a prebiotic soup, a prechemical soup . . .), at the level of the accumulating epistrata, or at the level of the abutting parastrata: everywhere there arise simultaneous accelerations and blockages, comparative speeds, differences in deterritorialization creating relative fields of reterritorialization.

These relative movements should most assuredly not be confused with the possibility of absolute deterritorialization, an absolute line of flight, absolute drift. The former are stratic or interstratic, whereas the latter concern the plane of consistency and its destratification (its "combustion," as Geoffroy would say). There is no doubt that mad physical particles crash through the strata as they accelerate, leaving minimal trace of their passage, escaping spatiotemporal and even existential coordinates as they tend toward a state of absolute deterritorialization, the state of unformed matter on the plane of consistency. In a certain sense, the acceleration of relative deterritorializations reaches the sound barrier: if the particles bounce off this wall, or allow themselves to be captured by black holes, they fall back onto the strata, into the strata's relations and milieus; but if they cross the barrier they reach the unformed, destratified element of the plane of consistency. *We may even say that the abstract machines that emit and combine particles have two very different modes of existence: the Ecumenon and the Planomenon.* Either the abstract machines remain prisoner to stratifications, are enveloped in a certain specific stratum whose program or unity of composition they define (the abstract Animal, the abstract chemical Body, Energy in itself) and whose movements of relative deterritorialization they regulate. Or, on the contrary, the abstract machine cuts across all stratifications, develops alone and in its own right on the plane of consistency whose diagram it constitutes, the same machine at work in astrophysics and in microphysics, in the natural and in the artificial, piloting flows of absolute deterritorialization (in no sense, of course, is unformed matter chaos of any kind). But this presentation is still too simplified.

First, one does not go from the relative to the absolute simply by acceleration, even though increases in speed tend to have this comparative and global result. Absolute deterritorialization is not defined as a giant accelerator; its absoluteness does not hinge on how fast it goes. It is actually possible to reach the absolute by way of phenomena of relative slowness or delay. Retarded development is an example. What qualifies a deterritorialization is not its speed (some are very slow) but its nature, whether it constitutes epistrata and parastrata and proceeds by articulated segments or, on the contrary, jumps from one singularity to another following a nondecomposable, nonsegmentary line drawing a metastratum of the plane of consistency. Second, under no circumstances must it be thought that absolute deterritorialization comes suddenly or afterward, is in excess or beyond. That would preclude any understanding of why the strata themselves are animated by movements of relative deterritorialization and decoding that are not like accidents occurring on them. In fact, what is primary is an absolute deterritorializa- tion, an absolute line of flight, however complex or multiple—that of the plane of consistency or body without organs (the Earth, the absolutely deterritorialized). This absolute deterritorialization becomes relative only after stratification occurs on that plane or body: It is the strata that are always residue, not the opposite. The question is not how something manages to leave the strata but how things get into them in the first place. There is a perpetual immanence of absolute deterritorialization within relative deterritorialization; and the machinic assemblages between strata that regulate the differential relations and relative movements also have cutting edges of deterritorialization oriented toward the absolute. The plane of consistency is always immanent to the strata; the two states of the abstract machine always coexist as two different states of intensities.

Most of the audience had left (the first to go were the Marinetians with their double articulation, followed by the Hjelmslevians with their content and expression, and the biologists with their proteins and nucleic acids). The only ones left were the mathematicians, accustomed to other follies, along with a few astrologers, archaeologists, and scattered individuals. Challenger, moreover, had changed since the beginning of his talk. His voice had become hoarser, broken occasionally by an apish cough. His dream was not so much to give a lecture to humans as to provide a program for pure computers. Or else he was dreaming of an axiomatic, for axiomatics deals essentially with stratification. Challenger was addressing himself to memory only. Now that we had discussed what was constant and what varied in a stratum from the standpoint of substances and forms, the question remaining to be answered was what varied between strata from the standpoint of content and expression. For if it is true that there is always a real distinction constitutive of double articulation, a reciprocal presupposition of content and expression, then what varies from one stratum to another is the nature of this real distinction, and the nature and respective positions of the terms distinguished. Let us start with a certain group of strata that can be characterized summarily as follows: on these strata, content (form and substance) is molecular, and expression (form and substance) is molar. The difference between the two is primarily one of order of magnitude or scale. Resonance, or the communication occurring between the two independent orders, is what institutes the stratified system. The molecular content of that system has its own form corresponding to the distribution of elemental masses and the action of one molecule upon another; similarly, expression has a form manifesting the statistical aggregate and state of equilibrium existing on the macroscopic level. Expression is like an "operation of amplifying structuration carrying the active properties of the originally microphysical discontinuity to the macrophysical level."

We took as our point of departure cases of this kind on the geological stratum, the crystalline stratum, and physicochemical strata, wherever the molar can be said to express microscopic molecular interactions ("the crystal is the macroscopic expression of a microscopic structure"; the "crystalline form expresses certain atomic or molecular characteristics of the constituent chemical categories"). Of course, this still leaves numerous possibilities, depending on the number and nature of the intermediate

states, and also on the impact of exterior forces on the formation of expression. There may be a greater or lesser number of intermediate states between the molecular and the molar; there may be a greater or lesser number of exterior forces or organizing centers participating in the molar form. Doubtless, these two factors are in an inverse relation to each other and indicate limit-cases. For example, the molar form of expression may be of the "mold" type, mobilizing a maximum of exterior forces; or it may be of the "modulation" type, bringing into play only a minimum number of them. Even in the case of the mold, however, there are nearly instantaneous, interior intermediate states between the molecular content that assumes its own specific forms and the determinate molar expression of the outside by the form of the mold. Conversely, even when the multiplication and temporalization of the intermediate states testify to the endogenous character of the molar form (as with crystals), a minimum of exterior forces still intervene in each of the stages.[19] We must therefore say that the relative independence of content and expression, the real distinction between molecular content and molar expression with their respective forms, has a special status enjoying a certain amount of latitude between the limit-cases.

Since strata are judgments of God, one should not hesitate to apply all the subtleties of medieval Scholasticism and theology. There is a real distinction between content and expression because the corresponding forms are effectively distinct in the "thing" itself, and not only in the mind of the observer. But this real distinction is quite special; it is only *formal* since the two forms compose or shape a single thing, a single stratified subject. Various examples of formal distinction can be cited: between scales or orders of magnitude (as between a map and its model; or, in a different fashion, between the micro- and macrophysical levels, as in the parable of Eddington's two offices); between the various states or formal reasons through which a thing passes; between the thing in one form, and as affected by a possibly exterior causality giving it a different form; and so forth. (There is a proliferation of distinct forms because, in addition to content and expression each having its own forms, intermediate states introduce forms of expression proper to content and forms of content proper to expression.)

As diverse and real as formal distinctions are, on the organic stratum the very nature of the distinction changes. As a result, the entire distribution between content and expression is different. The organic stratum nevertheless preserves, and even amplifies, the relation between the molecular and the molar, with all kinds of intermediate states. We saw this in the case of morphogenesis, where double articulation is inseparable from a communication between two orders of magnitude. The same thing applies to cellular chemistry. But the organic stratum has a unique character that must account for the amplifications. In a preceding discussion, expression was dependent upon the expressed molecular content in all directions and in every dimension and had independence only to the extent that it appealed to a higher order of magnitude and to exterior forces: The real distinction was between forms, but forms belonging to the same aggregate, the same thing or subject. *Now, however, expression becomes independent in its own right, in other words, autonomous.* Before, the coding of a stratum was coextensive with that stratum; on the organic stratum, on the other hand, it takes place on an autonomous and independent line that detaches as much as possible from the second and third dimensions. Expression ceases to be voluminous or superficial, becoming linear, unidimensional (even in its segmentarity). The essential thing is *the linearity of the nucleic sequence.*[20] The real distinction between content and expression, therefore, is not simply formal. It is strictly speaking real, and passes into the molecular, without regard to order of magnitude. It is between two classes of molecules, nucleic acids of expression and proteins of content, nucleic elements or nucleotides and protein elements or amino acids. Both expression and content are now molecular *and* molar. The distinction no longer concerns a single aggregate or subject; linearity takes us further in the direction of flat multiplicities, rather than unity. Expression involves nucleotides and nucleic acids as well as molecules that, in their substance and form, are entirely independent not only of molecules of content but of any directed action in the exterior milieu. Thus invariance is a characteristic of certain molecules and is not found exclusively on the molar scale. Conversely, proteins, in their substance and form of content, are equally independent of nucleotides: the only thing univocally determined is that one amino acid rather than another corresponds to a sequence of three nucleotides.[21] What the linear form of expression determines is therefore a derivative form of expression, one that is relative to content and that, through a folding back upon itself of the protein sequence of the amino acids, finally yields the characteristic three-dimensional structures. In short, what is specific to the organic stratum is *this alignment of expression, this exhaustion or detachment of a line of expression*, this reduction of form and substance of expression to a unidimensional line, guaranteeing their reciprocal independence from content without having to account for orders of magnitude.

This has many consequences. The new configuration of expression and content conditions not only the organism's power to reproduce but also its power to deterritorialize or accelerate deterritorialization. The alignment of the code or linearity of the nucleic sequence in fact marks a threshold of deterritorialization of the "sign" that gives it a new ability to be copied and makes the organism more deterritorialized than a crystal: only something deterritorialized is capable of reproducing itself. When content and expression are divided along the lines of the molecular and the molar, substances move from state to state, from the preceding state to the following state, or from layer to layer, from an already constituted layer to a layer in the process of forming, while forms install themselves at the limit between the last layer or last state and the exterior milieu. Thus the stratum develops into epistrata and parastrata; this is accomplished through a set of *inductions* from layer to layer and state to state, or at the limit. A crystal displays this process in its pure state, since its form expands in all directions, but always as a function of the surface layer of the substance, which can be emptied of most of its interior without interfering with the growth. It is the crystal's subjugation to three-dimensionality, in other words its index of territoriality, that makes the structure incapable of formally reproducing and expressing itself; only the accessible surface can reproduce itself, since it is the only deterritorializable part. On the contrary, the detachment of a pure line of expression on the organic stratum makes it possible for the organism to attain a much higher threshold of deterritorialization, gives it a mechanism of reproduction covering all the details of its complex spatial structure, and enables it to put all of its interior layers "topologically in contact" with the exterior, or rather with the polarized limit (hence the special role of the living membrane). The development of the stratum into epistrata and parastrata occurs not through simple inductions but through *transductions* that account for the amplification of the resonance between the molecular and the molar, independently of order of magnitude; for the functional efficacy of the interior substances, independently of distance; and for the possibility of a proliferation and even interlacing of forms, independently of codes (surplus values of code or phenomena of transcoding or aparallel evolution).[22]

There is a third major grouping of strata, defined less by a human essence than, once again, by a new distribution of content and expression. Form of content becomes "alloplastic" rather than "homoplastic"; in other words, it brings about modifications in the external world. Form of expression becomes linguistic rather than genetic; in other words, it operates with symbols that are comprehensible, transmittable, and modifiable from outside. What some call the properties of human beings—technology and language, tool and symbol, free hand and supple larynx, "gesture and speech"—are in fact properties of this new distribution. It would be difficult to maintain that the emergence of human beings marked the absolute origin of this distribution. Leroi-Gourhan's analyses give us an understanding of how contents came to be linked with the hand-tool couple and expressions with the face-language couple.[23] In this context, the hand must not be thought of simply as an organ but instead as a coding (the digital code), a dynamic structuration, a dynamic formation (the manual form, or manual formal traits). The hand as a general form of content is extended in tools, which are themselves active forms implying substances, or formed matters; finally, products are formed matters, or substances, which in turn serve as tools. Whereas manual formal traits constitute the unity of composition of the stratum, the forms and substances of tools and products are organized into parastrata and epistrata that themselves function as veritable strata and mark discontinuities, breakages, communications and diffusions, nomadisms and sedentarities, multiple thresholds and speeds of relative deterritorialization in human populations. For with the hand as a formal trait or general form of content a major threshold of deterritorialization is reached and opens, an accelerator that in itself permits a shifting interplay of comparative deterritorializations and reterritorializations—what makes this acceleration possible is, precisely, phenomena of "retarded development" in the organic substrata. Not only is the hand a deterritorialized back paw; the hand thus freed is itself deterritorialized in relation to the grasping and locomotive hand of the monkey. The synergistic deterritorializations of other organs (for example, the foot) must be taken into account. So must correlative deterritorializations of the milieu: the steppe as an associated milieu more deterritorialized than the forest, exerting a selective pressure of deterritorialization upon the body and technology (it was on the steppe, not in the forest, that the hand was able to appear as a free form, and fire as a technologically formable matter). Finally, complementary reterritorializations must be taken into account (the foot as a compensatory reterritorialization for the hand, also occurring on the steppe). Maps should be made of these things, organic, ecological, and technological maps one can lay out on the plane of consistency.

On the other hand, language becomes the new form of expression, or rather the set of formal traits defining the new expression in operation throughout the stratum. Just as manual traits exist only in forms and formed matters that shatter their continuity and determine the distribution of their effects, formal traits of expression exist only in a diversity of formal languages and imply one or several formable substances. The substance involved is fundamentally vocal substance, which brings into play various organic elements: not only the larynx, but the mouth and lips, and the overall motricity of the face. Once again, a whole intensive map must be accounted for: the mouth as a deterritorialization of the snout (the whole "conflict between the mouth and the brain," as Perrier called it); the lips as a deterritorialization of the mouth (only humans have lips, in other words, an outward curling of the interior mucous membranes; only human females have breasts, in other words, deterritorialized mammary glands:

the extended nursing period advantageous for language learning is accompanied by a complementary reterritorialization of the lips on the breasts, and the breasts on the lips). What a curious deterritorialization, filling one's mouth with words instead of food and noises. The steppe, once more, seems to have exerted strong pressures of selection: the "supple larynx" is a development corresponding to the free hand and could have arisen only in a deforested milieu where it is no longer necessary to have gigantic laryngeal sacks in order for one's cries to be heard above the constant din of the forest. To articulate, to speak, is to speak softly. Everyone knows that lumberjacks rarely talk.[24] Physiological, acoustic, and vocal substance are not the only things that undergo all these deterritorializations. The form of expression, as language, also crosses a threshold.

Vocal signs have temporal linearity, and it is this superlinearity that constitutes their specific deterritorialization and differentiates them from genetic linearity. Genetic linearity is above all spatial, even though its segments are constructed and reproduced in succession; thus at this level it does not require effective overcoding of any kind, only phenomena of end-to-end connection, local regulations, and partial interactions (overcoding takes place only at the level of integrations implying different orders of magnitude). That is why Jacob is reluctant to compare the genetic code to a language; in fact, the genetic code has neither emitter, receiver, comprehension, nor translation, only redundancies and surplus values.[25] The temporal linearity of language expression relates not only to a succession but to a formal synthesis of succession in which time constitutes a process of linear overcoding and engenders a phenomenon unknown on the other strata: *translation*, translatability, as opposed to the previous inductions and transductions. Translation should not be understood simply as the ability of one language to "represent" in some way the givens of another language, but beyond that as the ability of language, with its own givens on its own stratum, to represent all the other strata and thus achieve a scientific conception of the world. The scientific world (*Welt*, as opposed to the *Umwelt* of the animal) is the translation of all of the flows, particles, codes, and territorialities of the other strata into a sufficiently deterritorialized system of signs, in other words, into an overcoding specific to language. This property of *overcoding* or *superlinearity* explains why, in language, not only is expression independent of content, but form of expression is independent of substance: translation is possible because the same form can pass from one substance to another, which is not the case for the genetic code, for example, between RNA and DNA chains. We will see later on how this situation gives rise to certain imperialist pretentions on behalf of language, which are naively expressed in such formulas as: "Every semiology of a nonlinguistic system must use the medium of language. . . . Language is the interpreter of all the other systems, linguistic and nonlinguistic." This amounts to defining an abstract character of language and then saying that the other strata can share in that character only by being spoken in language. That is stating the obvious. More positively, it must be noted that the immanence within language of universal translation means that its epistrata and parastrata, with respect to superpositions, diffusions, communications, and abutments, operate in an entirely different manner than those of other strata: all human movements, even the most violent, imply translations.

We have to hurry, Challenger said, we're being rushed by the line of time on this third stratum. So we have a new organization of content and expression, each with its own forms and substances: technological content, semiotic or symbolic expression. Content should be understood not simply as the hand and tools but as a technical social machine that preexists them and constitutes states of force or formations of power. Expression should be understood not simply as the face and language, or individual languages, but as a semiotic collective machine that preexists them and constitutes regimes of signs. A formation of power is much more than a tool; a regime of signs is much more than a language. Rather, they act as determining and selective agents, as much in the constitution of languages and tools as in their usages and mutual or respective diffusions and communications. The third stratum sees the emergence of Machines that are fully a part of that stratum but at the same time rear up and stretch their pincers out in all directions at all the other strata. *Is this not like an intermediate state between the two states of the abstract Machine*?—the state in which it remains enveloped in a corresponding stratum (ecumenon), and the state in which it develops in its own right on the destratified plane of consistency (planomenon). The abstract machine begins to unfold, to stand to full height, producing an illusion exceeding all strata, even though the machine itself still belongs to a determinate stratum. This is, obviously, the illusion constitutive of man (who does man think he is?). This illusion derives from the overcoding immanent to language itself. But what is not illusory are the new distributions between content and expression: technological content characterized by the hand-tool relation and, at a deeper level, tied to a social Machine and formations of power; symbolic expression characterized by face-language relations and, at a deeper level, tied to a semiotic Machine and regimes of signs. On both sides, the epistrata and parastrata, the superposed degrees and abutting forms, attain more than ever before the status of autonomous strata in their own right. In cases where we can discern two different regimes of signs or two different formations of power, we shall say that they are in fact two different strata in human populations.

What precisely is the relation now between content and expression, and what type of distinction is there between them? It's all in the head. Yet never was a distinction more real. What we are trying to say is that there is indeed one exterior milieu for the entire stratum, permeating the entire stratum: the cerebral-nervous milieu. It comes from the organic substratum, but of course that substratum does not merely play the role of a substratum or passive support. It is no less complex in organization. Rather, it constitutes the prehuman soup immersing us. Our hands and faces are immersed in it. The brain is a population, a set of tribes tending toward two poles. In Leroi-Gourhan's analyses of the constitution of these two poles in the soup—one of which depends on the actions of the face, the other on the hand—their correlation or relativity does not preclude a real distinction between them; quite the contrary, it entails one, as the reciprocal presupposition of two articulations, the manual articulation of content and the facial articulation of expression. And the distinction is not simply real, as between molecules, things, or subjects; it has become *essential* (as they used to say in the Middle Ages), as between attributes, genres of being, or irreducible categories: things and words. Yet we find that the most general of movements, the one by which each of the distinct articulations is already double in its own right, carries over onto this level; certain formal elements of content play the role of expression in relation to content proper, and certain formal elements of expression play the role of content in relation to expression proper. In the first case, Leroi-Gourhan shows how the hand creates a whole world of symbols, a whole pluridimensional language, not to be confused with unilinear verbal language, which constitutes a radiating expression specific to content (he sees this as the origin of writing).[26] The second case is clearly displayed in the double articulation specific to language itself, since phonemes form a radiating content specific to the expression of monemes as linear significant segments (it is only under these conditions that double articulation as a general characteristic of strata has the linguistic meaning Martinet attributes to it). Our discussion of the relations between content and expression, the real distinction between them, and the variations of those relations and that distinction on the major types of strata, is now provisionally complete.

Challenger wanted to go faster and faster. No one was left, but he went on anyway. The change in his voice, and in his appearance, was growing more and more pronounced. Something animalistic in him had begun to speak when he started talking about human beings. You still couldn't put your finger on it, but Challenger seemed to be deterritorializing on the spot. He still had three problems he wanted to discuss. The first seemed primarily terminological: Under what circumstances may we speak of signs? Should we say they are everywhere on all the strata and that there is a sign whenever there is a form of expression? We may summarily distinguish three kinds of signs: *indexes (territorial signs), symbols (deterritorialized signs), and icons (signs of reterritorialization)*. Should we say that there are signs on all the strata, under the pretext that every stratum includes territorialities and movements of deterritorialization and reterritorialization? This kind of expansive method is very dangerous, because it lays the groundwork for or reinforces the imperialism of language, if only by relying on its function as universal translator or interpreter. It is obvious that there is no system of signs common to all strata, not even in the form of a semiotic "chora" theoretically prior to symbolization.[27] It would appear that we may accurately speak of signs only when there is a distinction between forms of expression and forms of content that is not only real but also categorical. Under these conditions, there is a semiotic system on the corresponding stratum because the abstract machine has precisely that fully erect posture that permits it to "write," in other words, to treat language and extract a *regime* of signs from it. But before it reaches that point, in so-called natural codings, the abstract machine remains enveloped in the strata: It does not write in any way and has no margin of latitude allowing it to recognize something as a sign (except in the strictly territorial sense of animal signs). After that point, the abstract machine develops on the plane of consistency and no longer has any way of making a categorical distinction between signs and particles; for example, it writes, but flush with the real, it inscribes directly upon the plane of consistency. It therefore seems reasonable to reserve the word "sign" in the strict sense for the last group of strata. This terminological discussion would be entirely without interest if it did not bring us to yet another danger: not the imperialism of language affecting all of the strata, but the imperialism of the signifier affecting language itself, affecting all regimes of signs and the entire expanse of the strata upon which they are located. The question here is not whether there are signs on every stratum but whether all signs are signifiers, whether all signs are endowed with signifiance, whether the semiotic of signs is necessarily linked to a semiology of the signifier. Those who take this route may even be led to forgo the notion of the sign, for the primacy of the signifier over language guarantees the primacy of language over all of the strata even more effectively than the simple expansion of the sign in all directions. What we are saying is that the illusion specific to *this* posture of the abstract Machine, the illusion that one can grasp and shuffle all the strata between one's pincers, can be better secured through the erection of the signifier than through the extension of the sign (thanks to signifiance, language can claim to be in direct contact with the strata without having to go through the supposed signs on each one). But we're still going in the same circle, we're still spreading the same canker.

The linguistic relation between the signifier and signified has, of course, been conceived in many different ways. It has been said that they are arbitrary; that they are as necessary to each other as the two sides of the same leaf; that they correspond term by term, or else globally; and that they are so ambivalent as to be indistinguishable. In any event, the signified is thought not to exist outside of its relationship with signifier, and the ultimate signified is the very existence of the signifier, extrapolated beyond the sign. There is only one thing that can be said about the signifier: it is Redundancy, it is the Redundant. Hence its incredible despotism, and its success. Theories of arbitrariness, necessity, term-by-term or global correspondence, and ambivalence serve the same cause: the reduction of expression to the signifier. Yet forms of content and forms of expression are highly relative, always in a state of reciprocal presupposition. The relations between their respective segments are biunivocal, exterior, and "deformed." There is never conformity between the two, or from one to the other. There is always real independence and a real distinction; even to fit the forms together, and to determine the relations between them, requires a specific, variable assemblage. None of these characteristics applies to the signifier-signified relation, even though some seem to coincide with it partially and accidentally. Overall, these characteristics stand in radical opposition to the scenario of the signifier. A form of content is not a signified, any more than a form of expression is a signifier.[28] This is true for all the strata, including those on which language plays a role.

Signifier enthusiasts take an oversimplified situation as their implicit model: word and thing. From the word they extract the signifier, and from the thing a signified in conformity with the word, and therefore subjugated to the signifier. They operate in a sphere interior to and homogeneous with language. Let us follow Foucault in his exemplary analysis, which, though it seems not to be, is eminently concerned with linguistics. Take a thing like the prison: the prison is a form, the "prison-form"; it is a form of content on a stratum and is related to other forms of content (school, barracks, hospital, factory). This thing or form does not refer back to the word "prison" but to entirely different words and concepts, such as "delinquent" and "delinquency," which express a new way of classifying, stating, translating, and even committing criminal acts. "Delinquency" is the form of expression in reciprocal presupposition with the form of content "prison." Delinquency is in no way a signifier, even a juridical signifier, the signified of which would be the prison. That would flatten the entire analysis. Moreover, the form of expression is reducible not to words but to a set of statements arising in the social field considered as a stratum (that is what a regime of signs is). The form of content is reducible not to a thing but to a complex state of things as a formation of power (architecture, regimentation, etc.). We could say that there are two constantly intersecting multiplicities, "discursive multiplicities" of expression and "nondiscursive multiplicities" of content. It is even more complex than that because the prison as a form of content has a relative expression all its own; there are all kinds of statements specific to it that do not necessarily coincide with the statements of delinquency. Conversely, delinquency as a form of expression has an autonomous content all its own, since delinquency expresses not only a new way of evaluating crimes but a new way of committing them. Form of content and form of expression, prison and delinquency: each has its own history, microhistory, segments. At most, along with other contents and expressions, they imply a shared state of the abstract Machine acting not at all as a signifier but as a kind of diagram (a single abstract machine for the prison and the school and the barracks and the hospital and the factory . . .). Fitting the two types of forms together, segments of content and segments of expression, requires a whole double-pincered, or rather double-headed, concrete assemblage taking their real distinction into account. It requires a whole organization articulating formations of power and regimes of signs, and operating on the molecular level (societies characterized by what Foucault calls disciplinary power).[29] In short, we should never oppose words to things that supposedly correspond to them, nor signifiers to signifieds that are supposedly in conformity with them. What should be opposed are distinct formalizations, in a state of unstable equilibrium or reciprocal presupposition. "*It is in vain that we say what we see; what we see never resides in what we say.*"[30] As in school: there is not just one writing lesson, that of the great redundant Signifier for any and all signifieds. There are two distinct formalizations in reciprocal presupposition and constituting a double-pincer: the formalization of expression in the reading and writing lesson (with its own relative contents), and the formalization of content in the lesson of things (with their own relative expressions). We are never signifier or signified. We are stratified.

The preferred method would be severely restrictive, as opposed to the expansive method that places signs on all strata or signifier in all signs (although at the limit it may forgo signs entirely). First, there exist forms of expression without signs (for example, the genetic code has nothing to do with a language). It is only under certain conditions that strata can be said to include signs; signs cannot be equated with language in general but are defined by regimes of statements that are so many real usages or functions of language. Then why retain the word *sign* for these regimes, which formalize an expression without designating or signifying the simultaneous contents, which are formalized in a different way? Signs are not signs of a thing; they are signs of deterritorialization and reterritorialization, they mark a certain threshold crossed in the course of these movements, and it is for this reason that the word should be retained (as we have seen, this applies even to animal "signs").

Next, if we consider regimes of signs using this restrictive definition, we see that they are not, or not necessarily, signifiers. Just as signs designate only a certain formalization of expression in a determinate group of strata, signifiance itself designates only one specific regime among a number of regimes existing in that particular formalization. Just as there are asemiotic expressions, or expressions without signs, there are asemiological regimes of signs, asignifying signs, both on the strata and on the plane of consistency. The most that can be said of signifiance is that it characterizes *one* regime, which is not even the most interesting or modern or contemporary one, but is perhaps only more pernicious, cancerous, and despotic than the others, and more steeped in illusion than they.

In any case, content and expression are never reducible to signified-signifier. And (this is the second problem) neither are they reducible to base-superstructure. One can no more posit a primacy of content as the determining factor than a primacy of expression as a signifying system. Expression can never be made into a form reflecting content, even if one endows it with a "certain" amount of independence and a certain potential for reacting, if only because so-called economic content already has a form and even forms of expression that are specific to it. Form of content and form of expression involve two parallel formalizations in presupposition: it is obvious that their segments constantly intertwine, embed themselves in one another; but this is accomplished by the abstract machine from which the two forms derive, and by machinic assemblages that regulate their relations. If this parallelism is replaced by a pyramidal image, then content (including its form) becomes an economic base of production displaying all of the characteristics of the Abstract; the assemblages become the first story of a superstructure that, as such, is necessarily situated within a State apparatus; the regimes of signs and forms of expression become the second story of the superstructure, defined by ideology. It isn't altogether clear where language should go, since the great Despot decided that it should be reserved a special place, as the common good of the nation and the vehicle for information. Thus one misconstrues the nature of language, which exists only in heterogeneous regimes of signs, and rather than circulating information distributes contradictory orders. It misconstrues the nature of regimes of signs, which express organizations of power or assemblages and have nothing to do with ideology as the supposed expression of a content (ideology is a most execrable concept obscuring all of the effectively operating social machines). It misconstrues the nature of organizations of power, which are in no way located within a State apparatus but rather are everywhere, effecting formalizations of content and expression, the segments of which they intertwine. Finally, it misconstrues the nature of content, which is in no way economic "in the last instance," since there are as many directly economic signs or expressions as there are noneconomic contents. Nor can the status of social formations be analyzed by throwing some signifier into the base, or vice versa, or a bit of phallus or castration into political economy, or a bit of economics or politics into psychoanalysis.

There is a third problem. It is difficult to elucidate the system of the strata without seeming to introduce a kind of cosmic or even spiritual evolution from one to the other, as if they were arranged in stages and ascended degrees of perfection. Nothing of the sort. The different figures of content and expression are not stages. There is no biosphere or noosphere, but everywhere the same Mechanosphere. If one begins by considering the strata in themselves, it cannot be said that one is less organized than another. This even applies to a stratum serving as a substratum: there is no fixed order, and one stratum can serve directly as a substratum for another without the intermediaries one would expect there to be from the standpoint of stages and degrees (for example, microphysical sectors can serve as an immediate substratum for organic phenomena). Or the apparent order can be reversed, with cultural or technical phenomena providing a fertile soil, a good soup, for the development of insects, bacteria, germs, or even particles. The industrial age defined as the age of insects . . . It's even worse nowadays: you can't even tell in advance which stratum is going to communicate with which other, or in what direction. Above all, there is no lesser, no higher or lower, organization; the substratum is an integral part of the stratum, is bound up with it as the milieu in which change occurs, and not an increase in organization.[31] Furthermore, if we consider the plane of consistency we note that the most disparate of things and signs move upon it: a semiotic fragment rubs shoulders with a chemical interaction, an electron crashes into a language, a black hole captures a genetic message, a crystallization produces a passion, the wasp and the orchid cross a letter . . . There is no "like" here, we are not saying "like an electron," "like an interaction," etc. The plane of consistency is the abolition of all metaphor; all that consists is Real. These are electrons in person, veritable black holes, actual organites, authentic sign sequences. It's just that they have been uprooted from their strata, destratified, decoded, deterritorialized, and that is what makes their proximity and interpenetration in the plane of consistency possible. A silent dance. *The plane of consistency knows nothing of differences in level, orders of magnitude, or distances. It knows nothing of the difference between the artificial and the natural. It knows nothing of the distinction between contents and expressions, or that between forms and formed substances*; these things exist only by means of and in relation to the strata.

But how can one still identify and name things if they have lost the strata that qualified them, if they have gone into absolute deterritorialization? Eyes are black holes, but what are black holes and eyes outside their strata and territorialities? What it comes down to is that we cannot content ourselves with a dualism or summary opposition between the strata and the destratified plane of consistency. The strata themselves are animated and defined by relative speeds of deterritorialization; moreover, absolute deterritorialization is there from the beginning, and the strata are spinoffs, thickenings on a plane of consistency that is everywhere, always primary and always immanent. In addition, the plane of consistency is occupied, drawn by the abstract Machine; the abstract Machine exists *simultaneously* developed on the destratified plane it draws, and enveloped in each stratum whose unity of composition it defines, and even half-erected in certain strata whose form of prehension it defines. That which races or dances upon the plane of consistency thus carries with it the aura of its stratum, an undulation, a memory or tension. The plane of consistency retains just enough of the strata to extract from them variables that operate in the plane of consistency as its own functions. The plane of consistency, or planomenon, is in no way an undifferentiated aggregate of unformed matters, but neither is it a chaos of formed matters of every kind. It is true that on the plane of consistency there are no longer forms or substances, content or expression, respective and relative deterritorializations. But beneath the forms and substances of the strata the plane of consistency (or the abstract machine) *constructs continuums of intensity*: it creates continuity for intensities that it extracts from distinct forms and substances. Beneath contents and expressions the plane of consistency (or the abstract machine) *emits and combines particles-signs* that set the most asignifying of signs to functioning in the most deterritorialized of particles. Beneath relative movements the plane of consistency (or the abstract machine) *performs conjunctions of flows of deterritorialization* that transform the respective indexes into absolute values. The only intensities known to the strata are discontinuous, bound up in forms and substances; the only particles are divided into particles of content and articles of expression; the only deterritorialized flows are disjointed and reterritorialized. Continuum of intensities, combined emission of particles or signs-particles, conjunction of deterritorialized flows: these are the three factors proper to the plane of consistency; they are brought about by the abstract machine and are constitutive of destratification. Now there is no hint in all of this of a chaotic white night or an undifferentiated black night. There are rules, rules of "plan(n)ing," of diagramming, as we will see later on, or elsewhere. The abstract machine is not random; the continuities, emissions and combinations, and conjunctions do not occur in just any fashion.

A final distinction must now be noted. Not only does the abstract machine have different simultaneous states accounting for the complexity of what takes place on the plane of consistency, but the abstract machine should not be confused with what we call a concrete machinic assemblage. The *abstract machine* sometimes develops upon the plane of consistency, whose continuums, emissions, and conjugations it constructs, and sometimes remains enveloped in a stratum whose unity of composition and force of attraction or prehension it defines. The *machinic assemblage* is something entirely different from the abstract machine, even though it is very closely connected with it. First, on a stratum, it performs the coadaptations of content and expression, ensures biunivocal relationships between segments of content and segments of expression, and guides the division of the stratum into epistrata and parastrata. Next, between strata, it ensures the relation to whatever serves as a substratum and brings about the corresponding changes in organization. Finally, it is in touch with the plane of consistency because it necessarily effectuates the abstract machine on a particular stratum, between strata, and in the relation between the strata and the plane. An assemblage (for example, the smith's anvil among the Dogons) is necessary for the articulations of the organic stratum to come about. An assemblage is necessary for the relation between two strata to come about. And an assemblage is necessary for organisms to be caught within and permeated by a social field that utilizes them: Must not the Amazons amputate a breast to adapt the organic stratum to a warlike technological stratum, as though at the behest of a fearsome woman-bow-steppe assemblage? Assemblages are necessary for states of force and regimes of signs to intertwine their relations. Assemblages are necessary in order for the unity of composition enveloped in a stratum, the relations between a given stratum and the others, and the relation between these strata and the plane of consistency to be organized rather than random. In every respect, machinic assemblages *effectuate* the abstract machine insofar as it is developed on the plane of consistency or enveloped in a stratum. The most important problem of all: given a certain machinic assemblage, what is its relation of effectuation with the abstract machine? How does it effectuate it, with what adequation? Classify assemblages. What we call the mechanosphere is the set of all abstract machines and machinic assemblages outside the strata, on the strata, or between strata.

The system of the strata thus has nothing to do with signifier and signified, base and superstructure, mind and matter. All of these are ways of reducing the strata to a single stratum, or of closing the system in on itself by cutting it off from the plane of consistency as destratification. We had to summarize before we lost our voice. Challenger was finishing up. His voice had become unbearably shrill. He was suffocating. His hands were becoming elongated pincers that had become incapable of grasping anything but could still vaguely point to things. Some kind of matter seemed to be pouring out from the double mask, the two heads; it was impossible to tell whether it was getting thicker or more watery. Some of the audience had returned, but only shadows and prowlers. "You hear that? It's an animal's voice." So the summary would have to be quick, the terminology would have to be set down as well as possible, for no good reason. There was a first group of notions: the Body without Organs or the destratified Plane of Consistency; the Matter of the Plane, that which occurs on the body or plane (singular, nonsegmented multiplicities composed of intensive continuums, emissions of particles-signs, conjunctions of flows); and the abstract Machine, or abstract Machines, insofar as they construct that body or draw that plane or "diagram" what occurs (lines of flight, or absolute deterritorializations).

Then there was the system of the strata. On the intensive continuum, the strata fashion forms and form matters into substances. In combined emissions, they make the distinction between expressions and contents, units of expression and units of content, for example, signs and particles. In conjunctions, they separate flows, assigning them relative movements and diverse territorialities, relative deterritorializations and complementary reterritorializations. Thus the strata set up everywhere double articulations animated by movements: forms and substances of content and forms and substances of expression constituting segmentary multiplicities with relations that are determinable in every case. Such are the *strata*. Each stratum is a double articulation of content and expression, both of which are really distinct and in a state of reciprocal presupposition. Content and expression intermingle, and it is two-headed machinic assemblages that place their segments in relation. What varies from stratum to stratum is the nature of the real distinction between content and expression, the nature of the substances as formed matters, and the nature of the relative movements. We may make a summary distinction between three major types of real distinction: the real-formal distinction between orders of magnitude, with the establishment of a resonance of expression (induction); the real-real distinction between different subjects, with the establishment of a linearity of expression (transduction); and the real-essential distinction between different attributes or categories, with the establishment of a superlinearity of expression (translation).

Each stratum serves as the substratum for another stratum. Each stratum has a unity of composition defined by its milieu, substantial elements, and formal traits (Ecumenon). But it divides into *parastrata* according to its irreducible forms and associated milieus, and into *epistrata* according to its layers of formed substances and intermediary milieus. Epistrata and parastrata must themselves be thought of as strata. A machinic assemblage is an *interstratum* insofar as it regulates the relations between strata, as well as the relations between contents and expressions on each stratum, in conformity with the preceding divisions. A single assemblage can borrow from different strata, and with a certain amount of apparent disorder; conversely, a stratum or element of a stratum can join others in functioning in a different assemblage. Finally, the machinic assemblage is a *metastratum* because it is also in touch with the plane of consistency and necessarily effectuates the abstract machine. The abstract machine exists enveloped in each stratum, whose Ecumenon or unity of composition it defines, and developed on the plane of consistency, whose destratification it performs (the Planomenon). Thus when the assemblages fit together the variables of a stratum as a function of its unity, they also bring about a specific effectuation of the abstract machine as it exists outside the strata. Machinic assemblages are simultaneously located at the intersection of the contents and expression on each stratum, and at the intersection of all of the strata with the plane of consistency. They rotate in all directions, like beacons.

It was over. Only later on would all of this take on concrete meaning. The double-articulated mask had come undone, and so had the gloves and the tunic, from which liquids escaped. As they streamed away they seemed to eat at the strata of the lecture hall, which was filled with fumes of olibanum and "hung with strangely figured arras." Disarticulated, deterritorialized, Challenger muttered that he was taking the earth with him, that he was leaving for the mysterious world, his poison garden. He whispered something else: it is by headlong flight that things progress and signs proliferate. Panic is creation. A young woman cried out, her face "convulsed with a wilder, deeper, and more hideous epilepsy of stark panic than they had seen on human countenance before." No one had heard the summary, and no one tried to keep Challenger from leaving. Challenger, or what remained of him, slowly hurried toward the *plane of consistency*, following a bizarre trajectory with nothing relative left about it. He tried to slip into an assemblage serving as a drum-gate, the particle Clock with its intensive clicking and conjugated rhythms hammering out the absolute: "The figure slumped oddly into a posture scarcely human, and began a curious, fascinated sort of shuffle toward the coffin-shaped clock. . . . The figure had now reached the abnormal clock, and the watchers saw through the dense fumes a blurred black claw fumbling with the tall, hieroglyphed door. The fumbling made a queer, clicking sound. Then the figure entered the coffin-shaped case and pulled the door shut after it. . . . The abnormal clicking went on, beating out the dark, cosmic rhythm which underlies all mystical gate-openings"[32]—the Mechanosphere, or rhizosphere.

4. November 20, 1923—Postulates of Linguistics

The Order-word Assemblage

I. "Language Is Informational and Communicational"

When the schoolmistress instructs her students on a rule of grammar or arithmetic, she is not informing them, any more than she is informing herself when she questions a student. She does not so much instruct as "insign," give orders or commands. A teacher's commands are not external or additional to what he or she teaches us. They do not flow from primary significations or result from information: an order always and already concerns prior orders, which is why ordering is redundancy. The compulsory education machine does not communicate information; it imposes upon the child semiotic coordinates possessing all of the dual foundations of grammar (masculine-feminine, singular-plural, noun-verb, subject of the statement-subject of enunciation, etc.). The elementary unit of language—the statement—is the order-word.[1] Rather than common sense, a faculty for the centralization of information, we must define an abominable faculty consisting in emitting, receiving, and transmitting order-words. Language is made not to be believed but to be obeyed, and to compel obedience. "The baroness has not the slightest intention of convincing me of her sincerity; she is simply indicating that she prefers to see me pretend to agree."[2] We see this in police or government announcements, which often have little plausibility or truthfulness, but say very clearly what should be observed and retained. The indifference to any kind of credibility exhibited by these announcements often verges on provocation. This is proof that the issue lies elsewhere. Let people say . . . : that is all language demands. Spengler notes that the fundamental forms of speech are not the statement of a judgment or the expression of a feeling, but "the command, the expression of obedience, the assertion, the question, the affirmation or negation," very short phrases that command life and are inseparable from enterprises and large-scale projects: "Ready?" "Yes." "Go ahead."[3] Words are not tools, but we give children language, pens, and notebooks as we give workers shovels and pickaxes. A rule of grammar is a power marker before it is a syntactical marker. The order does not refer to prior significations or to a prior organization of distinctive units. Quite the opposite. Information is only the strict minimum necessary for the emission, transmission, and observation of orders as commands. One must be just informed enough not to confuse "Fire!" with "Fore!" or to avoid the unfortunate situation of the teacher and the student as described by Lewis Carroll (the teacher, at the top of the stairs, asks a question that is passed on by servants, who distort it at each step of the way, and the student, below in the courtyard, returns an answer that is also distorted at each stage of the trip back). Language is not life; it gives life orders. Life does not speak; it listens and waits.[4] Every order-word, even a father's to his son, carries a little death sentence—a Judgment, as Kafka put it.

The hard part is to specify the status and scope of the order-word. It is not a question of the origin of language, since the order-word is only a language-function, a function coextensive with language. If language always seems to presuppose itself, if we cannot assign it a nonlinguistic point of departure, it is because language does not operate between something seen (or felt) and something said, but always goes from saying to saying. We believe that narrative consists not in communicating what one has seen but in transmitting what one has heard, what someone else said to you. Hearsay. It does not even suffice to invoke a vision distorted by passion. The "first" language, or rather the first determination of language, is not the trope or metaphor but *indirect discourse*. The importance some have accorded metaphor and metonymy proves disastrous for the study of language. Metaphors and metonymies are merely effects; they are a part of language only when they presuppose indirect discourse. There are many passions in a passion, all manner of voices in a voice, murmurings, speaking in tongues: that is why all discourse is indirect, and the translative movement proper to language is that of indirect discourse.[5] Benveniste denies that the bee has language, even though it has an organic coding process and *even uses tropes*. It has no language because it can communicate what it has seen but not transmit what has been communicated to it. A bee that has seen a food source can communicate the message to bees that did not see it, but a bee that has not seen it cannot transmit the message to others that did not see it.[6] Language is not content to go from a first party to a second party, from one who has seen to one who has not, but necessarily goes from a second party to a third party, neither of whom has seen. It is in this sense that language is the transmission of the word as order-word, not the communication of a sign as information. Language is a map, not a tracing. But how can the order-word be a function coextensive with language when the order, the command, seems tied to a restricted type of explicit proposition marked by the imperative?

Austin's famous theses clearly demonstrate that the various extrinsic relations between action and speech by which a statement can describe an action in an indicative mode or incite it in an imperative mode, etc., are not all there is. There are also intrinsic relations between speech and certain actions that are accomplished by *saying* them (the performative: I swear by saying "I swear"), and more generally between speech and certain actions that are accomplished in speaking (the illocutionary: I ask a question by saying "Is . . . ?" I make a promise by saying "I love you . . ."; I give a command by using the imperative, etc.). These acts internal to speech, these immanent relations between statements and acts, have been termed *implicit or nondiscursive presuppositions*, as opposed to the potentially explicit assumptions by which a statement refers to other statements or an external action (Ducrot). The theory of the performative sphere, and the broader sphere of the illocutionary, has had three important and immediate consequences: (1) It has made it impossible to conceive of language as a code, since a code is the condition of possibility for all explanation. It has also made it impossible to conceive of speech as the communication of information: to order, question, promise, or affirm is not to inform someone about a command, doubt, engagement, or assertion but to effectuate these specific, immanent, and necessarily implicit acts. (2) It has made it impossible to define semantics, syntactics, or even phonematics as scientific zones of language independent of *pragmatics*. Pragmatics ceases to be a "trash heap," pragmatic determinations cease to be subject to the alternative: fall outside language, or answer to explicit conditions that syntacticize and semanticize pragmatic determinations. Instead, pragmatics becomes the presupposition behind all of the other dimensions and insinuates itself into everything. (3) It makes it impossible to maintain the distinction between language and speech because speech can no longer be defined simply as the extrinsic and individual use of a primary signification, or the variable application of a preexisting syntax. Quite the opposite, the meaning and syntax of language can no longer be defined independently of the speech acts they presuppose.[7]

It is true that it is still difficult to see how speech acts or implicit presuppositions can be considered a function coextensive with language. It is all the more difficult if one starts with the performative (that which one does by saying it) and moves by extension to the illocutionary (that which one does in speaking). For it is always possible to thwart that move. The performative can be walled in by explaining it by specific syntactic and semantic characteristics avoiding any recourse to a generalized pragmatics. According to Benveniste, for example, the performative relates not to acts but instead to a property of *self-referentiality* of terms (the true personal pronouns, I, YOU . . . , defined as shifters). By this account, a preexistent structure of subjectivity, or intersubjectivity, in language, rather than presupposing speech acts, is adequate to account for them.[8] Benveniste thus defines language as communicational rather than informational; this properly linguistic intersubjectivity, or subjectification, explains all the rest, in other words, everything that is brought into being by saying it. The question is whether subjective communication is any better a linguistic notion than ideal information. Oswald Ducrot has set forth the reasons that have led him to reverse Benveniste's schema: The phenomenon of self-referentiality cannot account for the performative. The opposite is the case; it is "the fact that certain statements are socially devoted to the accomplishment of certain actions" that explains self-referentiality. The performative itself is explained by the illocutionary, not the opposite. It is the illocutionary that constitutes the nondiscursive or implicit presuppositions. And the illocutionary is in turn explained by collective assemblages of enunciation, by juridical acts or equivalents of juridical acts, which, far from depending on subjectification proceedings or assignations of subjects in language, in fact determine their distribution. Communication is no better a concept than information; intersubjectivity gets us no further than signifiance in accounting for these "statements-acts" assemblages that in each language delimit the role and range of subjective morphemes.[9] (We will see that the analysis of indirect discourse confirms this point of view since it shows that subjectifications are not primary but result from a complex assemblage.)

We call *order-words*, not a particular category of explicit statements (for example, in the imperative), but the relation of every word or every statement to implicit presuppositions, in other words, to speech acts that are, and can only be, accomplished in the statement. Order-words do not concern commands only, but every act that is linked to statements by a "social obligation." Every statement displays this link, directly or indirectly. Questions, promises, are order-words. The only possible definition of language is the set of all order-words, implicit presuppositions, or speech acts current in a language at a given moment.

The relation between the statement and the act is internal, immanent, but it is not one of identity. Rather, it is a relation of *redundancy*. The order-word itself is the redundancy of the act and the statement. Newspapers, news, proceed by redundancy, in that they tell us what we "must" think, retain, expect, etc. Language is neither informational nor communicational. It is not the communication of information but something quite different: the transmission of order-words, either from one statement to another or within each statement, insofar as each statement accomplishes an act and the act is accomplished in the statement. The most general schema of information science posits in principle an ideal state of maximum information and makes redundancy merely a limitative condition serving to decrease this theoretical maximum in order to prevent it from being drowned out by noise. We are saying that the redundancy of the order-word is instead primary and that information is only the minimal condition for the transmission of order-words (which is why the opposition to be made is not between noise and information but between all the indisciplines at work in language, and the order-word as discipline or "grammaticality"). Redundancy has two forms, *frequency* and *resonance;* the first concerns the signifiance of information, the second (I = I) concerns the subjectivity of communication. It becomes apparent that information and communication, and even signifiance and subjectification, are subordinate to redundancy. A distinction is sometimes made between information and communication; some authors envision an abstract signifiance of information and an abstract subjectification of communication. None of this, however, yields an implicit or primary form of language. There is no signifiance independent of dominant significations, nor is there subjectification independent of an established order of subjection. Both depend on the nature and transmission of order-words in a given social field.

There is no individual enunciation. There is not even a subject of enunciation. Yet relatively few linguists have analyzed the necessarily social character of enunciation.[10] The problem is that it is not enough to establish that enunciation has this social character, since it could be extrinsic; therefore too much or too little is said about it. The social character of enunciation is intrinsically founded only if one succeeds in demonstrating how enunciation in itself implies *collective assemblages*. It then becomes clear that the statement is individuated, and enunciation subjectified, only to the extent that an impersonal collective assemblage requires it and determines it to be so. It is for this reason that indirect discourse, *especially "free" indirect discourse*, is of exemplary value: there are no clear, distinctive contours; what comes first is not an insertion of variously individuated statements, or an interlocking of different subjects of enunciation, but a collective assemblage resulting in the determination of relative subjectification proceedings, or assignations of individuality and their shifting distributions within discourse. Indirect discourse is not explained by the distinction between subjects; rather, it is the assemblage, as it freely appears in this discourse, that explains all the voices present within a single voice, the glimmer of girls in a monologue by Charlus, the languages in a language, the order-words in a word. The American murderer "Son of Sam" killed on the prompting of an ancestral voice, itself transmitted through the voice of a dog. The notion of collective assemblage of enunciation takes on primary importance since it is what must account for the social character. We can no doubt define the collective assemblage as the redundant complex of the act and the statement that necessarily accomplishes it. But this is still only a nominal definition; it does not even enable us to justify our previous position that redundancy is irreducible to a simple identity (or that there is no simple identity between the statement and the act). If we wish to move to a real definition of the collective assemblage, we must ask of what consist these acts immanent to language that are in redundancy with statements or constitute order-words.

These acts seem to be defined as the set of all *incorporeal transformations* current in a given society and *attributed* to the bodies of that society. We may take the word "body" in its broadest sense (there are mental bodies, souls are bodies, etc.). We must, however, distinguish between the actions and passions affecting those bodies, and acts, which are only noncorporeal attributes or the "expressed" of a statement. When Ducrot asks what an act consists of, he turns precisely to the juridical assemblage, taking the example of the judge's sentence that transforms the accused into a convict. In effect, what takes place beforehand (the crime of which someone is accused), and what takes place after (the carrying out of the penalty), are actions-passions affecting bodies (the body of the property, the body of the victim, the body of the convict, the body of the prison); but the transformation of the accused into a convict is a pure instantaneous act or incorporeal attribute that is the expressed of the judge's sentence.[11] Peace and war are states or interminglings of very different kinds of bodies, but the declaration of a general mobilization expresses an instantaneous and incorporeal transformation of bodies. Bodies have an age, they mature and grow old; but majority, retirement, any given age category, are incorporeal transformations that are immediately attributed to bodies in particular societies. "You are no longer a child": this statement concerns an incorporeal transformation, even if it applies to bodies and inserts itself into their actions and passions. The incorporeal transformation is recognizable by its instantaneousness, its immediacy, by the simultaneity of the statement expressing the transformation and the effect the transformation produces; that is why order-words are precisely dated, to the hour, minute, and second, and take effect the moment they are dated. Love is an intermingling of bodies that can be represented by a heart with an arrow through it, by a union of souls, etc., but the declaration "I love you" expresses a noncorporeal attribute of bodies, the lover's as well as that of the loved one. Eating bread and drinking wine are interminglings of bodies; communing with Christ is also an intermingling of bodies, properly spiritual bodies that are no less "real" for being spiritual. But the transformation of the body of the bread and the wine into the body and blood of Christ is the pure expressed of a statement attributed to the bodies. In an airplane hijacking, the threat of a hijacker brandishing a revolver is obviously an action; so is the execution of the hostages, if it occurs. But the transformation of the passengers into hostages, and of the plane-body into a prison-body, is an instantaneous incorporeal transformation, a "mass media act" in the sense in which the English speak of "speech acts." The order-words or assemblages of enunciation in a given society (in short, the illocutionary) designate this instantaneous relation between statements and the incorporeal transformations or noncorporeal attributes they express.

The instantaneousness of the order-word, which can be projected to infinity, placed at the origin of society, is quite strange; for Rousseau, for example, the passage from the state of nature to the social state is like a leap in place, an incorporeal transformation occurring at zero hour. Real history undoubtedly recounts the actions and passions of the bodies that develop in a social field; it communicates them in a certain fashion; but it also transmits order-words, in other words, pure acts intercalated into that development. History will never be rid of dates. Perhaps economics or financial analysis best demonstrates the presence and instantaneousness of these decisive acts in an overall process (that is why statements definitely do not belong to ideology, but are already at work in what is supposedly the domain of the economic base). The galloping inflation in Germany after 1918 was a crisis affecting the monetary body, and many other bodies besides; but the sum of the "circumstances" suddenly made possible a semiotic transformation that, although indexed to the body of the earth and material assets, was still a pure act or incorporeal transformation—*November 20, 1923 . . .*[12]

The assemblages are in constant variation, are themselves constantly subject to transformations. First, the circumstances must be taken into account: Benveniste clearly demonstrates that a performative statement is nothing outside of the circumstances that make it performative. Anybody can shout, "I declare a general mobilization," but in the absence of an effectuated variable giving that person the right to make such a statement it is an act of peurility or insanity, not an act of enunciation. This is also true of "I love you," which has neither meaning nor subject nor addressee outside of circumstances that not only give it credibility but make it a veritable assemblage, a power marker, even in the case of an unhappy love (it is still by a will to power that one obeys . . .). The general term "circumstances" should not leave the impression that it is a question only of external circumstances. "I swear" is not the same when said in the family, at school, in a love affair, in a secret society, or in court: it is not the same thing, and neither is it the same statement; it is not the same bodily situation, and neither is it the same incorporeal transformation. The transformation applies to bodies but is itself incorporeal, internal to enunciation. There are variables of expression *that establish a relation between language and the outside, but precisely because they are immanent to language.* As long as linguistics confines itself to constants, whether syntactical, morphological, or phonological, it ties the statement to a signifier and enunciation to a subject and accordingly botches the assemblage; it consigns circumstances to the exterior, closes language in on itself, and makes pragmatics a residue. Pragmatics, on the other hand, does not simply appeal to external circumstances: it brings to light variables of expression or of enunciation that are so many internal reasons for language not to close itself off. As Vološinov [Bakhtin] says, as long as linguistics extracts constants, it is incapable of helping us understand how a single word can be a complete enunciation; there must be "an extra something" that "remains outside of the scope of the entire set of linguistic categories and definitions," even though it is still entirely within the purview of the theory of enunciation or language.[13] The order-word is precisely that variable that makes the word as such an enunciation. The instantaneousness of the order-word, its immediacy, gives it a power of variation in relation to the bodies to which the transformation is attributed.

Pragmatics is a politics of language. A study such as Jean-Pierre Faye's on the constitution of Nazi statements in the German social field is in this respect exemplary (and cannot be directly transferred to the constitution of Fascist statements in Italy). Transformational research of this kind is concerned with the variation of the order-words and noncorporeal attributes linked to social bodies and effectuating immanent acts. We may take as another example, under different conditions, the formation of a properly Leninist type of statement in Soviet Russia, basing ourselves on a text by Lenin entitled "On Slogans" (1917). This text constituted an incorporeal transformation that extracted from the masses a proletarian class as an assemblage of enunciation *before* the conditions were present for the proletariat to exist as a body. A stroke of genius from the First Marxist International, which "invented" a new type of class: Workers of the world, unite![14] Taking advantage of the break with the Social Democrats, Lenin invented or decreed yet another incorporeal transformation that extracted from the proletarian class a vanguard as an assemblage of enunciation and was attributed to the "Party," a new type of party as a distinct body, at the risk of falling into a properly bureaucratic system of redundancy. The Leninist wager, an act of audacity? Lenin declared that the slogan (*mot d'ordre*) "All power to the Soviets" was valid only from the 27th of February to the 4th of July for the peacetime development of the Revolution, and no longer held in the state of war; the passage from peace to war implied this transformation, not just from the masses to a guiding proletariat, but from the proletariat to a directing vanguard. *July 4 exactly* the power of the Soviets came to an end. All of the external circumstances can be assigned: the war as well as the insurrection that forced Lenin to flee to Finland. But the fact remains that the incorporeal transformation was uttered on the 4th of July, prior to the organization of the body to which it would be attributed, namely, the Party itself. "Every particular slogan must be deduced from the totality of the specific features of a definite political situation."[15] If the objection is leveled that these specific features pertain to politics and not linguistics, it must be observed how thoroughly politics works language from within, causing not only the vocabulary but also the structure and all of the phrasal elements to vary as the order-words change. A type of statement can be evaluated only as a function of its pragmatic implications, in other words, in relation to the implicit presuppositions, immanent acts, or incorporeal transformations it expresses and which introduce new configurations of bodies. True intuition is not a judgment of grammaticality but an evaluation of internal variables of enunciation in relation to the aggregate of the circumstances.

We have gone from explicit commands to order-words as implicit presuppositions; from order-words to the immanent acts or incorporeal transformations they express; and from there to the assemblages of enunciation whose variables they are. To the extent these variables enter at a given moment into determinable relations, the assemblages combine in *a regime of signs or a semiotic machine*. It is obvious that a society is plied by several semiotics, that its regimes are in fact mixed. Moreover, at a later time there will arise new order-words that will modify the variables and will not yet be part of a known regime. Thus the order-word is redundancy in several ways: as a function of the process of transmission essential to it, and in itself, from the time it is emitted, in its "immediate" relation with the act or transformation it effectuates. The order-word is already redundancy even when it is in rupture with a particular semiotic. That is why every statement of a collective assemblage of enunciation belongs to indirect discourse. Indirect discourse is the presence of a reported statement within the reporting statement, the presence of an order-word within the word. Language in its entirety is indirect discourse. Indirect discourse in no way supposes direct discourse; rather, the latter is extracted from the former, to the extent that the operations of signifiance and proceedings of subjectification in an assemblage are distributed, attributed, and assigned, or that the variables of the assemblage enter into constant relations, however temporarily. Direct discourse is a detached fragment of a mass and is born of the dismemberment of the collective assemblage; but the collective assemblage is always like the murmur from which I take my proper name, the constellation of voices, concordant or not, from which I draw my voice. I always depend on a molecular assemblage of enunciation that is not given in my conscious mind, any more than it depends solely on my apparent social determinations, which combine many heterogeneous regimes of signs. Speaking in tongues. To write is perhaps to bring this assemblage of the unconscious to the light of day, to select the whispering voices, to gather the tribes and secret idioms from which I extract something I call my Self (*Moi*). *I* is an order-word. A schizophrenic said: "I heard voices say: *he is conscious of life*."[16] In this sense, there is indeed a schizophrenic cogito, but it is a cogito that makes self-consciousness the incorporeal transformation of an order-word, or a result of indirect discourse. My direct discourse is still the free indirect discourse running through me, coming from other worlds or other planets. That is why so many artists and writers have been tempted by the séance table. When we ask what faculty is specific to the order-word, we must indeed attribute to it some strange characteristics: a kind of instantaneousness in the emission, perception, and transmission of order-words; a wide variability, and a power of forgetting permitting one to feel absolved of the order-words one has followed and then abandoned in order to welcome others; a properly ideal or ghostly capacity for the apprehension of incorporeal transformations; an aptitude for grasping language as an immense indirect discourse.[17] The faculty of the cuer and the cued, of the song that always holds a tune within a tune in a relation of redundancy; a faculty that is in truth mediumistic, glossolalic, or xenoglossic.

Let us return to the question of how this defines a language-function, a function coextensive with language. It is evident that order-words, collective assemblages, or regimes of signs cannot be equated with language. But they effectuate its condition of possibility (*the superlinearity of expression*), they fulfill in each instance this condition of possibility; without them, language would remain a pure virtuality (the superlinear character of indirect discourse). Doubtless, the assemblages vary, undergo transformation. But they do not necessarily vary by language, they do not correspond to the various languages. A language seems to be defined by the syntactical, semantic, phonological constants in its statements; the collective assemblage, on the contrary, concerns the usage of these constants in relation to variables internal to enunciation itself (variables of expression, immanent acts, or incorporeal transformations). Different constants, different languages, may have the same usage; the same constants in a given language may have different usages, successively or even simultaneously. We cannot content ourselves with a duality between constants as linguistic factors that are explicit or potentially explicit, and variables as extrinsic, nonlinguistic factors. For the pragmatic variables of usage are internal to enunciation and constitute the implicit presuppositions of language. Thus if the collective assemblage is in each instance coextensive with the linguistic system considered, and to language as a whole, it is because it expresses the set of incorporeal transformations that effectuate the condition of possibility of language and utilize the elements of the linguistic system. The language-function thus defined is neither informational nor communicational; it has to do neither with signifying information nor with intersubjective communication. And it is useless to abstract a signifiance outside information, or a subjectivity outside communication. For the subjectification proceedings and movement of signifiance relate to regimes of signs, or collective assemblages. The language-function is the transmission of order-words, and order-words relate to assemblages, just as assemblages relate to the incorporeal transformations constituting the variables of the function. Linguistics is nothing without a pragmatics (semiotic or political) to define the effectuation of the *condition of possibility* of language and the *usage* of linguistic elements.

II. "There Is an Abstract Machine of Language That Does Not Appeal to Any 'Extrinsic' Factor"

If in a social field we distinguish the set of corporeal modifications and the set of incorporeal transformations, we are presented, despite the variety in each of the sets, with two formalizations, one of *content*, the other of *expression*. For content is not opposed to form but has its own formalization: the hand-tool pole, or the lesson of things. It is, however, opposed to expression, inasmuch as expression also has its own formalization: the face-language pole, the lesson of signs. Precisely because content, like expression, has a form of its own, one can never assign the form of expression the function of simply representing, describing, or averring a corresponding content: there is neither correspondence nor conformity. The two formalizations are not of the same nature; they are independent, heterogeneous. The Stoics were the first to theorize this independence: they distinguished between the actions and passions of bodies (using the word "body" in the broadest sense, as applying to any formed content) and incorporeal acts (the "expressed" of the statements). The form of expression is constituted by the warp of expresseds, and the form of content by the woof of bodies. When knife cuts flesh, when food or poison spreads through the body, when a drop of wine falls into water, there is an *intermingling of bodies*; but the statements, "The knife is cutting the flesh," "I am eating," "The water is turning red," express *incorporeal transformations* of an entirely different nature (events).[18] The genius of the Stoics was to have taken this paradox as far as it could go, up to the point of insanity and cynicism, and to have grounded it in the most serious of principles: their reward was to be the first to develop a philosophy of language.

The paradox gets us nowhere unless, like the Stoics, we add that incorporeal transformations, incorporeal attributes, apply to bodies, and only to bodies. They are the expressed of statements but are *attributed* to bodies. The purpose is not to describe or represent bodies; bodies already have proper qualities, actions and passions, souls, in short forms, which are themselves bodies. Representations are bodies too! If noncorporeal attributes apply to bodies, if there are good grounds for making a distinction between the incorporeal expressed "to become red" and the corporeal quality "red," etc., it has nothing to with representation. We cannot even say that the body or state of things is the "referent" of the sign. In expressing the noncorporeal attribute, and by that token attributing it to the body, one is not representing or referring but *intervening* in a way; it is a speech act. The independence of the two kinds of forms, forms of expression and forms of content, is not contradicted but confirmed by the fact that the expressions or expresseds are inserted into or intervene in contents, not to represent them but to anticipate them or move them back, slow them down or speed them up, separate or combine them, delimit them in a different way. The warp of the instantaneous transformations is always inserted into the woof of the continuous modifications. (Hence the significance of dates for the Stoics. From what moment can it be said that someone is bald? In what sense does a statement of the type "There will be a naval battle tomorrow" constitute a date or order-word?) The night of August 4, July 4, 1917, November 20, 1923: What incorporeal transformation is expressed by these dates, incorporeal yet attributed to bodies, inserted into them? The independence of the form of expression and the form of content is not the basis for a parallelism between them or a representation of one by the other, but on the contrary a parceling of the two, a manner in which expressions are inserted into contents, in which we ceaselessly jump from one register to another, in which signs are at work in things themselves just as things extend into or are deployed through signs. An assemblage of enunciation does not speak "of" things; it speaks *on the same level as* states of things and states of content. So that the same x, the same particle, may function either as a body that acts and undergoes actions or as a sign constituting an act or order-word, depending on which form it is taken up by (for example, the theoretico-experimental aggregate of physics). In short, the functional independence of the two forms is only the form of their reciprocal presupposition, and of the continual passage from one to the other. We are never presented with an interlinkage of order-words and a causality of contents each in its own right; nor do we see one represent the other, with the second serving as referent. On the contrary, the independence of the two lines is distributive, such that a segment of one always forms a relay with a segment of the other, slips into, introduces itself into the other. We constantly pass from order-words to the "silent order" of things, as Foucault puts it, and vice versa.

But when we use a word as vague as "intervene," when we say that expressions intervene or insert themselves into contents, are we not still prey to a kind of idealism in which the order-word instantaneously falls from the sky? What we must determine is not an origin but points of intervention or insertion in the framework of the reciprocal presupposition of the two forms. Both forms of content and forms of expression are inseparable from a movement of deterritorialization that carries them away. Both expression and content are more or less deterritorialized, relatively deterritorialized, according to the particular state of their form. In this respect, one cannot posit a primacy of expression over content, or content over expression. Sometimes the semiotic components are more deterritorialized than the material components, and sometimes the reverse. For example, a mathematical complex of signs may be more deterritorialized than a set of particles; conversely, the particles may have experimental effects that deterritorialize the semiotic system. A criminal action may be deterritorializing in relation to the existing regime of signs (the earth cries for revenge and crumbles beneath my feet, my offense is too great); but the sign that expresses the act of condemnation may in turn be deterritorializing in relation to all actions and reactions ("a fugitive and a vagabond shalt thou be in the earth" [Gen. 4:12], you cannot even be killed). In short, there are degrees of deterritorialization that quantify the respective forms and according to which contents and expression are conjugated, feed into each other, accelerate each other, or on the contrary become stabilized and perform a reterritorialization. What we call circumstances or variables are these degrees themselves. There are *variables of content*, or proportions in the interminglings or aggregations of bodies, and there are *variables of expression*, factors internal to enunciation. Germany, toward November 20, 1923: on the one hand, the deterritorializing inflation of the monetary body and, on the other, in response to the inflation, a semiotic transformation of the reichsmark into the rentenmark, making possible a reterritorialization. Russia, toward July 4, 1917: on the one hand proportions of a state of "bodies" Soviets-provisional government, and on the other the elaboration of a Bolshevik incorporeal semiotic, accelerating things and contributing to the action of the detonating body of the Party. In short, the way an expression relates to a content is not by uncovering or representing it. Rather, forms of expression and forms of content communicate through a conjunction of their quanta of relative deterritorialization, each intervening, operating in the other.

We may draw some general conclusions on the nature of Assemblages from this. On a first, horizontal, axis, an assemblage comprises two segments, one of content, the other of expression. On the one hand it is a *machinic assemblage* of bodies, of actions and passions, an intermingling of bodies reacting to one another; on the other hand it is a *collective assemblage of enunciation*, of acts and statements, of incorporeal transformations attributed to bodies. Then on a vertical axis, the assemblage has both *territorial sides*, or reterritorialized sides, which stabilize it, and *cutting edges of deterritorialization,* which carry it away. No one is better than Kafka at differentiating the two axes of the assemblage and making them function together. On the one hand, the ship-machine, the hotel-machine, the circus-machine, the castle-machine, the court-machine, each with its own intermingled pieces, gears, processes, and bodies contained in one another or bursting out of containment (see the head bursting through the roof).[19] On the other hand, the regime of signs or of enunciation: each regime with its incorporeal transformations, acts, death sentences and judgments, proceedings, "law." It is obvious that statements do not represent machines: the Stoker's discourse does not describe stoking as a body; it has its own form, and a development without resemblance.[20] Yet it is attributed to bodies, to the whole ship as a body. A discourse of submission to order-words; a discourse of discussion, claims, accusation, and defense. On the second axis, what is compared or combined of the two aspects, what always inserts one into the other, are the sequenced or conjugated degrees of deterritorialization, and the operations of reterritorialization that stabilize the aggregate at a given moment. K., the K.-function, designates the line of flight or deterritorialization that carries away all of the assemblages but also undergoes all kinds of reterritorializations and redundancies—redundancies of childhood, village-life, love, bureaucracy, etc.

The tetravalence of the assemblage. Taking the feudal assemblage as an example, we would have to consider the interminglings of bodies defining feudalism: the body of the earth and the social body; the body of the overlord, vassal, and serf; the body of the knight and the horse and their new relation to the stirrup; the weapons and tools assuring a symbiosis of bodies—a whole machinic assemblage. We would also have to consider statements, expressions, the juridical regime of heraldry, all of the incorporeal transformations, in particular, oaths and their variables (the oath of obedience, but also the oath of love, etc.): the collective assemblage of enunciation. On the other axis, we would have to consider the feudal territorialities and reterritorializations, and at the same time the line of deterritorialization that carries away both the knight and his mount, statements and acts. We would have to consider how all this combines in the Crusades.

It would be an error to believe that content determines expression by causal action, even if expression is accorded the power not only to "reflect" content but to react upon it in an active way. This kind of ideological conception of the statement, which subordinates it to a primary economic content, runs into all kinds of difficulties inherent to dialectics. First, although it may be possible to conceive of a causal action moving from content to expression, the same cannot be said for the respective *forms*, the form of content and the form of expression. We must recognize that expression is independent and that this is precisely what enables it to react upon contents. This independence, however, has been poorly conceived. If contents are said to be economic, the form of content cannot be said to be economic and is reduced to a pure abstraction, namely, the production of goods and the means of that production considered in themselves. Similarly, if expressions are said to be ideological, the form of expression is not said to be ideological and is reduced to language as abstraction, as the availability of a good shared by all. Those who take this approach claim to characterize contents and expressions by all the struggles and conflicts pervading them in two different forms, but these forms themselves are exempt from struggle and conflict, and the relation between them remains entirely indeterminate.[21] The only way to define the relation is to revamp the theory of ideology by saying that expressions and statements intervene directly in productivity, in the form of a production of meaning or sign-value. The category of production doubtless has the advantage of breaking with schemas of representation, information, and communication. But is it any more adequate than these schemas? Its application to language is very ambiguous in that it appeals to an ongoing dialectical miracle of the transformation of matter into meaning, content into expression, the social process into a signifying system.

We think the material or machinic aspect of an assemblage relates not to the production of goods but rather to a precise state of intermingling of bodies in a society, including all the attractions and repulsions, sympathies and antipathies, alterations, amalgamations, penetrations, and expansions that affect bodies of all kinds in their relations to one another. What regulates the obligatory, necessary, or permitted interminglings of bodies is above all an alimentary regime and a sexual regime. Even technology makes the mistake of considering tools in isolation: tools exist only in relation to the interminglings they make possible or that make them possible. The stirrup entails a new man-horse symbiosis that at the same time entails new weapons and new instruments. Tools are inseparable from symbioses or amalgamations defining a Nature-Society machinic assemblage. They presuppose a social machine that selects them and takes them into its "phylum": a society is defined by its amalgamations, not by its tools. Similarly, the semiotic or collective aspect of an assemblage relates not to a productivity of language but to regimes of signs, to a machine of expression whose variables determine the usage of language elements. These elements do not stand on their own any more than tools do. There is a primacy of the machinic assemblage of bodies over tools and goods, a primacy of the collective assemblage of enunciation over language and words. The articulation of the two aspects of the assemblage is effected by the movements of deterritorialization that quantify their forms. That is why a social field is defined less by its conflicts and contradictions than by the lines of flight running through it. An assemblage has neither base nor superstructure, neither deep structure nor superficial structure; it flattens all of its dimensions onto a single plane of consistency upon which reciprocal presuppositions and mutual insertions play themselves out.

The other mistake (which is combined with the first as needed) is to believe in the adequacy of the form of expression as a linguistic system. This system may be conceived as a signifying phonological structure, or as a deep syntactical structure. In either case, it is credited with engendering semantics, therefore of fulfilling expression, whereas contents are relegated to the arbitrariness of a simple "reference" and pragmatics to the exteriority of nonlinguistic factors. What all of these undertakings have in common is to erect an *abstract machine of language*, but as a synchronic set of constants. We will not object that the machine thus conceived is too abstract. On the contrary, it is not abstract enough, it remains "linear." It remains on an intermediate level of abstraction allowing it to consider linguistic factors in themselves, independently of nonlinguistic factors, and to treat those linguistic factors as constants. But if the abstraction is taken further, one necessarily reaches a level where the pseudoconstants of language are superseded by variables of expression internal to enunciation itself; these variables of expression are then no longer separable from the variables of content with which they are in perpetual interaction. *If the external pragmatics of nonlinguistic factors must be taken into consideration, it is because linguistics itself is inseparable from an internal pragmatics involving its own factors.* It is not enough to take into account the signified, or even the referent, because the very notions of signification and reference are bound up with a supposedly autonomous and constant structure. There is no use constructing a semantics, or even recognizing a certain validity to pragmatics, if they are still pretreated by a phonological or syntactical machine. For a true abstract machine pertains to an assemblage in its entirety: it is defined as the diagram of that assemblage. It is not language based but diagrammatic and superlinear. Content is not a signified nor expression a signifier; rather, both are variables of the assemblage. We get nowhere until the pragmatic, but also semantic, syntactical, and phonological determinations are directly linked to the assemblages of enunciation upon which they depend. Chomsky's abstract machine retains an arborescent model and a linear ordering of linguistic elements in sentences and sentence combinations. But as soon as pragmatic values or internal variables are taken into account, in particular with respect to indirect discourse, one is obliged to bring "hypersentences" into play or to construct "abstract objects" (incorporeal transformations). This implies superlinearity, in other words, a plane whose elements no longer have a fixed linear order: the rhizome model.[22] From this standpoint, the interpenetration of language and the social field and political problems lies at the deepest level of the abstract machine, not at the surface. The abstract machine as it relates to the diagram of the assemblage is never purely a matter of language, except for lack of sufficient abstraction. It is language that depends on the abstract machine, not the reverse. At most, we may distinguish in the abstract machine two states of the diagram, one in which variables of content and expression are distributed according to their heterogeneous forms in reciprocal presupposition on a plane of consistency, and another in which it is no longer even possible to distinguish between variables of content and expression because the variability of that same plane has prevailed over the duality of forms, rendering them "indiscernible." (The first state relates to still relative movements of deterritorialization; in the second, an absolute threshold of deterritorialization has been reached.)

III. "There Are Constants or Universals of Language That Enable Us to Define It as a Homogeneous System"

The question of structural invariants—and the very idea of structure is inseparable from invariants, whether atomic or relational—is essential to linguistics. It is what allows linguistics to claim a basis in pure scientificity, to be nothing but science . . . safe from any supposedly external or pragmatic factor. The question of invariants assumes several closely connected forms: (1) the constants of a language (phonological, by commutativity; syntactical, by transformativity; semantic, by generativity); (2) the universals of language (by decomposition of the phoneme into distinctive features; of syntax into fundamental constituents; of signification into minimal semantic elements); (3) trees linking constants to one another, with binary relations between trees (see Chomsky's linear arborescent method); (4) competence, in principle coextensive with language and defined by judgments of grammaticality; (5) homogeneity, bearing on elements and relations as well as intuitive judgments; (6) synchrony, which erects an "in-itself" and a "for-itself" of language, perpetually moving from the objective system to the subjective consciousness that apprehends its principle (that of the linguist himself or herself).

One can juggle all of these factors, subtract some or even add new ones. They go together, however, because the essentials of all of them are present on the level of any one. For example, the distinction between speech and language is recapitulated in the distinction between competence and performance, but at the level of grammaticality. If it is objected that the distinction between competence and performance is entirely relative (a linguistic competence can be economic, religious, political, or aesthetic, etc.; the teaching competence of a grade school teacher may be only a performance in relation to the judgment of an inspector or government regulations), linguists respond that they are willing to multiply levels of competence, and even to introduce pragmatic values into the system. Brekle, for example, proposes adding an "idiosyncratic performatory competence" factor tied to a whole constellation of linguistic, psychological, or sociological factors. But what use is this injection of pragmatics if pragmatics is in turn considered to have constants or universals of its own? And in what way are expressions like "I," "promise," "know" more universal than "greet," "name," or "condemn"?[23] Similarly, when efforts are made to make Chomsky's trees bud and to shatter linear order, as long as the pragmatic components marking the ruptures are placed above the tree or effaced from the derivation nothing has really been accomplished, one has failed to constitute a rhizome.[24] In truth, the nature of the abstract machine is the most general problem: there is no reason to tie the abstract to the universal or the constant, or to efface the singularity of abstract machines insofar as they are built around variables and variations.

The debate between Chomsky and Labov will give us a better understanding of what the issue is. Every language is an essentially heterogeneous reality; linguists know this and say so. But this is a *factual* remark. Chomsky asks only that one carve from this aggregate a homogeneous or standard system as a basis for abstraction or idealization, making possible a scientific study of *principles*. Limiting oneself to standard English is thus not the issue, for even a linguist who studies Black English or the English of the ghettos is obliged to extract a standard system guaranteeing the constancy and homogeneity of the object under study (no science can operate any other way, they say). Thus Chomsky pretends to believe that by asserting his interest in the variable features of language, Labov is situating himself in a de facto pragmatics external to linguistics.[25] Labov, however, has other ambitions. When he brings to light lines of *inherent variation*, he does not see them simply as "free variants" pertaining to pronunciation, style, or nonpertinent features that lie outside the system and leave the homogeneity of the system intact; neither does he see them as a de facto mix between two systems, each homogeneous in its own right, as if the speaker moved from one to the other. He refuses the alternative linguistics set up for itself: assigning variants to different systems, or relegating them to a place outside the structure. It is the variation itself that is systematic, in the sense in which musicians say that "the theme is the variation." Labov sees variation as a de jure component affecting each system from within, sending it cascading or leaping on its own power and forbidding one to close it off, to make it homogeneous in principle. Labov does consider variables of all kinds, phonetic, phonological, syntactical, semantic, stylistic. Yet it would seem difficult to accuse him of missing the distinction between the de jure and the de facto—or between linguistics and stylistics, or synchrony and diachrony, or pertinent and nonpertinent features, or competence and performance, or the grammaticality of language and the agrammaticality of speech. Although this may be hardening his positions, we would say rather that Labov proposes a different distribution of the de facto and the de jure, and especially a different conception of the de jure itself and of abstraction. He takes the example of a young black person who, in a very short series of phrases, seems to pass from the Black English system to the standard system eighteen times. Is it not the abstract distinction between the two systems that proves arbitrary and insufficient? For the majority of the forms belongs to one or the other only by virtue of the fortuities of a given sequence. Must it not be admitted that every system is in variation and is defined not by its constants and homogeneity but on the contrary by a variability whose characteristics are immanent, continuous, and regulated in a very specific mode (*variable or optional* rules)?[26]

How can we conceptualize this continuous variation at work within a language, even if it means overstepping the limits Labov sets for himself as well as the conditions of scientificity invoked by linguistics? In the course of a single day, an individual repeatedly passes from language to language. He successively speaks as "father to son" and as a boss; to his lover, he speaks an infantilized language; while sleeping he is plunged into an oniric discourse, then abruptly returns to a professional language when the telephone rings. It will be objected that these variations are extrinsic, that it is still the same language. But that is to prejudge the question. First, it is not certain that the phonology is the same, nor the syntax, nor the semantics. Second, the whole question is whether this supposedly identical language is defined by invariants or, on the contrary, by the line of continuous variation running through it. Some linguists have suggested that linguistic change occurs less by systemic rupture than by a gradual modification of frequency, by a coexistence and continuity of different usages. Take as an example the statement, "I swear!" It is a different statement depending on whether it is said by a child to his or her father, by a man in love to his loved one, or by a witness before the court. These are like three sequences. (Or Messiaen's four "amen"s stretched over seven sequences.) Once again, there is no reason to say that the variables are merely situational, and that the statement remains constant in principle. Not only are there as many statements as there are effectuations, but all of the statements are present in the effectuation of one among them, so that the line of variation is virtual, in other words, real without being actual, and consequently continuous regardless of the leaps the statement makes. To place the statement in continuous variation is to send it through all the prosodic, semantic, syntactical, and phonological variables that can affect it in the shortest moment of time (the smallest interval). Build the *continuum* of "I swear!" with the corresponding transformations. This is the standpoint of pragmatics, but a pragmatics internal to language, immanent, including variations of linguistic elements of all kinds. For example, Kafka's line of the three proceedings: the father's proceedings in the family; the engagement proceedings at the hotel; and the court proceedings. There is a constant tendency to seek a "reduction": everything is explained by the situation of the child in relation to its father, or of the man in relation to castration, or of the citizen in relation to the law. But this is to content oneself with extracting a pseudoconstant of content, which is no better than extracting a pseudoconstant of expression. Placing-in-variation allows us to avoid these dangers, because it builds a continuum or medium without beginning or end. Continuous variation should not be confused with the continuous or discontinuous character of the variable itself: the order-word, a continuous variation for a discontinuous variable . . . A variable can be continuous over a portion of its trajectory, then leap or skip, without that affecting its continuous variation; what this does is impose an absent development as an "alternative continuity" that is virtual yet real.

A constant or invariant is defined less by its permanence and duration than by its function as a center, if only relative. In the tonal or diatonic system of music, laws of resonance and attraction determine centers valid for all modes and endowed with stability and attractive power (*pouvoir*). These centers therefore organize distinct, distinctive, forms that are clearly established for a certain amount of time: a linear, codified, centered system of the arborescent type. It is true that the minor "mode" gives tonal music a decentered, runaway, fugitive character due to the nature of its intervals and the lesser stability of its chords. This mode thus has the ambiguity of undergoing operations that align it to a major model or standard at the same time as it continues to display a certain modal power (*puissance*) irreducible to tonality, as though music set out on a journey and garnered all resurgences, phantoms of the Orient, imaginary lands, traditions from all over. But temperament, tempered chromaticism has an even greater ambiguity: stretching the action of the center to the most distant tones, but also preparing the disaggregation of the central principle, replacing the centered forms of continuous development with a form that constantly dissolves and transforms itself. When development subordinates form and spans the whole, as in Beethoven, variation begins to free itself and becomes identified with creation. But when chromaticism is unleashed, becomes a generalized chromaticism, turns back against temperament, affecting not only pitches but all sound components—durations, intensities, timbre, attacks—it becomes impossible to speak of a sound form organizing matter; it is no longer even possible to speak of a continuous development of form. Rather, it is a question of a highly complex and elaborate material making audible nonsonorous forces. The couple matter-form is replaced by the coupling material-forces. The synthesizer has taken the place of the old "a priori synthetic judgment," and all functions change accordingly. By placing all its components in continuous variation, music itself becomes a superlinear system, a rhizome instead of a tree, and enters the service of a virtual cosmic continuum of which even holes, silences, ruptures, and breaks are a part. Thus the important thing is certainly not to establish a pseudobreak between the tonal system and atonal music; the latter, on the contrary, in breaking away from the tonal system, only carried temperament to its ultimate conclusion (although no Viennese stopped there). The essential thing is almost the opposite movement: the ferment in the tonal system itself (during much of the nineteenth and twentieth centuries) that dissolved temperament and widened chromaticism while preserving a relative tonality, which reinvented new modalities, brought a new amalgamation of major and minor, and in each instance conquered realms of continuous variation for this variable or that. This ferment came to the forefront and made itself heard in its own right; and, through the molecular material thus wrought, it made audible the nonsonorous forces of the cosmos that have always agitated music—a bit of Time in the pure state,[27] a grain of absolute Intensity. . . The words "tonal," "modal," "atonal" do not mean much. Music is not alone in being art as cosmos and in drawing the virtual lines of an infinite variation.

Once again, the objection will be raised that music is not a language, that the components of sound are not pertinent features of language, that there is no correspondence between the two. We are not suggesting any correspondence. We keep asking that the issue be left open, that any presupposed distinction be rejected. This especially applies to the language-speech distinction, which is used to relegate all kinds of variables at work within expression and enunciation to a position outside language. The Voice-Music relation proposed by Jean-Jacques Rousseau, on the other hand, could have taken not only phonetics and prosody but all of linguistics in a different direction. The voice in music has always been a privileged axis of experimentation, playing simultaneously on language and sound. Music has linked the voice to instruments in various ways; but as long as the voice is song, its main role is to "hold" sound, it functions as a constant circumscribed on a note and *accompanied* by the instrument. Only when the voice is tied to timbre does it reveal a tessitura that renders it heterogeneous to itself and gives it a power of continuous variation: it is then no longer accompanied, but truly "machined," it belongs to a musical machine that prolongs or superposes on a single plane parts that are spoken, sung, achieved by special effects, instrumental, or perhaps electronically generated. This is the sound plane of a generalized "glissando" implying the constitution of a statistical space in which each variable has, not an average value, but a probability of frequency that places it in continuous variation with the other variables.[28] Luciano Berio's *Visage* (Face) and Dieter Schnebel's *Glossolalie* (Speaking in tongues) are typical examples of this. And despite what Berio himself says, it is less a matter of using pseudoconstants to produce a simulacrum of language or a metaphor for the voice than of attaining that secret neuter language without constants and entirely in indirect discourse where the synthesizer and the instrument speak no less than the voice, and the voice plays no less than the instrument. It should not be thought that music has forgotten how to sing in a now mechanical and atomized world; rather, an immense coefficient of variation is affecting and carrying away all of the phatic, aphatic, linguistic, poetic, instrumental, or musical parts of a single sound assemblage—"a simple scream suffusing all degrees" (Thomas Mann). There are many procedures for placing the voice in variation, not only *Sprechgesang* (speech-song), which constantly leaves pitch behind by descent or ascent, but also circular breathing techniques and zones of resonance in which several voices seem to issue from the same mouth. Secret languages are very significant in this connection, in learned as well as popular music. Certain ethnomusicologists have found extraordinary cases (in Dahomey, for example) where a first, diatonic, vocal part is superseded by a chromatic descent into a secret language that slips from one sound to the next in a continuous fashion, modulating a sound continuum into smaller and smaller intervals until it becomes a "parlando" all of the intervals of which blur together—and then the diatonic part is itself transposed according to the chromatic levels of a terraced architecture, the song sometimes interrupted by a parlando, by a simple conversation lacking definite pitch.[29] It is perhaps characteristic of secret languages, slangs, jargons, professional languages, nursery rhymes, merchants' cries to stand out less for their lexical inventions or rhetorical figures than for the way in which they effect continuous variations of the common elements of language. They are chromatic languages, close to a musical notation. A secret language does not merely have a hidden cipher or code still operating by constants and forming a subsystem; *it places the public language's system of variables in a state of variation.*

This is what we are getting at: a generalized chromaticism. Placing elements of any nature in continuous variation is an operation that will perhaps give rise to new distinctions, but takes none as final and has none in advance. On the contrary, this operation in principle bears on the voice, speech, language, and music simultaneously. There is no reason to make prior, principled distinctions. Linguistics in general is still in a kind of major mode, still has a sort of diatonic scale and a strange taste for dominants, constants, and universals. All languages, in the meantime, are in immanent continuous variation: neither synchrony nor diachrony, but asynchrony, chromaticism as a variable and continuous state of language. For a chromatic linguistics according pragmatism its intensities and values.

What is called a style can be the most natural thing in the world; it is nothing other than the procedure of a continuous variation. Of the dualisms established by linguistics, there are few with a more shaky foundation than the separation between linguistics and stylistics: Because a style is not an individual psychological creation but an assemblage of enunciation, it unavoidably produces a language within a language. Take an arbitrary list of authors we are fond of: Kafka once again, Beckett, Ghérasim Luca, Jean-

Luc Godard. It will be noted that they are all more or less in a bilingual situation: Kafka, the Czechoslovakian Jew writing in German; Beckett, the Irishman writing in English and French; Luca, originally from Romania; Godard and his will to be Swiss. But this is only circumstantial, an opportunity, and the opportunity can be found elsewhere. It will also be noted that many of them are not only or not primarily writers (Beckett and theater and television, Godard and film and television, Luca and his audiovisual machines). The reason for this is that when one submits linguistic elements to a treatment producing continuous variation, when one introduces an internal pragmatics into language, one is necessarily led to treat nonlinguistic elements such as gestures and instruments in the same fashion, as if the two aspects of pragmatics joined on the same line of variation, in the same continuum. Moreover, the idea perhaps comes first from outside, with language following only later, as with the necessarily exterior sources of a style. But the essential thing is that each of these authors has his own procedure of variation, his own widened chromaticism, his own mad production of speeds and intervals. The creative stammering of Ghérasim Luca, in the poem "Passionnément" (Passionately).[30] Godard's is another kind of stammering. In theater: Robert Wilson's whispering, without definite pitch, and Carmelo Bene's ascending and descending variations.[31] It's easy to stammer, but making language itself stammer is a different affair; it involves placing all linguistic, and even nonlinguistic, elements in variation, both variables of expression and variables of content. A new form of redundancy. AND . . . AND . . . AND . . . There has always been a struggle in language between the verb *être* (to be) and the conjunction *et* (and) between *est* and *et* (is and and [which in French are identical in pronunciation—Trans.]) It is only in appearance that these two terms are in accord and combine, for the first acts in language as a constant and forms the diatonic scale of language, while the second places everything in variation, constituting the lines of a generalized chromaticism. From one to the other, everything shifts. Writers in British or American English have been more conscious than the French of this struggle and the stakes involved, and of the valence of the "and."[32] It was Proust who said that "masterpieces are written in a kind of foreign language." That is the same as stammering, making language stammer rather than stammering in speech. To be a foreigner, but in one's own tongue, not only when speaking a language other than one's own. To be bilingual, multilingual, but in one and the same language, without even a dialect or patois. To be a bastard, a half-breed, but through a purification of race. That is when style becomes a language. That is when language becomes intensive, a pure continuum of values and intensities. That is when all of language becomes secret, yet has nothing to hide, as opposed to when one carves out a secret subsystem within language. One attains this result only by sobriety, creative subtraction. Continuous variation has only ascetic lines, a touch of herb and pure water.

It is possible to take any linguistic variable and place it in variation following a necessarily virtual continuous line between two of its states. We are no longer in the situation of linguists who expect the constants of language to experience a kind of mutation or undergo the effects of changes accumulated in speech alone. Lines of change or creation are fully and directly a part of the abstract machine. Hjelmslev remarked that a language necessarily includes unexploited possibilities or potentialities and that the abstract machine must include these possibilities or potentialities.[33] "Potential" and "virtual" are not at all in opposition to "real"; on the contrary, the reality of the creative, or the placing-in-continuous variation of variables, is in opposition only to the actual determination of their constant relations. Each time we draw a line of variation, the variables are of a particular nature (phonological, syntactical or grammatical, semantic, and so on), but the line itself is apertinent, asyntactic or agrammatical, asemantic. Agrammaticality, for example, is no longer a contingent characteristic of speech opposed to the grammaticality of language; rather, it is the ideal characteristic of a line placing grammatical variables in a state of continuous variation. Let us take Nicolas Ruwet's examples of certain singular expressions of Cummings's: "he danced his did," or "they went their came." It is possible to reconstitute the variations through which the grammatical variables pass in virtuality in order to end up as agrammatical expressions of this kind ("he did his dance," "he danced his dance," "he danced what he did," . . . ; "they went as they came," "they went their way," . . .).[34] In spite of Ruwet's structural interpretation, we should avoid taking the view that the atypical expression is produced by the successive correct forms. It is instead the atypical expression that produces the placing-in-variation of the correct forms, uprooting them from their state as constants. The atypical expression constitutes a cutting edge of deterritorialization of language, it plays the role of *tensor;* in other words, it causes language to tend toward the limit of its elements, forms, or notions, toward a near side or a beyond of language. The tensor effects a kind of transitivization of the phrase, causing the last term to react upon the preceding term, back through the entire chain. It assures an intensive and chromatic treatment of language. An expression as simple as AND . . . can play the role of tensor for all of language. In this sense, AND is less a conjunction than the atypical expression of all of the possible conjunctions it places in continuous variation. The tensor, therefore, is not reducible either to a constant or a variable, but assures the variation of the variable by subtracting in each instance the value of the constant ($n - 1$). Tensors coincide with no linguistic category; nevertheless they are pragmatic values essential to both assemblages of enunciation and indirect discourses.[35]

Some believe that these variations do not express the usual labor of creation in language and remain marginal, confined to poets, children, and lunatics. That is because they wish to define the abstract machine by constants that can be modified only secondarily, by a cumulative effect or syntagmatic mutation. But the abstract machine of language is not universal, or even general, but singular; it is not actual, but virtual-real; it has, not invariable or obligatory rules, but optional rules that ceaselessly vary with the variation itself, as in a game in which each move changes the rules. That is why abstract machines and assemblages of enunciation are complementary, and present in each other. The abstract machine is like the diagram of an assemblage. It draws lines of continuous variation, while the concrete assemblage treats variables and organizes their highly diverse relations as a function of those lines. The assemblage negotiates variables at this or that level of variation, according to this or that degree of deterritorialization, and determines which variables will enter into constant relations or obey obligatory rules and which will serve instead as a fluid matter for variation. We should not conclude from this that the assemblage brings only a certain resistance or inertia to bear against the abstract machine; for even "constants" are essential to the determination of the virtualities through which the variation passes, they are themselves optionally chosen. There is indeed braking and resistance at a certain level, but at another level of the assemblage there is nothing but a come-and-go between different types of variables, and corridors of passage traveled in both directions: the variables effectuate the machine in unison, in the sum of their relations. There is therefore no basis for a distinction between a constant and collective language, and variable and individual speech acts. The abstract machine is always singular, designated by the proper name of a group or individual, while the assemblage of enunciation is always collective, in the individual as in the group. The Lenin abstract machine, and the Bolshevik collective assemblage . . . The same goes for literature, for music. There is no primacy of the individual; there is instead an indissolubility of a singular Abstract and a collective Concrete. The abstract machine does not exist independently of the assemblage, any more than the assemblage functions independently of the machine.

VI. "Language Can Be Scientifically Studied Only under the Conditions of a Standard or Major Language"

Since everybody knows that language is a heterogeneous, variable reality, what is the meaning of the linguists' insistence on carving out a homogeneous system in order to make a scientific study possible? It is a question of extracting a set of constants from the variables, or of determining constant relations between variables (this is already evident in the phonologists' concept of commutativity). But the scientific model taking language as an object of study is one with the political model by which language is homogenized, centralized, standardized, becoming a language of power, a major or dominant language. Linguistics can claim all it wants to be science, nothing but pure science—it wouldn't be the first time that the order of pure science was used to secure the requirements of another order. What is grammaticality, and the sign S, the categorical symbol that dominates statements? It is a power marker before it is a syntactical marker, and Chomsky's trees establish constant relations between power variables. Forming grammatically correct sentences is for the normal individual the prerequisite for any submission to social laws. No one is supposed to be ignorant of grammaticality; those who are belong in special institutions. The unity of language is fundamentally political. There is no mother tongue, only a power takeover by a dominant language that at times advances along a broad front, and at times swoops down on diverse centers simultaneously. We can conceive of several ways for a language to homogenize, centralize: the republican way is not necessarily the same as the royal way, and is not the least harsh.[36] The scientific enterprise of extracting constants and constant relations is always coupled with the political enterprise of imposing them on speakers and transmitting order-words.

> Speak white and loud
> yes what a wonderful language
> for hiring
> giving orders
> appointing the hour of death in the works
> and of the break that refreshes . . .

Must a distinction then be made between two kinds of languages, "high" and "low," major and minor? The first would be defined precisely by the power (*pouvoir*) of constants, the second by the power (*puissance*) of variation. We do not simply wish to make an opposition between the unity of a major language and the multiplicity of dialects. Rather, each dialect has a zone of transition and variation; or better, each minor language has a properly dialectical zone of variation. According to Malmberg, it is rare to find clear boundaries on dialect maps; instead, there are transitional and limitrophe zones, zones of indiscernibility. It is also said that "the Québecois language is so rich in modulations and variations of regional accents and in games with tonic accents that it sometimes seems, with no exaggeration, that it would be better preserved by musical notation than by any system of spelling."[37] The very notion of dialect is quite questionable. Moreover, it is relative because one needs to know in relation to what major language it exercises its function: for example, the Québecois language must be evaluated not only in relation to standard French but also in relation to major English, from which it borrows all kinds of phonetic and syntactical elements, in order to set them in variation. The Bantu dialects must be evaluated not only in relation to the mother tongue but also in relation to Afrikaans as a major language, and English as a counter-major language preferred by blacks.[38] In short, the notion of dialect does not elucidate that of minor language, but the other way around; it is the minor language that defines dialects through its own possibilities for variation. Should we identify major and minor languages on the basis of regional situations of bilingualism or multilingualism including at least one dominant language and one dominated language, or a world situation giving certain languages an imperialist power over others (for example, the role of American English today)?

At least two things prevent us from adopting this point of view. As Chomsky notes, a dialect, ghetto language, or minor language is not immune to the kind of treatment that draws a homogeneous system from it and extracts constants: Black English has its own grammar, which is not defined by a sum of mistakes or infractions against standard English; but that grammar can be studied only by applying to it the same rules of study that are applied to standard English. In this sense, the notions of major and minor seem to have no linguistic relevance. When French lost its worldwide major function it lost nothing of its constancy and homogeneity, its centralization. Conversely, Afrikaans attained homogeneity when it was a locally minor language struggling against English. Even politically, especially politically, it is difficult to see how the upholders of a minor language can operate if not by giving it (if only by writing in it) a constancy and homogeneity making it a locally major language capable of forcing official recognition (hence the political role of writers who assert the rights of a minor language). But the opposite argument seems more compelling: the more a language has or acquires the characteristics of a major language, the more it is affected by continuous variations that transpose it into a "minor" language. It is futile to criticize the worldwide imperialism of a language by denouncing the corruptions it introduces into other languages (for example, the purists' criticisms of English influences in French, the petit-bourgeois or academic denunciation of "Franglais"). For if a language such as British English or American English is major on a world scale, it is necessarily worked upon by all the minorities of the world, using very diverse procedures of variation. Take the way Gaelic and Irish English set English in variation. Or the way Black English and any number of "ghetto languages" set American English in variation, to the point that New York is virtually a city without a language. (Furthermore, American English could not have *constituted* itself without this linguistic labor of the minorities.) Or the linguistic situation in the old Austrian empire: German was a major language in relation to the minorities, but as such it could not avoid being treated by those minorities in a way that made it a minor language in relation to the German of the Germans. There is no language that does not have intralinguistic, endogenous, internal minorities. So at the most general level of linguistics, Chomsky's and Labov's positions are constantly passing and converting into each other. Chomsky can say that even a minor, dialectical, or ghetto language cannot be studied unless invariants are extracted from it and "extrinsic or mixed" variables are eliminated; and Labov can respond that even a standard or major language cannot be studied independently of "inherent" variations, which are precisely neither mixed nor extrinsic. *You will never find a homogeneous system that is not still or already affected by a regulated, continuous, immanent process of variation* (why does Chomsky pretend not to understand this?).

There are not, therefore, two kinds of languages but two possible treatments of the same language. Either the variables are treated in such a way as to extract from them constants and constant relations or in such a way as to place them in continuous variation. We were wrong to give the impression at times that constants existed alongside variables, linguistic constants alongside variables of enunciation: that was only for convenience of presentation. For it is obvious that the constants are drawn from the variables themselves; universals in linguistics have no more existence in themselves than they do in economics and are always concluded from a universalization or a rendering-uniform involving variables. *Constant is not opposed to variable;* it is a treatment of the variable opposed to the other kind of treatment, or continuous variation. So-called obligatory rules correspond to the first kind of treatment, whereas optional rules concern the construction of a continuum of variation. Moreover, there are a certain number of categories or distinctions that cannot be invoked, that are inapplicable and useless as a basis for objections because they presuppose the first treatment and are entirely subordinated to the quest for constants: for example, language as opposed to speech; synchrony as opposed to diachrony; competence as opposed to performance; distinctive features as opposed to nondistinctive (or secondarily distinctive) features. For nondistinctive features, whether prosodic, stylistic, or pragmatic, are not only omnipresent variables, in contrast to the presence or absence of a constant; they are not only superlinear and "suprasegmental" elements, in contrast to linear segmental elements; their very characteristics give them the power to place all the elements of language in a state of continuous variation—for example, the impact of tone on phonemes, accent on morphemes, or intonation on syntax. These are not secondary features but another treatment of language that no longer operates according to the preceding categories.

"Major" and "minor" do not qualify two different languages but rather two usages or functions of language. Bilingualism, of course, provides a good example, but once again we use it simply for the sake of convenience. Doubtless, in the Austrian empire Czech was a minor language in relation to German; but the German of Prague already functioned as a potentially minor language in relation to the German of Vienna or Berlin; and Kafka, a Czechoslovakian Jew writing in German, submits German to creative treatment as a minor language, constructing a continuum of variation, negotiating all of the variables both to constrict the constants and to expand the variables: make language stammer, or make it "wail," stretch tensors through all of language, even written language, and draw from it cries, shouts, pitches, durations, timbres, accents, intensities. Two conjoined tendencies in so-called minor languages have often been noted: an impoverishment, a shedding of syntactical and lexical forms; but simultaneously a strange proliferation of shifting effects, a taste for overload and paraphrase. This applies to the German of Prague, Black English, and Québecois. But with rare exceptions, the interpretation of the linguists has been rather malevolent, invoking a consubstantial poverty and preciosity. The alleged poverty is in fact a restriction of constants and the overload an extension of variations functioning to deploy a continuum sweeping up all components. The poverty is not a lack but a void or ellipsis allowing one to sidestep a constant instead of tackling it head on, or to approach it from above or below instead of positioning oneself within it. And the overload is not a rhetorical figure, a metaphor, or symbolic structure; it is a mobile paraphrase bearing witness to the unlocalized presence of an indirect discourse at the heart of every statement. From both sides we see a rejection of reference points, a dissolution of constant form in favor of differences in dynamic. The closer a language gets to this state, the closer it comes not only to a system of musical notation, but also to music itself.[39]

Subtract and place in variation, remove and place in variation: a single operation. Minor languages are characterized not by overload and poverty in relation to a standard or major language, but by a sobriety and variation that are like a minor treatment of the standard language, a becoming-minor of the major language. The problem is not the distinction between major and minor language; it is one of a becoming. It is a question not of reterritorializing oneself on a dialect or a patois but of deterritorializing the major language. Black Americans do not oppose Black to English, they transform the American English that is their own language into Black

English. Minor languages do not exist in themselves: they exist only in relation to a major language and are also investments of that language for the purpose of making it minor. One must find the minor language, the dialect or rather idiolect, on the basis of which one can make one's own major language minor. That is the strength of authors termed "minor," who are in fact the greatest, the only greats: having to conquer one's own language, in other words, to attain that sobriety in the use of a major language, in order to place it in a state of continuous variation (the opposite of regionalism). It is in one's own language that one is bilingual or multilingual. Conquer the major language in order to delineate in it as yet unknown minor languages. Use the minor language to *send the major language racing*. Minor authors are foreigners in their own tongue. If they are bastards, if they experience themselves as bastards, it is due not to a mixing or intermingling of languages but rather to a subtraction and variation of their own language achieved by stretching tensors through it.

The notion of *minority* is very complex, with musical, literary, linguistic, as well as juridical and political, references. The opposition between minority and majority is not simply quantitative. Majority implies a constant, of expression or content, serving as a standard measure by which to evaluate it. Let us suppose that the constant or standard is the average adult-white-heterosexual-European-male-speaking a standard language (Joyce's or Ezra Pound's Ulysses). It is obvious that "man" holds the majority, even if he is less numerous than mosquitoes, children, women, blacks, peasants, homosexuals, etc. That is because he appears twice, once in the constant and again in the variable from which the constant is extracted. Majority assumes a state of power and domination, not the other way around. It assumes the standard measure, not the other way around. Even Marxism "has almost always translated hegemony from the point of view of the national worker, qualified, male and over thirty-five."[40] A determination different from that of the constant will therefore be considered minoritarian, by nature and regardless of number, in other words, a subsystem or an outsystem. This is evident in all the operations, electoral or otherwise, where you are given a choice, but on the condition that your choice conform to the limits of the constant ("you mustn't choose to change society . . ."). But at this point, everything is reversed. For the majority, insofar as it is analytically included in the abstract standard, is never anybody, it is always Nobody—Ulysses—whereas the minority is the becoming of everybody, one's potential becoming to the extent that one deviates from the model. There is a majoritarian "fact," but it is the analytic fact of Nobody, as opposed to the becoming-minoritarian of everybody. That is why we must distinguish between: the majoritarian as a constant and homogeneous system; minorities as subsystems; and the minoritarian as a potential, creative and created, becoming. The problem is never to acquire the majority, even in order to install a new constant. There is no becoming-majoritarian; majority is never becoming. All becoming is minoritarian. Women, regardless of their numbers, are a minority, definable as a state or subset; but they create only by making possible a becoming over which they do not have ownership, into which they themselves must enter; this is a becoming-woman affecting all of humankind, men and women both. The same goes for minor languages: they are not simply sublanguages, idiolects or dialects, but potential agents of the major language's entering into a becoming-minoritarian of all of its dimensions and elements. We should distinguish between minor languages, the major language, and the becoming-minor of the major language. Minorities, of course, are objectively definable states, states of language, ethnicity, or sex with their own ghetto territorialities, but they must also be thought of as seeds, crystals of becoming whose value is to trigger uncontrollable movements and deterritorializations of the mean or majority. That is why Pasolini demonstrated that the essential thing, precisely in free indirect discourse, is to be found neither in language A, nor in language B, but "in language X, which is none other than language A in the actual process of becoming language B."[41] There is a universal figure of minoritarian consciousness as the becoming of everybody, and that becoming is creation. One does not attain it by acquiring the majority. The figure to which we are referring is continuous variation, as an amplitude that continually oversteps the representative threshold of the majoritarian standard, by excess or default. In erecting the figure of a universal minoritarian consciousness, one addresses powers (*puissances*) of becoming that belong to a different realm from that of Power (*Pouvoir*) and Domination. Continuous variation constitutes the becoming-minoritarian of everybody, as opposed to the majoritarian Fact of Nobody. Becoming-minoritarian as the universal figure of consciousness is called autonomy. It is certainly not by using a minor language as a dialect, by regionalizing or ghettoizing, that one becomes revolutionary; rather, by using a number of minority elements, by connecting, conjugating them, one invents a specific, unforeseen, autonomous becoming.[42]

The major and minor mode are two different treatments of language, one of which consists in extracting constants from it, the other in placing it in continuous variation. The order-word is the variable of enunciation that effectuates the condition of possibility of language and defines the usage of its elements according to one of the two treatments; we must therefore return to it as the only "metalanguage" capable of accounting for this double direction, this double treatment of variables. The problem of the functions of language is in general poorly formulated because this order-word variable, which subsumes all possible functions, is overlooked. Following Canetti's suggestions, we may begin from the following pragmatic situation: the order-word is a death sentence; it always implies a death sentence, even if it has been considerably softened, becoming symbolic, initiatory, temporary, etc. Order-words bring immediate death to those who receive the order, or potential death if they do not obey, or a death they must themselves inflict, take elsewhere. A father's orders to his son, "You will do this," "You will not do that," cannot be separated from the little death sentence the son experiences on a point of his person. Death, death; it is the only judgment, and it is what makes judgment a system. The verdict. *But the order-word is also something else*, inseparably connected: it is like a warning cry or a message to flee. It would be oversimplifying to say that flight is a reaction against the order-word; rather, it is included in it, as its other face in a complex assemblage, its other component. Canetti is right to invoke the lion's roar, which enunciates flight and death simultaneously.[43] The order-word has two tones. The prophet receives order-words just as much in taking flight as in longing for death: Jewish prophetism fused the wish to be dead and the flight impulse with the divine order-word.

Now if we consider the first aspect of the order-word, in other words, death as the expressed of the statement, it clearly meets the preceding requirements: even though death essentially concerns bodies, is attributed to bodies, its immediacy, its instantaneousness, lends it the authentic character of an incorporeal transformation. What precedes and follows it may be an extensive system of actions and passions, a slow labor of bodies; in itself, it is neither action nor passion, but a pure act, a pure transformation that enunciation fuses with the statement, the sentence. That man is dead . . . You are already dead when you receive the order-word . . . In effect, death is everywhere, as that ideal, uncrossable boundary separating bodies, their forms, and states, and as the condition, even initiatory, even symbolic, through which a subject must pass in order to change its form or state. This is the sense in which Canetti speaks of "enantiomorphosis":[44] a regime that involves a hieratic and immutable Master who at every moment legislates by constants, prohibiting or strictly limiting metamorphoses, giving figures clear and stable contours, setting forms in opposition two by two and requiring subjects to die in order to pass from one form to the other. It is always by means of something incorporeal that a body separates and distinguishes itself from another. The figure, insofar as it is the extremity of a body, is the noncorporeal attribute that limits and completes that body: death is the Figure. It is through death that a body reaches completion not only in time but in space, and it is through death that its lines form or outline a shape. There are dead spaces just as there are dead times. "If [enantiomorphosis is] practiced often the whole world shrivels. . . .

Social prohibitions against metamorphosis are perhaps the most important of all. . . . Death itself, the strictest of all boundaries, is what is interposed between classes."[45] In a regime of this kind, any new body requires the erection of an opposable form, as well as the formation of distinct subjects; death is the general incorporeal transformation attributed to all bodies from the standpoint of their forms and substances (for example, the body of the Party cannot come into its own without an operation of enantiomorphosis, and without the formation of new activists, which assumes the elimination of the first generation).

It is true that we are bringing in considerations of content as well as expression. For even at the moment when the two planes are most distinct, as the regime of bodies and the regime of signs in an assemblage, they are still in reciprocal presupposition. The incorporeal transformation is the expressed of order-words, but also the attribute of bodies. Not only do linguistic variables of expression enter into relations of formal opposition or distinction favorable to the extraction of constants; nonlinguistic variables of content do also. As Hjelmslev notes, an expression is divided, for example, into phonic units in the same way a content is divided into social, zoological, or physical units ("calf" divides into young-bovine-male).[46] The network of binarities, or arborescences, is applicable to both sides. There is, however, no analytic resemblance, correspondence, or conformity between the two planes. But their independence does not preclude isomorphism, in other words, the existence of the same kind of constant relations on both sides. It is by virtue of this type of relations that linguistic and nonlinguistic elements are inseparable from the start, despite their absence of correspondence. The elements of content give the interminglings of bodies clear contours at the same time as the elements of expression give the noncorporeal expresseds a power of sentencing or judgment. These elements are all abstract or deterritorialized to different degrees, but in each instance they effect a reterritorialization of the overall assemblage on certain order-words and contours. Indeed, the significance of the doctrine of synthetic judgment is to have demonstrated that there is an a priori link (isomorphism) between Sentence and Figure, form of expression and form of content.

If we consider the other aspect of the order-word, flight rather than death, it appears that variables are in a new state, that of continuous variation. An incorporeal transformation is still attributed to bodies, but it is now a passage to the limit: that is the only way, not to eliminate death, but to reduce it or make it a variation itself. This movement pushes language to its own limits, while bodies are simultaneously caught up in a movement of metamorphosis of their contents or a process of exhaustion causing them to reach or overstep the limit of their figures. This is an appropriate place to bring up the opposition between minor sciences and major sciences: for example, the tendency of the broken line to become a curve, a whole operative geometry of the trait and movement, a pragmatic science of placings-in-variation that operates in a different manner than the royal or major science of Euclid's invariants and travels a long history of suspicion and even repression (we will return to this question later).[47] The smallest interval is always diabolical: the master of metamorphoses is opposed to the invariant hieratic king. It is as though an intense matter or a continuum of variation were freed, here in the internal tensors of language, there in the internal tensions of content. The idea of the smallest interval does not apply to figures of the same nature; it implies at least a curve and a straight line, a circle and a tangent. We witness a transformation of substances and a dissolution of forms, a passage to the limit or flight from contours in favor of fluid forces, flows, air, light, and matter, such that a body or a word does not end at a precise point. We witness the incorporeal power of that intense matter, the material power of that language. A matter more immediate, more fluid, and more ardent than bodies or words. In continuous variation the relevant distinction is no longer between a form of expression and a form of content but between two inseparable planes in reciprocal presupposition. The relativity of the distinction between them is now fully realized on the plane of consistency, where the assemblage is swept up by a now absolute deterritorialization. Absolute, however, does not mean undifferentiated: differences, now "infinitely small," are constituted in a single matter serving both for expression as incorporeal power and for content as limitless corporeality. The relation of presupposition between variables of content and expression no longer requires two forms: the placing-in-variation of the variables instead draws the two forms together and effects the conjunction of cutting edges of deterritorialization on both sides; this occurs on the plane of a single liberated matter that contains no figures, is deliberately unformed, and retains in expression and in content only those cutting edges, tensors, and tensions. Gestures and things, voices and sounds, are caught up in the same "opera," swept away by the same shifting effects of stammering, vibrato, tremolo, and overspilling. A synthesizer places all of the parameters in continuous variation, gradually making "fundamentally heterogeneous elements end up turning into each other in some way." The moment this conjunction occurs there is a common matter. It is only at this point that one reaches the abstract machine, or the diagram of the assemblage. The synthesizer has replaced judgment, and matter has replaced the figure or formed substance. It is no longer even appropriate to group biological, physicochemical, and energetic intensities on the one hand, and mathematical, aesthetic, linguistic, informational, semiotic intensities, etc., on the other. The multiplicity of systems of intensities conjugates or forms a rhizome throughout the entire assemblage the moment the assemblage is swept up by these vectors or tensions of flight. For the question was not how to elude the order-word but how to elude the death sentence it envelops, how to develop its power of escape, how to prevent escape from veering into the imaginary or falling into a black hole, how to maintain or draw out the revolutionary potentiality of the order-word. Hofmannsthal adopts the order-word, "Germany, Germany!", or the need to reterritorialize, even in a "melancholy mirror." But beneath this order-word he hears another, as if the old German "figures" were mere constants that were then effaced to uncover a relation with nature and life all the more profound for being variable. When should this relation to life be a hardening, when submission? At what moment is rebellion called for and at what moment surrender or impassibility? When is dry speech necessary and when exuberance or amusement?[48] Whatever the breaks and ruptures, only continuous variation brings forth this virtual line, this virtual continuum of life, "the essential element of the real beneath the everyday." There is a splendid statement in one of Herzog's films. The main character asks himself a question and then says, Who will answer this answer? Actually, there is no question, answers are all one ever answers. To the answer already contained in a question (cross-examination, competition, plebiscite, etc.) one should respond with questions from another answer. One should bring forth the order-word of the order-word. In the order-word, life must answer the answer of death, not by fleeing, but by making flight act and create. There are pass-words beneath order-words. Words that pass, words that are components of passage, whereas order-words mark stoppages or organized, stratified compositions. A single thing or word undoubtedly has this twofold nature: it is necessary to extract one from the other—to transform the compositions of order into components of passage.

5. 587 B.C.–A.D. 70: On Several Regimes of Signs

The Order of the Ark of the Israelites

A New Regime

We call any specific formalization of expression a regime of signs, at least when the expression is linguistic. A regime of signs constitutes a semiotic system. But it appears difficult to analyze semiotic systems in themselves: there is always a form of content that is simultaneously inseparable from and independent of the form of expression, and the two forms pertain to assemblages that are not principally linguistic. However, one can proceed as though the formalization of expression were autonomous and self-sufficient. Even if that is done, there is such diversity in the forms of expression, such a mixture of these forms, that it is impossible to attach any particular privilege to the form or regime of the "signifier." If we call the signifying semiotic system semiology, then semiology is only one regime of signs among others, and not the most important one. Hence the necessity of a return to pragmatics, in which language never has universality in itself, self-sufficient formalization, a general semiology, or a metalanguage. Thus it is the study of the signifying regime that first testifies to the inadequacy of linguistic presuppositions, and in the very name of regimes of signs.

There is a simple general formula for the signifying regime of the sign (the signifying sign): every sign refers to another sign, and only to another sign, ad infinitum. That is why, at the limit, one can forgo the notion of the sign, for what is retained is not principally the sign's relation to a state of things it designates, or to an entity it signifies, but only the formal relation of sign to sign insofar as it defines a so-called signifying chain. The limitlessness of signifiance replaces the sign. When denotation (here, designation and signification taken together) is assumed to be part of connotation, one is wholly within this signifying regime of the sign. Not much attention is paid to *indexes*, in other words, the territorial states of things constituting the designatable. Not much attention is paid to *icons*, that is, operations of reterritorialization constituting the signifiable. Thus the sign has already attained a high degree of relative deterritorialization; it is thought of as a *symbol* in a constant movement of referral from sign to sign. The signifier is the sign in redundancy with the sign. All signs are signs of signs. The question is not yet what a given sign signifies but to which other signs it refers, or which signs add themselves to it to form a network without beginning or end that projects its shadow onto an amorphous atmospheric continuum. It is this amorphous continuum that for the moment plays the role of the "signified," but it continually glides beneath the signifier, for which it serves only as a medium or wall: the specific forms of all contents dissolve in it. The atmospherization or mundanization of contents. Contents are abstracted. This is the situation Lévi-Strauss describes: the world begins to signify before anyone knows *what* it signifies; the signified is given without being known.[1] Your wife looked at you with a funny expression. And this morning the mailman handed you a letter from the IRS and crossed his fingers. Then you stepped in a pile of dog shit. You saw two sticks on the sidewalk positioned like the hands of a watch. They were whispering behind your back when you arrived at the office. It doesn't matter what it means, it's still signifying. The sign that refers to other signs is struck with a strange impotence and uncertainty, but mighty is the signifier that constitutes the chain. The paranoiac shares this impotence of the deterritorialized sign assailing him from every direction in the gliding atmosphere, but that only gives him better access to the superpower of the signifier, through the royal feeling of wrath, as master of the network spreading through the atmosphere. The paranoid despotic regime: they are attacking me and making me suffer, but I can guess what they're up to, I'm one step ahead of them, I've always known, I have power even in my impotence. "I'll get them."

Nothing is ever over and done with in a regime of this kind. It's made for that, it's the tragic regime of infinite debt, to which one is simultaneously debtor and creditor. A sign refers to another sign, into which it passes and which carries it into still other signs. "To the point that it returns in a circular fashion . . ." Not only do signs form an infinite network, but the network of signs is infinitely circular. The statement survives its object, the name survives its owner. Whether it passes into other signs or is kept in reserve for a time, the sign survives both its state of things and its signified; it leaps like an animal or a dead person to regain its place in the chain and invest a new state, a new signified, from which it will in turn extricate itself.[2] A hint of the eternal return. There is a whole regime of roving, floating statements, suspended names, signs lying in wait to return and be propelled by the chain. The signifier as the self-redundancy of the deterritorialized sign, a funereal world of terror.

But what counts is less this circularity of signs than the multiplicity of the circles or chains. The sign refers not only to other signs in the same circle, but to signs in other circles or spirals as well. Robert Lowie describes how Crow and Hopi men react differently when their wives cheat on them (the Crow are nomadic hunters and the Hopi sedentaries with an imperial tradition): "A Crow Indian whose wife has cheated on him slashes her face, whereas the Hopi who has fallen victim to the same misfortune, without losing his calm, withdraws and prays for drought and famine to descend on the village." It is easy to see where the paranoia resides, the despotic element or signifying regime, or again, as Lévi-Strauss says, "the bigotry": "In effect, for a Hopi everything is connected: a social disturbance or a domestic incident calls into question the system of the universe, the levels of which are united by multiple correspondences; a disruption on one plane is only intelligible, and morally tolerable, as a projection of other disruptions involving other levels."[3] The Hopi jump from one circle to another, or from one sign to another on a different spiral. One leaves the village or the city, only to return. The jumps may be regulated not only by presignifying rituals but also by a whole imperial bureaucracy passing judgment on their legitimacy. The jumps are not made at random, they are not without rules. Not only are they regulated, but some are prohibited: Do not overstep the outermost circle, do not approach the innermost circle . . . There is a distinction between circles because, although all signs refer to each other only to the extent that they are deterritorialized, oriented toward the same center of signifiance, distributed throughout an amorphous continuum, they have different speeds of deterritorialization attesting to a place of origin (temple, palace, house, street, village, bush, etc.), and they have differential relations maintaining the distinction between circles or constituting thresholds in the atmosphere of the continuum (private and public, family incident and social disorder). Moreover, the distribution of these thresholds and circles changes according to the case. Deception is fundamental to the system. Jumping from circle to circle, always moving the scene, playing it out somewhere else: such is the hysteric operation of the deceiver as subject, answering to the paranoid operation of the despot installed in his center of signifiance.

There is one other aspect: the signifying regime is not simply faced with the task of organizing into circles signs emitted from every direction; it must constantly assure the expansion of the circles or spiral, it must provide the center with more signifier to overcome the entropy inherent in the system and to make new circles blossom or replenish the old. Thus a secondary mechanism in the service of signifiance is necessary: interpretance or interpretation. This time the signifier assumes a new figure: it is no longer the amorphous continuum that is given without being known and across which the network of signs is strung. A portion of signified is made to correspond to a sign or group of signs for which that signified has been deemed suitable, thus making it knowable. To the syntagmatic axis of the sign referring to other signs is added a paradigmatic axis on which the sign, thus formalized, fashions for itself a suitable signified (once again there is abstraction of the content, but in a new way). The interpretive priest, the seer, is one of the despot-god's bureaucrats. A new aspect of deception arises, the deception of the priest: interpretation is carried to infinity and never encounters anything to interpret that is not already itself an interpretation. The signified constantly reimparts signifier, recharges it or produces more of it. The form always comes from the signifier. The ultimate signified is therefore the signifier itself, in its redundancy or "excess." It is perfectly futile to claim to transcend interpretation or even communication through the production of signifier, because communication and interpretation are what always serve to reproduce and produce signifier. That is certainly not the way to revive the notion of production. The discovery of the psychoanalyst-priests (a discovery every kind of priest or seer made in their time) was that interpretation had to be subordinated to signifiance, to the point that the signifier would impart no signified without the signified reimparting signifier in its turn. Actually, there is no longer even any need to interpret, but that is because the best interpretation, the weightiest and most radical one, is an eminently significant silence. It is well known that although psychoanalysts have ceased to speak, they interpret even more, or better yet, fuel interpretation on the part of the subject, who jumps from one circle of hell to the next. In truth, signifiance and interpretosis are the two diseases of the earth or the skin, in other words, humankind's fundamental neurosis.

There is not much to say about the center of signifiance, or the Signifier in person, because it is a pure abstraction no less than a pure principle; in other words, it is nothing. Lack or excess, it hardly matters. It comes to the same thing to say that the sign refers to other signs ad infinitum and that the infinite set of all signs refers to a supreme signifier. At any rate, this pure formal redundancy of the signifier could not even be conceptualized if it did not have its own substance of expression, for which we must find a name: *faciality*. Not only is language always accompanied by faciality traits, but the face crystallizes all redundancies, it emits and receives, releases and recaptures signifying signs. It is a whole body unto itself: it is like the body of the center of signifiance to which all of the deterritorialized signs affix themselves, and it marks the limit of their deterritorialization. The voice emanates from the face; that is why, however fundamentally important the writing machine is in the imperial bureaucracy, what is written retains an oral or nonbook character. The face is the Icon proper to the signifying regime, the reterritorialization internal to the system. The signifier reterritorializes on the face. The face is what gives the signifier substance; it is what fuels interpretation, and it is what changes, changes traits, when interpretation reimparts signifier to its substance. Look, his expression changed. The signifier is always facialized. Faciality reigns materially over that whole constellation of signifiances and interpretations (psychologists have written extensively on the baby's relations to the mother's face, and sociologists on the role of the face in mass media and advertising). The despot-god has never hidden his face, far from it: he makes himself one, or even several. The mask does not hide the face, it *is* the face. The priest administers the face of the god. With the despot, everything is public, and everything that is public is so by virtue of the face. Lies and deception may be a fundamental part of the signifying regime, but secrecy is not.[4] Conversely, when the face is effaced, when the faciality traits disappear, we can be sure that we have entered another regime, other zones infinitely muter and more imperceptible where subterranean becomings-animal occur, becomings-molecular, nocturnal deterritorializations overspilling the limits of the signifying system. The despot or god brandishes the solar face that is his entire body, as the body of the signifier. He looked at me queerly, he knitted his brow, what did I do to make him change expression? I have her picture in front of me, it's as if she were watching me . . . Surveillance by the face, as Strindberg said. Overcoding by the signifier, irradiation in all directions, unlocalized omnipresence.

Finally, the face or body of the despot or god has something like a counterbody: the body of the tortured, or better, of the excluded. There is no question that these two bodies communicate, for the body of the despot is sometimes subjected to trials of humiliation or even torture, or of exile and exclusion. "At the opposite pole one might imagine placing the body of the condemned man; he, too, has his legal status; he gives rise to his own ceremonial . . . not in order to ground the surplus power possessed by the person of the sovereign, but in order to code the lack of power with which those subjected to punishment are marked. In the darkest region of the political field the condemned man outlines the symmetrical, inverted figure of the king."[5] The one who is tortured is fundamentally one who loses his or her face, entering into a becoming-animal, a becoming-molecular the ashes of which are thrown to the wind. But it appears that the one who is tortured is not at all the final term, but rather the first step before exclusion. Oedipus, at least, understood that. He tortured himself, gouged out his own eyes, then went away. The rite, the becoming-animal of the scapegoat clearly illustrates this: a first expiatory animal is sacrificed, but a second is driven away, sent out into the desert wilderness. In the signifying regime, the scapegoat represents a new form of increasing entropy in the system of signs: it is charged with everything that was "bad" in a given period, that is, everything that resisted signifying signs, everything that eluded the referral from sign to sign through the different circles; it also assumes everything that was unable to recharge the signifier at its center and carries off everything that spills beyond the outermost circle. Finally, and especially, it incarnates that line of flight the signifying regime cannot tolerate, in other words, an absolute deterritorialization; the regime must block a line of this kind or define it in an entirely negative fashion precisely because it exceeds the degree of deterritorialization of the signifying sign, however high it may be. The line of flight is like a tangent to the circles of signifiance and the center of the signifier. It is under a curse. The goat's anus stands opposite the face of the despot or god. Anything that threatens to put the system to flight will be killed or put to flight itself. Anything that exceeds the excess of the signifier or passes beneath it will be marked with a negative value. Your only choice will be between a goat's ass and the face of the god, between sorcerers and priests. The complete system, then, consists of the paranoid face or body of the despot-god in the signifying center of the temple; the interpreting priests who continually recharge the signified in the temple, transforming it into signifier; the hysterical crowd of people outside, clumped in tight circles, who jump from one circle to another; the faceless, depressive scapegoat emanating from the center, chosen, treated, and adorned by the priests, cutting across the circles in its headlong flight into the desert. This excessively hasty overview is applicable not only to the imperial despotic regime but to all subjected, arborescent, hierarchical, centered groups: political parties, literary movements, psychoanalytic associations, families, conjugal units, etc. The photo, faciality, redundancy, signifiance, and interpretation are at work everywhere. The dreary world of the signifier; its archaism with an always contemporary function;

its essential deception, connoting all of its aspects; its profound antics. The signifier reigns over every domestic squabble, and in every State apparatus.

The signifying regime of the sign is defined by eight aspects or principles: (1) the sign refers to another sign, ad infinitum (the limitlessness of signifiance, which deterritorializes the sign); (2) the sign is brought back by other signs and never ceases to return (the circularity of the deterritorialized sign); (3) the sign jumps from circle to circle and constantly displaces the center at the same time as it ties into it (the metaphor or hysteria of signs); (4) the expansion of the circles is assured by interpretations that impart signified and reimpart signifier (the interpretosis of the priest); (5) the infinite set of signs refers to a supreme signifier presenting itself as both lack and excess (the despotic signifier, the limit of the system's deterritorialization); (6) the form of the signifier has a substance, or the signifier has a body, namely, the Face (the principle of faciality traits, which constitute a reterritorialization); (7) the system's line of flight is assigned a negative value, condemned as that which exceeds the signifying regime's power of deterritorialization (the principle of the scapegoat); (8) the regime is one of universal deception, in its jumps, in the regulated circles, in the seer's regulation of interpretations, in the publicness of the facialized center, and in the treatment of the line of flight.

Not only is this semiotic system not the first, but we see no reason to accord it any particular privilege from the standpoint of an abstract evolutionism. We would like to indicate very briefly certain characteristics of the other two semiotic systems. First, the so-called primitive, *presignifying semiotic*, which is much closer to "natural" codings operating without signs. There is no reduction to faciality as the sole substance of expression: there is no elimination of forms of content through abstraction of the signified. To the extent that there is still abstraction of content from a strictly semiotic point of view, it fosters a pluralism or polyvocality of forms of expression that prevents any power takeover by the signifier and preserves expressive forms particular to content; thus forms of corporeality, gesturality, rhythm, dance, and rite coexist heterogeneously with the vocal form.[6] A variety of forms and substances of expression intersect and form relays. It is a segmentary but plurilinear, multidimensional semiotic that wards off any kind of signifying circularity. Segmentarity is the law of the lineages. Here, the sign owes its degree of relative deterritorialization not to a perpetual referral to other signs but rather to a confrontation between the territorialities and compared segments from which each sign is extracted (the camp, the bush, the moving of the camp). Not only is the polyvocality of statements preserved, but it is possible to finish with a statement: A name that has been used up is abolished, a situation quite unlike the placing in reserve or transformation occurring in the signifying semiotic. The meaning of cannibalism in a presignifying regime is precisely this: eating the name, a semiography that is fully a part of a semiotic in spite of its relation to content (the relation is an expressive one).[7] It should not be thought that a semiotic of this kind functions by ignorance, repression, or foreclosure of the signifier. On the contrary, it is animated by a keen presentiment of what is to come. It does not need to understand it to fight against it. It is wholly destined by its very segmentarity and polyvocality to avert the already-present threat: universalizing abstraction, erection of the signifier, circularity of statements, and their correlates, the State apparatus, the instatement of the despot, the priestly caste, the scapegoat, etc. Every time they eat a dead man, they can say: one more the State won't get.

There is another semiotic, the *countersignifying* semiotic (whose most notable representatives are the fearsome, warlike, and animal-raising nomads, as opposed to hunter nomads, who belong to the previous semiotic). This time, the semiotic proceeds less by segmentarity than by arithmetic and numeration. Of course, the number already played a role of great importance in the division and union of segmentary lineages; it also had a function of decisive importance in the signifying imperial bureaucracy. But that was a kind of number that represented or signified, a number "incited, produced, caused by something other than itself." On the contrary, a numerical sign that is not produced by something outside the system of marking it institutes, which marks a mobile and plural distribution, which itself determines functions and relations, which arrives at arrangements rather than totals, distributions rather than collections, which operates more by breaks, transitions, migration, and accumulation than by combining units—a sign of this kind would appear to belong to the semiotic of a nomad war machine directed against the State apparatus. The numbering number.[8] Its numerical organization into tens, fifties, hundreds, thousands, etc., and the associated spatial organization were obviously adopted by State armies, but basically bear witness to a military system specific to the great nomads of the steppes, from the Hyksos to the Mongols. They were superposed upon the principle of lineage. Secrecy and spying are important elements of the war machine's semiotic of Numbers. The role of Numbers in the Bible is not unrelated to the nomads, since Moses got the idea from his father-in-law, Jethro the Kenite: he used it as an organizational principle for the march and migration, and applied it himself to the military domain. In this countersignifying regime, the imperial despotic line of flight is replaced by a line of abolition that turns back against the great empires, cuts across them and destroys them, or else conquers them and integrates with them to form a mixed semiotic.

We would like to go into greater detail on a fourth regime of signs, the *postsignifying* regime, which has different characteristics opposing it to signifiance and is defined by a unique procedure, that of "subjectification."

There are many regimes of signs. Our own list is arbitrarily limited. There is no reason to identify a regime or a semiotic system with a people or historical moment. There is such mixture within the same period or the same people that we can say no more than that a given people, language, or period assures the relative dominance of a certain regime. Perhaps all semiotics are mixed and not only combine with various forms of content but also combine different regimes of signs. Presignifying elements are always active in the signifying regime; countersignifying elements are always present and at work within it; and postsignifying elements are already there. Even that is to mark too much temporality. The semiotics and their mixtures may appear in a history of confrontation and intermingling of peoples, but also in languages in which there are several competing functions, or in a psychiatric hospital in which different forms of insanity coexist among the patients or even combine in a single patient; or in an ordinary conversation in which people are speaking the same tongue but different languages (all of a sudden a fragment of an unexpected semiotic surfaces). We are not suggesting an evolutionism, we are not even doing history. Semiotic systems depend on assemblages, and it is the assemblages that determine that a given people, period, or language, and even a given style, fashion, pathology, or minuscule event in a limited situation, can assure the predominance of one semiotic or another. We are trying to make maps of regimes of signs: we can turn them around or retain selected coordinates or dimensions, and depending on the case we will be dealing with a social formation, a pathological delusion (*délire*), a historical event, etc. We will see this on another occasion when we deal with a dated social system, "courtly love," and then switch to a private enterprise called "masochism." We can also combine maps or separate them. To make the distinction between two types of semiotics (for example, the postsignifying regime and the signifying regime), we must consider very diverse domains simultaneously.

In the first years of the twentieth century, psychiatry, at the height of its clinical skills, confronted the problem of nonhallucinatory delusions in which mental integrity is retained without "intellectual diminishment." There was a first major grouping, paranoid or interpretive delusions, which already subsumed various aspects. But the question of the possible independence of another group was prefigured in Esquirol's monomania and Kraepelin's querulous delusion, and later defined by Sérieux and Capgras as grievance delusion, and by Clérambault as passional delusion ("querulousness or seeking redress, jealousy, erotomania"). Basing ourselves on very fine studies of Sérieux and Capgras on the one hand, and Clérambault on the other (the latter took the distinction furthest), we will contrast a paranoid-interpretive ideal regime of signifiance with a passional, postsignifying subjective regime. The first regime is defined by an insidious onset and a hidden center bearing witness to endogenous forces organized around an idea; by the development of a network stretching across an amorphous continuum, a gliding atmosphere into which the slightest incident may be carried; by an organization of radiating circles expanding by circular irradiation in all directions, and in which the individual jumps from one point to another, one circle to another, approaches the center then moves away, operates prospectively and retrospectively; and by a transformation of the atmosphere, as a function of variable traits or secondary centers clustered around a principal nucleus. The second regime, on the contrary, is defined by a decisive external occurrence, by a relation with the outside that is expressed more as an emotion than an idea, and more as effort or action than imagination ("active delusion rather than ideational delusion"); by a limited constellation operating in a single sector; by a "postulate" or "concise formula" serving as the point of departure for a linear series or proceeding that runs its course, at which point a new proceeding begins. In short, it operates *by the linear and temporal succession of finite proceedings, rather than by the simultaneity of circles in unlimited expansion.*[9]

This story of two kinds of delusions without intellectual diminishment is of great importance. For it is not a disruption of a preexisting discipline of psychiatry; it lies at the heart of the constitution of the psychiatrist in the nineteenth century and explains why he or she was from the start what he or she has been ever since: the psychiatrist was born cornered, caught between legal, police, humanitarian demands, accused of not being a true doctor, suspected of mistaking the sane for mad and the mad for sane, prey to quandaries of conscience, the last Hegelian *belle âme*. If we consider the two types of intact delusions, we can say that people in the first group seem to be completely mad, but aren't: President Schreber developed his radiating paranoia and relations with God in every direction, but he was not mad in that he remained capable of managing his wealth wisely and distinguishing between circles. At the other pole are those who do not seem mad in any way, but are, as borne out by their sudden actions, such as quarrels, arsons, murders (Esquirol's four great monomanias, erotic, intellectual, arson, and homocidal, already belong in this category). In short, psychiatry was not at all constituted in relation to the concept of madness, or even as a modification of that concept, but rather by *its split in these two opposite directions.* And is it not our own double image, all of ours, that psychiatry thus reveals: seeming mad without being it, then being it without seeming it? (This twofold assertion is also psychoanalysis's point of departure, its way of linking into psychiatry: we seem to be mad but aren't, observe the dream; we are mad but don't seem to be, observe everyday life.) Thus psychiatrists were alternately in the position of on the one hand pleading for tolerance and understanding, underscoring the uselessness of confinement, appealing for open-door asylums; and on the other arguing for stepped-up surveillance and special high-security asylums, stricter measures necessitated by the fact that the mad seemed not to be.[10] Is it by chance that the distinction between the two major kinds of delusions, ideational and active, in many ways recapitulates the distinction between the classes (paranoiacs do not particularly need to be committed, they are usually bourgeois, whereas monomaniacs, passional redress-seekers, are most often from the working and rural classes, or are marginal, as in the case of political assassins).[11] A class with radiant, irradiating ideas (but of course!) against a class reduced to linear, sporadic, partial, local actions . . . All paranoiacs are not bourgeois, all passionals or monomaniacs are not proletarian. But God and his psychiatrists are charged with recognizing, among these de facto mixes, those who preserve, even in delusion, the class-based social order, and those who sow disorder, even strictly localized, such as haystack fires, parental murders, déclassé love and aggression.

We are trying, then, to make a distinction between a paranoid, signifying, despotic regime of signs and a passional or subjective, postsignifying, authoritarian regime. Authoritarian is assuredly not the same as despotic, passional is not the same as paranoid, and subjective is not the same as signifying. What happens in the second regime, by comparison with the signifying regime as we have already defined it? In the first place, *a sign or packet of signs detaches from the irradiating circular network* and sets to work on its own account, starts running a straight line, as though swept into a narrow, open passage. Already the signifying system drew a line of flight or deterritorialization exceeding the specific index of its deterritorialized signs, but the system gave that line a negative value and sent the scapegoat fleeing down it. Here, it seems that the line receives a positive sign, as though it were effectively occupied and followed by a people who find in it their reason for being or destiny. Once again, we are not, of course, doing history: we are not saying that a people invents this regime of signs, only that at a given moment a people effectuates the assemblage that assures the relative dominance of that regime under certain historical conditions (and that regime, that dominance, that assemblage may be assured under other conditions, for example, pathological, literary, romantic, or entirely mundane). We are not saying that a people is possessed by a given type of delusion but that the map of a delusion, its coordinates considered, may coincide with the map of a people, its coordinates considered. The paranoid Pharaoh and the passional Hebrew? In the case of the Jewish people, a group of signs detaches from the Egyptian imperial network of which it was a part and sets off down a line of flight into the desert, pitting the most authoritarian of subjectivities against despotic signifiance, the most passional and least interpretive of delusions against interpretational paranoid delusion, in short, a linear "proceeding and grievance" against the irradiating circular network. *Your grievance, your proceeding*: that is Moses' word to his people, and the proceedings come one after the other along a line of Passion.[12] From this Kafka derives his own conception of querulousness or the proceeding, and the succession of linear segments: the father-proceeding, hotel-proceeding, ship-proceeding, court-proceeding . . .

We cannot overlook the most fundamental or extensive event in the history of the Jewish people: the destruction of the Temple, in two stages (587 B.C. and A.D. 70). The whole history of the Temple—the mobility and fragility of the ark, then the construction of a House by Solomon, its reconstruction under Darius, etc.—has meaning only in relation to renewed proceedings of destruction, the two supreme moments of which came with Nebuchadnezzar and Titus. A temple, mobile, fragile, or destroyed: the ark is no more than a little portable packet of signs. An entirely negative line of flight occupied by the animal or scapegoat laden with all the dangers threatening the signifier has become an impossibility. Let misfortune befall us: this formula punctuates Jewish history. It is we who must follow the most deterritorialized line, the line of the scapegoat, but we will change its sign, we will turn it into the positive line of our subjectivity, our Passion, our proceeding or grievance. We will be our own scapegoat. We will be the lamb: "The God who, like a lion, was given blood sacrifice must be shoved into the background, and the sacrificed god must occupy the foreground. . . . God became the animal that was slain, instead of the animal that does the slaying."[13] We will follow, we will wed the tangent separating the land from the waters, we will separate the circular network from the gliding continuum, we will make the line of separation our own, in order to forge our path along it and dissociate the elements of the signifier (the dove of the ark). A narrow line of march, an in-between that is not a mean but a slender line. There is a Jewish specificity, immediately affirmed in a semiotic system. This semiotic, however, is no less mixed than any other. On the one hand, it is intimately related to the countersignifying regime of the nomads (the Hebrews had a nomadic past, a continuing relationship with the nomadic numerical organization that inspired them, and their own particular becoming-nomad; their line of deterritorialization owed much to the military line of nomadic destruction).[14] On the other hand, it has an essential relation to the signifying semiotic itself, for which the Hebrews and their God would always be nostalgic: reestablish an imperial society and integrate with it, enthrone a king like everybody else (Samuel), rebuild a temple that would finally be solid (David and Solomon, Zachariah), erect the spiral of the Tower of Babel and find the face of God again; not just bring the wandering to a halt, but overcome the diaspora, which itself exists only as a function of an ideal regathering. We only have space to indicate what, in this mixed semiotic, bears witness to the new postsignifying subjective or passional regime.

Faciality undergoes a profound transformation. The god averts his face, which must be seen by no one; and the subject, gripped by a veritable fear of the god, averts his or her face in turn. The averted faces, in profile, replace the frontal view of the radiant face. It is this double turning away that draws the positive line of flight. The prophet is the main figure in this assemblage; he needs a sign to guarantee the word of God, he is himself marked by a sign indicating the special regime to which he belongs. It is Spinoza who has elaborated the profoundest theory of prophetism, taking into account the semiotic proper to it. Cain, who turns away from the God who turns away from him, already follows the line of deterritorialization, protected by a sign allowing him to escape death. The mark of Cain. A punishment worse than imperial death? The Jewish God invented the reprieve, existence in reprieve, *indefinite postponement*.[15] But He also invented the positivity of alliance, or the covenant, as the new relation with the deity, since the subject remains alive. Abel, whose name is vanity, is nothing; Cain is the true man. This is very different from the system of rigging or deception animating the face of the signifier, the interpretation of the seer and the displacements of the subject. It is the regime of betrayal, universal betrayal, in which the true man never ceases to betray God just as God betrays man, with the wrath of God defining the new positivity. Before his death, Moses receives the words of the great song of betrayal. Even the prophet, unlike the seer-priest, is fundamentally a traitor and thus fulfills God's order better than anyone who remained faithful could. God calls upon Jonah to go to Nineveh to entreat the inhabitants, who had repeatedly betrayed God, to mend their ways. But Jonah's first act is to take off in the opposite direction; he also betrays God, fleeing "far from the face of Adonai."[16] He takes a ship for Tarshish and sleeps, like a righteous man. The tempest sent by God causes him to be thrown into the sea, where he is swallowed by the great fish and vomited out at the boundary between land and water, the limit of separation or line of flight earlier occupied by the dove of the Ark (Jonah, precisely, is the word for dove). But Jonah, in fleeing from the face of God, did exactly what God had wanted: he took the evil of Nineveh upon himself; he did it even more effectively than God had wanted, he anticipated God. That is why he slept like a righteous man. God let him live, temporarily protected by the tree of Cain, but then made the tree die because Jonah had renewed the covenant by occupying the line of flight.[17] Jesus universalizes the system of betrayal: he betrays the God of the Jews, he betrays the Jews, he is betrayed by God ("Why hast thou forsaken me?" [Matthew 27:46; Mark 15:34—Trans.]), he is betrayed by Judas, the true man. He took evil upon himself, but the Jews who kill him also take it upon themselves. Jesus is asked for a sign of his divine descendance: he invokes the sign of Jonah [Luke 11:29—Trans.]. Cain, Jonah, and Jesus constitute three great linear proceedings along which signs rush and form relays. There are many others. Everywhere a double turning away on a line of flight.

When a prophet declines the burden God entrusts to him (Moses, Jeremiah, Isaiah, etc.), it is not because the burden would have been too heavy. as with an imperial oracle or seer who refuses a dangerous mission. It is instead a case like Jonah's, who by hiding and fleeing and betraying anticipates the will of God more effectively than if he had obeyed. The prophet is always being forced by God, literally violated by him, much more than inspired by him. The prophet is not a priest. The prophet does not know how to talk, God puts the words in his mouth: word-ingestion, a new form of semiophagy. Unlike the seer, the prophet interprets nothing: *his delusion is active rather than ideational or imaginative*, his relation to God is passional and authoritative rather than despotic and signifying; he anticipates and detects the powers (*puissances*) of the future rather than applying past and present powers (*pouvoirs*). Faciality traits no longer function to prevent the formation of a line of flight, or to form a body of signifiance controlling that line and sending only a faceless goat down it. Rather, it is faciality itself that organizes the line of flight, in the face-off between two countenances that become gaunt and turn away in profile. Betrayal has become an idée fixe, the main obsession, replacing the deceit of the paranoiac and the hysteric. The "persecutor-persecuted" relation has no relevance whatsoever: its meaning is altogether different in the authoritarian passional regime than in the despotic paranoid regime.

Something is still bothering us: the story of Oedipus. Oedipus is almost unique in the Greek world. The whole first part is imperial, despotic, paranoid, interpretive, divinatory. But the whole second part is Oedipus's wandering, his line of flight, the double turning away of his own face and that of God. Rather than very precise limits to be crossed in order, or which one does not have the right to cross (*hybris*), there is a concealed limit toward which Oedipus is swept. Rather than interpretive signifying irradiation, there is a subjective linear proceeding permitting Oedipus to keep a secret, but only as a residue capable of starting a new linear proceeding. Oedipus, his name is *atheos*: he invents something worse than death or exile, he wanders and survives on a strangely positive line of separation or deterritorialization. Hölderlin and Heidegger see this as the birth of the *double turning away*, the change of face, and also the birth of modern tragedy, for which they bizarrely credit the Greeks: the outcome is no longer murder or sudden death but survival under reprieve, unlimited postponement.[18] Nietzsche suggests that Oedipus, as opposed to Prometheus, was the Semitic myth of the Greeks, the glorification of Passion or passivity.[19] Oedipus: Greek Cain. Let us return to psychoanalysis. It was not by chance that Freud pounced upon Oedipus. Psychoanalysis is a definite case of a mixed semiotic: a despotic regime of signifiance and interpretation, with irradiation of the face, but also an authoritarian regime of subjectification and prophetism, with a turning away of the face (the positioning of the psychoanalyst behind the patient suddenly assumes its full significance). Recent efforts to explain that a "signifier represents the subject for another signifier" are typically syncretic: a linear proceeding of subjectivity along with a circular development of the signifier and interpretation. Two absolutely different regimes of signs in a mix. But the worst, most underhanded of powers are founded on it.

One more remark on the story of authoritarian passional betrayal, as opposed to despotic paranoid deception. Everything is infamy, but Borges botched his history of universal infamy.[20] He should have distinguished between the great realm of deceptions and the great realm of betrayals. And also between the various figures of betrayal. There is, in effect, a second figure of betrayal that springs up at certain places at certain times, but always as a function of a variable assemblage with new components. Christianity is a particularly important case of a mixed semiotic, with its signifying imperial combination together with its postsignifying Jewish subjectivity. It transforms both the ideal signifying system and the postsignifying passional system. It invents a new assemblage. Heresies are still a part of deception, just as orthodoxy is a part of signifiance. But there are heresies that are more than heresies and profess pure treason, for example, the Buggers; it is not by chance that the Bulgars played a special role.[21] Beware the Bulgars, as Monsieur Plume would say. The problem is one of territorialities in relation to deep movements of deterritorialization. England, another territoriality or another deterritorialization: Cromwell, everywhere a traitor, a straight line of passional subjectification opposed to the royal center of signifiance and the intermediary circles: the dictator against the despot. Richard III, the deformed, the twisted, whose ideal is to betray everything: he confronts Lady Anne in a face-off in which the two countenances turn away, but each knows she or he is the other's, destined for the other. This is unlike Shakespeare's other historical dramas, in which kings and assassins deceive in order to take power but then become good kings. That kind are men of the State. Richard III comes from elsewhere: his ventures, including those with women, derive more from a war machine than from a State apparatus. He is the traitor, springing from the great nomads and their secrecy. He says so from the beginning, when he mentions a secret project infinitely surpassing the conquest of power. He wants to return the war machine both to the fragile State and pacified couples. The only one to guess is Lady Anne, fascinated, terrified, consenting. Elizabethan theater is full of these traitorous characters who aspire to be absolute traitors, in opposition to the deceptions of the man of the court or even of the State.

How many betrayals accompanied the great discoveries of Christendom, the discovery of new lands and continents! Lines of deterritorialization on which small groups betray everything, their companions, the king, the indigenous peoples, the neighboring explorer, in the mad hope of founding, with a woman of their family, a race that would finally be pure and represent a new beginning. Herzog's film, *Aguirre*, is very Shakespearean. Aguirre asks, How can one be a traitor everywhere and in everything? I'm the only traitor here. No more deception, it's time for betrayal. What a grandiose dream! I will be the last traitor, the total traitor, and therefore the last man.

Then there was the Reformation: the extraordinary figure of Luther, as traitor to all things and all people; his personal relation with the Devil resulting in betrayal, through good deeds as well as bad.

These new figures of betrayal always return to the Old Testament: I am the wrath of God. But betrayal has become humanist, it does not fall between God and his own men; it relies on God, but falls between the men of God and the others, denounced as deceivers. In the end, there is only one man of God or of the wrath of God, a single betrayer against all deceivers. But every deceiver is mixed, and which does not take him- or herself to be the one? And what betrayer does not say to him- or herself at some point that he or she was nothing but a deceiver after all? (See the strange case of Maurice Sachs.)

It is clear that the book, or what takes its place, has a different meaning in the signifying paranoid regime than in the postsignifying passional regime. In the first case, there is an emission of the despotic signifier, and its interpretation by scribes and priests, which fixes the signified and reimparts signifier; but there is also, from sign to sign, a movement from one territory to another, a circulation assuring a certain speed of deterritorialization (for example, the circulation of an epic, or the rivalry between several cities for the birth of a hero, or, once again, the role of scribe-priests in exchanges of territorialities and genealogies).[22] What takes the place of the book always has an external model, a referent, face, family, or territory that preserves the book's oral character. On the contrary, in the passional regime the book seems to be internalized, and to internalize everything: it becomes the sacred written Book. It takes the place of the face and God, who hides his face and gives Moses the inscribed stone tablets. God manifests himself through trumpets and the Voice, but what is heard in sound is the nonface, just as what is seen in the book are words. *The book has become the body of passion,* just as the face was the body of the signifier. It is now the book, the most deterritorialized of things, that fixes territories and genealogies. The latter are what the book says, and the former the place at which the book is said. The function of interpretation has totally changed. Or it disappears entirely in favor of a pure and literal recitation forbidding the slightest change, addition, or commentary (the famous "stultify yourself" of the Christians belongs to this passional line; the Koran goes the furthest in this direction). Or else interpretation survives but becomes internal to the book itself, which loses its circulatory function for outside elements: for example, the different types of coded interpretation are fixed according to axes internal to the book; interpretation is organized according to correspondences between two books, such as the Old and New Testaments, and may even induce a third book suffused by the same element of interiority.[23] Finally, interpretation may reject all intermediaries or specialists and become direct, since the book is written both in itself and in the heart, once as a point of subjectification and again in the subject (the Reformation conception of the book). In any case, this is the point of departure for the delusional passion of the book as origin and finality of the world. The unique book, the total work, all possible combinations *inside* the book, the tree-book, the cosmos-book: all of these platitudes so dear to the avant-gardes, which cut the book off from its relations with the outside, are even worse than the chant of the signifier. Of course, they are entirely bound up with a mixed semiotic. But in truth they have a particularly pious origin. Wagner, Mallarmé, and Joyce, Marx and Freud: still Bibles. If passional delusion is profoundly monomaniacal, monomania for its part found a fundamental element of its assemblage in monotheism and the Book. The strangest cult.

This is how things are in the passional regime, or the regime of subjectification. There is no longer a center of signifiance connected to expanding circles or an expanding spiral, but a point of subjectification constituting the point of departure of the line. There is no longer a signifier-signified relation, but a subject of enunciation issuing from the point of subjectification and a subject of the statement in a determinable relation to the first subject. There is no longer sign-to-sign circularity, but a linear proceeding into which the sign is swept via subjects. We may consider these three diverse realms.

1. *The Jews as opposed to the empires.* God withdraws his face, becoming a point of subjectification for the drawing of a line of flight or deterritorialization; Moses is the subject of enunciation, constituted on the basis of the tablets of God that replace the face; the Jewish people constitute the subject of the statement, for betrayal as well as for a new land, and enter an ever-renewed covenant or linear "proceeding" rather than a circular expansion.

2. *So-called modern, or Christian, philosophy*: Descartes as opposed to ancient philosophy. There is a primacy of the idea of the infinite as an absolutely necessary point of subjectification. The Cogito, consciousness, the "I think" is the subject of enunciation that reflects its own use and conceives of itself following a line of deterritorialization represented by methodical doubt. The subject of the statement is the union of the soul and the body, or feeling, guaranteed in a complex way by the cogito, and performs the necessary reterritorializations. The cogito is a proceeding that must always be recommenced, haunted by the possibility of betrayal, a deceitful God, and an evil Genius. When Descartes says, I can infer "I think therefore I am" but not "I walk therefore I am," he is initiating the distinction between the two subjects (what still-Cartesian contemporary linguists call a shifter, even though they find traces of the second subject in the first).

3. *Nineteenth-century psychiatry*: monomania distinguished from mania; subjective delusion separated from ideational delusions; "possession" replacing sorcery; a slow elaboration of passional delusion, as distinct from paranoia . . . The schema of passional delusion according to Clérambault is as follows: the Postulate as the point of subjectification (*He* loves me); pride as the tonality of the subject of enunciation (delusional pursuit of the loved one); Spite, Rancor (a result of a reversion to the subject of the statement). Passional delusion is a veritable cogito. In the foregoing example of erotomania, as well as in jealousy and querulous delusion, Clérambault stresses that a sign must follow a segment or linear proceeding through to the end before it can begin another, whereas the signs in paranoid delusion form an endless, self-adjusting network developing in all directions. The cogito also follows a linear temporal proceeding needing to be recommenced. The history of the Jews is punctuated by catastrophes after each of which there were just enough survivors to start a new proceeding. In the course of a proceeding, while there is linear movement the plural is often used, whereas there is a return to the Singular as soon as there is a pause or stoppage marking the end of one movement before another begins.[24] Fundamental segmentarity: one proceeding must end (and its termination must be marked) before another begins, to enable another to begin.

The point of subjectification is the origin of the passional line of the postsignifying regime. The point of subjectification can be anything. It must only display the following characteristic traits of the subjective semiotic: the double turning away, betrayal, and existence under reprieve. For anorexics, food plays this role (anorexics do not confront death but save themselves by betraying food, which is equally a traitor since it is suspected of containing larvae, worms, and microbes). A dress, an article of underwear, a shoe are points of subjectification for a fetishist. So is a faciality trait for someone in love, but the meaning of faciality has changed; it is no longer the body of the signifier but has become the point of departure for a deterritorialization that puts everything else to flight. A thing, an animal, will do the trick. There are cogitos on everything. "A pair of eyes set far apart, a head hewn of quartz, a haunch that seemed to live its own life. . . . Whenever the beauty of the female becomes irresistible, it is traceable to a single quality":[25] a point of subjectification in the departure of a passional line. Moreover, several points coexist in a given individual or group, which are always engaged in several distinct and not always compatible linear proceedings. The various forms of education or "normalization" imposed upon an individual consist in making him or her change points of subjectification, always moving toward a higher, nobler one in closer conformity with the supposed ideal. Then from the point of subjectification issues a subject of enunciation, as a function of a mental reality determined by that point. Then from the subject of enunciation issues a subject of the statement, in other words, a subject bound to statements in conformity with a dominant reality (of which the mental reality just mentioned is a part, even when it seems to oppose it). What is important, what makes the postsignifying passional line a line of subjectification or subjection, is the constitution, the doubling of the two subjects, and the recoiling of one into the other, of the subject of enunciation into the subject of the statement (the linguists acknowledge this when they speak of the "imprint of the process of enunciation in the statement"). Signifiance brought about uniformity in the substance of enunciation; now subjectivity effects an individuation, collective or particular. Substance has become subject, as they say. *The subject of enunciation recoils into the subject of the statement, to the point that the subject of the statement resupplies subject of enunciation for another proceeding.* The subject of the statement has become the "respondent" or guarantor of the subject of enunciation, through a kind of reductive echolalia, in a biunivocal relation. This relation, this recoiling, is also that of mental reality into the dominant reality. There is always an appeal to a dominant reality that functions from within (already in the Old Testament, and during the Reformation, with trade and capitalism). There is no longer even a need for a transcendent center of power; power is instead immanent and melds with the "real," operating through normalization. A strange invention: as if in one form the doubled subject were the *cause* of the statements of which, in its other form, it itself is a part. This is the paradox of the legislator-subject replacing the signifying despot: the more you obey the statements of the dominant reality, the more in command you are as subject of enunciation in mental reality, for in the end you are only obeying yourself! You are the one in command, in your capacity as a rational being. A new form of slavery is invented, namely, being slave to oneself, or to pure "reason," the Cogito. Is there anything more passional than pure reason? Is there a colder, more extreme, more self-interested passion than the Cogito?

Althusser clearly brings out this constitution of social individuals as subjects: he calls it interpellation ("Hey you, over there!") and calls the point of subjectification the Absolute Subject; he analyzes the "specular doubling" of subjects and for purposes of demonstration uses the example of God, Moses, and the Jewish people.[26] Linguists like Benveniste adopt a curious linguistic personology that is very close to the Cogito: the *You*, which can doubtless designate the person one is addressing, but more importantly, a point of subjectification on the basis of which each of us is constituted as a subject. The *I* as subject of enunciation, designating the person that utters and reflects its own use in the statement ("the empty nonreferential sign"); this is the I appearing in propositions of the type "I believe, I assume, I think . . ." Finally, the I as subject of the statement, indicating a state for which a *She* or *He* could always be substituted ("I suffer, I walk, I breathe, I feel . . .").[27] This is not, however, a question of a linguistic operation, for a subject is never the condition of possibility of language or the cause of the statement: there is no subject, only collective assemblages of enunciation. Subjectification is simply one such assemblage and designates a formalization of expression or a regime of signs rather than a condition internal to language. Neither is it a question of a movement characteristic of ideology, as Althusser says: subjectification as a regime of signs or a form of expression is tied to an assemblage, in other words, an organization of power that is already fully functioning in the economy, rather than superposing itself upon contents or relations between contents determined as real in the last instance. Capital is a point of subjectification par excellence.

The psychoanalytic cogito: the psychoanalyst presents him- or herself as an ideal point of subjectification that brings the patient to abandon old, so-called neurotic, points. The patient is partially a subject of enunciation in all he or she says to the psychoanalyst, and under the artificial mental conditions of the session: the patient is therefore called the "analysand."

But in everything else the patient says or does, he or she is a subject of the statement, eternally psychoanalyzed, going from one linear proceeding to another, perhaps even changing analysts, growing increasingly submissive to the normalization of a dominant reality. In this sense, psychoanalysis, with its mixed semiotic, fully participates in a line of subjectification. The psychoanalyst does not even have to speak anymore, the analysand assumes the burden of interpretation; as for the psychoanalyzed patient, the more he or she thinks about "his" or "her" next session, or the preceding one, in segments, the better a subject he or she is.

Just as the paranoid regime had two axes—one sign referring to another (making the sign a signifier), and the signifier referring to the signified—so too the passional regime, the line of subjectification, has two axes, one syntagmatic and the other paradigmatic: as we have just seen, the first axis is consciousness. Consciousness as passion is precisely that doubling of subjects, of the subject of enunciation and the subject of the statement, and the recoiling of one into the other. But the second form of subjectification is love as passion, love-passion, another type of double, of doubling and recoiling. Here again, a variable point of subjectification serves to distribute two subjects that as much conceal their faces as reveal them to each other, that wed a line of flight, a line of deterritorialization forever drawing them together and driving them apart. But everything changes: there is a celibate side to this doubled consciousness, and there is a passional love couple that no longer has any use for consciousness or reason. Yet it is the same regime, even in betrayal and even if the betraying is done by a third party. Adam and Eve, and Cain's wife (about whom the Bible should have said more). Richard III, the traitor, is in the end given consciousness in a dream, but only the strange face-off with Lady Anne, a meeting of two countenances that conceal themselves knowing that they have promised themselves to each other following the same line that will nonetheless separate them. The most loyal and tender, or intense, love assigns subject of enunciation and a subject of the statement that constantly switch places, wrapped in the sweetness of being a naked statement in the other's mouth, and of the other's being a naked enunciation in my own mouth. But there is always a traitor in the making. What love is not betrayed? What cogito lacks its evil genius, the traitor it will never be rid of? "Tristan . . . Isolde . . . Isolde . . . Tristan": the cry of the two subjects climbs the scale of intensities until it reaches the summit of a suffocating consciousness, whereas the ship follows the line of the waters, the line of death and the unconscious, betrayal, a continuous melody line. Passional love is a cogito built for two, just as the cogito is a passion for the self alone. There is a potential couple in the cogito, just as there is a doubling of a single virtual subject in love-passion. Klossowski has created the strangest figures on the basis of this complementarity between an over intense thought and an over feverish couple. The line of subjectification is thus entirely occupied by the Double, but it has two figures since there are two kinds of doubles: the syntagmatic figure of consciousness, or the consciousness-related double, relating to form (Self = Self [*Moi* = *Moi*]); and the paradigmatic figure of the couple, or the passional double, relating to substance (Man = Woman; here, the double is immediately the difference between the sexes).

We can follow the becoming of these doubles in mixed semiotics, which are interminglings as well as degradations. On the one hand, the passional love double, the couple in love-passion, falls into a conjugal relation or even a "domestic squabble" situation: Which is the subject of enunciation? Which is the subject of the statement? The battle of the sexes: *You're stealing my thoughts*. The domestic squabble has always been a cogito for two, a war cogito. Strindberg took this fall of love-passion into despotic conjugality and hysterico-paranoid squabbling to its extreme ("she" says she found it all by herself when in fact she owes it all to me, echo, thought theft, O Strindberg!).[28] On the other hand, the consciousness-related double of pure thought, the couple of the legislating subject, falls into a bureaucratic relation and a new form of persecution in which one double takes over the role of subject of enunciation while the other is reduced to a subject of the statement; the cogito itself becomes an "office squabble," a bureaucratic love delusion. A new form of bureaucracy replaces or conjugates with the old imperial bureaucracy, the bureaucrat says *I think* (Kafka goes the furthest in this direction, as in the example of Sortini and Sordini in *The Castle*, or the many subjectifications of Klamm).[29] Conjugality is the development of the couple, and bureaucracy the development of the cogito. But one is contained in the other: amorous bureaucracy, bureaucratic couple. Too much has been written on the double, haphazardly, metaphysically, finding it everywhere, in any old mirror, without noticing the specific regime it possesses both in a mixed semiotic where it introduces new phases, and in the pure semiotic of subjectification where it inscribes itself on a line of flight and introduces very particular figures. Once again: the two figures of thought-consciousness and love-passion in the postsignifying regime; the two moments of bureaucratic consciousness and conjugal relation in the mixed fall or combination. But even in a mixed state, the original line is easily discovered by semiotic analysis.

There is a redundancy of consciousness and love that is not the same as the signifying redundancy of the other regime. In the signifying regime, redundancy is a phenomenon of objective *frequency* involving signs or elements of signs (the phonemes, letters, and groups of letters in a language): there is both a maximum frequency of the signifier in relation to each sign, and a comparative frequency of one sign in relation to another. In any case, it could be said that this regime develops a kind of "wall" on which signs are inscribed, in relation to one another and in relation to the signifier. In the postsignifying regime, on the other hand, the redundancy is one of *subjective resonance* involving above all shifters, personal pronouns and proper names. Here again, we may distinguish between the maximum resonance of self-consciousness (Self = Self [*Moi* = *Moi*]) and a comparative resonance of names (Tristan . . . Isolde . . .). This time, however, there is no longer a wall upon which the frequency is tallied but instead a black hole attracting consciousness and passion and in which they resonate. Tristan calls Isolde, Isolde calls Tristan, both drawn toward the black hole of a self-consciousness, carried by the tide toward death. When the linguists distinguish between two forms of redundancy, frequency and resonance, they often ascribe the latter a merely derivative status.[30] In fact, it is a question of two semiotics that mix but retain their own distinct principles (similarly, one could define other forms of redundancy, such as rhythmic, gestural, or numerical, relating to the other regimes of signs). The most essential distinction between the signifying regime and the subjective regime and their respective redundancies is the *movement of deterritorialization* they effectuate. Since the signifying sign refers only to other signs, and the set of all signs to the signifier itself, the corresponding semiotic enjoys a high level of deterritorialization; but it is a deterritorialization that is still *relative*, expressed as frequency. In this system, the line of flight remains negative, it is assigned a negative sign. As we have seen, the subjective regime proceeds entirely differently: precisely because the sign breaks its relation of signifiance with other signs and sets off racing down a positive line of flight, it attains an *absolute* deterritorialization expressed in the black hole of consciousness and passion. The absolute deterritorialization of the cogito. That is why subjective redundancy seems both to graft itself onto signifying redundancy and to derive from it, as second-degree redundancy.

Things are even more complicated than we have let on. Subjectification assigns the line of flight a positive sign, it carries deterritorialization to the absolute, intensity to the highest degree, redundancy to a reflexive form, etc. But it has its own way of repudiating the positivity it frees, or of relativizing the absoluteness it attains, without, however, falling back to the preceding regime. In this redundancy of resonance, the absolute of consciousness is the absolute of impotence and the intensity of passion, the heat of the void. This is because subjectification essentially constitutes finite linear proceedings, one of which ends before the next begins: thus the cogito is always recommenced, a passion or grievance is always recapitulated. Every consciousness pursues its own death, every love-passion its own end, attracted by a black hole, and all the black holes resonate together.

Thus subjectification imposes on the line of flight a segmentarity that is forever repudiating that line, and upon absolute deterritorialization a point of abolition that is forever blocking that deterritorialization or diverting it. The reason for this is simple: forms of expression and regimes of signs are still *strata* (even considered in themselves, after abstracting forms of content); subjectification is no less a stratum than signifiance.

The principal strata binding human beings are the organism, signifiance and interpretation, and subjectification and subjection. These strata together are what separates us from the plane of consistency and the abstract machine, where there is no longer any regime of signs, where the line of flight effectuates its own potential positivity and deterritorialization its absolute power. The problem, from this standpoint, is to tip the most favorable assemblage from its side facing the strata to its side facing the plane of consistency or the body without organs. Subjectification carries desire to such a point of excess and unloosening that it must either annihilate itself in a black hole or change planes. Destratify, open up to a new function, a *diagrammatic* function. Let consciousness cease to be its own double, and passion the double of one person for another. Make consciousness an experimentation in life, and passion a field of continuous intensities, an emission of particles-signs. Make the body without organs of consciousness and love. Use love and consciousness to abolish subjectification: "To become the great lover, the magnetizer and catalyzer . . . one has to first experience the profound wisdom of being an utter fool."[31] Use the *I think* for a becoming-animal, and love for a becoming-woman of man. Desubjectify consciousness and passion. Are there not diagrammatic redundancies distinct from both signifying redundancies and subjective redundancies? Redundancies that would no longer be knots of arborescence but resumptions and upsurges in a rhizome? Stammer language, be a foreigner in one's own tongue:

> do domi not passi do not dominate
> do not dominate your passive passions not
> . . . .
> do devouring not not dominate
> your rats your rations your rats rations not not . . .[32]

It seems necessary to distinguish between three types of deterritorialization: the first type is relative, proper to the strata, and culminates in signifiance; the second is absolute, but still negative and stratic, and appears in subjectification (*Ratio et Passio*); finally, there is the possibility of a positive absolute deterritorialization on the plane of consistency or the body without organs.

We have not, of course, managed to eliminate forms of content (for example, the role of the Temple, or the position of a dominant Reality, etc.). What we have done is to isolate, under artificial conditions, a certain number of semiotics displaying very diverse characteristics. The *presignifying semiotic*, in which the "overcoding" marking the privileged status of language operates diffusely: enunciation is collective, statements themselves are polyvocal, and substances of expression are multiple; relative deterritorialization is determined by the confrontation between the territorialities and segmentary lineages that ward off the State apparatus. The *signifying semiotic:* overcoding is fully effectuated by the signifier, and by the State apparatus that emits it; there is uniformity of enunciation, unification of the substance of expression, and control over statements in a regime of circularity; relative deterritorialization is taken as far as it can go by a redundant and perpetual referral from sign to sign. The *countersignifying semiotic:* here, overcoding is assured by the Number as form of expression or enunciation, and by the War Machine upon which it depends; deterritorialization follows a line of active destruction or abolition. The *postsignifying semiotic*, in which overcoding is assured by the redundancy of consciousness; a subjectification of enunciation occurs on a passional line that makes the organization of power (*pouvoir*) immanent and raises deterritorialization to the absolute, although in a way that is still negative.

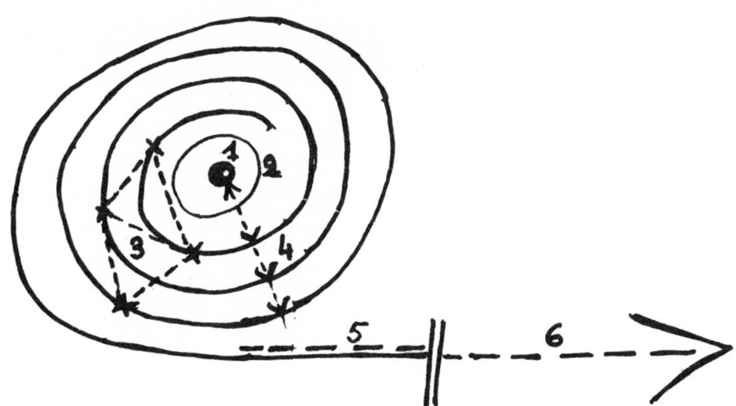

(1) The Center or the Signifier; the faciality of the god or despot. (2) The Temple or Palace, with priests and bureaucrats. (3) The organization in circles and the sign referring to other signs on the same circle or on different circles. (4) The interpretive development of signifier into signified, which then reimparts signifier. (5) The expiatory animal; the blocking of the line of flight. (6) The scapegoat, or the negative sign of the line of flight.

Yet we must consider two aspects: on the one hand, these semiotics are still concrete even after forms of content have been abstracted, but only to the extent that they are mixed, that they constitute mixed combinations. Every semiotic is mixed and only functions as such; each one necessarily captures fragments of one or more other semiotics (surplus value of code). Even from this perspective, the signifying semiotic has no privileged status to apply toward the formation of a general semiology: in particular, the way in which it combines with the passional semiotic of subjectification ("the signifier for the subject") implies nothing that would privilege it over other combinations, for example, the combination of the passional semiotic and the countersignifying semiotic, or of the countersignifying semiotic and the signifying semiotic itself (when the Nomads turn imperial), etc. There is no general semiology.

For example, without privileging one regime over another, it is possible to construct schemas of the signifying and postsignifying semiotics that clearly illustrate the possibilities for concrete mixture.

The second aspect, complementary but very different, consists in the possibility of transforming one abstract or pure semiotic into another, by virtue of the translatability ensuing from overcoding as the special characteristic of language. This time, it is no longer a question of concrete mixed semiotics but of transformations of one abstract semiotic into another (even though that transformation is not itself abstract, in other words, effectively takes place without being performed by a "translator" in the role of pure knower). All transformations taking a given semiotic into the presignifying regime may be called *analogical transformations;* those that take it into the signifying regime are *symbolic;* into the countersignifying regime, *polemical or strategic;* into the postsignifying regime, *consciousness-related or mimetic;* finally, transformations that blow apart semiotics systems or regimes of signs on the plane of consistency of a positive absolute deterritorialization are called *diagrammatic.* A transformation is not the same thing as a statement in a pure semiotic; nor even an ambiguous statement requiring a whole pragmatic analysis to determine the semiotic it belongs to; nor a statement belonging to a mixed semiotic (although the transformation may have that effect). A transformational statement marks the way in which a semiotic translates for its own purposes a statement originating elsewhere, and in so doing diverts it, leaving untransformable residues and actively resisting the inverse transformation. Furthermore, transformations are not limited to the ones we just listed. It is always through transformation that a new semiotic is created in its own right. Translations can be creative. New pure regimes of signs are formed through transformation and translation. Again, there is no general semiology but rather a transsemiotic.

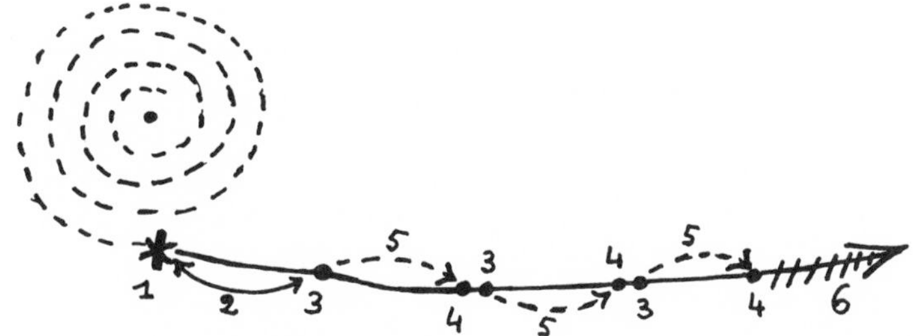

(1) The point of subjectification, replacing the center of signfiance. (2) The two faces turned away from each other. (3) The subject of enunciation resulting from the point of subjectification and the turning away. (4) The subject of the statement, into which the subject of enunciation recoils. (5) The succession of finite linear proceedings accompanied by a new form of priest and a new bureaucracy. (6) The line of flight, which is freed but still segmented, remaining negative and blocked.

In analogical transformations, we often see sleep, drugs, and amorous rapture form expressions that translate into presignifying regimes the subjective or signifying regimes one wishes to impose upon the expressions, but which they resist by themselves imposing upon these regimes an unexpected segmentarity and polyvocality. Christianity underwent strange creative translations in its transmission to "barbarian" or even "savage" peoples. The introduction of monetary signs into certain commercial circuits in Africa caused those signs to undergo an analogical transformation that was very difficult to control (except when the circuits underwent a destructive transformation instead).[33] The songs of black Americans, including, especially, the words, would be a better example, since they show how the slaves "translated" the English signifier and made presignifying or even countersignifying use of the language, blending it with their own African languages just as they blended old African work songs with their new forced labor; these songs also show how, with Christianization and the abolition of slavery, the slaves underwent a proceeding of "subjectification" or even "individuation" that transformed their music, while the music simultaneously transformed the proceeding by analogy; and also how unique problems of "faciality" were posed when whites in "blackface" appropriated the words and songs and blacks responded by darkening their faces another hue, taking back their dances and songs, even transforming or translating those of the whites.[34] Of course, the crudest and most visible transformations were in the other direction: the symbolic translations occurring when the signifier takes power. The preceding examples concerning monetary signs and rhythmic regimes can be repeated in the opposite direction. The passage from an African dance to a white dance often exhibits a consciousness-related or mimetic translation, accompanied by a power takeover by signifiance and subjectification. ("In Africa the dance is impersonal, sacred and obscene. When the phallus becomes erect and is handled like a banana it is not a 'personal hard-on' we see but a tribal erection. . . . The hoochie-koochie dancer of the big city dances alone—a fact of staggering significance. The law forbids response, forbids participation. Nothing is left of the primitive rite but the 'suggestive' movements of the body. What they suggest varies with *the individual observer.*")[35]

It is not simply linguistic, lexical, or even syntactic transformations that determine the importance of a true semiotic translation but the opposite. Crazy talk is not enough. In each case we must judge whether what we see is an adaptation of an old semiotic, a new variety of a particular mixed semiotic, or the process of creation of an as yet unknown regime. For example, it is relatively easy to stop saying "I," but that does not mean that you have gotten away from the regime of subjectification; conversely, you can keep on saying "I," just for kicks, and already be in another regime in which personal pronouns function only as fictions. Signifiance and interpretation are so thick-skinned, they form such a sticky mixture with subjectification, that it is easy to believe that you are outside them when you are in fact still secreting them. People sometimes denounce interpretation yet show so signifying a face that they simultaneously impose interpretation upon the subject, which continues to nourish itself on it in order to survive. Who can really believe that psychoanalysis is capable of changing a semiotic amassing every deception? The only change there has been is a role switch. Instead of a patient who signifies and a psychoanalyst who interprets, we now have a signifying analyst and it is the patient who does all the interpreting. In the antipsychiatric experiment of Kingsley Hall, Mary Barnes, a former nurse turned "schizophrenic," embraces the new semiotic of the Voyage, only to arrogate to herself a veritable power in the community and reintroduce as a collective delusion the worst kind of psychoanalytic regime of interpretation ("She *interpreted* everything that was done for her, or for anyone else for that matter . . .").[36] A highly stratified semiotic is difficult to get away from. Even a presignifying, or countersignifying, semiotic, even an asignifying diagram, harbors knots of coincidence just waiting to form virtual centers of signifiance and points of subjectification. Of course, an operation of translation is not easy when it is a question of destroying a dominant atmospheric semiotic. One of the things of profound interest in Castaneda's books, under the influence of drugs, or other things, and of a change of atmosphere, is precisely that they show how the Indian manages to combat the mechanisms of interpretation and instill in the disciple a presignifying semiotic, or even an asignifying diagram: Stop! You're making me tired! Experiment, don't signify and interpret! Find your own places, territorialities, deterritorializations, regime, lines of flight! Semiotize yourself instead of rooting around in your prefab childhood and Western semiology. "Don Juan stated that in order to arrive at 'seeing' one first had to 'stop the world.' 'Stopping the world' was indeed an appropriate rendition of certain states of awareness in which the reality of everyday life is altered because the flow of interpretation, which ordinarily runs uninterruptedly, has been stopped by a set of circumstances alien to the flow."[37] In short, a true semiotic transformation appeals to all kinds of variables, not only external ones, but also variables implicit to language, internal to statements.

Pragmatics, then, already displays two components. The first could be called *generative* since it shows how the various abstract regimes form concrete mixed semiotics, with what variants, how they combine, and which one is predominant. The second is the *transformational* component, which shows how these regimes of signs are translated into each other, especially when there is a creation of a new regime. Generative pragmatics makes tracings of mixed semiotics; transformational pragmatics makes maps of transformations. Although a mixed semiotic does not necessarily imply effective creativity, and may content itself with combinatory possibilities without veritable transformation, it is still the transformational component that accounts for the originality of a regime as well as for the novelty of the mixes it enters at a given moment in a given domain. This second component is therefore the more profound, and it is the only means of measuring the elements of the first component.[38] For example, we may ask when statements of the Bolshevik type first appeared, and how Leninism, at the time of the break with the social democrats, effected a veritable transformation that created an original semiotic, even if its fall into the mixed semiotic of Stalinist organization was inevitable. In an exemplary study, Jean-Pierre Faye did a detailed analysis of the transformations that produced Nazism, viewed as a system of new statements in a given social field. At what moment is a regime of signs established, and in what domain? Throughout an entire people? In a fraction of that people? In a more or less localizable margin inside a psychiatric hospital? (For as we have seen we can find a semiotic of subjectification in the ancient history of the Jews, but also in psychiatric diagnosis in the nineteenth century, with, of course, profound variations and even veritable transformations in the corresponding semiotic.) All of these questions fall within the purview of pragmatics. There is no question that the most profound transformations and translations of our time are not occurring in Europe. Pragmatics should reject the idea of an invariant immune from transformation, even if it is the invariant of a dominant "grammaticality." For language is a political affair before it is an affair for linguistics; even the evaluation of degrees of grammaticality is a political matter.

What is a semiotic, in other words, a regime of signs or a formalization of expression? They are simultaneously more and less than language. Language as a whole is defined by "superlinearity," its condition of possibility; individual languages are defined by constants, elements, and relations of a phonological, syntactical, and semantic nature. Doubtless, every regime of signs effectuates the condition of possibility of language and utilizes language elements, but that is all. No regime can be identical to that condition of possibility, and no regime has the property of constants. As Foucault clearly shows, regimes of signs are only *functions of existence* of language that sometimes span a number of languages and are sometimes distributed within a single language; they coincide neither with a structure nor with units of a given order, but rather intersect them and cause them to appear in space and time. This is the sense in which regimes of signs are assemblages of enunciation, which cannot be adequately accounted for by any linguistic category: *what makes a proposition or even a single word a "statement"* pertains to implicit presuppositions that cannot be made explicit, that mobilize pragmatic variables proper to enunciation (incorporeal transformations). This precludes explaining an assemblage in terms of the signifier or the subject, because both pertain to variables of enunciation within the assemblage. It is signifiance and subjectification that presuppose the assemblage, not the reverse. The names we gave to the regimes of signs ("presignifying," "signifying," "countersignifying," "postsignifying") would remain evolutionist if heterogeneous functions or varieties of assemblages did not effectively correspond to them (segmentarization, signifiance and interpretation, numeration, subjectification). Regimes of signs are thus defined by variables that are internal to enunciation but remain external to the constants of language and irreducible to linguistic categories.

But at this point, everything turns around, and the reasons why a regime of signs is less than language also become the reasons why it is more than language. Only one side of the assemblage has to do with enunciation or formalizes expression; on its other side, inseparable from the first, it formalizes contents, it is a machinic assemblage or an assemblage of bodies. Now contents are not "signifieds" dependent upon a signifier in any way, nor are they "objects" in any kind of relation of causality with the subject. They have their own formalization and have no relation of symbolic correspondence or linear causality with the form of expression: the two forms are in reciprocal presupposition, and they can be abstracted from each other only in a very relative way because they are two sides of a single assemblage. We must therefore arrive at something in the assemblage itself that is still more profound than these sides and can account for both of the forms in presupposition, forms of expression or regimes of signs (semiotic systems) and forms of content or regimes of bodies (physical systems). This is what we call the *abstract machine*, which constitutes and conjugates all of the assemblage's cutting edges of deterritorialization.[39] We must say that the abstract machine is necessarily "much more" than language. When linguists (following Chomsky) rise to the idea of a purely language-based abstract machine, our immediate objection is that their machine, far from being too abstract, is not abstract enough because it is limited to the form of expression and to alleged universals that presuppose language. Abstracting content is an operation that appears all the more relative and inadequate when seen from the viewpoint of abstraction itself. A true abstract machine has no way of making a distinction within itself between a plane of expression and a plane of content because it draws a single plane of consistency, which in turn formalizes contents and expressions according to strata and reterritorializations. The abstract machine in itself is destratified, deterritorialized; it has no form of its own (much less substance) and makes no distinction within itself between content and expression, even though outside itself it presides over that distinction and distributes it in strata, domains, and territories. An abstract machine in itself is not physical or corporeal, any more than it is semiotic; it is *diagrammatic* (it knows nothing of the distinction between the artificial and the natural either). It operates by *matter*, not by substance; by *function*, not by form. Substances and forms are of expression "or" of content. But functions are not yet "semiotically" formed, and matters are not yet "physically" formed. The abstract machine is pure Matter-Function—a diagram independent of the forms and substances, expressions and contents it will distribute.

We define the abstract machine as the aspect or moment at which nothing but functions and matters remain. A diagram has neither substance nor form, neither content nor expression.[40] Substance is a formed matter, and matter is a substance that is unformed either physically or semiotically. Whereas expression and content have distinct forms, are really distinct from each other, function has only "traits," of content and of expression, between which it establishes a connection: it is no longer even possible to tell whether it is a particle or a sign. A matter-content having only degrees of intensity, resistance, conductivity, heating, stretching, speed, or tardiness; and a function-expression having only "tensors," as in a system of mathematical, or musical, writing. Writing now functions on the same level as the real, and the real materially writes. The diagram retains the most deterritorialized content and the most deterritorialized expression, in order to conjugate them. Maximum deterritorialization sometimes starts from a trait of content and sometimes from a trait of expression; that trait is said to be "deterritorializing" in relation to the other precisely because it diagrams it, carries it off, raises it to its own power. The most deterritorialized element causes the other element to cross a threshold enabling a conjunction of their respective deterritorializations, a shared acceleration. This is the abstract machine's absolute, positive deterritorialization. That is why *diagrams* must be distinguished from *indexes*, which are territorial signs, but also from *icons*, which pertain to reterritorialization, and from *symbols*, which pertain to relative or negative deterritorialization.[41] Defined diagrammatically in this way, an abstract machine is neither an infrastructure that is determining in the last instance nor a transcendental Idea that is determining in the supreme instance. Rather, it plays a piloting role. The diagrammatic or abstract machine does not function to represent, even something real, but rather constructs a real that is yet to come, a new type of reality. Thus when it constitutes points of creation or potentiality it does not stand outside history but is instead always "prior to" history. Everything escapes, everything creates—never alone, but through an abstract machine that produces continuums of intensity, effects conjunctions of deterritorialization, and extracts expressions and contents. This Real-Abstract is totally different from the fictitious abstraction of a supposedly pure machine of expression. It is an Absolute, but one that is neither undifferentiated nor transcendent. Abstract machines thus have proper names (as well as dates), which of course designate not persons or subjects but matters and functions. The name of a musician or scientist is used in the same way as a painter's name designates a color, nuance, tone, or intensity: it is always a question of a conjunction of Matter and Function. The double deterritorialization of the voice and the instrument is marked by a Wagner abstract machine, a Webern abstract machine, etc. In physics and mathematics, we may speak of a Riemann abstract machine, and in algebra of a Galois abstract machine (defined precisely by an arbitrary line, called the adjunctive line, which conjugates with a body taken as a starting point), etc. There is a diagram whenever a singular abstract machine functions directly in a matter.

Strictly speaking, therefore, there are no regimes of signs on the diagrammatic level, or on the plane of consistency, because form of expression is no longer really distinct from form of content. The diagram knows only traits and cutting edges that are still elements of content insofar as they are material and of expression insofar as they are functional, but which draw one another along, form relays, and meld in a shared deterritorialization: particles-signs. There is nothing surprising in this, for the real distinction between form of expression and form of content appears only with the strata, and is different on each one. It is on the strata that the double articulation appears that formalizes traits of expression and traits of content, each in its own right, turning matters into physically or semiotically formed substances and functions into forms of expression or content. Expression then constitutes indexes, icons, or symbols that enter regimes or semiotic systems. Content then constitutes bodies, things, or objects that enter physical systems, organisms, and organizations. The deeper movement for conjugating matter and function—absolute deterritorialization, identical to the earth itself—appears only in the form of respective territorialities, negative or relative deterritorializations, and complementary reterritorializations. All of this culminates in a language stratum that installs an abstract machine on the level of expression and takes the abstraction of content even further, tending to strip it of any form of its own (the imperialism of language, the pretensions to a general semiology). In short, the strata substantialize diagrammatic matters and separate a formed plane of content from a formed plane of expression. They hold expressions and contents, separately substantialized and formalized, in the pincers of a double articulation assuring their independence and real distinction and enthroning a dualism that endlessly reproduces and redivides. They shatter the continuums of intensity, introducing breaks between different strata and within each stratum. They prevent conjunctions of flight from forming and crush the cutting edges of deterritorialization, either by effecting reterritorializations that make these movements merely relative, or by assigning certain of the lines an entirely negative value, or again by segmenting them, blocking them, plugging them, or plunging them into a kind of black hole.

Above all, diagrammaticism should not be confused with an operation of the axiomatic type. Far from drawing creative lines of flight and conjugating traits of positive deterritorialization, axiomatics blocks all lines, subordinates them to a punctual system, and halts the geometric and algebraic writing systems that had begun to run off in all directions. This happened in relation to the question of indeterminism in physics: a "reordering" was undertaken to reconcile it with physical determinism. Mathematical writing systems were axiomatized, in other words, restratified, resemiotized, and material flows were rephysicalized. It is as much a political as a scientific affair: science must not go crazy. Hilbert and de Broglie were as much politicians as scientists: they reestablished order. An axiomatization, a semiotization, a physicalization, is not a diagram but in fact the opposite of a diagram. The program of a stratum, against the diagram of the plane of consistency. This does not, however, preclude the diagram's heading back down the road to escape and scattering new, singular abstract machines (the mathematical creation of improbable functions was carried out in opposition to axiomatization, and the material invention of unfindable particles in opposition to physicalization). Science as such is like everything else; madness is as intrinsic to it as reorderings. The same scientists may participate in both aspects, having their own madness, police, signifiances, or subjectifications, as well as their own abstract machines, all in their capacity as scientists. The phrase "the politics of science" is a good designation for these currents, which are internal to science and not simply circumstances and State factors that act upon it from the outside, leading it to make an atomic bomb here and embark upon a space program there. These political influences or determinations would not exist if science itself did not have its own poles, oscillations, strata, and destratifications, its own lines of flight and reorderings, in short, the more or less potential events of its own politics, its own particular "polemics," its own internal war machine (of which thwarted, persecuted, or hindered scientists are historically a part). It is not enough to say that axiomatics does not take invention and creation into account: it possesses a deliberate will to halt or stabilize the diagram, to take its place by lodging itself on the level of a coagulated abstraction too gross for the concrete but too fine for the real. We will see in what sense this is the "capitalist" level.

We cannot, however, content ourselves with a dualism between the plane of consistency and its diagrams and abstract machines on the one hand, and the strata and their programs and concrete assemblages on the other. Abstract machines do not exist only on the plane of consistency, upon which they develop diagrams; they are already present enveloped or "encasted" in the strata in general, or even erected on particular strata upon which they simultaneously organize a form of expression and a form of content. What is illusory in the second case is the idea of an exclusively expressive or language-based abstract machine, not the idea of an abstract machine internal to the stratum and accounting for the relativity of those two distinct forms. Thus there are two complementary movements, one by which abstract machines work the strata and are constantly setting things loose, another by which they are effectively stratified, effectively captured by the strata. *On the one hand*, strata could never organize themselves if they did not harness diagrammatic matters or functions and formalize them from the standpoint of both expression and content; every regime of signs, and even signifiance and subjectification, is still a diagrammatic effect (although relativized and negativized). *On the other hand*, abstract machines would never be present, even on the strata, if they did not have the power or potentiality to extract and accelerate destratified particles-signs (the passage to the absolute). Consistency is neither totalizing nor structuring; rather, it is deterritorializing (a biological stratum, for example, evolves not according to statistical phenomena but rather according to cutting edges of deterritorialization). The security, tranquillity, and homeostatic equilibrium of the strata are thus never completely guaranteed:

to regain a plane of consistency that inserts itself into the most diverse systems of stratification and jumps from one to the other, it suffices to prolong the lines of flight working the strata, to connect the dots, to conjugate the processes of deterritorialization. We have seen that signifiance and interpretation, consciousness and passion, can prolong themselves following these lines, and at the same time open out onto a properly diagrammatic experience. All of these states or modes of the abstract machine coexist in what we call the *machinic assemblage.* The assemblage has two poles or vectors: one vector is oriented toward the strata, upon which it distributes territorialities, relative deterritorializations, and reterritorializations; the other is oriented toward the plane of consistency or destratification, upon which it conjugates processes of deterritorialization, carrying them to the absolute of the earth. It is along its stratic vector that the assemblage differentiates a form of expression (from the standpoint of which it appears as a collective assemblage of enunciation) from a form of content (from the standpoint of which it appears as a machinic assemblage of bodies); it fits one form to the other, one manifestation to the other, placing them in reciprocal presupposition. But along its diagrammatic or destratified vector, it no longer has two sides; all it retains are traits of expression and content from which it extracts degrees of deterritorialization that add together and cutting edges that conjugate.

A regime of signs has more than just two components. It has, in fact, four of them, which form the object of Pragmatics. The first was the *generative* component, which shows how a form of expression located on the language stratum always appeals to several combined regimes, in other words, how every regime of signs or semiotic is concretely mixed. On the level of this component, one *can* abstract forms of content, most successfully if emphasis is placed on the mixture of regimes in the form of expression: one should not, however, conclude from this the predominance of a regime constituting a general semiology and unifying forms. The second, *transformational,* component, shows how one abstract regime can be translated, transformed into another, and especially how it can be created from other regimes. This second component is obviously more profound, because all mixed regimes presuppose these transformations from one regime to another, past, present, or potential (as a function of the creation of new regimes). Once again, one abstracts, or can abstract, content, since the analysis is limited to metamorphoses internal to the form of expression, even though the form of expression is not adequate to account for them. The third component is *diagrammatic:* it consists in taking regimes of signs or forms of expression and extracting from them particles-signs that are no longer formalized but instead constitute unformed traits capable of combining with one another. This is the height of abstraction, but also the moment at which abstraction becomes real; everything operates through abstract-real machines (which have names and dates). One can abstract forms of content, but one must simultaneously abstract forms of expression; for what is retained of each are only unformed traits. That is why an abstract machine that would operate purely on the level of language is an absurdity. It is clear that this diagrammatic component is in turn more profound than the transformational component: the creations-transformations of a regime of signs operate by the emergence of ever-new abstract machines. Finally, the last, properly *machinic*, component is meant to show how abstract machines are effectuated in concrete assemblages; it is these assemblages that give distinct form to traits of expression, but not without doing the same for traits of content—the two forms being in reciprocal presupposition, or having a necessary, unformed relation that once again prevents the form of expression from behaving as though it were self-sufficient (although it is independent or distinct in a strictly formal way).

Thus pragmatics (or schizoanalysis) can be represented by four circular components that bud and form rhizomes.

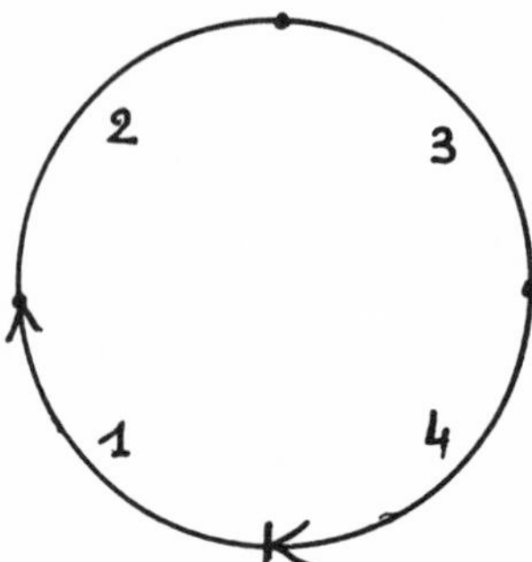

(1) The generative component: the study of concrete mixed semiotics; their mixtures and variations. (2) The transformational component: the study of pure semiotics; their transformations-translations and the creation of new semiotics. (3) The diagrammatic component: the study of abstract machines, from the standpoint of semiotically unformed matters in relation to physically unformed matters. (4) The machinic component: the study of the assemblages that effectuate abstract machines, simultaneously semiotizing matters of expression and physicalizing matters of content.

Pragmatics as a whole would consist in this: making a *tracing* of the mixed semiotics, under the generative component; making the transformational *map* of the regimes, with their possibilities for translation and creation, for budding along the lines of the tracings; making the *diagram* of the abstract machines that are in play in each case, either as potentialities or as effective emergences; outlining the *program* of the assemblages that distribute everything and bring a circulation of movement with alternatives, jumps, and mutations.

For example, in considering a given "proposition," in other words, a verbal aggregate defined syntactically, semantically, and logically as the expression of an individual or group ("I love you" or "I am jealous"), one would begin by asking to which "statement" this proposition corresponds in the group or individual (for the same proposition can be tied to completely different statements). This question means: What regime of signs is the proposition taken up by and without which its syntactical, semantic, and logical elements would remain totally empty universal conditions? What nonlinguistic element, or variable of enunciation, gives it consistency? There is a presignifying "I love you" of the collective type in which, as Miller says, a dance weds all the women of the tribe; there is a countersignifying "I love you" of the distributive and polemical type that has to do with war and relations of force (the "I love you" of Penthesilea and Achilles); there is an "I love you" that is addressed to a center of signifiance and uses interpretation to make a whole series of signifieds correspond to the signifying chain; and there is a postsignifying or passional "I love you" that constitutes a proceeding beginning from a point of subjectification, then another, and yet another. Similarly, the proposition "I am jealous" is clearly not the same statement in the passional regime of subjectification as in the paranoid regime of signifiance: these are two distinct delusions. Second, once it has been determined which statement the proposition corresponds to in a given group or individual at a given time, one would look into the possibilities not only of mixture but also of translation and transformation into another regime, or into statements belonging to other regimes; one would look at what passes and does not pass in such a transformation, what remains irreducible and what flows. Third, one could try to create new, as yet unknown statements for that proposition, even if the result were a patois of sensual delight, physical and semiotic systems in shreds, asubjective affects, signs without signifiance where syntax, semantics, and logic are in collapse. This research should go from the worst to the best since it would cover precious, metaphorical, or stultifying regimes as well as cries-whispers, feverish improvisations, becomings-animal, becomings-molecular, real transsexualities, continuums of intensity, constitutions of bodies without organs . . . These two poles are inseparable; they entertain perpetual relations of transformation, conversion, jumping, falling, and rising. This final research simultaneously brings into play, on the one hand, abstract machines, diagrams and diagrammatic functions, and, on the other hand, machinic assemblages, the formal distinctions they make between expression and content, and their investments of words and organs according to a relation of reciprocal presupposition. For example, the "I love you" of courtly love: What is its diagram, what abstract machine emerges, and what is the new assemblage? These questions apply as much to destratification as to the organization of strata. In short, there are no syntactically, semantically, or logically definable propositions that transcend or loom above statements. All methods for the transcendentalization of language, all methods for endowing language with universals, from Russell's logic to Chomsky's grammar, have fallen into the worst kind of abstraction, in the sense that they validate a level that is both too abstract and not abstract enough. Regimes of signs are not based on language, and language alone does not constitute an abstract machine, whether structural or generative. The opposite is the case. It is language that is based on regimes of signs, and regimes of signs on abstract machines, diagrammatic functions, and machinic assemblages that go beyond any system of semiology, linguistics, or logic. There is no universal propositional logic, nor is there grammaticality in itself, any more than there is signifier for itself. "Behind" statements and semioticizations there are only machines, assemblages, and movements of deterritorialization that cut across the stratification of the various systems and elude both the coordinates of language and of existence. That is why pragmatics is not a complement to logic, syntax, or semantics; on the contrary, it is the fundamental element upon which all the rest depend.

6. November 28, 1947: How Do You Make Yourself a Body without Organs?

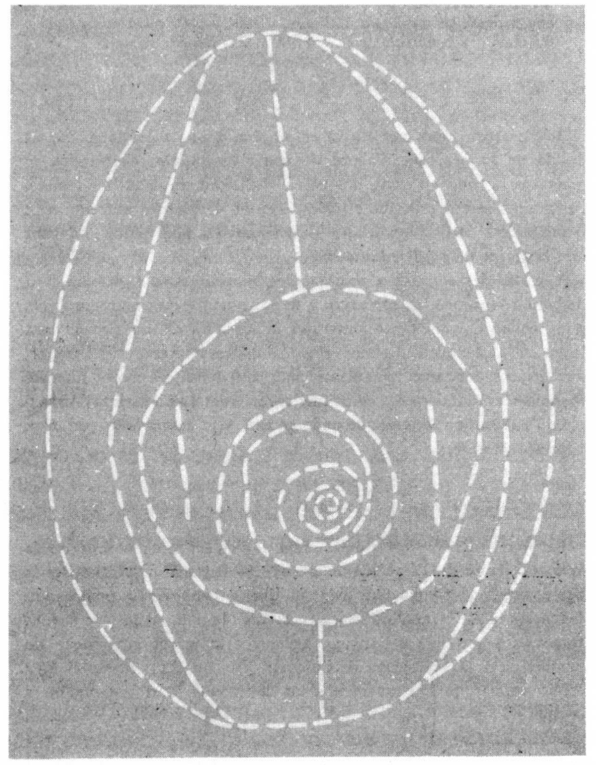

The Dogon Egg and the Distribution of Intensities

At any rate, you have one (or several). It's not so much that it preexists or comes ready-made, although in certain respects it is preexistent. At any rate, you make one, you can't desire without making one. And it awaits you; it is an inevitable exercise or experimentation, already accomplished the moment you undertake it, unaccomplished as long as you don't. This is not reassuring, because you can botch it. Or it can be terrifying, and lead you to your death. It is nondesire as well as desire. It is not at all a notion or a concept but a practice, a set of practices. You never reach the Body without Organs, you can't reach it, you are forever attaining it, it is a limit. People ask, So what is this BwO?—But you're already on it, scurrying like a vermin, groping like a blind person, or running like a lunatic: desert traveler and nomad of the steppes. On it we sleep, live our waking lives, fight—fight and are fought—seek our place, experience untold happiness and fabulous defeats; on it we penetrate and are penetrated; on it we love. On November 28, 1947, Artaud declares war on the organs: *To be done with the judgment of God*, "for you can tie me up if you wish, but there is nothing more useless than an organ."[1] Experimentation: not only radiophonic but also biological and political, incurring censorship and repression. Corpus and Socius, politics and experimentation. They will not let you experiment in peace.

The BwO: it is already under way the moment the body has had enough of organs and wants to slough them off, or loses them. A long procession. The *hypochondriac body:* the organs are destroyed, the damage has already been done, nothing happens anymore. "Miss X claims that she no longer has a brain or nerves or chest or stomach or guts. All she has left is the skin and bones of a disorganized body. These are her own words."[2] The *paranoid body:* the organs are continually under attack by outside forces, but are also restored by outside energies. ("He lived for a long time without a stomach, without intestines, almost without lungs, with a torn oesophagus, without a bladder, and with shattered ribs, he used sometimes to swallow part of his own larynx with his food, etc. But divine miracles ('rays') always restored what had been destroyed.")[3] The *schizo body,* waging its own active internal struggle against the organs, at the price of catatonia. Then the *drugged body,* the experimental schizo: "The human body is scandalously inefficient. Instead of a mouth and an anus to get out of order why not have one all-purpose hole to eat *and* eliminate? We could seal up nose and mouth, fill in the stomach, make an air hole direct into the lungs where it should have been in the first place."[4] The *masochist body:* it is poorly understood in terms of pain; it is fundamentally a question of the BwO. It has its sadist or whore sew it up; the eyes, anus, urethra, breasts, and nose are sewn shut. It has itself strung up to stop the organs from working; flayed, as if the organs clung to the skin; sodomized, smothered, to make sure everything is sealed tight.

Why such a dreary parade of sucked-dry, catatonicized, vitrified, sewn-up bodies, when the BwO is also full of gaiety, ecstasy, and dance? So why these examples, why must we start there? Emptied bodies instead of full ones. What happened? Were you cautious enough? Not wisdom, caution. In doses. As a rule immanent to experimentation: injections of caution. Many have been defeated in this battle. Is it really so sad and dangerous to be fed up with seeing with your eyes, breathing with your lungs, swallowing with your mouth, talking with your tongue, thinking with your brain, having an anus and larynx, head and legs? Why not walk on your head, sing with your sinuses, see through your skin, breathe with your belly: the simple Thing, the Entity, the full Body, the stationary Voyage, Anorexia, cutaneous Vision, Yoga, Krishna, Love, Experimentation. Where psychoanalysis says, "Stop, find your self again," we should say instead, "Let's go further still, we haven't found our BwO yet, we haven't sufficiently dismantled our self." Substitute forgetting for anamnesis, experimentation for interpretation. Find your body without organs. Find out how to make it. It's a question of life and death, youth and old age, sadness and joy. It is where everything is played out.

"Mistress, 1) You may tie me down on the table, ropes drawn tight, for ten to fifteen minutes, time enough to prepare the instruments; 2) One hundred lashes at least, a pause of several minutes; 3) You begin sewing, you sew up the hole in the glans; you sew the skin around the glans to the glans itself, preventing the top from tearing; you sew the scrotum to the skin of the thighs. You sew the breasts, securely attaching a button with four holes to each nipple. You may connect them with an elastic band with buttonholes—*Now you go on to the second phase:* 4) You can choose either to turn me over on the table so I am tied lying on my stomach, but with my legs together, or to bind me to the post with my wrists together, and my legs also, my whole body tightly bound; 5) You whip my back buttocks thighs, a hundred lashes at least; 6) You sew my buttocks together, all the way up and down the crack of my ass. Tightly, with a doubled thread, each stitch knotted. If I am on the table, now tie me to the post; 7) You give me fifty thrashes on the buttocks; 8) If you wish to intensify the torture and carry out your threat from last time, stick the pins all the way into my buttocks as far as they go; 9) Then you may tie me to the chair; you give me thirty thrashes on the breasts and stick in the smaller pins; if you wish, you may heat them red-hot beforehand, all or some. I should be tightly bound to the chair, hands behind my back so my chest sticks out. I haven't mentioned burns, only because I have a medical exam coming up in awhile, and they take a long time to heal." This is not a phantasy, it is a program: There is an essential difference between the psychoanalytic interpretation of the phantasy and the antipsychiatric experimentation of the program. Between the phantasy, an interpretation that must itself be interpreted, and the motor program of experimentation.[5] The BwO is what remains when you take everything away. What you take away is precisely the phantasy, and signifiances and subjectifications as a whole. Psychoanalysis does the opposite: it translates everything into phantasies, it converts everything into phantasy, it retains the phantasy. It royally botches the real, because it botches the BwO.

Something will happen. Something is already happening. But what comes to pass on the BwO is not exactly the same as how you make yourself one. However, one is included in the other. Hence the two phases set forth in the preceding letter. *Why two clearly distinguished phases*, when the same thing is done in both cases—sewing and flogging? One phase is for the fabrication of the BwO, the other to make something circulate on it or pass across it; the same procedures are nevertheless used in both phases, but they must be done over, done twice. What is certain is that the masochist has made himself a BwO under such conditions that the BwO can no longer be populated by anything but intensities of pain, *pain waves*. It is false to say that the masochist is looking for pain but just as false to say that he is looking for pleasure in a particularly suspensive or roundabout way. The masochist is looking for a type of BwO that only pain can fill, or travel over, due to the very conditions under which that BwO was constituted. Pains are populations, packs, modes of king-masochist-in-the-desert that he engenders and augments. The same goes for the drugged body and intensities of cold, *refrigerator waves*. For each type of BwO, we must ask: (1) What type is it, how is it fabricated, by what procedures and means (predetermining what will come to pass)? (2) What are its modes, what comes to pass, and with what variants and what surprises, what is unexpected and what expected? In short, there is a very special relation of synthesis and analysis between a given type of BwO and what happens on it: an *a priori* synthesis by which something will necessarily be produced in a given mode (but what it will be is not known) and an infinite analysis by which what is produced on the BwO is already part of that body's production, is already included in the body, is already on it (but at the price of an infinity of passages, divisions, and secondary productions). It is a very delicate experimentation since there must not be any stagnation of the modes or slippage in type: the masochist and the drug user court these ever-present dangers that empty their BwO's instead of filling them.

You can fail twice, but it is the same failure, the same danger. Once at the level of the constitution of the BwO and again at the level of what passes or does not pass across it. You think you have made yourself a good BwO, that you chose the right Place, Power (*Puissance*), and Collectivity (there is always a collectivity, even when you are alone), and then nothing passes, nothing circulates, or something prevents things from moving. A paranoid point, a point of blockage, an outburst of delirium: it comes across clearly in *Speed*, by William Burroughs, Jr. Is it possible to locate this danger point, should the block be expelled, or should one instead "love, honor, and serve degeneracy wherever it surfaces"? To block, to be blocked, is that not still an intensity? In each case, we must define what comes to pass and what does not pass, what causes passage and prevents it. As in the meat circuit according to Lewin, something flows through channels whose sections are delimited by doors with gatekeepers, passers-on.[6] Door openers and trap closers, Malabars and Fierabras. The body is now nothing more than a set of valves, locks, floodgates, bowls, or communicating vessels, each with a proper name: a peopling of the BwO, a Metropolis that has to be managed with a whip. What peoples it, what passes across it, what does the blocking?

A BwO is made in such a way that it can be occupied, populated only by intensities. Only intensities pass and circulate. Still, the BwO is not a scene, a place, or even a support upon which something comes to pass. It has nothing to do with phantasy, there is nothing to interpret. The BwO causes intensities to pass; it produces and distributes them in a *spatium* that is itself intensive, lacking extension. It is not space, nor is it in space; it is matter that occupies space to a given degree—to the degree corresponding to the intensities produced. It is nonstratified, unformed, intense matter, the matrix of intensity, intensity = 0; but there is nothing negative about that zero, there are no negative or opposite intensities. Matter equals energy. Production of the real as an intensive magnitude starting at zero. That is why we treat the BwO as the full egg before the extension of the organism and the organization of the organs, before the formation of the strata; as the intense egg defined by axes and vectors, gradients and thresholds, by dynamic tendencies involving energy transformation and kinematic movements involving group displacement, by migrations: all independent of *accessory forms* because the organs appear and function here only as pure intensities.[7] The organ changes when it crosses a threshold, when it changes gradient. "No organ is constant as regards either function or position, . . . sex organs sprout anywhere, . . . rectums open, defecate and close, . . . the entire organism changes color and consistency in split-second adjustments."[8] The tantric egg.

After all, is not Spinoza's *Ethics* the great book of the BwO? The attributes are types or genuses of BwO's, substances, powers, zero intensities as matrices of production. The modes are everything that comes to pass: waves and vibrations, migrations, thresholds and gradients, intensities produced in a given type of substance starting from a given matrix. The masochist body as an attribute or genus of substance, with its production of intensities and pain modes based on its degree 0 of being sewn up. The drugged body as a different attribute, with its production of specific intensities based on absolute Cold = 0. ("Junkies always beef about *The Cold* as they call it, turning up their black coat collars and clutching their withered necks . . . pure junk con. A junky does not want to be warm, he wants to be cool-cooler-COLD. But he wants The Cold like he wants His Junk—NOT OUTSIDE where it does him no good but INSIDE so he can sit around with a spine like a frozen hydraulic jack . . . his metabolism approaching Absolute

BwO- Smooth space- speeds

Zero.")[9] Etc. The problem of whether there is a substance of all substances, a single substance for all attributes, becomes: *Is there a totality of all BwO's*? If the BwO is already a limit, what must we say of the totality of all BwO's? It is a problem not of the One and the Multiple but of a fusional multiplicity that effectively goes beyond any opposition between the one and the multiple. A formal multiplicity of substantial attributes that, as such, constitutes the ontological unity of substance. There is a continuum of all of the attributes or genuses of intensity under a single substance, and a continuum of the intensities of a certain genus under a single type or attribute. A continuum of all substances in intensity and of all intensities in substance. The uninterrupted continuum of the BwO. BwO, immanence, immanent limit. Drug users, masochists, schizophrenics, lovers—all BwO's pay homage to Spinoza. The BwO is the *field of immanence* of desire, the *plane of consistency* specific to desire (with desire defined as a process of production without reference to any exterior agency, whether it be a lack that hollows it out or a pleasure that fills it).

Every time desire is betrayed, cursed, uprooted from its field of immanence, a priest is behind it. The priest cast the triple curse on desire: the negative law, the extrinsic rule, and the transcendent ideal. Facing north, the priest said, Desire is lack (how could it not lack what it desires?). The priest carried out the first sacrifice, named castration, and all the men and women of the north lined up behind him, crying in cadence, "Lack, lack, it's the common law." Then, facing south, the priest linked desire to pleasure. For there are hedonistic, even orgiastic, priests. Desire will be assuaged by pleasure; and not only will the pleasure obtained silence desire for a moment but the process of obtaining it is already a way of interrupting it, of instantly discharging it and unburdening oneself of it. Pleasure as discharge: the priest carries out the second sacrifice, named masturbation. Then, facing east, he exclaimed: *Jouissance* is impossible, but impossible *jouissance* is inscribed in desire. For that, in its very impossibility, is the Ideal, the "*manque-à-jouir* that is life."[10] The priest carried out the third sacrifice, phantasy or the thousand and one nights, the one hundred twenty days, while the men of the East chanted: Yes, we will be your phantasy, your ideal and impossibility, yours and also our own. The priest did not turn to the west. He knew that in the west lay a plane of consistency, but he thought that the way was blocked by the columns of Hercules, that it led nowhere and was uninhabited by people. But that is where desire was lurking, west was the shortest route east, as well as to the other directions, rediscovered or deterritorialized.

The most recent figure of the priest is the psychoanalyst, with his or her three principles: Pleasure, Death, and Reality. Doubtless, psychoanalysis demonstrated that desire is not subordinated to procreation, or even to genitality. That was its modernism. But it retained the essentials; it even found new ways of inscribing in desire the negative law of lack, the external rule of pleasure, and the transcendent ideal of phantasy. Take the interpretation of masochism: when the ridiculous death instinct is not invoked, it is claimed that the masochist, like everybody else, is after pleasure but can only get it through pain and phantasied humiliations whose function is to allay or ward off deep anxiety. This is inaccurate; the masochist's suffering is the price he must pay, not to achieve pleasure, but to untie the pseudobond between desire and pleasure as an extrinsic measure. Pleasure is in no way something that can be attained only by a detour through suffering; it is something that must be delayed as long as possible because it interrupts the continuous process of positive desire. There is, in fact, a joy that is immanent to desire as though desire were filled by itself and its contemplations, a joy that implies no lack or impossibility and is not measured by pleasure since it is what distributes intensities of pleasure and prevents them from being suffused by anxiety, shame, and guilt. In short, the masochist uses suffering as a way of constituting a body without organs and bringing forth a plane of consistency of desire. That there are other ways, other procedures than masochism, and certainly better ones, is beside the point; it is enough that some find this procedure suitable for them.

Take a masochist who did not undergo psychoanalysis: "PROGRAM . . . At night, put on the bridle and attach my hands more tightly, either to the bit with the chain, or to the big belt right after returning from the bath. Put on the entire harness right away also, the reins and thumbscrews, and attach the thumbscrews to the harness. My penis should be in a metal sheath. Ride the reins for two hours during the day, and in the evening as the master wishes. Confinement for three or four days, hands still tied, the reins alternately tightened and loosened. The master will never approach her horse without the crop, and without using it. If the animal should display impatience or rebelliousness, the reins will be drawn tighter, the master will grab them and give the beast a good thrashing."[11] What is this masochist doing? He seems to be imitating a horse, *Equus eroticus*, but that's not it. Nor are the horse and the master-trainer or mistress images of the mother or father. Something entirely different is going on: a becoming-animal essential to masochism. It is a question of forces. The masochist presents it this way: *Training axiom—destroy the instinctive forces in order to replace them with transmitted forces.* In fact, it is less a destruction than an exchange and circulation ("what happens to a horse can also happen to me"). Horses are trained: humans impose upon the horse's instinctive forces transmitted forces that regulate the former, select, dominate, overcode them. The masochist effects an inversion of signs: the horse transmits its transmitted forces to him, so that the masochist's innate forces will in turn be tamed. There are two series, the horse's (innate force, force transmitted by the human being), and the masochist's (force transmitted by the horse, innate force of the human being). One series explodes into the other, forms a circuit with it: an increase in power or a circuit of intensities. The "master," or rather the mistress-rider, the equestrian, ensures the conversion of forces and the inversion of signs. The masochist constructs an entire assemblage that simultaneously draws and fills the field of immanence of desire; he constitutes a body without organs or plane of consistency using himself, the horse, and the mistress. "Results to be obtained: that I am kept in continual expectancy of actions and orders, and that little by little all opposition is replaced by a *fusion* of my person with yours. . . . Thus at the mere thought of your boots, without even acknowledging it, I must feel fear. In this way, *it will no longer be women's legs that have an effect on me*, and if it pleases you to command me to receive your caresses, when you have had them and if you make me feel them, you will give me the imprint of your body as I have never had it before and never would have had it otherwise."[12] Legs are still organs, but the boots now only determine a zone of intensity as an imprint or zone on a BwO.

Similarly, or actually in a different way, it would be an error to interpret courtly love in terms of a law of lack or an ideal of transcendence. The renunciation of external pleasure, or its delay, its infinite regress, testifies on the contrary to an achieved state in which desire no longer lacks anything but fills itself and constructs its own field of immanence. Pleasure is an affection of a person or a subject; it is the only way for persons to "find themselves" in the process of desire that exceeds them; pleasures, even the most artificial, are reterritorializations. But the question is precisely whether it is necessary to find oneself. Courtly love does not love the self, any more than it loves the whole universe in a celestial or religious way. It is a question of making a body without organs upon which intensities pass, self and other—not in the name of a higher level of generality or a broader extension, but by virtue of singularities that can no longer be said to be personal, and intensities that can no longer be said to be extensive. The field of immanence is not internal to the self, but neither does it come from an external self or a nonself. Rather, it is like the absolute Outside that knows no Selves because interior and exterior are equally a part of the immanence in which they have fused. "Joy" in courtly love, the exchange of hearts, the test or "assay": everything is allowed, as long as it is not external to desire or transcendent to its plane, or else internal to persons. The slightest caress may be as strong as an orgasm; orgasm is a mere fact, a rather deplorable one, in relation to desire in pursuit of its principle. Everything is allowed: all that counts is for pleasure to be the flow of desire itself, Immanence, instead of a measure that interrupts it or delivers it to the three phantoms, namely, internal lack, higher transcendence, and apparent exteriority.[13] If pleasure is not the norm of desire, it is not by virtue of a lack that is impossible to fill but, on the contrary, by virtue of its positivity, in other words, the plane of consistency it draws in the course of its process.

A great Japanese compilation of Chinese Taoist treatises was made in A.D. 982-984. We see in it the formation of a circuit of intensities between female and male energy, with the woman playing the role of the innate or instinctive force (Yin) stolen by or transmitted to the man in such a way that the transmitted force of the man (Yang) in turn becomes innate, all the more innate: an augmentation of powers.[14] The condition for this circulation and multiplication is that the man not ejaculate. It is not a question of experiencing desire as an internal lack, nor of delaying pleasure in order to produce a kind of externalizable surplus value, but instead of constituting an intensive body without organs, Tao, a field of immanence in which desire lacks nothing and therefore cannot be linked to any external or transcendent criterion. It is true that the whole circuit can be channeled toward procreative ends (ejaculation when the energies are right); that is how Confucianism understood it. But this is true only for one side of the assemblage of desire, the side facing the strata, organisms, State, family . . . It is not true for the other side, the Tao side of destratification that draws a plane of consistency proper to desire. Is the Tao masochistic? Is courtly love Taoist? These questions are largely meaningless. The field of immanence or plane of consistency must be constructed. This can take place in very different social formations through very different assemblages (perverse, artistic, scientific, mystical, political) with different types of bodies without organs. It is constructed piece by piece, and the places, conditions, and techniques are irreducible to one another. The question, rather, is whether the pieces can fit together, and at what price. Inevitably, there will be monstrous crossbreeds. The plane of consistency would be the totality of all BwO's, a pure multiplicity of immanence, one piece of which may be Chinese, another American, another medieval, another petty perverse, but all in a movement of generalized deterritorialization in which each person takes and makes what she or he can, according to tastes she or he will have succeeded in abstracting from a Self [*Moi*], according to a politics or strategy successfully abstracted from a given formation, according to a given procedure abstracted from its origin.

We distinguish between: (1) BwO's, which are different types, genuses, or substantial attributes. For example, the Cold of the drugged BwO, the Pain of the masochist BwO. Each has its degree 0 as its principle of production (*remissio*). (2) What happens on each type of BwO, in other words, the modes, the intensities that are produced, the waves that pass (*latitudo*). (3) The potential totality of all BwO's, the plane of consistency (*Omnitudo*, sometimes called the BwO). There are a number of questions. Not only how to make oneself a BwO, and how to produce the corresponding intensities without which it would remain empty (not exactly the same question). But also how to reach the plane of consistency. How to sew up, cool down, and tie together all the BwO's. If this is possible to do, it is only by conjugating the intensities produced on each BwO, by producing a continuum of all intensive continuities. Are not assemblages necessary to fabricate each BwO, is not a great abstract Machine necessary to construct the plane of consistency? Gregory Bateson uses the term *plateau* for continuous regions of intensity constituted in such a way that they do not allow themselves to be interrupted by any external termination, any more than they allow themselves to build toward a climax; examples are certain sexual, or aggressive, processes in Balinese culture.[15] A plateau is a piece of immanence. Every BwO is made up of plateaus. Every BwO is itself a plateau in communication with other plateaus on the plane of consistency. The BwO is a component of passage.

A rereading of *Hèliogabale* and *Les Tarahumaras*. For Heliogabalus is Spinoza, and Spinoza is Heliogabalus revived. And the Tarahumaras are experimentation, peyote. Spinoza, Heliogabalus, and experimentation have the same formula: anarchy and unity are one and the same thing, not the unity of the One, but a much stranger unity that applies only to the multiple.[16] These two books by Artaud express the multiplicity of fusion, fusionability as infinite zero, the plane of consistency, Matter where no gods go; principles as forces, essences, substances, elements, remissions, productions; manners of being or modalities as produced intensities, vibrations, breaths, Numbers. Finally, the difficulty of reaching this world of crowned Anarchy if you go no farther than the organs ("the liver that turns the skin yellow, the brain wracked by syphilis, the intestines that expel filth") and if you stay locked into the organism, or into a stratum that blocks the flows and anchors us in this, our world.

We come to the gradual realization that the BwO is not at all the opposite of the organs. The organs are not its enemies. The enemy is the organism. The BwO is opposed not to the organs but to that organization of the organs called the organism. It is true that Artaud wages a struggle against the organs, but at the same time what he is going after, what he has it in for, is the organism: *The body is the body. Alone it stands. And in no need of organs. Organism it never is. Organisms are the enemies of the body.*[17] The BwO is not opposed to the organs; rather, the BwO and its "true organs," which must be composed and positioned, are opposed to the organism, the organic organization of the organs. The *judgment of God*, the system of the judgment of God, the theological system, is precisely the operation of He who makes an organism, an organization of organs called the organism, because He cannot bear the BwO, because He pursues it and rips it apart so He can be first, and have the organism be first. The organism is already that, the judgment of God, from which medical doctors benefit and on which they base their power. The organism is not at all the body, the BwO; rather, it is a stratum on the BwO, in other words, a phenomenon of accumulation, coagulation, and sedimentation that, in order to extract useful labor from the BwO, imposes upon it forms, functions, bonds, dominant and hierarchized organizations, organized transcendences. The strata are bonds, pincers. "Tie me up if you wish." We are continually stratified. But who is this we that is not me, for the subject no less than the organism belongs to and depends on a stratum? Now we have the answer: the BwO is that glacial reality where the alluvions, sedimentations, coagulations, foldings, and recoilings that compose an organism—and also a signification and a subject—occur. For the judgment of God weighs upon and is exercised against the BwO; it is the BwO that undergoes it. It is in the BwO that the organs enter into the relations of composition called the organism. The BwO howls: "They've made me an organism! They've wrongfully folded me! They've stolen my body!" The judgment of God uproots it from its immanence and makes it an organism, a signification, a subject. It is the BwO that is stratified. It swings between two poles, the surfaces of stratification into which it is recoiled, on which it submits to the judgment, and the plane of consistency in which it unfurls and opens to experimentation. If the BwO is a limit, if one is forever attaining it, it is because behind each stratum, encasted in it, there is always another stratum. For many a stratum, and not only an organism, is necessary to make the judgment of God. A perpetual and violent combat between the plane of consistency, which frees the BwO, cutting across and dismantling all of the strata, and the surfaces of stratification that block it or make it recoil.

Let us consider the three great strata concerning us, in other words, the ones that most directly bind us: the organism, signifiance, and subjectification. The surface of the organism, the angle of signifiance and interpretation, and the point of subjectification or subjection. You will be organized, you will be an organism, you will articulate your body—otherwise you're just depraved. You will be signifier and signified, interpreter and interpreted—otherwise you're just a deviant. You will be a subject, nailed down as one, a subject of the enunciation recoiled into a subject of the statement—otherwise you're just a tramp. To the strata as a whole, the BwO opposes disarticulation (or *n* articulations) as the property of the plane of consistency, experimentation as the operation on that plane (no signifier, never interpret!), and nomadism as the movement (keep moving, even in place, never stop moving, motionless voyage, desubjectification). What does it mean to disarticulate, to cease to be an organism? How can we convey how easy it is, and the extent to which we do it every day? And how necessary caution is, the art of dosages, since overdose is a danger. You don't do it with a sledgehammer, you use a very fine file. You invent self-destructions that have nothing to do with the death drive. Dismantling the organism has never meant killing yourself, but rather opening the body to connections that presuppose an entire assemblage, circuits, conjunctions, levels and thresholds, passages and distributions of intensity, and territories and deterritorializations measured with the craft of a surveyor. Actually, dismantling the organism is no more difficult than dismantling the other two strata, signifiance and subjectification. Signifiance clings to the soul just as the organism clings to the body, and it is not easy to get rid of either. And how can we unhook ourselves from the points of subjectification that secure us, nail us down to a dominant reality? Tearing the conscious away from the subject in order to make it a means of exploration, tearing the unconscious away from signifiance and interpretation in order to make it a veritable production: this is assuredly no more or less difficult than tearing the body away from the organism. Caution is the art common to all three; if in dismantling the organism there are times one courts death, in slipping away from signifiance and subjection one courts falsehood, illusion and hallucination and psychic death. Artaud weighs and measures every word: the conscious "knows what is good for it and what is of no value to it: it knows which thoughts and feelings it can receive without danger and with profit, and which are harmful to the exercise of its freedom. Above all, it knows just how far its own being goes, and just how far it has not yet gone or does not have the right to go without sinking into the unreal, the illusory, the unmade, the unprepared . . . a *Plane* which normal consciousness does not reach but which *Ciguri* allows us to reach, and which is the very mystery of all poetry. But there is in human existence another plane, obscure and formless, where consciousness has not entered, and which surrounds it like an unilluminated extension or a menace, as the case may be. And which itself gives off adventurous sensations, perceptions. These are those shameless fantasies which affect an unhealthy conscious. . . . I too have had false sensations and perceptions and I have believed in them."[18]

You have to keep enough of the organism for it to reform each dawn; and you have to keep small supplies of signifiance and subjectification, if only to turn them against their own systems when the circumstances demand it, when things, persons, even situations, force you to; and you have to keep small rations of subjectivity in sufficient quantity to enable you to respond to the dominant reality. Mimic the strata. You don't reach the BwO, and its plane of consistency, by wildly destratifying. That is why we encountered the paradox of those emptied and dreary bodies at the very beginning: *they had emptied themselves of their organs* instead of looking for the point at which they could patiently and momentarily dismantle the organization of the organs we call the organism. There are, in fact, several ways of botching the BwO: either one fails to produce it, or one produces it more or less, but nothing is produced on it, intensities do not pass or are blocked. This is because the BwO is always swinging between the surfaces that stratify it and the plane that sets it free. If you free it with too violent an action, if you blow apart the strata without taking precautions, then instead of drawing the plane you will be killed, plunged into a black hole, or even dragged toward catastrophe. Staying stratified—organized, signified, subjected—is not the worst that can happen; the worst that can happen is if you throw the strata into demented or suicidal collapse, which brings them back down on us heavier than ever. This is how it should be done: Lodge yourself on a stratum, experiment with the opportunities it offers, find an advantageous place on it, find potential movements of deterritorialization, possible lines of flight, experience them, produce flow conjunctions here and there, try out continuums of intensities segment by segment, have a small plot of new land at all times. It is through a meticulous relation with the strata that one succeeds in freeing lines of flight, causing conjugated flows to pass and escape and bringing forth continuous intensities for a BwO. Connect, conjugate, continue: a whole "diagram," as opposed to still signifying and subjective programs. We are in a social formation; first see how it is stratified for us and in us and at the place where we are; then descend from the strata to the deeper assemblage within which we are held; gently tip the assemblage, making it pass over to the side of the plane of consistency. It is only there that the BwO reveals itself for what it is: connection of desires, conjunction of flows, continuum of intensities. You have constructed your own little machine, ready when needed to be plugged into other collective machines. Castaneda describes a long process of experimentation (it makes little difference whether it is with peyote or other things): let us recall for the moment how the Indian forces him first to find a "place," already a difficult operation, then to find "allies," and then gradually to give up interpretation, to construct flow by flow and segment by segment lines of experimentation, becoming-animal, becoming-molecular, etc. For the BwO is all of that: necessarily a Place, necessarily a Plane, necessarily a Collectivity (assembling elements, things, plants, animals, tools, people, powers, and fragments of all of these; for it is not "my" body without organs, instead the "me" (*moi*) is on it, or what remains of me, unalterable and changing in form, crossing thresholds).

In the course of Castaneda's books, the reader may begin to doubt the existence of the Indian Don Juan, and many other things besides. But that has no importance. So much the better if the books are a syncretism rather than an ethnographical study, and the protocol of an experiment rather than an account of an initiation. The fourth book, *Tales of Power*, is about the living distinction between the "Tonal" and the "Nagual." The *tonal* seems to cover many disparate things: It is the organism, and also all that is organized and organizing; but it is also signifiance, and all that is signifying or signified, all that is susceptible to interpretation, explanation, all that is memorizable in the form of something recalling something else; finally, it is the Self (*Moi*), the subject, the historical, social, or individual person, and the corresponding feelings. In short, the tonal is everything, including God, the judgment of God, since it "makes up the rules by which it apprehends the world. So, in a manner of speaking, it creates the world."[19] Yet the tonal is only an island. For the *nagual* is also everything. And it is the same everything, but under such conditions that the body without organs has replaced the organism and experimentation has replaced all interpretation, for which it no longer has any use. Flows of intensity, their fluids, their fibers, their continuums and conjunctions of affects, the wind, fine segmentation, microperceptions, have replaced the world of the subject. Becomings, becomings-animal, becomings-molecular, have replaced history, individual or general. In fact, the tonal is not as disparate as it seems: it includes all of the strata and everything that can be ascribed to the strata, the organization of the organism, the interpretations and explanations of the signifiable, the movements of subjectification. The nagual, on the contrary, dismantles the strata. It is no longer an organism that functions but a BwO that is constructed. No longer are there acts to explain, dreams or phantasies to interpret, childhood memories to recall, words to make signify; instead, there are colors and sounds, becomings and intensities (and when you become-dog, don't ask if the dog you are playing with is a dream or a reality, if it is "your goddam mother" or something else entirely). There is no longer a Self [*Moi*] that feels, acts, and recalls; there is "a glowing fog, a dark yellow mist" that has affects and experiences movements, speeds.[20] The important thing is not to dismantle the tonal by destroying it all of a sudden. You have to diminish it, shrink it, clean it, and that only at certain moments. You have to keep it in order to survive, to ward off the assault of the nagual. For a nagual that erupts, that destroys the tonal, a body without organs that shatters all the strata, turns immediately into a body of nothingness, pure self-destruction whose only outcome is death: "The tonal must be protected at any cost."[21]

We still have not answered the question of why there are so many dangers, and so many necessary precautions. It is not enough to set up an abstract opposition between the strata and the BwO. For the BwO already exists in the strata as well as on the destratified plane of consistency, but in a totally different manner. Take the organism as a stratum: there is indeed a

BwO that opposes the organization of the organs we call the organism, but there is also a BwO of the organism that belongs to that stratum. *Cancerous tissue:* each instant, each second, a cell becomes cancerous, mad, proliferates and loses its configuration, takes over everything; the organism must resubmit it to its rule or restratify it, not only for its own survival, but also to make possible an escape from the organism, the fabrication of the "other" BwO on the plane of consistency. Take the stratum of signifiance: once again, there is a cancerous tissue, this time of signifiance, a burgeoning body of the despot that blocks any circulation of signs, as well as preventing the birth of the asignifying sign on the "other" BwO. Or take a stifling body of subjectification, which makes a freeing all the more unlikely by forbidding any remaining distinction between subjects. Even if we consider given social formations, or a given stratic apparatus within a formation, we must say that every one of them has a BwO ready to gnaw, proliferate, cover, and invade the entire social field, entering into relations of violence and rivalry as well as alliance and complicity. A BwO of money (inflation), but also a BwO of the State, army, factory, city, Party, etc. If the strata are an affair of coagulation and sedimentation, all a stratum needs is a high sedimentation rate for it to lose its configuration and articulations, and to form its own specific kind of tumor, within itself or in a given formation or apparatus. The strata spawn their own BwO's, totalitarian and fascist BwO's, terrifying caricatures of the plane of consistency. It is not enough to make a distinction between full BwO's on the plane of consistency and empty BwO's on the debris of strata destroyed by a too-violent destratification. We must also take into account cancerous BwO's in a stratum that has begun to proliferate. *The three-body problem.* Artaud said that outside the "plane" is another plane surrounding us with "an unilluminated extension or a menace, as the case may be." It is a struggle and as such is never sufficiently clear. How can we fabricate a BwO for ourselves without its being the cancerous BwO of a fascist inside us, or the empty BwO of a drug addict, paranoiac, or hypochondriac? How can we tell the three Bodies apart? Artaud was constantly grappling with this problem. The extraordinary composition of *To Be Done with the Judgment of God*: he begins by cursing the cancerous body of America, the body of war and money; he denounces the strata, which he calls "caca"; to the strata he opposes the true Plane, even if it is only peyote, the little trickle of the Tarahumaras; but he also knows about the dangers of a too-sudden, careless destratification. Artaud was constantly grappling with all of that, and flowed with it. *Letter to Hitler*: "Dear Sir, In 1932 in the Ider Café in Berlin, on one of the evenings when I made your acquaintance and shortly before you took power, I showed you roadblocks on *a map that was not just a map of geography*, roadblocks against me, an act of force aimed in a certain number of directions you indicated to me. Today Hitler I lift the roadblocks I set down! The Parisians need gas. Yours, A.A.—P.S. Be it understood, dear sir, that this is hardly an invitation, it is above all a warning."[22] That map that is not only a map of geography is something like a BwO intensity map, where the roadblocks designate thresholds and the gas, waves or flows. Even if Artaud did not succeed for himself, it is certain that through him something has succeeded for us all.

The BwO is the egg. But the egg is not regressive; on the contrary, it is perfectly contemporary, you always carry it with you as your own milieu of experimentation, your associated milieu. The egg is the milieu of pure intensity, spatium not extension, Zero intensity as principle of production. There is a fundamental convergence between science and myth, embryology and mythology, the biological egg and the psychic or cosmic egg: the egg always designates this intensive reality, which is not undifferentiated, but is where things and organs are distinguished solely by gradients, migrations, zones of proximity. The egg is the BwO. The BwO is not "before" the organism; it is adjacent to it and is continually in the process of constructing itself. If it is tied to childhood, it is not in the sense that the adult regresses to the child and the child to the Mother, but in the sense that the child, like the Dogon twin who takes a piece of the placenta with him, tears from the organic form of the Mother an intense and destratified matter that on the contrary constitutes his or her perpetual break with the past, his or her present experience, experimentation. The BwO is a childhood block, a becoming, the opposite of a childhood memory. It is not the child "before" the adult, or the mother "before" the child: it is the strict contemporaneousness of the adult, of the adult and the child, their map of comparative densities and intensities, and all of the variations on that map. The BwO is precisely this intense germen where there are not and cannot be either parents or children (organic representation). This is what Freud failed to understand about Weissmann: the child as the germinal contemporary of its parents. Thus the BwO is never yours or mine. It is always *a* body. It is no more projective than it is regressive. It is an involution, but always a contemporary, creative involution. The organs distribute themselves on the BwO, but they distribute themselves independently of the form of the organism; forms become contingent, organs are no longer anything more than intensities that are produced, flows, thresholds, and gradients. "A" stomach, "an" eye, "a" mouth: the indefinite article does not lack anything; it is not indeterminate or undifferentiated, but expresses the pure determination of intensity, intensive difference. The indefinite article is the conductor of desire. It is not at all a question of a fragmented, splintered body, of organs without the body (OwB). The BwO is exactly the opposite. There are not organs in the sense of fragments in relation to a lost unity, nor is there a return to the undifferentiated in relation to a differentiable totality. There is a distribution of intensive principles of organs, with their positive indefinite articles, within a collectivity or multiplicity, inside an assemblage, and according to machinic connections operating on a BwO. *Logos spermaticos.* The error of psychoanalysis was to understand BwO phenomena as regressions, projections, phantasies, in terms of an *image* of the body. As a result, it only grasps the flipside of the BwO and immediately substitutes family photos, childhood memories, and part-objects for a worldwide intensity map. It understands nothing about the egg nor about indefinite articles nor about the contemporaneousness of a continually self-constructing milieu.

The BwO is desire; it is that which one desires and by which one desires. And not only because it is the plane of consistency or the field of immanence of desire. Even when it falls into the void of too-sudden destratification, or into the proliferation of a cancerous stratum, it is still desire. Desire stretches that far: desiring one's own annihilation, or desiring the power to annihilate. Money, army, police, and State desire, fascist desire, even fascism is desire. There is desire whenever there is the constitution of a BwO under one relation or another. It is a problem not of ideology but of pure matter, a phenomenon of physical, biological, psychic, social, or cosmic matter. That is why the material problem confronting schizoanalysis is knowing whether we have it within our means to make the selection, to distinguish the BwO from its doubles: empty vitreous bodies, cancerous bodies, totalitarian and fascist. The test of desire: not denouncing false desires, but distinguishing within desire between that which pertains to stratic proliferation, or else too-violent destratification, and that which pertains to the construction of the plane of consistency (keep an eye out for all that is fascist, even inside us, and also for the suicidal and the demented). The plane of consistency is not simply that which is constituted by the sum of all BwO's. There are things it rejects; the BwO chooses, as a function of the abstract machine that draws it. Even within a BwO (the masochist body, the drugged body, etc.), we must distinguish what can be composed on the plane and what cannot. There is a fascist use of drugs, or a suicidal use, but is there also a possible use that would be in conformity with the plane of consistency? Even paranoia: Is there a possibility of using it that way in part? When we asked the question of the totality of all BwO's, considered as substantial attributes of a single substance, it should have been understood, strictly speaking, to apply only to the plane. The plane is the totality of the full BwO's that have been selected (there is no positive totality including the cancerous or empty bodies). What is the nature of this totality? Is it solely logical? Or must we say that each BwO, from a basis in its own genus, produces effects identical or analogous to the effects other

BwO's produce from a basis in their genera? Could what the drug user or masochist obtains also be obtained in a different fashion in the conditions of the plane, so it would even be possible to use drugs without using drugs, to get soused on pure water, as in Henry Miller's experimentations? Or is it a question of a real passage of substances, an intensive continuum of all the BwO's? Doubtless, anything is possible. All we are saying is that the identity of effects, the continuity of genera, the totality of all BwO's, can be obtained on the plane of consistency only by means of an abstract machine capable of covering and even creating it, by assemblages capable of plugging into desire, of effectively taking charge of desires, of assuring their continuous connections and transversal tie-ins. Otherwise, the BwO's of the plane will remain separated by genus, marginalized, reduced to means of bordering, while on the "other plane" the emptied or cancerous doubles will triumph.

7. Year Zero: Faciality

Earlier, we encountered two axes, signifiance and subjectification. We saw that they were two very different semiotic systems, or even two strata. Signifiance is never without a white wall upon which it inscribes its signs and redundancies. Subjectification is never without a black hole in which it lodges its consciousness, passion, and redundancies. Since all semiotics are mixed and strata come at least in twos, it should come as no surprise that a very special mechanism is situated at their intersection. Oddly enough, it is a face: the *white wall/black hole* system. A broad face with white cheeks, a chalk face with eyes cut in for a black hole. Clown head, white clown, moon-white mime, angel of death, Holy Shroud. The face is not an envelope exterior to the person who speaks, thinks, or feels. The form of the signifier in language, even its units, would remain indeterminate if the potential listener did not use the face of the speaker to guide his or her choices ("Hey, he seems angry . . ."; "He couldn't say it . . ."; "You see my face when I'm talking to you . . ."; "look at me carefully . . ."). A child, woman, mother, man, father, boss, teacher, police officer, does not speak a general language but one whose signifying traits are indexed to specific faciality traits. Faces are not basically individual; they define zones of frequency or probability, delimit a field that neutralizes in advance any expressions or connections unamenable to the appropriate significations. Similarly, the form of subjectivity, whether consciousness or passion, would remain absolutely empty if faces did not form loci of resonance that select the sensed or mental reality and make it conform in advance to a dominant reality. The face itself is redundancy. It is itself in redundancy with the redundancies of signifiance or frequency, and those of resonance or subjectivity. The face constructs the wall that the signifier needs in order to bounce off of; it constitutes the wall of the signifier, the frame or screen. The face digs the hole that subjectification needs in order to break through; it constitutes the black hole of subjectivity as consciousness or passion, the camera, the third eye.

Or should we say things differently? It is not exactly the face that constitutes the wall of the signifier or the hole of subjectivity. The face, at least the concrete face, vaguely begins to take shape *on* the white wall. It vaguely begins to appear *in* the black hole. In film, the close-up of the face can be said to have two poles: make the face reflect light or, on the contrary, emphasize its shadows to the point of engulfing it "in pitiless darkness."[1] A psychologist once said that the face is a visual percept that crystallizes out of "different varieties of vague luminosity without form or dimension." A suggestive whiteness, a hole that captures, a face. According to this account, the dimensionless black hole and formless white wall are already there to begin with. And there are already a number of possible combinations in the system: either black holes distribute themselves on the white wall, or the white wall unravels and moves toward a black hole combining all black holes, hurtling them together or making them "crest." Sometimes faces appear on the wall, with their holes; sometimes they appear in the hole, with their linearized, rolled-up wall. A horror story, the face is a horror story. It is certain that the signifier does not construct the wall that it needs all by itself; it is certain that subjectivity does not dig its hole all alone. Concrete faces cannot be assumed to come ready-made. They are engendered by an *abstract machine of faciality* (*visagéité*), which produces them at the same time as it gives the signifier its white wall and subjectivity its black hole. Thus the black hole/white wall system is, to begin with, not a face but the abstract machine that produces faces according to the changeable combinations of its cogwheels. Do not expect the abstract machine to resemble what it produces, or will produce.

The abstract machine crops up when you least expect it, at a chance juncture when you are just falling asleep, or into a twilight state or hallucinating, or doing an amusing physics experiment . . . Kafka's novella, "Blumfeld":[2] the bachelor returns home in the evening to find two little ping-pong balls jumping around by themselves on the "wall" constituted by the floor. They bounce everywhere and even try to hit him in the face. They apparently contain other, still smaller, electric balls. Blumfeld finally manages to lock them up in the black hole of a wardrobe. The scene continues the next day when Blumfeld tries to give the balls to a small, feebleminded boy and two grimacing little girls, and then at the office, where he encounters his two grimacing and feebleminded assistants, who want to make off with a broom. In a wonderful ballet by Debussy and Nijinsky, a little tennis ball comes bouncing onto the stage at dusk, and at the end another ball appears in a similar fashion. This time, between the two balls, two girls and a boy who watches them develop passional dance and facial traits in vague luminosities (curiosity, spite, irony, ecstasy . . .).[3] There is nothing to explain, nothing to interpret. It is the pure abstract machine of a twilight state. White wall/black hole? But depending on the combinations, the wall could just as well be black, and the hole white. The balls can bounce off of a wall or spin into a black hole. Even upon impact they can have the relative role of a hole in relation to the wall, just as when they are rolling straight ahead they can have the relative role of a wall in relation to the hole they are heading for. They circulate in the white wall/black hole system. Nothing in all of this resembles a face, yet throughout the system faces are distributed and faciality traits organized. Nevertheless, the abstract machine can be effectuated in other things besides faces, but not in any order, and not without the necessary foundation (*raisons*).

The face has been a major concern of American psychology, in particular the relation between the mother and the child through eye-to-eye contact. Four-eye machine? Let us recall certain stages in the research: (1) Isakower's studies on falling asleep, in which so-called proprioceptive sensations of a manual, buccal, cutaneous, or even vaguely visual nature recall the infantile mouth-breast relation. (2) Lewin's discovery of a *white screen* of the dream, which is ordinarily covered by visual contents but remains white when the only dream contents are proprioceptive sensations (this screen or white wall, once again, is the breast as it approaches, getting larger and then pressing flat). (3) Spitz's interpretation according to which the white screen, rather than being a representation of the breast itself as an object of tactile sensation or contact, is a visual percept implying a minimum of distance and upon which the mother's face appears for the child to use as a guide in finding the breast. Thus there is a combination of two very different kinds of elements: manual, buccal, or cutaneous proprioceptive sensations; and the visual perception of the face seen from the front against the white screen, with the shape of the eyes drawn in for black holes. This visual perception very quickly assumes decisive importance for the act of eating, in relation to the breast as a volume and the mouth as a cavity, both experienced through touch.[4]

We can now propose the following distinction: the face is part of a surface-holes, holey surface, system. This system should under no circumstances be confused with the volume-cavity system proper to the (proprioceptive) body. The head is included in the body, but the face is not. The face is a surface: facial traits, lines, wrinkles; long face, square face, triangular face; the face is a map, even when it is applied to and wraps a volume, even when it surrounds and borders cavities that are now no more than holes. The head, even the human head, is not necessarily a face. The face is produced only when the head ceases to be a part of the body, when it ceases to be coded by the body, when it ceases to have a multidimensional, polyvocal corporeal code—when the body, head included, has been decoded and has to be *overcoded* by something we shall call the Face. This amounts to saying that the head, all the volume-cavity elements of the head, have to be facialized. What accomplishes this is the screen with holes, the white wall/black hole, the abstract machine producing faciality. But the operation does not end there: if the head and its elements are facialized, the entire body also can be facialized, comes to be facialized as part of an inevitable process. When the mouth and nose, but first the eyes, become a holey surface, all the other volumes and cavities of the body follow. An operation worthy of Doctor Moreau: horrible and magnificent. Hand, breast, stomach, penis and vagina, thigh, leg and foot, all come to be facialized. Fetishism, erotomania, etc., are inseparable from these processes of facialization. It is not at all a question of taking a part of the body and making it *resemble* a face, or making a dream-face dance in a cloud. No anthropomorphism here. Facialization operates not by resemblance but by an order of reasons. It is a much more unconscious and machinic operation that draws the entire body across the holey surface, and in which the role of the face is not as a model or image, but as an overcoding of all of the decoded parts. Everything remains sexual; there is no sublimation, but there are new coordinates. *It is precisely because the face depends on an abstract machine that it is not content to cover the head,* but touches all other parts of the body, and even, if necessary, other objects without resemblance. *The question then becomes what circumstances trigger the machine* that produces the face and facialization. Although the head, even the human head, is not necessarily a face, the face is produced in humanity. But it is produced by a necessity that does not apply to human beings "in general." The face is not animal, but neither is it human in general; there is even something absolutely inhuman about the face. It would be an error to proceed as though the face became inhuman only beyond a certain threshold: close-up, extreme magnification, recondite expression, etc. The inhuman in human beings: that is what the face is from the start. It is by nature a close-up, with its inanimate white surfaces, its shining black holes, its emptiness and boredom. Bunker-face. To the point that if human beings have a destiny, it is rather to escape the face, to dismantle the face and facializations, to become imperceptible, to become clandestine, not by returning to animality, nor even by returning to the head, but by quite spiritual and special becomings-animal, by strange true becomings that get past the wall and get out of the black holes, that make *faciality traits* themselves finally elude the organization of the face—freckles dashing toward the horizon, hair carried off by the wind, eyes you traverse instead of seeing yourself in or gazing into in those glum face-to-face encounters between signifying subjectivities. "I no longer look into the eyes of the woman I hold in my arms but I swim through, head and arms and legs, and I see that behind the sockets of the eyes there is a region unexplored, the world of futurity, and here there is no logic whatsoever. . . . I have broken the wall. . . . My eyes are useless, for they render back only the image of the known. My whole body must become a constant beam of light, moving with an ever greater rapidity, never arrested, never looking back, never dwindling. . . . *Therefore I close my ears, my eyes, my mouth.*"[5] BwO. Yes, the face has a great future, but only if it is destroyed, dismantled. On the road to the asignifying and asubjective. But so far we have explained nothing of what we sense.

The move from the body-head system to the face system has nothing to do with an evolution or genetic stages. Nor with phenomenological positions. Nor with integrations of part-objects, or structural or structuring systems. Nor can there be any appeal to a preexisting subject, or one brought into existence, except by this machine specific to faciality. In the literature of the face, Sartre's text on the look and Lacan's on the mirror make the error of appealing to a form of subjectivity or humanity reflected in a phenomenological field or split in a structural field. *The gaze is but secondary in relation to the gazeless eyes, to the black hole of faciality. The mirror is but secondary in relation to the white wall of faciality.* Neither will we speak of a genetic axis, or the integration of part-objects. Any approach based on stages in ontogenesis is arbitrary: it is thought that what is fastest is primary, or even serves as a foundation or springboard for what comes next. An approach based on part-objects is even worse; it is the approach of a demented experimenter who flays, slices, and anatomizes everything in sight, and then proceeds to sew things randomly back together again. You can make any list of part-objects you want: hand, breast, mouth, eyes . . . It's still Frankenstein. What we need to consider is not fundamentally organs without bodies, or the fragmented body; it is the body without organs, animated by various intensive movements that determine the nature and emplacement of the organs in question and make that body an organism, or even a system of strata of which the organism is only a part. It becomes apparent that the slowest of movements, or the last to occur or arrive, is not the least intense. And the fastest may already have converged with it, connected with it, in the disequilibrium of a nonsynchronic development of strata that have different speeds and lack a sequence of stages but are nevertheless simultaneous. The question of the body is not one of part-objects but of differential speeds.

These movements are movements of deterritorialization. They are what "make" the body an animal or human organism. For example, the prehensile hand implies a *relative* deterritorialization not only of the front paw but also of the locomotor hand. It has a correlate, the use-object or tool: the club is a deterritorialized branch. The breast of the woman, with her upright posture, indicates a deterritorialization of the animal's mammary gland; the mouth of the child, adorned with lips by an outfolding of the mucous membranes, marks a deterritorialization of the snout and mouth of the animal. Lips-breast: each serves as a correlate of the other.[6] The human head implies a deterritorialization in relation to the animal and has as its correlate the organization of a world, in other words, a milieu that has itself been deterritorialized (the steppe is the first "world," in contrast to the forest milieu). But the face represents a far more intense, if slower, deterritorialization. We could say that it is an *absolute* deterritorialization: it is no longer relative because it removes the head from the stratum of the organism, human or animal, and connects it to other strata, such as signifiance and subjectification. Now the face has a correlate of great importance: the landscape, which is not just a milieu but a deterritorialized world. There are a number of face-landscape correlations, on this "higher" level. Christian education exerts spiritual control over both faciality and landscapity (*paysagéité*): Compose them both, color them in, complete them, arrange them according to a complementarity linking landscapes to faces.[7] Face and landscape manuals formed a pedagogy, a strict discipline, and were an inspiration to the arts as much as the arts were an inspiration to them. Architecture positions its ensembles—houses, towns or cities, monuments or factories—to function like faces in the landscape they transform. Painting takes up the same movement but also reverses it, positioning a landscape as a face, treating one like the other: "treatise on the face and the landscape." The close-up in film treats the face primarily as a landscape; that is the definition of film, black hole and white wall, screen and camera. But the same goes for the earlier arts, architecture, painting, even the novel: close-ups animate and invent all of their correlations. So, is your mother a landscape or a face? A face or a factory? (Godard.) All faces envelop an unknown, unexplored landscape; all landscapes are populated by a loved or dreamed-of face, develop a face to come or already past. What face has not called upon the landscapes it amalgamated, sea and hill; what landscape has not evoked the face that would have completed it, providing an unexpected complement for its lines and traits? Even when painting becomes abstract, all it does is rediscover the black hole and white wall, the great composition of the white canvas and black slash. Tearing, but also stretching of the canvas along an axis of escape (*fuite*), at a vanishing point (*point de fuite*), along a diagonal, by a knife slice, slash, or hole: the machine is already in place that always functions to produce faces and landscapes, however abstract. Titian began his paintings in black and white, not to make outlines to fill in, but as the matrix for each of the colors to come.

The novel—*A flock of geese flew which the snow had dazzled. [Perceval] saw them and heard them, for they were going away noisily because of a falcon which came drawing after them at a great rate until he found abandoned one separated from the flock, and he struck it so and bruised it that he knocked it down to earth. . . . When Perceval saw the trampled snow on which the goose had lain, and the blood which appeared around, he leaned upon his lance and looked at that image, for the blood and the snow together seemed to him like the fresh color which was on the face of his friend, and he thinks until he forgets himself; for the vermilion seated on white was on her face just the same as these three drops of blood on the white snow. . . . We have seen a knight who is dozing on his charger.* Everything is there: the redundancy specific to the face and landscape, the snowy white wall of the landscape-face, the black hole of the falcon and the three drops distributed on the wall; and, simultaneously, the silvery line of the landscape-face spinning toward the black hole of the knight deep in catatonia. Cannot the knight, at certain times and under certain conditions, push the movement further still, crossing the black hole, breaking through the white wall, dismantling the face—even if the attempt may backfire?[8] All of this is in no way characteristic of the genre of the novel only at the end of its history; it is there from the beginning, it is an essential part of the genre. It is false to see Don Quixote as the end of the chivalric novel, invoking the hero's hallucinations, harebrained ideas, and hypnotic or cataleptic states. It is false to see novels such as Beckett's as the end of the novel in general, invoking the black holes, the characters' line of deterritorialization, the schizophrenic promenades of Molloy or the Unnameable, their loss of their names, memory, or purpose. The novel does have an evolution, but that is surely not it. The novel has always been defined by the adventure of lost characters who no longer know their name, what they are looking for, or what they are doing, amnesiacs, ataxics, catatonics. They differentiate the genre of the novel from the genres of epic or drama (when the dramatic or epic hero is stricken with folly or forgetting, etc., it is in an entirely different way). *La princesse de*

Clèves is a novel precisely by virtue of what seemed paradoxical to the people of the time: the states of absence or "rest," the sleep that overtakes the characters. There is always a Christian education in the novel. Molloy is the beginning of the genre of the novel. When the novel began, with Chrétien de Troyes, for example, the essential character that would accompany it over the entire course of its history was already there: The knight of the novel of courtly love spends his time forgetting his name, what he is doing, what people say to him, he doesn't know where he is going or to whom he is speaking, he is continually drawing a line of absolute deterritorialization, but also losing his way, stopping, and falling into black holes. "He awaits chivalry and adventure." Open Chrétien de Troyes to any page and you will find a catatonic knight seated on his steed, leaning on his lance, waiting, seeing the face of his loved one in the landscape; you have to hit him to make him respond. Lancelot, in the presence of the queen's white face, doesn't notice his horse plunge into the river; or he gets into a passing cart and it turns out to be the cart of disgrace. There is a face-landscape aggregate proper to the novel, in which black holes sometimes distribute themselves on a white wall, and the white line of the horizon sometimes spins toward a black hole, or both simultaneously.

Theorems of Deterritorialization, or Machinic Propositions[9]

First theorem: One never deterritorializes alone; there are always at least two terms, hand-use object, mouth-breast, face-landscape. And each of the two terms reterritorializes on the other. Reterritorialization must not be confused with a return to a primitive or older territoriality: it necessarily implies a set of artifices by which one element, itself deterritorialized, serves as a new territoriality for another, which has lost its territoriality as well. Thus there is an entire system of horizontal and complementary reterritorializations, between hand and tool, mouth and breast, face and landscape. *Second theorem*: The fastest of two elements or movements of deterritorialization is not necessarily the most intense or most deterritorialized. Intensity of deterritorialization must not be confused with speed of movement or development. The fastest can even connect its intensity to the slowest, which, as an intensity, does not come after the fastest but is simultaneously at work on a different stratum or plane (for example, the way the breast-mouth relation is guided from the start by a plane of faciality). *Third theorem*: It can even be concluded from this that the *least* deterritorialized reterritorializes on the *most* deterritorialized. This is where the second system of reterritorializations comes in, the vertical system running from bottom to top. This is the sense in which not only the mouth but also the breast, hand, the entire body, even the tool, are "facialized." As a general rule, relative deterritorializations (transcoding) reterritorialize on a deterritorialization that is in certain respects absolute (overcoding). We have seen that the deterritorialization of the head into a face is absolute but remains negative in that it passes from one stratum to another, from the stratum of the organism to those of signifiance and subjectification. The hand and breast reterritorialize on the face and in the landscape: they are facialized at the same time as they are landscapified. Even a use-object may come to be facialized: you might say that a house, utensil, or object, an article of clothing, etc., is *watching me*, not because it resembles a face, but because it is taken up in the white wall/black hole process, because it connects to the abstract machine of facialization. The close-up in film pertains as much to a knife, cup, clock, or kettle as to a face or facial element, for example, Griffith's "the kettle is watching me." Is it not fair to say, then, that there are close-ups in novels, as when Dickens writes the opening line of *The Cricket on the Hearth*: "The kettle began it . . .",[10] and in painting, when a utensil becomes a face-landscape from within, or when a cup on a tablecloth or a teapot is facialized, in Bonnard, Vuillard? *Fourth theorem*: The abstract machine is therefore effectuated not only in the faces that produce it but also to varying degrees in body parts, clothes, and objects that it facializes following an order of reasons (rather than an organization of resemblances).

Yet the question remains: When does the abstract machine of faciality enter into play? When is it triggered? Take some simple examples: the maternal power operating through the face during nursing; the passional power operating through the face of the loved one, even in caresses; the political power operating through the face of the leader (streamers, icons, and photographs), even in mass actions; the power of film operating through the face of the star and the close-up; the power of television. It is not the individuality of the face that counts but the efficacy of the ciphering it makes possible, and in what cases it makes it possible. This is an affair not of ideology but of economy and the organization of power (*pouvoir*). We are certainly not saying that the face, the power of the face (*la puissance du visage*), engenders and explains social power (*pouvoir*). *Certain assemblages of power* (*pouvoir*) *require the production of a face*, others do not. If we consider primitive societies, we see that there is very little that operates through the face: their semiotic is nonsignifying, nonsubjective, essentially collective, polyvocal, and corporeal, playing on very diverse forms and substances. This polyvocality operates through bodies, their volumes, their internal cavities, their variable exterior connections and coordinates (territorialities). A fragment from a manual semiotic, a manual sequence, may be coordinated, without subordination or unification, with an oral sequence, or a cutaneous one, or a rhythmic one, etc. Lizot, for example, shows how "the dissociation of duty, ritual and daily life is almost total . . . it is strange, inconceivable to us": during mourning behavior, certain people make obscene jokes while others cry; or an Indian abruptly stops crying and begins to repair his flute; or everybody goes to sleep.[11] The same goes for incest. There is no incest prohibition; instead, there are sequences of incest that connect with sequences of prohibition following specific coordinates. Paintings, tattoos, or marks on the skin embrace the multidimensionality of bodies. Even masks ensure the head's belonging to the body, rather than making it a face. Doubtless, there are profound movements of deterritorialization that shake up the coordinates of the body and outline particular assemblages of power; however, they connect the body not to faciality but to becomings-animal, in particular with the help of drugs. Of course, there is no less spirituality for that, for these becomings-animal involve an animal Spirit—a jaguar-spirit, bird-spirit, ocelot-spirit, toucan-spirit—that takes possession of the body's interior, enters its cavities, and fills its volumes instead of making a face for it. Possession expresses a direct relation between Voices and the body rather than a relation to the face. Shaman, warrior, and hunter organizations of power, fragile and precarious, are all the more spiritual by virtue of the fact that they operate through corporeality, animality, and vegetality. When we said earlier that the human head still belongs to the stratum of the organism, we obviously were not denying the existence of culture and society among these peoples; we were merely saying that these cultures' and societies' codes pertain to bodies, to the belonging of heads to bodies, to the ability of the body-head system to *become* and receive souls, and to receive them as friends while repulsing enemy souls. "Primitives" may have the most human of heads, the most beautiful and most spiritual, but they have no face and need none.

The reason is simple. The face is not a universal. It is not even that of the white man; it is White Man himself, with his broad white cheeks and the black hole of his eyes. The face is Christ. The face is the typical European, what Ezra Pound called the average sensual man, in short, the ordinary everyday Erotomaniac (nineteenth-century psychiatrists were right to say that erotomania, unlike nymphomania, often remains pure and chaste; this is because it operates through the face and facialization). Not a universal, but *facies totius universi*. Jesus Christ superstar: he invented the facialization of the entire body and spread it everywhere (the Passion of Joan of Arc, in close-up). Thus the face is by nature an entirely specific idea, which did not preclude its acquiring and exercising the most general of functions: the function of biunivocalization, or binarization. It has two aspects: the abstract machine of faciality, insofar as it is composed by a black hole/white wall system, functions in two ways, one of which concerns the units or elements, the other the choices. Under the first aspect, the black hole acts as a central computer, Christ, the third eye that moves across the wall or the white screen serving as general surface of reference. Regardless of the content one gives it, the machine constitutes a facial unit, an elementary face in biunivocal relation with another: it is a man *or* a woman, a rich person or a poor one, an adult or a child, a leader or a subject, "an x *or* a y." The movement of the black hole across the screen, the trajectory of the third eye over the surface of reference, constitutes so many dichotomies or arborescences, like four-eye machines made of elementary faces linked together two by two. The face of a teacher and a student, father and son, worker and boss, cop and citizen, accused and judge ("the judge had a stern expression, his eyes were horizonless . . ."): concrete individualized faces are produced and transformed on the basis of these units, these combinations of units—like the face of a rich child in which a military calling is already discernible, that West Point chin. You don't so much have a face as slide into one.

Under the second aspect, the abstract machine of faciality assumes a role of selective response, or choice: given a concrete face, the machine judges whether it passes or not, whether it goes or not, on the basis of the elementary facial units. This time, the binary relation is of the "yes-no" type. The empty eye or black hole absorbs or rejects, like a half-doddering despot who can still give a signal of acquiescence or refusal. The face of a given teacher is contorted by tics and bathed in an anxiety that makes it "no go." A defendant, a subject, displays an overaffected submission that turns into insolence. Or someone is too polite to be honest. A given face is neither a man's nor a woman's. Or it is neither a poor person's nor a rich person's. Is it someone who lost his fortune? At every moment, the machine rejects faces that do not conform, or seem suspicious. But only at a given level of choice. For it is necessary to produce successive divergence-types of deviance for everything that eludes biunivocal relationships, and to establish binary relations between what is accepted on first choice and what is only tolerated on second, third choice, etc. The white wall is always expanding, and the black hole functions repeatedly. The teacher has gone mad, but madness is a face conforming to the *n*th choice (not the last, however, since there are mad faces that do not conform to what one assumes madness should be). A ha! It's not a man and it's not a woman, so it must be a transvestite: The binary relation is between the "no" of the first category and the "yes" of the following category, which under certain conditions may just as easily mark a tolerance as indicate an enemy to be mowed down at all costs. At any rate, you've been recognized, the abstract machine has you inscribed in its overall grid. It is clear that in its new role as deviance detector, the faciality machine does not restrict itself to individual cases but operates in just as general a fashion as it did in its first role, the computation of normalities. If the face is in fact Christ, in other words, your average ordinary White Man, then the first deviances, the first divergence-types, are racial: yellow man, black man, men in the second or third category. They are also inscribed on the wall, distributed by the hole. They must be Christianized, in other words, facialized. European racism as the white man's claim has never operated by exclusion, or by the designation of someone as Other: it is instead in primitive societies that the stranger is grasped as an "other."[12] Racism operates by the determination of degrees of deviance in relation to the White-Man face, which endeavors to integrate nonconforming traits into increasingly eccentric and backward waves, sometimes tolerating them at given places under given conditions, in a given ghetto, sometimes erasing them from the wall, which never abides alterity (it's a Jew, it's an Arab, it's a Negro, it's a lunatic . . .). From the viewpoint of racism, there is no exterior, there are no people on the outside. There are only people who should be like us and whose crime it is not to be. The dividing line is not between inside and outside but rather is internal to simultaneous signifying chains and successive subjective choices. Racism never detects the particles of the other; it propagates waves of sameness until those who resist identification have been wiped out (or those who only allow themselves to be identified at a given degree of divergence). Its cruelty is equaled only by its incompetence and naïveté.

On the brighter side, painting has exploited all the resources of the Christ-face. Painting has taken the abstract white wall/black hole machine of faciality in all directions, using the face of Christ to produce every kind of facial unit and every degree of deviance. In this respect, there is an exultation in the painting of the Middle Ages to the Renaissance, like an unbridled freedom. Not only did Christ preside over the facialization of the entire body (his own) and the landscapification of all milieus (his own), but he composed all of the elementary faces and had every divergence at his disposal: Christ-athlete at the fair, Christ-Mannerist queer, Christ-Negro, or at least a Black Virgin at the edge of the wall. The most prodigious strokes of madness appear on canvas under the auspices of the Catholic code. A single example chosen from many [Giotto, *The Life of St. Francis*, scene XII, *The Transfiguration*—Trans.]: against the white background of the landscape and the black-blue hole of the sky, the crucified Christ-turned-kite-machine sends stigmata to Saint Francis by rays; the stigmata effect the facialization of the body of the saint, in the image of the body of Christ; but the rays carrying the stigmata to the saint are also the strings Francis uses to pull the divine kite. It was under the sign of the cross that people learned to steer the face and processes of facialization in all directions.

Information theory takes as its point of departure a homogeneous set of ready-made *signifying* messages that are already functioning as elements in biunivocal relationships, or the elements of which are biunivocally organized between messages. Second, the picking of a combination depends on a certain number of *subjective* binary choices that increase proportionally to the number of elements. But the problem is that all of this biunivocalization and binarization (which is not just the result of an increase in calculating skills, as some say) assumes the deployment of a wall or screen, the installation of a central computing hole without which no message would be discernible and no choice could be implemented. The black hole/white wall system must already have gridded all of space and outlined its arborescences or dichotomies for those of signifier and subjectification even to be conceivable. The mixed semiotic of signifiance and subjectification has an exceptional need to be protected from any intrusion from the outside. In fact, there must not be any exterior: no nomad machine, no primitive polyvocality must spring up, with their combinations of heterogeneous substances of expression. Translatability of any kind requires a single substance of expression. One can constitute signifying chains operating with deterritorialized, digitalized, discrete elements only if there is a semiological screen available, a wall to protect them. One can make subjective choices between two chains or at each point in a chain only if no outside tempest sweeps away the chains and subjects. One can form a web of subjectivities only if one possesses a central eye, a black hole capturing everything that would exceed or transform either the assigned affects or the dominant significations. Moreover, it is absurd to believe that language as such can convey a message. A language is always embedded in the faces that announce its statements and ballast them in relation to the signifiers in progress and subjects concerned. Choices are guided by faces, elements are organized around faces: a common grammar is never separable from a facial education. The face is a veritable megaphone. Thus not only must the abstract machine of faciality provide a protective screen and a computing black hole; in addition, the faces it produces draw all kinds of arborescences and dichotomies without which the signifying and the subjective would not be able to make the arborescences and dichotomies function that fall within their purview in language. Doubtless, the binarities and biunivocalities of the face are not the same as those of language, of its elements and subjects. There is no resemblance between them. But the former subtend the latter. When the faciality machine translates formed contents of whatever kind into a single substance of expression, it already subjugates them to the exclusive form of signifying and subjective expression. It carries out the prior gridding that makes it possible for the signifying elements to become discernible, and for the subjective choices to be implemented. The faciality machine is not an annex to the signifier and the subject; rather, it is subjacent (*connexe*) to them and is their condition of possibility. Facial biunivocalities and binarities double the others; facial redundancies are in redundancy with signifying and subjective redundancies. It is precisely because the face depends on an abstract machine that it does not assume a preexistent subject or signifier; but it is subjacent to them and provides the substance necessary to them. What chooses the faces is not a subject, as in the Szondi test; it is faces that choose their subjects. What interprets the black blotch/white hole figure, or the white page/black hole, is not a signifier, as in the Rorschach test; it is that figure which programs the signifiers.

We have made some progress toward answering the question of what triggers the abstract machine of faciality, for it is not in operation all the time or in just any social formation. *Certain* social formations need face, and also landscape.[13] There is a whole history behind it. At very different dates, there occurred a generalized collapse of all of the heterogeneous, polyvocal, primitive semiotics in favor of a semiotic of signifiance and subjectification. Whatever the differences between signifiance and subjectification, whichever prevails over the other in this case or that, whatever the varying figures assumed by their de facto mixtures—they have it in common to crush all polyvocality, set up language as a form of exclusive expression, and operate by signifying biunivocalization and subjective binarization. The superlinearity proper to language is no longer coordinated with multidimensional figures: it now flattens out all volumes and subordinates all lines. Is it by chance that linguistics always, and very quickly, encounters the problem of homonymy, or ambiguous statements that it then subjects to a set of binary reductions? More generally, linguistics can tolerate no polyvocality or rhizome traits: a child who runs around, plays, dances, and draws cannot concentrate attention on language and writing, and will never be a good subject. In short, the new semiotic needs systematically to destroy the whole range of primitive semiotic systems, even if it retains some of their debris in well-defined enclosures.

However, there is more to the picture than semiotic systems waging war on one another armed only with their own weapons. *Very specific assemblages of power impose signifiance and subjectification* as their determinate form of expression, in reciprocal presupposition with new contents: there is no signifiance without a despotic assemblage, no subjectification without an authoritarian assemblage, and no mixture between the two without assemblages of power that act through signifiers and act upon souls and subjects. It is these assemblages, these despotic or authoritarian formations, that give the new semiotic system the means of its imperialism, in other words, the means both to crush the other semiotics and protect itself against any threat from outside. A concerted effort is made to do away with the body and corporeal coordinates through which the multidimensional or polyvocal semiotics operated. Bodies are disciplined, corporeality dismantled, becomings-animal hounded out, deterritorialization pushed to a new threshold—a jump is made from the organic strata to the strata of signifiance and subjectification. A single substance of expression is produced. The white wall/black hole system is constructed, or rather the abstract machine is triggered that must allow and ensure the almightiness of the signifier as well as the autonomy of the subject. You will be pinned to the white wall and stuffed in the black hole. This machine is called the faciality machine because it is the social production of face, because it performs the facialization of the entire body and all its surroundings and objects, and the landscapification of all worlds and milieus. The deterritorialization of the body implies a reterritorialization on the face; the decoding of the body implies an overcoding by the face; the collapse of corporeal coordinates or milieus implies the constitution of a landscape. The semiotic of the signifier and the subjective never operates through bodies. It is absurd to claim to relate the signifier to the body. At any rate it can be related only to a body that has already been entirely facialized. The difference between our uniforms and clothes and primitive paintings and garb is that the former effect a facialization of the body, with buttons for black holes against the white wall of the material. Even the mask assumes a new function here, the exact opposite of its old one. For there is no unitary function of the mask, except a negative one (in no case does the mask serve to dissimulate, to hide, even while showing or revealing). Either the mask assures the head's belonging to the body, its becoming-animal, as was the case in primitive societies. Or, as is the case now, the mask assures the erection, the construction of the face, the facialization of the head and the body: the mask is now the face itself, the abstraction or operation of the face. The inhumanity of the face. Never does the face assume a prior signifier or subject. The order is totally different: despotic and authoritarian concrete assemblage of power → triggering of the abstract machine of faciality, white wall/black hole → installation of the new semiotic of signifiance and subjectification on that holey surface. That is why we have been addressing just two problems exclusively: the relation of the face to the abstract machine that produces it, and the relation of the face to the assemblages of power that require that social production. The face is a politics.

Of course, we have already seen that signifiance and subjectification are semiotic systems that are entirely distinct in their principles and have different regimes (circular irradiation versus segmentary linearity) and different apparatuses of power (despotic generalized slavery versus authoritarian contract-proceeding). Neither begins with Christ, or the White Man as Christian universal: there are Indian, African, and Asiatic despotic formations of signifiance; the authoritarian process of subjectification appears most purely in the destiny of the Jewish people. But however different these semiotics are, they still form a de facto *mix*, and it is at the level of this mixture that they assert their imperialism, in other words, their common endeavor to crush all other semiotics. There is no signifiance that does not harbor the seeds of subjectivity; there is no subjectification that does not drag with it remnants of signifier. If the signifier bounces above all off a wall, if subjectivity spins above all toward a hole, then we must say that the wall of the signifier already includes holes and the black hole of subjectivity already carries scraps of wall. The mix, therefore, has a solid foundation in the indissociable white wall/black hole machine, and the two semiotics intermingle through intersection, splicing, and the plugging of one into the other, as with the "Hebrew and the Pharaoh." But there is more because the nature of the mixtures may vary greatly. If it is possible to assign the faciality machine a date—the year zero of Christ and the historical development of the White Man—it is because that is when the mixture ceased to be a splicing or an intertwining, becoming a total interpenetration in which each element suffuses the other like drops of red-black wine in white water. Our semiotic of modern White Men, the semiotic of capitalism, has attained this state of mixture in which signifiance and subjectification effectively interpenetrate. Thus it is in this semiotic that faciality, or the white wall/black hole system, assumes its full scope. We must, however, assess the states of mixture and the varying proportions of the elements. Whether in the Christian or pre-Christian state, one element may dominate another, one may be more or less powerful than the other. We are thus led to define *limit-faces*, which are different from both the facial units and the degrees of facial divergence previously defined.

1. The black hole is on the white wall. It is not a unit, since the black hole is in constant movement on the wall and operates by binarization. Two black holes, four black holes, *n* black holes distribute themselves like eyes. Faciality is always a multiplicity. The landscape will be populated with eyes or black holes, as in an Ernst painting, or a drawing by Aloïse or Wölfli. Circles are drawn around a hole on the white wall; an eye can be placed in each of the circles. We can even propose the following law: the more circles there are around a hole, the more the bordering effect acts to increase the surface over which the hole slides and to give that surface a force of capture. Perhaps the purest case is to be found in popular Ethiopian scrolls representing demons: on the white surface of the parchment, two black holes are

drawn, or an outline of round or rectangular faces; but the black holes spread and reproduce, they enter into redundancy, and each time a secondary circle is drawn, a new black hole is constituted, an eye is put in it.[14] An effect of capturing a surface that becomes more enclosed the more it expands. This is the signifying despotic face and the multiplication proper to it, its proliferation, its redundancy of frequency. A multiplication of eyes. The despot or his representatives are everywhere. This is the face as seen from the front, by a subject who does not so much see as get snapped up by black holes. This is a figure of destiny, *terrestrial* destiny, objective signifying destiny. The close-up in film knows this figure well: the Griffith close-up of a face, an element of a face or a facialized object, which then assumes an anticipatory temporal value (the hands of the clock foreshadow something).

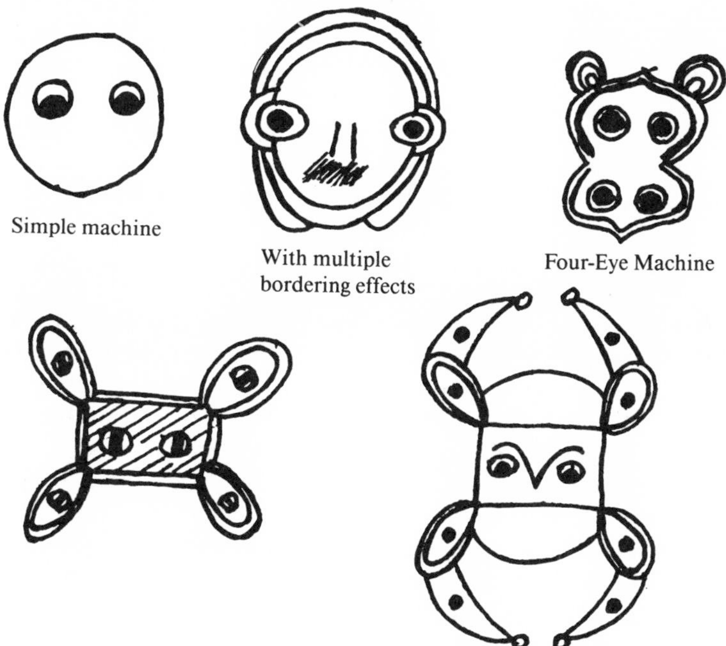

Proliferation of Eyes By Multiplication of Border

Terrestrial Signifying Despotic Face

2. Now, on the contrary, the white wall has unraveled, becoming a silver thread moving toward the black hole. One black hole "crests" all the other black holes, all of the eyes and faces, while the landscape becomes a thread

whose far end coils around the hole. It is still a multiplicity but constitutes a different figure of destiny: reflexive, passional, subjective destiny. It is the *maritime* face or landscape: it follows the line separating the sky from the waters, or the land from the waters. This authoritarian face is in profile and spins toward the black hole. Or else there are two faces facing each other, but in profile to the observer, and their union is already marked by a limitless separation. Or else the faces turn away from each other, swept away by betrayal. Tristan, Isolde, Isolde, Tristan, in the boat carrying them to the black hole of betrayal and death. A faciality of consciousness and passion, a redundancy of resonance and coupling. This time, the effect of the close-up is no longer to expand a surface while simultaneously closing it off; its only function is to have an anticipatory temporal value. It marks the origin of a scale of intensity, or is part of that scale; the closer the faces get to the black hole as termination point, the more the close-up heats the line they follow. Eisenstein's close-ups versus Griffith's (the intensive heightening of shame, or anger, in the close-ups in *Potemkin*).[15] Here again, it is clear that any combination is possible between the two limit-figures of the face. In Pabst's *Lulu*, the despotic face of the fallen Lulu is associated with the image of a bread knife, which has the anticipatory value of foreshadowing the murder; but the authoritarian face of Jack the Ripper also ascends a whole scale of intensities leading to the knife and Lulu's murder.

More generally, we may note characteristics common to the two limit-figures. First, although the white wall, the broad cheeks, is the substantial element of the signifier, and the black hole the reflexive element of subjectivity, they always go together. But in one of two modes: either the black holes distribute themselves and multiply on the white wall, or the wall, reduced to its crest or horizon thread, hurtles toward a black hole that crests them all. There is no wall without black holes, and no black hole without a wall. Second, in both cases the black hole is necessarily surrounded by a border, or even bordered more than once: the effect of this border is either to expand the surface of the wall or to intensify the line. The black hole is never in the eyes (pupil); it is always inside the border, and the eyes are always inside the hole: dead eyes, which see all the better for being in a black hole.[16] These common characteristics do not preclude the existence of a limit-difference between the two figures of the face, and proportions according to which first one then the other dominates in the mixed semiotic. The terrestrial signifying despotic face, the maritime subjective passional authoritarian face (the desert can also be a sea of land). Two figures of destiny, two states of the faciality machine. Jean Paris has clearly shown how these poles operate in painting, the pole of the despotic Christ and that of the passional Christ: on the one hand, the face of Christ seen from the front, as in a Byzantine mosaic, with the black hole of the eyes against a gold background, all depth projected forward; and on the other hand, faces that cross glances and turn away from each other, seen half-turned or in profile, as in a quattrocento painting, their sidelong glances drawing multiple lines, integrating depth into the painting itself (arbitrary examples of transition and mixture can be cited, such as Duccio's *Calling of Saint Peter and Saint Andrew*, against the background of an aquatic landscape; the second formula has already overtaken Christ and the first fisherman, while the second fisherman remains within the Byzantine code).[17]

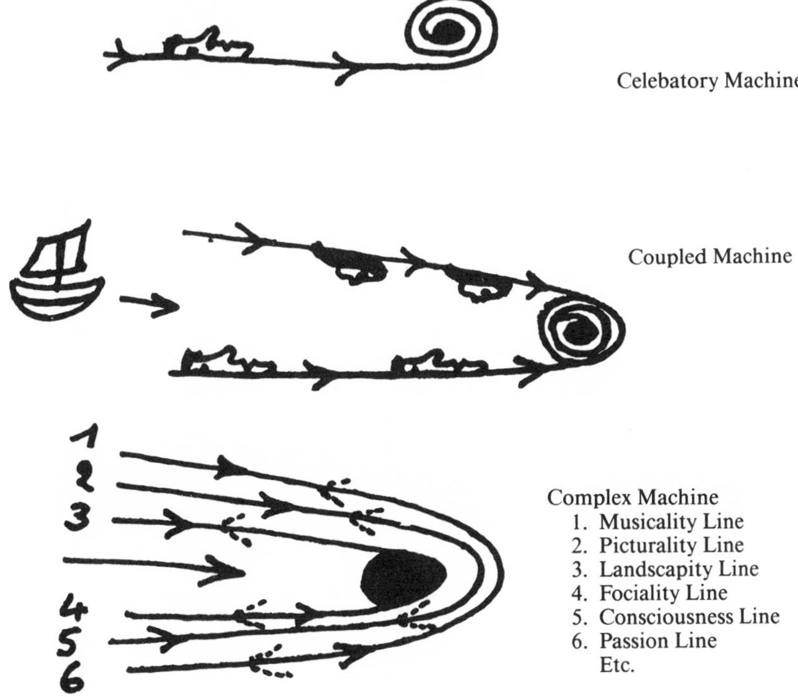

Maritime Subjective Authoritarian Face (ater Tristan and Isolde)

Swann's Love: Proust was able to make the face, landscape, painting, music, etc., resonate together. Three moments in the story of Swann and Odette. First, a whole signifying mechanism is set up. The face of Odette with her broad white or yellow cheeks, and her eyes as black holes. But this face continually refers back to other things, also arrayed on the wall. That is Swann's aestheticism, his amateurism: a thing must always recall something else, in a network of interpretations under the sign of the signifier. A face refers back to a landscape. A face must "recall" a painting, or a fragment of a painting. A piece of music must let fall a little phrase that connects with Odette's face, to the point that the little phrase becomes only a signal. The white wall becomes populous, the black holes are arrayed. This entire mechanism of signifiance, with its referral of interpretations, prepares the way for the second, passional subjective, moment, during which Swann's jealousy, querulous delusion, and erotomania develop. Now Odette's face races down a line hurtling toward a single black hole, that of Swann's Passion. The other lines, of landscapity, picturality, and musicality, also rush toward this catatonic hole and coil around it, bordering it several times.

But in the third moment, at the end of his long passion, Swann attends a reception where he sees the faces of the servants and guests *disaggregate* into autonomous aesthetic traits, as if the line of picturality regained its independence, both beyond the wall and outside the black hole. Then Vinteuil's little phrase regains its transcendence and renews its connection with a still more intense, asignifying, and asubjective line of pure musicality. And Swann knows that he no longer loves Odette and, above all, that Odette will never again love him.

Was this salvation through art necessary? For neither Swann nor Proust was saved. Was it necessary to break through the wall and out of the hole in *this* way, by renouncing love? Was not that love rotten from the start, made of signifiance and jealousy? Was it possible to do anything else, considering Odette's mediocrity and Swann's aestheticism? In a way, the madeleine is the same story. The narrator munches his madeleine: redundancy, the black hole of involuntary memory. How can he get out of that? And it is, above all, something one has to get out of, escape from. Proust knows that quite well, even if his commentators do not. But the way he gets out is through art, uniquely through art.

How do you get out of the black hole? How do you break through the wall? How do you dismantle the face? Whatever genius there may be in the French novel, that is not its affair. It is too concerned with measuring the wall, or even with building it, with plumbing the depths of black holes and composing faces. The French novel is profoundly pessimistic and idealistic, "critical of life rather than creative of life." It stuffs its characters down the hole and bounces them off the wall. It can only conceive of organized voyages, and of salvation only through art, a still Catholic salvation, in other words, salvation through eternity. It spends its time plotting points instead of drawing lines, active lines of flight or of positive deterritorialization. The Anglo-American novel is totally different. "To get away. To get away, out! . . . To cross a horizon . . ."[18] From Hardy to Lawrence, from Melville to Miller, the same cry rings out: Go across, get out, break through, make a beeline, don't get stuck on a point. Find the line of separation, follow it or create it, to the point of treachery. That is why their relationship to other civilizations, to the Orient or South America, and also to drugs and voyages in place, is entirely different from that of the French. They know how difficult it is to get out of the black hole of subjectivity, of consciousness and memory, of the couple and conjugality. How tempting it is to let yourself get caught, to lull yourself into it, to latch back onto a *face*. "[Being] locked away in the black hole . . . gave her a molten copperish glow, the words coming out of her mouth like lava, her flesh clutching ravenously for a hold, a perch on something solid and substantial, something in which to reintegrate and repose for a few moments. . . . At first I mistook it for passion, for ecstasy. . . . I thought I had found a living volcano, a female Vesuvius. I never thought I had found a human ship going down in an ocean of despair, in a Sargasso of impotence. Now I think of that black star gleaming through the hole in the ceiling, that fixed star which hung above our conjugal cell, more fixed, more remote than the Absolute, and I know it was her, emptied of all that was properly herself: a dead black sun without aspect."[19] A copperish glow like the face at the bottom of a black hole. The point is to get out of it, not in art, in other words, in spirit, but in life, in real life. *Don't take away my power to love.* These English and American authors also know how hard it is to break through the wall of the signifier. Many people have tried since Christ, beginning with Christ. But Christ himself botched the crossing, the jump, he *bounced* off the wall. "As if by a great recoil, this negative backwash rolled up and stayed his death. The whole negative impulse of humanity seemed to coil up into a monstrous inert mass to create the human integer, the figure one, one and indivisible"—the Face.[20] Cross the wall, the Chinese perhaps, but at what price? At the price of a *becoming-animal*, a *becoming-flower or rock*, and beyond that a strange *becoming-imperceptible*, a *becoming-hard now one with loving*.[21] It is a question of speed, even if the movement is in place. Is this also to dismantle the face, or as Miller says, no longer to look at or into the eyes but to swim through them, to close your own eyes and make your body a beam of light moving at ever-increasing speed? Of course, this requires all the resources of art, and art of the highest kind. It requires a whole line of writing, picturality, musicality . . . For it is through writing that you become animal, it is through color that you become imperceptible, it is through music that you become hard and memoryless, simultaneously animal and imperceptible: in love. But art is never an end in itself; it is only a tool for blazing life lines, in other words, all of those real becomings that are not produced only *in* art, and all of those active escapes that do not consist in fleeing *into* art, taking refuge in art, and all of those positive deterritorializations that never reterritorialize on art, but instead sweep it away with them toward the realms of the asignifying, asubjective, and faceless.

Dismantling the face is no mean affair. Madness is a definite danger: Is it by chance that schizos lose their sense of the face, their own and others', their sense of the landscape, and the sense of language and its dominant significations all at the same time? The organization of the face is a strong one. We could say that the face holds within its rectangle or circle a whole set of traits, *faciality traits*, which it subsumes and places at the service of signifiance and subjectification. What is a tic? It is precisely the continually refought battle between a faciality trait that tries to escape the sovereign organization of the face and the face itself, which clamps back down on the trait, takes hold of it again, blocks its line of flight, and reimposes its organization upon it. (There is a medical distinction between the clonic or convulsive tic and the tonic or spasmodic tic; perhaps we can say that in the first case the faciality trait that is trying to escape has the upper hand, whereas in the second case the facial organization that is trying to clamp back down or immobilize itself has the upper hand.) But if dismantling the face is a major affair, it is because it is not simply a question of tics, or an amateur's or aesthete's adventure. If the face is a politics, dismantling the face is also a politics involving real becomings, an entire becoming-clandestine. Dismantling the face is the same as breaking through the wall of the signifier and getting out of the black hole of subjectivity. Here, the program, the slogan, of schizoanalysis is: Find your black holes and white walls, know them, know your faces; it is the only way you will be able to dismantle them and draw your lines of flight.[22]

It is time once again to multiply practical warnings. First, it is never a question of a return to . . . It is not a question of "returning" to the presignifying and presubjective semiotics of primitive peoples. We will always be failures at playing African or Indian, even Chinese, and no voyage to the South Seas, however arduous, will allow us to cross the wall, get out of the hole, or lose our face. We will never succeed in making ourselves a new primitive head and body, human, spiritual, and faceless. It would only be taking more photos and bouncing off the wall again. We will always find ourselves reterritorialized again. O my little desert island, on you I am in the Closerie des Lilas again, O my deep ocean, you reflect the lake in the Bois de Boulogne, O little phrase of Vinteuil, you recall a sweet moment. These are Eastern physical and spiritual exercises, but for a couple, like a conjugal bed tucked with a Chinese sheet: you did do your exercises today, didn't you? Lawrence has only one grudge against Melville: he knew better than anyone how to get across the face, the eyes and horizon, the wall and hole, but he mistook that crossing, that creative line, for an "impossible return," a return to the savages in *Typee*, for a way of staying an artist and hating life, of maintaining a nostalgia for the Home Country. ("He ever pined for Home and Mother, the two things he had run away from as far as ships would carry him. . . . Melville came home to face out the rest of his life. . . . He refused life. But he stuck to his ideal of perfect relationship, possible perfect love. . . . A truly perfect relationship is one in which each party leaves great tracts unknown in the other party. . . . Melville was, at the core, a mystic and an idealist. . . . And he stuck to his ideal guns. I abandon mine. I say, let the old guns rot. *Get new ones, and shoot straight.*")[23]

We can't turn back. Only neurotics, or, as Lawrence says, "renegades," deceivers, attempt a regression. The white wall of the signifier, the black hole of subjectivity, and the facial machine are impasses, the measure of our submissions and subjections; but we are born into them, and it is there we must stand battle. Not in the sense of a necessary stage, but in the sense of a tool for which a new use must be invented. Only across the wall of the signifier can you run lines of asignifiance that void all memory, all return, all possible signification and interpretation. Only in the black hole of subjective consciousness and passion do you discover the transformed, heated, captured particles you must relaunch for a nonsubjective, living love in which each party connects with unknown tracts in the other without entering or conquering them, in which the lines composed are broken lines. Only on your face and at the bottom of your black hole and upon your white wall will you be able to set faciality traits free like birds, not in order to return to a primitive head, but to invent the combinations by which those traits connect with landscapity traits that have themselves been freed from the landscape and with traits of picturality and musicality that have also been freed from their respective codes. With what joy the painters used the face of Christ himself, taking it in every sense and direction; and it was not simply the joy of a desire to paint, but the joy of all desires. Is it possible to tell, when the knight of the courtly novel is in his catatonic state, whether he is deep in his black hole or already astride the particles that will carry him out of it to begin a new journey? Lawrence, who has been compared to Lancelot, writes: "To be alone, mindless and memoryless beside the sea . . . As alone and as absent and as present as an aboriginal dark on the sand in the sun . . . Far off, far off, as if he had landed on another planet, as a man might after death . . . The landscape?—he cared not a thing about the landscape. . . . Humanity?—there was none. Thought?—fallen like a stone into the sea. The great, the glamorous past?—worn thin, frail, like a frail translucent film of shell thrown up on the shore."[24] The uncertain moment at which the white wall/black hole, black point/white shore system, as on a Japanese print, itself becomes one with the act of leaving it, breaking away from and crossing through it.

We have seen that the abstract machine has two very different states: sometimes it is taken up in strata where it brings about deterritorializations that are merely relative, or deterritorializations that are absolute but remain negative; sometimes it is developed on a plane of consistency giving it a "diagrammatic" function, a positive value of deterritorialization, the ability to form new abstract machines. Sometimes the abstract machine, as the faciality machine, forces flows into signifiances and subjectifications, into knots of aborescence and holes of abolition; sometimes, to the extent that it performs a veritable "defacialization," it frees something like *probe-heads* (*têtes chercheuses*, guidance devices) that dismantle the strata in their wake, break through the walls of signifiance, pour out of the holes of subjectivity, fell trees in favor of veritable rhizomes, and steer the flows down lines of positive deterritorializaton or creative flight. There are no more concentrically organized strata, no more black holes around which lines coil to form borders, no more walls to which dichotomies, binarities, and bipolar values cling. There is no more face to be in redundancy with a landscape, painting, or little phrase of music, each perpetually bringing the other to mind, on the unified surface of the wall or the central swirl of the black hole. Each freed faciality trait forms a rhizome with a freed trait of landscapity, picturality, or musicality. This is not a collection of part-objects but a living block, a connecting of stems by which the traits of a face enter a real multiplicity or diagram with a trait of an unknown landscape, a trait of painting or music that is thereby effectively produced, created, according to quanta of absolute, positive deterritorialization—not evoked or recalled according to systems of reterritorialization. A wasp trait and an orchid trait. Quanta marking so many mutations of abstract machines, each of which operates as a function of the other. Thus opens a rhizomatic realm of possibility effecting the potentialization of the possible, as opposed to arborescent possibility, which marks a closure, an impotence.

The face, what a horror. It is naturally a lunar landscape, with its pores, planes, matts, bright colors, whiteness, and holes: there is no need for a close-up to make it inhuman; it is naturally a close-up, and naturally inhuman, a monstrous hood. Necessarily so because it is produced by a machine and in order to meet the requirements of the special apparatus of power that triggers the machine and takes deterritorialization to the absolute while keeping it negative. Earlier, when we contrasted the primitive, spiritual, human head with the inhuman face, we were falling victim to a nostalgia for a return or regression. In truth, there are only inhumanities, humans are made exclusively of inhumanities, but very different ones, of very different natures and speeds. Primitive inhumanity, prefacial inhumanity, has all the polyvocality of a semiotic in which the head is a part of the body, a body that is already deterritorialized relatively and plugged into becomings-spiritual/animal. Beyond the face lies an altogether different inhumanity: no longer that of the primitive head, but of "probe-heads";

here, cutting edges of deterritorialization become operative and lines of deterritorialization positive and absolute, forming strange new becomings, new polyvocalities. Become clandestine, make rhizome everywhere, for the wonder of a nonhuman life to be created. *Face, my love,* you have finally become a probe-head . . . Year zen, year omega, year ω . . . Must we leave it at that, three states, and no more: primitive heads, Christ-face, and probe-heads?

8. 1874: Three Novellas, or "What Happened?"

It is not very difficult to determine the essence of the "novella" as a literary genre: Everything is organized around the question, "What happened? Whatever could have happened?" The tale is the opposite of the novella, because it is an altogether different question that the reader asks with bated breath: What is going to happen? Something is always going to happen, come to pass. Something always happens in the novel also, but the novel integrates elements of the novella and the tale into the variation of its perpetual living present (*duration*). The detective novel is a particularly hybrid genre in this respect, since most often the something = *X* that has happened is on the order of a murder or theft, but exactly what it is that has happened remains to be discovered, and in the present determined by the model detective. Yet it would be an error to reduce these different aspects to the three dimensions of time. Something happened, something is going to happen, can designate a past so immediate, a future so near, that they are one (as Husserl would say) with retentions and protentions of the present itself. Nevertheless, the distinction is legitimate, in view of the different movements that animate the present, are contemporaneous with it: One moves with it, another already casts it into the past *from the moment* it is present (novella), while another *simultaneously* draws it into the future (tale). We are lucky to have treatments of the same subject by a tale writer and a novella writer: two lovers, one of whom dies suddenly in the other's room. In Maupassant's tale, "Une ruse" (An artifice), everything revolves around these questions: What is going to happen? How will the survivor extricate himself from the situation? What will the third party-savior, in this case a doctor, think of? In Barbey d'Aurevilly's novella, "Le rideau cramoisi" (The crimson curtain), everything revolves around: Something happened, but what? That is the question, not only because it is really not known what the cold young woman just died from, but also because it will never be known why she gave herself to the petty officer, or how the third party-savior, here the colonel of the regiment, was able to arrange things.[1] It should not be thought that it is easier to leave things open-ended: for there to be something that has happened that we will never know about, or even several things in a row, requires no less minute attention and precision than the contrary case, when the author must invent the details of what will need to be known. You will never know what just happened, or you will always know what is going to happen: these are the reasons for the reader's two bated breaths, in the novella and the tale, respectively, and they are two ways in which the living present is divided at every instant. In the novella, we do not wait for something to happen, we expect something to have just happened. The novella is a last novella, whereas the tale is a first tale. The "presence" of the tale writer is completely different from that of the novella writer (and both are different from that of the novelist). Let us not dwell too much on the dimensions of time: the novella has little to do with a memory of the past or an act of reflection; quite to the contrary, it plays upon a fundamental forgetting. It evolves in the element of "what happened" because it places us in a relation with something unknowable and imperceptible (and not the other way around: it is not because it speaks of a past about which it can no longer provide us knowledge). It may even be that nothing has happened, but it is precisely that nothing that makes us say, Whatever could have happened to make me forget where I put my keys, or whether I mailed that letter, etc.? What little blood vessel in my brain could have ruptured? What is this nothing that makes something happen? The novella has a fundamental relation to *secrecy* (not with a secret matter or object to be discovered, but with the form of the secret, which remains impenetrable), whereas the tale has a relation to *discovery* (the form of discovery, independent of what can be discovered). The novella also enacts *postures* of the body and mind that are like folds or envelopments, whereas the tale puts into play *attitudes or positions* that are like unfoldings and developments, however unexpected. Barbey has an evident fondness for body posture, in other words, states of the body when it is surprised by something that just happened. In the preface to the *Diaboliques*, Barbey even suggests that there is a diabolism of body postures, a sexuality, pornography, and scatology of postures quite different from those that also, and simultaneously, mark body attitudes or positions. Posture is like inverse suspense. Thus it is not a question of saying that the novella relates to the past and the tale to the future; what we should say instead is that the novella relates, in the present itself, to the formal dimension of something that has happened, even if that something is nothing or remains unknowable. Similarly, one should not try to make the distinction between the novella and the tale coincide with categories such as the fantastic, the fabulous, etc.; that is another problem, there is no reason why it should overlap. The links of the novella are: What happened? (the modality or expression), Secrecy (the form), Body Posture (the content).

Take Fitzgerald. He is a tale and novella writer of genius. He is a novella writer when he asks himself, *Whatever could have happened for things to have come to this?* He is the only one who has been able to carry this question to such a point of intensity. It is not a question of memory, reflection, old age, or fatigue, whereas the tale would deal with childhood, action, or impulse. Yet it is true that Fitzgerald only asks himself the question of the novella writer when he is personally worn-out, fatigued, sick, or even worse off. But once again, there is not necessarily a connection: it can also be a question of vigor, or love. It still is, even in desperate conditions. It is better to think of it as an affair of perception: you enter a room and perceive something as already there, as just having happened, even though it has not yet been done. Or you know that what is in the process of happening is happening for the last time, it's already over with. You hear an "I love you" you know is the last one. Perceptual semiotics. God, whatever could have happened, even though everything is and remains imperceptible, and in order for everything to be and remain imperceptible forever?

Not only is there a specificity of the novella, but there is also a specific way in which the novella treats a universal matter. For we are made of lines. We are not only referring to lines of writing. Lines of writing conjugate with other lines, life lines, lines of luck or misfortune, lines productive of the variation of the line of writing itself, lines that are *between the lines* of writing. Perhaps the novella has its own way of giving rise to and combining these lines, which nonetheless belong to everyone and every genre. Vladimir Propp has said, with great solemnity, that the folktale must be defined in terms of external and internal *movements* that it qualifies, formalizes, and combines in its own specific way.[2] We would like to demonstrate that the novella is defined by living *lines*, flesh lines, about which it brings a special revelation. Marcel Arland is correct to say that the novella "is nothing but pure lines right down to the nuances, *and* nothing but the pure and conscious power of the word."[3]

First Novella: "In the Cage," Henry James

The heroine, a young telegrapher, leads a very clear-cut, calculated life proceeding by delimited segments: the telegrams she takes one after the other, day after day; the people to whom she sends the telegrams; their social class and the different ways they use telegraphy; the words to be counted. Moreover, her telegraphist's cage is like a contiguous segment to the grocery store next door, where her fiancé works. Contiguity of territories. And the fiancé is constantly plotting out their future, work, vacations, house. Here, as for all of us, there is a line of rigid segmentarity on which everything seems calculable and foreseen, the beginning and end of a segment, the passage from one segment to another. Our lives are made like that: Not only are the great molar aggregates segmented (States, institutions, classes), but so are people as elements of an aggregate, as are feelings as relations between people; they are segmented, not in such a way as to disturb or disperse, but on the contrary to ensure and control the identity of each agency, including personal identity. The fiancé can say to the young woman, Even though there are differences between our segments, we have the same tastes and we are alike. I am a man, you are a woman; you are a telegraphist, I am a grocer; you count words, I weigh things; our segments fit together, conjugate. Conjugality. A whole interplay of well-determined, well-planned territories. They have a future but no becoming. This is the first life line, the *molar or rigid line of segmentarity;* in no sense is it dead, for it occupies and pervades our life, and always seems to prevail in the end. It even includes much tenderness and love. It would be too easy to say, "This is a bad line," for you find it everywhere, and in all the other lines.

A rich couple comes into the post office and reveals to the young woman, or at least confirms, the existence of another life: coded, multiple telegrams, signed with pseudonyms. It is hard to tell who is who anymore, or what anything means. Instead of a rigid line composed of well-determined segments, telegraphy now forms a supple flow marked by *quanta* that are like so many little segmentations-in-progress grasped at the moment of their birth, as on a moonbeam, or on an intensive scale. Thanks to her "prodigious talent for interpretation," the young woman grasps that the man has a secret that has placed him in danger, deeper and deeper in danger, in a dangerous posture. It does not just have to do with his love relations with the woman. James has reached the stage in his work when it is no longer the matter of the secret that interests him, even if he has succeeded in rendering it entirely banal and unimportant. Now what counts is the form of the secret; the matter no longer even has to be discovered (we never find out, there are several possibilities, there is an objective indetermination, a kind of molecularization of the secret). In relation to this man, directly with him, the young telegraphist develops a strange passional complicity, a whole intense molecular life that does not even enter into rivalry with the life she leads with her fiancé. What has happened, whatever could have happened? This life, however, is not in her head, it is not imaginary. Rather, we should say that there are two *politics* involved, as the young woman suggests in a remarkable conversation with her fiancé: a macropolitics and a micropolitics that do not envision classes, sexes, people, or feelings in at all the same way. Or again, there are two very different types of relations: intrinsic relations of *couples* involving well-determined aggregates or elements (social classes, men and women, this or that particular person), and less localizable relations that are always external to themselves and instead concern flows and particles eluding those classes, sexes, and persons. Why are the latter relations of *doubles* rather than of couples? "She was literally afraid of the alternate self who might be waiting outside. He might be waiting; it was he who was her alternate self, and of him she was afraid."[4] In any case, this line is very different from the previous one; it is a *line of molecular or supple segmentation* the segments of which are like quanta of deterritorialization. It is on this line that a present is defined whose very form is the form of something that has already happened, however close you might be to it, since the ungraspable matter of that something is entirely molecularized, traveling at speeds beyond the ordinary thresholds of perception. Yet we will not say that it is necessarily better.

There is no question that the two lines are constantly interfering, reacting upon each other, introducing into each other either a current of suppleness or a point of rigidity. Nathalie Sarraute, in her essay on the novel, praises English novelists, not only for discovering (as did Proust and Dostoyevsky) the great movements, territories, and points of the unconscious that allow us to regain time or revive the past, but also for inopportunely following these molecular lines, simultaneously present and imperceptible. She shows that dialogue or conversation does indeed comply with the breaks of a fixed segmentarity, with vast movements of regulated distribution corresponding to the attitudes and positions of each of us; but also that they are run through and swept up by *micromovements*, fine segmentations distributed in an entirely different way, unfindable particles of an anonymous matter, tiny cracks and postures operating by different agencies even in the unconscious, secret lines of disorientation or deterritorialization: as she puts it, a whole subconversation within conversation, in other words, a micropolitics of conversation.[5]

Then James's heroine reaches a sort of maximum quantum in her supple segmentarity or line of flow beyond which she cannot go (even if she wanted to, there is no going further). There is a danger that these vibrations traversing us may be aggravated beyond our endurance. What happened? The molecular relation between the telegraphist and the telegraph sender dissolved in the form of the secret—because nothing happened. Each of them is propelled toward a rigid segmentarity: he will marry the now-widowed lady, she will marry her fiancé. And yet everything has changed. She has reached something like a new line, a third type, a kind of *line of flight* that is just as real as the others even if it occurs in place: this line no longer tolerates segments; rather, it is like an exploding of the two segmentary series. She has broken through the wall, she has gotten out of the black holes. She has attained a kind of absolute deterritorialization. "She ended up knowing so much that she could no longer interpret anything. *There were no longer shadows to help her see more clearly, only glare.*"[6] You cannot go further in life than this sentence by James. The nature of the secret has changed once again. Undoubtedly, the secret always has to do with love, and sexuality. But previously it was either only a hidden matter given in the past (the better hidden the more ordinary it was), and we did not exactly know what form to give it: See, I am bending under the burden of my secret, see what mystery resides within me. It was a way of seeming interesting, what D. H. Lawrence called "the dirty little secret," *my* Oedipus, in a way. Or else the secret became the form of something whose matter was molecularized, imperceptible, unassignable: not a given of the past but the ungivable "What happened?" But on this third line there is no longer even any form—nothing but a pure abstract line. It is because we no longer have anything to hide that we can no longer be apprehended. To become imperceptible oneself, to have dismantled love in order to become capable of loving. To have dismantled one's self in order finally to be alone and meet the true double at the other end of the line. A clandestine passenger on a motionless voyage. To become like everybody else; but this, precisely, is a becoming only for one who knows how to be nobody, to no longer be anybody. To paint oneself gray on gray. As Kierkegaard says, nothing distinguishes the knight of the faith from a bourgeois German going home or to the post office: he sends off no special telegraphic sign; he constantly produces or reproduces finite segments, yet he is already moving on a line no one even suspects.[7] In any case, the telegraphic line is not a symbol, and it is not simple. There are at least three of them: a line of rigid and clear-cut segmentarity; a line of molecular segmentarity; and an abstract line, a line of flight no less deadly and no less alive than the others. On the first line, there are many words and conversations, questions and answers, interminable explanations, precisions; the second is made of silences, allusions, and hasty innuendos inviting interpretation. But if the third line flashes, if the line of flight is like a train in motion, it is because one jumps linearly on it, one can finally speak "literally" of anything at all, a blade of grass, a catastrophe or sensation, calmly accepting that which occurs when it is no longer possible for anything to stand for anything else. The three lines, however, continually intermingle.

Second Novella: "The Crack-up," F. Scott Fitzgerald

What happened? This is the question Fitzgerald keeps coming back to toward the end, having remarked that "of course all life is a process of breaking down."[8] How should we understand this "of course"? We can say, first of all, that life is always drawn into an increasingly rigid and desiccated segmentarity. For the writer Fitzgerald, voyages, with their clear-cut segments, had lost their usefulness. There was also, from segment to segment, the depression, loss of wealth, fatigue and growing old, alcoholism, the failure of conjugality, the rise of the cinema, the advent of fascism and Stalinism, and the loss of success and talent—at the very moment Fitzgerald would find his genius. "*The big sudden blows that come, or seem to come, from outside*" (p. 69), and proceed by oversignificant *breaks*, moving us from one term to the other according to successive binary "choices": rich/poor . . . Even when change runs in the other direction, there is nothing to compensate for the rigidification, the aging that overcodes everything that occurs. This is a line of rigid segmentarity bringing masses into play, even if it was supple to begin with.

But Fitzgerald says that there is another type of cracking, with an entirely different segmentarity. Instead of great breaks, these are microcracks, as in a dish; they are much more subtle and supple, and *occur when things are going well on the other side*. If there is aging on this line, it is not of the same kind: when you age on this line you don't feel it on the other line, you don't notice it on the other line until after "it" has already happened on this line. At such a moment, which does not correspond to any of the ages of the other line, you reach a degree, a quantum, an intensity beyond which you cannot go. (It's a very delicate business, these intensities: the finest intensity becomes harmful if it overtaxes your strength at a given moment; you have to be able to take it, you have to be in shape.) But what exactly happened? In truth, nothing assignable or perceptible: molecular changes, redistributions of desire such that when something occurs, the self that awaited it is already dead, or the one that would await it has not yet arrived. This time, there are outbursts and crackings in the immanence of a rhizome, rather than great movements and breaks determined by the transcendence of a tree. The crack-up "happens almost without your knowing it but is realized suddenly indeed" (p. 69). This molecular line, more supple but no less disquieting, in fact, much more disquieting, is not simply internal or personal: it also brings everything into play, but on a different scale and in different forms, with segmentations of a different nature, rhizomatic instead of arborescent. A micropolitics.

There is, in addition, a third line, which is like a line of rupture or a "clean break" and marks the exploding of the other two, their shake-up . . . in favor of something else? "This led me to the idea that the ones who had survived had made some sort of clean break. This is a big word and is no parallel to a jailbreak when one is probably headed for a new jail or will be forced back to the old one" (p. 81). Here, Fitzgerald contrasts rupture with structural pseudobreaks in so-called signifying chains. But he also distinguishes it from more supple, more subterranean links or stems of the "voyage" type, or even from molecular conveyances. "The famous 'Escape' or 'run away from it all' is an excursion in a trap even if the trap includes the South Seas, which are only for those who want to paint them or sail them. A clean break is something you cannot come back from; that is irretrievable because it makes the past cease to exist" (p. 81). Can it be that voyages are always a return to rigid segmentarity? Is it always your daddy and mommy that you meet when you travel, even as far away as the South Seas, like Melville? Hardened muscles? Must we say that supple segmentarity itself reconstructs the great figures it claimed to escape, but under the microscope, in miniature? Beckett's unforgettable line is an indictment of all voyages: "*We don't travel for the fun of it, as far as I know; we're foolish, but not that foolish.*"

In rupture, not only has the matter of the past volitized; the form of what happened, of an imperceptible something that happened in a volatile matter, no longer even exists. One has become imperceptible and clandestine in motionless voyage. Nothing can happen, or can have happened, any longer. Nobody can do anything for or against me any longer. My territories are out of grasp, not because they are imaginary, but the opposite: because I am in the process of drawing them. Wars, big and little, are behind me. Voyages, always in tow to something else, are behind me. I no longer have any secrets, having lost my face, form, and matter. I am now no more than a line. I have become capable of loving, not with an abstract, universal love, but a love I shall choose, and that shall choose me, blindly, my double, just as selfless as I. One has been saved by and for love, by abandoning love and self. Now one is no more than an abstract line, like an arrow crossing the void. Absolute deterritorialization. One has become like everybody/the whole world (*tout le monde*), but in a way that can become like everybody/the whole world. One has painted the world on oneself, not oneself on the world. It should not be said that the genius is an extraordinary person, *nor* that everybody has genius. The genius is someone who knows how to make everybody/the whole world a becoming (Ulysses, perhaps: Joyce's failed ambition, Pound's near-success). One has entered becomings-animal, becomings-molecular, and finally becomings-imperceptible. "I was off the dispensing end of the relief roll forever. The heady villainous feeling continued. . . . I will try to be a correct animal though, and if you throw me a bone with enough meat on it I may even lick your hand."[9] Why such a despairing tone? Does not the line of rupture or true flight have its own danger, one worse than the others? Time to die. In any case, Fitzgerald proposes a distinction between the three lines traversing us and composing "a life" (after Maupassant). *Break line, crack line, rupture line.* The line of rigid segmentarity with molar breaks; the line of supple segmentation with molecular cracks; the line of flight or rupture, abstract, deadly and alive, nonsegmentary.

Third Novella: "The Story of the Abyss and the Spyglass," Pierrette Fleutiaux[10]

Some segments are more or less near, and others more or less distant. The segments seem to encircle an abyss, a kind of huge black hole. On each segment there are two kinds of lookouts, near-seers and far-seers. What they watch for are the movements, outbursts, infractions, disturbances, and rebellions occurring in the abyss. But there is a major difference between the two types of lookouts. The near-seers have a simple spyglass. In the abyss, they see the outline of gigantic cells, great binary divisions, dichotomies, well-defined segments of the type "classroom, barracks, low-income housing project, or even countryside seen from an airplane." They see branches, chains, rows, columns, dominoes, striae. Once in a while along the edges they discover a misshapen figure or a shaky contour. Then they bring out the terrible Ray Telescope. It is used not to see with but to cut with, to cut out shapes. This geometrical instrument, which emits a laser beam, assures the dominion of the great signifying break everywhere and restores the momentarily threatened molar order. The cutting telescope *overcodes* everything; it acts on flesh and blood, but itself is nothing but pure geometry, as a State affair, and the near-seers' physics in the service of that machine. What is geometry, what is the State, and what are the near-seers? These are meaningless questions ("I am speaking literally") because it is not so much a question of defining something as effectively drawing a line; not a line of writing but a line of rigid segmentarity along which everyone will be judged and rectified according to his or her contours, individual or collective.

Very different is the situation of those with long-distance vision, the far-seers, with all their ambiguities. There are very few of them, at most one per segment. Their telescopes are complex and refined. But they are in no way leaders. And what they see is entirely different from what the others see. They see a whole microsegmentarity, details of details, "a roller coaster of possibilities," tiny movements that have not reached the edge, lines or vibrations that start to form long before there are outlined shapes, "segments that move by jerks." A whole rhizome, a molecular segmentarity that does not permit itself to be overcoded by a signifier like the cutting machine, or even to be attributed to a given figure, a given aggregate or element. This second line is inseparable from the anonymous segmentation that produces it and challenges everything all the time, without goal or reason: "What happened?" The far-seers can divine the future, but always in the form of a becoming of something that has already happened in a molecular matter; unfindable particles. The situation is the same in biology: the great cellular divisions and dichotomies, with their contours, are accompanied by migrations, invaginations, displacements, and morphogenetic impulses whose segments are marked not by localizable points but by thresholds of intensity passing underneath, mitoses that scramble everything, and molecular lines that intersect each other within the large-scale cells and between their breaks. The situation is the same in a society: rigid segments and overcutting segments are crosscut underneath by segmentations of another nature. But this is neither one nor the other, neither biology nor a society; nor is it a resemblance between the two: "I am speaking literally," I am drawing lines, lines of writing, and life passes between the lines. A line of supple segmentarity formed and became entangled with the other, but it was a very different kind of line, shakily drawn by the micropolitics of the far-seers. It is a political affair, as worldwide in scope as the other, but on a scale and in a form that is incommensurable, nonsuperposable. It is also a perceptual affair, for perception always goes hand in hand with semiotics, practice, politics, theory. One sees, speaks and thinks on a given scale, and according to a given line that may or may not conjugate with the other's line, even if the other is still oneself. If it does not, then you should not insist, you should not argue; you should flee, flee, even saying as you go, "Okay, okay, you win." It's no use talking; you first have to change telescopes, mouths, and teeth, all of the segments. Not only does one speak literally, one also lives literally, in other words, following lines, whether connectable or not, even heterogeneous ones. Sometimes it doesn't work when they are homogeneous.[11]

The ambiguity of the far-seers' situation is that they are able to detect the slightest microinfraction in the abyss, things the others do not see; they also observe, beneath its apparent geometrical justice, the dreadful damage caused by the Cutting Telescope. They feel as though they foresee things and are ahead of the others because they see the smallest thing as already having happened; but they know that their warnings are to no avail because the cutting telescope will set everything straight without being warned, without the need for or possibility of prediction. At times they feel that they do indeed see something the others do not, but at other times that what they see differs only in degree and serves no purpose. Although they are collaborators with the most rigid and cruelest project of control, how could they not feel a vague sympathy for the subterranean activity revealed to them? An ambiguity in the molecular line, *as if it vacillated between two sides*. One day (what will have happened?), a far-seer will abandon his or her segment and start walking across a narrow overpass above the dark abyss, will break his or her telescope and depart on a line of flight to meet a blind Double approaching from the other side.

Individual or group, we are traversed by lines, meridians, geodesics, tropics, and zones marching to different beats and differing in nature. We said that we are composed of lines, three kinds of lines. Or rather, of bundles of lines, for each kind is multiple. We may be more interested in a certain line than in the others, and perhaps there is indeed one that is, not determining, but of greater importance . . . if it is there. For some of these lines are imposed on us from outside, at least in part. Others sprout up somewhat by chance, from a trifle, why we will never know. Others can be invented, drawn, without a model and without chance: we must invent our lines of flight, if we are able, and the only way we can invent them is by effectively drawing them, in our lives. Aren't lines of flight the most difficult of all? Certain groups or people have none and never will. Certain groups or people lack a given kind of line, or have lost it. The painter Florence Julien has a special interest in lines of flight: she invented a procedure by which she extracts from photographs lines that are nearly abstract and formless. But once again, there is a bundle of very diverse lines: the line of flight of children leaving school at a run is different from that of demonstrators chased by the police, or of a prisoner breaking out. There are different animal lines of flight: each species, each individual, has its own. Fernand Deligny transcribes the lines and paths of autistic children by means of *maps*: he carefully distinguishes "lines of drift" and "customary lines." This does not only apply to walking; he also makes maps of perceptions and maps of gestures (cooking or collecting wood) showing customary gestures and gestures of drift. The same goes for language, if it is present. Deligny opened his lines of writing to life lines. The lines are constantly crossing, intersecting for a moment, following one another. A line of drift intersects a customary line, and at that point the child does something not quite belonging to either one: he or she finds something he or she lost—what happened?—or jumps and claps his or her hands, a slight and rapid movement—and that gesture in turn emits several lines.[12] In short, *there is a line of flight, which is already complex since it has singularities; and there a customary or molar line with segments; and between the two (?), there is a molecular line with quanta that cause it to tip to one side or the other.*

As Deligny says, it should be borne in mind that these lines mean nothing. It is an affair of cartography. They compose us, as they compose our map. They transform themselves and may even cross over into one another. Rhizome. It is certain that they have nothing to do with language; it is, on the contrary, language that must follow them, it is writing that must take sustenance from them, *between* its own lines. It is certain that they have nothing to do with a signifier, the determination of a subject by the signifier; instead, the signifier arises at the most rigidified level of one of the lines, and the subject is spawned at the lowest level. It is certain that they have nothing to do with a structure, which is never occupied by anything more than points and positions, by arborescences, and which always forms a closed system, precisely in order to prevent escape. Deligny invokes a common Body upon which these lines are inscribed as so many segments, thresholds, or quanta, territorialities, deterritorializations, or reterritorializations. The lines are inscribed on a Body without Organs, upon which everything is drawn and flees, which is itself an abstract line with neither imaginary figures nor symbolic functions: the real of the BwO. *This body is the only practical object of schizoanalysis:* What is your body without organs? What are your lines? What map are you in the process of making or rearranging? What abstract line will you draw, and at what price, for yourself and for others? What is your line of flight? What is your BwO, merged with that line? Are you cracking up? Are you going to crack up? Are you deterritorializing? Which lines are you severing, and which are you extending or resuming? Schizoanalysis does not pertain to elements or aggregates, nor to subjects, relations, or structures. It pertains only to *lineaments* running through groups as well as individuals. Schizoanalysis, as the analysis of desire, is immediately practical and political, whether it is a question of an individual, group, or society. For politics precedes being. Practice does not come after the emplacement of the terms and their relations, but actively participates in the drawing of the lines; it confronts the same dangers and the same variations as the emplacement does. Schizoanalysis is like the art of the new. Or rather, there is no problem of application: the lines it brings out could equally be the lines of a life, a work of literature or art, or a society, depending on which system of coordinates is chosen.

Line of molar or rigid segmentarity, line of molecular or supple segmentation, line of flight—many problems arise. The first concerns the *particular character of each line*. It might be thought that rigid segments are socially determined, predetermined, overcoded by the State; there may be a tendency to construe supple segmentarity as an interior activity, something imaginary or phantasmic. As for the line of flight, would it not be entirely personal, the way in which an individual escapes on his or her own account, escapes "responsibilities," escapes the world, takes refuge in the desert, or else in art . . . ? False impression. Supple segmentarity has nothing to do with the imaginary, and micropolitics is no less extensive or real than macropolitics. Politics on the grand scale can never administer its molar segments without also dealing with the microinjections or infiltrations that work in its favor or present an obstacle to it; indeed, the larger the molar aggregates, the greater the molecularization of the agencies they put into play. Lines of flight, for their part, never consist in running away from the world but rather in causing runoffs, as when you drill a hole in a pipe; there is no social system that does not leak from all directions, even if it makes its segments increasingly rigid in order to seal the lines of flight. There is nothing imaginary, nothing symbolic, about a line of flight. There is nothing more active than a line of flight, among animals or humans.[13] Even History is forced to take that route rather than proceeding by "signifying breaks." What is escaping in a society at a given moment? It is on lines of flight that new weapons are invented, to be turned against the heavy arms of the State. "I may be running, but I'm looking for a gun as I go" (George Jackson). It was along lines of flight that the nomads swept away everything in their path and found new weapons, leaving the Pharaoh thunderstruck. It is possible for a single group, or a single individual even, to exhibit all the lines we have been discussing simultaneously. But it is most frequently the case that a single group or individual functions as a line of flight; that group or individual creates the line rather than following it, is itself the living weapon it forges rather than stealing one. Lines of flight are realities; they are very dangerous for societies, although they can get by without them, and sometimes manage to keep them to a minimum.

The second problem concerns *the respective importance of the lines*. You can begin with the rigid segmentarity, it's the easiest, it's pregiven; and then you can look at how and to what extent it is crosscut by a supple segmentarity, a kind of rhizome surrounding its roots. Then you can look at how the line of flight enters in. And alliances and battles. But it is also possible to begin with the line of flight: perhaps this is the primary line, with its absolute deterritorialization. It is clear that the line of flight *does not come afterward*; it is there from the beginning, even if it awaits its hour, and waits for the others to explode. Supple segmentarity, then, is only a kind of compromise operating by relative deterritorializations and permitting reterritorializations that cause blockages and reversions to the rigid line. It is odd how supple segmentarity is caught between the two other lines, ready to tip to one side or the other; such is its ambiguity. It is also necessary to look at the various combinations: it is quite possible that one group or individual's line of flight may not work to benefit that of another group or individual; it may on the contrary block it, plug it, throw it even deeper into rigid segmentarity. It can happen in love that one person's creative line is the other's imprisonment. The composition of the lines, of one line with another, is a problem, even of two lines of the same type. There is no assurance that two lines of flight will prove compatible, compossible. There is no assurance that the body without organs will be easy to compose. There is no assurance that a love, or a political approach, will withstand it.

Third problem: there is a *mutual immanence* of the lines. And it is not easy to sort them out. No one of them is transcendent, each is at work within the others. Immanence everywhere. Lines of flight are immanent to the social field. Supple segmentarity continually dismantles the concretions of rigid segmentarity, but everything that it dismantles it reassembles on its own level: micro-Oedipuses, microformations of power, microfascisms. The line of flight blasts the two segmentary series apart; but it is capable of the worst, of bouncing off the wall, falling into a black hole, taking the path of greatest regression, and in its vagaries reconstructing the most rigid of segments. Have you sown your wild oats? That is worse than not escaping at all: See Lawrence's reproach to Melville.[14] Between the matter of a dirty little secret in rigid segmentarity, the empty form of "What happened?" in supple segmentarity, and clandestinity of what can no longer happen on the line of flight, how can we fail to see the upheavals caused by a monster force, the Secret, threatening to bring everything tumbling down? Between the Couple of the first kind of segmentarity, the Double of the second, and the Clandestine of the line of flight, there are so many possible mixtures and passages.

There is one last problem, the most anguishing one, concerning *the dangers specific to each line*. There is not much to say about the danger confronting the first, for the chances are slim that its rigidification will fail. There is not much to say about the ambiguity of the second. But why is the line of flight, even aside from the danger it runs of reverting to one of the other two lines, imbued with such singular despair in spite of its message of joy, as if at the very moment things are coming to a resolution its undertaking were threatened by something reaching down to its core, by a death, a demolition? Shestov said of Chekhov, a great creator of novellas: "There can be practically no doubt that Chekhov exerted himself, and something broke inside him. And the overstrain came not from hard and heavy labor; no mighty overpowering exploit broke him: he stumbled and fell, he slipped. . . . The old Chekhov of gaiety and mirth is no more. . . . Instead, a morose and overshadowed man, a 'criminal.' "[15] *What happened?* Once again, this is the question facing all of Chekhov's characters. Is it not possible to exert oneself, and even break something, without falling into a black hole of bitterness and sand? But did Chekhov really fall? Is that not to judge him entirely from the outside? Was Chekhov not correct in saying that however grim his characters are, he still carries "a hundred pounds of love"? Of course, nothing is easy on the lines that compose us, and that constitute the essence of the Novella (*la Nouvelle*), and sometimes of Good News (*la Bonne Nouvelle*).

What are your couples, your doubles, your clandestines, and what are their mixes? When one person says to another, love the taste of whiskey on my lips like I love the gleam of madness in your eyes, what lines are they in the process of composing, or, on the contrary, making incompossible? Fitzgerald: "Perhaps fifty percent of our friends and relations will tell you in good faith that it was my drinking that drove Zelda mad, and the other half would assure you that it was her madness that drove me to drink. Neither of these judgments means much of anything. These two groups of friends and relations would be unanimous in saying that each of us would have been much better off without the other. The irony is that we have never been more in love with each other in all of our lives. She loves the alcohol on my lips. I cherish her most extravagant hallucinations." "In the end, nothing really had much importance. We destroyed ourselves. But in all honesty, I never thought we destroyed each other." Beautiful texts. All of the lines are there: the lines of family and friends, of all those who speak, explain, and psychoanalyze, assigning rights and wrongs, of the whole binary machine of the Couple, united or divided, in rigid segmentarity (50 percent). Then there is the line of supple segmentation, from which the alcoholic and the madwoman extract, as from a kiss on the lips and eyes, the multiplication of a double at the limit of what they can endure in their state and with the tacit understandings serving them as internal messages. Finally, there is a line of flight, all the more shared now that they are separated, or vice versa, each of them the clandestine of the other, a double all the more successful now that nothing has importance any longer, now that everything can begin anew, since they have been destroyed but not by each other. Nothing will enter memory, everything was on the lines, between the lines, in the AND that made one *and* the other imperceptible, without disjunction or conjunction but only a line of flight forever in the process of being drawn, toward a new acceptance, the opposite of renunciation or resignation—a new happiness?

9. 1933: Micropolitics and Segmentarity

Segmentarities (Overview of the Types)

We are segmented from all around and in every direction. The human being is a segmentary animal. Segmentarity is inherent to all the strata composing us. Dwelling, getting around, working, playing: life is spatially and socially segmented. The house is segmented according to its rooms' assigned purposes; streets, according to the order of the city; the factory, according to the nature of the work and operations performed in it. We are segmented in a *binary* fashion, following the great major dualist oppositions: social classes, but also men-women, adults-children, and so on. We are segmented in a *cir-*

cular fashion, in ever larger circles, ever wider disks or coronas, like Joyce's "letter": my affairs, my neighborhood's affairs, my city's, my country's, the world's . . . We are segmented in a *linear* fashion, along a straight line or a number of straight lines, of which each segment represents an episode or "proceeding": as soon as we finish one proceeding we begin another, forever proceduring or procedured, in the family, in school, in the army, on the job. School tells us, "You're not at home anymore"; the army tells us, "You're not in school anymore" . . . Sometimes the various segments belong to different individuals or groups, and sometimes the same individual or group passes from one segment to another. But these figures of segmentarity, the binary, circular, and linear, are bound up with one another, even cross over into each other, changing according to the point of view. This is already evident among "savage" peoples: Lizot shows how the communal House is organized in circular fashion, going from interior to exterior in a series of coronas within which certain types of localizable activities take place (worship and ceremonies, followed by exchange of goods, followed by family life, followed by trash and excrement); at the same time "each of these coronas is itself transversally divided, each segment devolves upon a particular lineage and is subdivided among different kinship groups."[1] In a more general context, Lévi-Strauss shows that the dualist organization of primitive peoples has a circular form, and also takes a linear form encompassing "any number of groups" (at least three).[2]

Why return to the primitives, when it is a question of our own life? The fact is that the notion of segmentarity was constructed by ethnologists to account for so-called primitive societies, which have no fixed, central State apparatus and no global power mechanisms or specialized political institutions. In these societies, the social segments have a certain leeway, between the two extreme poles of fusion and scission, depending on the task and the situation; there is also considerable communicability between heterogeneous elements, so that one segment can fit with another in a number of different ways; and they have a local construction excluding the prior determination of a base domain (economic, political, juridical, artistic); they have extrinsic and situational properties, or relations irreducible to the intrinsic properties of a structure; activity is continuous, so segmentarity is not grasped as something separate from a segmentation-in-progress operating by outgrowths, detachments, and mergings. Primitive segmentarity is characterized by a polyvocal *code* based on lineages and their varying situations and relations, and an itinerant *territoriality* based on local, overlapping divisions. Codes and territories, clan lineages and tribal territorialities, form a fabric of relatively supple segmentarity.[3]

However, it seems to us difficult to maintain that State societies, even our modern States, are any less segmentary. The classical opposition between segmentarity and centralization hardly seems relevant.[4] Not only does the State exercise power over the segments it sustains or permits to survive, but it possesses, and imposes, its own segmentarity. Perhaps the opposition sociologists establish between the segmentary and the central is biological deep down: the ringed worm, and the central nervous system. But the central brain itself is a worm, even more segmented than the others, in spite of and including all of its vicarious actions. There is no opposition between the central and the segmentary. The modern political system is a global whole, unified and unifying, but is so because it implies a constellation of juxtaposed, imbricated, ordered subsystems; the analysis of decision making brings to light all kinds of compartmentalizations and partial processes that interconnect, but not without gaps and displacements. Technocracy operates by the segmentary division of labor (this applies to the international division of labor as well). Bureaucracy exists only in compartmentalized offices and functions only by "goal displacements" and the corresponding "dysfunctions." Hierarchy is not simply pyramidal; the boss's office is as much at the end of the hall as on top of the tower. In short, we would say that modern life has not done away with segmentarity but has on the contrary made it exceptionally rigid.

Instead of setting up an opposition between the segmentary and the centralized, we should make a distinction between two types of segmentarity, one "primitive" and supple, the other "modern" and rigid. This distinction reframes each of the figures previously discussed.

1. Binary oppositions (men/women, those on top/those on the bottom, etc.) are very strong in primitive societies, but seem to be the result of machines and assemblages that are not in themselves binary. The social binarity between men and women in a group applies rules according to which both sexes must take their respective spouses from different groups (which is why there are at least three groups). Thus Lévi-Strauss can demonstrate that dualist organization never stands on its own in this kind of society. On the contrary, it is a particularity of modern societies, or rather State societies, to bring into their own duality machines that function as such, and proceed simultaneously by biunivocal relationships and successively by binarized choices. Classes and sexes come in twos, and phenomena of tripartition result from a transposition of the dual, not the reverse. We have already encountered this, notably in the case of the Face machine, which differs in this respect from primitive head machines. It seems that modern societies elevated dual segmentarity to the level of a self-sufficient organization. The question, therefore, is not whether the status of women, or those on the bottom, is better or worse, but the type of organization from which that status results.

2. Similarly, we may note that in primitive societies circular segmen-

tarity does not necessarily imply that the circles are concentric, or have the same center. In a supple regime, centers already act as so many *knots, eyes,* or *black holes*; but they do not all resonate together, they do not fall on the same point, they do not converge in the same black hole. There is a multiplicity of animist eyes, each of which is assigned, for example, a particular animal spirit (snake-spirit, woodpecker-spirit, cayman-spirit . . .). Each black hole is occupied by a different animal eye. Doubtless, we see operations of rigidification and centralization take shape here and there: all of the centers must collect on a single circle, which itself has a single center. The shaman draws lines between all the points or spirits, outlines a constellation, a radiating set of roots tied to a central tree. This is the birth of a centralized power with an arborescent system to discipline the outgrowths of the primitive rhizome.[5] Here, the tree simultaneously plays the role of a principle of dichotomy or binarity, and an axis of rotation. But the power of the shaman is still entirely localized, strictly dependent upon a particular segment, contingent upon drugs, and each point continues to emit independent sequences. The same cannot be said of modern societies, or even of States. Of course, the centralized is not opposed to the segmentary, and the circles remain distinct. But they become concentric, definitively arborified. The segmentarity becomes rigid, to the extent that all centers resonate in, and all black holes fall on, a single point of accumulation that is like a point of intersection somewhere behind the eyes. The face of the father, teacher, colonel, boss, enter into redundancy, refer back to a center of signifiance that moves across the various circles and passes back over all of the segments. The supple microheads with animal facializations are replaced by a macroface whose center is everywhere and circumference nowhere. There are no longer *n* eyes in the sky, or in becomings-animal and -vegetable, but a central computing eye scanning all of the radii. The central State is constituted not by the abolition of circular segmentarity but by a concentricity of distinct circles, or the organization of a resonance among centers. *There are already just as many power centers in primitive societies; or, if one prefers, there are still just as many in State societies.* The latter, however, behave as apparatuses of resonance; they organize resonance, whereas the former inhibit it.[6]

3. Finally, in the case of linear segmentarity, we would say that each segment is underscored, rectified, and homogenized in its own right, but also in relation to the others. Not only does each have its own unit of measure, but there is an equivalence and translatability between units. The central eye has as its correlate a space through which it moves, but it itself remains invariant in relation to its movements. With the Greek city-state and Cleisthenes' reform, a homogeneous and isotopic space appears that overcodes the lineal segments, at the same time as distinct focal points

begin to resonate in a center acting as their common denominator.[7] Paul Virilio shows that after the Greek city-state, the Roman Empire imposes a geometrical or *linear reason of State* including a general outline of camps and fortifications, a universal art of "marking boundaries by lines," a laying-out of territories, a substitution of space for places and territorialities, and a transformation of the world into the city; in short, an increasingly rigid segmentarity.[8] The segments, once underscored or overcoded, seem to lose their ability to bud, they seem to lose their dynamic relation to segmentations-in-progress, or in the act of coming together or coming apart. If there exists a primitive "geometry" (a protogeometry), it is an operative geometry in which figures are never separable from the affectations befalling them, the lines of their becoming, the segments of their segmentation: there is "roundness," but no circle, "alignments," but no straight line, etc. On the contrary, State geometry, or rather the bond between the State and geometry, manifests itself in the primacy of the theorem-element, which substitutes fixed or ideal essences for supple morphological formations, properties for affects, predetermined segments for segmentations-in-progress. Geometry and arithmetic take on the power of the scalpel. Private property implies a space that has been overcoded and gridded by surveying. Not only does each line have its segments, but the segments of one line correspond to those of another; for example, the wage regime establishes a correspondence between monetary segments, production segments, and consumable-goods segments.

We may summarize the principal differences between rigid segmentarity and supple segmentarity. In the rigid mode, binary segmentarity stands on its own and is governed by great machines of direct binarization, whereas in the other mode, binarities result from "multiplicities of *n* dimensions." Second, circular segmentarity tends to become concentric, in other words, causes all of its focal points to coincide in a single center that is in constant movement but remains invariant through its movements, and is part of a machine of resonance. Finally, linear segmentarity feeds into a machine of overcoding that constitutes *more geometrico* homogeneous space and extracts segments that are determinate as to their substance, form, and relations. It will be noted that this rigid segmentarity is always expressed by the Tree. The Tree is the knot of arborescence or principle of dichotomy; it is the axis of rotation guaranteeing concentricity; it is the structure or network gridding the possible. This opposition between arborified and rhizomatic segmentarity is not just meant to indicate two states of a single process, but also to isolate two different processes. For primitive societies operate essentially by codes and territorialities. It is in fact the distinction between these two elements, the tribal system of territories and the clan system of lineages, that prevents resonance.[9] Modern, or State, societies, on the other hand, have replaced the declining codes with a univocal overcoding, and the lost territories with a specific reterritorialization (which takes place in an overcoded geometrical space). Segmentarity is always the result of an abstract machine, but different abstract machines operate in the rigid and the supple.

It is not enough, therefore, to oppose the centralized to the segmentary. Nor is it enough to oppose two kinds of segmentarity, one supple and primitive, the other modern and rigidified. There is indeed a distinction between the two, but they are inseparable, they overlap, they are entangled. Primitive societies have nuclei of rigidity or arborification that as much anticipate the State as ward it off. Conversely, our societies are still suffused by a supple fabric without which their rigid segments would not hold. Supple segmentarity cannot be restricted to primitive peoples. It is not the vestige of the savage within us but a perfectly contemporary function, inseparable from the other. Every society, and every individual, are thus plied by both segmentarities simultaneously: one molar, the other *molecular.* If they are distinct, it is because they do not have the same terms or the same relations or the same nature or even the same type of multiplicity. If they are inseparable, it is because they coexist and cross over into each other. The configurations differ, for example, between the primitives and us, but the two segmentarities are always in presupposition. In short, everything is political, but every politics is simultaneously a *macropolitics* and a *micropolitics.* Take aggregates of the perception or feeling type: their molar organization, their rigid segmentarity, does not preclude the existence of an entire world of unconscious micropercepts, unconscious affects, fine segmentations that grasp or experience different things, are distributed and operate differently. There is a micropolitics of perception, affection, conversation, and so forth. If we consider the great binary aggregates, such as the sexes or classes, it is evident that they also cross over into molecular assemblages of a different nature, and that there is a double reciprocal dependency between them. For the two sexes imply a multiplicity of molecular combinations bringing into play not only the man in the woman and the woman in the man, but the relation of each to the animal, the plant, etc.: a thousand tiny sexes. And social classes themselves imply "masses" that do not have the same kind of movement, distribution, or objectives and do not wage the same kind of struggle. Attempts to distinguish mass from class effectively tend toward this limit: *the notion of mass is a molecular notion* operating according to a type of segmentation irreducible to the molar segmentarity of class. Yet classes are indeed fashioned from masses; they crystallize them. And masses are constantly flowing or leaking from classes. Their reciprocal presupposition, however, does not preclude a difference in viewpoint, nature, scale, and function (understood in this way, the notion of mass has entirely different connotations than Canetti's "crowd").

It is not sufficient to define bureaucracy by a rigid segmentarity with compartmentalization of contiguous offices, an office manager in each segment, and the corresponding centralization at the end of the hall or on top of the tower. For at the same time there is a whole bureaucratic segmentation, a suppleness of and communication between offices, a bureaucratic perversion, a permanent inventiveness or creativity practiced even against administrative regulations. If Kafka is the greatest theorist of bureaucracy, it is because he shows how, at a certain level (but which one? it is not localizable), the barriers between offices cease to be "a definite dividing line" and are immersed in a molecular medium (*milieu*) that dissolves them and simultaneously makes the office manager proliferate into microfigures impossible to recognize or identify, discernible only when they are centralizable: another regime, coexistent with the separation *and* totalization of the rigid segments.[10] We would even say that fascism implies a molecular regime that is distinct both from molar segments and their centralization. Doubtless, fascism invented the concept of the totalitarian State, but there is no reason to define fascism by a concept of its own devising: there are totalitarian States, of the Stalinist or military dictatorship type, that are not fascist. The concept of the totalitarian State applies only at the macropolitical level, to a rigid segmentarity and a particular mode of totalization and centralization. But fascism is inseparable from a proliferation of molecular focuses in interaction, which skip from point to point, *before* beginning to resonate together in the National Socialist State. Rural fascism and city or neighborhood fascism, youth fascism and war veteran's fascism, fascism of the Left and fascism of the Right, fascism of the couple, family, school, and office: every fascism is defined by a micro-black hole that stands on its own and communicates with the others, before resonating in a great, generalized central black hole.[11] There is fascism when a *war machine* is installed in each hole, in every niche. Even after the National Socialist State had been established, microfascisms persisted that gave it unequaled ability to act upon the "masses." Daniel Guérin is correct to say that if Hitler took power, rather then taking over the German State administration, it was because from the beginning he had at his disposal microorganizations giving him "an unequaled, irreplaceable ability to penetrate every cell of society," in other words, a molecular and supple segmentarity, flows capable of suffusing every kind of cell. Conversely, if capitalism came to consider the fascist experience as catastrophic, if it preferred to ally itself with Stalinist totalitarianism, which from its point of view was much more sensible and manageable, it was because the segmentarity and centralization of the latter was more classical and less fluid. What makes fascism dangerous is its molecular or micropolitical power, for it is a mass movement: a cancerous body rather than a totalitarian organism. American film has often depicted these molecular focal points; band, gang, sect, family, town, neighborhood, vehicle fascisms spare no one. Only microfascism provides an answer to the global question: Why does desire desire its own repression, how can it desire its own repression? The masses certainly do not passively submit to power; nor do they "want" to be repressed, in a kind of masochistic hysteria; nor are they tricked by an ideological lure. Desire is never separable from complex assemblages that necessarily tie into molecular levels, from microformations already shaping postures, attitudes, perceptions, expectations, semiotic systems, etc. Desire is never an undifferentiated instinctual energy, but itself results from a highly developed, engineered setup rich in interactions: a whole supple segmentarity that processes molecular energies and potentially gives desire a fascist determination. Leftist organizations will not be the last to secrete microfascisms. It's too easy to be antifascist on the molar level, and not even see the fascist inside you, the fascist you yourself sustain and nourish and cherish with molecules both personal and collective.

Four errors concerning this molecular and supple segmentarity are to be avoided. The first is axiological and consists in believing that a little suppleness is enough to make things "better." But microfascisms are what make fascism so dangerous, and fine segmentations are as harmful as the most rigid of segments. The second is psychological, as if the molecular were in the realm of the imagination and applied only to the individual and interindividual. But there is just as much social-Real on one line as on the other. Third, the two forms are not simply distinguished by size, as a small form and a large form; although it is true that the molecular works in detail and operates in small groups, this does not mean that it is any less coextensive with the entire social field than molar organization. Finally, the qualitative difference between the two lines does not preclude their boosting or cutting into each other; there is always a proportional relation between the two, directly or inversely proportional.

In the first case, the stronger the molar organization is, the more it induces a molecularization of its own elements, relations, and elementary apparatuses. When the machine becomes planetary or cosmic, there is an increasing tendency for assemblages to miniaturize, to become micro-assemblages. Following André Gorz's formula, the only remaining element of work left under world capitalism is the molecular, or molecularized, individual, in other words, the "mass" individual. The administration of a great organized molar security has as its correlate a whole micromanagement of petty fears, a permanent molecular insecurity, to the point that the motto of domestic policymakers might be: a macropolitics of society by and for a micropolitics of insecurity.[12] However, the second case is even more important: molecular movements do not complement but rather thwart and break through the great worldwide organization. That is what French President Valéry Giscard d'Estaing was saying in his military and political geography lesson: the more balanced things are between East and West, in an overcoding and overarmed dualist machine, the more "destabilized" they become along the other, North-South, line. There is always a Palestinian or Basque or Corsican to bring about a "regional destabilization of security."[13] The two great molar aggregates of the East and West are perpetually being undermined by a molecular segmentation causing a zigzag crack, making it difficult for them to keep their own segments in line. It is as if a line of flight, perhaps only a tiny trickle to begin with, leaked between the segments, escaping their centralization, eluding their totalization. The profound movements stirring in a society present themselves in this fashion, even if they are necessarily "represented" as a confrontation between molar segments. It is wrongly said (in Marxism in particular) that a society is defined by its contradictions. That is true only on the larger scale of things. From the viewpoint of micropolitics, a society is defined by its lines of flight, which are molecular. There is always something that flows or flees, that escapes the binary organizations, the resonance apparatus, and the overcoding machine: things that are attributed to a "change in values," the youth, women, the mad, etc. May 1968 in France was molecular, making what led up to it all the more imperceptible from the viewpoint of macropolitics. It happens that people who are very limited in outlook or are very old grasp the event better than the most advanced politicians, or politicians who consider themselves advanced from the viewpoint of organization. As Gabriel Tarde said, what one needs to know is which peasants, in which areas of the south of France, stopped greeting the local landowners. A very old, outdated landowner can in this case judge things better than a modernist. It was the same with May '68: those who evaluated things in macropolitical terms understood nothing of the event because something unaccountable was escaping. The politicians, the parties, the unions, many leftists, were utterly vexed; they kept repeating over and over again that "conditions" were not ripe. It was as though they had been temporarily deprived of the entire dualism machine that made them valid spokespeople. Bizarrely, de Gaulle, and even Pompidou, understood much more than the others. A molecular flow was escaping, minuscule at first, then swelling, without, however, ceasing to be unassignable. The reverse, however, is also true: molecular escapes and movements would be nothing if they did not return to the molar organizations to reshuffle their segments, their binary distributions of sexes, classes, and parties.

The issue is that the molar and the molecular are distinguished not by size, scale, or dimension but by the nature of the system of reference envisioned. Perhaps, then, the words "line" and "segment" should be reserved for molar organization, and other, more suitable, words should be sought for molecular composition. And in fact, whenever we can identify a well-defined *segmented line*, we notice that it continues in another form, as a *quantum flow*. And in every instance, we can locate a "power center" at the border between the two, defined not by an absolute exercise of power within its domain but by the relative adaptations and conversions it effects between the line and the flow. Take a monetary flow with segments. These segments can be defined from several points of view, for example, from the viewpoint of a corporate budget (real wages, net profit, management salaries, interest on assets, reserves, investments, etc.). Now this line of payment-money is linked to another aspect, namely, the flow of financing-money, which has, not segments, but rather poles, singularities, and quanta (the poles of the flow are the creation of money and its destruction; the singularities are nominal liquid assets; the quanta are inflation, deflation, stagflation, etc.). This has led some to speak of a "mutant, convulsive, creative and circulatory flow" tied to desire and always subjacent to the solid line and its segments determining interest rates and supply and demand.[14] In a balance of payment, we again encounter a binary segmentarity that distinguishes, for example, so-called autonomous operations from so-called compensatory operations. But movements of capital do not allow themselves to be segmented in this way; because they are "*the most thoroughly broken down*, according to their nature, duration, and the personality of the creditor or debtor," one "no longer has any idea where to draw the line when dealing with these flows."[15] Yet there is always a correlation between the two aspects since linearization and segmentation are where flows run dry, but are also their point of departure for a new creation. When we talk about banking power, concentrated most notably in the central banks, it is indeed a question of the relative power to regulate "as much as" possible the communication, conversion, and coadaptation of the two parts of the circuit. That is why power centers are defined much more by what escapes them or by their impotence than by their zone of power. In short, the molecular, or microeconomics, micropolitics, is defined not by the smallness of its elements but by the nature of its "mass"—the quantum flow as opposed to the molar segmented line.[16] The task of making the segments correspond to the quanta, of adjusting the segments to the quanta, implies hit-and-miss changes in rhythm and mode rather than any omnipotence; and something always escapes.

We could take other examples, such as the power of the Church. Church power has always been associated with a certain administration of sin possessing a strong segmentarity (the seven deadly sins), units of measure (how many times?), and rules of equivalence and atonement (confession, penance . . .). But there is also what might be called the molecular flow of sinfulness, something quite different yet complementary: it hugs close to the linear zone, as though negotiated through it, but itself has only poles (original sin-redemption or grace) and quanta ("that sin which is the default of consciousness of sin"; the sin of having a consciousness of sin; the sin of the consequence of having a consciousness of sin).[17] The same could be said of a flow of criminality, in contrast to the molar line of a legal code and its divisions. Or to take another example, discussions of military power, or the power of the army, consider a segmentable line broken down into types of war corresponding exactly to the States waging war and the political goals those States assign themselves (from "limited" war to "total" war). But following Clausewitz's intuition, the war machine is very different; it is a flow of *absolute* war stretching between an offensive and a defensive pole, and is marked only by quanta (psychic and material forces that are like the nominal liquid assets of war). We may say of the pure flow that it is abstract yet real; ideal yet effective; absolute yet "differentiated." It is true that the flow and its quanta can be grasped only by virtue of indexes on the segmented line, but conversely, that line and those indexes exist only by virtue of the flow suffusing them. In every case, it is evident that the segmented line (macropolitics) is immersed in and prolonged by quantum flows (micropolitics) that continually reshuffle and stir up its segments.

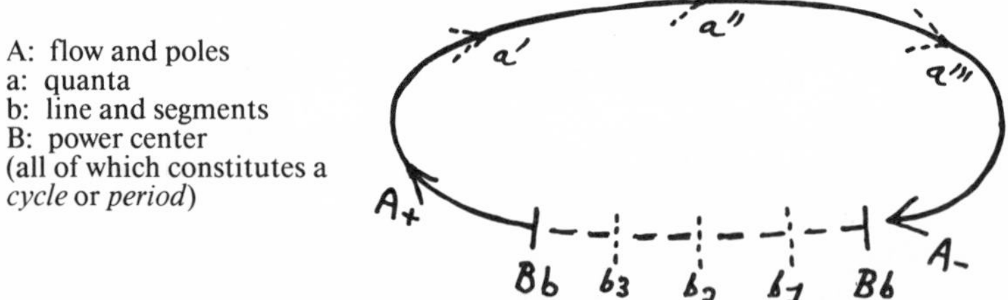

In homage to Gabriel Tarde (1843-1904): his long-forgotton work has assumed new relevance with the influence of American sociology, in particular microsociology. It had been quashed by Durkheim and his school (in polemics similar to and as harsh as Cuvier's against Geoffroy Saint-Hilaire). Durkheim's preferred objects of study were the great collective representations, which are generally binary, resonant, and overcoded. Tarde countered that collective representations presuppose exactly what needs explaining, namely, "the similarity of millions of people." That is why Tarde was interested instead in the world of detail, or of the infinitesimal: the little *imitations*, *oppositions*, and *inventions* constituting an entire realm of subrepresentative matter. Tarde's best work was his analyses of a minuscule bureaucratic innovation, or a linguistic innovation, etc. The Durkheimians answered that what Tarde did was psychology or interpsychology, not sociology. But that is true only in appearance, as a first approximation: a microimitation does seem to occur between two individuals. But at the same time, and at a deeper level, it has to do not with an individual but with a flow or a wave. *Imitation is the propagation of a flow; opposition is binarization, the making binary of flows; invention is a conjugation or connection of different flows.* What, according to Tarde, is a flow? It is belief or desire (the two aspects of every assemblage); a flow is always of belief and of desire. Beliefs and desires are the basis of every society, because they are flows and as such are "quantifiable"; they are veritable social Quantities, whereas sensations are qualitative and representations are simple resultants.[18] Infinitesimal imitation, opposition, and invention are therefore like flow quanta marking a propagation, binarization, or conjugation of beliefs and desires. Hence the importance of statistics, providing it concerns itself with the cutting edges and not only with the "stationary" zone of representations. For in the end, the difference is not at all between the social and the individual (or interindividual), but between the molar realm of representations, individual or collective, and the molecular realm of beliefs and desires in which the distinction between the social and the individual loses all meaning since flows are neither attributable to individuals nor overcodable by collective signifiers. Representations already define large-scale aggregates, or determine segments on a line; beliefs and desires, on the other hand, are flows marked by quanta, flows that are created, exhausted, or transformed, added to one another, subtracted or combined. Tarde invented microsociology and took it to its full breadth and scope, denouncing in advance the misinterpretations to which it would later fall victim.

This is how you tell the difference between the segmented line and the quantum flow. A mutant flow always implies something tending to elude or escape the codes; quanta are precisely signs or degrees of deterritorialization in the decoded flow. The rigid line, on the other hand, implies an overcoding that substitutes itself for the faltering codes; its segments are like reterritorializations on the overcoding or overcoded line. Let us return to the case of original sin: it is the very act of a flow marking a decoding in relation to creation (with just one last island preserved for the Virgin), and a deterritorialization in relation to the land of Adam; but it simultaneously performs an overcoding by binary organizations and resonance (Powers, Church, empires, rich-poor, men-women, etc.) and complementary reterritorializations (on the land of Cain, on work, on reproduction, on money . . .). Now the two systems of reference are in inverse relation to each other, in the sense that the first eludes the second, or the second arrests the first, prevents it from flowing further; but at the same time, they are strictly complementary and coexistent, because one exists only as a function of the other; yet they are different and in direct relation to each other, although corresponding term by term, because the second only effectively arrests the first on a "plane" that is not the plane specific to the first, while the momentum of the first continues on its own plane.

A social field is always animated by all kinds of movements of decoding and deterritorialization affecting "masses" and operating at different speeds and paces. These are not contradictions but escapes. At this level, everything is a question of *mass*. For example, from the tenth to the fourteenth centuries we see an acceleration of factors of decoding and deterritorialization: the masses of the last invaders swooping down from north, east, and south; military masses turned into pillaging bands; ecclesiastical masses confronted with infidels and heretics, and adopting increasingly deterritorialized objectives; peasant masses leaving the seigneurial domains; seigneurial masses forced to find means of exploitation less territorial than serfdom; urban masses breaking away from the backcountry and finding increasingly less territorialized social arrangements in the cities; women's masses detaching themselves from the old passional and conjugal code; monetary masses that cease to be a hoard object and inject themselves into great commercial circuits.[19] We may cite the Crusades as effecting a connection of flows, each boosting and accelerating the others (even the flow of femininity in the "faraway Princess," even the flow of children in the Crusades of the thirteenth century). But at the same time, and inseparably, there occur overcodings and reterritorializations. The Crusades were overcoded by the pope and assigned territorial objectives. The Holy Land, the Peace of God, a new type of abbey, new figures of money, new modes of exploitation of the peasant through leasehold and the wage system (or revivals of slavery), urban reterritorializations, etc., form a complex system. At this point, we must introduce a distinction between the two notions of *connection* and *conjugation* of flows. "Connection" indicates the way in which decoded and deterritorialized flows boost one another, accelerate their shared escape, and augment or stoke their quanta; the "conjugation" of these same flows, on the other hand, indicates their relative stoppage, like a point of accumulation that plugs or seals the lines of flight, performs a general reterritorialization, and brings the flows under the dominance of a single flow capable of overcoding them. But it is precisely the most deterritorialized flow, under the first aspect, that always brings about the accumulation or conjunction of the processes, determines the overcoding, and serves as the basis for reterritorialization under the second aspect (we have already encountered a theorem according to which it is always *on* the most deterritorialized element that reterritorialization takes place). For example, the merchant bourgeoisie of the cities conjugated or capitalized a domain of knowledge, a technology, assemblages and circuits into whose dependency the nobility, Church, artisans, and even peasants *would enter*. It is precisely because the bourgeoisie was a cutting edge of deterritorialization, a veritable particle accelerator, that it also performed an overall reterritorialization.

The task of the historian is to designate the "period" of coexistence or simultaneity of these two movements (decoding-deterritorialization and overcoding-reterritorialization). For the duration of this period, one distinguishes between the molecular aspect and the molar aspect: on the one hand, *masses or flows*, with their mutations, quanta of deterritorialization, connections, and accelerations; on the other hand, *classes or segments*, with their binary organization, resonance, conjunction or accumulation, and line of overcoding favoring one line over the others.[20] The difference between macrohistory and microhistory has nothing to do with the length of the durations envisioned, long or short, but rather concerns distinct systems of reference, depending on whether it is an overcoded segmented line that is under consideration or the mutant quantum flow. The rigid system does not bring the other system to a halt: the flow continues beneath the line, forever mutant, while the line totalizes. *Mass* and *class* do not have the same contours or the same dynamic, even though the same group can be assigned both signs. The bourgeoisie considered as a mass *and* as a class . . . The relations of a mass to other masses are not the same as the relations of the "corresponding" class to the other classes. Of course, there are just as many relations of force, and just as much violence, on one side as the other. The point is that the same struggle assumes two very different aspects, in relation to which the victories and defeats differ. Mass movements accelerate and feed into one another (or dim for a long while, enter long stupors), but jump from one class to another, undergo mutation, emanate or emit new quanta that then modify class relations, bring their overcoding and reterritorialization into question, and run new lines of flight in new directions. Beneath the self-reproduction of classes, there is always a variable map of masses. Politics operates by macrodecisions and binary choices, binarized interests; but the realm of the decidable remains very slim. Political decision making necessarily descends into a world of microdeterminations, attractions, and desires, which it must sound out or evaluate in a different fashion. Beneath linear conceptions and segmentary decisions, an evaluation of flows and their quanta. A curious passage by Michelet reproaches François I for having badly evaluated the flow of emigration bringing to France large numbers of people in struggle against the Church: François saw it only as an influx of potential soldiers, instead of perceiving a mass molecular flow which France could have used to its own advantage by leading a different Reformation than the one that occurred.[21] Problems are always like this. Good or bad, politics and its judgments are always molar, but it is the molecular and its assessment that makes it or breaks it.

Now we are in a better position to draw a map. If we return to a very general sense of the word "line," we see that there are not just two kinds of lines but three. First, a relatively supple line of interlaced codes and territorialities; that is why we started with so-called *primitive* segmentarity, in which the social space is constituted by territorial and lineal segmentations. Second, a rigid line, which brings about a dualist organization of segments, a concentricity of circles in resonance, and generalized overcoding; here, the social space implies a *State apparatus*. This system is different from the primitive system precisely because overcoding is not a stronger code, but a specific procedure different from that of codes (similarly, reterritorialization is not an added territory, but takes place in a different space than that of territories, namely, overcoded geometrical space). Third, one or several lines of flight, marked by quanta and defined by decoding and deterritorialization (there is always something like a *war machine* functioning on these lines).

This way of presenting things still has the disadvantage of making it seem as though primitive societies came first. In truth, codes are never separable from the movement of decoding, nor are territories from the vectors of deterritorialization traversing them. And overcoding and reterritorialization do not come after. It would be more accurate to say that there is a space in which the three kinds of closely intermingled lines coexist, tribes, empires, and war machines. We could also put it this way: lines of flight are primary, *or* the already-rigid segments are, and supple segmentations swing between the two. Take a proposition like the following one by the historian Pirenne about barbarian tribes: "The Barbarians did not spontaneously hurl themselves upon the Empire. They were pushed forward by the flood of the Hunnish advance, which in this way caused the whole series of invasions."[22] On one side, we have the rigid segmentarity of the Roman Empire, with its center of resonance and periphery, its State, its *pax romana*, its geometry, its camps, its *limes* (boundary lines). Then, on the horizon, there is an entirely different kind of line, the line of the nomads who come in off the steppes, venture a fluid and active escape, sow deterritorialization everywhere, launch flows whose quanta heat up and are swept along by a Stateless war machine. The migrant barbarians are indeed between the two: they come and go, cross and recross frontiers, pillage and ransom, but also integrate themselves and reterritorialize. At times they will subside into the empire, assigning themselves a segment of it, becoming mercenaries or confederates, settling down, occupying land or carving out their own State (the wise Visigoths). At other times, they will go over to the nomads, allying with them, becoming indiscernible (the brilliant Ostrogoths). Perhaps because they were constantly being defeated by the Huns and Visigoths, the Vandals ("zone-two Goths") drew a line of flight that made them as strong as their masters; they were the only band or mass to cross the Mediterranean. But they were also the ones who produced the most startling reterritorialization: an empire in Africa.[23] Thus it seems that the three lines do not only coexist, but transform themselves into one another, cross over into one another. Again, we have taken a summary example in which the lines are illustrated by different groups. What we have said applies all the more to cases in which all of the lines are in a single group, a single individual.

In view of this, it would be better to talk about simultaneous states of the abstract Machine. There is on the one hand an *abstract machine of overcoding:* it defines a rigid segmentarity, a macrosegmentarity, because it produces or rather reproduces segments, opposing them two by two, making all the centers resonate, and laying out a divisible, homogeneous space striated in all directions. This kind of abstract machine is linked to the State apparatus. We do not, however, equate it with the State apparatus itself. The abstract machine may be defined, for example, *more geometrico*, or under other conditions by an "axiomatic"; but the State apparatus is neither geometry nor axiomatics: it is only the assemblage of reterritorialization effectuating the overcoding machine within given limits and under given conditions. The most we can say is that the State apparatus tends increasingly to identify with the abstract machine it effectuates. This is where the notion of the totalitarian State becomes meaningful: a State becomes totalitarian when, instead of effectuating, within its own limits, the worldwide overcoding machine, it identifies with it, creating the conditions for "autarky," producing a reterritorialization by "closed vessel," in the artifice of the void (this is never an ideological operation, but rather an economic and political one).[24]

On the other hand, at the other pole, there is an abstract machine of mutation, which operates by decoding and deterritorialization. It is what draws the lines of flight: it steers the quantum flows, assures the connection-creation of flows, and emits new quanta. It itself is in a state of flight, and erects war machines on its lines. If it constitutes another pole, it is because molar or rigid segments always seal, plug, block the lines of flight, whereas this machine is always making them flow, "between" the rigid segments and in another, submolecular, direction. But between the two poles there is also a whole realm of properly molecular negotiation, translation, and transduction in which at times molar lines are already undermined by fissures and cracks, and at other times lines of flight are already drawn toward black holes, flow connections are already replaced by limitative conjunctions, and quanta emissions are already converted into center-points. All of this happens at the same time. It is at the same time that lines of flight connect and continue their intensities, whip particles-signs out of black holes; and also retreat into the swirl of micro-black holes or molecular conjunctions that interrupt them; or again, enter overcoded, concentricized, binarized, stable segments arrayed around a central black hole.

What is a center or focal point of power? Answering this question will illustrate the entanglement of the lines. We speak of the power of the army, Church, and school, of public and private power . . . Power centers obviously involve rigid segments. Each molar segment has one or more centers. It might be objected that the segments themselves presuppose a power center, as what distinguishes and unites them, sets them in opposition and makes them resonate. But there is no contradiction between the segmentary parts and the centralized apparatus. On the one hand, the most rigid of segmentarities does not preclude centralization: this is because the common central point is not where all the other points melt together, but instead acts as a point of resonance on the horizon, behind all the other points. The State is not a point taking all the others upon itself, but a resonance chamber for them all. Even when the State is totalitarian, its function as resonator for distinct centers and segments remains unchanged: the only difference is that it takes place under closed-vessel conditions that increase its internal reach, or couples "resonance" with a "forced movement." On the other hand, and conversely, the strictest of centralizations does not eradicate the distinctiveness of the centers, segments, and circles. When the overcoding line is drawn, it assures the prevalence of one segment, as such, over the other (in the case of binary segmentarity), gives a certain center a power of relative resonance over the others (in the case of circular segmentarity), and underscores the dominant segment through which it itself passes (in the case of linear segmentarity). Thus centralization is always hierarchical, but hierarchy is always segmentary.

Each power center is also molecular and exercises its power on a micrological fabric in which it exists only as diffuse, dispersed, geared down, miniaturized, perpetually displaced, acting by fine segmentation, working in detail and in the details of detail. Foucault's analysis of "disciplines" or micropowers (school, army, factory, hospital, etc.) testifies to these "focuses of instability" where groupings and accumulations confront each other, but also confront breakaways and escapes, and where inversions occur.[25] What we have is no longer The Schoolmaster but the monitor, the best student, the class dunce, the janitor, etc. No longer the general, but the junior officers, the noncommissioned officers, the soldier inside me, and also the malcontent: all have their own tendencies, poles, conflicts, and relations of force. Even the warrant officer and janitor are only invoked for explanatory purposes; for they have a molar side *and* a molecular side, and make us realize that the general or the landlord also had both sides all along. We would not say that the proper name loses its power when it enters these zones of indiscernibility, but that it takes on a new kind of power. To talk like Kafka, what we have is no longer the public official Klamm, but maybe his secretary Momus, or other molecular Klamms the differences between which, and with Klamm, are all the greater for no longer being assignable. ("[The officials] don't always stick to the same book, yet it isn't the books they change, but their places, and [they] have to squeeze past one another when they change places, because there's so little room." "This official is rarely very like Klamm, and if he were sitting in his own office at his own desk with his name on the door I would have no more doubt at all,"[26] says Barnabas, whose dream would be a uniquely molar segmentarity, no matter how rigid and horrendous, as the only guarantee of certainty and security. But he cannot but notice that the molar segments are necessarily immersed in the molecular soup that nourishes them and makes their outlines waver.) And every power center has this microtexture. The microtextures—not masochism—are what explain how the oppressed can take an active role in oppression: the workers of the rich nations actively participate in the exploitation of the Third World, the arming of dictatorships, and the pollution of the atmosphere.

This is not surprising since the texture lies between the line of overcoding with rigid segments and the ultimate quantum line. It continually swings between the two, now channeling the quantum line back into the segmented line, now causing flows and quanta to escape from the segmented line. This is the third aspect of power centers, or their limit. For the only purpose these centers have is to translate as best they can flow quanta into line segments (only segments are totalizable, in one way or another). But this is both the principle of their power and the basis of their impotence. Far from being opposites, power and impotence complement and reinforce each other in a kind of fascinating satisfaction that is found above all in the most mediocre Statesmen, and defines their "glory." For they extract glory from their shortsightedness, and power from their impotence, because it confirms that there is no choice. The only "great" Statesmen are those who connect with flows, like pilot-signs or particles-signs, and who emit quanta that get out of the black holes: it is not by chance that these men encounter each other only on lines of flight, in the act of drawing them, sounding them out, following them, or forging ahead of them, even though they may make a mistake and take a fall (Moses the Hebrew, Genseric the Vandal, Genghis the Mongol, Mao the Chinese . . .). But there is no Power regulating the flows themselves. No one dominates the growth of the "monetary mass," or money supply. If an image of the master or an idea of the State is projected outward to the limits of the universe, as if something had domination over flows as well as segments, and in the same manner, the result is a fictitious and ridiculous representation. The stock exchange gives a better image of flows and their quanta than does the State. Capitalists may be the masters of surplus value and its distribution, but they do not dominate the flows from which surplus value derives. Rather, power centers function at the points where flows are converted into segments: they are exchangers, converters, oscillators. Not that the segments themselves are governed by a decision-making power. We have seen, on the contrary, that segments (classes, for example) form at the conjunction of masses and deterritorialized flows and that the most deterritorialized flow determines the dominant segment; thus the dollar segment dominates currency, the bourgeoisie dominates capitalism, etc. Segments, then, are themselves governed by an abstract machine. But what power centers govern are the assemblages that effectuate that abstract machine, in other words, that continually adapt variations in mass and flow to the segments of the rigid line, as a function of a dominant segment and dominated segments. Much perverse invention can enter into the adaptations.

This is the sense in which we would speak, for example, of banking power (the World Bank, central banks, credit banks): if the flow of financing-money, or credit money, involves the mass of economic transactions, what banks govern is the conversion of the credit money that has been *created* into segmentary payment-money that is *appropriated*, in other words, coinage or State money for the purchase of goods that are themselves segmented (the importance of the interest rate in this respect). What banks govern is the conversion between the two kinds of money, and the conversion of the segments of the second kind into any given good.[27] The same could be said of every central power. Every central power has three aspects or zones: (1) its zone of power, relating to the segments of a solid rigid line; (2) its zone of indiscernibility, relating to its diffusion throughout a microphysical fabric; (3) its zone of impotence, relating to the flows and quanta it can only convert without being able to control or define. It is always from the depths of its impotence that each power center draws its power, hence their extreme maliciousness, and vanity. Better to be a tiny quantum flow than a molar converter, oscillator, or distributor! Returning to the example of money, the first zone is represented by the public central banks; the second by the "indefinite series of private relations between banks and borrowers"; the third by the desiring flow of money, whose quanta are defined by the mass of economic transactions. It is true that the same problems are reformulated at the level of these very transactions, in relation to other power centers. But the first zone of the power center is always defined by the State apparatus, which is the assemblage that effectuates the abstract machine of molar overcoding; the second is defined in the molecular fabric immersing this assemblage; the third by the abstract machine of mutation, flows, and quanta.

We cannot say that one of these three lines is bad and another good, by nature and necessarily. The study of the dangers of each line is the object of pragmatics or schizoanalysis, to the extent that it undertakes not to represent, interpret, or symbolize, but only to make maps and draw lines, marking their mixtures as well as their distinctions. According to Nietzsche's Zarathustra and Castaneda's Indian Don Juan, there are three or even four dangers: first, Fear, then Clarity, then Power, and finally the great Disgust, the longing to kill and to die, the Passion for abolition.[28] We can guess what fear is. We are always afraid of losing. Our security, the great molar organization that sustains us, the arborescences we cling to, the binary machines that give us a well-defined status, the resonances we enter into, the system of overcoding that dominates us—we desire all that. "The values, morals, fatherlands, religions and private certitudes our vanity and self-complacency generously grant us are so many abodes the world furnishes for those who think on that account that they stand and rest amid stable things; they know nothing of the enormous rout they are heading for . . . *in flight from flight*."[29] We flee from flight, rigidify our segments, give ourselves over to binary logic; the harder they have been to us on one segment, the harder we will be on another; we reterritorialize on anything available; the only segmentarity we know is molar, at the level of the large-scale aggregates we belong to, as well as at the level of the little groups we get into, as well as at the level of what goes on in our most intimate and private recesses. Everything is involved: modes of perception, kinds of actions, ways of moving, life-styles, semiotic regimes. A man comes home and says, "Is the grub ready?", and the wife answers, "What a scowl! Are you in a bad mood?": two rigid segments in confrontation. The more rigid the segmentarity, the more reassuring it is for us. That is what fear is, and how it makes us retreat into the first line.

The second danger, Clarity, seems less obvious. Clarity, in effect, concerns the molecular. Once again, everything is involved, even perception, even the semiotic regime, but this time on the second line. Castaneda illustrates, for example, the existence of a molecular perception to which drugs give us access (but so many things can be drugs): we attain a visual and sonorous microperception revealing spaces and voids, like holes in the molar structure. That is precisely what clarity is: the distinctions that appear in what used to seem full, the holes in what used to be compact; and conversely, where just before we saw end points of clear-cut segments, now there are indistinct fringes, encroachments, overlappings, migrations, acts of segmentation that no longer coincide with the rigid segmentarity. Everything now appears supple, with holes in fullness, nebulas in forms, and flutter in lines. Everything has the clarity of the microscope. We think we have understood everything, and draw conclusions. We are the new knights; we even have a mission. A microphysics of the migrant has replaced the macrogeometry of the sedentary. But this suppleness and clarity do not only present dangers, they are themselves a danger. First, supple segmentarity runs the risk of reproducing in miniature the affections, the affectations, of the rigid: the family is replaced by a community, conjugality by a regime of exchange and migration; worse, micro-Oedipuses crop up, microfascisms lay down the law, the mother feels obliged to titillate her child, the father becomes a mommy. A dark light that falls from no star and emanates such sadness: this shifting segmentarity derives directly from the most rigid, for which it is indirect compensation. The more molar the aggregates become, the more molecular become their elements and the relations between their elements: molecular man for molar humanity. One deterritorializes, massifies, but only in order to knot and annul the mass movements and movements of deterritorialization, to invent all kinds of marginal reterritorializations even worse than the others. But above all, supple segmentarity brings dangers of its own that do not merely reproduce in small scale the dangers of molar segmentarity, which do not derive from them or compensate for them. As we have seen, microfascisms have a specificity of their own that can crystallize into a macrofascism, but may also float along the supple line on their own account and suffuse every little cell. A multitude of black holes may very well not become centralized, and acts instead as viruses adapting to the most varied situations, sinking voids in molecular perceptions and semiotics. Interactions without resonance. Instead of the great paranoid fear, we are trapped in a thousand little monomanias, self-evident truths, and clarities that gush from every black hole and no longer form a system, but are only rumble and buzz, blinding lights giving any and everybody the mission of self-appointed judge, dispenser of justice, policeman, neighborhood SS man. We have overcome fear, we have sailed from the shores of security, only to enter a system that is no less concentricized, no less organized: the system of petty insecurities that leads everyone to their own black hole in which to turn dangerous, possessing a clarity on their situation, role, and mission even more disturbing than the certitudes of the first line.

Power (*Pouvoir*) is the third danger, because it is on both lines simultaneously. It stretches from the rigid segments with their overcoding and resonance to the fine segmentations with their diffusion and interactions, and back again. Every man of power jumps from one line to the other, alternating between a petty and a lofty style, the rogue's style and the grandiloquent style, drugstore demagoguery and the imperialism of the high-ranking government man. But this whole chain and web of power is immersed in a world of mutant flows that eludes them. It is precisely its impotence that makes power so dangerous. The man of power will always want to stop the lines of flight, and to this end to trap and stabilize the mutation machine in the overcoding machine. But he can do so only by creating a void, in other words, by first stabilizing the overcoding machine itself by containing it within the local assemblage charged with effectuating it, in short, by giving the assemblage the dimensions of the machine. This is what takes place in the artificial conditions of totalitarianism or the "closed vessel."

But there is a fourth danger as well, and this is the one that interests us most, because it concerns the lines of flight themselves. We may well have presented these lines as a sort of mutation or creation drawn not only in the imagination but also in the very fabric of social reality; we may well have attributed to them the movement of the arrow and the speed of an absolute—but it would be oversimplifying to believe that the only risk they fear and confront is allowing themselves to be recaptured in the end, letting themselves be sealed in, tied up, reknotted, reterritorialized. They themselves emanate a strange despair, like an odor of death and immolation, a state of war from which one returns broken: they have their own dangers distinct from the ones previously discussed. This is exactly what led Fitzgerald to say: "I had a feeling that I was standing at twilight on a deserted range, with an empty rifle in my hands and the targets down. No problem set—simply a silence with only the sound of my own breathing. . . . My self-immolation was something sodden-dark."[30] Why is the line of flight a war one risks coming back from defeated, destroyed, after having destroyed everything one could? This, precisely, is the fourth danger: the line of flight crossing the wall, getting out of the black holes, but instead of connecting with other lines and each time augmenting its valence, *turning to destruction, abolition pure and simple, the passion of abolition.* Like Kleist's line of flight, and the strange war he wages; like suicide, double suicide, a way out that turns the line of flight into a line of death.

We are not invoking any kind of death drive. There are no internal drives in desire, only assemblages. Desire is always assembled; it is what the assemblage determines it to be. The assemblage that draws lines of flight is on the same level as they are, and is of the war machine type. Mutations spring from this machine, *which in no way has war as its object*, but rather the emission of quanta of deterritorialization, the passage of mutant flows (in this sense, every creation is brought about by a war machine). There are many reasons to believe that the war machine is of a different origin, is a different assemblage, than the State apparatus. It is of nomadic origin and is directed against the State apparatus. One of the fundamental problems of the State is to appropriate this war machine that is foreign to it and make it a piece in its apparatus, in the form of a stable military institution; and the State has always encountered major difficulties in this. It is precisely when the war machine has reached the point that it has no other object but war, it is when it substitutes destruction for mutation, that it frees the most catastrophic charge. Mutation is in no way a transformation of war; on the contrary, war is like the fall or failure of mutation, the only object left for the war machine after it has lost its power to change. War, it must be said, is only the abominable residue of the war machine, either after it has allowed itself to be appropriated by the State apparatus, or even worse, has constructed itself a State apparatus capable only of destruction. When this happens, the war machine no longer draws mutant lines of flight, but a pure, cold line of abolition. (Later, we will propose a theory of the complex relation between the war machine and war.)[31]

This brings us back to the paradox of fascism, and the way in which fascism differs from totalitarianism. For totalitarianism is a State affair: it essentially concerns the relation between the State as a localized assemblage and the abstract machine of overcoding it effectuates. Even in the case of a military dictatorship, it is a State army, not a war machine, that takes power and elevates the State to the totalitarian stage. Totalitarianism is quintessentially conservative. Fascism, on the other hand, involves a war machine. When fascism builds itself a totalitarian State, it is not in the sense of a State army taking power, but of a war machine taking over the State. A bizarre remark by Virilio puts us on the trail: in fascism, the State is far less totalitarian than it is *suicidal*. There is in fascism a realized nihilism. Unlike the totalitarian State, which does its utmost to seal all possible lines of flight, fascism is constructed on an intense line of flight, which it transforms into a line of pure destruction and abolition. It is curious that from the very beginning the Nazis announced to Germany what they were bringing: at once wedding bells and death, including their own death, and the death of the Germans. They thought they would perish but that their undertaking would be resumed, all across Europe, all over the world, throughout the solar system. And the people cheered, not because they did not understand, but because they wanted that death through the death of others. Like a will to wager everything you have every hand, to stake your own death against the death of others, and measure everything by "deleometers." Klaus Mann's novel, *Mephisto*, gives samplings of entirely ordinary Nazi speeches and conversations: "Heroism was something that was being ruled out of our lives. . . . In reality, we are not marching forward, we are reeling, staggering. Our beloved Führer is dragging us toward the shades of darkness and everlasting nothingness. How can we poets, we who have a special affinity for darkness and lower depths, not admire him? . . . Fires blazing on the horizon; rivers of blood in all the streets; and the frenzied dancing of the survivors, of *those who are still spared, around the bodies of the dead*!"[32] Suicide is presented not as a punishment but as the crowning glory of the death of others. One can always say that it is just a matter of foggy talk and ideology, nothing but ideology. But that is not true. The insufficiency of economic and political definitions of fascism does not simply imply a need to tack on vague, so-called ideological determinations. We prefer to follow Faye's inquiry into the precise formation of Nazi statements, which are just as much in evidence in politics and economics as in the most absurd of conversations. They always contain the "stupid and repugnant" cry, *Long live death!*, even at the economic level, where the arms expansion replaces growth in consumption and where investment veers from the means of production toward the means of pure destruction. Paul Virilio's analysis strikes us as entirely correct in defining fascism not by the notion of the totalitarian State but by the notion of the suicidal State: so-called total war seems less a State undertaking than an undertaking of a war machine that appropriates the State and channels into it a flow of absolute war whose only possible outcome is the suicide of the State itself. "The triggering of a hitherto unknown material process, one that is limitless and aimless. . . . Once triggered, its mechanism cannot stop at peace, for the indirect strategy effectively places the dominant powers outside the usual categories of space and time. . . . It was in the horror of daily life and its environment that Hitler finally found his surest means of governing, the legitimation of his policies and military strategy; and it lasted right up to the end, for the ruins and horrors and crimes and chaos of total war, far from discharging the repulsive nature of its power, normally only increase its scope. Telegram 71 is the normal outcome: *If the war is lost, may the nation perish.* Here, Hitler decides to join forces with his enemies in order to complete the destruction of his own people, by obliterating the last remaining resources of its life-support system, civil reserves of every kind (potable water, fuel, provisions, etc.)."[33] It was this reversion of the line of flight into a line of destruction that already animated the molecular focuses of fascism, and made them interact in a war machine instead of resonating in a State apparatus. *A war machine that no longer had war as its object* and would rather annihilate its own servants than stop the destruction. All the dangers of the other lines pale by comparison.

10. 1730: Becoming-Intense, Becoming-Animal, Becoming-Imperceptible . . .

Memories of a Moviegoer. I recall the fine film *Willard* (1972, Daniel Mann). A "B" movie perhaps, but a fine unpopular film: unpopular because the heroes are rats. My memory of it is not necessarily accurate. I will recount the story in broad outline. Willard lives with his authoritarian mother in the old family house. Dreadful Oedipal atmosphere. His mother orders him to destroy a litter of rats. He spares one (or two or several). After a violent argument, the mother, who "resembles" a dog, dies. The house is coveted by a businessman, and Willard is in danger of losing it. He likes the principal rat he saved, Ben, who proves to be of prodigious intelligence. There is also a white female rat, Ben's companion. Willard spends all his free time with them. They multiply. Willard takes the rat pack, led by Ben, to the home of the businessman, who is put to a terrible death. But he foolishly takes his two favorites to the office with him and has no choice but to let the employees kill the white rat. Ben escapes, after throwing Willard a long, hard glare. Willard then experiences a pause in his destiny, in his *becoming-rat*. He tries with all his might to remain among humans. He even responds to the advances of a young woman in the office who bears a strong "resemblance" to a rat—but it is only a resemblance. One day when he has invited the young woman over, all set to be conjugalized, reoedipalized, Ben suddenly reappears, full of hate. Willard tries to drive him away, but succeeds only in driving away the young woman: he then is lured to the basement by Ben, where a pack of countless rats is waiting to tear him to shreds. It is like a tale; it is never disturbing.

It is all there: there is a becoming-animal not content to proceed by resemblance and for which resemblance, on the contrary, would represent an obstacle or stoppage; the proliferation of rats, the pack, brings a becoming-molecular that undermines the great molar powers of family, career, and conjugality; there is a sinister choice since there is a "favorite" in the pack with which a kind of contract of alliance, a hideous pact, is made; there is the institution of an assemblage, a war machine or criminal machine, which can reach the point of self-destruction; there is a circulation of impersonal affects, an alternate current that disrupts signifying projects as well as subjective feelings, and constitutes a nonhuman sexuality; and there is an irresistible deterritorialization that forestalls attempts at professional, conjugal, or Oedipal reterritorialization. (Are there Oedipal animals with which one can "play Oedipus," play family, my little dog, my little cat, and then other animals that by contrast draw us into an irresistible becoming? Or another hypothesis: Can the same animal be taken up by two opposing functions and movements, depending on the case?)

Memories of a Naturalist. One of the main problems of natural history was to conceptualize the relationships between animals. It is very different in this respect from later evolutionism, which defined itself in terms of genealogy, kinship, descent, and filiation. As we know, evolutionism would arrive at the idea of an evolution that does not necessarily operate by filiation. But it was unavoidable that it begin with the genealogical motif. Darwin himself treats the evolutionist theme of kinship and the naturalist theme of the sum and value of differences or resemblances as very separate things: groups that are equally related can display highly variable degrees of difference with respect to the ancestor. Precisely because natural history is concerned primarily with the sum and value of differences, it can conceive of progressions and regressions, continuities and major breaks, but not an evolution in the strict sense, in other words, the possibility of a descent the *degrees* of modification of which depend on external conditions. Natural history can think only in terms of relationships (between A and B), not in terms of production (from A to *x*).

But something very important transpires at the level of relationships. For natural history conceives of the relationships between animals in two ways: series and structure. In the case of a series, I say *a* resembles *b*, *b* resembles *c*, etc.; all of these terms conform in varying degrees to a single, eminent term, perfection, or quality as the principle behind the series. This is exactly what the theologians used to call an analogy of proportion. In the case of a structure, I say *a* is to *b* as *c* is to *d;* and each of these relationships realizes after its fashion the perfection under consideration: gills are to breathing under water as lungs are to breathing air; or the heart is to gills as the absence of a heart is to tracheas [in insects] . . . This is an analogy of proportionality. In the first case, I have resemblances that differ from one another in a single series, and between series. In the second case, I have differences that resemble each other within a single structure, and between structures. The first form of analogy passes for the most sensible and popular, and requires imagination; but the kind of imagination it requires is a studious one that has to take branchings in the series into account, fill in apparent ruptures, ward off false resemblances and graduate the true ones, and take both progressions and regressions or degraduations into account. The second form of analogy is considered royal because it requires instead all the resources of understanding (*entendement*), in order to define equivalent relations by discovering, on the one hand, the independent variables that can be combined to form a structure and, on the other hand, the correlates that entail one another within each structure. As different as they are, the two themes of series and structure have always coexisted in natural history; in appearance contradictory, in practice they have reached a more or less stable compromise.[1] In the same way, the two figures of analogy coexisted in the minds of the theologians in various equilibriums. This is because in both cases Nature is conceived as an enormous *mimesis:* either in the form of a chain of beings perpetually imitating one another, progressively and regressively, and tending toward the divine higher term they all imitate by graduated resemblance, as the model for and principle behind the series; or in the form of a mirror Imitation with nothing left to imitate because it itself is the model everything else imitates, this time by ordered difference. (This mimetic or mimological vision is what made the idea of an evolution-production possible at that moment.)

This problem is in no way behind us. Ideas do not die. Not that they survive simply as archaisms. At a given moment they may reach a scientific stage, and then lose that status or emigrate to other sciences. Their application and status, even their form and content, may change; yet they retain something essential throughout the process, across the displacement, in the distribution of a new domain. Ideas are always reusable, because they have been usable before, but in the most varied of actual modes. For, on the one hand, the relationships between animals are the object not only of science but also of dreams, symbolism, art and poetry, practice and practical use. And on the other hand, the relationships between animals are bound up with the relations between man and animal, man and woman, man and child, man and the elements, man and the physical and microphysical universe. The twofold idea "series-structure" crosses a scientific threshold at a certain moment; but it did not start there and it does not stay there, or else crosses over into other sciences, animating, for example, the human sciences, serving in the study of dreams, myths, and organizations. The history of ideas should never be continuous; it should be wary of resemblances, but also of descents or filiations; it should be content to mark the thresholds through which an idea passes, the journeys it takes that change its nature or object. Yet the objective relationships between animals have been applied to certain subjective relations between man and animal, from the standpoint of a collective imagination or a faculty of social understanding.

Jung elaborated a theory of the Archetype as collective unconscious; it assigns the animal a particularly important role in dreams, myths, and human collectivities. The animal is inseparable from a *series* exhibiting the double aspect of progression-regression, in which each term plays the role of a possible transformer of the libido (metamorphosis). A whole approach to the dream follows from this; given a troubling image, it becomes a question of integrating it into its archetypal series. That series may include feminine, masculine, or infantile sequences, as well as animal, vegetable, even elementary or molecular sequences. In contrast to natural history, man is now no longer the eminent term of the series; that term may be an animal for man, the lion, crab, bird of prey, or louse, in relation to a given act or function, in accordance with a given demand of the unconscious.

Bachelard wrote a fine Jungian book when he elaborated the ramified series of Lautréamont, taking into account the speed coefficient of the metamorphoses and the degree of perfection of each term in relation to a pure aggressiveness as the principle of the series: the serpent's fang, the horn of the rhinoceros, the dog's tooth, the owl's beak; and higher up, the claw of the eagle or the vulture, the pincer of the crab, the legs of the louse, the suckers of the octopus. Throughout Jung's work a process of mimesis brings nature and culture together in its net, by means of analogies of proportion in which the series and their terms, and above all the animals occupying a middle position, assure cycles of conversion nature-culture-nature: archetypes as "analogical representations."[2]

Is it by chance that structuralism so strongly denounced the prestige accorded the imagination, the establishment of resemblances in a series, the imitation pervading the entire series and carrying it to its term, and the identification with this final term? Nothing is more explicit than Lévi-Strauss's famous texts on totemism: transcend external resemblances to arrive at *internal homologies*.[3] It is no longer a question of instituting a serial organization of the imaginary, but instead a symbolic and structural order of understanding. It is no longer a question of graduating resemblances, ultimately arriving at an identification between Man and Animal at the heart of a mystical participation. It is a question of ordering differences to arrive at a correspondence of relations. The animal is distributed according to differential relations or distinctive oppositions between species; the same goes for human beings, according to the groups considered. When analyzing the institution of the totem, we do not say that this group of people identifies with that animal species. We say that what group A is to group B, species A′ is to species B′. This method is profoundly different from the preceding one: given two human groups, each with its totem animal, we must discover the way in which the two totems entertain relations analogous to those between the two groups—the Crow is to the Falcon . . .

The method also applies to Man-child, man-woman relations, etc. If we note, for example, that the warrior has a certain astonishing relation to the young woman, we refrain from establishing an imaginary series tying the two together; instead, we look for a term effecting an equivalence of relations. Thus Vernant can say that marriage is to the woman what war is to the man. The result is a homology between the virgin who refuses marriage and the warrior who disguises himself as a woman.[4] In short, symbolic understanding replaces the analogy of proportion with an analogy of proportionality; the serialization of resemblances with a structuration of differences; the identification of terms with an equality of relations; the metamorphoses of the imagination with conceptual metaphors; the great continuity between nature and culture with a deep rift distributing correspondences without resemblance between the two; the imitation of a primal model with a mimesis that is itself primary and without a model. A man can never say: "I am a bull, a wolf . . ." But he can say: "I am to a woman what the bull is to a cow, I am to another man what the wolf is to the sheep." Structuralism represents a great revolution; the whole world becomes more rational. Lévi-Strauss is not content to grant the structural model all the prestige of a true classification system; he relegates the serial model to the dark domain of sacrifice, which he depicts as illusory, even devoid of good sense. The *serial theme of sacrifice* must yield to the *structural theme of the institution of the totem*, correctly understood. But here, as in natural history, many compromises are reached between archetypal series and symbolic structures.[5]

Memories of a Bergsonian. None of the preceding satisfies us, from our restricted viewpoint. We believe in the existence of very special becomings-animal traversing human beings and sweeping them away, affecting the animal no less than the human. "From 1730 to 1735, all we hear about are vampires." Structuralism clearly does not account for these becomings, since it is designed precisely to deny or at least denigrate their existence: a correspondence of relations does not add up to a becoming. When structuralism encounters becomings of this kind pervading a society, it sees them only as phenomena of degradation representing a deviation from the true order and pertaining to the adventures of diachrony. Yet in his study of myths, Lévi-Strauss is always encountering these rapid acts by which a human becomes animal at the same time as the animal becomes . . . (Becomes what? Human, or something else?). It is always possible to try to explain these *blocks of becoming* by a correspondence between two relations, but to do so most certainly impoverishes the phenomenon under study. Must it not be admitted that myth as a frame of classification is quite incapable of registering these becomings, which are more like fragments of tales? Must we not lend credence to Jean Duvignaud's hypothesis that there are "anomic" phenomena pervading societies that are not degradations of the mythic order but irreducible dynamisms drawing lines of flight and implying other forms of expression than those of myth, even if myth recapitulates them in its own terms in order to curb them?[6] Does it not seem that alongside the two models, sacrifice and series, totem institution and structure, there is still room for something else, something more secret, more subterranean: *the sorcerer* and becomings (expressed in tales instead of myths or rites)?

A becoming is not a correspondence between relations. But neither is it a resemblance, an imitation, or, at the limit, an identification. The whole structuralist critique of the series seems irrefutable. To become is not to progress or regress along a series. Above all, becoming does not occur in the imagination, even when the imagination reaches the highest cosmic or dynamic level, as in Jung or Bachelard. Becomings-animal are neither dreams nor phantasies. They are perfectly real. But which reality is at issue here? For if becoming animal does not consist in playing animal or imitating an animal, it is clear that the human being does not "really" become an animal any more than the animal "really" becomes something else. Becoming produces nothing other than itself. We fall into a false alternative if we say that you either imitate or you are. What is real is the becoming itself, the block of becoming, not the supposedly fixed terms through which that which becomes passes. Becoming can and should be qualified as becoming-animal even in the absence of a term that would be the animal become. The becoming-animal of the human being is real, even if the animal the human being becomes is not; and the becoming-other of the animal is real, even if that something other it becomes is not. This is the point to clarify: that a becoming lacks a subject distinct from itself; but also that it has no term, since its term in turn exists only as taken up in another becoming of which it is the subject, and which coexists, forms a block, with the first. This is the principle according to which there is a reality specific to becoming (the Bergsonian idea of a coexistence of very different "durations," superior or inferior to "ours," all of them in communication).

Finally, becoming is not an evolution, at least not an evolution by descent and filiation. Becoming produces nothing by filiation; all filiation is imaginary. Becoming is always of a different order than filiation. It concerns alliance. If evolution includes any veritable becomings, it is in the domain of *symbioses* that bring into play beings of totally different scales and kingdoms, with no possible filiation. There is a block of becoming that snaps up the wasp and the orchid, but from which no wasp-orchid can ever descend. There is a block of becoming that takes hold of the cat and baboon, the alliance between which is effected by a C virus. There is a block of becoming between young roots and certain microorganisms, the alliance between which is effected by the materials synthesized in the leaves (rhizosphere). If there is originality in neoevolutionism, it is attributable in part to phenomena of this kind in which evolution does not go from something less differentiated to something more differentiated, in which it ceases to be a hereditary filiative evolution, becoming communicative or contagious. Accordingly, the term we would prefer for this form of evolution between heterogeneous terms is "involution," on the condition that involution is in no way confused with regression. Becoming is involutionary, involution is creative. To regress is to move in the direction of something less differentiated. But to involve is to form a block that runs its own line "between" the terms in play and beneath assignable relations.

Neoevolutionism seems important for two reasons: the animal is defined not by characteristics (specific, generic, etc.) but by populations that vary from milieu to milieu or within the same milieu; movement occurs not only, or not primarily, by filiative productions but also by transversal communications between heterogeneous populations. Becoming is a rhizome, not a classificatory or genealogical tree. Becoming is certainly not imitating, or identifying with something; neither is it regressing-progressing; neither is it corresponding, establishing corresponding relations; neither is it producing, producing a filiation or producing through filiation. Becoming is a verb with a consistency all its own; it does not reduce to, or lead back to, "appearing," "being," "equaling," or "producing."

Memories of a Sorcerer, I. A becoming-animal always involves a pack, a band, a population, a peopling, in short, a multiplicity. We sorcerers have always known that. It may very well be that other agencies, moreover very different from one another, have a different appraisal of the animal. One may retain or extract from the animal certain characteristics: species and genera, forms and functions, etc. Society and the State need animal characteristics to use for classifying people; natural history and science need characteristics in order to classify the animals themselves. Serialism and structuralism either graduate characteristics according to their resemblances, or order them according to their differences. Animal characteristics can be mythic or scientific. But we are not interested in characteristics; what interests us are modes of expansion, propagation, occupation, contagion, peopling. I am legion. The Wolf-Man fascinated by several wolves watching him. What would a lone wolf be? Or a whale, a louse, a rat, a fly? Beelzebub is the Devil, but the Devil as lord of the flies. The wolf is not fundamentally a characteristic or a certain number of characteristics; it is a wolfing. The louse is a lousing, and so on. What is a cry independent of the population it appeals to or takes as its witness? Virginia Woolfs experiences herself not as a monkey or a fish but as a troop of monkeys, a school of fish, according to her variable relations of becoming with the people she approaches. We do not wish to say that certain animals live in packs. We want nothing to do with ridiculous evolutionary classifications à la Lorenz, according to which there are inferior packs and superior societies. What we are saying is that every animal is fundamentally a band, a pack. That it has pack modes, rather than characteristics, even if further distinctions within these modes are called for. It is at this point that the human being encounters the animal. We do not become animal without a fascination for the pack, for multiplicity. A fascination for the outside? Or is the multiplicity that fascinates us already related to a multiplicity dwelling within us? In one of his masterpieces, H. P. Lovecraft recounts the story of Randolph Carter, who feels his "self" reel and who experiences a fear worse than that of annihilation: "Carters of forms both human and non-human, vertebrate and invertebrate, conscious and mindless, animal and vegetable. And more, there were Carters having nothing in common with earthly life, but moving outrageously amidst backgrounds of other planets and systems and galaxies and cosmic continua. . . . Merging with nothingness is peaceful oblivion; but to be aware of existence and yet to know that one is no longer a definite being distinguished from other beings," nor from all of the becomings running through us, "that is the nameless summit of agony and dread."[7] Hofmannsthal, or rather Lord Chandos, becomes fascinated with a "people" of dying rats, and it is in him, through him, in the interstices of his disrupted self that the "soul of the animal bares its teeth at monsterous fate":[8] not pity, but *unnatural participation*. Then a strange imperative wells up in him: either stop writing, or write like a rat . . . If the writer is a sorcerer, it is because writing is a becoming, writing is traversed by strange becomings that are not becomings-writer, but becomings-rat, becomings-insect, becomings-wolf, etc. We will have to explain why. Many suicides by writers are explained by these unnatural participations, these unnatural nuptials. Writers are sorcerers because they experience the animal as the only population before which they are responsible in principle. The German preromantic Karl Philipp Moritz feels responsible not for the calves that die but before the calves that die and give him the incredible feeling of an unknown Nature—*affect*.[9] For the affect is not a personal feeling, nor is it a characteristic; it is the effectuation of a power of the pack that throws the self into upheaval and makes it reel. Who has not known the violence of these animal sequences, which uproot one from humanity, if only for an instant, making one scrape at one's bread like a rodent or giving one the yellow eyes of a feline? A fearsome involution calling us toward unheard-of becomings. These are not regressions, although fragments of regression, sequences of regression may enter in.

We must distinguish three kinds of animals. First, individuated animals, family pets, sentimental, Oedipal animals each with its own petty history, "my" cat, "my" dog. These animals invite us to regress, draw us into a narcissistic contemplation, and they are the only kind of animal psychoanalysis understands, the better to discover a daddy, a mommy, a little brother behind them (when psychoanalysis talks about animals, animals learn to laugh): *anyone who likes cats or dogs is a fool*. And then there is a second kind: animals with characteristics or attributes; genus, classification, or State animals; animals as they are treated in the great divine myths, in such a way as to extract from them series or structures, archetypes or models (Jung is in any event profounder than Freud). Finally, there are more demonic animals, pack or affect animals that form a multiplicity, a becoming, a population, a tale . . . Or once again, cannot any animal be treated in all three ways? There is always the possibility that a given animal, a louse, a cheetah or an elephant, will be treated as a pet, my little beast. And at the other extreme, it is also possible for any animal to be treated in the mode of the pack or swarm; that is our way, fellow sorcerers. Even the cat, even the dog. And the shepherd, the animal trainer, the Devil, may have a favorite animal in the pack, although not at all in the way we were just discussing. Yes, any animal is or can be a pack, but to varying degrees of vocation that make it easier or harder to discover the multiplicity, or multiplicity-grade, an animal contains (actually or virtually according to the case). Schools, bands, herds, populations are not inferior social forms; they are affects and powers, involutions that grip every animal in a becoming just as powerful as that of the human being with the animal.

Jorge Luis Borges, an author renowned for his excess of culture, botched at least two books, only the titles of which are nice: first, *A Universal History of Infamy*, because he did not see the sorcerer's fundamental distinction between deception and treason (becomings-animal are there from the start, on the treason side); second, his *Manual de zoología fantástica*, where he not only adopts a composite and bland image of myth but also eliminates all of the problems of the pack and the corresponding becoming-animal of the human being: "We have deliberately excluded from this manual legends of transformations of the human being, the *lobizón*, the werewolf, etc."[10] Borges is interested only in characteristics, even the most fantastic ones, whereas sorcerers know that werewolves are bands, and vampires too, and that bands transform themselves into one another. But what exactly does that mean, the animal as band or pack? Does a band not imply a filiation, bringing us back to the reproduction of given characteristics? How can we conceive of a peopling, a propagation, a becoming that is without filiation or hereditary production? A multiplicity without the unity of an ancestor? It is quite simple; everybody knows it, but it is discussed only in secret. We oppose epidemic to filiation, contagion to heredity, peopling by contagion to sexual reproduction, sexual production. Bands, human or animal, proliferate by contagion, epidemics, battlefields, and catastrophes. Like hybrids, which are in themselves sterile, born of a sexual union that will not reproduce itself, but which begins over again every time, gaining that much more ground. Unnatural participations or nuptials are the true Nature spanning the kingdoms of nature. Propagation by epidemic, by contagion, has nothing to do with filiation by heredity, even if the two themes intermingle and require each other. The vampire does not filiate, it infects. The difference is that contagion, epidemic, involves terms that are entirely heterogeneous: for example, a human being, an animal, and a bacterium, a virus, a molecule, a microorganism. Or in the case of the truffle, a tree, a fly, and a pig. These combinations are neither genetic nor structural; they are interkingdoms, unnatural participations. That is the only way Nature operates—against itself. This is a far cry from filiative production or hereditary reproduction, in which the only differences retained are a simple duality between sexes within the same species, and small modifications across generations. For us, on the other hand, there are as many sexes as there are terms in symbiosis, as many differences as elements contributing to a process of contagion. We know that many beings pass between a man and a woman; they come from different worlds, are borne on the wind, form rhizomes around roots; they cannot be understood in terms of production, only in terms of becoming. The Universe does not function by filiation. All we are saying is that animals are packs, and that packs form, develop, and are transformed by contagion.

These multiplicities with heterogeneous terms, cofunctioning by contagion, enter certain *assemblages;* it is there that human beings effect their becomings-animal. But we should not confuse these dark assemblages, which stir what is deepest within us, with organizations such as the institution of the family and the State apparatus. We could cite hunting societies, war societies, secret societies, crime societies, etc. Becomings-animal are proper to them. We will not expect to find filiative regimes of the family type or modes of classification and attribution of the State or pre-State type or even serial organizations of the religious type. Despite appearances and possible confusions, this is not the site of origin or point of application for myths. These are tales, or narratives and statements of becoming. It is therefore absurd to establish a hierarchy even of animal collectivities from the standpoint of a whimsical evolutionism according to which packs are lower on the scale and are superseded by State or familial societies. On the contrary, there is a difference in nature. The origin of packs is entirely different from that of families and States; they continually work them from within and trouble them from without, with other forms of content, other forms of expression. The pack is simultaneously an animal reality, and the reality of the becoming-animal of the human being; contagion is simultaneously an animal peopling, and the propagation of the animal peopling of the human being. The hunting machine, the war machine, the crime machine entail all kinds of becomings-animal that are not articulated in myth, *still less in totemism.* Dumézil showed that becomings of this kind pertain essentially to the man of war, but only insofar as he is external to families and States, insofar as he upsets filiations and classifications. The war machine is always exterior to the State, even when the State uses it, appropriates it. The man of war has an entire becoming that implies multiplicity, celerity, ubiquity, metamorphosis and treason, the power of affect. Wolf-men, bear-men, wildcat-men, men of every animality, secret brotherhoods, animate the battlefields. But so do the animal packs used by men in battle, or which trail the battles and take advantage of them. And together they spread contagion.[11] There is a complex aggregate: the becoming-animal of men, packs of animals, elephants and rats, winds and tempests, bacteria sowing contagion. A single *Furor.* War contained zoological sequences before it became bacteriological. It is in war, famine, and epidemic that werewolves and vampires proliferate. Any animal can be swept up in these packs and the corresponding becomings; cats have been seen on the battlefield, and even in armies. That is why the distinction we must make is less between kinds of animals than between the different states according to which they are integrated into family institutions, State apparatuses, war machines, etc. (and what is the relation of the writing machine and the musical machine to becomings-animal?)

Memories of a Sorcerer, II. Our first principle was: pack and contagion, the contagion of the pack, such is the path becoming-animal takes. But a second principle seemed to tell us the opposite: wherever there is multiplicity, you will also find an exceptional individual, and it is with that individual that an alliance must be made in order to become-animal. There may be no such thing as a lone wolf, but there is a leader of the pack, a master of the pack, or else the old deposed head of the pack now living alone, there is the Loner, and there is the Demon. Willard has his favorite, the rat Ben, and only becomes-rat through his relation with him, in a kind of alliance of love, then of hate. *Moby-Dick* in its entirety is one of the greatest masterpieces of becoming; Captain Ahab has an irresistible becoming-whale, but one that bypasses the pack or the school, operating directly through a monstrous alliance with the Unique, the Leviathan, Moby-Dick. There is always a pact with a demon; the demon sometimes appears as the head of the band, sometimes as the Loner on the sidelines of the pack, and sometimes as the higher Power (*Puissance*) of the band. The exceptional individual has many possible positions. Kafka, another great author of real becomings-animal, sings of mouse society; but Josephine, the mouse singer, sometimes holds a privileged position in the pack, sometimes a position outside the pack, and sometimes slips into and is lost in the anonymity of the collective statements of the pack.[12] In short, every Animal has its Anomalous. Let us clarify that: every animal swept up in its pack or multiplicity has its anomalous. It has been noted that the origin of the word *anomal* ("anomalous"), an adjective that has fallen into disuse in French, is very different from that of *anormal* ("abnormal"): *a-normal,* a Latin adjective lacking a noun in French, refers to that which is outside rules or goes against the rules, whereas *an-omalie*, a Greek noun that has lost its adjective, designates the unequal, the coarse, the rough, the cutting edge of deterritorialization.[13] The abnormal can be defined only in terms of characteristics, specific or generic; but the anomalous is a position or set of positions in relation to a multiplicity. Sorcerers therefore use the old adjective "anomalous" to situate the positions of the exceptional individual in the pack. It is always with the Anomalous, Moby-Dick or Josephine, that one enters into alliance to become-animal.

It does seem as though there is a contradiction: between the pack and the loner; between mass contagion and preferential alliance; between pure multiplicity and the exceptional individual; between the aleatory aggregate and a predestined choice. And the contradiction is real: Ahab chooses Moby-Dick, in a choosing that exceeds him and comes from elsewhere, and in so doing breaks with the law of the whalers according to which one should first pursue the pack. Penthesilea shatters the law of the pack, the pack of women, the pack of she-dogs, by choosing Achilles as her favorite enemy. Yet it is by means of this anomalous choice that each enters into his or her becoming-animal, the becoming-dog of Penthesilea, the becoming-whale of Captain Ahab. We sorcerers know quite well that the contradictions are real but that real contradictions are not just for laughs. For the whole question is this: What exactly is the nature of the anomalous? What function does it have in relation to the band, to the pack? It is clear that the anomalous is not simply an exceptional individual; that would be to equate it with the family animal or pet, the Oedipalized animal as psychoanalysis sees it, as the image of the father, etc. Ahab's Moby-Dick is not like the little cat or dog owned by an elderly woman who honors and cherishes it. Lawrence's becoming-tortoise has nothing to do with a sentimental or domestic relation. Lawrence is another of the writers who leave us troubled and filled with admiration because they were able to tie their writing to real and unheard-of becomings. But the objection is raised against Lawrence: "Your tortoises aren't real!" And he answers: Possibly, but my becoming is, my becoming is real, even and especially if you have no way of judging it, because you're just little house dogs . . .[14] The anomalous, the preferential element in the pack, has nothing to do with the preferred, domestic, and psychoanalytic individual. Nor is the anomalous the bearer of a species presenting specific or generic characteristics in their purest state; nor is it a model or unique specimen; nor is it the perfection of a type incarnate; nor is it the eminent term of a series; nor is it the basis of an absolutely harmonious correspondence. The anomalous is neither an individual nor a species; it has only affects, it has neither familiar or subjectified feelings, nor specific or significant characteristics. Human tenderness is as foreign to it as human classifications. Lovecraft applies the term "Outsider" to this thing or entity, the Thing, which arrives and passes at the edge, which is linear yet multiple, "teeming, seething, swelling, foaming, spreading like an infectious disease, this nameless horror."

If the anomalous is neither an individual nor a species, then what is it? It is a phenomenon, but a phenomenon of bordering. This is our hypothesis: a multiplicity is defined not by the elements that compose it in extension, not by the characteristics that compose it in comprehension, but by the lines and dimensions it encompasses in "intension." If you change dimensions, if you add or subtract one, you change multiplicity. Thus there is a borderline for each multiplicity; it is in no way a center but rather the enveloping line or farthest dimension, as a function of which it is possible to count the others, all those lines or dimensions constitute the pack at a given moment (beyond the borderline, the multiplicity changes nature). That is what Captain Ahab says to his first mate: I have no personal history with Moby-Dick, no revenge to take, any more than I have a myth to play out; but I do have a becoming! Moby-Dick is neither an individual nor a genus; he is the borderline, and I have to strike him to get at the pack as a whole, to reach the pack as a whole and pass beyond it. The elements of the pack are only imaginary "dummies," the characteristics of the pack are only symbolic entities; all that counts is the borderline—the anomalous. "To me, the white whale is that wall, shoved near to me." The white wall. "Sometimes I think there is naught beyond. But 'tis enough."[15] That the anomalous is the borderline makes it easier for us to understand the various positions it occupies in relation to the pack or the multiplicity it borders, and the various positions occupied by a fascinated Self (*Moi*). It is now even possible to establish a classification system for packs while avoiding the pitfalls of an evolutionism that sees them only as an inferior collective stage (instead of taking into consideration the particular assemblages they bring into play). In any event, the pack has a borderline, and an anomalous position, whenever in a given space an animal is on the line or in the act of drawing the line in relation to which all the other members of the pack will fall into one of two halves, left or right: a peripheral position, such that it is impossible to tell if the anomalous is still in the band, already outside the band, or at the shifting boundary of the band. Sometimes each and every animal reaches this line or occupies this dynamic position, as in a swarm of mosquitoes, where "each individual moves randomly unless it sees the rest of [the swarm] in the same half-space; then it hurries to re-enter the group. Thus stability is assured in catastrophe by a *barrier*."[16] Sometimes it is a specific animal that draws and occupies the borderline, as leader of the pack. Sometimes the borderline is defined or doubled by a being of another nature that no longer belongs to the pack, or never belonged to it, and that represents a power of another order, potentially acting as a threat as well as a trainer, outsider, etc. In any case, no band is without this phenomenon of bordering, or the anomalous. It is true that bands are also undermined by extremely varied forces that establish in them interior centers of the conjugal, familial, or State type, and that make them pass into an entirely different form of sociability, replacing pack affects with family feelings or State intelligibilities. The center, or internal black holes, assumes the principal role. This is what evolutionism sees as progress, this adventure also befalls bands of humans when they reconstitute group familialism, or even authoritarianism or pack fascism.

Sorcerers have always held the anomalous position, at the edge of the fields or woods. They haunt the fringes. They are at the borderline of the village, or *between* villages. The important thing is their affinity with alliance, with the pact, which gives them a status opposed to that of filiation. The relation with the anomalous is one of alliance. The sorcerer has a relation of alliance with the demon as the power of the anomalous. The old-time theologians drew a clear distinction between two kinds of curses against sexuality. The first concerns sexuality as a process of filiation transmitting the original sin. But the second concerns it as a power of alliance inspiring illicit unions or abominable loves. This differs significantly from the first in that it tends to prevent procreation; since the demon does not himself have the ability to procreate, he must adopt indirect means (for example, being the female succubus of a man and then becoming the male incubus of a woman, to whom he transmits the man's semen). It is true that the relations between alliance and filiation come to be regulated by laws of marriage, but even then alliance retains a dangerous and contagious power. Leach was able to demonstrate that despite all the exceptions that seemingly disprove the rule, the sorcerer belongs first of all to a group united to the group over which he or she exercises influence only by alliance: thus in a matrilineal group we look to the father's side for the sorcerer or witch. And there is an entire evolution of sorcery depending on whether the relation of alliance acquires permanence or assumes political weight.[17] In order to produce werewolves in your own family it is not enough to resemble a wolf, or to live like a wolf: the pact with the Devil must be coupled with an alliance with another family, and it is the return of this alliance to the first family, the reaction of this alliance on the first family, that produces werewolves by feedback effect. A fine tale by Erckmann and Chatrian, *Hugues-le-loup*, assembles the traditions concerning this complex situation.[18]

The contradiction between the two themes, "contagion through the animal as pack," and "pact with the anomalous as exceptional being," is progressively fading. It is with good reason that Leach links the two concepts of alliance and contagion, pact and epidemic. Analyzing Kachin sorcery, he writes: "Witch influence was thought to be transmitted in the food that the women prepared. . . . Kachin witchcraft is contagious rather than hereditary . . . it is associated with affinity, not filiation."[19] Alliance or the pact is the form of expression for an infection or epidemic constituting the form of content. In sorcery, blood is of the order of contagion and alliance. It can be said that becoming-animal is an affair of sorcery because (1) it implies an initial relation of alliance with a demon; (2) the demon functions as the borderline of an animal pack, into which the human being passes or in which his or her becoming takes place, by contagion; (3) this becoming itself implies a second alliance, with another human group; (4) this new borderline between the two groups guides the contagion of animal and human being within the pack. There is an entire politics of becomings-animal, as well as a politics of sorcery, which is elaborated in assemblages that are neither those of the family nor of religion nor of the State. Instead, they express minoritarian groups, or groups that are oppressed, prohibited, in revolt, or always on the fringe of recognized institutions, groups all the more secret for being extrinsic, in other words, anomic. If becoming-animal takes the form of a Temptation, and of monsters aroused in the imagination by the demon, it is because it is accompanied, at its origin as in its undertaking, by a rupture with the central institutions that have established themselves or seek to become established.

Let us cite pell-mell, not as mixes to be made, but as different cases to be studied: becomings-animal in the war machine, wildmen of all kinds (the war machine indeed comes from without, it is extrinsic to the State, which treats the warrior as an anomalous power); becomings-animal in crime societies, leopard-men, crocodile-men (when the State prohibits tribal and local wars); becomings-animal in riot groups (when the Church and State are faced with peasant movements containing a sorcery component, which they repress by setting up a whole trial and legal system designed to expose pacts with the Devil); becomings-animal in asceticism groups, the grazing anchorite or wild-beast anchorite (the asceticism machine is in an anomalous position, on a line of flight, off to the side of the Church, and disputes the Church's pretension to set itself up as an imperial institution);[20] becomings-animal in societies practicing sexual initiation of the "sacred deflowerer" type, wolf-men, goat-men, etc. (who claim an Alliance superior and exterior to the order of families; families have to win from them the right to regulate their own alliances, to determine them according to relations of complementary lines of descent, and to domesticate this unbridled power of alliance).[21]

The politics of becomings-animal remains, of course, extremely ambiguous. For societies, even primitive societies, have always appropriated these becomings in order to break them, reduce them to relations of totemic or symbolic correspondence. States have always appropriated the war machine in the form of national armies that strictly limit the becomings of the warrior. The Church has always burned sorcerers, or reintegrated anchorites into the toned-down image of a series of saints whose only remaining relation to animals is strangely familiar, domestic. Families have always warded off the demonic Alliance gnawing at them, in order to regulate alliances among themselves as they see fit. We have seen sorcerers serve as leaders, rally to the cause of despotism, create the countersorcery of exorcism, pass over to the side of the family and descent. But this spells the death of the sorcerer, and also the death of becoming. We have seen becoming spawn nothing more than a big domestic dog, as in Henry Miller's damnation ("it would be better to feign, to pretend to be an animal, a dog for example, and catch the bone thrown to me from time to time") or Fitzgerald's ("I will try to be a correct animal though, and if you throw me a bone with enough meat on it I may even lick your hand"). Invert Faust's formula: So that is what it was, the form of the traveling scholar? A mere poodle?[22]

Memories of a Sorcerer, III. Exclusive importance should not be attached to becomings-animal. Rather, they are segments occupying a median region. On the near side, we encounter becomings-woman, becomings-child (becoming-woman, more than any other becoming, possesses a special introductory power; it is not so much that women are witches, but that sorcery proceeds by way of this becoming-woman). On the far side, we find becomings-elementary, -cellular, -molecular, and even becomings-imperceptible. Toward what void does the witch's broom lead? And where is Moby-Dick leading Ahab so silently? Lovecraft's hero encounters strange animals, but he finally reaches the ultimate regions of a Continuum inhabited by unnameable waves and unfindable particles. Science fiction has gone through a whole evolution taking it from animal, vegetable, and mineral becomings to becomings of bacteria, viruses, molecules, and things imperceptible.[23] The properly musical content of music is plied by becomings-woman, becomings-child, becomings-animal; however, it tends, under all sorts of influences, having to do also with the instruments, to become progressively more molecular in a kind of cosmic lapping through which the inaudible makes itself heard and the imperceptible appears as such: no longer the songbird, but the sound molecule.

If the experimentation with drugs has left its mark on everyone, even nonusers, it is because it changed the perceptive coordinates of space-time and introduced us to a universe of microperceptions in which becomings-molecular take over where becomings-animal leave off. Carlos Castaneda's books clearly illustrate this evolution, or rather this involution, in which the affects of a becoming-dog, for example, are succeeded by those of a becoming-molecular, microperceptions of water, air, etc. A man totters from one door to the next and disappears into thin air: "All I can tell you is that we are fluid, luminous beings made of fibers."[24] All so-called initiatory journeys include these thresholds and doors where becoming itself becomes, and where one changes becoming depending on the "hour" of the world, the circles of hell, or the stages of a journey that sets scales, forms, and cries in variation. From the howling of animals to the wailing of elements and particles.

Thus packs, or multiplicities, continually transform themselves into each other, cross over into each other. Werewolves become vampires when they die. This is not surprising, since becoming and multiplicity are the same thing. A multiplicity is defined not by its elements, nor by a center of unification or comprehension. It is defined by the number of dimensions it has; it is not divisible, it cannot lose or gain a dimension *without changing its nature.* Since its variations and dimensions are immanent to it, *it amounts to the same thing to say that each multiplicity is already composed of heterogeneous terms in symbiosis, and that a multiplicity is continually transforming itself into a string of other multiplicities, according to its thresholds and doors.* For example, the Wolf-Man's pack of wolves also becomes a swarm of bees, and a field of anuses, and a collection of small holes and tiny ulcerations (the theme of contagion): all these heterogeneous elements compose "the" multiplicity of symbiosis and becoming. If we imagined the position of a fascinated Self, it was because the multiplicity toward which it leans, stretching to the breaking point, is the continuation of another multiplicity that works it and strains it from the inside. In fact, the self is only a threshold, a door, a becoming between two multiplicities. Each multiplicity is defined by a borderline functioning as Anomalous, but there is a string of borderlines, a continuous line of borderlines (*fiber*) following which the multiplicity changes. And at each threshold or door, a new pact? A fiber stretches from a human to an animal, from a human or an animal to molecules, from molecules to particles, and so on to the imperceptible. Every fiber is a Universe fiber. A fiber strung across borderlines constitutes a line of flight or of deterritorialization. It is evident that the Anomalous, the Outsider, has several functions: not only does it border each multiplicity, of which it determines the temporary or local stability (with the highest number of dimensions possible under the circumstances), not only is it the precondition for the alliance necessary to becoming, but it also carries the transformations of becoming or crossings of multiplicities always farther down the line of flight. Moby-Dick is the *White Wall* bordering the pack; he is also the demonic *Term of the Alliance;*

not so in Spinoza

finally, he is the terrible *Fishing Line* with nothing on the other end, the line that crosses the wall and drags the captain . . . where? Into the void . . .

The error we must guard against is to believe that there is a kind of logical order to this string, these crossings or transformations. It is already going too far to postulate an order descending from the animal to the vegetable, then to molecules, to particles. Each multiplicity is symbiotic; its becoming ties together animals, plants, microorganisms, mad particles, a whole galaxy. Nor is there a preformed logical order to these heterogeneities, the Wolf-Man's wolves, bees, anuses, little scars. Of course, sorcery always codifies certain transformations of becomings. Take a novel steeped in the traditions of sorcery, Alexandre Dumas's *Meneur de loups;* in a first pact, the man of the fringes gets the Devil to agree to make his wishes come true, with the stipulation that a lock of his hair turn red each time he gets a wish. We are in the hair-multiplicity, hair is the borderline. The man himself takes a position on the wolves' borderline, as leader of the pack. Then when he no longer has a single human hair left, a second pact makes him become-wolf himself; it is an endless becoming since he is only vulnerable one day in the year. We are aware that between the hair-multiplicity and the wolf-multiplicity it is always possible to induce an order of resemblance (red like the fur of a wolf); but the resemblance remains quite secondary (the wolf of the transformation is black, with one white hair). In fact, there is a first multiplicity, of hair, taken up in a becoming-red fur; and a second multiplicity, of wolves, which in turn takes up the becoming-animal of the man. Between the two, there is threshold and fiber, symbiosis of or passage between heterogeneities. That is how we sorcerers operate. Not following a logical order, but following alogical consistencies or compatibilities. The reason is simple. It is because no one, not even God, can say in advance whether two borderlines will string together or form a fiber, whether a given multiplicity will or will not cross over into another given multiplicity, or even if given heterogeneous elements will enter symbiosis, will form a consistent, or cofunctioning, multiplicity susceptible to transformation. No one can say where the line of flight will pass: Will it let itself get bogged down and fall back to the Oedipal family animal, a mere poodle? Or will it succumb to another danger, for example, turning into a line of abolition, annihilation, self-destruction, Ahab, Ahab . . . ? We are all too familiar with the dangers of the line of flight, and with its ambiguities. The risks are ever-present, but it is always possible to have the good fortune of avoiding them. Case by case, we can tell whether the line is consistent, in other words, whether the heterogeneities effectively function in a multiplicity of symbiosis, whether the multiplicities are effectively transformed through the becomings of passage. Let us take an example as simple as: *x* starts practicing piano again. Is it an Oedipal return to childhood? Is it a way of dying, in a kind of sonorous abolition? Is it a new borderline, an active line that will bring other becomings entirely different from becoming or rebecoming a pianist, that will induce a transformation of all of the preceding assemblages to which *x* was prisoner? Is it a way out? Is it a pact with the Devil? Schizoanalysis, or pragmatics, has no other meaning: Make a rhizome. But you don't know what you can make a rhizome with, you don't know which subterranean stem is effectively going to make a rhizome, or enter a becoming, people your desert. So experiment.

That's easy to say? Although there is no preformed logical order to becomings and multiplicities, there are *criteria*, and the important thing is that they not be used after the fact, that they be applied in the course of events, that they be sufficient to guide us through the dangers. If multiplicities are defined and transformed by the borderline that determines in each instance their number of dimensions, we can conceive of the possibility of laying them out on a plane, the borderlines succeeding one another, forming a broken line. It is only in appearance that a plane of this kind "reduces" the number of dimensions; for it gathers in all the dimensions to the extent that *flat multiplicities*—which nonetheless have *an increasing or decreasing number of dimensions*—are inscribed upon it. It is in grandiose and simplified terms that Lovecraft attempted to pronounce sorcery's final word: "Then the waves increased in strength and sought to improve his understanding, reconciling him to the multiform entity of which his present fragment was an infinitesimal part. They told him that every figure of space is but the result of the intersection by a plane of some corresponding figure of one more dimension—as a square is cut from a cube, or a circle from a sphere. The cube and sphere, of three dimensions, are thus cut from corresponding forms of four dimensions, which men know only through guesses and dreams; and these in turn are cut from forms of five dimensions, and so on up to the dizzy and reachless heights of archetypal infinity."[25] Far from reducing the multiplicities' number of dimensions to two, the *plane of consistency* cuts across them all, intersects them in order to bring into coexistence any number of multiplicities, with any number of dimensions. The plane of consistency is the intersection of all concrete forms. Therefore all becomings are written like sorcerers' drawings on this plane of consistency, which is the ultimate Door providing a way out for them. This is the only criterion to prevent them from bogging down, or veering into the void. The only question is: Does a given becoming reach that point? Can a given multiplicity flatten and conserve all its dimensions in this way, like a pressed flower that remains just as alive dry? Lawrence, in his becoming-tortoise, moves from the most obstinate animal dynamism to the abstract, pure geometry of scales and "cleavages of division," without, however, losing any of the dynamism: he pushes becoming-tortoise all the way to the plane of consistency.[26] Everything becomes imperceptible, everything is becoming-imperceptible on the plane of consistency, which is nevertheless precisely where the imperceptible is seen and heard. It is the Planomenon, or the Rhizosphere, the Criterium (and still other names, as the number of dimensions increases). At *n* dimensions, it is called the Hypersphere, the Mechanosphere. It is the abstract Figure, or rather, since it has no form itself, the abstract Machine of which each concrete assemblage is a multiplicity, a becoming, a segment, a vibration. And the abstract machine is the intersection of them all.

Waves are vibrations, shifting borderlines inscribed on the plane of consistency as so many abstractions. The abstract machine of the waves. In *The Waves*, Virginia Woolf—who made all of her life and work a passage, a becoming, all kinds of becomings between ages, sexes, elements, and kingdoms—intermingles seven characters, Bernard, Neville, Louis, Jinny, Rhoda, Suzanne, and Percival. But each of these characters, with his or her name, its individuality, designates a multiplicity (for example, Bernard and the school of fish). Each is simultaneously in this multiplicity and at its edge, and crosses over into the others. Percival is like the ultimate multiplicity enveloping the greatest number of dimensions. But he is not yet the plane of consistency. Although Rhoda thinks she sees him rising out of the sea, no, it is not he. "When the white arm rests upon the knee it is a triangle; now it is upright—a column; now a fountain. . . . Behind it roars the sea. It is beyond our reach."[27] Each advances like a wave, but on the plane of consistency they are a single abstract Wave whose vibration propagates following a line of flight or deterritorialization traversing the entire plane (each chapter of Woolf's novel is preceded by a meditation on an aspect of the waves, on one of their hours, on one of their becomings).

Memories of a Theologian. Theology is very strict on the following point: there are no werewolves, human beings cannot become animal. That is because there is no transformation of essential forms; they are inalienable and only entertain relations of analogy. The Devil and the witch, and the pact between them, are no less real for that, for there is in reality a *local movement* that is properly diabolical. Theology distinguishes two cases, used as models during the Inquisition: that of Ulysses' companions, and that of Diomedes' companions, the imaginary vision and the spell. In the first, the subject believes him- or herself to be transformed into an animal, pig, ox, or wolf, and the observers believe it too; but this is an internal local movement bringing sensible images back to the imagination and bouncing them off external meanings. In the second, the Devil "assumes" real animal bodies, even transporting the accidents and affects befalling them to other bodies (for example, a cat or a wolf that has been taken over by the

Devil can receive wounds that are relayed to an exactly corresponding part of a human body).[28] This is a way of saying that the human being does not become animal in reality, but that there is nevertheless a demonic reality of the becoming-animal of the human being. Therefore it is certain that the demon performs local transports of all kinds. The Devil is a transporter; he transports humors, affects, or even bodies (the Inquisition brooks no compromises on this power of the Devil: the witch's broom, or "the Devil take you"). But these transports cross neither the barrier of essential forms nor that of substances or subjects.

There is another, altogether different, problem concerning the laws of nature that has to do not with demonology but with alchemy, and above all physics. It is the problem of accidental forms, distinct from both essential forms and determined subjects. For accidental forms are susceptible to *more and less:* more or less charitable, but also more or less white, more or less warm. A degree of heat is a perfectly individuated warmth distinct from the substance or the subject that receives it. A degree of heat can enter into composition with a degree of whiteness, or with another degree of heat, to form a third unique individuality distinct from that of the subject. What is the individuality of a day, a season, an event? A shorter day and a longer day are not, strictly speaking, extensions but degrees proper to extension, just as there are degrees proper to heat, color, etc. An accidental form therefore has a "latitude" constituted by a certain number of composable individuations. A degree, an intensity, is an individual, a *Haecceity* that enters into composition with other degrees, other intensities, to form another individual. Can latitude be explained by the fact that the subject participates more or less in the accidental form? But do these degrees of participation not imply a flutter, a vibration in the form itself that is not reducible to the properties of a subject? Moreover, if intensities of heat are not composed by addition, it is because one must add their respective subjects; it is the subjects that prevent the heat of the whole from increasing. All the more reason to effect distributions of intensity, to establish latitudes that are "deformedly deformed," speeds, slownesses, and degrees of all kinds corresponding to a body or set of bodies taken as longitude: a cartography.[29] In short, between substantial forms and determined subjects, *between the two*, there is not only a whole operation of demonic local transports but a natural play of haecceities, degrees, intensities, events, and accidents that compose individuations totally different from those of the well-formed subjects that receive them.

Memories of a Spinozist, I. Substantial or essential forms have been critiqued in many different ways. Spinoza's approach is radical: Arrive at elements that no longer have either form or function, that are abstract in this sense even though they are perfectly real. They are distinguished solely by movement and rest, slowness and speed. They are not atoms, in other words, finite elements still endowed with form. Nor are they indefinitely divisible. They are infinitely small, ultimate parts of an actual infinity, laid out on the same plane of consistency or composition. They are not defined by their number since they always come in infinities. However, depending on their degree of speed or the relation of movement and rest into which they enter, they belong to a given Individual, which may itself be part of another Individual governed by another, more complex, relation, and so on to infinity. There are thus smaller and larger infinities, not by virtue of their number, but by virtue of the composition of the relation into which their parts enter. Thus each individual is an infinite multiplicity, and the whole of Nature is a multiplicity of perfectly individuated multiplicities. The plane of consistency of Nature is like an immense Abstract Machine, abstract yet real and individual; its pieces are the various assemblages and individuals, each of which groups together an infinity of particles entering into an infinity of more or less interconnected relations. There is therefore a unity to the plane of nature, which applies equally to the inanimate and the animate, the artificial and the natural. This plane has nothing to do with a form or a figure, nor with a design or a function. Its unity has nothing to do with a ground buried deep within things, nor with an end or a project in the mind of God. Instead, it is a plane upon which everything is laid out, and which is like the intersection of all forms, the machine of all functions; its dimensions, however, increase with those of the multiplicities or individualities it cuts across. It is a fixed plane, upon which things are distinguished from one another only by speed and slowness. A plane of immanence or univocality opposed to analogy. The One expresses in a single meaning all of the multiple. (*"L'un se dit en un seul et même sens de tout le multiple."*) Being expresses in a single meaning all that differs. What we are talking about is not the unity of substance but the infinity of the modifications that are part of one another on this unique plane of life.

The never-ending debate between Cuvier and Geoffroy Saint-Hilaire: both agree at least in denouncing resemblances, or imaginary, sensible analogies. But in Cuvier, scientific definition concerns the relations between organs, and between organs and functions. Cuvier thus takes analogy to the scientific stage, making it an analogy of proportionality. The unity of the plane, according to him, can only be a unity of analogy, therefore a transcendent unity that cannot be realized without fragmenting into distinct branches, according to irreducible, uncrossable, heterogeneous compositions. Baer would later add: according to noncommunicating types of development and differentiation. The plane is a hidden plan(e) of organization, a structure or genesis. Geoffroy has an entirely different point of view because he goes beyond organs and functions to abstract elements he terms "anatomical," even to particles, pure materials that enter into various combinations, forming a given organ and assuming a given function depending on their degree of speed or slowness. Speed and slowness, movement and rest, tardiness and rapidity subordinate not only the forms of structure but also the types of development. This approach later reappears in an evolutionist framework, with Perrier's tachygenesis and differential rates of growth in allometry: species as kinematic entities that are either precocious or retarded. (Even the question of fertility is less one of form and function than speed; do the paternal chromosomes arrive early enough to be incorporated into the nuclei?) In any case, there is a pure plane of immanence, univocality, composition, upon which everything is given, upon which unformed elements and materials dance that are distinguished from one another only by their speed and that enter into this or that individuated assemblage depending on their connections, their relations of movement. A fixed plane of life upon which everything stirs, slows down or accelerates. A single abstract Animal for all the assemblages that effectuate it. A unique plane of consistency or composition for the cephalopod and the vertebrate; for the vertebrate to become an Octopus or Cuttlefish, all it would have to do is fold itself in two fast enough to fuse the elements of the halves of its back together, then bring its pelvis up to the nape of its neck and gather its limbs together into one of its extremities, like "a clown who throws his head and shoulders back and walks on his head and hands."[30] *Plication*. It is no longer a question of organs and functions, and of a transcendent Plane that can preside over their organization only by means of analogical relations and types of divergent development. It is a question not of organization but of composition; not of development or differentiation but of movement and rest, speed and slowness. It is a question of elements and particles, which do or do not arrive fast enough to effect a passage, a becoming or jump on the same plane of pure immanence. And if there are in fact jumps, rifts between assemblages, it is not by virtue of their essential irreducibility but rather because there are always elements that do not arrive on time, or arrive after everything is over; thus it is necessary to pass through fog, to cross voids, to have lead times and delays, which are themselves part of the plane of immanence. Even the failures are part of the plane. We must try to conceive of this world in which a single fixed plane—which we shall call a plane of absolute immobility *or* absolute movement—is traversed by nonformal elements of relative speed that enter this or that individuated assemblage depending on their degrees of speed and slowness. A plane of consistency peopled by anonymous matter, by infinite bits of impalpable matter entering into varying connections.

Children are Spinozists. When Little Hans talks about a "peepee-maker," he is referring not to an organ or an organic function but basically to a material, in other words, to an aggregate whose elements vary according to its connections, its relations of movement and rest, the different individuated assemblages it enters. Does a girl have a peepee-maker? The boy says yes, and not by analogy, nor in order to conjure away a fear of castration. It is obvious that girls have a peepee-maker because they effectively pee: a machinic functioning rather than an organic function. Quite simply, the same material has different connections, different relations of movement and rest, enters different assemblages in the case of the boy and the girl (a girl does not pee standing or into the distance). Does a locomotive have a peepee-maker? Yes, in yet another machinic assemblage. Chairs don't have them: but that is because the elements of the chair were not able to integrate this material into their relations, or decomposed the relation with that material to the point that it yielded something else, a rung, for example. It has been noted that for children an organ has "a thousand vicissitudes," that it is "difficult to localize, difficult to identify, it is in turn a bone, an engine, excrement, the baby, a hand, daddy's heart . . ." This is not at all because the organ is experienced as a part-object. It is because the organ is exactly what its elements make it according to their relation of movement or rest, and the way in which this relation combines with or splits off from that of neighboring elements. This is not animism, any more than it is mechanism; rather, it is universal machinism: a plane of consistency occupied by an immense abstract machine comprising an infinite number of assemblages. Children's questions are poorly understood if they are not seen as question-machines; that is why indefinite articles play so important a role in these questions (*a* belly, a child, a horse, a chair, "how is *a* person made?"). Spinozism is the becoming-child of the philosopher. We call the *longitude* of a body the particle aggregates belonging to that body in a given relation; these aggregates are part of each other depending on the composition of the relation that defines the individuated assemblage of the body.

Memories of a Spinozist, II. There is another aspect to Spinoza. To every relation of movement and rest, speed and slowness grouping together an infinity of parts, there corresponds a degree of power. To the relations composing, decomposing, or modifying an individual there correspond intensities that affect it, augmenting or diminishing its power to act; these intensities come from external parts or from the individual's own parts. Affects are becomings. Spinoza asks: What can a body do? We call the *latitude* of a body the affects of which it is capable at a given degree of power, or rather within the limits of that degree. *Latitude is made up of intensive parts* *falling under a capacity, and longitude of extensive parts falling under a relation.* In the same way that we avoided defining a body by its organs and functions, we will avoid defining it by Species or Genus characteristics; instead we will seek to count its affects. This kind of study is called ethology, and this is the sense in which Spinoza wrote a true Ethics. A racehorse is more different from a workhorse than a workhorse is from an ox. Von Uexküll, in defining animal worlds, looks for the active and passive affects of which the animal is capable in the individuated assemblage of which it is a part. For example, the Tick, attracted by the light, hoists itself up to the tip of a branch; it is sensitive to the smell of mammals, and lets itself fall when one passes beneath the branch; it digs into its skin, at the least hairy place it can find. Just three affects; the rest of the time the tick sleeps, sometimes for years on end, indifferent to all that goes on in the immense forest. Its degree of power is indeed bounded by two limits: the optimal limit of the feast after which it dies, and the pessimal limit of the fast as it waits. It will be said that the tick's three affects assume generic and specific characteristics, organs and functions, legs and snout. This is true from the standpoint of physiology, but not from the standpoint of Ethics. Quite the contrary, in Ethics the organic characteristics derive from longitude and its relations, from latitude and its degrees. We know nothing about a body until we know what it can do, in other words, what its affects are, how they can or cannot enter into composition with other affects, with the affects of another body, either to destroy that body or to be destroyed by it, either to exchange actions and passions with it or to join with it in composing a more powerful body.

Once again, we turn to children. Note how they talk about animals, and are moved by them. They make a list of affects. Little Hans's horse is not representative but affective. It is not a member of a species but an element or individual in a machinic assemblage: draft horse-omnibus-street. It is defined by a list of active and passive affects in the context of the individuated assemblage it is part of: having eyes blocked by blinders, having a bit and a bridle, being proud, having a big peepee-maker, pulling heavy loads, being whipped, falling, making a din with its legs, biting, etc. These affects circulate and are transformed within the assemblage: what a horse "can do." They indeed have an optimal limit at the summit of horsepower, but also a pessimal threshold: a horse falls down in the street! It can't get back on its feet with that heavy load on its back, and the excessive whipping; a horse is going to die!—this was an ordinary sight in those days (Nietzsche, Dostoyevsky, Nijinsky lamented it). So just what is the becoming-horse of Little Hans? Hans is also taken up in an assemblage: his mother's bed, the paternal element, the house, the café across the street, the nearby warehouse, the street, the right to go out onto the street, the winning of this right, the pride of winning it, but also the dangers of winning it, the fall, shame . . . These are not phantasies or subjective reveries: it is not a question of imitating a horse, "playing" horse, identifying with one, or even experiencing feelings of pity or sympathy. Neither does it have to do with an objective analogy between assemblages. The question is whether Little Hans can endow his own elements with the relations of movement and rest, the affects, that would make it become horse, forms and subjects aside. Is there an as yet unknown assemblage that would be neither Hans's nor the horse's, but that of the becoming-horse of Hans? An assemblage, for example, in which the horse would bare its teeth and Hans might show something else, his feet, his legs, his peepee-maker, whatever? And in what way would that ameliorate Hans's problem, to what extent would it open a way out that had been previously blocked? When Hofmannsthal contemplates the death throes of a rat, it is in him that the animal "bares his teeth at monstrous fate." *This is not a feeling of pity*, as he makes clear; still less an identification. It is a composition of speeds and affects involving entirely different individuals, a symbiosis; it makes the rat become a thought, a feverish thought in the man, at the same time as the man becomes a rat gnashing its teeth in its death throes. The rat and the man are in no way the same thing, but Being expresses them both in a single meaning in a language that is no longer that of words, in a matter that is no longer that of forms, in an affectability that is no longer that of subjects. *Unnatural participation*. But the plane of composition, the plane of Nature, is precisely for participations of this kind, and continually makes and unmakes their assemblages, employing every artifice.

This is not an analogy, or a product of the imagination, but a composition of speeds and affects on the plane of consistency: a plan(e), a program, or rather a diagram, a problem, a question-machine. Vladimir Slepian formulates the "problem" in a thoroughly curious text: I'm hungry, always hungry, a man should not be hungry, so I'll have to become a dog—but how? This will not involve imitating a dog, nor an analogy of relations. I must succeed in endowing the parts of my body with relations of speed and slowness that will make it become dog, in an original assemblage proceeding neither by resemblance nor by analogy. For I cannot become dog without the dog itself becoming something else. Slepian gets the idea of using shoes to solve this problem, the artifice of the shoes. If I wear shoes on my hands, then their elements will enter into a new relation, resulting in the affect or becoming I seek. But how will I be able to tie the shoe on my second hand, once the first is already occupied? With my mouth, which in turn receives an investment in the assemblage, becoming a dog muzzle, insofar as a dog muzzle is now used to tie shoes. At each stage of the problem, what needs to be done is not to compare two organs but to place elements or materials in a relation that uproots the organ from its specificity, making it become "with" the other organ. But this becoming, which has already taken in feet, hands, and mouth, will nevertheless fail. It founders on the tail. The tail would have had to have been invested, forced to exhibit elements common to the sexual organ and the caudal appendage, so that the former would be taken up in the becoming-dog of the man at the same time as the latter were taken up in a becoming *of* the dog, in another becoming that would also be part of the assemblage. The plan(e) fails, Slepian falters on this point. The tail remains an organ of the man on the one hand and an appendage of the dog on the other; their relations do not enter into composition in the new assemblage. This is where psychoanalytic drift sets in, bringing back all the clichés about the tail, the mother, the childhood memory of the mother threading needles, all those concrete figures and symbolic analogies.[31] But this is the way Slepian wants it in this fine text. For there is a way in which the failure of the plan(e) is part of the plan(e) itself: The plan(e) is infinite, you can start it in a thousand different ways; you will always find something that comes too late or too early, forcing you to recompose all of your relations of speed and slowness, all of your affects, and to rearrange the overall assemblage. An infinite undertaking. But there is another way in which the plan(e) fails; this time, it is because *another plan(e)* returns full force, breaking the becoming-animal, folding the animal back onto the animal and the person onto the person, recognizing only resemblances between elements and analogies between relations. Slepian confronts both dangers.

We wish to make a simple point about psychoanalysis: from the beginning, it has often encountered the question of the becomings-animal of the human being: in children, who continually undergo becomings of this kind; in fetishism and in particular masochism, which continually confront this problem. The least that can be said is that the psychoanalysts, even Jung, did not understand, or did not want to understand. They killed becoming-animal, in the adult as in the child. They saw nothing. They see the animal as a representative of drives, or a representation of the parents. They do not see the reality of a becoming-animal, that it is affect in itself, the drive in person, and represents nothing. There exist no other drives than the assemblages themselves. There are two classic texts in which Freud sees nothing but the father in the becoming-horse of Hans, and Ferenczi sees the same in the becoming-cock of Arpad. The horse's blinders are the father's eyeglasses, the black around its mouth is his mustache, its kicks are the parents' "lovemaking." Not one word about Hans's relation to the street, on how the street was forbidden to him, on what it is for a child to see the spectacle "a horse is proud, a blinded horse pulls, a horse falls, a horse is whipped . . ." Psychoanalysis has no feeling for unnatural participations, nor for the assemblages a child can mount in order to solve a problem from which all exits are barred him: a *plan(e)*, not a phantasy. Similarly, fewer stupidities would be uttered on the topic of pain, humiliation, and anxiety in masochism if it were understood that it is the becomings-animal that lead the masochism, not the other way around. There are always apparatuses, tools, engines involved, there are always artifices and constraints used in taking Nature to the fullest. That is because it is necessary to annul the organs, to shut them away so that their liberated elements can enter into the new relations from which the becoming-animal, and the circulation of affects within the machinic assemblage, will result. As we have seen elsewhere, this was the case for the mask, the bridle, the bit, and the penis sheath in *Equus eroticus:* paradoxically, in the becoming-horse assemblage the man subdues his own "instinctive" forces while the animal transmits to him its "acquired" forces. Reversal, unnatural participation. And the boots of the woman-master function to annul the leg as a human organ, to make the elements of the leg enter a relation suited to the overall assemblage: "In this way, it will no longer be women's legs that have an effect on me . . ."[32] But to break the becoming-animal all that is needed is to extract a segment from it, to abstract one of its moments, to fail to take into account its internal speeds and slownesses, to arrest the circulation of affects. Then nothing remains but imaginary resemblances between terms, or symbolic analogies between relations. This segment refers to the father, that relation of movement and rest refers to the primal scene, etc. It must be recognized that psychoanalysis alone is not enough to bring about this breakage. It only brings out a danger inherent in becoming. There is always the danger of finding yourself "playing" the animal, the domestic Oedipal animal, Miller going bowwow and taking a bone, Fitzgerald licking your hand, Slepian returning to his mother, or the old man playing horse or dog on an erotic postcard from 1900 (and "playing" at being a wild animal would be no better). Becomings-animal continually run these dangers.

Memories of a Haecceity. A body is not defined by the form that determines it nor as a determinate substance or subject nor by the organs it possesses or the functions it fulfills. On the plane of consistency, *a body is defined only by a longitude and a latitude:* in other words the sum total of the material elements belonging to it under given relations of movement and rest, speed and slowness (longitude); the sum total of the intensive affects it is capable of at a given power or degree of potential (latitude). Nothing but affects and local movements, differential speeds. The credit goes to Spinoza for calling attention to these two dimensions of the Body, and for having defined the plane of Nature as pure longitude and latitude. Latitude and longitude are the two elements of a cartography.

There is a mode of individuation very different from that of a person, subject, thing, or substance. We reserve the name *haecceity* for it.[33] A season, a winter, a summer, an hour, a date have a perfect individuality lacking nothing, even though this individuality is different from that of a thing or a subject. They are haecceities in the sense that they consist entirely of relations of movement and rest between molecules or particles, capacities to affect and be affected. When demonology expounds upon the diabolical art of local movements and transports of affect, it also notes the importance of rain, hail, wind, pestilential air, or air polluted by noxious particles, favorable conditions for these transports. Tales must contain haecceities that are not simply emplacements, but concrete individuations that have a status of their own and direct the metamorphosis of things and subjects. Among types of civilizations, the Orient has many more individuations by haecceity than by subjectivity or substantiality: the haiku, for example, must include indicators as so many floating lines constituting a complex individual. In Charlotte Brontë, everything is in terms of *wind*, things, people, faces, loves, words. Lorca's "five in the evening," when love falls and fascism rises. That awful five in the evening! We say, "What a story!" "What heat!" "What a life!" to designate a very singular individuation. The hours of the day in Lawrence, in Faulkner. A degree of heat, an intensity of white, are perfect individualities; and a degree of heat can combine in latitude with another degree to form a new individual, as in a body that is cold here and hot there depending on its longitude. Norwegian omelette. A degree of heat can combine with an intensity of white, as in certain white skies of a hot summer. This is in no way an individuality of the instant, as opposed to the individuality of permanences or durations. A tear-off calendar has just as much time as a perpetual calendar, although the time in question is not the same. There are animals that live no longer than a day or an hour; conversely, a group of years can be as long as the most durable subject or object. We can conceive of an abstract time that is equal for haecceities and for subjects or things. Between the extreme slownesses and vertiginous speeds of geology and astronomy, Michel Tournier places meteorology, where meteors live at our pace: "A cloud forms in the sky like an image in my brain, the wind blows like I breathe, a rainbow spans the horizon for as long as my heart needs to reconcile itself to life, the summer passes like vacation drifts by." But is it by chance that in Tournier's novel this certitude can come only to a twin hero who is deformed and desubjectified, and has acquired a certain ubiquity?[34] Even when times are abstractly equal, the individuation of a life is not the same as the individuation of the subject that leads it or serves as its support. It is not the same Plane: in the first case, it is the plane of consistency or of composition of haecceities, which knows only speeds and affects; and in the second case, it is the altogether different plane of forms, substances, and subjects. And it is not in the same time, the same temporality. *Aeon:* the indefinite time of the event, the floating line that knows only speeds and continually divides that which transpires into an already-there that is at the same time not-yet-here, a simultaneous too-late and too-early, a something that is both going to happen and has just happened. *Chronos:* the time of measure that situates things and persons, develops a form, and determines a subject.[35] Boulez distinguishes tempo and nontempo in music: the "pulsed time" of a formal and functional music based on values versus the "nonpulsed time" of a floating music, both floating *and* machinic, which has nothing but speeds or differences in dynamic.[36] In short, the difference is not at all between the ephemeral and the durable, nor even between the regular and the irregular, but between two modes of individuation, two modes of temporality.

We must avoid an oversimplified conciliation, as though there were on the one hand formed subjects, of the thing or person type, and on the other hand spatiotemporal coordinates of the haecceity type. For you will yield nothing to haecceities unless you realize that that is what you are, and that you are nothing but that. When the face becomes a haecceity: "It seemed a curious mixture that simply made do with time, weather and these people."[37] You are longitude and latitude, a set of speeds and slownesses between unformed particles, a set of nonsubjectified affects. You have the individuality of a day, a season, a year, *a life* (regardless of its duration)—a climate, a wind, a fog, a swarm, a pack (regardless of its regularity). Or at least you can have it, you can reach it. A cloud of locusts carried in by the wind at five in the evening; a vampire who goes out at night, a werewolf at full moon. It should not be thought that a haecceity consists simply of a decor or backdrop that situates subjects, or of appendages that hold things and people to the ground. It is the entire assemblage in its individuated aggregate that is a haecceity; it is this assemblage that is defined by a longitude and a latitude, by speeds and affects, independently of forms and subjects, which belong to another plane. It is the wolf itself, and the horse, and the child, that cease to be subjects to become events, in assemblages that are inseparable from an hour, a season, an atmosphere, an air, a life. The street enters into composition with the horse, just as the dying rat enters into composition with the air, and the beast and the full moon enter into composition with each other. At most, we may distinguish assemblage haecceities (a body considered only as longitude and latitude) and interassemblage haecceities, which also mark the potentialities of becoming within each assemblage (the milieu of intersection of the longitudes and latitudes). But the two are strictly inseparable. Climate, wind, season, hour are not of another nature than the things, animals, or people that populate them, follow them, sleep and awaken within them. This should be read without a pause: the animal-stalks-at-five-o'clock. The becoming-evening, becoming-night of an animal, blood nuptials. Five o'clock is this animal! This animal is this place! "The thin dog is running in the road, this dog is the road," cries Virginia Woolf. That is how we need to feel. Spatiotemporal relations, determinations, are not predicates of the thing but dimensions of multiplicities. The street is as much a part of the omnibus-horse assemblage as the Hans assemblage the becoming-horse of which it initiates. We are all five o'clock in the evening, or another hour, or rather two hours simultaneously, the optimal and the pessimal, noon-midnight, but distributed in a variable fashion. The plane of consistency contains only haecceities, along intersecting lines. Forms and subjects are not of that world. Virginia Woolf's walk through the crowd, among the taxis. Taking a walk is a haecceity; never again will Mrs. Dalloway say to herself, "I am this, I am that, he is this, he is that." And "She felt very young; at the same time unspeakably aged. She sliced like a knife through everything; at the same time was outside, looking on. . . . She always had the feeling that it was very, very dangerous to live even one day."[38] Haecceity, fog, glare. A haecceity has neither beginning nor end, origin nor destination; it is always in the middle. It is not made of points, only of lines. It is a rhizome.

And it is not the same language, at least not the same usage of language. For if the plane of consistency only has haecceities for content, it also has its own particular semiotic to serve as expression. A plane of content and a plane of expression. This semiotic is composed above all of proper names, verbs in the infinitive and indefinite articles or pronouns. *Indefinite article + proper name + infinitive verb* constitutes the basic chain of expression, correlative to the least formalized contents, from the standpoint of a semiotic that has freed itself from both formal signifiances and personal subjectifications. In the first place, the verb in the infinitive is in no way indeterminate with respect to time; it expresses the floating, nonpulsed time proper to Aeon, in other words, the time of the pure event or of becoming, which articulates relative speeds and slownesses independently of the chronometric or chronological values that time assumes in the other modes. There is good reason to oppose the infinitive as mode and tense of becoming to all of the other modes and tenses, which pertain to Chronos since they form pulsations or values of being (the verb "to be" is precisely the only one that has no infinitive, or rather the infinitive of which is only an indeterminate, empty expression, taken abstractly to designate the sum total of definite modes and tenses).[39] Second, the proper name is no way the indicator of a subject; thus it seems useless to ask whether its operation resembles the nomination of a species, according to whether the subject is considered to be of another nature than that of the Form under which it is classified, or only the ultimate act of that Form, the limit of classification.[40] The proper name does not indicate a subject; nor does a noun take on the value of a proper name as a function of a form or a species. The proper name fundamentally designates something that is of the order of the event, of becoming or of the haecceity. It is the military men and meteorologists who hold the secret of proper names, when they give them to a strategic operation or a hurricane. The proper name is not the subject of a tense but the agent of an infinitive. It marks a longitude and a latitude. If Tick, Wolf, Horse, etc., are true proper names, they are so not by virtue of the specific and generic denominators that characterize them but of the speeds that compose them and the affects that fill them; it is by virtue of the event they are in themselves and in the assemblages—the becoming-horse of Little Hans, the becoming-wolf of the Were [which etymologically means "man"—Trans.], the becoming-tick of the Stoic (other proper names).

Third, the indefinite article and the indefinite pronoun are no more indeterminate than the infinitive. Or rather they are lacking a determination only insofar as they are applied to a form that is itself indeterminate, or to a determinable subject. On the other hand, they lack nothing when they introduce haecceities, events, the individuation of which does not pass into a form and is not effected by a subject. The indefinite then has maximum determination: once upon a time; a child is being beaten; a horse is falling . . . Here, the elements in play find their individuation in the assemblage of which they are a part, independent of the form of their concept and the subjectivity of their person. We have remarked several times the extent to which children use the indefinite not as something indeterminate but, on the contrary, as an individuating function within a collectivity. That is why we are dumbfounded by the efforts of psychoanalysis, which desperately wants there to be something definite hidden behind the indefinite, a possessive, a person. When the child says "*a* belly," "*a* horse," "how do *people* grow up?" "*someone* is beating *a* child," the psychoanalyst hears "my belly," "the father," "will I grow up to be like daddy?" The psychoanalyst asks: Who is being beaten, and by whom?[41] Even linguistics is not immune from the same prejudice, inasmuch as it is inseparable from a personology; according to linguistics, in addition to the indefinite article and the pronoun, the third-person pronoun also lacks the determination of subjectivity that is proper to the first two persons and is supposedly the necessary condition for all enunciation.[42]

We believe on the contrary that the third person indefinite, HE, THEY, implies no indetermination from this point of view; it ties the statement to a collective assemblage, as its necessary condition, rather than to a subject of the enunciation. Blanchot is correct in saying that ONE and HE—*one* is dying, *he* is unhappy—in no way take the place of a subject, but instead do away with any subject in favor of an assemblage of the haecceity type that carries or brings out the event insofar as it is unformed and incapable of being effectuated by persons ("something happens to them that they can only get a grip on again by letting go of their ability to say I").[43] The HE does not represent a subject but rather makes a diagram of an assemblage. It does not overcode statements, it does not transcend them as do the first two persons; on the contrary, it prevents them from falling under the tyranny of subjective or signifying constellations, under the regime of empty redundancies. The contents of the chains of expression it articulates are those that can be assembled for a maximum number of occurrences and becomings. "They arrive like fate . . . where do they come from, how have they pushed this far . . .?"[44] He or one, indefinite article, proper name, infinitive verb: A HANS TO BECOME HORSE, A PACK NAMED WOLF TO LOOK AT HE, ONE TO DIE, WASP TO MEET ORCHID, THEY ARRIVE HUNS. Classified ads, telegraphic machines on the plane of consistency (once again, we are reminded of the procedures of Chinese poetry and the rules for translation suggested by the best commentators).[45]

Memories of a Plan(e) Maker. Perhaps there are two planes, or two ways of conceptualizing the plane. The plane can be a hidden principle, which makes visible what is seen and audible what is heard, etc., which at every instant causes the given to be given, in this or that state, at this or that moment. But the plane itself is not given. It is by nature hidden. It can only be inferred, induced, concluded from that to which it gives rise (simultaneously or successively, synchronically or diachronically). A plane of this kind is as much a plan(e) of organization as of development: it is structural or genetic, and both at once, structure and genesis, the structural plan(e) of formed organizations with their developments, the genetic plan(e) of evolutionary developments with their organizations. These are only nuances of this first conception of the plane. To accord these nuances too much importance would prevent us from grasping something more important; that the plan(e), conceived or made in this fashion, always concerns the development of forms and the formation of subjects. A hidden structure necessary for forms, a secret signifier necessary for subjects. It ensues that the plan(e) itself will not be given. It exists only in a supplementary dimension to that to which it gives rise ($n+1$). This makes it a teleological plan(e), a design, a mental principle. It is a plan(e) of transcendence. It is a plan(e) of analogy, either because it assigns the eminent term of a development or because it establishes the proportional relations of a structure. It may be in the mind of a god, or in the unconscious of life, of the soul, or of language: it is always concluded from its own effects. It is always inferred. *Even if it is said to be immanent*, it is so only by absence, analogically (metaphorically, metonymically, etc.). The tree is given in the seed, but as a function of a plan(e) that is not given. The same applies to music. The developmental or organizational principle does not appear in itself, in a direct relation with that which develops or is organized: There is a transcendent compositional principle that is not of the nature of sound, that is not "audible" by itself or for itself. This opens the way for all possible interpretations. Forms and their developments, and subjects and their formations, relate to a plan(e) that operates as a transcendent unity or hidden principle. The plan(e) can always be described, but as a part aside, as ungiven in that to which it gives rise. Is this not how even Balzac, even Proust, describe their work's plan(e) of organization or development, as though in a metalanguage? Is not Stockhausen also obliged to describe the structure of his sound forms as existing "alongside" them, since he is unable to make it audible? Life plan(e), music plan(e), writing plan(e), it's all the same: a plan(e) that cannot be given as such, that can only be inferred from the forms it develops and the subjects it forms, since it is *for* these forms and these subjects.

Then there is an altogether different plane, or an altogether different conception of the plane. Here, there are no longer any forms or developments of forms; nor are there subjects or the formation of subjects. There is no structure, any more than there is genesis. There are only relations of movement and rest, speed and slowness between unformed elements, or at least between elements that are relatively unformed, molecules and particles of all kinds. There are only haecceities, affects, subjectless individuations that constitute collective assemblages. Nothing develops, but things arrive late or early, and form this or that assemblage depending on their compositions of speed. Nothing subjectifies, but haecceities form according to compositions of nonsubjectified powers or affects. We call this plane, which knows only longitudes and latitudes, speeds and haecceities, the plane of consistency or composition (as opposed to the plan(e) of organization or development). It is necessarily a plane of immanence and univocality. We therefore call it the plane of Nature, although nature has nothing to do with it, since on this plane there is no distinction between the natural and the artificial. However many dimensions it may have, it never has a supplementary dimension to that which transpires upon it. That alone makes it natural and immanent. The same goes for the principle of contradiction: this plane could also be called the plane of noncontradiction. The plane of consistency could be called the plane of nonconsistency. It is a geometrical plane, no longer tied to a mental design but to an abstract design. Its number of dimensions continually increases as what happens happens, but even so it loses nothing of its planitude. It is thus a plane of proliferation, peopling, contagion; but this proliferation of material has nothing to do with an evolution, the development of a form or the filiation of forms. Still less is it a regression leading back to a principle. It is on the contrary an *involution*, in which form is constantly being dissolved, freeing times and speeds. It is a fixed plane, a fixed sound plane, or visual plane, or writing plane, etc. Here, fixed does not mean immobile: it is the absolute state of movement as well as of rest, from which all relative speeds and slownesses spring, and nothing but them. Certain modern musicians oppose the transcendent plan(e) of organization, which is said to have dominated all of Western classical music, to the immanent sound plane, which is always given along with that to which it gives rise, brings the imperceptible to perception, and carries only differential speeds and slownesses in a kind of molecular lapping: *the work of art must mark seconds, tenths and hundredths of seconds.*[46] Or rather it is a question of a freeing of time, Aeon, a nonpulsed time for a floating music, as Boulez says, an electronic music in which forms are replaced by pure modifications of speed. It is undoubtedly John Cage who first and most perfectly deployed this fixed sound plane, which affirms a process against all structure and genesis, a floating time against pulsed time or tempo, experimentation against any kind of interpretation, and in which silence as sonorous rest also marks the absolute state of movement. The same could be said of the fixed visual plane: Godard, for example, effectively carries the fixed plane of cinema to this state where forms dissolve, and all that subsists are tiny variations of speed between movements in composition. Nathalie Sarraute, for her part, proposes a clear distinction between two planes of writing: a transcendent plan(e) that organizes and develops forms (genres, themes, motifs) and assigns and develops subjects (personages, characters, feelings); and an altogether different plane that liberates the particles of an anonymous matter, allowing them to communicate through the "envelope" of forms and subjects, retaining between them only relations of movement and rest, speed and slowness, floating affects, so that the plane itself is perceived at the same time as it allows us to perceive the imperceptible (the microplane, the molecular plane).[47] So from the point of view of a well-founded abstraction, we can make it seem as though the two planes, the two conceptions of the plane, were in clear and absolute opposition. From this point of view, we can say, You can see the difference between the following two types of propositions: (1) forms develop and subjects form as a function of a plan(e) that can only be inferred (the plan[e] of organization-development); (2) there are only speeds and slownesses between unformed elements, and affects between nonsubjectified powers, as a function of a plane that is necessarily given at the same time as that to which it gives rise (the plane of consistency or composition).[48]

Let us consider three major cases from nineteenth-century German literature, Hölderlin, Kleist, and Nietzsche. First, Hölderlin's extraordinary composition, *Hyperion*, as analyzed by Robert Rovini: the importance of haecceities of the season type. These constitute, in two different ways, the "frame of the narrative" (plan[e]) and the details of what happens within that frame (the assemblages and interassemblages).[49] He also notes how the succession of the seasons and the superposition of the same season from different years dissolves forms and persons and gives rise to movements, speeds, delays, and affects, as if as the narrative progressed something were escaping from an impalpable matter. And perhaps also the relation to a "realpolitik," to a war machine, to a musical machine of dissonance.

Kleist: everything with him, in his writing as in his life, becomes speed and slowness. A succession of catatonic freezes and extreme velocities, fainting spells and shooting arrows. Sleep on your steed, then take off at a gallop. Jump from one assemblage to another, with the aid of a faint, by crossing a void. Kleist multiplies "life plan(e)s," but his voids and failures, his leaps, earthquakes, and plagues are always included on a single plane. The plane is not a principle of organization but a means of transportation. No form develops, no subject forms; affects are displaced, becomings catapult forward and combine into blocks, like the becoming-woman of Achilles and the becoming-dog of Penthesilea. Kleist offers a wonderful explanation of how forms and persons are only appearances produced by the displacement of a center of gravity on an abstract line, and by the conjunction of these lines on a plane of immanence. He is fascinated by bears; they are impossible to fool because their cruel little eyes see through appearances to the true "soul of movement," the *Gemüt* or nonsubjective affect: the becoming-bear of Kleist. Even death can only be conceptualized as the intersection of elementary reactions of different speeds. *A skull exploding*, one of Kleist's obsessions. All of Kleist's work is traversed by a war machine invoked against the State, by a musical machine invoked against painting or the "picture." It is odd how Goethe and Hegel hated this new kind of writing. Because for them the plan(e) must indissolubly be a harmonious development of Form and a regulated formation of the Subject, personage, or character (the sentimental education, the interior and substantial solidity of the character, the harmony or analogy of the forms and continuity of development, the cult of the State, etc.). Their conception of the Plane is totally opposed to that of Kleist. The anti-Goetheism, anti-Hegelianism of Kleist, and already of Hölderlin. Goethe gets to the crux of the matter when he reproaches Kleist for simultaneously setting up a pure "stationary process" that is like the fixed plane, introducing voids and jumps that prevent any development of a central character, and mobilizing a violence of affects that causes an extreme confusion of feelings.[50]

Nietzsche does the same thing by different means. There is no longer any development of forms or formation of subjects. He criticizes Wagner for retaining too much harmonic form, and too many pedagogical personages, or "characters": too much Hegel and Goethe. Now Bizet, on the other hand, Nietzsche says . . . It seems to us that fragmentary writing is not so much the issue in Nietzsche. It is instead speeds and slownesses: not writing slowly or rapidly, but rather writing, and everything else besides, as a production of speeds and slownesses between particles. No form will resist that, no character or subject will survive it. Zarathustra is only speeds and slownesses, and the eternal return, the life of the eternal return, is the first great concrete freeing of nonpulsed time. *Ecce Homo* has only individuations by haecceities. It is inevitable that the Plan(e), thus conceived, will always fail, but that the failures will be an integral part of the plan(e): See the multitude of plans for *The Will to Power.* For a given aphorism, it is always possible, even necessary, to introduce new relations of speed and slowness between its elements that truly make it change assemblages, jump from one assemblage to the next (the issue is therefore not the fragment). As Cage says, it is of the nature of the plan(e) that it fail.[51] Precisely because it is not a plan(e) of organization, development, or formation, but of nonvoluntary transmutation. Or Boulez: "Program the machine so that each time a tape is played on it, it produces different time characteristics." So the plan(e)—life plan(e), writing plan(e), music plan(e)—must necessarily fail for it is impossible to be faithful to it; but the failures are a part of the plan(e) for the plan(e) expands or shrinks along with the dimensions of that which it deploys in each instance (planitude of *n* dimensions). A strange machine that is simultaneously a machine of war, music, and contagion-proliferation-involution.

Why does the opposition between the two kinds of planes lead to a still more abstract hypothesis? Because one continually passes from one to the other, by unnoticeable degrees and without being aware of it, or one becomes aware of it only afterward. Because one continually reconstitutes one plane atop another, or extricates one from the other. For example, all we need to do is to sink the floating plane of immanence, bury it in the depths of Nature instead of allowing it to play freely on the surface, for it to pass to the other side and assume the role of a ground that can no longer be anything more than a principle of analogy from the standpoint of organization, and a law of continuity from the standpoint of development.[52] The plane of organization or development effectively covers what we have called stratification: Forms and subjects, organs and functions, are "strata" or relations between strata. The plane of consistency or immanence, on the other hand, implies a destratification of all of Nature, by even the most artificial of means. The plane of consistency is the body without organs. Pure relations of speed and slowness between particles imply movements of deterritorialization, just as pure affects imply an enterprise of desubjectification. Moreover, the plane of consistency does not preexist the movements of deterritorialization that unravel it, the lines of flight that draw it and cause it to rise to the surface, the becomings that compose it. The plane of organization is constantly working away at the plane of consistency, always trying to plug the lines of flight, stop or interrupt the movements of deterritorialization, weigh them down, restratify them, reconstitute forms and subjects in a dimension of depth. Conversely, the plane of consistency is constantly extricating itself from the plane of organization, causing particles to spin off the strata, scrambling forms by dint of speed or slowness, breaking down functions by means of assemblages or microassemblages. But once again, so much caution is needed to prevent the plane of consistency from becoming a pure plane of abolition or death, to prevent the involution from turning into a regression to the undifferentiated. Is it not necessary to retain a minimum of strata, a minimum of forms and functions, a minimal subject from which to extract materials, affects, and assemblages?

In fact, the opposition we should set up between the two planes is that between two abstract poles: for example, to the transcendent, organizational plane of Western music based on sound forms and their development, we oppose the immanent plane of consistency of Eastern music, composed of speeds and slownesses, movements and rest. In keeping with our concrete hypothesis, the whole becoming of Western music, all musical becoming, implies a minimum of sound forms and even of melodic and harmonic functions; speeds and slownesses are made to pass across them, and it is precisely these speeds and slownesses that reduce the forms and functions to the minimum. Beethoven produced the most astonishing polyphonic richness with relatively scanty themes of three or four notes. There is a material proliferation that goes hand in hand with a dissolution of form (involution) but is at the same time accompanied by a continuous development of form. Perhaps Schumann's genius is the most striking case of form being developed only for the relations of speed and slowness one materially and emotionally assigns it. Music has always submitted its forms and motifs to temporal transformations, augmentations or diminutions, slowdowns or accelerations, which do not occur solely according to laws of organization or even of development. Expanding and contracting microintervals are at play within coded intervals. Wagner and the post-Wagnerians free variations of speed between sound particles to an even greater extent. Ravel and Debussy retain just enough form to shatter it, affect it, modify it through speeds and slownesses. *Bolero* is the classic example, nearly a caricature, of a machinic assemblage that preserves a minimum of form in order to take it to the bursting point. Boulez speaks of proliferations of little motifs, accumulations of little notes that proceed kinematically and affectively, sweeping away a simple form by adding indications of speed to it; this allows one to produce extremely complex dynamic relations on the basis of intrinsically simple formal relations. Even a rubato by Chopin cannot be reproduced because it will have different time characteristics at each playing.[53] It is as though an immense plane of consistency of variable speed were forever sweeping up forms and functions, forms and subjects, extracting from them particles and affects. A clock keeping a whole assortment of times.

What is a girl, what is a group of girls? Proust at least has shown us once and for all that their individuation, collective or singular, proceeds not by subjectivity but by haecceity, pure haecceity. "Fugitive beings." They are pure relations of speeds and slownesses, and nothing else. A girl is late on account of her speed: she did too many things, crossed too many spaces in relation to the relative time of the person waiting for her. Thus her apparent slowness is transformed into the breakneck speed of our waiting. It must be said in this connection, and for the whole of the *Recherche du temps perdu*, that Swann does not at all occupy the same position as the narrator. Swann is not a rough sketch or precursor of the narrator, except secondarily and at rare moments. They are not at all on the same *plane*. Swann is always thinking and feeling in terms of subjects, forms, resemblances between subjects, and correspondences between forms. For him, one of Odette's lies is a form whose secret subjective content must be discovered, provoking amateur detective activity. To him Vinteuil's music is a form that must evoke something else, fall back on something else, echo other forms, whether paintings, faces, or landscapes. Although the narrator may follow in Swann's footsteps, he is nonetheless in a different element, on a different plane. One of Albertine's lies is nearly devoid of content; it tends on the contrary to merge with the emission of a particle issuing from the eyes of the beloved, a particle that stands only for itself and travels too fast through the narrator's auditory or visual field. This molecular speed is unbearable because it indicates a distance, a *proximity* where Albertine would like to be, and already is.[54] So that the narrator's pose is not principally that of the investigating detective but (a very different figure) that of the jailer. How can he become master of speed, how can he stand it nervously (as a headache) and perceptually (as a flash)? How can he build a prison for Albertine? Jealousy is different in Swann and the narrator, as is the perception of music: Vinteuil gradually ceases to be apprehended in terms of forms and comparable subjects, and assumes incredible speeds and slownesses that combine on a plane of consistency of variation, the plane of music and of the *Recherche* (just as Wagnerian motifs abandon all fixity of form and all assignation of personages). It is as though Swann's desperate efforts to reterritorialize the flow of things (to reterritorialize Odette on a secret, painting on a face, music on the Bois de Boulogne) were replaced by the sped-up movement of deterritorialization, by a linear speedup of the abstract machine, sweeping away faces and landscapes, and then love, jealousy, painting, and music itself, according to increasingly stronger coefficients that nourish the Work at risk of dissolving everything and dying. For the narrator, despite partial victories, fails in his project; that project was not at all to regain time or to force back memories, but to become master of speeds to the rhythm of his asthma. It was to face annihilation. But another outcome was possible, or was made possible by Proust.

Memories of a Molecule. Becoming-animal is only one becoming among others. A kind of order or apparent progression can be established for the segments of becoming in which we find ourselves; becoming-woman, becoming-child; becoming-animal, -vegetable, or -mineral; becomings-molecular of all kinds, becomings-particles. Fibers lead us from one to the other, transform one into the other as they pass through doors and across thresholds. Singing or composing, painting, writing have no other aim: to unleash these becomings. Especially music; music is traversed by a becoming-woman, becoming-child, and not only at the level of themes and motifs: the little refrain, children's games and dances, childhood scenes. Instrumentation and orchestration are permeated by becomings-animal, above all becomings-bird, but many others besides. The lapping, wailing of molecular discordances have always been present, even if instrumental evolution with other factors is now giving them growing importance, as the value of a new threshold for a properly musical content: the sound molecule, relations of speed and slowness between particles. Becomings-animal plunge into becomings-molecular. This raises all kinds of questions.

In a way, we must start at the end: all becomings are already molecular. That is because becoming is not to imitate or identify with something or someone. Nor is it to proportion formal relations. Neither of these two figures of analogy is applicable to becoming: neither the imitation of a subject nor the proportionality of a form. Starting from the forms one has, the subject one is, the organs one has, or the functions one fulfills, becoming is to extract particles between which one establishes the relations of movement and rest, speed and slowness that are *closest* to what one is becoming, and through which one becomes. This is the sense in which becoming is the process of desire. This principle of proximity or approximation is entirely particular and reintroduces no analogy whatsoever. It indicates as rigor-ously as possible a *zone of proximity*[55] *or copresence* of a particle, the movement into which any particle that enters the zone is drawn. Louis Wolfson embarks upon a strange undertaking: a schizophrenic, he translates as quickly as possible each phrase in his maternal language into foreign words with similar sound and meaning; an anorexic, he rushes to the refrigerator, tears open the packages and snatches their contents, stuffing himself as quickly as possible.[56] It would be false to believe that he needs to borrow "disguised" words from foreign languages. Rather, he snatches from his own language verbal particles that can no longer belong to the form of that language, just as he snatches from food alimentary particles that no longer act as formed nutritional substances; the two kinds of particles enter into proximity. We could also put it this way: Becoming is to emit particles that take on certain relations of movement and rest because they enter a particular zone of proximity. Or, it is to emit particles that enter that zone because they take on those relations. A haecceity is inseparable from the fog and mist that depend on a molecular zone, a corpuscular space. Proximity is a notion, at once topological and quantal, that marks a belonging to the same molecule, independently of the subjects considered and the forms determined.

Schérer and Hocquenghem made this essential point in their reconsideration of the problem of wolf-children. Of course, it is not a question of a real production, as if the child "really" became an animal; nor is it a question of a resemblance, as if the child imitated animals that really raised it; nor is it a question of a symbolic metaphor, as if the autistic child that was abandoned or lost merely became the "analogue" of an animal. Schérer and Hocquenghem are right to expose this false reasoning, which is based on a culturalism or moralism upholding the irreducibility of the human order: Because the child has not been transformed into an animal, it must only have a metaphorical relation to it, induced by the child's illness or rejection. For their own part, they appeal to an objective zone of indetermination or uncertainty, "something shared or indiscernible," a proximity "that makes it impossible to say where the boundary between the human and animal lies," not only in the case of autistic children, but for all children; it is as though, independent of the evolution carrying them toward adulthood, there were room in the child for other becomings, "other contemporaneous possibilities" that are not regressions but creative involutions bearing witness to "*an inhumanity immediately experienced in the body as such*," unnatural nuptials "outside the programmed body." There is a reality of becoming-animal, even though one does not in reality become animal. It is useless, then, to raise the objection that the dog-child only plays dog within the limits of his formal constitution, and does nothing canine that another human being could not have done if he or she had so desired. For what needs to be explained is precisely the fact that all children, and even many adults, do it to a greater or lesser degree, and in so doing bear witness to an inhuman connivance with the animal, rather than an Oedipal symbolic community.[57] Neither should it be thought that children who graze, or eat dirt or raw flesh, are merely getting the vitamins and minerals they need. It is a question of composing a body with the animal, a body without organs defined by zones of intensity or proximity. Where does this objective indetermination or indiscernibility of which Schérer and Hocquenghem speak come from?

An example: Do not imitate a dog, but make your organism enter into composition with *something else* in such a way that the particles emitted from the aggregate thus composed will be canine as a function of the relation of movement and rest, or of molecular proximity, into which they enter. Clearly, this something else can be quite varied, and be more or less directly related to the animal in question: it can be the animal's natural food (dirt and worm), or its exterior relations with other animals (you can become-dog with cats, or become-monkey with a horse), or an apparatus or prosthesis to which a person subjects the animal (muzzle and reindeer, etc.), or something that does not even have a localizable relation to the animal in question. For this last case, we have seen how Slepian bases his attempt to become-dog on the idea of tying shoes to his hands using his mouth-muzzle. Philippe Gavi cites the performances of Lolito, an eater of bottles, earthenware, porcelains, iron, and even bicycles, who declares: "I consider myself half-animal, half-man. More animal than man. I love animals, dogs especially, I feel a bond with them. My teeth have adapted; in fact, when I don't eat glass or iron, my jaw aches like a young dog's that craves to chew a bone."[58] If we interpret the word "like" as a metaphor, or propose a structural analogy of relations (man-iron = dog-bone), we understand nothing of becoming. The word "like" is one of those words that change drastically in meaning and function when they are used in connection with haecceities, when they are made into expressions of becomings instead of signified states or signifying relations. A dog may exercise its jaw on iron, but when it does it is using its jaw as a molar organ. When Lolito eats iron, it is totally different: he makes his jaw enter into composition with the iron in such a way that he himself becomes the jaw of a molecular dog. The actor Robert De Niro walks "like" a crab in a certain film sequence; but, he says, it is not a question of his imitating a crab; it is a question of making something that has to do with the crab enter into composition with the image, with the speed of the image.[59] That is the essential point for us: you become-animal only if, by whatever means or elements, you emit corpuscles that enter the relation of movement and rest of the animal particles, or what amounts to the same thing, that enter the zone of proximity of the animal molecule. You become animal only molecularly. You do not become a barking molar dog, but by barking, if it is done with enough feeling, with enough necessity and composition, you emit a molecular dog. Man does not become wolf, or vampire, as if he changed molar species; the vampire and werewolf are becomings of man, in other words, proximities between molecules in composition, relations of movement and rest, speed and slowness between emitted particles. Of course there are werewolves and vampires, we say this with all our heart; but do not look for a resemblance or analogy to the animal, for this is becoming-animal in action, the production of the molecular animal (whereas the "real" animal is trapped in its molar form and subjectivity). It is within us that the animal bares its teeth like Hofmannsthal's rat, or the flower opens its petals; but this is done by corpuscular emission, by molecular proximity, and not by the imitation of a subject or a proportionality of form. Albertine can always imitate a flower, but it is when she is sleeping and enters into composition with the particles of sleep that her beauty spot and the texture of her skin enter a relation of rest and movement that place her in the zone of a molecular vegetable: the becoming-plant of Albertine. And it is when she is held prisoner that she emits the particles of a bird. And it is when she flees, launches down a line of flight, that she becomes-horse, even if it is the horse of death.

Yes, all becomings are molecular: the animal, flower, or stone one becomes are molecular collectivities, haecceities, not molar subjects, objects, or form that we know from the outside and recognize from experience, through science, or by habit. If this is true, then we must say the same of things human: there is a becoming-woman, a becoming-child, that do not resemble the woman or the child as clearly distinct molar entities (although it is possible—only possible—for the woman or child to occupy privileged positions in relation to these becomings). What we term a molar entity is, for example, the woman as defined by her form, endowed with organs and functions and assigned as a subject. Becoming-woman is not imitating this entity or even transforming oneself into it. We are not, however, overlooking the importance of imitation, or moments of imitation, among certain homosexual males, much less the prodigious attempt at a real transformation on the part of certain transvestites. All we are saying is that these indissociable aspects of becoming-woman must first be understood as a function of something else: not imitating or assuming the female form, but emitting particles that enter the relation of movement and rest, or the zone of proximity, of a microfemininity, in other words, that produce in us a molecular woman, create the molecular woman. We do not mean to say that a creation of this kind is the prerogative of the man, but on the contrary that the woman as a molar entity *has to become-woman* in order that the man also becomes- or can become-woman. It is, of course, indispensable for women to conduct a molar politics, with a view to winning back their own organism, their own history, their own subjectivity: "we as women . . ." makes its appearance as a subject of enunciation. But it is dangerous to confine oneself to such a subject, which does not function without drying up a spring or stopping a flow. The song of life is often intoned by the driest of women, moved by *ressentiment*, the will to power and cold mothering. Just as a dessicated child makes a much better child, there being no childhood flow emanating from it any longer. It is no more adequate to say that each sex contains the other and must develop the opposite pole in itself. Bisexuality is no better a concept than the separateness of the sexes. It is as deplorable to miniaturize, internalize the binary machine as it is to exacerbate it; it does not extricate us from it. It is thus necessary to conceive of a molecular women's politics that slips into molar confrontations, and passes under or through them.

When Virginia Woolf was questioned about a specifically women's writing, she was appalled at the idea of writing "as a woman." Rather, writing should produce a becoming-woman as atoms of womanhood capable of crossing and impregnating an entire social field, and of contaminating men, of sweeping them up in that becoming. Very soft particles—but also very hard and obstinate, irreducible, indomitable. The rise of women in English novel writing has spared no man: even those who pass for the most virile, the most phallocratic, such as Lawrence and Miller, in their turn continually tap into and emit particles that enter the proximity or zone of indiscernibility of women. In writing, they become-women. The question is not, or not only, that of the organism, history, and subject of enunciation that oppose masculine to feminine in the great dualism machines. The question is fundamentally that of the body—the body they *steal* from us in order to fabricate opposable organisms. This body is stolen first from the girl: Stop behaving like that, you're not a little girl anymore, you're not a tomboy, etc. The girl's becoming is stolen first, in order to impose a history, or prehistory, upon her. The boy's turn comes next, but it is by using the girl as an example, by pointing to the girl as the object of his desire, that an opposed organism, a dominant history is fabricated for him too. The girl is the first victim, but she must also serve as an example and a trap. That is why, conversely, the reconstruction of the body as a Body without Organs, the anorganism of the body, is inseparable from a becoming-woman, or the production of a molecular woman. Doubtless, the girl becomes a woman in the molar or organic sense. But conversely, becoming-woman or the molecular woman is the girl herself. The girl is certainly not defined by virginity; she is defined by a relation of movement and rest, speed and slowness, by a combination of atoms, an emission of particles: haecceity. She never ceases to roam upon a body without organs. She is an abstract line, or a line of flight. Thus girls do not belong to an age group, sex, order, or kingdom: they slip in everywhere, between orders, acts, ages, sexes; they produce *n* molecular sexes on the line of flight in relation to the dualism machines they cross right through. The only way to get outside the dualisms is to be-between, to pass between, the intermezzo—that is what Virginia Woolf lived with all her energies, in all of her work, never ceasing to become. The girl is like the block of becoming that remains contemporaneous to each opposable term, man, woman, child, adult. It is not the girl who becomes a woman; it is becoming-woman that produces the universal girl. Trost, a mysterious author, painted a portrait of the girl, to whom he linked the fate of the revolution: her speed, her freely machinic body, her intensities, her abstract line or line of flight, her molecular production, her indifference to memory, her nonfigurative character—"the nonfigurative of desire."[60] Joan of Arc? The special role of the girl in Russian terrorism: the girl with the bomb, guardian of dynamite? It is certain that molecular politics proceeds via the girl and the child. But it is also certain that girls and children draw their strength neither from the molar status that subdues them nor from the organism and subjectivity they receive; they draw their strength from the becoming-molecular they cause to pass between sexes and ages, the becoming-child of the adult as well as of the child, the becoming-woman of the man as well as of the woman. The girl and the child do not become; it is becoming itself that is a child or a girl. The child does not become an adult any more than the girl becomes a woman; the girl is the becoming-woman of each sex, just as the child is the becoming-young of every age. Knowing how to age does not mean remaining young; it means extracting from one's age the particles, the speeds and slownesses, the flows that constitute the youth of *that* age. Knowing how to love does not mean remaining a man or a woman; it means extracting from one's sex the particles, the speeds and slownesses, the flows, the *n* sexes that constitute the girl of *that* sexuality. It is Age itself that is a becoming-child, just as Sexuality, any sexuality, is a becoming-woman, in other words, a girl. This by way of response to the stupid question, Why did Proust make Albert Albertine?

Although all becomings are already molecular, including becoming-woman, it must be said that all becomings begin with and pass through becoming-woman. It is the key to all the other becomings. When the man of war disguises himself as a woman, flees disguised as a girl, hides as a girl, it is not a shameful, transitory incident in his life. To hide, to camouflage oneself, is a warrior function, and the line of flight attracts the enemy, traverses something and puts what it traverses to flight; the warrior arises in the infinity of a line of flight. Although the femininity of the man of war is not accidental, it should not be thought of as structural, or regulated by a correspondence of relations. It is difficult to see how the correspondence between the two relations "man-war" and "woman-marriage" could entail an equivalence between the warrior and the girl as a woman who refuses to marry.[61] It is just as difficult to see how the general bisexuality, or even homosexuality, of military societies could explain this phenomenon, which is no more imitative than it is structural, representing instead an essential *anomie* of the man of war. This phenomenon can only be understood in terms of becoming. We have seen how the man of war, by virtue of his *furor* and celerity, was swept up in irresistible becomings-animal. These are becomings that have as their necessary condition the becoming-woman of the warrior, or his alliance with the girl, his contagion with her. The man of war is inseparable from the Amazons. The union of the girl and the man of war does not produce animals, but simultaneously produces the becoming-woman of the latter and the becoming-animal of the former, in a single "block" in which the warrior in turn becomes animal by contagion with the girl at the same time as the girl becomes warrior by contagion with the animal. Everything ties together in an asymmetrical block of becoming, an instantaneous zigzag. It is in the vestiges of a double war machine—that of the Greeks, soon to be supplanted by the State, and that of the Amazons, soon to be dissolved—that Achilles and Penthesilea, the last man of war and the last queen of the girls, choose one another, Achilles in a becoming-woman, Penthesilea in a becoming-dog.

The rites of transvestism or female impersonation in primitive societies in which a man becomes a woman are not explainable by a social organization that places the given relations in correspondence, or by a psychic organization that makes the woman desire to become a man just as the man desires to become a woman.[62] Social structure and psychic identification leave too many special factors unaccounted for: the linkage, unleashing, and communication of the becomings triggered by the transvestite; the power (*puissance*) of the resultant becoming-animal; and above all the participation of these becomings in a specific war machine. The same applies for sexuality: it is badly explained by the binary organization of the sexes, and just as badly by a bisexual organization within each sex. Sexuality brings into play too great a diversity of conjugated becomings; these are like *n* sexes, an entire war machine through which love passes. This is not a return to those appalling metaphors of love and war, seduction and conquest, the battle of the sexes and the domestic squabble, or even the Strindberg-war: it is only after love is done with and sexuality has dried up that things appear this way. What counts is that love itself is a war machine endowed with strange and somewhat terrifying powers. Sexuality is the production of a thousand sexes, which are so many uncontrollable becomings. *Sexuality proceeds by way of the becoming-woman of the man and the becoming-animal of the human*: an emission of particles. There is no need for bestialism in this, although it may arise, and many psychiatric anecdotes document it in ways that are interesting, if oversimplified and consequently off the track, too beastly. It is not a question of "playing" the dog, like an elderly gentleman on a postcard; it is not so much a question of making love with animals. Becomings-animal are basically of another power, since their reality resides not in an animal one imitates or to which one corresponds but in themselves, in that which suddenly sweeps us up and makes us become—a *proximity, an indiscernibility* that extracts a shared element from the animal far more effectively than any domestication, utilization, or imitation could: "the Beast."

If becoming-woman is the first quantum, or molecular segment, with the becomings-animal that link up with it coming next, what are they all rushing toward? Without a doubt, toward becoming-imperceptible. The imperceptible is the immanent end of becoming, its cosmic formula. For example, Matheson's *Shrinking Man* passes through the kingdoms of nature, slips between molecules, to become an unfindable particle in infinite meditation on the infinite. Paul Morand's *Monsieur Zéro* flees the larger countries, crosses the smallest ones, descends the scale of States, establishes an anonymous society in Lichtenstein of which he is the only member, and dies imperceptible, forming the particle 0 with his fingers: "I am a man who flees by swimming under water, and at whom all the world's rifles fire. . . . I must no longer offer a target." But what does becoming-imperceptible signify, coming at the end of all the molecular becomings that begin with becoming-woman? Becoming-imperceptible means many things. What is the relation between the (anorganic) imperceptible, the (asignifying) indiscernible, and the (asubjective) impersonal?

A first response would be: to be like everybody else. That is what Kierkegaard relates in his story about the "knight of the faith," the man of becoming: to look at him, one would notice nothing, a bourgeois, nothing but a bourgeois. That is how Fitzgerald lived: after a real rupture, one succeeds . . . in being just like everybody else. To go unnoticed is by no means easy. To be a stranger, even to one's doorman or neighbors. If it is so difficult to be "like" everybody else, it is because it is an affair of becoming. Not everybody becomes everybody [and everything: *tout le monde*—Trans.], makes a becoming of everybody/everything. This requires much asceticism, much sobriety, much creative involution: an English elegance, an English fabric, blend in with the walls, eliminate the too-perceived, the too-much-to-be-perceived. "Eliminate all that is waste, death, and superfluity," complaint and grievance, unsatisfied desire, defense or pleading, everything that roots each of us (everybody) in ourselves, in our molarity. For everybody/everything is the molar aggregate, but *becoming everybody/*

everything is another affair, one that brings into play the cosmos with its molecular components. Becoming everybody/everything (*tout le monde*) is to world (*faire monde*), to make a world (*faire un monde*). By process of elimination, one is no longer anything more than an abstract line, or a piece in a puzzle that is itself abstract. It is by conjugating, by continuing with other lines, other pieces, that one makes a world that can overlay the first one, like a transparency. Animal elegance, the camouflage fish, the clandestine: this fish is crisscrossed by abstract lines that resemble nothing, that do not even follow its organic divisions; but thus disorganized, disarticulated, it worlds with the lines of a rock, sand, and plants, becoming imperceptible. The fish is like the Chinese poet: not imitative or structural, but cosmic. François Cheng shows that poets do not pursue resemblance, any more than they calculate "geometric proportions." They retain, extract only the essential lines and movements of nature; they proceed only by continued or superposed "traits," or strokes.[63] It is in this sense that becoming-everybody/everything, making the world a becoming, is to world, to make a world or worlds, in other words, to find one's proximities and zones of indiscernibility. The Cosmos as an abstract machine, and each world as an assemblage effectuating it. If one reduces oneself to one or several abstract lines that will prolong itself in and conjugate with others, producing immediately, directly *a* world in which it is *the* world that becomes, then one becomes-everybody/everything. Kerouac's dream, and already Virginia Woolf's, was for the writing to be like the line of a Chinese poem-drawing. She says that it is necessary to "saturate every atom," and to do that it is necessary to eliminate, to eliminate all that is resemblance and analogy, but also "to put everything into it": eliminate everything that exceeds the moment, but put in everything that it includes—and the moment is not the instantaneous, it is the haecceity into which one slips and that slips into other haecceities by transparency.[64] To be present at the dawn of the world. Such is the link between imperceptibility, indiscernibility, and impersonality—the three virtues. To reduce oneself to an abstract line, a trait, in order to find one's zone of indiscernibility with other traits, and in this way enter the haecceity and impersonality of the creator. One is then like grass: one has made the world, everybody/everything, into a becoming, because one has made a necessarily communicating world, because one has suppressed in oneself everything that prevents us from slipping between things and growing in the midst of things. One has combined "everything" (*le "tout"*): the indefinite article, the infinitive-becoming, and the proper name to which one is reduced. Saturate, eliminate, put everything in.

Movement has an essential relation to the imperceptible; it is by nature imperceptible. Perception can grasp movement only as the displacement of a moving body or the development of a form. Movements, becomings, in other words, pure relations of speed and slowness, pure affects, are below and above the threshold of perception. Doubtless, thresholds of perception are relative; there is always a threshold capable of grasping what eludes another: the eagle's eye . . . But the adequate threshold can in turn operate only as a function of a perceptible form and a perceived, discerned subject. So that movement in itself *continues* to occur elsewhere: if we serialize perception, the movement always takes place above the maximum threshold and below the minimum threshold, in expanding or contracting intervals (microintervals). Like huge Japanese wrestlers whose advance is too slow and whose holds are too fast to see, so that what embraces are less the wrestlers than the infinite slowness of the wait (what is going to happen?) and the infinite speed of the result (what happened?). What we must do is reach the photographic or cinematic threshold; but in relation to the photograph, movement and affect once again took refuge above and below. When Kierkegaard adopts the marvelous motto, "I look only at the movements,"[65] he is acting astonishingly like a precursor of the cinema, multiplying versions of a love scenario (between Agnes and the merman) according to variable speeds and slownesses. He has all the more reason to say that there is no movement that is not infinite; that the movement of the infinite can occur only by means of affect, passion, love, in a becoming that is the girl, but without reference to any kind of "mediation"; and that this movement as such eludes any mediating perception because it is already effectuated at every moment, and the dancer or lover finds him- or herself already "awake and walking" the second he or she falls down, and even the instant he or she leaps.[66] Movement, like the girl as a fugitive being, cannot be perceived.

However, we are obliged to make an immediate correction: movement also "must" be perceived, it cannot but be perceived, the imperceptible is also the *percipiendum*. There is no contradiction in this. If movement is imperceptible by nature, it is so always in relation to a given threshold of perception, which is by nature relative and thus plays the role of a mediation on the plane that effects the distribution of thresholds and percepts and makes forms perceivable to perceiving subjects. It is the plane of organization and development, the plane of transcendence, that renders perceptible without itself being perceived, without being capable of being perceived. But on the *other* plane, the plane of immanence or consistency, the principle of composition itself must be perceived, cannot but be perceived at the same time as that which it composes or renders. In this case, movement is no longer tied to the mediation of a relative threshold that it eludes ad infinitum; it has reached, regardless of its speed or slowness, an absolute but differentiated threshold that is one with the construction of this or that region of the continued plane. It could also be said that movement ceases to be the procedure of an always relative deterritorialization, becoming the process of absolute deterritorialization. The difference between the two planes accounts for the fact that what cannot be perceived on one cannot but be perceived on the other. It is in jumping from one plane to the other, or from the relative thresholds to the absolute threshold that coexists with them, that the imperceptible becomes necessarily perceived. Kierkegaard shows that the plane of the infinite, which he calls the plane of faith, must become a pure plane of immanence that continually and immediately imparts, reimparts, and regathers the finite: unlike the man of infinite resignation, the knight of the faith or man of becoming will get the girl, he will have all of the finite and perceive the imperceptible, as "heir apparent to the finite."[67] Perception will no longer reside in the relation between a subject and an object, but rather in the movement serving as the limit of that relation, in the period associated with the subject and object. Perception will confront its own limit; it will be in the midst of things, throughout its own proximity, as the presence of one haecceity in another, the prehension of one by the other or the passage from one to the other: Look only at the movements.

It is odd that the word "faith" should be used to designate a plane that works by immanence. But if the knight is the man of becoming, then there are all kinds of knights. Are there not even knights of narcotics, in the sense that faith is a drug (in a way very different from the sense in which religion is an opiate)? These knights claim that drugs, under necessary conditions of caution and experimentation, are inseparable from the deployment of a plane. And on this plane not only are becomings-woman, becomings-animal, becomings-molecular, becomings-imperceptible conjugated, but the imperceptible itself becomes necessarily perceived at the same time as perception becomes necessarily molecular: arrive at holes, microintervals between matters, colors and sounds engulfing lines of flight, world lines, lines of transparency and intersection.[68] *Change perception;* the problem has been formulated correctly because it presents "drugs" as a pregnant whole free of secondary distinctions (hallucinatory or nonhallucinatory, hard or soft, etc.). All drugs fundamentally concern speeds, and modifications of speed. What allows us to describe an overall Drug assemblage in spite of the differences between drugs is a line of perceptive causality that makes it so that (1) the imperceptible is perceived; (2) perception is molecular; (3) desire directly invests the perception and the perceived. The Americans of the beat generation had already embarked on this path, and spoke of a molecular revolution specific to drugs. Then came Castaneda's broad synthesis. Leslie Fiedler set forth the poles of the American Dream: cornered between two nightmares, the genocide of the Indians and the slavery of the blacks, Americans constructed a psychically repressed image of the black as the force of affect, of the multiplication of affects, but a socially repressed image of the Indian as subtlety of perception, perception made increasingly keen and more finely divided, infinitely slowed or accelerated.[69] In Europe, Henri Michaux tended to be more willing to free himself of rites and civilizations, establishing admirable and minute protocols of experience, doing away with the question of causality with respect to drugs, delimiting drugs as well as possible, separating them from delirium and hallucination. But at this point everything reconnects: again, the problem is well formulated if we say that drugs eliminate forms and persons, if we bring into play the mad speeds of drugs and the extraordinary posthigh slownesses, if we clasp one to the other like wrestlers, if we confer upon perception the molecular power to grasp microperceptions, microoperations, and upon the perceived the force to emit accelerated or decelerated particles in a floating time that is no longer our time, and to emit haecceities that are no longer of this world: deterritorialization, "I was disoriented . . ." (a perception of things, thoughts, desires in which desire, thought, and the thing have invaded all of perception: the imperceptible finally perceived). Nothing left but the world of speeds and slownesses without form, without subject, without a face. Nothing left but the zigzag of a line, like "the lash of the whip of an enraged cart driver" shredding faces and landscapes.[70] A whole rhizomatic labor of perception, the moment when desire and perception meld.

This problem of specific causality is an important one. Invoking causalities that are too general or are extrinsic (psychological or sociological) is as good as saying nothing. There is a discourse on drugs current today that does no more than dredge up generalities on pleasure and misfortune, on difficulties in communication, on causes that always come from somewhere else. The more incapable people are of grasping a specific causality in extension, the more they pretend to understand the phenomenon in question. There is no doubt that an assemblage never contains a causal infrastructure. It does have, however, and to the highest degree, an abstract line of creative or specific causality, its *line of flight or of deterritorialization*; this line can be effectuated only in connection with general causalities of another nature, but is in no way explained by them. It is our belief that the issue of drugs can be understood only at the level where desire directly invests perception, and perception becomes molecular at the same time as the imperceptible is perceived. Drugs then appear as the agent of this becoming. This is where pharmacoanalysis would come in, which must be both compared and contrasted to psychoanalysis. For psychoanalysis must be taken simultaneously as a model, a contrasting approach, and a betrayal. Psychoanalysis can be taken as a model of reference because it was able, with respect to essentially affective phenomena, to construct the schema of a specific causality divorced from ordinary social or psychological generalities. But this schema still relies on a plane of organization that can never be apprehended in itself, that is always concluded from something else, that is always inferred, concealed from the system of perception: it is called the Unconscious. Thus the plane of the Unconscious remains a plane of transcendence guaranteeing, justifying, the existence of psychoanalysis and the necessity of its interpretations. This plane of the Unconscious stands in molar opposition to the perception-consciousness system, and because desire must be *translated* onto this plane, it is itself linked to gross molarities, like the submerged part of an iceberg (the Oedipal structure, or the rock of castration). The imperceptible thus remains all the more imperceptible because it is opposed to the perceived in a dualism machine. Everything is different on the plane of consistency or immanence, which is necessarily perceived in its own right in the course of its construction: experimentation replaces interpretation, now molecular, nonfigurative, and nonsymbolic, the unconscious as such is given in microperceptions; desire directly invests the field of perception, where the imperceptible appears as the perceived object of desire itself, "the nonfigurative of desire." The unconscious no longer designates the hidden principle of the transcendent plane of organization, but the process of the immanent plane of consistency as it appears on itself in the course of its construction. For the unconscious must be constructed, not rediscovered. There is no longer a conscious-unconscious dualism machine, because the unconscious is, or rather is produced, there where consciousness goes, carried by the plane.[71] Drugs give the unconscious the immanence and plane that psychoanalysis has consistently botched (perhaps the famous cocaine episode marked a turning point that forced Freud to renounce a direct approach to the unconscious).

But if it is true that drugs are linked to this immanent, molecular perceptive causality, we are still faced with the question of whether they actually succeed in drawing the plane necessary for their action. The causal line, or the line of flight, of drugs is constantly being segmentarized under the most rigid of forms, that of dependency, the hit and the dose, the dealer. Even in its supple form, it can mobilize gradients and thresholds of perception toward becomings-animal, becomings-molecular, but even this is done in the context of a relativity of thresholds that restrict themselves to imitating a plane of consistency rather than drawing it on an absolute threshold. What good does it do to perceive as fast as a quick-flying bird if speed and movement continue to escape somewhere else? The deterritorializations remain relative, compensated for by the most abject reterritorializations, so that the imperceptible and perception continually pursue or run after each other without ever truly coupling. Instead of holes in the world allowing the world lines themselves to run off, the lines of flight coil and start to swirl in black holes; to each addict a hole, group or individual, like a snail. Down, instead of high. The molecular microperceptions are overlaid in advance, depending on the drug, by hallucinations, delusions, false perceptions, phantasies, or paranoid outbursts; they restore forms and subjects every instant, like so many phantoms or doubles continually blocking construction of the plane. Moreover, as we saw in our enumeration of the dangers, not only is the plane of consistency in danger of being betrayed or thrown offtrack through the influence of other causalities that intervene in an assemblage of this kind, but the plane itself engenders dangers of its own, by which it is dismantled at the same time as it is constructed. We are no longer, it itself is no longer *master of speeds*. Instead of making a body without organs sufficiently rich or full for the passage of intensities, drug addicts erect a vitrified or emptied body, or a cancerous one: the causal line, creative line, or line of flight immediately turns into a line of death and abolition. The abominable vitrification of the veins, or the purulence of the nose—the glassy body of the addict. Black holes and lines of death, Artaud's and Michaux's warnings converge (they are more technical, more consistent than the informational, psychoanalytic, or sociopsychological discourse of treatment and assistance centers). Artaud: You will not avoid hallucinations, erroneous perceptions, shameless phantasies, or bad feelings, like so many black holes on the plane of consistency, because your conscious will also go in that booby-trapped direction.[72] Michaux: You will no longer be master of your speeds, you will get stuck in a mad race between the imperceptible and perception, a race all the more circular now that everything is relative.[73] You will be full of yourself, you will lose control, you will be on a plane of consistency, in a body without organs, but at a place where you will always botch them, empty them, undo what you do, motionless rags. These words are so much simpler than "erroneous perceptions" (Artaud) or "bad feelings" (Michaux), but say the most technical of things: that the immanent molecular and perceptive causality of desire fails in the drug-assemblage. Drug addicts continually fall back into what they wanted to escape: a segmentarity all the more rigid for being marginal, a territorialization all the more artificial for being based on chemical substances, hallucinatory forms, and phantasy subjectifications. Drug addicts may be considered as precursors or experimenters who tirelessly blaze new paths of life, but their cautiousness lacks the foundation for caution. So they either join the legion of false heroes who follow the conformist path of a little death and a long fatigue. Or, what is worse, all they will have done is make an attempt only nonusers or former users can resume and benefit from, secondarily rectifying the always aborted plane of drugs, discovering through drugs what drugs lack for the construction of a plane of consistency. Is the mistake drug users make always to start over again from ground zero, either going on the drug again or quitting, when what they should do is make it a stopover, to start from the "middle," bifurcate from the middle? To succeed in getting drunk, but on pure water (Henry Miller). To succeed in getting high, but by abstention, "to take and abstain, especially abstain," I am a drinker of water (Michaux). To reach the point where "to get high or not to get high" is no longer the question, but rather whether drugs have sufficiently changed the general conditions of space and time perception so that nonusers can succeed in passing through the holes in the world and following the lines of flight at the very place where means other than drugs become necessary. Drugs do not guarantee immanence; rather, the immanence of drugs allows one to forgo them. Is it cowardice or exploitation to wait until others have taken the risks? No, it is joining an undertaking in the middle, while changing the means. It is necessary to choose the right molecule, the water, hydrogen, or helium molecule. This has nothing to do with models, all models are molar: it is necessary to determine the molecules and particles in relation to which "proximities" (indiscernibilities, becomings) are engendered and defined. The vital assemblage, the life-assemblage, is *theoretically or logically* possible with all kinds of molecules, silicon, for example. But it so happens that this assemblage is not *machinically* possible with silicon: the abstract machine does not let it pass because it does not distribute zones of proximity that construct the plane of consistency.[74] We shall see that machinic reasons are entirely different from logical reasons or possibilities. One does not conform to a model, one straddles the right horse. Drug users have not chosen the right molecule or the right horse. Drugs are too unwieldy to grasp the imperceptible and becomings-imperceptible; drug users believed that drugs would grant them the plane, when in fact the plane must distill its own drugs, remaining master of speeds and proximities.

Memories of the Secret. The secret has a privileged, but quite variable, relation to perception and the imperceptible. The secret relates first of all to certain contents. The content is *too big* for its form . . . or else the contents themselves have a form, but that form is covered, doubled, or replaced by a simple container, envelope, or box whose role it is to suppress formal relations. These are contents it has been judged fitting to isolate or disguise for various reasons. Drawing up a list of these reasons (shame, treasure, divinity, etc.) has limited value as long as the secret is opposed to its discovery as in a binary machine having only two terms, the secret and disclosure, the secret and desecration. For on the one hand, the secret as content is superseded by a perception of the secret, which is no less secret than the secret. It matters little what the goal is, and whether the aim of the perception is a denunciation, final divulging, or disclosure. From an anecdotal standpoint, the perception of the secret is the opposite of the secret, but from the standpoint of the concept, it is a part of it. What counts is that the perception of the secret must necessarily be secret itself: the spy, the voyeur, the blackmailer, the author of anonymous letters are no less secretive than what they are in a position to disclose, regardless of their ulterior motives. There is always a woman, a child, a bird to secretly perceive the secret. There is always a perception finer than yours, a perception of your imperceptible, of what is in your box. We can even envision a profession of secrecy for those who are in a position to perceive the secret. The protector of the secret is not necessarily in on it, but is also tied to a perception, since he or she must perceive and detect those who wish to discover the secret (counterespionage). There is thus a first direction, in which the secret moves toward an equally secretive perception, a perception that seeks to be imperceptible itself. A wide variety of very different figures may revolve around this first point. And then there is a second point, just as inseparable from the secret as its content: the way in which it imposes itself and spreads. Once again, whatever the finalities or results, the secret has a way of spreading that is in turn shrouded in secrecy. The secret as secretion. The secret must sneak, insert, or introduce itself into the arena of public forms; it must pressure them and prod known subjects into action (we are referring to influence of the "lobby" type, even if the lobby is not in itself a secret society).

In short, the secret, defined as a content that has hidden its form in favor of a simple container, is inseparable from two movements that can accidentally interrupt its course or betray it, but are nonetheless an essential part of it: something must ooze from the box, something will be perceived through the box or in the half-opened box. The secret was invented by society; it is a sociological or social notion. Every secret is a collective assemblage. The secret is not at all an immobilized or static notion. Only becomings are secrets; the secret has a becoming. The secret has its origin in the war machine; it is the war machine and its becomings-woman, becomings-child, becomings-animal that bring the secret.[75] A secret society always acts in society as a war machine. Sociologists who have studied secret societies have determined many of their laws: protection, equalization and hierarchy, silence, ritual, deindividuation, centralization, autonomy, compartmentalization, etc.[76] But perhaps they have not given enough weight to the principal laws governing the movement of content: (1) every secret society has a still more secret hindsociety, which either perceives the secret, protects it, or metes out the punishment for its disclosure (it is not at all begging the question to define the secret society by the presence of a secret hindsociety: a society is secret when it exhibits this doubling, has this special section); (2) every secret society has its own mode of action, which is in turn secret; the secret society may act by influence, creeping, insinuation, oozing, pressure, or invisible rays; "passwords" and secret languages (there is no contradiction here; the secret society cannot live without the universal project of permeating all of society, of creeping into all of the forms of society, disrupting its hierarchy and segmentation; the secret hierarchy conjugates with a conspiracy of equals, it commands its members to swim in society as fish in water, but conversely society must be like water around fish; it needs the complicity of the entire surrounding society). This is evident in cases as diverse as the mob groups of the United States and the animal-men of Africa: on the one hand, there is the mode of influence of the secret society and its leaders on the political or public figures of its surroundings; and on the other hand, there is the secret society's mode of doubling itself with a hindsociety, which may constitute a special section of killers or guards.[77] Influence and doubling, secretion and concretion, every secret operates between two "discreets" [*discrets*: also "discrete (terms)"—Trans.] that can, moreover, link or meld in certain cases. The child's secret combines these elements to marvelous effect: the secret as a content in a box, the secret influence and propagation of the secret, the secret perception of the secret (the child's secret is not composed of miniaturized adult secrets but is necessarily accompanied by a secret perception of the adult secret). A child discovers a secret . . .

But the becoming of the secret compels it not to content itself with concealing its form in a simple container, or with swapping it for a container. The secret, as secret, must now acquire its own form. The secret is elevated from a finite content to the infinite form of secrecy. This is the point at which the secret attains absolute imperceptibility, instead of being linked to a whole interplay of relative perceptions and reactions. We go from a content that is well defined, localized, and belongs to the past, to the a priori general form of a nonlocalizable *something* that has happened. We go from the secret defined as a hysterical childhood content to secrecy defined as an eminently virile paranoid form. And this form displays the same two concomitants of the secret, the secret perception and the mode of action by secret influence; but these concomitants have become "traits" of a form they ceaselessly reconstitute, reform, recharge. On the one hand, paranoiacs denounce the international plot of those who steal their secrets, their most intimate thoughts; or they declare that they have the gift of perceiving the secrets of others before they have formed (someone with paranoid jealousy does not apprehend the other in the act of escaping; they divine or foresee the slightest intention of it). On the other hand, paranoiacs act by means of, or else suffer from, rays they emit or receive (Raymond

Roussel and Schreber). Influence by rays, and doubling by flight or echo, are what now give the secret its infinite form, in which perceptions as well as actions pass into imperceptibility. Paranoid judgment is like an anticipation of perception replacing empirical research into boxes and their contents: *guilty* a priori, and in any event! (for example, the evolution of the narrator of the *Recherche* in relation to Albertine). We can say, in summary fashion, that psychoanalysis has gone from a hysterical to an increasingly paranoid conception of the secret.[78] Interminable analysis: the Unconscious has been assigned the increasingly difficult task of itself being the infinite form of secrecy, instead of a simple box containing secrets. You will tell all, but in saying everything you will say nothing because all the "art" of psychoanalysis is required in order to measure your contents against the pure form. At this point, however, after the secret has been raised to the level of a form in this way, an inevitable adventure befalls it. When the question "What happened?" attains this infinite virile form, the answer is necessarily that nothing happened, and both form and content are destroyed. The news travels fast that the secret of men is nothing, in truth nothing at all. Oedipus, the phallus, castration, "the splinter in the flesh"—that was the secret? It is enough to make women, children, lunatics, and molecules laugh.

The more the secret is made into a structuring, organizing form, the thinner and more ubiquitous it becomes, the more its content becomes molecular, at the same time as its form dissolves. It really wasn't much, as Jocasta says. The secret does not as a result disappear, but it does take on a more feminine status. What was behind President Schreber's paranoid secret all along, if not a becoming-feminine, a becoming-woman? For women do not handle the secret in at all the same way as men (except when they reconstitute an inverted image of virile secrecy, a kind of secrecy of the gyneceum). Men alternately fault them for their indiscretion, their gossiping, and for their solidarity, their betrayal. Yet it is curious how a woman can be secretive while at the same time hiding nothing, by virtue of transparency, innocence, and speed. The complex assemblage of secrecy in courtly love is properly feminine and operates in the most complete transparency. Celerity against gravity. The celerity of a war machine against the gravity of a State apparatus. Men adopt a grave attitude, knights of the secret: "You see what burden I bear: my seriousness, my discretion." But they end up telling everything—and it turns out to be nothing. There are women, on the other hand, who tell everything, sometimes in appalling technical detail, but one knows no more at the end than at the beginning; they have hidden everything by celerity, by limpidity. They have no secret because they have become a secret themselves. Are they more politic than we? Iphigenia. *Innocent* a priori. That is the girl's defense against the judgment proferred by men: "guilty a priori" . . . This is where the secret reaches its ultimate state: its content is molecularized, it has become molecular, at the same time as its form has been dismantled, becoming a pure moving line—in the sense in which it can be said a given line is the "secret" of a painter, or a given rhythmic cell, a given sound molecule (which does not constitute a theme or form) the "secret" of a musician.

If ever there was a writer who dealt with the secret, it was Henry James. In this respect, he went through an entire evolution, like a perfecting of his art. For he began by looking for the secret in contents, even insignificant, half-opened ones, contents briefly glimpsed. Then he raised the possibility of there being an infinite form of secrecy that no longer even requires a content and that has conquered the imperceptible. But he raises this possibility only in order to ask the question, Is the secret in the content or in the form? And the answer is already apparent: *neither.*[79] James is one of those writers who is swept up in an irresistible becoming-woman. He never stopped pursuing his goal, inventing the necessary technical means. Molecularize the content of the secret and linearize its form. James explored it all, from the becoming-child of the secret (there is always a child who discovers secrets: *What Maisie Knew*) to the becoming-woman of the secret (secrecy by a transparency that is no longer anything more than a pure line that scarcely leaves any traces of its own passage; the admirable *Daisy Miller*). James is not as close to Proust as people say; it is he who raises the cry, "Innocent a priori!" (all Daisy asked for was a little respect, she would have given her love for that . . .) in opposition to the "Guilty a priori" that condemns Albertine. What counts in the secret is less its three states (child's content, virile infinite form, pure feminine line) than the becomings attached to them, the becoming-child of the secret, its becoming-feminine, its becoming-molecular—which occur precisely at the point where the secret has lost both its content and its form, where the imperceptible, the clandestine with nothing left to hide, has finally been perceived. From the gray eminence to the gray immanence. *Oedipus passes through all three secrets*: the secret of the sphinx whose box he penetrates; the secret that weighs upon him as the infinite form of his own guilt; and finally, the secret at Colonus that makes him inaccessible and melds with the pure line of his flight and exile, he who has nothing left to hide, or, like an old No actor, has only a girl's mask with which to cover his lack of a face. Some people can talk, hide nothing, not lie: they are secret by transparency, as impenetrable as water, in truth incomprehensible. Whereas the others have a secret that is always breached, even though they surround it with a thick wall or elevate it to an infinite form.

Memories and Becomings, Points and Blocks. Why are there so many becomings of man, but no becoming-man? First because man is majoritarian par excellence, whereas becomings are minoritarian; all becoming is a becoming-minoritarian. When we say majority, we are referring not to a greater relative quantity but to the determination of a state or standard in relation to which larger quantities, as well as the smallest, can be said to be minoritarian: white-man, adult-male, etc. Majority implies a state of domination, not the reverse. It is not a question of knowing whether there are more mosquitoes or flies than men, but of knowing how "man" constituted a standard in the universe in relation to which men necessarily (analytically) form a majority. The majority in a government presupposes the right to vote, and not only is established among those who possess that right but is exercised over those who do not, however great their numbers; similarly, the majority in the universe assumes as pregiven the right and power of man.[80] In this sense women, children, but also animals, plants, and molecules, are minoritarian. It is perhaps the special situation of women in relation to the man-standard that accounts for the fact that becomings, being minoritarian, always pass through a becoming-woman. It is important not to confuse "minoritarian," as a becoming or process, with a "minority", as an aggregate or a state. Jews, Gypsies, etc., may constitute minorities under certain conditions, but that in itself does not make them becomings. One reterritorializes, or allows oneself to be reterritorialized, on a minority as a state; but in a becoming, one is deterritorialized. Even blacks, as the Black Panthers said, must become-black. Even women must become-woman. Even Jews must become-Jewish (it certainly takes more than a state). But if this is the case, then becoming-Jewish necessarily affects the non-Jew as much as the Jew. Becoming-woman necessary affects men as much as women. In a way, the subject in a becoming is always "man," but only when he enters a becoming-minoritarian that rends him from his major identity. As in Arthur Miller's novel, *Focus*, or Losey's film, *Mr. Klein:* it is the non-Jew who becomes Jewish, who is swept up in, carried off by, this becoming after being rent from his standard of measure. Conversely, if Jews themselves must become-Jewish, if women must become-woman, if children must become-child, if blacks must become-black, it is because only a minority is capable of serving as the active medium of becoming, but under such conditions that it ceases to be a definable aggregate in relation to the majority. Becoming-Jewish, becoming-woman, etc., therefore imply two simultaneous movements, one by which a term (the subject) is withdrawn from the majority, and another by which a term (the medium or agent) rises up from the minority. There is an asymmetrical and indissociable block of becoming, a block of alliance: the two "Mr. Kleins," the Jew and the non-Jew, enter into a becoming-Jewish (the same thing happens in *Focus*).

A woman has to become-woman, but in a becoming-woman of all man. A Jew becomes Jewish, but in a becoming-Jewish of the non-Jew. A becoming-minoritarian exists only by virtue of a deterritorialized medium and subject that are like its elements. There is no subject of the becoming except as a deterritorialized variable of the majority; there is no medium of becoming except as a deterritorialized variable of a minority. We can be thrown into a becoming by anything at all, by the most unexpected, most insignificant of things. You don't deviate from the majority unless there is a little detail that starts to swell and carries you off. It is because the hero of *Focus*, the average American, needs glasses that give his nose a vaguely Semitic air, it is "because of the glasses" that he is thrown into this strange adventure of the becoming-Jewish of the non-Jew. Anything at all can do the job, but it always turns out to be a political affair. Becoming-minoritarian is a political affair and necessitates a labor of power (*puissance*), an active micropolitics. This is the opposite of macropolitics, and even of History, in which it is a question of knowing how to win or obtain a majority. As Faulkner said, to avoid ending up a fascist there was no other choice but to become-black.[81] Unlike history, becoming cannot be conceptualized in terms of past and future. Becoming-revolutionary remains indifferent to questions of a future and a past of the revolution; it passes between the two. Every becoming is a block of coexistence. The so-called ahistorical societies set themselves outside history, not because they are content to reproduce immutable models or are governed by a fixed structure, but because they are societies of becoming (war societies, secret societies, etc.). There is no history but of the majority, or of minorities as defined in relation to the majority. And yet "how to win the majority" is a totally secondary problem in relation to the advances of the imperceptible.

Let us try to say it another way: There is no becoming-man because man is the molar entity par excellence, whereas becomings are molecular. The faciality function showed us the form under which man constitutes the majority, or rather the standard upon which the majority is based: white, male, adult, "rational," etc., in short, the average European, the subject of enunciation. Following the law of arborescence, it is this central Point that moves across all of space or the entire screen, and at every turn nourishes a certain distinctive opposition, depending on which faciality trait is retained: male-(female), adult-(child), white-(black, yellow, or red); rational-(animal). The central point, or third eye, thus has the property of organizing binary distributions within the dualism machines, and of reproducing itself in the principal term of the opposition; the entire opposition at the same time resonates in the central point. The constitution of a "majority" as redundancy. Man constitutes himself as a gigantic memory, through the position of the central point, its frequency (insofar as it is necessarily reproduced by each dominant point), and its resonance (insofar as all of the points tie in with it). Any line that goes from one point to another in the aggregate of the molar system, and is thus defined by points answering to these mnemonic conditions of frequency and resonance, is a part of the arborescent system.[82]

What constitutes arborescence is the submission of the line to the point. Of course, the child, the woman, the black have memories; but the Memory that collects those memories is still a virile majoritarian agency treating them as "childhood memories," as conjugal, or colonial memories. It is possible to operate by establishing a conjunction or collocation of contiguous points rather than a relation between distant points: you would then have phantasies rather than memories. For example, a woman can have a female point alongside a male point, and a man a male point alongside a female one. The constitution of these hybrids, however, does not take us very far in the direction of a true becoming (for example, bisexuality, as the psychoanalysts note, in no way precludes the prevalence of the masculine or the majority of the "phallus"). One does not break with the arborescent schema, one does not reach becoming or the molecular, as long as a line is connected to two distant points, or is composed of two contiguous points. A line of becoming is not defined by points that it connects, or by points that compose it; on the contrary, it passes *between* points, it comes up through the middle, it runs perpendicular to the points first perceived, transversally to the localizable relation to distant or contiguous points.[83] A point is always a point of origin. But a line of becoming has neither beginning nor end, departure nor arrival, origin nor destination; to speak of the absence of an origin, to make the absence of an origin the origin, is a bad play on words. A line of becoming has only a middle. The middle is not an average; it is fast motion, it is the absolute speed of movement. A becoming is always in the middle; one can only get it by the middle. A becoming is neither one nor two, nor the relation of the two; it is the in-between, the border or line of flight or descent running perpendicular to both. If becoming is a block (a line-block), it is because it constitutes a zone of proximity and indiscernibility, a no-man's-land, a nonlocalizable relation sweeping up the two distant or contiguous points, carrying one into the proximity of the other—and the border-proximity is indifferent to both contiguity and to distance. The line or block of becoming that unites the wasp and the orchid produces a shared deterritorialization: of the wasp, in that it becomes a liberated piece of the orchid's reproductive system, but also of the orchid, in that it becomes the object of an orgasm in the wasp, also liberated from its own reproduction. A coexistence of two asymmetrical movements that combine to form a block, down a line of flight that sweeps away selective pressures. The line, or the block, does not link the wasp to the orchid, any more than it conjugates or mixes them: it passes between them, carrying them away in a shared proximity in which the discernibility of points disappears. The line-system (or block-system) of becoming is opposed to the point-system of memory. Becoming is the movement by which the line frees itself from the point, and renders points indiscernible: the rhizome, the opposite of arborescence; break away from arborescence. *Becoming is an antimemory.* Doubtless, there exists a molecular memory, but as a factor of integration into a majoritarian or molar system. Memories always have a reterritorialization function. On the other hand, a vector of deterritorialization is in no way indeterminate; it is directly plugged into the molecular levels, and the more deterritorialized it is, the stronger is the contact: it is deterritorialization that makes the aggregate of the molecular components "hold together." From this point of view, one may contrast a *childhood block*, or a becoming-child, with the *childhood memory*: "a" molecular child is produced . . . "a" child coexists with us, in a zone of proximity or a block of becoming, on a line of deterritorialization that carries us both off—as opposed to the child we once were, whom we remember or phantasize, the molar child whose future is the adult. "This will be childhood, but it must not be my childhood," writes Virginia Woolf. (*Orlando* already does not operate by memories, but by blocks, blocks of ages, block of epochs, blocks of the kingdoms of nature, blocks of sexes, forming so many becomings between things, or so many lines of deterritorialization.)[84] Wherever we used the word "memories" in the preceding pages, we were wrong to do so; we meant to say "becoming," we were saying becoming.

If the line is opposed to the point (or blocks to memories, becoming to the faculty of memory), it is not in an absolute way: a punctual system includes a certain utilization of lines, and the block itself assigns the point new functions. In a punctual system, a point basically refers to linear coordinates. Not only are a horizontal line and a vertical line represented, but the vertical moves parallel to itself, and the horizontal superposes other horizontals upon itself; every point is assigned in relation to the two base coordinates, but is also marked on a horizontal line of superposition and on a vertical line or plane of displacement. Finally, two points are connected when any line is drawn from one to the other. *A system is termed punctual* when its lines are taken as coordinates in this way, or as localizable connections; for example, systems of arborescence, or molar and mnemonic systems in general, are punctual. Memory has a punctual organization because every present refers simultaneously to the horizontal line of the *flow* of time (kinematics), which goes from an old present to the actual present, and the vertical line of the *order* of time (stratigraphy), which goes from the present to the past, or to the representation of the old present. This is, of course, a basic schema that cannot be developed further without running into major complications, but it is the one found in representations of art forming a "didactic" system, in other words, a mnemotechnics. Musical representation, on the one hand, draws a horizontal, melodic line, the bass line, upon which other melodic lines are superposed; points are assigned that enter into relations of counterpoint between lines. On the other hand, it draws a vertical, harmonic line or plane, which moves along the horizontals but is no longer dependent upon them; it runs from high to low and defines a chord capable of linking up with the following chords. Pictorial representation has an analogous form, with means of its own: this is not only because the painting has a vertical and a horizontal, but because the traits and colors, each on its own account, relate to verticals of displacement and horizontals of superposition (for example, the vertical cold form, or white, light and tonality; the horizontal warm form, or black, chromatics and modality, etc.). To cite only relatively recent examples, this is evident in the didactic systems of Kandinsky, Klee, and Mondrian, which necessarily imply an encounter with music.

Let us summarize the principal characteristics of a punctual system: (1) Systems of this kind comprise two base lines, horizontal and vertical; they serve as coordinates for assigning points. (2) The horizontal line can be superposed vertically and the vertical line can be moved horizontally, in such a way that new points are produced or reproduced, under conditions of horizontal frequency and vertical resonance. (3) From one point to another, a line can (or cannot) be drawn, but if it can it takes the form of a localizable connection; diagonals thus play the role of connectors between points of different levels or moments, instituting in their turn frequencies and resonances on the basis of these points of variable horizon or verticon, contiguous or distant.[85] These systems are arborescent, mnemonic, molar, structural; they are systems of territorialization or reterritorialization. The line and the diagonal remain totally subordinated to the point because they serve as coordinates for a point or as localizable connections for two points, running from one point to another.

Opposed to the punctual system are linear, or rather multilinear, systems. Free the line, free the diagonal: every musician or painter has this intention. One elaborates a punctual system or a didactic representation, but with the aim of making it snap, of sending a tremor through it. A punctual system is most interesting when there is a musician, painter, writer, philosopher to oppose it, who even fabricates it in order to oppose it, like a springboard to jump from. History is made only by those who oppose history (not by those who insert themselves into it, or even reshape it). This is not done for provocation but happens because the punctual system they found ready-made, or themselves invented, must have allowed this operation: free the line and the diagonal, draw the line instead of plotting a point, produce an imperceptible diagonal instead of clinging to an even elaborated or reformed vertical or horizontal. When this is done it always goes down in History but never comes from it. History may try to break its ties to memory; it may make the schemas of memory more elaborate, superpose and shift coordinates, emphasize connections, or deepen breaks. The dividing line, however, is not there. The dividing line passes not between history and memory but between punctual "history-memory" systems and diagonal or multilinear assemblages, which are in no way eternal: they have to do with becoming; they are a bit of becoming in the pure state; they are transhistorical. There is no act of creation that is not transhistorical and does not come up from behind or proceed by way of a liberated line. Nietzsche opposes history not to the eternal but to the subhistorical or superhistorical: the Untimely, which is another name for haecceity, becoming, the innocence of becoming (in other words, forgetting as opposed to memory, geography as opposed to history, the map as opposed to the tracing, the rhizome as opposed to arborescence). "The unhistorical is like an atmosphere within which alone life can germinate and with the destruction of which it must vanish. . . . What deed would man be capable of if he had not first entered into that vaporous region of the unhistorical?"[86] Creations are like mutant abstract lines that have detached themselves from the task of representing a world, precisely because they assemble a new type of reality that history can only recontain or relocate in punctual systems.

When Boulez casts himself in the role of historian of music, he does so in order to show how a great musician, in a very different manner in each case, invents a kind of diagonal running between the harmonic vertical and the melodic horizon. And in each case it is a different diagonal, a different technique, a creation. Moving along this transversal line, which is really a line of deterritorialization, there is a *sound block* that no longer has a point of origin, since it is always and already in the middle of the line; and no longer has horizontal and vertical coordinates, since it creates its own coordinates; and no longer forms a localizable connection from one point to another, since it is in "nonpulsed time": a deterritorialized rhythmic block that has abandoned points, coordinates, and measure, like a drunken boat that melds with the line or draws a plane of consistency. Speeds and slownesses inject themselves into musical form, sometimes impelling it to proliferation, linear microproliferations, and sometimes to extinction, sonorous abolition, involution, or both at once. The musician is in the best position to say: "I hate the faculty of memory, I hate memories." And that is because he or she affirms the power of becoming. The Viennese school is exemplary of this kind of diagonal, this kind of line-block. But it can equally be said that the Viennese school found a new system of territorialization, of points, verticals, and horizontals that position it in History. Another attempt, another creative act, came after it. The important thing is that all musicians have always proceeded in this way: drawing their own diagonal, however fragile, outside points, outside coordinates and localizable connections, in order to float a sound block down a created, liberated line, in order to unleash in space this mobile and mutant sound block, a haecceity (for example, chromaticism, aggregates, and complex notes, but already the resources and possibilities of polyphony, etc.).[87] Some have spoken of "oblique vectors" with respect to the organ. The diagonal is often composed of extremely complex lines and spaces of sound. Is that the secret of a little phrase or a rhythmic block? Undoubtedly, the point now assumes a new and essential creative function. It is no longer simply a question of an inevitable destiny reconstituting a punctual system; on the contrary, it is now the point that is subordinated to the line, the point now marks the proliferation of the line, or its sudden deviation, its acceleration, its slowdown, its furor or agony. Mozart's "microblocks." The block may even be reduced to a point, as though to a single note (point-block): Berg's B in *Wozzeck*, Schumann's A. Homage to Schumann, the madness of Schumann: the cello wanders across the grid of the orchestration, drawing its diagonal, along which the deterritorialized sound block moves; or an extremely sober kind of refrain is "treated" by a very elaborate melodic line and polyphonic architecture.

In a multilinear system, everything happens at once: the line breaks free of the point as origin; the diagonal breaks free of the vertical and the horizontal as coordinates; and the transversal breaks free of the diagonal as a localizable connection between two points. In short, a block-line passes amid (*au milieu des*) sounds and propels itself by its own nonlocalizable middle (*milieu*). The sound block is the *intermezzo*. It is a body without organs, an antimemory pervading musical organization, and is all the more sonorous: "The Schumannian body does not stay in place. . . . The intermezzo [is] consubstantial with the entire Schumannian oeuvre. . . . At the limit, there are only intermezzi. . . . The Schumannian body knows only bifurcations; it does not construct itself, it keeps diverging according to an accumulation of interludes. . . . Schumannian beating is panic, but it is also coded . . . and it is because the panic of the blows apparently keeps within the limits of a docile language that it is ordinarily not perceived. . . . Let us imagine for tonality two contradictory (and yet concomitant) statuses. On the one hand . . . a screen, a language intended to articulate the body . . . according to a known organization. . . . On the other hand, contradictorily . . . tonality becomes the ready servant of the beats within another level it claims to domesticate."[88]

Does the same thing, strictly the same thing, apply to painting? In effect, the point does not make the line; the line sweeps away the deterritorialized point, carries it off under its outside influence; the line does not go from one point to another, but runs *between points* in a different direction that renders them indiscernible. The line has become the diagonal, which has broken free from the vertical and the horizontal. But the diagonal has already become the transversal, the semidiagonal or free straight line, the broken or angular line, or the curve—always in the midst of themselves. Between the white vertical and the black horizontal lie Klee's gray, Kandinsky's red, Monet's purple; each forms a block of color. This line is without origin, since it always begins off the painting, which only holds it by the middle; it is without coordinates, because it melds with a plane of consistency upon which it floats and that it creates; it is without localizable connection, because it has lost not only its representative function but any function of outlining a form of any kind—by this token, the line has become abstract, truly abstract and mutant, a visual block; and under these conditions the point assumes creative functions again, as a color-point or line-point.[89] The line is between points, in their midst, and no longer goes from one point to another. It does not outline a shape. "He did not paint things, he painted between things." There is no falser problem in painting than depth and, in particular, perspective. For perspective is only a historical manner of *occupying* diagonals or transversals, lines of flight [*lignes de fuite:* here, the lines in a painting moving toward the vanishing point, or *point de fuite*—Trans.], in other words, of reterritorializing the moving visual block. We use the word "occupy" in the sense of "giving an occupation to," fixing a memory and a code, assigning a function. But the lines of flight, the transversals, are suitable for many other functions besides this molar function. Lines of flight as perspective lines, far from being made to represent depth, themselves invent the possibility of such a representation, which occupies them only for an instant, at a given moment. Perspective, and even depth, are the reterritorialization of lines of flight, which alone created painting by carrying it farther. What is called central perspective in particular plunged the multiplicity of escapes and the dynamism of lines into a punctual black hole. Conversely, it is true that problems of perspective triggered a whole profusion of creative lines, a mass release of visual blocks, at the very moment they claimed to have gained mastery over them. Is painting, in each of its acts of creation, engaged in a becoming as intense as that of music?

Becoming-Music. We have tried to define in the case of Western music (although the other musical traditions confront an analogous problem, under different conditions, to which they find different solutions) a block of becoming at the level of expression, or a block of expression: this block of becoming rests on transversals that continually escape from the coordinates or punctual systems functioning as musical codes at a given moment. It is obvious that there is a block of content corresponding to this block of expression. It is not really a correspondence; there would be no mobile "block" if a content, itself musical (and not a subject or a theme), were not always interfering with the expression. What does music deal with, what is the content indissociable from sound expression? It is hard to say, but it is something: *a* child dies, a child plays, a woman is born, a woman dies, a bird arrives, a bird flies off. We wish to say that these are not accidental themes in music (even if it is possible to multiply examples), much less imitative exercises; they are something essential. Why a child, a woman, a bird? It is because musical expression is inseparable from a becoming-woman, a becoming-child, a becoming-animal that constitute its content. Why does the child die, or the bird fall as though pierced by an arrow? Because of the "danger" inherent in any line that escapes, in any line of flight or creative deterritorialization: the danger of veering toward destruction, toward abolition. Mélisande [in Debussy's opera, *Pelléas et Mélisande*—Trans.], a child-woman, a secret, dies twice ("it's the poor little dear's turn now"). Music is never tragic, music is joy. But there are times it necessarily gives us a taste for death; not so much happiness as dying happily, being extinguished. Not as a function of a death instinct it allegedly awakens in us, but of a dimension proper to its sound assemblage, to its sound machine, the moment that must be confronted, the moment the transversal turns into a line of abolition. Peace *and* exasperation.[90] Music has a thirst for destruction, every kind of destruction, extinction, breakage, dislocation. Is that not its potential "fascism"? Whenever a musician writes *In Memoriam*, it is not so much a question of an inspirational motif or a memory, but on the contrary of a becoming that is only confronting its own danger, even taking a fall in order to rise again: a becoming-child, a becoming-woman, a becoming-animal, insofar as they are the content of music itself and continue to the point of death.

We would say that the *refrain* is properly musical content, the block of content proper to music. A child comforts itself in the dark or claps its hands or invents a way of walking, adapting it to the cracks in the sidewalk, or chants "Fort-Da" (psychoanalysts deal with the Fort-Da very poorly when they treat it as a phonological opposition or a symbolic component of the language-unconscious, when it is in fact a refrain). Tra la la. A woman sings to herself, "I heard her softly singing a tune to herself under her breath." A bird launches into its refrain. All of music is pervaded by bird songs, in a thousand different ways, from Jannequin to Messiaen. Frr, Frr. Music is pervaded by childhood blocks, by blocks of femininity. Music is pervaded by every minority, and yet composes an immense power. Children's, women's, ethnic, and territorial refrains, refrains of love and destruction: the birth of rhythm. Schumann's work is made of refrains, of childhood blocks, which he treats in a very special way: his own kind of becoming-child, his own kind of becoming-woman, Clara. It would be possible to catalogue the transversal or diagonal utilizations of the refrain in the history of music, all of the children's Games and *Kinderszenen*, all of the bird songs. But such a catalogue would be useless because it would seem like a multiplication of examples of themes, subjects, and motifs, when it is in fact a question of the most essential and necessary content of music. The motif of the refrain may be anxiety, fear, joy, love, work, walking, territory . . . but the refrain itself is the content of music.

We are not at all saying that the refrain is the origin of music, or that music begins with it. It is not really known when music begins. The refrain is rather a means of preventing music, warding it off, or forgoing it. But music exists because the refrain exists also, because music takes up the refrain, lays hold of it as a content in a form of expression, because it forms a block with it in order to take it somewhere else. *The child's refrain, which is not music, forms a block with the becoming-child of music:* once again, this asymmetrical composition is necessary. "Ah, vous dirai-je maman" ("Ah, mamma, now you shall know") in Mozart, Mozart's refrains. A theme in C, followed by twelve variations; not only is each note of the theme doubled, but the theme is doubled internally. Music submits the refrain to this very special treatment of the diagonal or transversal, it uproots the refrain from its territoriality. Music is a creative, active operation that consists in deterritorializing the refrain. Whereas the refrain is essentially territorial, territorializing, or reterritorializing, music makes it a deterritorialized content for a deterritorializing form of expression. Pardon that sentence: what musicians do should be musical, it should be written in music. Instead, we will give a figurative example: Mussorgsky's "Lullaby," in *Songs and Dances of Death*, presents an exhausted mother sitting up with her sick child; she is relieved by a visitor, Death, who sings a lullaby in which each couplet ends with an obsessive, sober refrain, a repetitive rhythm with only one note, a point-block: "Shush, little child, sleep my little child" (not only does the child die, but the deterritorialization of the refrain is doubled by Death in person, who replaces the mother).

Is the situation similar for painting, and if so, how? In no way do we believe in a fine-arts system; we believe in very diverse problems whose solutions are found in heterogeneous arts. To us, Art is a false concept, a solely nominal concept; this does not, however, preclude the possibility of a simultaneous usage of the various arts within a determinable multiplicity. The "problem" within which painting is inscribed is that of the *face-landscape*. That of music is entirely different: it is the problem of the *refrain*. Each arises at a certain moment, under certain conditions, on the line of its problem; but there is no possible structural or symbolic correspondence between the two, unless one translates them into punctual systems. We have distinguished the following three states of the landscape problem: (1) semiotic systems of corporeality, silhouettes, postures, colors, and lines (these semiotic systems are already present in profusion among animals; the head is part of the body, and the body has the milieu, the biotope as its correlate; these systems already display very pure lines as, for example, in the "grass stem" behavior); (2) an organization of the face, white wall/black holes, face/eyes, or facial profile/sideview of the eyes (this semiotic system of faciality has the landscape as its correlate: facialization of the entire body and landscapification of all the milieus, Christ as the European central point); (3) a deterritorialization of faces and landscapes, in favor of probe-heads whose lines no longer outline a form or form a contour, and whose colors no longer lay out a landscape (this is the pictorial semiotic system: Put the face and the landscape to flight. For example, what Mondrian correctly calls a "landscape": a pure, absolutely deterritorialized landscape).

For convenience, we presented three successive and distinct states, but only provisionally. We cannot decide whether animals have painting, even though they do not paint on canvas, and even when hormones induce their colors and lines; even here, there is little foundation for a clear-cut distinction between animals and human beings. Conversely, we must say that painting does not begin with so-called abstract art but recreates the silhouettes and postures of corporeality, and is already fully in operation in the face-landscape organization (the way in which painters "work" the face of Christ, and make it leak from the religious code in all directions). The aim of painting has always been the deterritorialization of faces and landscapes, either by a reactivation of corporeality, or by a liberation of lines or colors, or both at the same time. There are many becomings-animal, becomings-woman, and becomings-child in painting.

The problem of music is different, if it is true that its problem is the refrain. Deterritorializing the refrain, inventing lines of deterritorialization for the refrain, implies procedures and constructions that have nothing to do with those of painting (outside of vague analogies of the sort painters have often tried to establish). Again, it is not certain whether we can draw a dividing line between animals and human beings: Are there not, as Messiaen believes, musician birds and nonmusician birds? Is the bird's refrain necessarily territorial, or is it not already used for very subtle deterritorializations, for selective lines of flight? The difference between noise and sound is definitely not a basis for a definition of music, or even for the distinction between musician birds and nonmusician birds. Rather, it is the *labor of the refrain:* Does it remain territorial and territorializing, or is it carried away in a moving block that draws a transversal across all coordinates—and all of the intermediaries between the two? Music is precisely the adventure of the refrain: the way music lapses back into a refrain (in our head, in Swann's head, in the pseudo-probe-heads on TV and radio, the music of a great musician used as a signature tune, a ditty); the way it lays hold of the refrain, makes it more and more sober, reduced to a few notes, then takes it down a creative line that is so much richer, no origin or end of which is in sight . . .

Leroi-Gourhan established a distinction and correlation between two poles, "hand-tool" and "face-language." But there it was a question of distinguishing a form of content and a form of expression. Here we are considering expressions that hold their content within themselves, so we must make a different distinction: the face with its visual correlates (eyes) concerns painting; the voice with its auditory correlates (the ear is itself a refrain, it is shaped like one) concerns music. Music is a deterritorialization of the voice, which becomes less and less tied to language, just as painting is a deterritorialization of the face. Traits of vocability can indeed be indexed to traits of faciality, as in lipreading; they are not, however, in correspondence, especially when they are carried off by the respective movements of music and painting. The voice is far ahead of the face, very far ahead. Entitling a musical work *Visage* (Face) thus seems to be the greatest of sound paradoxes.[91] The only way to "line up" the two problems of painting and music is to take a criterion extrinsic to the fiction of the fine arts, to compare the forces of deterritorialization in each case. Music seems to have a much stronger deterritorializing force, at once more intense and much more collective, and the voice seems to have a much greater power of deterritorialization. Perhaps this trait explains the collective fascination exerted by music, and even the potentiality of the "fascist" danger we mentioned a little earlier: music (drums, trumpets) draws people and armies into a race that can go all the way to the abyss (much more so than banners and flags, which are paintings, means of classification and rallying). It may be that musicians are individually more reactionary than painters, more religious, less "social"; they nevertheless wield a collective force infinitely greater than that of painting: "The chorus formed by the assembly of the people is a very powerful bond . . ." It is always possible to explain this force by the material conditions of musical emission and reception, but it is preferable to take the reverse approach; these conditions are explained by the force of deterritorialization of music. It could be said that from the standpoint of the mutant abstract machine painting and music do not correspond to the same thresholds, or that the pictorial machine and the musical machine do not have the same index. There is a "backwardness" of painting in relation to music, as Klee, the most musicianly of painters, observed.[92] Maybe that is why many people prefer painting, or why aesthetics took painting as its privileged model: there is no question that it "scares" people less. Even its relations to capitalism and social formations are not at all of the same type.

Doubtless, in each case we must simultaneously consider factors of territoriality, deterritorialization, and reterritorialization. Animal and child refrains seem to be territorial: therefore they are not "music." But when music lays hold of the refrain and deterritorializes it, and deterritorializes the voice, when it lays hold of the refrain and sends it racing off in a rhythmic sound block, when the refrain "becomes" Schumann or Debussy, it is through a system of melodic and harmonic coordinates by means of which music reterritorializes upon itself, *qua* music. Conversely, we shall see that in certain cases even the animal refrain possesses forces of deterritorialization much more intense than animal silhouettes, postures, and colors. We must therefore take a number of factors into consideration: relative territorialities, their respective deterritorializations, and their correlative reterritorializations, several types of them (for example, intrinsic reterritorializations such as musical coordinates, and extrinsic ones such as the deterioration of the refrain into a hackneyed formula, or music into a ditty). The fact that there is no deterritorialization without a special reterritorialization should prompt us to rethink the abiding correlation between the molar and the molecular: no flow, no becoming-molecular escapes from a molar formation without molar components accompanying it, forming passages or perceptible landmarks for the imperceptible processes.

The becoming-woman, the becoming-child of music are present in the problem of the machining of the voice. Machining the voice was the first musical operation. As we know, the problem was resolved in Western music in two different ways, in Italy and in England: the head voice of the countertenor, who sings "above his voice," or whose voice operates inside the sinuses and at the back of the throat and the palate without relying on the diaphragm or passing through the bronchial tubes; and the stomach voice of the castrati, "stronger, more voluminous, more languid," as if they gave carnal matter to the imperceptible, impalpable, and aerial. Dominique Fernandez wrote a fine book on this subject; he shows, fortunately refraining from any psychoanalytic discussion of a link between music and castration, that the musical problem of the machinery of the voice necessarily implies the abolition of the overall dualism machine, in other words, the molar formation assigning voices to the "man or woman."[93] Being a man *or* a woman no longer exists in music. It is not certain, however, that the myth of the androgyne Fernandez invokes is adequate. It is a question not of myth but of real becoming. The voice itself must attain a becoming-woman or a becoming-child. That is the prodigious content of music. It is no longer a question, as Fernandez observes, of imitating a woman or a child, even if it is a child who is singing. The musical voice itself becomes-child at the same time as the child becomes-sonorous, purely sonorous. No child could ever have done that, or if one did, it would be by becoming in addition something other than a child, a child belonging to a different, strangely sensual and celestial, world. In short, the deterritorialization is double: the voice is deterritorialized in a becoming-child, but the child it becomes is itself deterritorialized, unengendered, becoming. "The child grew wings," said Schumann. We find the same zigzag movement in the becomings-animal of music: Marcel Moré shows that the music of Mozart is permeated by a becoming-horse, or becomings-bird. But no musician amuses himself by "playing" horse or bird. If the sound block has a becoming-animal as its content, then the animal simultaneously becomes, in sonority, something else, something absolute, night, death, joy—certainly not a generality or a simplification, but a haecceity, this death, that night. Music takes as its content a becoming-animal; but in that becoming-animal the horse, for example, takes as its expression soft kettledrum beats, winged like hooves from heaven or hell; and the birds find expression in *gruppeti*, appoggiaturas, staccato notes that transform them into so many souls.[94] It is the accents that form the diagonal in Mozart, the accents above all. If one does not follow the accents, if one does not observe them, one falls back into a relatively impoverished punctual system. The human musician is deterritorialized in the bird, but it is a bird that is itself deterritorialized, "transfigured," a celestial bird that has just as much of a becoming as that which becomes with it. Captain Ahab is engaged in an irresistible becoming-whale with Moby-Dick; but the animal, Moby-Dick, must simultaneously become an unbearable pure whiteness, a shimmering pure white wall, a silver thread that stretches out and supples up "like" a girl, or twists like a whip, or stands like a rampart. Can it be that literature sometimes catches up with painting, and even music? And that painting catches up with music? (Moré cites Klee's birds but on the other hand fails to understand what Messiaen says about bird song.) No art is imitative, no art can be imitative or figurative. Suppose a painter "represents" a bird; this is in fact a becoming-bird that can occur only to the extent that the bird itself is in the process of becoming something else, a pure line and pure color. Thus imitation self-destructs, since the imitator unknowingly enters into a becoming that conjugates with the unknowing becoming of that which he or she imitates. One imitates only if one fails, when one fails. The painter and musician do not imitate the animal, they become-animal at the same time as the animal becomes what they willed, at the deepest level of their concord with Nature.[95] Becoming is always double, that which one becomes becomes no less than the one that becomes—block is formed, essentially mobile, never in equilibrium. Mondrian's is the perfect square. It balances on one corner and produces a diagonal that half-opens its closure, carrying away both sides.

Becoming is never imitating. When Hitchcock does birds, he does not reproduce bird calls, he produces an electronic sound like a field of intensities or a wave of vibrations, a continuous variation, like a terrible threat welling up inside us.[96] And this applies not only to the "arts": *Moby-Dick*'s effect also hinges the pure lived experience of double becoming, and the book would not have the same beauty otherwise. The tarantella is a strange dance that magically cures or exorcises the supposed victims of a tarantula bite. But when the victim does this dance, can he or she be said to be imitating the spider, to be identifying with it, even in an identification through an "archetypal" or "agonistic" struggle? No, because the victim, the patient, the person who is sick, becomes a dancing spider only to the extent that the spider itself is supposed to become a pure silhouette, pure color and pure sound to which the person dances.[97] One does not imitate; one constitutes a block of becoming. Imitation enters in only as an adjustment of the block, like a finishing touch, a wink, a signature. But everything of importance happens elsewhere: in the becoming-spider of the dance, which occurs on the condition that the spider itself becomes sound and color, orchestra and painting. Take the case of the local folk hero, Alexis the Trotter, who ran "like" a horse at extraordinary speed, whipped himself with a short switch, whinnied, reared, kicked, knelt, lay down on the ground in the manner of a horse, competed against them in races, and against bicycles and trains. He imitated a horse to make people laugh. But he had a deeper zone of proximity or indiscernibility. Sources tell us that he was never as much of a horse as when he played the harmonica: precisely because he no longer needed a regulating or secondary imitation. It is said that he called his harmonica his "chops-destroyer" and played the instrument twice as fast as anyone else, doubled the beat, imposed a nonhuman tempo.[98] Alexis became all the more horse when the horse's bit became a harmonica, and the horse's trot went into double time. As always, the same must be said of the animals themselves. For not only do animals have colors and sounds, but they do not wait for the painter or musician to use those colors and sounds in a painting or music, in other words, to enter into determinate becomings-color and becomings-sounds by means of components of deterritorialization (we will return to this point later). Ethology is advanced enough to have entered this realm.

We are not at all arguing for an aesthetics of qualities, as if the pure quality (color, sound, etc.) held the secret of a becoming without measure, as in *Philebus*. Pure qualities still seem to us to be punctual systems: They are reminiscences, they are either transcendent or floating memories or seeds of phantasy. A functionalist conception, on the other hand, only considers the function a quality fulfills in a specific assemblage, or in passing from one assemblage to another. The quality must be considered from the standpoint of the becoming that grasps it, instead of becoming being considered from the standpoint of intrinsic qualities having the value of archetypes or phylogenetic memories. For example, whiteness, color, is gripped in a becoming-animal that can be that of the painter or of Captain Ahab, and at the same time in a becoming-color, a becoming-whiteness, that can be that of the animal itself. Moby-Dick's whiteness is the special index of his becoming-solitary. Colors, silhouettes, and animal refrains are indexes of becoming-conjugal or becoming-social that also imply components of deterritorialization. A quality functions only as a line of deterritorialization of an assemblage, or in going from one assemblage to another. This is why an animal-block is something other than a phylogenetic memory, and a childhood block something other than a childhood memory. In Kafka, a quality never functions for itself or as a memory, but rather rectifies an assemblage in which it is deterritorialized, and, conversely, for which it provides a line of deterritorialization; for example, the childhood steeple passes into the castle tower, takes it at the level of its zone of indiscernibility ("battlements that were irregular, broken, fumbling"), and launches down a line of flight (as if one of the tenants "had burst through the roof").[99] If things are more complicated and less sober for Proust, it is because for him qualities retain an air of reminiscence *or* phantasy, and yet with Proust as well these are functional blocks acting not as memories or phantasies but as a becoming-child, a becoming-woman, as components of deterritorialization passing from one assemblage to another.

To the theorems of simple deterritorialization we encountered earlier (in our discussion of the face),[100] we can now add others on generalized double deterritorialization. *Theorem Five:* deterritorialization is always double, because it implies the coexistence of a major variable and a minor variable in simultaneous becoming (the two terms of a becoming do not exchange places, there is no identification between them, they are instead drawn into an asymmetrical block in which both change to the same extent, and which constitutes their zone of proximity). *Theorem Six*: in nonsymmetrical double deterritorialization it is possible to assign a deterritorializing force and a deterritorialized force, even if the same force switches from one value to the other depending on the "moment" or aspect considered; furthermore, it is the least deterritorialized element that always triggers the deterritorialization of the most deterritorializing element, which then reacts back upon it in full force. *Theorem Seven*: the deterritorializing element has the relative role of expression, and the deterritorialized element the relative role of content (as evident in the arts); but not only does the content have nothing to do with an external subject or object, since it forms an asymmetrical block with the expression, but the deterritorialization carries the expression and the content to a proximity where the distinction between them ceases to be relevant, or where the deterritorialization creates their indiscernibility (example: the sound diagonal as the musical form of expression, and becomings-woman, -child, -animal as the contents proper to music, as refrains). *Theorem Eight*: one assemblage does not have the same forces or even speeds of deterritorialization as another; in each instance, the indices and coefficients must be calculated according to the block of becoming under consideration, and in relation to the mutations of an abstract machine (for example, there is a certain slowness, a certain viscosity, of painting in relation to music; but one cannot draw a symbolic boundary between the human being and animal. One can only calculate and compare powers of deterritorialization).

Fernandez demonstrates the presence of becomings-woman, becomings-child in vocal music. Then he decries the rise of instrumental and orchestral music; he is particularly critical of Verdi and Wagner for having resexualized the voice, for having restored the binary machine in response to the requirements of capitalism, which wants a man to be a man and a woman a woman, each with his or her own voice: Verdi-voices, Wagner-voices, are reterritorialized upon man *and* woman. He explains the premature disappearance of Rossini and Bellini (the retirement of the first and death of the second) by their hopeless feeling that the vocal becomings of the opera were no longer possible. However, Fernandez does not ask under what auspices, and with what new types of diagonals, this occurs. To begin with, it is true that the voice ceases to be machined for itself, with simple instrumental accompaniment; it ceases to be a stratum or a line of expression that stands on its own. But why? Music crossed a new threshold of deterritorialization, beyond which it is the instrument that machines the voice, and the voice and instrument are carried *on the same plane* in a relation that is sometimes one of confrontation, sometimes one of compensation, sometimes one of exchange and complementarity. The lied, in particular Schumann's lieder, perhaps marks the first appearance of this pure movement that places the voice and the piano on the same plane of consistency, makes the piano an instrument of delirium, and prepares the way for Wagnerian opera. Even a case like Verdi's: it has often been said that his opera remains lyrical and vocal in spite of its destruction of the bel canto, and in spite of the importance of orchestration in the final works; still, voices are instrumentalized and make extraordinary gains in tessitura or extension (the production of the Verdi-baritone, of the Verdi-soprano). At any rate, the issue is not a given composer, especially not Verdi, or a given genre, but the more general movement affecting music, the slow mutation of the musical machine. If the voice returns to a binary distribution of the sexes, this occurs in relation to binary groupings of instruments in orchestration. There are always molar systems in music that serve as coordinates; this dualist system of the sexes that reappears on the level of the voice, this molar and punctual distribution, serves as a foundation for new molecular flows that then intersect, conjugate, are swept up in a kind of instrumentation and orchestration that tend to be part of the creation itself. Voices may be reterritorialized on the distribution of the two sexes, but the continuous sound flow still passes between them as in a difference of potential.

This brings us to the second point: the principal problem concerning this new threshold of deterritorialization of the voice is no longer that of a properly vocal becoming-woman or becoming-child, but that of a becoming-molecular in which the voice itself is instrumentalized. Of course, becomings-woman and -child remain just as important, even take on new importance, but only to the extent that they convey another truth: what was produced was already a molecular child, a molecular woman . . . We need only think of Debussy: the becoming-child and the becoming-woman in his works are intense but are now inseparable from a molecularization of the motif, a veritable "chemistry" achieved through orchestration. The child and the woman are now inseparable from the sea and the water molecule (*Sirens*, precisely, represents one of the first complete attempts to integrate the voice with the orchestra). Already Wagner was reproached for the "elementary" character of his music, for its aquaticism, or its "atomization" of the motif, "a subdivision into infinitely small units." This becomes even clearer if we think of becoming-animal: birds are still just as important, yet the reign of birds seems to have been replaced by the age of insects, with its much more molecular vibrations, chirring, rustling, buzzing, clicking, scratching, and scraping. Birds are vocal, but insects are instrumental: drums and violins, guitars and cymbals.[101] A becoming-insect has replaced becoming-bird, or forms a block with it. The insect is closer, better able to make audible the truth that all becomings are molecular (cf. Martenot's waves, electronic music). The molecular has the capacity to make the *elementary* communicate with the *cosmic:* precisely because it effects a dissolution of form that connects the most diverse longitudes and latitudes, the most varied speeds and slownesses, which guarantees a continuum by stretching variation far beyond its formal limits. Rediscover Mozart, and that the "theme" was a variation from the start. Varèse explains that the sound molecule (the block) separates into elements arranged in different ways according to variable relations of speed, but also into so many waves or flows of a sonic energy irradiating the entire universe, a headlong line of flight. That is how he populated the Gobi desert with insects and stars constituting a becoming-music of the world, or a diagonal for a cosmos. Messiaen presents multiple chromatic durations in coalescence, "alternating between the longest and the shortest, in order to suggest the idea of the relations between the infinitely long durations of the stars and mountains and the infinitely short ones of the insects and atoms: a cosmic, elementary power that . . . derives above all from the labor of rhythm."[102] The same thing that leads a musician to discover the birds also leads him to discover the elementary and the cosmic. Both combine to form a block, a universe fiber, a diagonal or complex space. Music dispatches molecular flows. Of course, as Messiaen says, music is not the privilege of human beings: the universe, the cosmos, is made of refrains; the question in music is that of a power of deterritorialization permeating nature, animals, the elements, and deserts as much as human beings. The question is more what is not musical in human beings, and what already is musical in nature. Moreover, what Messiaen discovered in music is the same thing the ethologists discovered in animals: human beings are hardly at an advantage, except in the means of overcoding, of making punctual systems. That is even the opposite of having an advantage; through becomings-woman, -child, -animal, or -molecular, nature opposes its power, and the power of music, to the machines of human beings, the roar of factories and bombers. And it is necessary to reach that point, it is necessary for the nonmusical sound of the human being to form a block with the becoming-music of sound, for them to confront and embrace each other like two wrestlers who can no longer break free from each other's grasp, and slide down a sloping line: "Let the choirs represent the survivors . . . Faintly one hears the sound of cicadas. Then the notes of a lark, followed by the mockingbird. Someone laughs . . . A woman sobs . . . From a male a great shout: WE ARE LOST! A woman's voice: WE ARE SAVED! Staccato cries: Lost! Saved! Lost! Saved!"[103]

11. 1837: Of the Refrain

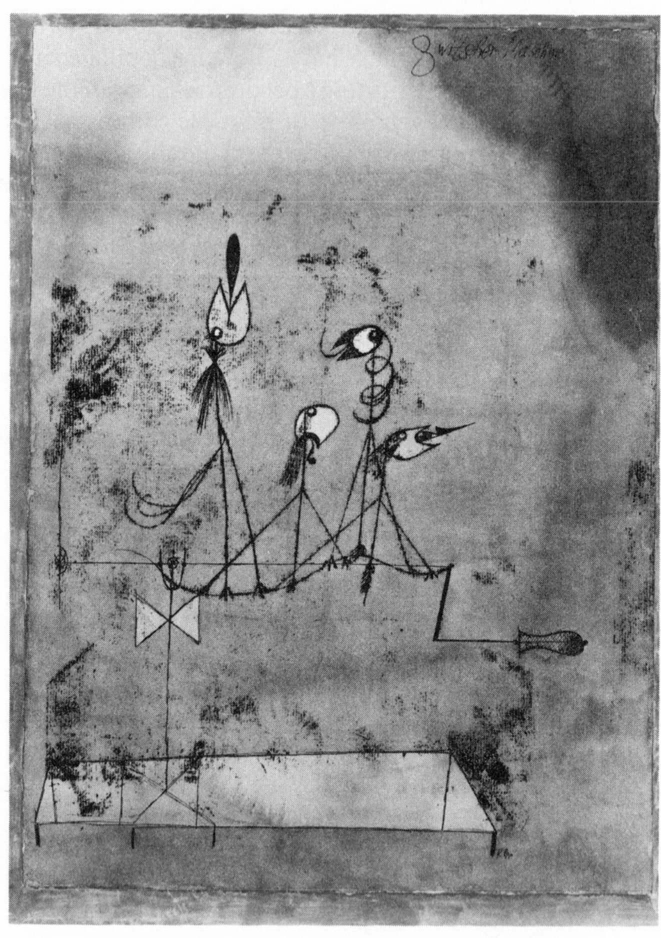

Paul Klee, *Twittering Machine*, 1922
Copyright © 1987 by Cosmopress, Geneva
Watercolor, pen and ink, 16¼ x 12″
Collection, The Museum of Modern Art, New York

I. A child in the dark, gripped with fear, comforts himself by singing under his breath. He walks and halts to his song. Lost, he takes shelter, or orients himself with his little song as best he can. The song is like a rough sketch of a calming and stabilizing, calm and stable, center in the heart of chaos. Perhaps the child skips as he sings, hastens or slows his pace. But the song itself is already a skip: it jumps from chaos to the beginnings of order in chaos and is in danger of breaking apart at any moment. There is always sonority in Ariadne's thread. Or the song of Orpheus.

II. Now we are at home. But home does not preexist: it was necessary to draw a circle around that uncertain and fragile center, to organize a limited space. Many, very diverse, components have a part in this, landmarks and marks of all kinds. This was already true of the previous case. But now the components are used for organizing a space, not for the momentary determination of a center. The forces of chaos are kept outside as much as possible, and the interior space protects the germinal forces of a task to fulfill or a deed to do. This involves an activity of selection, elimination and extraction, in order to prevent the interior forces of the earth from being submerged, to enable them to resist, or even to take something from chaos across the filter or sieve of the space that has been drawn. Sonorous or vocal components are very important: a wall of sound, or at least a wall with some sonic bricks in it. A child hums to summon the strength for the schoolwork she has to hand in. A housewife sings to herself, or listens to the radio, as she marshals the antichaos forces of her work. Radios and television sets are like sound walls around every household and mark territories (the neighbor complains when it gets too loud). For sublime deeds like the foundation of a city or the fabrication of a golem, one draws a circle, or better yet walks in a circle as in a children's dance, combining rhythmic vowels and consonants that correspond to the interior forces of creation as to the differentiated parts of an organism. A mistake in speed, rhythm, or harmony would be catastrophic because it would bring back the forces of chaos, destroying both creator and creation.

III. Finally, one opens the circle a crack, opens it all the way, lets someone in, calls someone, or else goes out oneself, launches forth. One opens the circle not on the side where the old forces of chaos press against it but in another region, one created by the circle itself. As though the circle tended on its own to open onto a future, as a function of the working forces it shelters. This time, it is in order to join with the forces of the future, cosmic forces. One launches forth, hazards an improvisation. But to improvise is to join with the World, or meld with it. One ventures from home on the thread of a tune. Along sonorous, gestural, motor lines that mark the customary path of a child and graft themselves onto or begin to bud "lines of drift" with different loops, knots, speeds, movements, gestures, and sonorities.[1]

These are not three successive moments in an evolution. They are three aspects of a single thing, the Refrain (*ritournelle*). They are found in tales (both horror stories and fairy tales), and in lieder as well. The refrain has all three aspects, it makes them simultaneous or mixes them: sometimes, sometimes, sometimes. Sometimes chaos is an immense black hole in which one endeavors to fix a fragile point as a center. Sometimes one organizes around that point a calm and stable "pace" (rather than a form): the black hole has become a home. Sometimes one grafts onto that pace a breakaway from the black hole. Paul Klee presented these three aspects, and their interlinkage, in a most profound way. He calls the black hole a "gray point" for pictorial reasons. The gray point starts out as nonlocalizable, nondimensional chaos, the force of chaos, a tangled bundle of aberrant lines. Then the point "jumps over itself" and radiates a dimensional space with horizontal layers, vertical cross sections, unwritten customary lines, a whole terrestrial interior force (this force also appears, at a more relaxed pace, in the atmosphere and in water). The gray point (black hole) has thus jumped from one state to another, and no longer represents chaos but the abode or home. Finally, the point launches out of itself, impelled by wandering centrifugal forces that fan out to the sphere of the cosmos: one "tries convulsively to fly from the earth, but at the following level one actually rises above it . . . powered by centrifugal forces that triumph over gravity."[2]

The role of the refrain has often been emphasized: it is territorial, a territorial assemblage. Bird songs: the bird sings to mark its territory. The Greek modes and Hindu rhythms are themselves territorial, provincial, regional. The refrain may assume other functions, amorous, professional or social, liturgical or cosmic: it always carries earth with it; it has a land (sometimes a spiritual land) as its concomitant; it has an essential relation to a Natal, a Native. A musical "nome" is a little tune, a melodic formula that seeks recognition and remains the bedrock or ground of polyphony (*cantus firmus*). The *nomos* as customary, unwritten law is inseparable from a distribution of space, a distribution in space. By that token, it is *ethos*, but the ethos is also the Abode.[3] Sometimes one goes from chaos to the threshold of a territorial assemblage: directional components, infra-assemblage. Sometimes one organizes the assemblage: dimensional components, intra-assemblage. Sometimes one leaves the territorial assemblage for other assemblages, or for somewhere else entirely: interassemblage, components of passage or even escape. And all three at once. Forces of chaos, terrestrial forces, cosmic forces: all of these confront each other and converge in the territorial refrain.

From chaos, *Milieus* and *Rhythms* are born. This is the concern of very ancient cosmogonies. Chaos is not without its own directional components, which are its own ecstasies. We have seen elsewhere how all kinds of milieus, each defined by a component, slide in relation to one another, over one another. Every milieu is vibratory, in other words, a block of space-time constituted by the periodic repetition of the component. Thus the living thing has an exterior milieu of materials, an interior milieu of composing elements and composed substances, an intermediary milieu of membranes and limits, and an annexed milieu of energy sources and actions-perceptions. Every milieu is coded, a code being defined by periodic repetition; but each code is in a perpetual state of transcoding or transduction. Transcoding or transduction is the manner in which one milieu serves as the basis for another, or conversely is established atop another milieu, dissipates in it or is constituted in it. The notion of the milieu is not unitary: not only does the living thing continually pass from one milieu to another, but the milieus pass into one another; they are essentially communicating. The milieus are open to chaos, which threatens them with exhaustion or intrusion. Rhythm is the milieus' answer to chaos. What chaos and rhythm have in common is the in-between—between two milieus, rhythm-chaos or the chaosmos: "*Between* night and day, between that which is constructed and that which grows naturally, between mutations from the inorganic to the organic, from plant to animal, from animal to humankind, yet without this series constituting a progression . . ." In this in-between, chaos becomes rhythm, not inexorably, but it has a chance to. Chaos is not the opposite of rhythm, but the milieu of all milieus. There is rhythm whenever there is a transcoded passage from one milieu to another, a communication of milieus, coordination between heterogeneous space-times. Drying up, death, intrusion have rhythm. It is well known that rhythm is not meter or cadence, even irregular meter or cadence: there is nothing less rhythmic than a military march. The tom-tom is not 1-2, the waltz is not 1, 2, 3, music is not binary or ternary, but rather forty-seven basic meters, as in Turkish music. Meter, whether regular or not, assumes a coded form whose unit of measure may vary, but in a noncommunicating milieu, whereas rhythm is the Unequal or the Incommensurable that is always undergoing transcoding. Meter is dogmatic, but rhythm is critical; it ties together critical moments, or ties itself together in passing from one milieu to another. It does not operate in a homogeneous space-time, but by heterogeneous blocks. It changes direction. Bachelard is right to say that "*the link between truly active moments (rhythm) is always effected on a different plane from the one upon which the action is carried out.*"[4] Rhythm is never on the same plane as that which has rhythm. Action occurs in a milieu, whereas rhythm is located between two milieus, or between two intermilieus, on the fence, between night and day, at dusk, *twilight* or *Zwielicht*, Haecceity. To change milieus, taking them as you find them: Such is rhythm. Landing, splashdown, takeoff . . . This easily avoids an aporia that threatened to introduce meter into rhythm, despite all the declarations of intent to the contrary: How can one proclaim the constituent inequality of rhythm while at the same time admitting implied vibrations, periodic repetitions of components? A milieu does in fact exist by virtue of a periodic repetition, but one whose only effect is to produce a difference by which the milieu passes into another milieu. It is the difference that is rhythmic, not the repetition, which nevertheless produces it: productive repetition has nothing to do with reproductive meter. This is the "critical solution of the antinomy."

One case of transcoding is particularly important: when a code is not content to take or receive components that are coded differently, and instead takes or receives fragments of a different code as such. The first case pertains to the leaf-water relation, the second to the spider-fly relation. It has often been noted that the spider web implies that there are sequences of the fly's own code in the spider's code; it is as though the spider had a fly in its head, a fly "motif," a fly "refrain." The implication may be reciprocal, as with the wasp and the orchid, or the snapdragon and the bumblebee. Jakob von Uexküll has elaborated an admirable theory of transcodings. He sees the components as melodies in counterpoint, each of which serves as a motif for another: Nature as music.[5] Whenever there is transcoding, we can be sure that there is not a simple addition, but the constitution of a new plane, as of a surplus value. A melodic or rhythmic plane, surplus value of passage or bridging. The two cases, however, are never pure; they are in reality mixed (for example, the relation of the leaf, this time not to water in general but to rain).

Still, we do not yet have a *Territory*, which is not a milieu, not even an additional milieu, nor a rhythm or passage between milieus. The territory is in fact an act that affects milieus and rhythms, that "territorializes" them. The territory is the product of a territorialization of milieus and rhythms. It amounts to the same thing to ask when milieus and rhythms become territorialized, and what the difference is between a nonterritorial animal and a territorial animal. A territory borrows from all the milieus; it bites into them, seizes them bodily (although it remains vulnerable to intrusions). It is built from aspects or portions of milieus. It itself has an exterior milieu, an interior milieu, an intermediary milieu, and an annexed milieu. It has the interior zone of a residence or shelter, the exterior zone of its domain, more or less retractable limits or membranes, intermediary or even neutralized zones, and energy reserves or annexes. It is by essence marked by "indexes," which may be components taken from any of the milieus: materials, organic products, skin or membrane states, energy sources, action-perception condensates. There is a territory precisely when milieu components cease to be directional, becoming dimensional instead, when they cease to be functional to become expressive. There is a territory when the rhythm has expressiveness. What defines the territory is the emergence of matters of expression (qualities). Take the example of color in birds or fish: color is a membrane state associated with interior hormonal states, but it remains functional and transitory as long as it is tied to a type of action (sexuality, aggressiveness, flight). It becomes expressive, on the other hand, when it acquires a temporal constancy and a spatial range that make it a territorial, or rather territorializing, mark: a signature.[6] The question is not whether color resumes its functions or fulfills new ones in the territory. It is clear that it does, but this reorganization of functions implies first of all that the component under consideration has become expressive and that its meaning, from this standpoint, is to mark a territory. The same species of birds may have colored and uncolored representatives; the colored birds have a territory, whereas the all-white ones are gregarious. We know what role urine and excrement play in marking, but territorial excrement, for example, in the rabbit, has a particular odor owing to specialized anal glands. Many monkeys, when serving as guards, expose their brightly colored sexual organs: the penis becomes a rhythmic and expressive color-carrier that marks the limits of the territory.[7] A milieu component becomes both a quality and a property, *quale* and *proprium*. It has been remarked how quick this becoming is in many cases, the rapidity with which a territory is constituted at the same time as expressive qualities are selected or produced. The brown stagemaker (*Scenopoeetes dentirostris*) lays down landmarks each morning by dropping leaves it picks from its tree, and then turning them upside down so the paler underside stands out against the dirt: inversion produces a matter of expression.[8]

The territory is not primary in relation to the qualitative mark; it is the mark that makes the territory. Functions in a territory are not primary; they presuppose a territory-producing expressiveness. In this sense, the territory, and the functions performed within it, are products of territorialization. Territorialization is an act of rhythm that has become expressive, or of milieu components that have become qualitative. The marking of a territory is dimensional, but it is not a meter, it is a rhythm. It retains the most general characteristic of rhythm, which is to be inscribed on a different plane than that of its actions. But now the distinction between the two planes is between territorializing expressions and territorialized functions. That is why we cannot accept a thesis like Lorenz's, *which tends to make aggressiveness the basis of the territory:* the territory would then be the product of the phylogenetic evolution of an instinct of aggression, starting at the point where that instinct became intraspecific, was turned against the animal's own kind. A territorial animal would direct its aggressiveness against members of its own species; the species would gain the selective advantage of distributing its members throughout a space where each would have its own place.[9] This ambiguous thesis, which has dangerous political overtones, seems to us to have little foundation. It is obvious that the function of aggression changes pace when it becomes intraspecific. But this reorganization of the function, rather than explaining the territory, presupposes it. There are numerous reorganizations within the territory, which also affect sexuality, hunting, etc.; there are even new functions, such as building a place to live. These functions are organized or created only because they are *territorialized*, and not the other way around. The T factor, the territorializing factor, must be sought elsewhere: precisely in the becoming-expressive of rhythm or melody, in other words, in the emergence of proper qualities (color, odor, sound, silhouette . . .).

Can this becoming, this emergence, be called Art? That would make the territory a result of art. The artist: the first person to set out a boundary stone, or to make a mark. Property, collective or individual, is derived from that, even when it is in the service of war and oppression. Property is fundamentally artistic because art is fundamentally *poster, placard.* As Lorenz says, coral fish are posters. The expressive is primary in relation to the possessive; expressive qualities, or matters of expression, are necessarily appropriative and constitute a having more profound than being.[10] Not in the sense that these qualities belong to a subject, but in the sense that they delineate a territory that will belong to the subject that carries or produces them. These qualities are signatures, but the signature, the proper name, is not the constituted mark of a subject, but the constituting mark of a domain, an abode. The signature is not the indication of a person; it is the chancy formation of a domain. Abodes have proper names, and are inspired. "The inspired and their abodes . . ."; it is with the abode that inspiration arises. No sooner do I like a color than I make it my standard or placard. One puts one's signature on something just as one plants one's flag on a piece of land. A high school monitor stamped all the leaves strewn about the school yard and then put them back in their places. He had signed. Territorial marks are readymades. And what is called *art brut* is not at all pathological or primitive; it is merely this constitution, this freeing, of matters of expression in the movement of territoriality: the base or ground of art. Take anything and make it a matter of expression. The stagemaker practices *art brut.* Artists are stagemakers, even when they tear up their own posters. Of course, from this standpoint art is not the privilege of human beings. Messiaen is right in saying that many birds are not only virtuosos but artists, above all in their territorial songs (if a robber "improperly wishes to occupy a spot which doesn't belong to it, the true owner sings and sings so well that the predator goes away. . . . If the robber sings better than the true proprietor, the proprietor yields his place").[11] The refrain is rhythm and melody that have been territorialized because they have become expressive—and have become expressive because they are territorializing. We are not going in circles. What we wish to say is that there is a self-movement of expressive qualities. Expressiveness is not reducible to the immediate effects of an impulse triggering an action in a milieu: effects of that kind are subjective impressions or emotions rather than expressions (as, for example, the temporary color a freshwater fish takes on under a given impulse). On the other hand, expressive qualities, the colors of the coral fish, for example, are auto-objective, in other words, find an objectivity in the territory they draw.

What is this objective movement? What does a matter *do* as a matter of expression? It is first of all a poster or placard, but that is not all it is. It merely takes that route. The signature becomes style. In effect, *expressive qualities or matters of expression enter shifting relations with one another that "express" the relation of the territory they draw to the interior milieu of impulses and exterior milieu of circumstances.* To express is not to depend upon; there is an autonomy of expression. On the one hand, expressive qualities entertain internal relations with one another that constitute *territorial motifs;* sometimes these motifs loom above the internal impulses, sometimes they are superposed upon them, sometimes they ground one impulse in another, sometimes they pass and cause a passage from one impulse to another, sometimes they insert themselves between them—but they are not themselves "pulsed." Sometimes these nonpulsed motifs arise in a fixed form, or seem to arise that way, but at other times the same ones, or others, take on variable speed and articulation; it is as much their variability as their fixity that makes them independent of the drives they combine or neutralize. "We know that our dogs go through motions of smelling, seeking, chasing, biting, and shaking to death with equal enthusiasm whether they are hungry or not."[12] Another example is the dance of the stickleback. Its zigzag is a motif in which the zig is tied to an aggressive drive toward the partner, and the zag to a sexual drive toward the nest; yet the zig and the zag are accented, or even oriented, differently. On the other hand, expressive qualities also entertain other internal relations that produce *territorial counterpoints:* this refers to the manner in which they constitute points in the territory that place the circumstances of the external milieu in counterpoint. For example, an enemy approaches or suddenly appears, or rain starts to fall, the sun rises, the sun sets . . . Here again, the points or counterpoints are autonomous in their fixity or variability in relation to the circumstances of the exterior milieu whose relation to the territory they express. For this relation can be given without the circumstances being given, just as the relation to the impulses can be given without the impulse being given. And even when the impulses and circumstances are given, the relation is prior to what it places in relation. Relations between matters of expression express relations of the territory to internal impulses and external circumstances: they have an autonomy within this very expression. In truth, territorial motifs and counterpoints explore potentialities of the interior or exterior milieu. Ethologists have grouped these phenomena under the concept of "ritualization" and have demonstrated the link between animal rituals and territory. But this word is not necessarily appropriate for these nonpulsed motifs and nonlocalized counterpoints, since it accounts for neither their variability nor their fixity. It is not one *or* the other, fixity or variability; certain motifs or points are fixed only if others are variable, or else they are fixed on one occasion and variable on another.

We should say, rather, that territorial motifs form *rhythmic faces or characters*, and that territorial counterpoints form *melodic landscapes*. There is a rhythmic character when we find that we no longer have the simple situation of a rhythm associated with a character, subject, or impulse. The rhythm itself is now the character in its entirety; as such, it may remain constant, or it may be augmented or diminished by the addition or subtraction of sounds or always increasing or decreasing durations, and by an amplification or elimination bringing death or resuscitation, appearance or disappearance. Similarly, the melodic landscape is no longer a melody associated with a landscape; the melody itself is a sonorous landscape in counterpoint to a virtual landscape. That is how we get beyond the placard stage: although each expressive quality, each matter of expression considered in itself, is a placard or poster, the analysis of them is nevertheless abstract. Expressive qualities entertain variable or constant relations with one another (that is what matters of expression *do*); they no longer constitute placards that mark a territory, but motifs and counterpoints that express the relation of the territory to interior impulses or exterior circumstances, whether or not they are given. No longer signatures, but a style. What objectively distinguishes a musician bird from a nonmusician bird is precisely this aptitude for motifs and counterpoints that, if they are variable, or even when they are constant, make matters of expression something other than a poster—a style—since they articulate rhythm and harmonize melody. We can then say that the musician bird goes from sadness to joy or that it greets the rising sun or endangers itself in order to sing or sings better than another, etc. None of these formulations carries the slightest risk of anthropomorphism, or implies the slightest interpretation. It is instead a kind of geomorphism. The relation to joy and sadness, the sun, danger, perfection, is given in the motif and counterpoint, even if the term of each of these relations is not given. In the motif and the counterpoint, the sun, joy or sadness, danger, become sonorous, rhythmic, or melodic.[13]

Human music also goes this route. For Swann, the art lover, Vinteuil's little phrase often acts as a placard associated with the Bois de Boulogne and the face and character of Odette: as if it reassured Swann that the Bois de Boulogne was indeed his territory, and Odette his possession. There is already something quite artistic in this way of hearing music. Debussy criticized Wagner, comparing his leitmotifs to signposts signaling the hidden circumstances of a situation, the secret impulses of a character. The criticism is accurate, on one level or at certain moments. But as the work develops, the motifs increasingly enter into conjunction, conquer *their own plane*, become autonomous from the dramatic action, impulses, and situations, and independent of characters and landscapes; they themselves become melodic landscapes and rhythmic characters continually enriching their internal relations. They may then remain relatively constant, or on the contrary grow or diminish, expand or contract, vary in the speed at which they unfold: in both cases, they are no longer pulsed and localized, and even the constants are in the service of variation; the more provisory they are, the more they display the continuous variation they resist, the more rigid they become.[14] Proust was among the first to underscore this life of the Wagnerian motif. Instead of the motif being tied to a character who appears, the appearance of the motif itself constitutes a rhythmic character in "the plenitude of a music that is indeed filled with so many strains, each of which is a being."[15] It is not by chance that the apprenticeship of the *Recherche* pursues an analogous discovery in relation to Vinteuil's little phrases: they do not refer to a landscape; they carry and develop within themselves landscapes that do not exist on the outside (the white sonata and red septet . . .). The discovery of the properly melodic landscape and the properly rhythmic character marks the moment of art when it ceases to be a silent painting on a signboard. This may not be art's last word, but art went that route, as did the bird: motifs and counterpoints that form an autodevelopment, in other words, a style. The interiorization of the melodic or sonorous landscape finds its exemplary form in Liszt and that of the rhythmic character in Wagner. More generally, the lied is the musical art of the landscape, the most pictorial, impressionist form of music. But the two poles are so closely bound that in the lied as well Nature appears as a rhythmic character with infinite transformations.

The territory is first of all the critical distance between two beings of the same species: Mark your distance. What is mine is first of all my distance; I possess only distances. Don't anybody touch me, I growl if anyone enters my territory, I put up placards. Critical distance is a relation based on matters of expression. It is a question of keeping at a distance the forces of chaos knocking at the door. *Mannerism:* the ethos is both abode and manner, homeland and style. This is evident in territorial dances termed baroque or mannerist, in which each pose, each movement, establishes a distance of this kind (sarabands, allemandes, bourrées, gavottes . . .).[16] There is a whole art of poses, postures, silhouettes, steps, and voices. Two schizophrenics converse or stroll according to laws of boundary and territory that may escape us. How very important it is, when chaos threatens, to draw an inflatable, portable territory. If need be, I'll put my territory on my own body, I'll territorialize my body: the house of the tortoise, the hermitage of the crab, but also tattoos that make the body a territory. Critical distance is not a meter, it is a rhythm. But the rhythm, precisely, is caught up in a becoming that sweeps up the distances between characters, making them rhythmic characters that are themselves more or less distant, more or less combinable (intervals). Two animals of the same sex and species confront each other: the rhythm of the first one "expands" when it approaches its territory or the center of its territory; the rhythm of the second contracts when it moves away from its territory. Between the two, at the boundaries, an oscillational constant is established: an active rhythm, a passively endured rhythm, and a witness rhythm?[17] Or else the animal opens its territory a crack for a partner of the opposite sex: a complex rhythmic character forms through duets, antiphonal or alternating singing, as in the case of African shrikes. Furthermore, we must simultaneously take into account two aspects of the territory: it not only ensures and regulates the coexistence of members of the same species by keeping them apart, but makes possible the coexistence of a maximum number of different species in the same milieu by specializing them. Members of the same species enter into rhythmic characters at the same time as different species enter into melodic landscapes; for the landscapes are peopled by characters and the characters belong to landscapes. An example is Messiaen's *Chronochromie*, with its eighteen bird songs forming autonomous rhythmic characters and simultaneously realizing an extraordinary landscape in complex counterpoint, with invented or implicit chords.

Not only does art not wait for human beings to begin, but we may ask if art ever appears among human beings, except under artificial and belated conditions. It has often been noted that human art was for a long time bound up with work and rites of a different nature. Saying this, however, perhaps has no more weight than saying that art begins with human beings. For it is true that a territory has two notable effects: *a reorganization of functions and a regrouping of forces.* On the one hand, when functional activities are territorialized they necessarily change pace (the creation of new functions such as building a dwelling, or the transformation of old functions, as when aggressiveness changes nature and becomes intraspecific). This is like a nascent theme of specialization or professionalism: if the territorial refrain so often passes into professional refrains, it is because professions assume that various activities are performed in the same milieu, and that the same activity has no other agents in the same territory. Professional refrains intersect in the milieu, like merchants' cries, but each marks a territory within which the same activity cannot be performed, nor the same cry ring out. In animals as in human beings, there are rules of critical distance for competition: my stretch of sidewalk. In short, a territorialization of functions is the condition for their emergence as "occupations" or "trades." Thus intraspecific or specialized aggressiveness is necessarily a territorialized aggressiveness; it does not explain the territory since it itself derives from it. It is immediately apparent that all activities within the territory adopt a new practical pace. But that is no reason to conclude that art in itself does not exist here, for it is present in the territorializing factor that is the necessary condition for the emergence of the work-function.

The situation is the same if we consider the other effect of territorialization. That other effect, which relates not to occupations but to rites and religions, consists in this: the territory groups all the forces of the different milieus together in a single sheaf constituted by the forces of the earth. The attribution of all the diffuse forces to the earth as receptacle or base takes place only at the deepest level of each territory. "The surrounding milieu was experienced as a unity; it is very hard to distinguish in these primal intuitions what belongs properly to the earth from what is merely manifested through the earth: mountains, forests, water, vegetation."[18] The forces of air and water, bird and fish, thus become forces of the earth. Moreover, although in extension the territory separates the interior forces of the earth from the exterior forces of chaos, the same does not occur in "intension," in the dimension of depth, where the two types of force clasp and are wed in a battle whose only criterion and stakes is the earth. There is always a place, a tree or grove, in the territory where all the forces come together in a hand-to-hand combat of energies. The earth is this close embrace.[19] This intense center is simultaneously inside the territory, and outside several territories that converge on it at the end of an immense pilgrimage (hence the ambiguities of the "natal"). Inside or out, the territory is linked to this intense center, which is like the unknown homeland, terrestrial source of all forces friendly and hostile, where everything is decided.[20] So we must once again acknowledge that religion, which is common to human beings and animals, occupies territory only because it depends on the raw aesthetic and territorializing factor as its necessary condition. It is this factor that at the same time organizes the functions of the milieu into occupations and binds the forces of chaos in rites and religions, which are forces of the earth. *Territorializing marks simultaneously develop into motifs and counterpoints, and reorganize functions and regroup forces.* But by virtue of this, the territory already unleashes something that will surpass it.

We always come back to this "moment": the becoming-expressive of rhythm, the emergence of expressive proper qualities, the formation of matters of expression that develop into motifs and counterpoints. We therefore need a notion, even an apparently negative one, that can grasp this fictional or raw moment. The essential thing is the disjunction noticeable between the code and the territory. The territory arises in a free margin of the code, one that is not indeterminate but rather is determined differently. Each milieu has its own code, and there is perpetual transcoding between milieus; the territory, on the other hand, seems to form at the level of a certain *decoding*. Biologists have stressed the importance of these determined margins, which are not to be confused with mutations, in other words, changes internal to the code: here, it is a question of duplicated genes or extra chromosomes that are not inside the genetic code, are free of function, and offer a free matter for variation.[21] But it is very unlikely that this kind of matter could create new species independently of mutations, unless it were accompanied by events of another order capable of multiplying the interactions of the organism with its milieus. Territorialization is precisely such a factor that lodges on the margins of the code of a single species and gives the separate representatives of that species the possibility of differentiating. It is because there is a disjunction between the territory and the code that the territory can indirectly induce new species. Wherever territoriality appears, it establishes an intraspecific *critical distance* between members of the same species; it is by virtue of its own disjunction in relation to *specific differences* that it becomes an oblique, indirect means of differentiation. From all of these standpoints, decoding appears as the "negative" of the territory, and the most obvious distinction between territorial animals and nonterritorial animals is that the former are much less coded than the latter. We have said enough bad things about the territory that we can now evaluate all the creations that tend toward it, occur within it, and result or will result from it.

We have gone from forces of chaos to forces of the earth. From milieus to territory. From functional rhythms to the becoming-expressive of rhythm. From phenomena of transcoding to phenomena of decoding. From milieu functions to territorialized functions. It is less a question of evolution than of passage, bridges and tunnels. We saw that milieus continually pass into one another. Now we see that the milieus pass into the territory. The expressive qualities we term aesthetic are certainly not "pure" or symbolic qualities but proper qualities, in other words, appropriative qualities, passages from milieu components to territory components. The territory itself is a place of passage. The territory is the first assemblage, the first thing to constitute an assemblage; the assemblage is fundamentally territorial. But how could it not already be in the process of passing into something else, into other assemblages? That is why we could not talk about the constitution of the territory without also talking about its internal organization. We could not describe the infra-assemblage (posters or placards) without also discussing the intra-assemblage (motifs and counterpoints). Nor can we say anything about the intra-assemblage without already being on the path to other assemblages, or elsewhere. The passage of the Refrain. The refrain moves in the direction of the territorial assemblage and lodges itself there or leaves. In a general sense, *we call a refrain any aggregate of matters of expression that draws a territory and develops into territorial motifs and landscapes* (there are optical, gestural, motor, etc., refrains). In the narrow sense, we speak of a refrain when an assemblage is sonorous or "dominated" by sound—but why do we assign this apparent privilege to sound?

We are now in the intra-assemblage. Its organization is very rich and complex. It includes not only the territorial assemblage but also assembled, territorialized functions. Take the Troglodytidae, the wren family: the male takes possession of his territory and produces a "music box refrain" as a warning to possible intruders; he builds his own nests in his territory, sometimes as many as a dozen; when a female arrives, he sits in front of a nest, invites her to visit, hangs his wings, and lowers the intensity of his song, reduced to a mere trill.[22] It seems that the nesting function is highly territorialized, since the nests are prepared by the male alone before the arrival of the female, who only visits and completes them; the "courtship" function is also territorialized, but to a lesser degree, since the territorial refrain becomes seductive by changing in intensity. All kinds of heterogeneous elements show up in the intra-assemblage: not only the assemblage marks that group materials, colors, odors, sounds, postures, etc., but also the various elements of given assembled behaviors that enter into a motif. For example, a display behavior is composed of a dance, clicking of the beak, an exhibition of colors, a posture with neck outstretched, cries, smoothing of the feathers, bows, a refrain . . . The first question to be asked is what holds these territorializing marks, territorial motifs, and territorialized functions together in the same intra-assemblage. This is a question of *consistency:* the "holding together" of heterogeneous elements. At first, they constitute no more than a fuzzy set, a discrete set that later takes on consistency.

But another question seems to interrupt or cut across the first one. For in many cases, a territorialized, assembled function acquires enough independence to constitute a new assemblage, one that is more or less deterritorialized, en route to deterritorialization. There is no need to effectively leave the territory to go this route; but what just a minute ago was a constituted function in the territorial assemblage has become the constituting element of another assemblage, the element of passage to another assemblage. As in courtly love, a color ceases to be territorial and enters a "courtship" assemblage. The territorial assemblage opens onto the courtship assemblage, which is a social assemblage that has gained autonomy. That is what happens when it is specifically the sexual partner or the members of a group that are recognized, rather than the territory: The partner is then said to be a *Tier mit der Heimvalenz*, "an animal with home value." There is therefore a distinction to be made between milieu groups and couples (without individual recognition), territorial groups and couples (in which there is only recognition inside the territory), and finally social groups and love couples (when there is recognition independent of place).[23] Courtship, or the group, is no longer a part of the territorial assemblage; a courtship or group assemblage takes on autonomy—even though it may stay inside the territory. Conversely, in the new assemblage there is a reterritorialization on the member of the couple or members of the group that have-the-value-of (valence). This opening of the assemblage onto other assemblages can be analyzed in detail, and varies widely. For example, when the male does not make the nest and confines himself to transporting materials or mimicking the construction of a nest (as in Australian grass finches), he either courts the female holding a piece of stubble in his beak (genus *Bathilda*), uses the grass stem only in the initial stages of courtship or even beforehand (genera *Aidemosyne* and *Lonchura*), or pecks at the grass without offering it (genus *Emblema*).[24] It could always be said that these "grass stem" behaviors are merely archaisms, or vestiges of nesting behavior. But the notion of behavior itself proves inadequate to this assemblage. For when the nest is no longer made by the male, nesting ceases to be a component of the territorial assemblage—it takes wing, so to speak, from the territory; furthermore, courtship, which now precedes nesting, itself becomes a relatively autonomous assemblage. In addition, the matter of expression, "grass stem," acts as a component of passage between the territorial assemblage and the courtship assemblage. The fact that the grass stem has an increasingly rudimentary function in certain species, the fact that it tends to cancel out in the series under consideration, is not enough to make it a vestige, much less a symbol. A matter of expression is never a vestige or a symbol. The grass stem is a deterritorialized component, or one en route to deterritorialization. It is neither an archaism nor a transitional or part-object. It is an operator, a vector. It is an *assemblage converter.* The stem cancels out precisely because it is a component of passage from one assemblage to another. This viewpoint is confirmed by the fact that if the stem cancels out, another relay component replaces it or assumes greater importance, namely, the refrain, which is not only territorial but becomes amorous and social, and changes accordingly.[25] The question of why, in the constitution of new assemblages, the sound component "refrain" has a stronger valence than the gestural component "grass stem" can be considered only later on. The important thing for now is to note this formation of new assemblages within the territorial assemblage, and this movement from the intra-assemblage to interassemblages by means of components of passage and relay: An innovative opening of the territory onto the female, or the group. Selective pressure proceeds by way of interassemblages. It is as though forces of deterritorialization affected the territory itself, causing us to pass from the territorial assemblage to other types of assemblages (courtship or sexuality assemblages, group or social assemblages). The grass stem and the refrain are two agents of these forces, two agents of deterritorialization.

The territorial assemblage continually passes into other assemblages. Likewise, the infra-assemblage is inseparable from the intra-assemblage, as is the intra-assemblage from interassemblages; yet these passages are not necessary but rather take place "on a case-by-case basis." The reason is simple: the intra-assemblage, the territorial assemblage, territorializes functions and forces (sexuality, aggressiveness, gregariousness, etc.), and in the process of territorializing them, transforms them. But these territorialized functions and forces can suddenly take on an autonomy that makes them swing over into other assemblages, compose other deterritorialized assemblages. In the intra-assemblage, sexuality may appear as a territorialized function, but it can just as easily draw a line of deterritorialization that describes another assemblage; there are therefore quite variable relations between sexuality and the territory, as if sexuality were keeping "its distance." Profession, trade, and specialty imply territorialized activities, but they can also take wing from the territory, building a new assemblage around themselves, and between professions. A territorial or territorialized component may set about budding, producing: this is the case for the refrain, so much so that we should perhaps call all cases of this kind of refrains. This ambiguity between the territory and deterritorialization is the ambiguity of the Natal. It is understood much more clearly if it is borne in mind that the territory has an intense center at its profoundest depths; but as we have seen, this intense center can be located outside the territory, at the point of convergence of very different and very distant territories. The Natal is outside. We may cite a certain number of troubling and well-known, more or less mysterious, cases illustrating prodigious takeoffs from the territory, displaying a vast movement of deterritorialization directly plugged into the territories and permeating them through and through: (1) pilgrimages to the source, as among salmon; (2) supernumerary assemblies, such as those of locusts or chaffinches, etc. (tens of millions of chaffinches near Thoune in 1950-1951); (3) magnetic or solar-guided migrations; (4) long marches, such as those of the lobsters.[26]

Whatever the causes of each of these movements, it is clear that the nature of the movement is different. It is no longer adequate to say that there is interassemblage, passage from a territorial assemblage to another type of assemblage; rather, we should say that one leaves all assemblages behind, that one exceeds the capacities of any possible assemblage, entering another plane. In effect, there is no longer a milieu movement or rhythm, nor a territorialized or territorializing movement or rhythm; there is something of the Cosmos in these more ample movements. The localization mechanisms are still extremely precise, but the localization has become cosmic. These are no longer territorialized forces bundled together as forces of the earth; they are the liberated or regained forces of a deterritorialized Cosmos. In migration, the sun is no longer the terrestrial sun reigning over a territory, even an aerial one; it is the celestial sun of the Cosmos, as in the two Jerusalems, the Apocalypse. Leaving aside these two grandiose cases where deterritorialization becomes absolute while losing nothing of its precision (because it weds cosmic variables), we must remark that the territory is constantly traversed by movements of deterritorialization that are relative and may even occur in place, by which one passes from the intra-assemblage to interassemblages, without, however, leaving the territory or issuing from the assemblages in order to wed the Cosmos. A territory is always en route to an at least potential deterritorialization, even though the new assemblage may operate a reterritorialization (something that "has-the-value-of" home). We saw that the territory constituted itself on a margin of decoding affecting the milieu; we now see that there is a margin of deterritorialization affecting the territory itself. There is a series of unclaspings. The territory is inseparable from certain coefficients of deterritorialization (which can be evaluated in each case) that place the relations of each territorialized function to the territory in variation, as well as the relations of the territory to each deterritorialized assemblage. It is the same "thing" that appears first as a territorialized function taken up in the intra-assemblage, and again as a deterritorialized or autonomous assemblage, as an interassemblage.

Refrains could accordingly be classified as follows: (1) territorial refrains that seek, mark, assemble a territory; (2) territorialized function refrains that assume a special function in the assemblage (the Lullaby that territorializes the child's slumber, the Lover's Refrain that territorializes the sexuality of the loved one, the Professional Refrain that territorializes trades and occupations, the Merchant Refrain that territorializes distribution and products); (3) the same, when they mark new assemblages, pass into new assemblages by means of deterritorialization-reterritorialization (nursery rhymes are a very complicated example: they are territorial refrains that are sung differently from neighborhood to neighborhood, sometimes from one street to the next; they distribute game roles and functions within the territorial assemblage; but they also cause the territory to pass into the game assemblage, which tends to become autonomous);[27] (4) refrains that collect or gather forces, either at the heart of the territory, or in order to go outside it (these are refrains of confrontation or departure that sometimes bring on a movement of absolute deterritorialization: "Goodbye, I'm leaving and I won't look back." At infinity, these refrains must rejoin the songs of the Molecules, the newborn wailing of the fundamental Elements, as Millikan put it. They cease to be terrestrial, becoming cosmic: when the religious Nome blooms and dissolves in a molecular pantheist Cosmos, when the singing of the birds is replaced by combinations of water, wind, clouds, and fog. "Outside, the wind and the rain . . ." The Cosmos as an immense deterritorialized refrain).

The problem of *consistency* concerns the manner in which the components of a territorial assemblage hold together. But it also concerns the manner in which different assemblages hold together, with components of passage and relay. It may even be the case that consistency finds the totality of its conditions only on a properly cosmic plane, where all the disparate and heterogeneous elements are convoked. However, from the moment heterogeneities hold together in an assemblage or interassemblages a problem of consistency is posed, in terms of coexistence or succession, and both simultaneously. Even in a territorial assemblage, it may be the most deterritorialized component, the deterritorializing vector, in other words, the refrain, that assures the consistency of the territory. If we ask the general question, "What holds things together?", the clearest, easiest answer seems to be provided by a formalizing, linear, hierarchized, centralized *arborescent* model. Take Tinbergen's schema, which presents a coded linkage of spatiotemporal forms in the central nervous system: a higher functional center goes automatically into operation and releases an appetitive behavior in search of specific stimuli (the migrational center); through the intermediary of the stimulus, a second center that had been inhibited up to this point is freed and releases a new appetitive behavior (the territorial center); then other subordinate centers are activated, centers of fighting, nesting, courtship . . . until stimuli are found that release the corresponding executive acts.[28] This kind of representation, however, is constructed of oversimplified binarities: inhibition-release, innate-acquired, etc. Ethologists have a great advantage over ethnologists: they did not fall into the structural danger of dividing an undivided "terrain" into forms of kinship, politics, economics, myth, etc. The ethologists have retained the integrality of a certain undivided "terrain." But by orienting it along the axes of inhibition-release, innate-acquired, they risk reintroducing souls and centers at each locus and stage of linkage. That is why even the authors who stress the role of the peripheral and the acquired at the level of releasing stimuli do not truly overturn the linear aborescent schema, even if they reverse the direction of the arrows.

It seems more important to us to underline a certain number of factors liable to suggest an entirely different schema, one favoring rhizomatic, rather than arborified, functioning, and no longer operating by these dualisms. First of all, what is called a functional center brings into play not only a localization but also a distribution of an entire population of neurons selected from throughout the central nervous system, as in a "cable network." This being the case, in considering the system as a whole we should speak less of automatism of a higher center than of coordination between centers, and of the cellular groupings or molecular populations that perform these couplings: there is no form or correct structure imposed from without or above but rather an articulation from within, as if oscillating molecules, oscillators, passed from one heterogeneous center to another, if only for the purpose of assuring the dominance of one among them.[29] This obviously excludes any linear relation from one center to another, in favor of packets of relations steered by molecules: the interaction or coordination may be positive *or* negative (release or inhibition), but it is never direct, as in a linear relation or chemical reaction; it always occurs between molecules with at least two heads, and each center taken separately.[30]

This represents a whole behavioral-biological "machinics," a whole molecular engineering that should help increase our understanding of the nature of problems of consistency. The philosopher Eugène Dupréel proposed a theory of *consolidation*; he demonstrated that life went not from a center to an exteriority but from an exterior to an interior, or rather from a discrete or fuzzy aggregate to its consolidation. This implies three things. First, that there is no beginning from which a linear sequence would derive, but rather densifications, intensifications, reinforcements, injections, showerings, like so many intercalary events ("there is growth only by intercalation"). Second, and this is not a contradiction, there must be an arrangement of intervals, a distribution of inequalities, such that it is sometimes necessary to make a hole in order to consolidate. Third, there is a superposition of disparate rhythms, an articulation from within of an interrhythmicity, with no imposition of meter or cadence.[31] Consolidation is not content to come after; it is creative. The fact is that the beginning always begins in-between, intermezzo. Consistency is the same as consolidation, it is the act that produces consolidated aggregates, of succession as well as of coexistence, by means of the three factors just mentioned: intercalated elements, intervals, and articulations of superposition. Architecture, as the art of the abode and the territory, attests to this: there are consolidations that are made afterward, and there are consolidations of the keystone type that are constituent parts of the ensemble. More recently, matters like reinforced concrete have made it possible for the architectural ensemble to free itself from arborescent models employing tree-pillars, branch-beams, foliage-vaults. Not only is concrete a heterogeneous matter whose degree of consistency varies according to the elements in the mix, but iron is intercalated following a rhythm; moreover, its *self-supporting surfaces* form a complex rhythmic personage whose "stems" have different sections and variable intervals depending on the intensity and direction of the force to be tapped (armature instead of structure). In this sense, the literary or musical work has an architecture: "Saturate every atom," as Virginia Woolf said;[32] or in the words of Henry James, it is necessary to "begin far away, as far away as possible," and to proceed by "blocks of wrought matter." It is no longer a question of imposing a form upon a matter but of elaborating an increasingly rich and consistent material, the better to tap increasingly intense forces. What makes a material increasingly rich is the same as what holds heterogeneities together without their ceasing to be heterogeneous. What holds them together in this way are intercalary oscillators, synthesizers with at least two heads; these are interval analyzers, rhythm synchronizers (the word "synchronizer" is ambiguous because molecular synchronizers do not proceed by homogenizing and equalizing measurement, but operate from within, between two rhythms). Is not consolidation the terrestrial name for consistency? The territorial assemblage is a milieu consolidation, a space-time consolidation, of coexistence and succession. And the refrain operates with these three factors.

The matters of expression themselves must present characteristics making this taking on of consistency possible. We have seen that they have an aptitude to enter into internal relations forming motifs and counterpoints: the territorializing marks become territorial motifs or counterpoints, the signatures and placards constitute a "style." These are the elements of a discrete or fuzzy aggregate; but they become consolidated, take on consistency. To this extent, they have effects, such as reorganizing functions and gathering forces. To get a better grasp on the mechanism of this aptitude, we may lay down certain conditions of homogeneity, beginning with marks or matters of the same kind, for example, a set of sonorous marks, the song of a bird. The song of the chaffinch normally has three distinct phases: the first has from four to fourteen notes rising in crescendo but decreasing in frequency; the second has from two to eight notes, lower than the first and of constant frequency; the third ends with a complex "flourish" or "ornament." From the standpoint of acquisition, this "full song" is preceded by a "subsong" that under normal conditions already assumes possession of the general tonal quality, overall duration and content of the stanzas, and even a tendency to end on a higher note.[33] But the organization into three stanzas, the order of the stanzas, the details and the ornament, are not pregiven; it is precisely the articulations from within that are missing, the intervals, the intercalary notes, everything making for motif and counterpoint. The distinction between subsong and full song could thus be presented as follows: the subsong as mark or placard, the full song as style or motif, and the aptitude to pass from one to the other, for one to consolidate itself in the other. Clearly, artificial isolation will have very different effects depending on whether it takes place before or after the acquisition of the components of the subsong.

Our present concern, however, is to find out what happens when these components effectively develop into the motifs and counterpoints of the full song. We must leave behind the conditions of qualitative homogeneity we set for ourselves. For as long as we confine ourselves to marks, marks of one kind coexist with marks of another kind, period: the sounds of an animal coexist with its colors, gestures, silhouettes; or else the sounds of a given species coexist with the sounds of other species, perhaps quite different but close in space. The organization of qualified marks into motifs and counterpoints necessarily entails a taking on of consistency, or a capture of the marks of another quality, a mutual branching of sounds-colors-gestures, or a capture of sounds from different animal species, etc. Consistency necessarily occurs between heterogeneities, not because it is the birth of a differentiation, but because heterogeneities that were formerly content to coexist or succeed one another become bound up with one another through the "consolidation" of their coexistence and succession. The intervals, intercalations, and articulations constitutive of motifs and counterpoints in the order of an expressive quality also envelop other qualities of a different order, or qualities of the same order but of another sex or even another species of animal. A color will "answer to" a sound. If a quality has motifs and counterpoints, if there are rhythmic characters and melodic landscapes in a given order, then there is the constitution of a veritable *machinic opera* tying together orders, species, and heterogeneous qualities. What we term machinic is precisely this synthesis of heterogeneities as such. Inasmuch as these heterogeneities are matters of *expression*, we say that their synthesis itself, their consistency or capture, forms a properly machinic "statement" or "enunciation." The varying relations into which a color, sound, gesture, movement, or position enters in the same species, and in different species, form so many machinic enunciations.

Let us return to the stagemaker, the magic bird or bird of the opera. He is not brightly colored (as though there were an inhibition). But his song, his refrain, can be heard from a great distance (is this a compensation, or on the contrary the prime factor?). He sings perched on his singing stick, a vine or branch located just above the display ground he has prepared by marking it with cut leaves turned upside down to contrast with the color of the earth. As he sings, he uncovers the yellow root of certain feathers underneath his beak: he makes himself visible at the same time as sonorous. His song forms a varied and complex motif interweaving his own notes and those of other birds that he imitates in the intervals.[34] This produces a consolidation that "consists" in species-specific sounds, sounds of other species, leaf hue, throat color: the stagemaker's machinic statement or assemblage of enunciation. Many birds "imitate" the songs of other species. But imitation may not be the best concept for these phenomena, which vary according to the assemblage into which they enter. The subsong contains elements that can enter into melodic and rhythmic organizations distinct from those of the species under consideration, supplying the full song with truly alien or added notes. If certain birds such as the chaffinch seem impervious to imitation, it is because any alien sounds appearing in their subsong are eliminated from the consistency of the full song. On the other hand, in cases where added phrases do get included in the full song, it may be because there is an interspecific assemblage of the parasitism type; or it may be because the bird's assemblage itself effectuates the counterpoints to its melody. Thorpe is not wrong to say that the problem is one of the occupation of frequency bands, as with radios (the sound aspect of territoriality).[35] It is less a question of imitating a song than of occupying corresponding frequencies; for there may be an advantage in being able to restrict oneself to a very determinate zone in some circumstances, and in others to widen or deepen the zone to assure oneself counterpoints and to invent chords that would otherwise remain diffuse, as, for example, in the rain forest, which is precisely where the greatest number of "imitative" birds are found.

From the standpoint of consistency, matters of expression must be considered not only in relation to their aptitude to form motifs and counterpoints but also in relation to the inhibitors and releasers that act on them, and the mechanisms of innateness or learning, heredity or acquisition, that modulate them. Ethology's mistake is to restrict itself to a binary distribution of these factors, even, and especially, when it is thought necessary to take both into account simultaneously, to intermix them at every level of a "tree of behaviors." Instead, what should be done is to start from a positive notion capable of accounting for the very particular character the innate and the acquired assume in the rhizome, and which is like the principle of their mixture. Such a notion cannot be arrived at in terms of behavior but rather only in terms of assemblage. Some authors emphasize autonomous developments encoded in centers (innateness); others emphasize acquired linkages regulated by peripheral sensations (learning). But Raymond Ruyer has demonstrated that the animal is instead prey to "musical rhythms" and "melodic and rhythmic themes" explainable neither as the encoding of a recorded phonograph disk nor by the movements of performance that effectuate them and adapt them to the circumstances.[36] The opposite is even true: the melodic or rhythmic themes precede their performance and recording. What is primary is the consistency of a refrain, a little tune, either in the form of a mnemic melody that has no need to be inscribed locally in a center, or in the form of a vague motif with no need to be pulsed or stimulated. There is perhaps more to be learned from a musical and poetic notion such as the Natal—in the lied, or in Hölderlin or Thomas Hardy—than from the slightly vapid and foggy categories of the innate and the acquired. For from the moment there is a territorial assemblage, we can say that the innate assumes a very particular figure, since it is inseparable from a movement of decoding and passes to the margins of the code, unlike the innate of the interior milieu; acquisition also assumes a very particular figure, since it is territorialized, in other words, regulated by matters of expression rather than by stimuli in the exterior milieu. The natal is the innate, but decoded; and it is the acquired, but territorialized. The natal is the new figure assumed by the innate and the acquired in the territorial assemblage. The affect proper to the natal, as heard in the lied: to be forever lost, or refound, or aspiring to the unknown homeland. In the natal, the innate tends to be displaced: as Ruyer says, it is in some way *prior to* or *downstream from* the act; it concerns less the act or the behavior than the matters of expression themselves, the perception that discerns and selects them, and the gesture that erects them, or itself constitutes them (that is why there are "critical periods" when the animal valorizes an object or situation, "is impregnated" by a matter of expression, long before being able to perform the corresponding act). This is not to say, however, that behavior is at the mercy of chance learning; for it is predetermined by this displacement, and finds rules of assemblage in its own territorialization. The natal, then, consists in a decoding of innateness and a territorialization of learning, one atop the other, one alongside the other. The natal has a consistency that cannot be explained as a mixture of the innate and the acquired, because it is instead what accounts for such mixtures in territorial assemblage and interassemblages. In short, the notion of behavior proves inadequate, too linear, in comparison with that of the assemblage. The natal stretches from what happens in the intra-assemblage all the way to the center that has been projected outside; it cuts across all the interassemblages and reaches all the way to the gates of the Cosmos.

The territorial assemblage is inseparable from lines or coefficients of deterritorialization, passages, and relays toward other assemblages. There have been many studies on the influence of artificial conditions on bird song, but the results vary both by species and according to the kind and timing of the artifice. Many birds are receptive to the songs of other species, if they are exposed to them during the critical period, and will reproduce the alien songs later on. The chaffinch, however, seems much more devoted to its own matters of expression and retains an innate sense of its own tonal quality even if exposed to synthetic sounds. The outcome also depends on whether the birds are isolated before or after the critical period. In the first case, chaffinches develop a nearly normal song; in the second, the subjects in the isolated group (who cannot hear each other) develop an abnormal, nonspecies-specific song that is nevertheless common to the group (see Thorpe). In any event, it is necessary to consider the effects of deterritorialization or denatalization on a given species at a given moment. Whenever a territorial assemblage is taken up by a movement that deterritorializes it (whether under so-called natural or artificial conditions), we say that a machine is released. That in fact is the distinction we would like to propose between *machine* and *assemblage:* a machine is like a set of cutting edges that insert themselves into the assemblage undergoing deterritorialization, and draw variations and mutations of it. For there are no mechanical effects; effects are always machinic, in other words, depend on a machine that is plugged into an assemblage and has been freed through deterritorialization. What we call *machinic statements* are machine effects that define consistency or enter matters of expression. Effects of this kind can be very diverse but are never symbolic or imaginary; they always have a real value of passage or relay.

As a general rule, a machine plugs into the territorial assemblage of a species and opens it to other assemblages, causes it to pass through the interassemblages of that species; for example, the territorial assemblage of a bird species opens onto interassemblages of courtship and gregariousness, moving in the direction of the partner or "socius." But the machine may also open the territorial assemblage to interspecific assemblages, as in the case of birds that adopt alien songs, and most especially in the case of parasitism.[37] Or it may go beyond all assemblages and produce an opening onto the Cosmos. Or, conversely, instead of opening up the deterritorialized assemblage onto something else, it may produce an effect of closure, as if the aggregate had fallen into and continues to spin in a kind of black hole. This is what happens under conditions of precocious or extremely sudden deterritorialization, and when specific, interspecific, and cosmic paths are blocked; the machine then produces "individual" group effects spinning in circles, as in the case of chaffinches that have been isolated too early, whose impoverished, simplified song expresses nothing more than the resonance of the black hole in which they are trapped. It is important to bring up this "black hole" function again because it can increase our understanding of phenomena of inhibition, and is in turn capable of breaking with the overnarrow inhibitor-releaser dualism. We saw earlier that an interassemblage could include lines of impoverishment and fixation leading to a black hole but could still perhaps lead into a richer and more positive line of deterritorialization (for example, the "grass stem" component among Australian grass finches falls into a black hole and leads into the "refrain" component).[38] Thus the black hole is a machine effect in assemblages and has a complex relation to other effects. It may be necessary for the release of innovative processes that they first fall into a catastrophic black hole: stases of inhibition are associated with the release of crossroads behaviors. On the other hand, when black holes resonate together or inhibitions conjugate and echo each other, instead of an opening onto consistency, we see a closure of the assemblage, as though it were deterritorialized in the void: young chaffinches. *Machines are always singular keys that open or close an assemblage, a territory.* Moreover, finding the machine in operation in a given territorial assemblage is not enough; it is already in operation in the emergence of matters of expression, in other words, in the constitution of the assemblage and in the vectors of deterritorialization that ply it from the start.

Thus consistency of matters of expression relates, on the one hand, to their aptitude to form melodic and rhythmic themes and, on the other hand, to the power of the natal. Finally, there is one other aspect: their very special relation to the molecular (the machine starts us down this road). The very words, "matters of expression," imply that expression has a primary relation to matter. As matters of expression take on consistency they constitute semiotic systems, but the *semiotic* components are inseparable from *material* components and are in exceptionally close contact with molecular levels. The whole question is thus whether or not the molar-molecular relation assumes a new figure here. In general, it has been possible to distinguish "molar-molecular" combinations that vary greatly depending on the direction followed. First, individual atoms can enter into probabilistic or statistical accumulations that tend to efface their individuality; this already happens on the level of the molecule, and then again in the molar aggregate. But they can become complicated in interactions and retain their individuality inside the molecule, then in the macromolecule, etc., setting up direct communications between individuals of different orders.[39] Second, it is clear that the distinction to be made is not between the individual and the statistical. In fact, it is always a question of populations; statistics concerns individual phenomena, and antistatistical individuality operates only in relation to molecular populations. The distinction is between two group movements, as in Alembert's equation, in which one group tends toward increasingly equilibrated, homogeneous, and probable states (the divergent wave and the delayed potential), and the other group tends toward less probable states of concentration (the convergent wave and the anticipated potential).[40] Third, the intramolecular internal forces that give an aggregate its molar form can be of two types: they are either covalent, arborescent, mechanical, linear, localizable relations subject to chemical conditions of action and reaction or to linked reactions, or they are indirect, noncovalent, machinic and nonmechanical, superlinear, nonlocalizable bonds operating by stereospecific *discernment or discrimination*, rather than by linkage.[41]

These are different ways of stating the same distinction, which seems much broader than the one we are looking for: it is, in effect, a distinction between matter and life, or rather, since there is only one matter, between two states, two tendencies of atomic matter (for example, there are bonds that immobilize the linked atoms in relation to one another, and other bonds that allow free rotation). Stating the distinction in the most general way, we could say that it is between stratified systems or systems of stratification on the one hand, and consistent, self-consistent aggregates on the other. But the point is that consistency, far from being restricted to complex life forms, fully pertains even to the most elementary atoms and particles. There is a coded system of stratification whenever, horizontally, there are linear causalities between elements; and, vertically, hierarchies of order between groupings; and, holding it all together in depth, a succession of framing forms, each of which informs a substance and in turn serves as a substance for another form. These causalities, hierarchies, and framings constitute a stratum, as well as the passage from one stratum to another, and the stratified combinations of the molecular and molar. On the other hand, we may speak of aggregates of consistency when instead of a regulated succession of forms-substances we are presented with consolidations of very heterogeneous elements, orders that have been short-circuited or even reverse causalities, and captures between materials and forces of a different nature: as if a *machinic phylum, a destratifying transversality,* moved through elements, orders, forms and substances, the molar and the molecular, freeing a matter and tapping forces.

Now if we ask ourselves where life fits into this distinction, we see that it undoubtedly implies a gain in consistency, in other words, a surplus value (surplus value of *destratification*). For example, it contains a greater number of self-consistent aggregates and processes of consolidation and gives them molar scope. It is destratifying from the outset, since its code is not distributed throughout the entire stratum but rather occupies an eminently specialized genetic line. But the question is almost contradictory, because asking where life fits in amounts to treating it as a particular stratum having its own order and befitting order, having its own forms and substances. It is true that it is both at once: a particularly complex system of stratification and an aggregate of consistency that disrupts orders, forms, and substances. As we have seen, the living thing performs a transcoding of milieus that can be considered both to constitute a stratum and to effect reverse causalities and transversals of destratification. The same question can be asked when life no longer restricts itself to mixing milieus but assembles territories as well. The territorial assemblage implies a *decoding* and is inseparable from its own *deterritorialization* (two new types of surplus value). "Ethology" then can be understood as a very privileged molar domain for demonstrating how the most varied components (biochemical, behavioral, perceptive, hereditary, acquired, improvised, social, etc.) can crystallize in assemblages that respect neither the distinction between orders nor the hierarchy of forms. What holds all the components together are *transversals*, and the transversal itself is only a component that has taken upon itself the specialized vector of deterritorialization. In effect, what holds an assemblage together is not the play of framing forms or linear causalities but, actually or potentially, its most deterritorialized component, a cutting edge of deterritorialization. An example is the refrain: it is more deterritorialized than the grass stem, but this does not preclude its being "determined," in other words, connected to biochemical and molecular components. The assemblage holds by its most deterritorialized component, but deterritorialized is not the same as indeterminate (the refrain may be narrowly connected to the presence of male hormones).[42] A component of this kind entering an assemblage may be among the most highly determined, even mechanized, of components, but it will still bring "play" to what it composes; it fosters the entry of new dimensions of the milieus by releasing processes of discernibility, specialization, contraction, and acceleration that open new possibilities, that open the territorial assemblage onto interassemblages. Back to the stagemaker: one of its acts consists in discerning and causing to be discerned both sides of the leaf. This act is connected to the determinism of the "toothed" beak. Assemblages are defined simultaneously by *matters of expression* that take on consistency independently of the form-substance relation; reverse causalities or "advanced" determinisms, decoded innate functions related to *acts of dis-*

cernment or election rather than to linked reactions; and *molecular combinations* that proceed by noncovalent bonding rather than by linear relations—in short, a new "pace" produced by the imbrication of the *semiotic* and the *material.* From this standpoint, we may oppose the consistency of assemblages to the stratification of milieus. But once again, this opposition is only relative, entirely relative. Just as milieus swing between a stratum state and a movement of destratification, assemblages swing between a territorial closure that tends to restratify them and a deterritorializing movement that on the contrary connects them with the Cosmos. Thus it is not surprising that the distinction we were seeking was not between assemblages and something else but between the two limits of any possible assemblage, in other words, between the system of strata and the plane of consistency. We should not forget that the strata rigidify and are organized on the plane of consistency, and that the plane of consistency is at work and is constructed in the strata, in both cases piece by piece, blow by blow, operation by operation.

We have gone from stratified milieus to territorialized assemblages and simultaneously, from the forces of chaos, as broken down, coded, transcoded by the milieus, to the forces of the earth, as gathered into the assemblages. Then we went from territorial assemblages to interassemblages, to the opening of assemblages along lines of deterritorialization; and simultaneously, the same from the ingathered forces of the earth to the deterritorialized, or rather deterritorializing, Cosmos. How does Paul Klee present this last movement, which is not a terrestrial "pace" but instead a cosmic "breakaway" [*échappée:* also "opening," "outlet," "vista"; in counterpoint, "escape tone"—Trans.]? And why so enormous a word, Cosmos, to discuss an operation that must be precise? Klee says that one "tries convulsively to fly from the earth," and that one "rises above it . . . powered by centrifugal forces that triumph over gravity." He adds that the artist begins by looking around him- or herself, into all the milieus, but does so in order to grasp the trace of creation in the created, of naturing nature in natured nature; then, adopting "an earthbound position,"[43] the artist turns his or her attention to the microscopic, to crystals, molecules, atoms, and particles, not for scientific conformity, but for movement, for nothing but immanent movement; the artist tells him- or herself that this world has had different aspects, will have still others, and that there are already others on other planets; finally, the artist opens up to the Cosmos in order to harness forces in a "work" (without which the opening onto the Cosmos would only be a reverie incapable of enlarging the limits of the earth); this work requires very simple, pure, almost childish means, but also the forces of a *people,* which is what is still lacking. "We still lack the ultimate force. . . .

We seek a people. We began over there in the Bauhaus. . . . More we cannot do."[44]

Classicism refers to form-matter relation, or rather a form-substance relation (substance is precisely a matter endowed with form). Matter is organized by a succession of forms that are compartmentalized, centralized, and hierarchized in relation to one another, each of which takes charge of a greater or lesser amount of matter. Each form is like the code of a milieu, and the passage from one form to another is a veritable transcoding. Even the seasons are milieus. Two coexistent operations are involved, one by which the form differentiates itself according to binary distinctions, the other by which the formed substantial parts, milieus or seasons, enter into an order of succession that can be the same in either direction. But beneath these operations, the classical artist hazards an extreme and dangerous adventure. He or she breaks down the milieus, separates them, harmonizes them, regulates their mixtures, passes from one to the other. What the artist confronts in this way is chaos, the forces of chaos, the forces of a raw and untamed matter upon which Forms must be imposed in order to make substances, and Codes in order to make milieus. Phenomenal agility. That is why no one has ever been able to draw a clear line between baroque and classical.[45] All of baroque lies brewing beneath classicism: the task of the classical artist is God's own, that of organizing chaos; and the artist's only cry is Creation! Creation! The Tree of Creation! An ancient wooden flute organizes chaos, but chaos reigns like the Queen of the Night. The classical artist proceeds with a One-Two: the one-two of the differentiation of form divided (man-woman, masculine and feminine rhythms, voices, families of instruments, all the binarities of the *ars nova*); and the one-two of the distinction between parts as they answer each other (the enchanted flute and the magic bell). The little tune, the bird refrain, is the binary unity of creation, the differentiating unity of the pure beginning: "At first the piano complained alone, like a bird deserted by its mate; the violin heard and answered it, as from a neighboring tree. It was as at the beginning of the world, as if there were as yet only the two of them on earth, *or rather* in this world closed to all the rest, fashioned by the logic of a creator, in which there would never be more than the two of them: this sonata."[46]

If we attempt an equally summary definition of romanticism, we see that everything is clearly different. A new cry resounds: the Earth, the territory and the Earth! With romanticism, the artist abandons the ambition of de jure universality and his or her status as creator: the artist territorializes, enters a territorial assemblage. The seasons are now territorialized. The earth is certainly not the same thing as the territory. The earth is the intense point at the deepest level of the territory or is projected outside it like a focal point, where all the forces draw together in close embrace. The earth is no longer one force among others, nor is it a substance endowed with form or a coded milieu, with bounds and an apportioned share. The earth has become that close embrace of all forces, those of the earth as well as of other substances, so that the artist no longer confronts chaos, but hell and the subterranean, the groundless. The artist no longer risks dissipation in the milieus but rather sinking too deeply into the earth: Empedocles. The artist no longer identifies with Creation but with the ground or foundation, the foundation has become creative. The artist is no longer God but the Hero who defies God: Found, Found, instead of Create. Faust, especially the second Faust, is impelled by this tendency. Criticism, the Protestantism of the earth, replaces dogmatism, the Catholicism of the milieus (code). It is certain that the Earth as an intense point in depth or in projection, as *ratio essendi*, is always in disjunction with the territory; and the territory as the condition of "knowledge," *ratio cognoscendi*, is always in disjunction with the earth. The territory is German, the Earth Greek. And this disjunction is precisely what determines the status of the romantic artist, in that she or he no longer confronts the gaping of chaos but the pull of the Ground (*Fond*). The little tune, the bird refrain, has changed: it is no longer the beginning of a world but draws a territorial assemblage upon the earth. It is then no longer made of two consonant parts that seek and answer one another; it addresses itself to a deeper singing that founds it, but also strikes against it and sweeps it away, making it ring dissonant. The refrain is indissolubly constituted by the territorial song and the singing of the earth that rises to drown it out. Thus at the end of *Das Lied von der Erde* (The song of the Earth) there are two coexistent motifs, one melodic, evoking the assemblages of the bird, the other rhythmic, evoking the deep, eternal breathing of the earth. Mahler says that the singing of the birds, the color of the flowers, and the fragrance of the forest are not enough to make Nature, that the god Dionysus and the great Pan are needed. The Ur-refrain of the earth harnesses all refrains whether territorial or not, and all milieu refrains. By the end of [Berg's] *Wozzeck*, the lullaby refrain, military refrain, drinking refrain, hunting refrain, child's refrain are so many admirable assemblages swept up by the powerful earth machine and its cutting edges: Wozzeck's voice, by which the earth becomes sonorous, Marie's death cry moving over the pond, the repeated B note, when the earth howled . . . It is owing to this disjunction, this decoding, that the romantic artist experiences the territory; but he or she experiences it as necessarily lost, and experiences him- or herself as an exile, a voyager, as deterritorialized, *driven back into the milieus*, like the Flying Dutchman or King Waldemar (whereas the classical artist inhabited the milieus). Yet this movement is still under earth's command, the repulsion from the territory is produced by the attraction of the earth. The signpost now only indicates the road of no return. This is the ambiguity of the natal, as it appears in the lied (as well as in symphony and opera): the lied is simultaneously the territory, the lost territory, and the earth vector. The intermezzo assumed increasing importance because it played on all the disjunctions between the earth and the territory, inserted itself into them, filled them after its fashion, "between night and day," "noon-midnight." From this standpoint, the fundamental innovations of romanticism can be said to be the following: There were no longer substantial parts corresponding to forms, milieus corresponding to codes, or a matter in chaos given order in forms and by codes. The parts were instead like assemblages produced and dismantled at the surface. Form itself became *a great form in continuous development*, a gathering of the forces of the earth taking all the parts up into a sheaf. Matter itself was no longer a chaos to subjugate and organize but rather *the moving matter of a continuous variation.* The universal had become a relation, variation. The continuous variation of matter and the continuous development of form. The assemblages thus placed matter and form in a new relation: matter ceased to be a matter of content, becoming instead a matter of expression, and form ceased to be a code subduing the forces of chaos, becoming a force itself, the sum of the forces of the earth. There was a new relation to danger, madness, limits: romanticism did not go further than baroque classicism; it went elsewhere, with other givens and other vectors.

What romanticism lacks most is a people. The territory is haunted by a solitary voice; the voice of the earth resonates with it and provides it percussion rather than answering it. Even when there is a people, it is mediatized by the earth, it rises up from the bowels of the earth and is apt to return there: more a subterranean than a terrestrial people. The hero is a hero of the earth; he is mythic, rather than being a hero of the people and historical. Germany, German romanticism, had a genius for experiencing the natal territory not as deserted but as "solitary," regardless of population density; for the population is only an emanation of the earth, and has the value of One Alone. The territory does not open onto a people, it half-opens onto the Friend, the Loved One; but the Loved One is already dead, and the Friend uncertain, disturbing.[47] As in the lied, everything in the territory occurs in relation to the One-Alone of the soul and the One-All of the earth. That is why romanticism takes on an entirely different aspect and even claims a different name, a different placard, in the Latin and Slavic countries, where on the contrary everything is put in terms of the theme of a people and the forces of a people. This time, it is the earth that is mediatized by the people, and exists only through the people. This time, the earth can be "deserted," an arid steppe, or a ravaged, dismembered territory; yet it is never solitary, it is always filled by a nomadic population that divides or regroups, contests or laments, attacks or suffers. This time, the hero is a hero of the people, and not of the earth; he is related to the *One-Crowd*, not the *One-All*. It certainly cannot be said that there is more or less nationalism on one side or the other because nationalism is everywhere in the figures of romanticism, sometimes as the driving force, sometimes as a black hole (fascism used Verdi much less than nazism did Wagner). The problem is a truly musical one, technically musical, and all the more political for that. The romantic hero, the voice of the romantic hero, acts as a subject, a subjectified individual with "feelings"; but this subjective vocal element is reflected in an orchestral and instrumental whole that on the contrary mobilizes nonsubjective "affects" and that reaches its height in romanticism. It should not be thought that the vocal element and the orchestral-instrumental whole are only in an extrinsic relation to one another: the orchestration imposes a given role on the voice, and the voice envelops a given mode of orchestration. Orchestration-instrumentation brings sound forces together or separates them, gathers or disperses them; but it changes, and the role of the voice changes too, depending on whether the forces are of the Earth or of the People, of the One-All or the One-Crowd. In the first case, it is a question of effecting *groupings of powers*, and these are what constitute affects; in the second case, it is *group individuations* that constitute affect and are the object of orchestration. Groupings of power are fully diversified, but they are like *the relations proper to the Universal;* we must use another word, the *Dividual*, to designate the type of musical relations and the intra- or intergroup passages occurring in group individuation. The sentimental or subjective element of the voice has a different role and even a different position depending on whether it internally confronts nonsubjectified groupings of power or nonsubjectified group individuations, the relations of the universal or the relations of the "dividual." Debussy formulated the problem of the One-Crowd well when he reproached Wagner for not knowing how to "do" a crowd or a people: a crowd must be fully individuated, but by group individuations that are not reducible to the individuality of the subjects that compose the crowd.[48] The people must be individualized, not according to the persons within it, but according to the affects it experiences, simultaneously or successively. The concepts of the One-Crowd and the Dividual are botched if the people is reduced to a juxtaposition, or if it is reduced to a power of the universal. In short, there are two very different conceptions of orchestration, depending on whether one is seeking to sonorize the forces of the Earth or the forces of the People. The simplest example of this difference is a doubtless Wagner-Verdi, in that Verdi puts increasing emphasis on the relations between the voice and instrumentation and orchestration. Even today, Stockhausen and Berio outline a new version of this difference, even though they are grappling with a musical problem different from that of romanticism (in Berio there is a search for a multiple cry, a cry of the population, in the dividual of the One-Crowd, and not for a cry of the Earth in the universal of the One-All). The idea of an Opera of the world, or cosmic music, changes drastically depending on which pole of orchestration is in play.[49] To avoid an oversimplified opposition between Wagner and Verdi, we would have to show how Berlioz had a genius for passing from one pole to the other in his orchestration, or even hesitating between them: a sonorous Nature *or* People. And how music like Mussorgsky's was able to do a crowd (despite what Debussy says). And how music like Bartók's was able to use popular, or population, airs to do populations, themselves sonorous, instrumental, and orchestral, which impose a Dividual scale, a prodigious new chromaticism.[50] And then there are all the non-Wagnerian paths . . .

If there is a modern age, it is, of course, the age of the cosmic. Paul Klee declared himself anti-Faustian. "As for animals and all the other creatures, I do not like them with a terrestrial cordiality; earthly things interest me less than cosmic things." The assemblage no longer confronts the forces of chaos, it no longer uses the forces of the earth or the people to deepen itself but instead opens onto the forces of the Cosmos. All this seems extremely general, and somewhat Hegelian, testifying to an absolute Spirit. Yet it is, should be, a question of technique, exclusively a question of technique. The essential relation is no longer matters-forms (or substances-attributes); neither is it the continuous development of form and the continuous variation of matter. It is now a direct relation *material-forces*. A material is a molecularized matter, which must accordingly "harness" forces; these forces are necessarily forces of the Cosmos. There is no longer a matter that finds its corresponding principle of intelligibility in form. It is now a question of elaborating a material charged with harnessing forces of a different order: the visual material must capture nonvisible forces. *Render visible*, Klee said; not render or reproduce the visible. From this perspective, philosophy follows the same movement as the other activities; whereas romantic philosophy still appealed to a formal synthetic identity ensuring a continuous intelligibility of matter (a priori synthesis), modern philosophy tends to elaborate a material of thought in order to capture forces that are not thinkable in themselves. This is Cosmos philosophy, after the manner of Nietzsche. The molecular material has even become so deterritorialized that we can no longer even speak of matters of expression, as we did in romantic territoriality. *Matters of expression are superseded by a material of capture.* The forces to be captured are no longer those of the earth, which still constitute a great expressive Form, but the forces of an immaterial, nonformal, and energetic Cosmos. The painter Millet used to say that what counts in painting is not, for example, what a peasant is carrying, whether it is a sacred object or a sack of potatoes, but its exact weight. This is the postromantic turning point: the essential thing is no longer forms and matters, or themes, but forces, densities, intensities. The earth itself swings over, tending to take on the value of pure material for a force of gravitation or weight. Perhaps it is not until Cézanne that rocks begin to exist uniquely through the forces of folding they harness, landscapes through thermal and magnetic forces, and apples through forces of germination: nonvisual forces that nevertheless have been rendered visible. When forces become necessarily cosmic, material becomes necessarily molecular, with enormous force operating in an infinitesimal space. The problem is no longer that of the beginning, any more than it is that of a foundation-ground. It is now a problem of consistency or consolidation: how to consolidate the material, make it consistent, so that it can harness unthinkable, invisible, nonsonorous forces. Debussy . . . Music molecularizes sound matter and in so doing becomes capable of harnessing nonsonorous forces such as Duration and Intensity.[51] *Render Duration sonorous.* Let us recall Nietzsche's idea of the eternal return as a little ditty, a refrain, but which captures the mute and unthinkable forces of the Cosmos. We thus leave behind the assemblages to enter the age of the Machine, the immense mechanosphere, the plane of cosmicization of forces to be harnessed. Varèse's procedure, at the dawn of this age, is exemplary: a musical machine of consistency, a *sound machine* (not a machine for reproducing sounds), which molecularizes and atomizes, ionizes sound matter, and harnesses a cosmic energy.[52] If this machine must have an assemblage, it is the synthesizer. By assembling modules, source elements, and elements for treating sound (oscillators, generators, and transformers), by arranging microintervals, the synthesizer makes audible the sound process itself, the production of that process, and puts us in contact with still other elements beyond sound matter.[53] It unites disparate elements in the material, and transposes the parameters from one formula to another. The synthesizer, with its operation of consistency, has taken the place of the ground in a priori synthetic judgment: its synthesis is of the molecular and the cosmic, material and force, not form and matter, *Grund* and territory. Philosophy is no longer synthetic judgment; it is like a thought synthesizer functioning to make thought travel, make it mobile, make it a force of the Cosmos (in the same way as one makes sound travel).

This synthesis of disparate elements is not without ambiguity. It has the same ambiguity, perhaps, as the modern valorization of children's drawings, texts by the mad, and concerts of noise. Sometimes one overdoes it, puts too much in, works with a jumble of lines and sounds; then instead of producing a cosmic machine capable of "rendering sonorous," one lapses back to a machine of reproduction that ends up reproducing nothing but a scribble effacing all lines, a scramble effacing all sounds. The claim is that one is opening music to all events, all irruptions, but one ends up reproducing a scrambling that prevents any event from happening. All one has left is a resonance chamber well on the way to forming a black hole. A material that is too rich remains too "territorialized": on noise sources, on the nature of the objects . . . (this even applies to Cage's prepared piano). One makes an aggregate fuzzy, instead of defining the fuzzy aggregate *by* the operations of consistency or consolidation pertaining to it. For this is the essential thing: *a fuzzy aggregate, a synthesis of disparate elements, is defined only by a degree of consistency that makes it possible to distinguish the disparate elements constituting that aggregate (discernibility).*[54] The material must be sufficiently deterritorialized to be molecularized and open onto something cosmic, instead of lapsing into a statistical heap. This condition is met only if there is a certain simplicity in the nonuniform material: a maximum of calculated sobriety in relation to the disparate elements and the parameters. The sobriety of the assemblages is what makes for the richness of the Machine's effects. People often have too much of a tendency to reterritorialize on the child, the mad, noise. If this is done, one *fuzzifies* instead of making the fuzzy aggregate consist, or harnessing cosmic forces in the deterritorialized material. That is why it infuriated Paul Klee when people would talk about the "childishness" of his drawings (and Varèse when they would talk about sound effects, etc.). According to Klee, what is needed in order to "render visible" or harness the Cosmos is a pure and simple line accompanied by the idea of an object, and nothing more: if you multiply the lines and take the whole object, you get nothing but a scramble, and visual sound effects.[55] According to Varèse, in order for the projection to yield a highly complex form, in other words, a cosmic distribution, what is necessary is a simple figure in motion and a plane that is itself mobile; otherwise, you get sound effects. Sobriety, sobriety: that is the common prerequisite for the deterritorialization of matters, the molecularization of material, and the cosmicization of forces. Maybe a child can do that. But the sobriety involved is the sobriety of a becoming-child that is not necessarily the becoming *of* the child, quite the contrary; the becoming-mad involved is not necessarily the becoming *of* the madman, quite the contrary. It is clear that what is necessary to make sound travel, and to travel around sound, is very pure and simple sound, an emission or wave without harmonics (La Monte Young has been successful at this). The more rarefied the atmosphere, the more disparate the elements you will find. Your synthesis of disparate elements will be all the *stronger* if you proceed with a sober gesture, an act of consistency, capture, or extraction that works in a material that is not meager but prodigiously simplified, creatively limited, selected. For there is no imagination outside of technique. The modern figure is not the child or the lunatic, still less the artist, but the cosmic artisan: a homemade atomic bomb—it's very simple really, it's been proven, it's been done. To be an artisan and no longer an artist, creator, or founder, is the only way to become cosmic, to leave the milieus and the earth behind. The invocation to the Cosmos does not at all operate as a metaphor; on the contrary, the operation is an effective one, from the moment the artist connects a material with forces of consistency or consolidation.

Material thus has three principal characteristics: it is a molecularized matter; it has a relation to forces to be harnessed; and it is defined by the operations of consistency applied to it. Finally, it is clear that the relation to the earth and the people has changed, and is no longer of the romantic type. The earth is now at its most deterritorialized: not only a point in a galaxy, but one galaxy among others. The people is now at its most molecularized: a molecular population, a people of oscillators as so many forces of interaction. The artist discards romantic figures, relinquishes both the forces of the earth and those of the people. The combat, if combat there is, has moved. The established powers have occupied the earth, they have built people's organizations. The mass media, the great people's organizations of the party or union type, are machines for reproduction, fuzzification machines that effectively scramble all the terrestrial forces of the people. The established powers have placed us in the situation of a combat at once atomic and cosmic, galactic. Many artists became aware of this situation long ago, even before it had been installed (Nietzsche, for example). They became aware of it because the same vector was traversing their own domain: a molecularization, an atomization of the material, coupled with a cosmicization of the forces taken up by that material. The question then became whether molecular or atomic "populations" of all natures (mass media, monitoring procedures, computers, space weapons) would continue to bombard the existing people in order to train it or control it or annihilate it—or if other molecular populations were possible, could slip into the first and give rise to a people yet to come. As Virilio says in his very rigorous analysis of the depopulation of the people and the deterritorialization of the earth, the question has become: "To dwell as a poet or as an assassin?"[56] The assassin is one who bombards the existing people with molecular populations that are forever closing all of the assemblages, hurling them into an ever wider and deeper black hole. The poet, on the other hand, is one who lets loose molecular populations in hopes that this will sow the seeds of, or even engender, the people to come, that these populations will pass into a people to come, open a cosmos. Once again, we must not make it seem as though the poet gorged on metaphors: it may be that the sound molecules of pop music are at this very moment implanting here and there a people of a new type, singularly indifferent to the orders of the radio, to computer safeguards, to the threat of the atomic bomb. In this respect, the relation of artists to the people has changed significantly: the artist has ceased to be the One-Alone withdrawn into him- or herself, but has also ceased to address the people, to invoke the people as a constituted force. Never has the artist been more in need of a people, while stating most firmly that the people is lacking—the people is what is most lacking. We are not referring to popular or populist artists. Mallarmé said that the Book needed a people. Kafka said that literature is the affair of the people. Klee said that the people is essential *yet lacking*. Thus the problem of the artist is that the modern depopulation of the people results in an open earth, and by means of art, or by means to which art contributes. Instead of being bombarded from all sides in a limiting cosmos, the people and the earth must be like the vectors of a cosmos that carries them off; then the cosmos itself will be art. From depopulation, make a cosmic people; from deterritorialization, a cosmic earth—that is the wish of the artisan-artist, here, there, locally. Our governments deal with the molecular and the cosmic, and our arts make them their affair also, with the same stakes, the people and the earth, and with unfortunately incomparable, but nevertheless competitive, means. Is it not of the nature of creations to operate in silence, locally, to seek consolidation everywhere, to go from the molecular to an uncertain cosmos, whereas the processes of destruction and conservation work in bulk, take center stage, occupy the entire cosmos in order to enslave the molecular and to stick it in a conservatory or a bomb?

These three "ages," the classical, romantic, and modern (for lack of a better term), should not be interpreted as an evolution, or as structures separated by signifying breaks. They are assemblages enveloping different Machines, or different relations to the Machine. In a sense, everything we attribute to an age was already present in the preceding age. Forces, for example: it has always been a question of forces, designated either as forces of chaos or forces of the earth. Similarly, for all of time painting has had the project of rendering visible, instead of reproducing the visible, and music of rendering sonorous, instead of reproducing the sonorous. Fuzzy aggregates have been constituting themselves and inventing their processes of consolidation all along. A *freeing of the molecular* was already found in classical matters of content, operating by destratification, and in romantic matters of expression, operating by decoding. The most we can say is that when forces appear as forces of the earth or of chaos, they are not grasped directly as forces but as reflected in relations between matter and form. Thus it is more a question of thresholds of perception, or thresholds of discernibility belonging to given assemblages. It is only after matter has been sufficiently deterritorialized that it itself emerges as molecular and brings forth pure forces attributable only to the Cosmos. It had been present "for all of time," but under different perceptual conditions. New conditions were necessary for what was buried or covered, inferred or concluded, presently to rise to the surface. What was composed in an assemblage, what was still only composed, becomes a component of a new assemblage. In this sense, all history is really the history of perception, and what we make history with is the matter of a becoming, not the subject matter of a story. Becoming is like the machine: present in a different way in every assemblage, passing from one to the other, opening one onto the other, outside any fixed order or determined sequence.

We are now ready to return to the refrain. We can propose a new classification system: milieu refrains, with at least two parts, one of which answers the other (the piano and the violin); natal refrains, refrains of the territory, where the part is related to the whole, to an immense refrain of the earth, according to relations that are themselves variable and mark in each instance the disjunction between the earth and the territory (the lullaby, the drinking song, hunting song, work song, military song, etc.); folk and popular refrains, themselves tied to an immense song of the people, according to variable relations of crowd individuations that simultaneously bring into play affects and nations (the Polish, Auvergnat, German, Magyar, or Romanian, but also the Pathetic, Panicked, Vengeful, etc.); molecularized refrains (the sea and the wind) tied to cosmic forces, the Cosmos refrain. For the Cosmos itself is a refrain, and the ear also (everything that has been taken for a labyrinth is in fact a refrain). But precisely why is the refrain eminently sonorous? Why this privileging of the ear, when even animals and birds present us with so many visual, chromatic, postural, and gestural refrains? Does the painter have fewer refrains than the musician? Are there fewer refrains in Cézanne or Klee than in Mozart, Schumann, or Debussy? Taking Proust's examples: Does Vermeer's little yellow span of wall, or a painter's flowers, Elstir's roses, constitute less of a refrain than Vinteuil's little phrase? There is surely no question here of declaring a given art supreme on the basis of a formal hierarchy of absolute criteria. Our problem is more modest: comparing the powers or coefficients of deterritorialization of sonorous and visual components. It seems that when sound deterritorializes, it becomes more and more refined; it becomes specialized and autonomous. Color clings more, not necessarily to the object, but to territoriality. When it deterritorializes, it tends to dissolve, to let itself be steered by other components. This is evident in phenomena of synesthesia, which are not reducible to a simple color-sound correspondence; sounds have a piloting role and induce colors that *are superposed* upon the colors we see, lending them a properly sonorous rhythm and movement.[57] Sound owes this power not to signifying or "communicational" values (which on the contrary presuppose that power), nor to physical properties (which would privilege light over sound), but to a phylogenetic line, a machinic phylum that operates in sound and makes it a cutting edge of deterritorialization. But this does not happen without great ambiguity: sound invades us, impels us, drags us, transpierces us. It takes leave of the earth, as much in order to drop us into a black hole as to open us up to a cosmos. It makes us want to die. Since its force of deterritorialization is the strongest, it also effects the most massive of reterritorializations, the most numbing, the most redundant. Ecstasy and hypnosis. Colors do not move a people. Flags can do nothing without trumpets. Lasers are modulated on sound. The refrain is sonorous par excellence, but it can as easily develop its force into a sickly sweet ditty as into the purest motif, or Vinteuil's little phrase. And sometimes the two combine: Beethoven used as a "signature tune." The potential fascism of music. Overall, we may say that music is plugged into a machinic phylum infinitely more powerful than that of painting: a line of selective pressure. That is why the musician has a different relation to the people, machines, and the established powers than does the painter. In particular, the established powers feel a keen need to control the distribution of black holes and lines of deterritorialization in this phylum of sounds, in order to ward off or appropriate the effects of musical machinism. Painters, at least as commonly portrayed, may be much more open socially, much more political, and less controlled from without and within. That is because each time they paint, they must create or recreate a phylum, and they must do so on the basis of bodies of light and color they themselves produce, whereas musicians have at their disposal a kind of germinal continuity, even if it is latent or indirect, on the basis of which they produce sound bodies. Two different movements of creation: one goes from *soma* to *germen*, and the other from *germen* to *soma*. The painter's refrain is like the flipside of the musician's, a negative of music.

So just what is a refrain? *Glass harmonica:* the refrain is a prism, a crystal of space-time. It acts upon that which surrounds it, sound or light, extracting from it various vibrations, or decompositions, projections, or transformations. The refrain also has a catalytic function: not only to increase the speed of the exchanges and reactions in that which surrounds it, but also to assure indirect interactions between elements devoid of so-called natural affinity, and thereby to form organized masses. The refrain is therefore of the crystal or protein type. The seed, or internal structure, then has two essential aspects: augmentations and diminutions, additions and withdrawals, amplifications and eliminations by unequal values, but also the presence of a retrograde motion running in both directions, as "in the side windows of a moving streetcar." The strange retrograde motion of *Joke*. It is of the nature of the refrain to become concentrated by elimination in a very short moment, as though moving from the extremes to a center, or, on the contrary, to develop by additions, moving from a center to the extremes, and also to travel these routes in both directions.[58] The refrain fabricates time (*du temps*). The refrain is the "implied tense" (*temps*) discussed by the linguist Gustave Guillaume. The ambiguity of the refrain is more evident now: for if the retrograde motion merely forms a closed circle, if the augmentations and diminutions are regular, proceeding, for example, by doubled or halved values, then this false spatiotemporal rigor leaves the exterior aggregate all the fuzzier; that aggregate now has only descriptive, indicative, or associative relations with the seed. It is "a worksite of inauthentic elements for the formation of impure crystals," rather than a pure crystal that harnesses cosmic forces. The refrain remains a formula evoking a character or landscape, instead of itself constituting a rhythmic character or melodic landscape. The refrain has two poles. These poles hinge not only on an intrinsic quality but also on a state of force on the part of the listener; thus the little phrase from Vinteuil's sonata is associated with Swann's love, the character of Odette, and the landscape of the Bois de Boulogne for a long time, until it turns back on itself, opens onto itself, revealing until then unheard-of potentialities, entering into other connections, setting love adrift in the direction of other assemblages. Here, Time is not an a priori form; rather, the refrain is the a priori form of time, which in each case fabricates different times [*temps:* also, "meters," "tempos"—Trans.].

It is odd how music does not eliminate the bad or mediocre refrain, or the bad usage of the refrain, but on the contrary carries it along, or uses it as a springboard. "Ah, vous dirai-je maman" ("Ah, mamma, now you shall know"), "Elle avait une jambe de bois" ("She had a wooden leg"), "Frère Jacques." Childhood or bird refrain, folk song, drinking song, Viennese waltz, cow bells: music uses anything and sweeps everything away. Not that a folk song, bird song, or children's song is reducible to the kind of closed and associative formula we just mentioned. Instead, what needs to be shown is that a musician requires a *first type* of refrain, a territorial or assemblage refrain, in order to transform it from within, deterritorialize it, producing a refrain of the *second type* as the final end of music: the cosmic refrain of a sound machine. Gisèle Brelet, discussing Bartók, gives a good formulation of the problem of the two types: beginning from popular and territorial *melodies* that are autonomous, self-sufficient, and closed in upon themselves, how can one construct a new chromaticism that places them in communication, thereby creating "*themes*" bringing about a development of Form, or rather a becoming of Forces? The problem is a general one because in many directions refrains will be planted by a new seed that brings back modes, makes those modes communicate, undoes temperament, melds major and minor, and cuts the tonal system loose, slipping through its net instead of breaking with it.[59] We may say long live Chabrier, as opposed to Schoenberg, just as Nietzsche said long live Bizet, and for the same reasons, with the same technical and musical intent. We go from modality to an untempered, widened chromaticism. We do not need to suppress tonality, we need to turn it loose. We go from assembled refrains (territorial, popular, romantic, etc.) to the great cosmic machined refrain. But the labor of creation is already under way in the first type; it is there in its entirety. Deformations destined to harness a great force are already present in the small-form refrain or rondo. Childhood scenes, children's games: the starting point is a childlike refrain, but the child has wings already, he becomes celestial. The becoming-child of the musician is coupled with a becoming-aerial of the child, in a nondecomposable block. The memory of an angel, or rather the becoming of a cosmos. Crystal: the becoming-bird of Mozart is inseparable from a becoming-initiate of the bird, and forms a block with it.[60] It is the extremely profound labor dedicated to the first type of refrain that creates the second type, or the little phrase of the Cosmos. In a concerto, Schumann requires all the assemblages of the orchestra to make the cello wander the way a light fades into the distance or is extinguished. In Schumann, a whole learned labor, at once rythmic, harmonic, and melodic, has this sober and simple result: *deterritorialize the refrain.*[61] Produce a deterritorialized refrain as the final end of music, release it in the Cosmos—that is more important than building a new system. Opening the assemblage onto a cosmic force. In the passage from one to the other, from the assemblage of sounds to the Machine that renders it sonorous, from the becoming-child of the musician to the becoming-cosmic of the child, many dangers crop up: black holes, closures, paralysis of the finger and auditory hallucinations, Schumann's madness, cosmic force gone *bad*, a note that pursues you, a sound that transfixes you. Yet one was already present in the other; the cosmic force was already present in the material, the great refrain in the little refrains, the great maneuver in the little maneuver. Except we can never be sure we will be strong enough, for we have no system, only lines and movements. Schumann.

12. 1227: Treatise on Nomadology—The War Machine

Nomad Chariot, Entirely of Wood, Altai, Fifth to Fourth Centuries B.C.

AXIOM I. *The war machine is exterior to the State apparatus.*

PROPOSITION I. *This exteriority is first attested to in mythology, epic, drama, and games.*

Georges Dumézil, in his definitive analyses of Indo-European mythology, has shown that political sovereignty, or domination, has two heads: the magician-king and the jurist-priest. Rex and flamen, raj and Brahman, Romulus and Numa, Varuna and Mitra, the despot and the legislator, the binder and the organizer. Undoubtedly, these two poles stand in opposition term by term, as the obscure and the clear, the violent and the calm, the quick and the weighty, the fearsome and the regulated, the "bond" and the "pact," etc.[1] But their opposition is only relative; they function as a pair, in alternation, as though they expressed a division of the One or constituted in themselves a sovereign unity. "At once antithetical and complementary, necessary to one another and consequently without hostility, lacking a mythology of conflict: a specification on any one level automatically calls forth a homologous specification on another. The two together exhaust the field of the function." They are the principal elements of a State apparatus that proceeds by a One-Two, distributes binary distinctions, and forms a milieu of interiority. It is a double articulation that makes the State apparatus into a *stratum*.

It will be noted that war is not contained within this apparatus. *Either* the State has at its disposal a violence that is not channeled through war—either it uses police officers and jailers in place of warriors, has no arms and no need of them, operates by immediate, magical capture, "seizes" and "binds," preventing all combat—*or*, the State acquires an army, but in a way that presupposes a juridical integration of war and the organization of a military function.[2] As for the war machine in itself, it seems to be irreducible to the State apparatus, to be outside its sovereignty and prior to its law: it comes from elsewhere. *Indra, the warrior god, is in opposition to Varuna no less than to Mitra.*[3] He can no more be reduced to one or the other than he can constitute a third of their kind. Rather, he is like a pure and immeasurable multiplicity, the pack, an irruption of the ephemeral and the power of metamorphosis. *He unties the bond just as he betrays the pact.* He brings a *furor* to bear against sovereignty, a celerity against gravity, secrecy against the public, a power (*puissance*) against sovereignty, a machine against the apparatus. He bears witness to another kind of justice, one of incomprehensible cruelty at times, but at others of unequaled pity as well (because he unties bonds . . .).[4] He bears witness, above all, to other relations with women, with animals, because he sees all things in relations of *becoming*, rather than implementing binary distributions between "states": a veritable becoming-animal of the warrior, a becoming-woman, which lies outside dualities of terms as well as correspondences between relations. In every respect, the war machine is of another species, another nature, another origin than the State apparatus.

Let us take a limited example and compare the war machine and the State apparatus in the context of the theory of games. Let us take chess and Go, from the standpoint of the game pieces, the relations between the pieces and the space involved. Chess is a game of State, or of the court: the emperor of China played it. Chess pieces are coded; they have an internal nature and intrinsic properties from which their movements, situations, and confrontations derive. They have qualities; a knight remains a knight, a pawn a pawn, a bishop a bishop. Each is like a subject of the statement endowed with a relative power, and these relative powers combine in a subject of enunciation, that is, the chess player or the game's form of interiority. Go pieces, in contrast, are pellets, disks, simple arithmetic units, and have only an anonymous, collective, or third-person function:

"It" makes a move. "It" could be a man, a woman, a louse, an elephant. Go pieces are elements of a nonsubjectified machine assemblage with no intrinsic properties, only situational ones. Thus the relations are very different in the two cases. Within their milieu of interiority, chess pieces entertain biunivocal relations with one another, and with the adversary's pieces: their functioning is structural. On the other hand, a Go piece has only a milieu of exteriority, or extrinsic relations with nebulas or constellations, according to which it fulfills functions of insertion or situation, such as bordering, encircling, shattering. All by itself, a Go piece can destroy an entire constellation synchronically; a chess piece cannot (or can do so diachronically only). Chess is indeed a war, but an institutionalized, regulated, coded war, with a front, a rear, battles. But what is proper to Go is war without battle lines, with neither confrontation nor retreat, without battles even: pure strategy, whereas chess is a semiology. Finally, the space is not at all the same: in chess, it is a question of arranging a closed space for oneself, thus of going from one point to another, of occupying the maximum number of squares with the minimum number of pieces. In Go, it is a question of arraying oneself in an open space, of holding space, of maintaining the possibility of springing up at any point: the movement is not from one point to another, but becomes perpetual, without aim or destination, without departure or arrival. The "smooth" space of Go, as against the "striated" space of chess. The *nomos* of Go against the State of chess, *nomos* against *polis*. The difference is that chess codes and decodes space, whereas Go proceeds altogether differently, territorializing or deterritorializing it (make the outside a territory in space; consolidate that territory by the construction of a second, adjacent territory; deterritorialize the enemy by shattering his territory from within; deterritorialize oneself by renouncing, by going elsewhere . . .). Another justice, another movement, another space-time.

"They come like fate, without reason, consideration, or pretext . . ." "In some way that is incomprehensible they have pushed right into the capital. At any rate, here they are; it seems that every morning there are more of them."[5] Luc de Heusch analyzes a Bantu myth that leads us to the same schema: Nkongolo, an indigenous emperor and administrator of public works, a man of the public and a man of the police, gives his half-sisters to the hunter Mbidi, who assists him and then leaves. Mbidi's son, a man of secrecy, joins up with his father, only to return from the outside with that inconceivable thing, an army. He kills Nkongolo and proceeds to build a new State.[6] "Between" the magical-despotic State and the juridical State containing a military institution, we see the flash of the war machine, arriving from without.

From the standpoint of the State, the originality of the man of war, his eccentricity, necessarily appears in a negative form: stupidity, deformity, madness, illegitimacy, usurpation, sin. Dumézil analyzes the three "sins" of the warrior in the Indo-European tradition: against the king, against the priest, against the laws originating in the State (for example, a sexual transgression that compromises the distribution of men and women, or even a betrayal of the laws of war as instituted by the State).[7] The warrior is in the position of betraying everything, including the function of the military, *or* of understanding nothing. It happens that historians, both bourgeois and Soviet, will follow this negative tradition and explain how Genghis Khan understood nothing: he "didn't understand" the phenomenon of the city. An easy thing to say. The problem is that the exteriority of the war machine in relation to the State apparatus is everywhere apparent but remains difficult to conceptualize. It is not enough to affirm that the war machine is external to the apparatus. It is necessary to reach the point of conceiving the war machine as itself a pure form of exteriority, whereas the State apparatus constitutes the form of interiority we habitually take as a model, or according to which we are in the habit of thinking. What complicates everything is that this extrinsic power of the war machine tends, under certain circumstances, to become confused with one of the two heads of the State apparatus. Sometimes it is confused with the magic violence of the State, at other times with the State's military institution. For instance, the war machine invents speed and secrecy; but there is all the same a certain speed and a certain secrecy that pertain to the State, relatively, secondarily. So there is a great danger of identifying the structural relation between the two poles of political sovereignty, and the dynamic interrelation of these two poles, with the power of war. Dumézil cites the lineage of the Roman kings: there is a Romulus-Numa relation that recurs throughout a series, with variants and an alternation between these two types of equally legitimate rulers; but there is also a relation with an "evil king," Tullus Hostilius, Tarquinius Superbus, an upsurge of the warrior as a disquieting and illegitimate character.[8] Shakespeare's kings could also be invoked: even violence, murders, and perversion do not prevent the State lineage from producing "good" kings; but a disturbing character like Richard III slips in, announcing from the outset his intention to reinvent a war machine and impose its line (deformed, treacherous and traitorous, he claims a "secret close intent"[9] totally different from the conquest of State power, and another —an *other*—relation with women). In short, whenever the irruption of war power is confused with the line of State domination, everything gets muddled; the war machine can then be understood only through the categories of the negative, since nothing is left that remains outside the State. But, returned to its milieu of exteriority, the war machine is seen to be of another species, of another nature, of another origin. One would have to say that it is located between the two heads of the State, between the two articulations, and that it is necessary in order to pass from one to the other. But "between" the two, in that instant, even ephemeral, if only a flash, it proclaims its own irreducibility. *The State has no war machine of its own;* it can only appropriate one in the form of a military institution, one that will continually cause it problems. This explains the mistrust States have toward their military institutions, in that the military institution inherits an extrinsic war machine. Karl von Clausewitz has a general sense of this situation when he treats the flow of absolute war as an Idea that States partially appropriate according to their political needs, and in relation to which they are more or less good "conductors."

Trapped between the two poles of political sovereignty, the man of war seems outmoded, condemned, without a future, reduced to his own fury, which he turns against himself. The descendants of Hercules, Achilles, then Ajax, have enough strength left to proclaim their independence from Agamemnon, a man of the old State. But they are powerless when it comes to Ulysses, a man of the nascent modern State, the first man of the modern State. And it is Ulysses who inherits Achilles' arms, only to convert them to other uses, submitting them to the laws of the State—not Ajax, who is condemned by the goddess he defied and against whom he sinned.[10] No one has portrayed the situation of the man of war, at once eccentric and condemned, better than Kleist. In *Penthesilea*, Achilles is already separated from his power: the war machine has passed over to the Amazons, a Stateless woman-people whose justice, religion, and loves are organized uniquely in a war mode. Descendants of the Scythians, the Amazons spring forth like lightning, "between" the two States, the Greek and the Trojan. They sweep away everything in their path. Achilles is brought before his double, Penthesilea. And in his ambiguous struggle, Achilles is unable to prevent himself from marrying the war machine, or from loving Penthesilea, and thus from betraying Agamemnon and Ulysses at the same time. Nevertheless, he already belongs enough to the Greek State that Penthesilea, for her part, cannot enter the passional relation of war with him without herself betraying the collective law of her people, the law of the pack that prohibits "choosing" the enemy and entering into one-to-one relationships or binary distinctions.

Throughout his work, Kleist celebrates the war machine, setting it against the State apparatus in a struggle that is lost from the start. Doubtless Arminius heralds a Germanic war machine that breaks with the imperial order of alliances and armies, and stands forever opposed to the Roman State. But the Prince of Homburg lives only in a dream and stands condemned for having reached victory in disobedience of the law of the State. As for Kohlhaas, his war machine can no longer be anything more than banditry. Is it the destiny of the war machine, when the State triumphs, to be caught in this alternative: either to be nothing more than the disciplined, military organ of the State apparatus, *or to turn against itself*, to become a double suicide machine for a solitary man and a solitary woman? Goethe and Hegel, State thinkers both, see Kleist as a monster, and Kleist has lost from the start. Why is it, then, that the most uncanny modernity lies with him? It is because the elements of his work are secrecy, speed, and affect.[11] And in Kleist the secret is no longer a content held within a form of interiority; rather, it becomes a form, identified with the form of exteriority that is always external to itself. Similarly, feelings become uprooted from the interiority of a "subject," to be projected violently outward into a milieu of pure exteriority that lends them an incredible velocity, a catapulting force: love or hate, they are no longer feelings but affects. And these affects are so many instances of the becoming-woman, the becoming-animal of the warrior (the bear, she-dogs). Affects transpierce the body like arrows, they are weapons of war. The deterritorialization velocity of affect. Even dreams (Homburg's, Pentheselea's) are externalized, by a system of relays and plug-ins, extrinsic linkages belonging to the war machine. Broken rings. This element of exteriority—which dominates everything, which Kleist invents in literature, which he is the first to invent—will give time a new rhythm: an endless succession of catatonic episodes or fainting spells, and flashes or rushes. Catatonia is: "This affect is too strong for me," and a flash is: "The power of this affect sweeps me away," so that the Self (*Moi*) is now nothing more than a character whose actions and emotions are desubjectified, perhaps even to the point of death. Such is Kleist's personal formula: a succession of flights of madness and catatonic freezes in which no subjective interiority remains. There is much of the East in Kleist: the Japanese fighter, interminably still, who then makes a move too quick to see. The Go player. Many things in modern art come from Kleist. Goethe and Hegel are old men next to Kleist. Could it be that it is at the moment the war machine ceases to exist, conquered by the State, that it displays to the utmost its irreducibility, that it scatters into thinking, loving, dying, or creating machines that have at their disposal vital or revolutionary powers capable of challenging the conquering State? Is the war machine already overtaken, condemned, appropriated as part of the same process whereby it takes on new forms, undergoes a metamorphosis, affirms its irreducibility and exteriority, and deploys that milieu of pure exteriority that the occidental man of the State, or the occidental thinker, continually reduces to something other than itself?

PROBLEM I. *Is there a way of warding off the formation of a State apparatus (or its equivalents in a group)?*

PROPOSITION II. *The exteriority of the war machine is also attested to by ethnology (a tribute to the memory of Pierre Clastres).*

Primitive, segmentary societies have often been defined as societies without a State, in other words, societies in which distinct organs of power do not appear. But the conclusion has been that these societies did not reach the degree of economic development, or the level of political differentiation, that would make the formation of the State apparatus both possible and inevitable: the implication is that primitive people "don't understand" so complex an apparatus. The prime interest in Pierre Clastres's theories is that they break with this evolutionist postulate. Not only does he doubt that the State is the product of an ascribable economic development, but he asks if it is not a potential concern of primitive societies to ward off or avert that monster they supposedly do not understand. Warding off the formation of a State apparatus, making such a formation impossible, would be the objective of a certain number of primitive social mechanisms, even if they are not consciously understood as such. To be sure, primitive societies have *chiefs*. But the State is not defined by the existence of chiefs; it is defined by the perpetuation or conservation of organs of power. The concern of the State is to conserve. Special institutions are thus necessary to enable a chief to become a man of State, but diffuse, collective mechanisms are just as necessary to prevent a chief from becoming one. Mechanisms for warding off, preventive mechanisms, are a part of chieftainship and keep an apparatus distinct from the social body from crystallizing. Clastres describes the situation of the chief, who has no instituted weapon other than his prestige, no other means of persuasion, no other rule than his sense of the group's desires. The chief is more like a leader or a star than a man of power and is always in danger of being disavowed, abandoned by his people. But Clastres goes further, identifying *war* in primitive societies as the surest mechanism directed against the formation of the State: war maintains the dispersal and segmentarity of groups, and the warrior himself is caught in a process of accumulating exploits leading him to solitude and a prestigious but powerless death.[12] Clastres can thus invoke natural Law while reversing its principal proposition: just as Hobbes saw clearly that *the State was against war, so war is against the State*, and makes it impossible. It should not be concluded that war is a state of nature, but rather that it is the mode of a social state that wards off and prevents the State. Primitive war does not produce the State any more than it derives from it. And it is no better explained by exchange than by the State: far from deriving from exchange, even as a sanction for its failure, war is what limits exchanges, maintains them in the framework of "alliances"; it is what prevents them from becoming a State factor, from fusing groups.

The importance of this thesis is first of all to draw attention to collective mechanisms of inhibition. These mechanisms may be subtle, and function as micromechanisms. This is easily seen in certain band or pack phenomena. For example, in the case of gangs of street children in Bogotá, Jacques Meunier cites three ways in which the leader is prevented from acquiring stable power: the members of the band meet and undertake their theft activity in common, with collective sharing of the loot, but they disperse to eat or sleep separately; also, and especially, each member of the band is paired off with one, two, or three other members, so if he has a disagreement with the leader, he will not leave alone but will take along his allies, whose combined departure will threaten to break up the entire gang; finally, there is a diffuse age limit, and at about age fifteen a member is inevitably induced to quit the gang.[13] These mechanisms cannot be understood without renouncing the evolutionist vision that sees bands or packs as a rudimentary, less organized, social form. Even in bands of animals, leadership is a complex mechanism that does not act to promote the strongest but rather inhibits the installation of stable powers, in favor of a fabric of immanent relations.[14] One could just as easily compare the form "high-society life" to the form "sociability" among the most highly evolved men and women: high-society groups are similar to gangs and operate by the diffusion of prestige rather than by reference to centers of power, as in social groupings (Proust clearly showed this noncorrespondence of high-society values and social values). Eugène Sue, a man of high society and a dandy, whom legitimists reproached for frequenting the Orléans family, used to say: "I'm not on the side of the family, I side with the pack." Packs, bands, are groups of the rhizome type, as opposed to the arborescent type that centers around organs of power. That is why bands in general, even those engaged in banditry or high-society life, are metamorphoses of a war machine formally distinct from all State apparatuses or their equivalents, which are instead what structure centralized societies. We certainly would not say that discipline is what defines a war machine: discipline is the characteristic required of armies after the State has appropriated them. The war machine answers to other rules. We are not saying that they are better, of course, only that they animate a fundamental indiscipline of the warrior, a questioning of hierarchy, perpetual blackmail by abandonment or betrayal, and a very volatile sense of honor, all of which, once again, impedes the formation of the State.

But why does this argument fail to convince us entirely? We follow Clastres when he demonstrates that the State is explained neither by a development of productive forces nor by a differentiation of political forces. It is the State, on the contrary, that makes possible the undertaking of large-scale projects, the constitution of surpluses, and the organization of the corresponding public functions. The State is what makes the distinction between governors and governed possible. We do not see how the State can be explained by what it presupposes, even with recourse to dialectics. The State seems to rise up in a single stroke, in an imperial form, and does not depend on progressive factors. Its on-the-spot emergence is like a stroke of genius, the birth of Athena. We also follow Clastres when he shows that the war machine is directed against the State, either against potential States whose formation it wards off in advance, or against actual States whose destruction it purposes. No doubt the war machine is realized more completely in the "barbaric" assemblages of nomadic warriors than in the "savage" assemblages of primitive societies. In any case, it is out of the question that the State could be the result of a war in which the conquerors imposed, by the very fact of their victory, a new law on the vanquished, because the organization of the war machine is directed against the State-form, actual or virtual. The State is no better accounted for as a result of war than by a progression of economic or political forces. This is where Clastres locates the break: between "primitive" counter-State societies and "monstrous" State societies whose formation it is no longer possible to explain. Clastres is fascinated by the problem of "voluntary servitude," in the manner of La Boétie: In what way did people want or desire servitude, which most certainly did not come to them as the outcome of an involuntary and unfortunate war? They did, after all, have counter-State mechanisms at their disposal: So how and why the State? Why did the State triumph? The more deeply Clastres delved into the problem, the more he seemed to deprive himself of the means of resolving it.[15] He tended to make primitive societies hypostases, self-sufficient entities (he insisted heavily on this point). He made their formal exteriority into a real independence. Thus he remained an evolutionist, and posited a state of nature. Only this state of nature was, according to him, a fully social reality instead of a pure concept, and the evolution was a sudden mutation instead of a development. For on the one hand, the State rises up in a single stroke, fully formed; on the other, the counter-State societies use very specific mechanisms to ward it off, to prevent it from arising. We believe that these two propositions are valid but that their interlinkage is flawed. There is an old scenario: "from clans to empires," or "from bands to kingdoms." But nothing says that this constitutes an evolution, since bands and clans are no less organized than empire-kingdoms. We will never leave the evolution hypothesis behind by creating a break between the two terms, that is, by endowing bands with self-sufficiency and the State with an emergence all the more miraculous and monstrous.

We are compelled to say that there has always been a State, quite perfect, quite complete. The more discoveries archaeologists make, the more empires they uncover. The hypothesis of the *Urstaat* seems to be verified: "The State clearly dates back to the most remote ages of humanity." It is hard to imagine primitive societies that would not have been in contact with imperial States, at the periphery or in poorly controlled areas. But of greater importance is the inverse hypothesis: that the State itself has always been in a relation with an outside and is inconceivable independent of that relationship. The law of the State is not the law of All or Nothing (State societies *or* counter-State societies) but that of interior and exterior. The State is sovereignty. But sovereignty only reigns over what it is capable of internalizing, of appropriating locally. Not only is there no universal State, but the outside of States cannot be reduced to "foreign policy," that is, to a set of relations among States. The outside appears simultaneously in two directions: huge worldwide machines branched out over the entire *ecumenon* at a given moment, which enjoy a large measure of autonomy in relation to the States (for example, commercial organization of the "multinational" type, or industrial complexes, or even religious formations like Christianity, Islam, certain prophetic or messianic movements, etc.); but also the local mechanisms of bands, margins, minorities, which continue to affirm the rights of segmentary societies in opposition to the organs of State power. The modern world can provide us today with particularly well developed images of these two directions: worldwide ecumenical machines, but also a neoprimitivism, a new tribal society as described by Marshall McLuhan. These directions are equally present in all social fields, in all periods. It even happens that they partially merge. For example, a commercial organization is also a band of pillage, or piracy, for part of its course and in many of its activities; or it is in bands that a religious formation begins to operate. What becomes clear is that bands, no less than worldwide organizations, imply a form irreducible to the State and that this form of exteriority necessarily presents itself as a diffuse and polymorphous war machine. It is a *nomos* very different from the "law." The State-form, as a form of interiority, has a tendency to reproduce itself, remaining identical to itself across its variations and easily recognizable within the limits of its poles, always seeking public recognition (there is no masked State). But the war machine's form of exteriority is such that it exists only in its own metamorphoses; it exists in an industrial innovation as well as in a technological invention, in a commercial circuit as well as in a religious creation, in all flows and currents that only secondarily allow themselves to be appropriated by the State. It is in terms not of independence, but of coexistence and competition *in a perpetual field of interaction*, that we must conceive of exteriority and interiority, war machines of metamorphosis and State apparatuses of identity, bands and kingdoms, megamachines and empires. The same field circumscribes its interiority in States, but describes its exteriority in what escapes States or stands against States.

PROPOSITION III. *The exteriority of the war ma chine is also attested to by epistemology, which intimates the existence and perpetuation of a "nomad" or "minor science."*

There is a kind of science, or treatment of science, that seems very difficult to classify, whose history is even difficult to follow. What we are referring to are not "technologies" in the usual sense of the term. But neither are they "sciences" in the royal or legal sense established by history. According to a recent book by Michel Serres, both the atomic physics of Democritus and Lucretius and the geometry of Archimedes are marked by it.[16] The characteristics of this kind of eccentric science would seem to be the following:

1. First of all, it uses a hydraulic model, rather than being a theory of solids treating fluids as a special case; ancient atomism is inseparable from flows, and flux is reality itself, or consistency.

2. The model in question is one of becoming and heterogeneity, as opposed to the stable, the eternal, the identical, the constant. It is a "paradox" to make becoming itself a model, and no longer a secondary characteristic, a copy; in the *Timaeus*, Plato raises this possibility, but only in order to exclude it and conjure it away in the name of royal science. By contrast, in atomism, just such a model of heterogeneity, and of passage or becoming in the heterogeneous, is furnished by the famed declination of the atom. The *clinamen*, as the minimum angle, has meaning only between a straight line and a curve, the curve and its tangent, and constitutes the original curvature of the movement of the atom. The clinamen is the smallest angle by which an atom deviates from a straight path.[17] It is a passage to the limit, an exhaustion, a paradoxical "exhaustive" model. The same applies to Archimedean geometry, in which the straight line, defined as "the shortest path between two points," is just a way of defining the length of a curve in a predifferential calculus.

3. One no longer goes from the straight line to its parallels, in a lamellar or laminar flow,[18] but from a curvilinear declination to the formation of spirals and vortices on an inclined plane: the greatest slope for the smallest angle. From *turba* to *turbo:* in other words, from bands or packs of atoms to the great vortical organizations.[19] The model is a vortical one; it operates in an open space throughout which things-flows are distributed, rather than plotting out a closed space for linear and solid things. It is the difference between a *smooth* (vectorial, projective, or topological) space and a *striated*

(metric) space: in the first case "space is occupied without being counted," and in the second case "space is counted in order to be occupied."[20]

4. Finally, the model is problematic, rather than theorematic: figures are considered only from the viewpoint of the *affections* that befall them: sections, ablations, adjunctions, projections. One does not go by specific differences from a genus to its species, or by deduction from a stable essence to the properties deriving from it, but rather from a problem to the accidents that condition and resolve it. This involves all kinds of deformations, transmutations, passages to the limit, operations in which each figure designates an "event" much more than an essence; the square no longer exists independently of a quadrature, the cube of a cubature, the straight line of a rectification. Whereas the theorem belongs to the rational order, the problem is affective and is inseparable from the metamorphoses, generations, and creations within science itself. Despite what Gabriel Marcel may say, the problem is not an "obstacle"; it is the surpassing of the obstacle, a pro-jection, in other words, a war machine. All of this movement is what royal science is striving to limit when it reduces as much as possible the range of the "problem-element" and subordinates it to the "theorem-element."[21]

This Archimedean science, or this conception of science, is bound up in an essential way with the war machine: the *problemata* are the war machine itself and are inseparable from inclined planes, passages to the limit, vortices, and projections. It would seem that the war machine is projected into an abstract knowledge formally different from the one that doubles the State apparatus. It would seem that a whole nomad science develops eccentrically, one that is very different from the royal or imperial sciences. Furthermore, this nomad science is continually "barred," inhibited, or banned by the demands and conditions of State science. Archimedes, vanquished by the Roman State, becomes a symbol.[22] The fact is that the two kinds of science have different modes of formalization, and State science continually imposes its form of sovereignty on the inventions of nomad science. State science retains of nomad science only what it can appropriate; it turns the rest into a set of strictly limited formulas without any real scientific status, or else simply represses and bans it. It is as if the "savants" of nomad science were caught between a rock and a hard place, between the war machine that nourishes and inspires them and the State that imposes upon them an order of reasons. The figure of the *engineer* (in particular the military engineer), with all its ambivalence, is illustrative of this situation. Most significant are perhaps borderline phenomena in which nomad science exerts pressure on State science, and, conversely, State science appropriates and transforms the elements of nomad science. This is true of the art of encampments, "castrametation," which has always mobilized projections and inclined planes: the State does not appropriate this dimension of the war machine without submitting it to civil and metric rules that strictly limit, control, localize nomad science, and without keeping it from having repercussions throughout the social field (in this respect, Vauban is like a repeat of Archimedes, and suffers an analogous defeat). It is true of descriptive and projective geometry, which royal science would like to turn into a mere practical dependency of analytic, or so-called higher, geometry (thus the ambiguous situation of Monge and Poncelet as "savants").[23] It is also true of differential calculus. For a long time, it had only parascientific status and was labeled a "Gothic hypothesis"; royal science only accorded it the value of a convenient convention or a well-founded fiction. The great State mathematicians did their best to improve its status, but precisely on the condition that all the dynamic, nomadic notions—such as becoming, heterogeneity, infinitesimal, passage to the limit, continuous variation —be eliminated and civil, static, and ordinal rules be imposed upon it (Carnot's ambiguous position in this respect). Finally, it is true of the hydraulic model, for it is certain that the State itself needs a hydraulic science (there is no going back on Wittfogel's theses on the importance of large-scale waterworks for an empire). But it needs it in a very different form, because the State needs to subordinate hydraulic force to conduits, pipes, embankments, which prevent turbulence, which constrain movement to go from one point to another, and space itself to be striated and measured, which makes the fluid depend on the solid, and flows proceed by parallel, laminar layers. The hydraulic model of nomad science and the war machine, on the other hand, consists in being distributed by turbulence across a smooth space, in producing a movement that holds space and simultaneously affects all of its points, instead of being held by space in a local movement from one specified point to another.[24] Democritus, Menaechmus, Archimedes, Vauban, Desargues, Bernoulli, Monge, Carnot, Poncelet, Perronet, etc.: in each case a monograph would be necessary to take into account the special situation of these savants whom State science used only after restraining or disciplining them, after repressing their social or political conceptions.

The sea as a smooth space is a specific problem of the war machine. As Virilio shows, it is at sea that the problem of the *fleet in being* is posed, in other words, the task of occupying an open space with a vortical movement that can rise up at any point. In this respect, the recent studies on rhythm, on the origin of that notion, do not seem entirely convincing. For we are told that rhythm has nothing to do with the movement of waves but rather that it designates "form" in general, and more specifically the form of a "measured, cadenced" movement.[25] However, rhythm is never the same as measure. And though the atomist Democritus is one of the authors who speak of rhythm in the sense of form, it should be borne in mind that he does so under very precise conditions of fluctuation and that the forms made by atoms are primarily large, nonmetric aggregates, smooth spaces such as the air, the sea, or even the earth (*magnae res*). There is indeed such a thing as measured, cadenced rhythm, relating to the coursing of a river between its banks or to the form of a striated space; but there is also a rhythm without measure, which relates to the upswell of a flow, in other words, to the manner in which a fluid occupies a smooth space.

This opposition, or rather this tension-limit between the two kinds of science—nomad, war machine science and royal, State science—reappears at different moments, on different levels. The work of Anne Querrien enables us to identify two of these moments; one is the construction of Gothic cathedrals in the twelfth century, the other the construction of bridges in the eighteenth and nineteenth centuries.[26] Gothic architecture is indeed inseparable from a will to build churches longer and taller than the Romanesque churches. Ever farther, ever higher . . . But this difference is not simply quantitative; it marks a qualitative change: the static relation, form-matter, tends to fade into the background in favor of a dynamic relation, material-forces. It is the cutting of the stone that turns it into material capable of holding and coordinating forces of thrust, and of constructing ever higher and longer vaults. The vault is no longer a form but the line of continuous variation of the stones. It is as if Gothic conquered a smooth space, while Romanesque remained partially within a striated space (in which the vault depends on the juxtaposition of parallel pillars). But stone cutting is inseparable from, on the one hand, a plane of projection at ground level, which functions as a plane limit, and, on the other hand, a series of successive approximations (squaring), or placings-in-variation of voluminous stones. Of course, one appealed to the theorematic science of Euclid in order to find a foundation for the enterprise: mathematical figures and equations were thought to be the intelligible form capable of organizing surfaces and volumes. But according to the legend, Bernard de Clairvaux quickly abandoned the effort as too "difficult," appealing to the specificity of an operative, Archimedean geometry, a projective and descriptive geometry defined as a minor science, more a mathegraphy than a matheology. His journeyman, the monk-mason Garin de Troyes, speaks of an operative logic of movement enabling the "initiate" to draw, then hew the volumes "in penetration in space," to make it so that "the cutting line propels the equation" (*le trait pousse le chiffre*).[27] One does not represent, one engenders and traverses. This science is characterized less by the absence of equations than by the very different role they play: instead of being good forms absolutely that organize matter, they are "generated" as "forces of thrust" (*poussées*) by the material, in a qualitative calculus of the optimum. This whole current of Archimedean geometry was taken to its highest expression, but was also brought to a temporary standstill, by the remarkable seventeenth-century mathematician Desargues. Like most of his kind, Desargues wrote little; he nevertheless exerted a great influence through his actions and left outlines, rough drafts, and projects, all centered on problem-events: "Lamentations," "draft project for the cutting of stones," "draft project for grappling with the events of the encounters of a cone and a plane, . . . Desargues, however, was condemned by the *parlement* of Paris, opposed by the king's secretary; his practices of perspective were banned.[28] Royal, or State, science only tolerates and appropriates stone cutting by means of *templates* (the opposite of squaring), under conditions that restore the primacy of the fixed model of form, mathematical figures, and measurement. Royal science only tolerates and appropriates perspective if it is static, subjected to a central black hole divesting it of its heuristic and ambulatory capacities. But the adventure, or event, of Desargues is the same one that had already occurred among the Gothic "journeymen" on a collective level. For not only did the Church, in its imperial form, feel the need to strictly control the movement of this nomad science (it entrusted the Templars with the responsibility of determining its locations and objects, governing the work sites, and regulating construction), but the secular State, in its royal form, turned against the Templars themselves, banning the guilds for a number of reasons, at least one of which was the prohibition of this operative or minor geometry.

Is Anne Querrien right to find yet another echo of the same story in the case of bridges in the eighteenth century? Doubtless, the conditions were very different, for the division of labor according to State norms was by then an accomplished fact. But the fact remains that in the government agency in charge of bridges and roadways, roadways were under a well-centralized administration while bridges were still the object of active, dynamic, and collective experimentation. Trudaine organized unusual, open "general assemblies" in his home. Perronet took as his inspiration a supple model originating in the Orient: The bridge should not choke or obstruct the river. To the heaviness of the bridge, to the striated space of thick and regular piles, he opposed a thinning and discontinuity of the piles, surbase, and vault, a lightness and continuous variation of the whole. But his attempt soon ran up against principled opposition; the State, in naming Perronet director of the school, followed a frequently used procedure that inhibited experimentation more than crowning its achievements. The whole history of the Ecole des Ponts et Chaussées (School of Bridges and Roadways) illustrates how this old, plebeian "corps" was subordinated to the Ecole des Mines, the Ecole des Travaux Publics, and the Ecole Polytechnique, at the same time as its activities were increasingly normalized.[29] We thus come to the question, What is a collective *body*? Undoubtedly, the great collective bodies of a State are differentiated and hierarchical organisms that on the one hand enjoy a monopoly over a power or function and on the other hand send out local representatives. They have a special relation to families, because they link the family model to the State model at both ends and regard themselves as "great families" of functionaries, clerks, intendants, or farmers. Yet it seems that in many of these collective bodies there is something else at work that does not fit into this schema. It is not just their obstinate defense of their privileges. It is also their aptitude—even caricatural or seriously deformed—to constitute themselves as a war machine, following other models, another dynamism, a nomadic ambition, over against the State. As an example, there is the very old problem of the *lobby*, a group with fluid contours, whose position is very ambiguous in relation to the State it wishes to "influence" and the war machine it wishes to promote, to whatever ends.[30]

A *body* (*corps*) is not reducible to an *organism*, any more than esprit de corps is reducible to the soul of an organism. Spirit is not better, but it is volatile, whereas the soul is weighted, a center of gravity. Must we invoke a military origin of the collective body and esprit de corps? "Military" is not the part that counts, but rather the distant nomadic origin. Ibn Khaldūn defines the nomad war machine by: families or lineages PLUS esprit de corps. The war machine entertains a relation to families that is very different from its relation to the State. In the war machine, the family is a band vector instead of a fundamental cell; a genealogy is transferred from one family to another according to the aptitude of a given family at a given time to realize the maximum of "agnatic solidarity." Here, it is not the public eminence of a family that determines its place in a State organism but the reverse; it is the secret power (*puissance*), or strength of solidarity, and the corresponding genealogical mobility that determine its eminence in a war body.[31] This has to do neither with the monopoly of an organic power (*pouvoir*) nor with local representation, but is related to the potential (*puissance*) of a vortical body in a nomad space. Of course, the great bodies of a modern State can hardly be thought of as Arab tribes. What we wish to say, rather, is that collective bodies always have fringes or minorities that reconstitute equivalents of the war machine—in sometimes quite unforeseen forms—in specific assemblages such as building bridges or cathedrals or rendering judgments or making music or instituting a science, a technology . . . A collective body of captains asserts its demands through the organization of the officers and the organism of the superior officers. There are always periods when the State as organism has problems with its own collective bodies, when these bodies, claiming certain privileges, are forced in spite of themselves to open onto something that exceeds them, a short revolutionary instant, an experimental surge. A confused situation: each time it occurs, it is necessary to analyze tendencies and poles, the nature of the movements. All of a sudden, it is as if the collective body of the notary publics were advancing like Arabs or Indians, then regrouping and reorganizing: a comic opera where you never know what is going to happen next (even the cry "The police are with us!" is sometimes heard).

Husserl speaks of a protogeometry that addresses *vague*, in other words, vagabond or nomadic, morphological essences. These essences are distinct from sensible things, as well as from ideal, royal, or imperial essences. Protogeometry, the science dealing with them, is itself vague, in the etymological sense of "vagabond": it is neither inexact like sensible things nor exact like ideal essences, but *anexact yet rigorous* ("essentially and not accidentally inexact"). The circle is an organic, ideal, fixed essence, but roundness is a vague and fluent essence, distinct both from the circle and things that are round (a vase, a wheel, the sun). A theorematic figure is a fixed essence, but its transformations, distortions, ablations, and augmentations, all of its variations, form problematic figures that are vague yet rigorous, "lens-shaped," "umbelliform," or "indented." It could be said that vague essences extract from things a determination that is more than thinghood (*choséité*), which is that of *corporeality* (*corporéité*), and which perhaps even implies an esprit de corps.[32] But why does Husserl see this as a protogeometry, a kind of halfway point and not a pure science? Why does he make pure essences dependent upon a passage to the limit, when any passage to the limit belongs as such to the vague? What we have, rather, are two formally different conceptions of science, and, ontologically, a single field of interaction in which royal science continually appropriates the contents of vague or nomad science while nomad science continually cuts the contents of royal science loose. At the limit, all that counts is the constantly shifting borderline. In Husserl (and also in Kant, though in the opposite direction: roundness as the "schema" of the circle), we find a very accurate appreciation of the irreducibility of nomad science, but simultaneously the concern of a man of the State, or one who sides with the State, to maintain a legislative and constituent primacy for royal science. Whenever this primacy is taken for granted, nomad science is portrayed as a prescientific or parascientific or subscientific agency. And most important, it becomes impossible to understand the relations between science and technology, science and practice, because nomad science is not a simple technology or practice, but a scientific field in which the problem of these relations is brought out and resolved in an entirely different way than from the point of view of royal science. The State is perpetually producing and reproducing ideal circles, but a war machine is necessary to make something round. Thus the specific characteristics of nomad science are what need to be determined in order to understand both the repression it encounters and the interaction "containing" it.

Nomad science does not have the same relation to work as royal science. Not that the division of labor in nomad science is any less thorough; it is different. We know of the problems States have always had with journeymen's associations, or *compagnonnages*, the nomadic or itinerant bodies of the type formed by masons, carpenters, smiths, etc. Settling, sedentarizing labor power, regulating the movement of the flow of labor, assigning it channels and conduits, forming corporations in the sense of organisms, and, for the rest, relying on forced manpower recruited on the spot (corvée) or among indigents (charity workshops)—this has always been one of the principal affairs of the State, which undertook to conquer both a *band vagabondage* and a *body nomadism*. Let us return to the example of Gothic architecture for a reminder of how extensively the journeymen traveled, building cathedrals near and far, scattering construction sites across the land, drawing on an active and passive power (mobility and the strike) that was far from convenient for the State. The State's response was to take over management of the construction sites, merging all the divisions of labor in the supreme distinction between the intellectual and the manual, the theoretical and the practical, modeled upon the difference between "governors" and "governed." In the nomad sciences, as in the royal sciences, we find the existence of a "plane," but not at all in the same way. The ground-level plane of the Gothic journeyman is opposed to the metric plane of the architect, which is on paper and off site. The plane of consistency or composition is opposed to another plane, that of organization or formation. Stone cutting by squaring is opposed to stone cutting using templates, which implies the erection of a model for reproduction. It can be said not only that there is no longer a need for skilled or qualified labor, but also that there is a need for unskilled or unqualified labor, for a dequalification of labor. The State does not give power (*pouvoir*) to the intellectuals or conceptual innovators; on the contrary, it makes them a strictly dependent organ with an autonomy that is only imagined yet is sufficient to divest those whose job it becomes simply to reproduce or implement of all of their power (*puissance*). This does not shield the State from more trouble, this time with the body of intellectuals it itself engendered, but which asserts new nomadic and political claims. In any case, if the State always finds it necessary to repress the nomad and minor sciences, if it opposes vague essences and the operative geometry of the trait, it does so not because the content of these sciences is inexact or imperfect, or because of their magic or initiatory character, but because they imply a division of labor opposed to the norms of the State. The difference is not extrinsic: the way in which a science, or a conception of science, participates in the organization of the social field, and in particular induces a division of labor, is part of that science itself. Royal science is inseparable from a "hylomorphic" model implying both a form that organizes matter and a matter prepared for the form; it has often been shown that this schema derives less from technology or life than from a society divided into governors and governed, and later, intellectuals and manual laborers. What characterizes it is that all matter is assigned to content, while all form passes into expression. It seems that nomad science is more immediately in tune with the connection between content and expression in themselves, each of these two terms encompassing both form and matter. Thus matter, in nomad science, is never prepared and therefore homogenized matter, but is essentially laden with singularities (which constitute a form of content). And neither is expression formal; it is inseparable from pertinent traits (which constitute a matter of expression). This is an entirely different schema, as we shall see. We can get a preliminary idea of this situation by recalling the most general characteristic of nomad art, in which a dynamic connection between support and ornament replaces the matter-form dialectic. From the point of view of nomad science, which presents itself as an art as much as a technique, the division of labor fully exists, but it does not employ the form-matter duality (even in the case of biunivocal correspondences). Rather, it *follows* the connections between singularities of matter and traits of expression, and lodges on the level of these connections, whether they be natural or forced.[33] This is another organization of work and of the social field through work.

It is instructive to contrast two models of science, after the manner of Plato in the *Timaeus*.[34] One could be called *Compars* and the other *Dispars*. The compars is the legal or legalist model employed by royal science. The search for laws consists in extracting constants, even if those constants are only relations between variables (equations). An invariable form for variables, a variable matter of the invariant: such is the foundation of the hylomorphic schema. But for the dispars as an element of nomad science the relevant distinction is material-forces rather than matter-form. Here, it is not exactly a question of extracting constants from variables but of placing the variables themselves in a state of continuous variation. If there are still equations, they are adequations, inequations, differential equations irreducible to the algebraic form and inseparable from a sensible intuition of variation. They seize or determine singularities in the matter, instead of constituting a general form. They effect individuations through events or haecceities, not through the "object" as a compound of matter and form; vague essences are nothing other than haecceities. In all these respects, there is an opposition between the *logos* and the *nomos*, the law and the *nomos*, prompting the comment that the law still "savors of morality."[35] This does not mean, however, that the legal model knows nothing of forces, the play of forces. That it does is evident in the homogeneous space corresponding to the compars. Homogeneous space is in no way a smooth space; on the contrary, it is the form of striated space. The space of *pillars*. It is striated by the fall of bodies, the verticals of gravity, the distribution of matter into parallel layers, the lamellar and laminar movement of flows. These parallel verticals have formed an independent dimension capable of spreading everywhere, of formalizing all the other dimensions, of striating all of space in all of its directions, so as to render it homogeneous. The vertical distance between two points provided the mode of comparison for the horizontal distance between two other points. Universal attraction became the law of all laws, in that it set the rule for the biunivocal correspondence between two bodies; and each time science discovered a new field, it sought to formalize it in the same mode as the field of gravity. Even chemistry became a royal science only by virtue of a whole theoretical elaboration of the notion of weight. Euclidean space is founded on the famous parallel postulate, but the parallels in question are in the first place gravitational parallels, and correspond to the forces exerted by gravity on all the elements of a body presumed to fill that space. It is the point of application of the resultant of all of these parallel forces that remains invariable when their common direction is changed or the body is rotated (the *center of gravity*). In short, it seems that the force of gravity lies at the basis of a laminar, striated, homogeneous, and centered space; it forms the foundation for those multiplicities termed metric, or arborescent, whose dimensions are independent of the situation and are expressed with the aid of units and points (movements from one point to another). It was not some metaphysical concern, but an effectively scientific one, that frequently led scientists in the nineteenth century to ask if all forces were not reducible to gravity, or rather to the form of attraction that gives gravity a universal value (a constant relation for all variables) and biunivocal scope (two bodies at a time, and no more). It is the form of interiority of all science.

The *nomos*, or the dispars, is altogether different. But this is not to say that the other forces refute gravity or contradict attraction. Although it is true that they do not go against them, they do not result from them either; they do not depend on them but testify to events that are always supplementary or of "variable affects." Each time a new *field* opened up in science—under conditions making this a far more important notion than that of form or object—it proved irreducible to the field of attraction and the model of the gravitational forces, although not contradictory to them. It affirmed a "more" or an excess, and lodged itself in that excess, that deviation. When chemistry took a decisive step forward, it was always by adding to the force of weight bonds of another type (for example, electric) that transformed the nature of chemical equations.[36] But it will be noted that the simplest considerations of velocity immediately introduce the difference between vertical descent and curvilinear motion, or more generally between the straight line and the curve, in the differential form of the clinamen, or the smallest deviation, the minimum excess. Smooth space is precisely the space of the smallest deviation: therefore it has no homogeneity, except between infinitely proximate points, and the linking of proximities is effected independently of any determined path. It is a space of contact, of small tactile or manual actions of contact, rather than a visual space like Euclid's striated space. Smooth space is a field without conduits or channels. A field, a heterogeneous smooth space, is wedded to a very particular type of multiplicity: nonmetric, acentered, rhizomatic multiplicities that occupy space without "counting" it and can "be explored only by legwork." They do not meet the visual condition of being observable from a point in space external to them; an example of this is the system of sounds, or even of colors, as opposed to Euclidean space.

When we oppose speed and slowness, the quick and the weighty, *Celeritas and Gravitas*, this must not be seen as a quantitative opposition, or as a mythological structure (although Dumézil has established the mythological importance of this opposition, precisely in relation to the State apparatus and its natural "gravity"). The opposition is both qualitative and scientific, in that speed is not merely an abstract characteristic of movement in general but is incarnated in a moving body that deviates, however slightly, from its line of descent or gravity. *Slow and rapid are not quantitative degrees of movement but rather two types of qualified movement*, whatever the speed of the former or the tardiness of the latter. Strictly speaking, it cannot be said that a body that is dropped has a speed, however fast it falls; rather it has an infinitely decreasing slowness in accordance with the law of falling bodies. Laminar movement that striates space, that goes from one point to another, is weighty; but rapidity, celerity, applies only to movement that deviates to the minimum extent and thereafter assumes a vortical motion, occupying a smooth space, actually drawing smooth space itself. In this space, matter-flow can no longer be cut into parallel layers, and movement no longer allows itself to be hemmed into biunivocal relations between points. In this sense, the role of the qualitative opposition gravity-celerity, heavy-light, slow-rapid is not that of a quantifiable scientific determination but of a condition that is coextensive to science and that regulates both the separation and the mixing of the two models, their possible interpenetration, the domination of one by the other, their alternative. And the best formulation, that of Michel Serres, is indeed couched in terms of an alternative, whatever mixes or compositions there may be: "Physics is reducible to two sciences, a general theory of routes and paths, and a global theory of waves."[37]

A distinction must be made between two types of science, or scientific procedures: one consists in "reproducing," the other in "following." The first involves reproduction, iteration and reiteration; the other, involving itineration, is the sum of the itinerant, ambulant sciences. Itineration is too readily reduced to a modality of technology, or of the application and verification of science. But this is not the case: *following is not at all the same thing as reproducing*, and one never follows in order to reproduce. The ideal of reproduction, deduction, or induction is part of royal science, at all times and in all places, and treats differences of time and place as so many variables, the constant form of which is extracted precisely by the law: for the same phenomena to recur in a gravitational and striated space it is sufficient for the same conditions to obtain, or for the same constant relation to hold between the differing conditions and the variable phenomena. Reproducing implies the permanence of a fixed point of *view* that is external to what is reproduced: watching the flow from the bank. But following is something different from the ideal of reproduction. Not better, just different. One is obliged to follow when one is in search of the "singularities" of a matter, or rather of a material, and not out to discover a form; when one escapes the force of gravity to enter a field of celerity; when one ceases to contemplate the course of a laminar flow in a determinate direction, to be carried away by a vortical flow; when one engages in a continuous variation of variables, instead of extracting constants from them, etc. And the meaning of Earth completely changes: with the legal model, one is constantly reterritorializing around a point of view, on a domain, according to a set of constant relations; but with the ambulant model, the process of deterritorialization constitutes and extends the territory itself. "Go first to your old plant and watch carefully the watercourse made by the rain. By now the rain must have carried the seeds far away. Watch the crevices made by the runoff, and from them determine the direction of the flow. Then find the plant that is growing at the farthest point from your plant. All the devil's weed plants that are growing in between are yours. Later . . . you can extend the size of your territory."[38] *There are itinerant, ambulant sciences that consist in following a flow in a vectorial field across which singularities are scattered like so many "accidents"* (problems). For example, why is primitive metallurgy necessarily an ambulant science that confers upon smiths a quasi-nomadic status? It could be objected that in these examples it is still a question of going from one point to another (even if they are singular points) through the intermediary of channels, and that it is still possible to cut the flow into layers. But this is only true to the extent that ambulant procedures and processes are necessarily tied to a striated space—always formalized by royal science—which deprives them of their model, submits them to its own model, and allows them to exist only in the capacity of "technologies" or "applied science." As a general rule, a smooth space, a vectorial field, a nonmetric multiplicity are always translatable, and necessarily translated, into a "compars": a fundamental operation by which one repeatedly overlays upon each point of smooth space a tangent Euclidean space endowed with a sufficient number of dimensions, by which one reintroduces parallelism between two vectors, treating multiplicity as though it were immersed in this homogeneous and striated space of reproduction, instead of continuing to follow it in an "exploration by legwork."[39] This is the triumph of the *logos* or the law over the *nomos*. But the complexity of the operation testifies to the existence of resistances it must overcome. Whenever ambulant procedure and process are returned to their own model, the points regain their position as singularities that exclude all biunivocal relations, the flow regains its curvilinear and vortical motion that excludes any parallelism between vectors, and smooth space reconquers the properties of contact that prevent it from remaining homogeneous and striated. There is always a current preventing the ambulant or itinerant sciences from being completely internalized in the reproductive royal sciences. There is a type of ambulant scientist whom State scientists are forever fighting or integrating or allying with, even going so far as to propose a minor position for them within the legal system of science and technology.

It is not that the ambulant sciences are more saturated with irrational procedures, with mystery and magic. They only get that way when they fall into abeyance. And the royal sciences, for their part, also surround themselves with much priestliness and magic. Rather, what becomes apparent in the rivalry between the two models is that the ambulant or nomad sciences do not destine science to take on an autonomous power, or even to have an autonomous development. They do not have the means for that because they subordinate all their operations to the sensible conditions of intuition and construction—*following* the flow of matter, *drawing and linking up* smooth space. Everything is situated in an objective zone of fluctuation that is coextensive with reality itself. However refined or rigorous, "approximate knowledge" is still dependent upon sensitive and sensible evaluations that pose more problems than they solve: problematics is still its only mode. In contrast, what is proper to royal science, to its theorematic or axiomatic power, is to isolate all operations from the conditions of intuition, making them true intrinsic concepts, or "categories." That is precisely why deterritorialization, in this kind of science, implies a reterritorialization in the conceptual apparatus. Without this categorical, apodictic apparatus, the differential operations would be constrained to follow the evolution of a phenomenon; what is more, since the experimentation would be open-air, and the construction at ground level, the coordinates permitting them to be erected as stable models would never become available. Certain of these requirements are translated in terms of "safety": the two cathedrals at Orléans and Beauvais collapsed at the end of the twelfth century, and control calculations are difficult to effect for the constructions of ambulant science. Although safety is a fundamental element in the theoretical norms of the State, and of the political ideal, there is also something else at issue as well. Due to all their procedures, the ambulant sciences quickly overstep the possibility of calculation: they inhabit that "more" that exceeds the space of reproduction and soon run into problems that are insurmountable from that point of view; they eventually resolve those problems by means of a real-life operation. The solutions are supposed to come from a set of activities that constitute them as nonautonomous. Only royal science, in contrast, has at its disposal a metric power that can define a conceptual apparatus or an autonomy of science (including the autonomy of experimental science). That is why it is necessary to couple ambulant spaces with a space of homogeneity, without which the laws of physics would depend on particular points in space. But this is less a translation than a constitution: precisely that constitution the ambulant sciences did not undertake, and do not have the means to undertake. In the field of interaction of the two sciences, the ambulant sciences confine themselves to *inventing problems* whose solution is tied to a whole set of collective, nonscientific activities but whose *scientific solution* depends, on the contrary, on royal science and the way it has transformed the problem by introducing it into its theorematic apparatus and its organization of work. This is somewhat like intuition and intelligence in Bergson, where only intelligence has the scientific means to solve formally the problems posed by intuition, problems that intuition would be content to entrust to the qualitative activities of a humanity engaged in *following* matter.[40]

PROBLEM II. *Is there a way to extricate thought from the State model?*
PROPOSITION IV. *The exteriority of the war machine is attested to, finally, by noology.*

Thought contents are sometimes criticized for being too conformist. But the primary question is that of form itself. Thought as such is already in conformity with a model that it borrows from the State apparatus, and which defines for it goals and paths, conduits, channels, organs, an entire *organon*. There is thus an image of thought covering all of thought; it is the special object of "noology" and is like the State-form developed in thought. This image has two heads, corresponding to the two poles of sovereignty: the *imperium* of true thinking operating by magical capture, seizure or binding, constituting the efficacy of a foundation (*mythos*); a republic of free spirits proceeding by pact or contract, constituting a legislative and juridical organization, carrying the sanction of a ground (*logos*). These two heads are in constant interference in the classical image of thought: a "republic of free spirits whose prince would be the idea of the Supreme Being." And if these two heads are in interference, it is not only because there are many intermediaries and transitions between them, and because the first prepares the way for the second and the second uses and retains the first, but also because, antithetical and complementary, they are necessary to one another. It is not out of the question, however, that in order to pass from one to the other there must occur, "between" them, an event of an entirely different nature, one that hides outside the image, takes place outside.[41] But confining ourselves to the image, it appears that it is not simply a metaphor when we are told of an *imperium* of truth and a republic of spirits. It is the necessary condition for the constitution of thought as principle, or as a form of interiority, as a stratum.

It is easy to see what thought gains from this: a gravity it would never have on its own, a center that makes everything, including the State, appear to exist by its own efficacy or on its own sanction. But the State gains just as much. Indeed, by developing in thought in this way the State-form gains something essential: a whole consensus. Only thought is capable of inventing the fiction of a State that is universal by right, of elevating the State to the level of de jure universality. It is as if the sovereign were left alone in the world, spanned the entire ecumenon, and now dealt only with actual or potential subjects. It is no longer a question of powerful, extrinsic organizations, or of strange bands: the State becomes the sole principle separating rebel subjects, who are consigned to the state of nature, from consenting subjects, who rally to its form of their own accord. If it is advantageous for thought to prop itself up with the State, it is no less advantageous for the State to extend itself in thought, and to be sanctioned by it as the unique, universal form. The particularity of States becomes merely an accident of fact, as is their possible perversity, or their imperfection. For the modern State defines itself in principle as "the rational and reasonable organization of a community": the only remaining particularity a community has is interior or moral (*the spirit of a people*), at the same time as the community is funneled by its organization toward the harmony of a universal (*absolute spirit*). The State gives thought a form of interiority, and thought gives that interiority a form of universality: "The goal of worldwide organization is the satisfaction of reasonable individuals within particular free States." The exchange that takes place between the State and reason is a curious one; but that exchange is also an analytic proposition, because realized reason is identified with the de jure State, just as the State is the becoming of reason.[42] In so-called modern philosophy, and in the so-called modern or rational State, everything revolves around the legislator and the subject. The State must realize the distinction between the legislator and the subject under formal conditions permitting thought, for its part, to conceptualize their identity. Always obey. The more you obey, the more you will be master, for you will only be obeying pure reason, in other words yourself... Ever since philosophy assigned itself the role of ground it has been giving the established powers its blessing, and tracing its doctrine of faculties onto the organs of State power. Common sense, the unity of all the faculties at the center constituted by the Cogito, is the State consensus raised to the absolute. This was most notably the great operation of the Kantian "critique," renewed and developed by Hegelianism. Kant was constantly criticizing bad usages, the better to consecrate the function. It is not at all surprising that the philosopher has become a public professor or State functionary. It was all over the moment the State-form inspired an image of thought. With full reciprocity. Doubtless, the image itself assumes different contours in accordance with the variations on this form: it has not always delineated or designated the philosopher, and will not always delineate him. It is possible to pass from a magical function to a rational function. The poet in the archaic imperial State was able to play the role of image trainer.[43] In modern States, the sociologist succeeded in replacing the philosopher (as, for example, when Durkheim and his disciples set out to give the republic a secular model of thought). Even today, psychoanalysis lays claim to the role of *Cogitatio universalis* as the thought of the Law, in a magical return. And there are quite a few other competitors and pretenders. Noology, which is distinct from ideology, is precisely the study of images of thought, and their historicity. In a sense, it could be said that all this has no importance, that thought has never had anything but laughable gravity. But that is all it requires: for us not to take it seriously. Because that makes it all the easier for it to think for us, and to be forever engendering new functionaries. Because the less people take thought seriously, the more they think in conformity with what the State wants. Truly, what man of the State has not dreamed of that paltry impossible thing—to be a thinker?

But noology is confronted by counterthoughts, which are violent in their acts and discontinuous in their appearances, and whose existence is mobile in history. These are the acts of a "private thinker," as opposed to the public professor: Kierkegaard, Nietzsche, or even Shestov. Wherever they dwell, it is the steppe or the desert. They destroy images. Nietzsche's *Schopenhauer as Educator* is perhaps the greatest critique ever directed against the image of thought and its relation to the State. "Private thinker," however, is not a satisfactory expression, because it exaggerates interiority, when it is a question of *outside thought*.[44] To place thought in an immediate relation with the outside, with the forces of the outside, in short to make thought a war machine, is a strange undertaking whose precise procedures can be studied in Nietzsche (the aphorism, for example, is very different from the maxim, for a maxim, in the republic of letters, is like an organic State act or sovereign judgment, whereas an aphorism always awaits its meaning from a new external force, a final force that must conquer or subjugate it, utilize it). There is another reason why "private thinker" is not a good expression. Although it is true that this counterthought attests to an absolute solitude, it is an extremely populous solitude, like the desert itself, a solitude already intertwined with a people to come, one that invokes and awaits that people, existing only through it, though it is not yet here. "We are lacking that final force, in the absence of a people to bear us. We are looking for that popular support." Every thought is already a tribe, the opposite of a State. And this form of exteriority of thought is not at all symmetrical to the form of interiority. Strictly speaking, symmetry exists only between different poles or focal points of interiority. But the form of exteriority of thought—the force that is always external to itself, or the final force, the *n*th power—is not at all *another image* in opposition to the image inspired by the State apparatus. It is, rather, a force that destroys both the image *and* its copies, the model *and* its reproductions, every possibility of subordinating thought to a model of the True, the Just, or the Right (Cartesian truth, Kantian just, Hegelian right, etc.). A "method" is the striated space of the *cogitatio universalis* and draws a path that must be followed from one point to another. But the form of exteriority situates thought in a smooth space that it must occupy without counting, and for which there is no possible method, no conceivable reproduction, but only relays, intermezzos, resurgences. Thought is like the Vampire; it has no image, either to constitute a model of or to copy. In the smooth space of Zen, the arrow does not go from one point to another but is taken up at any point, to be sent to any other point, and tends to permute with the archer and the target. The problem of the war machine is that of relaying, even with modest means, not that of the architectonic model or the monument. An ambulant people of relayers, rather than a model society. "Nature propels the philosopher into mankind like an arrow; it takes no aim but hopes the arrow will stick somewhere. But countless times it misses and is depressed at the fact. . . . The artist and the philosopher are evidence against the purposiveness of nature as regards the means it employs, though they are also first-rate evidence as to the wisdom of its purpose. They strike home at only a few, while they ought to strike home at everybody—and even these few are not struck with the force with which the philosopher and artist launch their shot."[45]

We have in mind in particular two pathetic texts, in the sense that in them thought is truly a *pathos* (an *antilogos* and an *antimythos*). One is a text by Artaud, in his letters to Jacques Rivière, explaining that thought operates on the basis of a *central breakdown*, that it lives solely by its own incapacity to take on form, bringing into relief only traits of expression in a material, developing peripherally, in a pure milieu of exteriority, as a function of singularities impossible to universalize, of circumstances impossible to interiorize. The other is the text by Kleist, "On the Gradual Formation of Ideas in Speech" ("Über die allmächliche Verfertigung der Gedanken beim Reden"), in which Kleist denounces the central interiority of the concept as a means of control—the control of speech, of language, but also of affects, circumstances and even chance. He distinguishes this from thought as a proceeding and a process, a bizarre anti-Platonic dialogue, an antidialogue between brother and sister where one speaks before knowing while the other relays before having understood: this, Kleist says, is the thought of the *Gemüt*, which proceeds like a general in a war machine should, or like a body charged with electricity, with pure intensity. "I mix inarticulate sounds, lengthen transitional terms, as well as using appositions when they are unnecessary." Gain some time, and then perhaps renounce, or wait. The necessity of not having control over language, of being a foreigner in one's own tongue, in order to draw speech to oneself and "bring something incomprehensible into the world." Such is the form of exteriority, the relation between brother and sister, the becoming-woman of the thinker, the becoming-thought of the woman: the *Gemüt* that refuses to be controlled, that forms a war machine. A thought grappling with exterior forces instead of being gathered up in an interior form, operating by relays instead of forming an image; an event-thought, a haecceity, instead of a subject-thought, a problem-thought instead of an essence-thought or theorem; a thought that appeals to a people instead of taking itself for a government ministry. Is it by chance that whenever a "thinker" shoots an arrow, there is a man of the State, a shadow or an image of a man of the State, that counsels and admonishes him, and wants to assign him a target or "aim"? Jacques Rivière does not hesitate to respond to Artaud: work at it, keep on working, things will come out all right, you will succeed in finding a method and in learning to express clearly what you think in essence (*cogitatio universalis*). Rivière is not a head of State, but he would not be the last in the *Nouvelle Revue Française* to mistake himself for the secret prince in a republic of letters or the gray eminence in a State of right. Lenz and Kleist confronted Goethe, that grandiose genius, of all men of letters a veritable man of the State. But that is not the worst of it: the worst is the way the texts of Kleist and Artaud themselves have ended up becoming monuments, inspiring a model to be copied—a model far more insidious than the others—for the artificial stammerings and innumerable tracings that claim to be their equal.

The classical image of thought, and the striating of mental space it effects, aspires to universality. It in effect operates with two "universals," the Whole as the final ground of being or all-encompassing horizon, and the Subject as the principle that converts being into being-for-us.[46] *Imperium* and republic. Between the two, all of the varieties of the real and the true find their place in a striated mental space, from the double point of view of Being and the Subject, under the direction of a "universal method." It is now easy for us to characterize the nomad thought that rejects this image and does things differently. It does not ally itself with a universal thinking subject but, on the contrary, with a singular race; and it does not ground itself in an all-encompassing totality but is on the contrary deployed in a horizonless milieu that is a smooth space, steppe, desert, or sea. An entirely different type of adequation is established here, between the race defined as "tribe" and smooth space defined as "milieu." A tribe in the desert instead of a universal subject within the horizon of all-encompassing Being. Kenneth White recently stressed this dissymmetrical complementarity between a race-tribe (the Celts, those who feel they are Celts) and a milieu-space (the Orient, the Gobi desert . . .). White demonstrates that this strange composite, the marriage of the Celt and the Orient, inspires a properly nomad thought that sweeps up English literature and constitutes American literature.[47] We immediately see the dangers, the profound ambiguities accompanying in this enterprise, as if each effort and each creation faced a possible infamy. For what can be done to prevent the theme of a race from turning into a racism, a dominant and all-encompassing fascism, or into a sect and a folklore, microfascisms? And what can be done to prevent the oriental pole from becoming a phantasy that reactivates all the fascisms in a different way, and also all the folklores, yoga, Zen, and karate? It is certainly not enough to travel to escape phantasy, and it is certainly not by invoking a past, real or mythical, that one avoids racism. But here again, the criteria for making the distinction are simple, whatever the de facto mixes that obscure them at a given level, at a given moment. The race-tribe exists only at the level of an oppressed race, and in the name of the oppression it suffers: there is no race but inferior, minoritarian; there is no dominant race; a race is defined not by its purity but rather by the impurity conferred upon it by a system of domination. Bastard and mixed-blood are the true names of race. Rimbaud said it all on this point: only he or she can invoke race who says, "I have always been of an inferior race . . . I am of an inferior race for all eternity . . . There I am on the Breton shore . . . I am a beast, a nigger . . . I am of a distant race: my ancestors were Norsemen."[48] In the same way that race is not something to be rediscovered, the Orient is not something to be imitated: it only exists in the construction of a smooth space, just as race only exists in the constitution of a tribe that peoples and traverses a smooth space. All of thought is a becoming, a double becoming, rather than the attribute of a Subject and the representation of a Whole.

AXIOM II. *The war machine is the invention of the nomads (insofar as it is exterior to the State apparatus and distinct from the military institution). As such, the war machine has three aspects, a spatiogeographic aspect, an arithmetic or algebraic aspect, and an affective aspect.*

PROPOSITION V. *Nomad existence necessarily effectuates the conditions of the war machine in space.*

The nomad has a territory; he follows customary paths; he goes from one point to another; he is not ignorant of points (water points, dwelling points, assembly points, etc.). But the question is what in nomad life is a principle and what is only a consequence. To begin with, although the points determine paths, they are strictly subordinated to the paths they determine, the reverse of what happens with the sedentary. The water point is reached only in order to be left behind; every point is a relay and exists only as a relay. A path is always between two points, but the in-between has taken on all the consistency and enjoys both an autonomy and a direction of its own. The life of the nomad is the intermezzo. Even the elements of his dwelling are conceived in terms of the trajectory that is forever mobilizing them.[49] The nomad is not at all the same as the migrant; for the migrant goes principally from one point to another, even if the second point is uncertain, unforeseen, or not well localized. But the nomad goes from point to point only as a consequence and as a factual necessity; in principle, points for him are relays along a trajectory. Nomads and migrants can mix in many ways, or form a common aggregate; their causes and conditions are no less distinct for that (for example, those who joined Mohammed at Medina had a choice between a nomadic or bedouin pledge, and a pledge of hegira or emigration).[50]

Second, even though the nomadic trajectory may follow trails or customary routes, it does not fulfill the function of the sedentary road, which is to *parcel out a closed space to people*, assigning each person a share and regulating the communication between shares. The nomadic trajectory does the opposite: it *distributes people (or animals) in an open space*, one that is indefinite and noncommunicating. The *nomos* came to designate the law, but that was originally because it was distribution, a mode of distribution. It is a very special kind of distribution, one without division into shares, in a space without borders or enclosure. The *nomos* is the consistency of a fuzzy aggregate: it is in this sense that it stands in opposition to the law or the *polis*, as the backcountry, a mountainside, or the vague expanse around a city ("either nomos or polis").[51] Therefore, and this is the third point, there is a significant difference between the spaces: sedentary space is striated, by walls, enclosures, and roads between enclosures, while nomad space is smooth, marked only by "traits" that are effaced and displaced with the trajectory. Even the lamellae of the desert slide over each other, producing an inimitable sound. The nomad distributes himself in a smooth space; he occupies, inhabits, holds that space; that is his territorial principle. It is therefore false to define the nomad by movement. Toynbee is profoundly right to suggest that the nomad is on the contrary *he who does not move.* Whereas the migrant leaves behind a milieu that has become amorphous or hostile, the nomad is one who does not depart, does not want to depart, who clings to the smooth space left by the receding forest, where the steppe or the desert advances, and who invents nomadism as a response to this challenge.[52] Of course, the nomad moves, but while seated, and he is only seated while moving (the Bedouin galloping, knees on the saddle, sitting on the soles of his upturned feet, "a feat of balance"). The nomad knows how to wait, he has infinite patience. Immobility and speed, catatonia and rush, a "stationary process," station as process—these traits of Kleist's are eminently those of the nomad. It is thus necessary to make a distinction between *speed* and *movement:* a movement may be very fast, but that does not give it speed; a speed may be very slow, or even immobile, yet it is still speed. Movement is extensive; speed is intensive. Movement designates the relative character of a body considered as "one," and which goes from point to point; *speed, on the contrary, constitutes the absolute character of a body whose irreducible parts (atoms) occupy or fill a smooth space in the manner of a vortex,* with the possibility of springing up at any point. (It is therefore not surprising that reference has been made to spiritual voyages effected without relative movement, but in intensity, in one place: these are part of nomadism.) In short, we will say by convention that only nomads have absolute movement, in other words, speed; vortical or swirling movement is an essential feature of their war machine.

It is in this sense that nomads have no points, paths, or land, even though they do by all appearances. If the nomad can be called the Deterritorialized par excellence, it is precisely because there is no reterritorialization *afterward* as with the migrant, or upon *something else* as with the sedentary (the sedentary's relation with the earth is mediatized by something else, a property regime, a State apparatus). With the nomad, on the contrary, it is deterritorialization that constitutes the relation to the earth, to such a degree that the nomad reterritorializes on deterritorialization itself. It is the earth that deterritorializes itself, in a way that provides the nomad with a territory. The land ceases to be land, tending to become simply ground (*sol*) or support. The earth does not become deterritorialized in its global and relative movement, but at specific locations, at the spot where the forest recedes, or where the steppe and the desert advance. Hubac is right to say that nomadism is explainable less by universal changes in climate (which relate instead to migrations) as by the "divagation of local climates."[53] The nomads are there, on the land, wherever there forms a smooth space that gnaws, and tends to grow, in all directions. The nomads inhabit these places; they remain in them, and they themselves make them grow, for it has been established that the nomads make the desert no less than they are made by it. They are vectors of deterritorialization. They add desert to desert, steppe to steppe, by a series of local operations whose orientation and direction endlessly vary.[54] The sand desert has not only oases, which are like fixed points, but also rhizomatic vegetation that is temporary and shifts location according to local rains, bringing changes in the direction of the crossings.[55] The same terms are used to describe ice deserts as sand deserts: there is no line separating earth and sky; there is no intermediate distance, no perspective or contour; visibility is limited; and yet there is an extraordinarily fine topology that relies not on points or objects but rather on haecceities, on sets of relations (winds, undulations of snow or sand, the song of the sand or the creaking of ice, the tactile qualities of both). It is a tactile space, or rather "haptic," a sonorous much more than a visual space.[56] The variability, the polyvocality of directions, is an essential feature of smooth spaces of the rhizome type, and it alters their cartography. The nomad, nomad space, is localized and not delimited. What is both limited and limiting is striated space, the *relative global*: it is limited in its parts, which are assigned constant directions, are oriented in relation to one another, divisible by boundaries, and can interlink; what is limiting (*limes* or wall, and no longer boundary) is this aggregate in relation to the smooth spaces it "contains," whose growth it slows or prevents, and which it restricts or places outside. Even when the nomad sustains its effects, he does not belong to this relative global, where one passes from one point to another, from one region to another. Rather, he is in a *local absolute*, an absolute that is manifested locally, and engendered in a series of local operations of varying orientations: desert, steppe, ice, sea.

Making the absolute appear in a particular place—is that not a very general characteristic of religion (recognizing that the nature of the appearance, and the legitimacy, or lack thereof, of the images that reproduce it are open to debate)? But the sacred place of religion is fundamentally a center that repels the obscure *nomos*. The absolute of religion is essentially a horizon that encompasses, and, if the absolute itself appears at a particular place, it does so in order to establish a solid and stable center for the global. The encompassing role of smooth spaces (desert, steppe, or ocean) in monotheism has been frequently noted. In short, religion converts the absolute. Religion is in this sense a piece in the State apparatus (in both of its forms, the "bond" and the "pact or alliance"), even if it has within itself the power to elevate this model to the level of the universal or to constitute an absolute *Imperium*. But for the nomad the terms of the question are totally different: locality is not delimited; the absolute, then, does not appear at a particular place but becomes a nonlimited locality; the coupling of the place and the absolute is achieved not in a centered, oriented globalization or universalization but in an infinite succession of local operations. Limiting ourselves to this opposition between points of view, it may be observed that nomads do not provide a favorable terrain for religion; the man of war is always committing an offense against the priest or the god. The nomads have a vague, literally vagabond "monotheism," and content themselves with that, and with their ambulant fires. The nomads have a sense of the absolute, but a singularly atheistic one. The universalist religions that have had dealings with nomads—Moses, Mohammed, even Christianity with the Nestorian heresy—have always encountered problems in this regard, and have run up against what they have termed obstinate impiety. These religions are not, in effect, separable from a firm and constant orientation, from an imperial de jure State, even, and especially, in the absence of a de facto State; they have promoted an ideal of sedentarization and addressed themselves more to the migrant components than the nomadic ones. Even early Islam favored the theme of the hegira, or migration, over nomadism; rather, it was through certain schisms (such as the Khārijī movement) that it won over the Arab or Berber nomads.[57]

However, it does not exhaust the question to establish a simple opposition between two points of view, religion-nomadism. For monotheistic religion, at the deepest level of its tendency to project a universal or spiritual State over the entire ecumenon, is not without ambivalence or fringe areas; it goes beyond even the ideal limits of the State, even the imperial State, entering a more indistinct zone, an outside of States where it has the possibility of undergoing a singular mutation or adaptation. We are referring to religion as an element in a war machine and the idea of holy war as the motor of that machine. The *prophet*, as opposed to the state personality of the king and the religious personality of the priest, directs the movement by which a religion becomes a war machine or passes over to the side of such a machine. It has often been said that Islam, and the prophet Mohammed, performed such a conversion of religion and constituted a veritable esprit de corps: in the formula of Georges Bataille, "early Islam, a society reduced to the military enterprise." This is what the West invokes in order to justify its antipathy toward Islam. Yet the Crusades were a properly Christian adventure of this type. The prophets may very well condemn nomad life; the war machine may very well favor the movement of migration and the ideal of establishment; religion in general may very well compensate for its specific deterritorialization with a spiritual and even physical reterritorialization, which in the case of the holy war assumes the well-directed character of a conquest of the holy lands as the center of the world. Despite all that, when religion sets itself up as a war machine, it mobilizes and liberates a formidable charge of nomadism or absolute deterritorialization; it doubles the migrant with an accompanying nomad, or with the potential nomad the migrant is in the process of becoming; and finally, it turns its dream of an absolute State back against the State-form.[58] And this turning-against is no less a part of the "essence" of religion than that dream. The history of the Crusades is marked by the most astonishing series of directional changes: the firm orientation toward the Holy Land as a center to reach often seems nothing more than a pretext. But it would be wrong to say that the play of self-interest, or economic, commercial, or political factors, diverted the crusade from its pure path. The idea of the crusade *in itself implies this variability of directions*, broken and changing, and intrinsically possesses all these factors or all these variables from the moment it turns religion into a war machine and simultaneously utilizes and gives rise to the corresponding nomadism.[59] The necessity of maintaining the most rigorous of distinctions between sedentaries, migrants, and nomads does not preclude de facto mixes; on the contrary, it makes them all the more necessary in turn. And it is impossible to think of the general process of sedentarization that vanquished the nomads without also envisioning the gusts of local nomadization that carried off sedentaries and doubled migrants (notably, to the benefit of religion).

Smooth or nomad space lies between two striated spaces: that of the forest, with its gravitational verticals, and that of agriculture, with its grids and generalized parallels, its now independent arborescence, its art of extracting the tree and wood from the forest. But being "between" also means that smooth space is controlled by these two flanks, which limit it, oppose its development, and assign it as much as possible a communicational role; or, on the contrary, it means that it turns against them, gnawing away at the forest on one side, on the other side gaining ground on the cultivated lands, affirming a noncommunicating force or a force of *divergence* like a "wedge" digging in. The nomads turn first against the forest and the mountain dwellers, then descend upon the farmers. What we have here is something like the flipside or the outside of the State-form—but in what sense? This form, as a global and relative space, implies a certain number of components: forest-clearing of fields; agriculture-grid laying; animal raising subordinated to agricultural work and sedentary food production; commerce based on a constellation of town-country (*polis-nomos*) communications. When historians inquire into the reasons for the victory of the West over the Orient, they primarily mention the following characteristics, which put the Orient in general at a disadvantage: deforestation rather than clearing for planting, making it extremely difficult to extract or even to find wood; cultivation of the type "rice paddy and garden" rather than arborescence and field; animal raising for the most part outside the control of the sedentaries, with the result that they lacked animal power and meat foods; the low communication content of the town-country relation, making commerce far less flexible.[60] The conclusion is not that the State-form is absent in the Orient. Quite to the contrary, a more rigid agency becomes necessary in order to retain and reunite the various components plied by escape vectors. States always have the same composition; if there is even one truth in the political philosophy of Hegel, it is that every State carries within itself the essential moments of its existence. States are made up not only of people but also of wood, fields, gardens, animals, and commodities. There is a unity of *composition* of all States, but States have neither the same *development* nor the same *organization*. In the Orient, the components are much more disconnected, disjointed, necessitating a great immutable Form to hold them together: "despotic formations," Asian or African, are rocked by incessant revolts, by secessions and dynastic changes, which nevertheless do not affect the immutability of the form. In the West, on the other hand, the interconnectedness of the components makes possible transformations of the State-form through revolution. It is true that the idea of revolution itself is ambiguous; it is Western insofar as it relates to a transformation of the State, but Eastern insofar as it envisions the destruction, the abolition of the State.[61] The great empires of the Orient, Africa, and America run up against wide-open smooth spaces that penetrate them and maintain gaps between their components (the *nomos* does not become countryside, the countryside does not communicate with the town, large-scale animal raising is the affair of the nomads, etc.): the oriental State is in direct confrontation with a nomad war machine. This war machine may fall back to the road of integration and proceed solely by revolt and dynastic change; nevertheless, it is the war machine, as nomad, that invents the abolitionist dream and reality. Western States are much more sheltered in their striated space and consequently have much more latitude in holding their components together; they confront the nomads only indirectly, through the intermediary of the migrations the nomads trigger or adopt as their stance.[62]

One of the fundamental tasks of the State is to striate the space over which it reigns, or to utilize smooth spaces as a means of communication in the service of striated space. It is a vital concern of every State not only to vanquish nomadism but to control migrations and, more generally, to establish a zone of rights over an entire "exterior," over all of the flows traversing the ecumenon. If it can help it, the State does not dissociate itself from a process of capture of flows of all kinds, populations, commodities or commerce, money or capital, etc. There is still a need for fixed paths in well-defined directions, which restrict speed, regulate circulation, relativize movement, and measure in detail the relative movements of subjects and objects. That is why Paul Virilio's thesis is important, when he shows that "the political power of the State is *polis*, police, that is, management of the public ways," and that "the gates of the city, its levies and duties, are barriers, filters against the fluidity of the masses, against the penetration power of migratory packs," people, animals, and goods.[63] Gravity, *gravitas*, such is the essence of the State. It is not at all that the State knows nothing of speed; but it requires that movement, even the fastest, cease to be the absolute state of a moving body occupying a smooth space, to become the relative characteristic of a "moved body" going from one point to another in a striated space. In this sense, the State never ceases to decompose, recompose, and transform movement, or to regulate speed. The State as town surveyor, converter, or highway interchange: the role of the engineer from this point of view. Speed and absolute movement are not without their laws, but they are the laws of the *nomos*, of the smooth space that deploys it, of the war machine that populates it. If the nomads formed the war machine, it was by inventing absolute speed, by being "synonymous" with speed. And each time there is an operation against the State—insubordination, rioting, guerrilla warfare, or revolution as act—it can be said that a war machine has revived, that a new nomadic potential has appeared, accompanied by the reconstitution of a smooth space or a manner of being in space as though it were smooth (Virilio discusses the importance of the riot or revolutionary theme of "holding the street"). It is in this sense that the response of the State against all that threatens to move beyond it is to striate space. The State does not appropriate the war machine without giving even it the form of relative movement: this was the case with the model of the *fortress* as a regulator of movement, which was precisely the obstacle the nomads came up against, the stumbling block and parry by which absolute vortical movement was broken. Conversely, when a State does not succeed in striating its interior or neighboring space, the flows traversing that State necessarily adopt the stance of a war machine directed against it, deployed in a hostile or rebellious smooth space (even if other States are able to slip their striations in). This was the adventure of China: toward the end of the fourteenth century, and in spite of its very high level of technology in ships and navigation, it turned its back on its huge maritime space, saw its commercial flows turn against it and ally themselves with piracy, and was unable to react except by a politics of immobility, of the massive restriction of commerce, which only reinforced the connection between commerce and the war machine.[64]

The situation is much more complicated than we have let on. The sea is perhaps principal among smooth spaces, the hydraulic model par excellence. But the sea is also, of all smooth spaces, the first one attempts were made to striate, to transform into a dependency of the land, with its fixed routes, constant directions, relative movements, a whole counterhydraulic of channels and conduits. One of the reasons for the hegemony of the West was the power of its State apparatuses to striate the sea by combining the technologies of the North and the Mediterranean and by annexing the Atlantic. But this undertaking had the most unexpected result: the multiplication of relative movements, the intensification of relative speeds in striated space, ended up reconstituting a smooth space or absolute movement. As Virilio emphasizes, the sea became the place of the *fleet in being*, where one no longer goes from one point to another, but rather holds space beginning from any point: instead of striating space, one occupies it with a vector of deterritorialization in perpetual motion. This modern strategy was communicated from the sea to the air, as the new smooth space, but also to the entire Earth considered as desert or sea. As converter and capturer, the State does not just relativize movement, it reimparts absolute movement. It does not just go from the smooth to the striated, it reconstitutes smooth space; it reimparts smooth in the wake of the striated. It is true that this new nomadism accompanies a worldwide war machine whose organization exceeds the State apparatuses and passes into energy, military-industrial, and multinational complexes. We say this as a reminder that smooth space and the form of exteriority do not have an irresistible revolutionary calling but change meaning drastically depending on the interactions they are part of and the concrete conditions of their exercise or establishment (for example, the way in which total war and popular war, and even guerrilla warfare, borrow one another's methods).[65]

PROPOSITION VI. *Nomad existence necessarily implies the numerical elements of a war machine.*

Tens, hundreds, thousands, myriads: all armies retain these decimal groupings, to the point that each time they are encountered it is safe to assume the presence of a military organization. Is this not the way an army deterritorializes its soldiers? An army is composed of units, companies, and divisions. The Numbers may vary in function, in combination; they may enter into entirely different strategies; but there is always a connection between the Number and the war machine. It is a question not of quantity but of organization or composition. When the State creates armies, it always applies this principle of numerical organization; but all it does is adopt the principle, at the same time as it appropriates the war machine. For so peculiar an idea—the numerical organization of people—came from the nomads. It was the Hyksos, conquering nomads, who brought it to Egypt; and when Moses applied it to his people in exodus, it was on the advice of his nomad father-in-law, Jethro the Kenite, and was done in such a way as to constitute a war machine, the elements of which are described in the biblical book of Numbers. The *nomos* is fundamentally numerical, arithmetic. When Greek geometrism is contrasted with Indo-Arab arithmetism, it becomes clear that the latter implies a nomos opposable to the logos: not that the nomads "do" arithmetic or algebra, but because arithmetic and algebra arise in a strongly nomad influenced world.

Up to now we have known three major types of human organization: *lineal*, *territorial*, and *numerical*. Lineal organization allows us to define so-called primitive societies. Clan lineages are essentially segments in action; they meld and divide, and vary according to the ancestor considered, the tasks, and the circumstances. Of course, number plays an important role in the determination of lineage, or in the creation of new lineages—as does the earth, since a clan segmentarity is doubled by a tribal segmentarity. The earth is before all else the matter upon which the dynamic of lineages is inscribed, and the number, a means of inscription: the lineages write upon the earth and with the number, constituting a kind of "geodesy." Everything changes with State societies: it is often said that the territorial principle becomes dominant. One could also speak of deterritorialization, since the earth becomes an object, instead of being an active material element in combination with lineage. Property is precisely the deterritorialized relation between the human being and the earth; this is so whether property constitutes a good belonging to the State, superposed upon continuing possession by a lineal community, or whether it itself becomes a good belonging to private individuals constituting a new community. In both cases (and according to the two poles of the State), something like an overcoding of the earth replaces geodesy. Of course, lineages remain very important, and numbers take on their own importance. But what moves to the forefront is a "territorial" organization, in the sense that all the segments, whether of lineage, land, or number, are taken up by *an astronomical space or a geometrical extension* that overcodes them—but certainly not in the same way in the archaic imperial State and in modern States. The archaic State envelops a *spatium* with a summit, a differentiated space with depth and levels, whereas modern States (beginning with the Greek city-state) develop a homogeneous *extensio* with an immanent center, divisible homologous parts, and symmetrical and reversible relations. Not only do the two models, the astronomical and the geometrical, enter into intimate mixes, but even when they are supposedly pure, both imply the subordination of lineages and numbers to this metric power, as it appears either in the *imperial spatium* or in the *political extensio*.[66] Arithmetic, the number, has always had a decisive role in the State apparatus: this is so even as early as the imperial bureaucracy, with the three conjoined operations of the census, taxation, and election. It is even truer of modern forms of the State, which in developing utilized all the calculation techniques that were springing up at the border between mathematical science and social technology (there is a whole social calculus at the basis of political economy, demography, the organization of work, etc.). This arithmetic element of the State found its specific power in the treatment of all kinds of matter: primary matters (raw materials), the secondary matter of wrought objects, or the ultimate matter constituted by the human population. Thus the number has always served to gain mastery over matter, to control its variations and movements, in other words, to submit them to the spatiotemporal framework of the State—either the imperial *spatium*, or the modern *extensio*.[67] The State has a territorial principle, or a principle of deterritorialization, that links the number to metric magnitudes (taking into account the increasingly complex metrics effecting the overcoding). We do not believe that the conditions of independence or autonomy of the Number are to be found in the State, even though all the factors of its development are present.

The *Numbering Number*, in other words, autonomous arithmetic organization, implies neither a superior degree of abstraction nor very large quantities. It relates only to conditions of possibility constituted by nomadism and to conditions of effectuation constituted by the war machine. It is in State armies that the problem of the treatment of large quantities arises, in relation to other matters; but the war machine operates with small quantities that it treats using numbering numbers. These numbers appear as soon as one distributes something in space, instead of dividing up space or distributing space itself. The number becomes a subject. The independence of the number in relation to space is a result not of abstraction but of the concrete nature of smooth space, which is occupied without itself being counted. The number is no longer a means of counting or measuring but of moving: it is the number itself that moves through smooth space. There is undoubtedly a geometry of smooth space: but as we have seen, it is a minor, operative geometry, a geometry of the trait. The more independent space is from a metrics, the more independent the number is from space. Geometry as a royal science has little importance for the war machine (its only importance is in State armies, and for sedentary fortification, but it leads generals to serious defeats).[68] The number becomes a principle whenever it occupies a smooth space, and is deployed within it as subject, instead of measuring a striated space. The number is the mobile occupant, the movable (*meuble*) in smooth space, as opposed to the geometry of the immovable (*immeuble*) in striated space. The nomadic numerical unit is the ambulant fire, and not the tent, which is still too much of an immovable: "The fire takes precedence over the yurt." The numbering number is no longer subordinated to metric determinations or geometrical dimensions, but has only a dynamic relation with geographical directions: it is a directional number, not a dimensional or metric one. Nomad organization is indissolubly arithmetic and directional; quantity is everywhere, tens, hundreds, direction is everywhere, left, right: the numerical chief is also the chief of the left or the right.[69] The numbering number is rhythmic, not harmonic. It is not related to cadence or measure: it is only in State armies, and for reasons of discipline and show, that one marches in cadence; but autonomous numerical organization finds its meaning elsewhere, whenever it is necessary to establish an *order of displacement* on the steppe, the desert—at the point where the lineages of the forest dwellers and the figures of the State lose their relevance. "He moved with the random walk which made only those sounds natural to the desert. Nothing in his passage would [indicate] that human flesh moved there. It was a way of walking so deeply conditioned in him that he didn't need to think about it. The feet moved of themselves, no measurable rhythm to their pacing."[70] In the war machine and nomadic existence, the number is no longer numbered, but becomes a Cipher (*Chiffre*), and it is in this capacity that it constitutes the "esprit de corps" and invents the secret and its outgrowths (strategy, espionage, war ruses, ambush, diplomacy, etc.).

A ciphered, rhythmic, directional, autonomous, movable, numbering number: the war machine is like the necessary consequence of nomadic organization (Moses experienced it, with all its consequences). Some people nowadays are too eager to criticize this numerical organization, denouncing it as a military or even concentration-camp society where people are no longer anything more than deterritorialized "numbers." But that is false. Horror for horror, the numerical organization of people is certainly no crueler than the lineal or State organizations. Treating people like numbers is not necessarily worse than treating them like trees to prune, or geometrical figures to shape and model. Moreover, the use of the number as a numeral, as a statistical element, is proper to the numbered number of the State, not to the numbering number. And the world of the concentration camp operates as much by lineages and territories as by numeration. The question is not one of good or bad but of specificity. The specificity of numerical organization rests on the nomadic mode of existence and the war machine function. The numbering number is distinct both from lineal codes and State overcoding. Arithmetic composition, on the one hand, selects, extracts from the lineages the elements that will enter into nomadism and the war machine and, on the other hand, directs them against the State apparatus, opposing a machine and an existence to the

State apparatus, drawing a deterritorialization that cuts across both the lineal territorialities and the territory or deterritoriality of the State.

A first characteristic of the numbering, nomadic or war, number is that it is always complex, that is, articulated. A complex of numbers every time. It is exactly for this reason that it in no way implies large, homogenized quantities, like State numbers or the numbered number, but rather produces its effect of immensity by its fine articulation, in other words, by its distribution of heterogeneity in a free space. Even State armies do not do away with this principle when they deal with large numbers (despite the predominance of "base" 10). The Roman legion was a number made up of numbers, articulated in such a way that the segments became mobile, and the figures geometrical, changing, transformational. The complex or articulated number comprises not only men but necessarily weapons, animals, and vehicles. The arithmetic base unit is therefore a unit of assemblage, for example, man-horse-bow, $1 \times 1 \times 1$, according to the formula that carried the Scythians to triumph; and the formula becomes more complicated to the extent that certain "weapons" assemble or articulate several men or animals, as in the case of the chariot with two horses and two men, one to drive and the other to throw, $2 \times 1 \times 2 = 1$; or in the case of the famous two-handled shield of the hoplite reform, which soldered together human chains. However small the unit, it is articulated. The numbering number always has several bases at the same time. It is also necessary to take into account arithmetic relations that are external yet still contained in the number, expressing the proportion of combatants among the members of a lineage or tribe, the role of reserves and stocks, the upkeep of people, things, and animals. *Logistics* is the art of these external relations, which are no less a part of the war machine than the internal relations of *strategy*, in other words, the composition of combat units in relation to one another. The two together constitute the science of the articulation of numbers of war. Every assemblage has this strategic aspect and this logistical aspect.

But the numbering number has a second, more secret, characteristic. Everywhere, the war machine displays a curious process of arithmetic replication or doubling, as if it operated along two nonsymmetrical and nonequal series. *On the one hand*, the lineages are indeed organized and reshuffled numerically; a numerical composition is superimposed upon the lineages in order to bring the new principle into predominance. But *on the other hand*, men are simultaneously extracted from each lineage to form a special numerical body—as if the new numerical composition of the lineage-body could not succeed without the constitution of a body proper to it, itself numerical. We believe that this is not an accidental phenomenon but rather an essential constituent of the war machine, a necessary operation for the autonomy of the number: the number of the body must have as its correlate a body of the number; the number must be doubled according to two complementary operations. For the social body to be numerized, the number must form a special body. When Genghis Khan undertook his great composition of the steppe, he numerically organized the lineages, and the fighters in each lineage, placing them under a cipher and a chief (groups of ten with decurions, groups of one hundred with centurions, groups of one thousand with chiliarchs). He also extracted from each arithmetized lineage a small number of men who were to constitute his personal guard, in other words, a dynamic formation comprising a staff, commissars, messengers, and diplomats ("antrustions").[71] One is never without the other: a double deterritorialization, the second of which is to a higher power. When Moses undertook his great composition of the desert—where the influence he felt from the nomads was necessarily stronger than that of Yahweh—he took a census of each tribe and organized them numerically; he also decreed a law according to which the firstborn of each tribe at that particular time belonged by right to Yahweh. As these firstborn were obviously still too young, their role in the Number was transferred to a special tribe, the Levites, who provided the body of the Number or the special guard of the ark; and as the Levites were less numerous than the new firstborn of the tribes taken together, the excess firstborn had to be bought back by the tribes in the form of taxes (bringing us back to a fundamental aspect of logistics). The war machine would be unable to function without this double series: it is necessary both that numerical composition replace lineal organization and that it conjure away the territorial organization of the State. Power in the war machine is defined according to this double series: power is no longer based on segments and centers, on the potential resonance of centers and overcoding of segments, but on these relations internal to the Number and independent of quantity. Tensions or power struggles are also a result of this: between Moses' tribes and the Levites, between Genghis's "noyans" and "antrustions." This is not simply a protest on the part of lineages wishing to regain their former autonomy; nor is it the prefiguration of a struggle for control over a State apparatus. It is a tension inherent in the war machine, in its special power, and in the particular limitations placed on the power of the "chief."

Thus numerical composition, or the numbering number, implies several operations: the arithmetization of the starting aggregates or sets (the lineages); the union of the extracted subsets (the constitution of groups of ten, one hundred, etc.); and the formation by substitution of another set in correspondence with the united set (the special body). It is this last operation that implies the most variety and originality in nomad existence. The same problem arises even in State armies, when the war machine is appropriated by the State. In effect, if the arithmetization of the social body has as its correlate the formation of a distinct special body, itself arithmetic, this special body may be constructed in several ways: (1) from a privileged lineage or tribe, the dominance of which subsequently takes on a new meaning (the case of Moses, with the Levites); (2) from representatives of each lineage, who subsequently serve also as hostages (the firstborn; this would actually be the Asian case, or the case of Genghis); (3) from a totally different element, one exterior to the base society, slaves, foreigners, or people of another religion (this was already the case as early as the Saxon regime, in which the king used Frankish slaves to compose his special body; but Islam is the prime example, even inspiring a specific sociological category, that of "military slavery": the Mameluks of Egypt, slaves from the steppe or the Caucasus who were purchased at a very early age by the sultan; or the Ottoman Janissaries, who came from Christian communities).[72]

Is this not the origin of an important theme, "the nomads as child stealers"? It is clear, especially in the last example, how the special body is instituted as an element determinant of power in the war machine. The war machine and nomadic existence have to ward off two things simultaneously: a return of the lineal aristocracy and the formation of imperial functionaries. What complicates everything is that the State itself has often been determined in such a way as to use slaves as high functionaries. As we shall see, the reasons for this varied, and although the two currents converged in armies, they came from two distinct sources. For the power of slaves, foreigners, or captives in a war machine of nomadic origin is very different from the power of lineal aristocracies, as well as from that of State functionaries and bureaucrats. They are "commissars," emissaries, diplomats, spies, strategists, and logisticians, sometimes smiths. They cannot be explained away as a "whim of the sultan." On the contrary, it is the possibility of the war chief having whims that is explained by the objective existence and necessity of this special numerical body, this Cipher that has value only in relation to a *nomos*. There is both a deterritorialization and a becoming proper to the war machine; the special body, in particular the slave-infidel-foreigner, is the one who *becomes* a soldier and believer while remaining deterritorialized in relation to the lineages and the State. You have to be born an infidel to become a believer; you have to be born a slave to become a soldier. Specific schools or institutions are needed for this purpose: the special body is an invention proper to the war machine, which States always utilize, adapting it so totally to their own ends that it becomes unrecognizable, or restituting it in bureaucratic staff form, or in the technocratic form of very special bodies, or in "esprit de corps" that serve the State as much as they resist it, or among the commissars who double the State as much as they serve it.

It is true that the nomads have no history; they only have a geography.

And the defeat of the nomads was such, so complete, that history is one with the triumph of States. We have witnessed, as a result, a generalized critique dismissing the nomads as incapable of any innovation, whether technological or metallurgical, political or metaphysical. Historians, bourgeois or Soviet (Grousset or Vladimirtsov), consider the nomads a pitiable segment of humanity that understands nothing: not technology, to which it supposedly remained indifferent; not agriculture, not the cities and States it destroyed or conquered. It is difficult to see, however, how the nomads could have triumphed in war if they did not possess strong metallurgical capabilities (the idea that the nomads received their technical weapons and political counseling from renegades from an imperial State is highly improbable). It is difficult to see how the nomads could have undertaken to destroy cities and States, except in the name of a nomad organization and a war machine defined not by ignorance but by their positive characteristics, by their specific space, by a composition all their own that broke with lineages and warded off the State-form. History has always dismissed the nomads. Attempts have been made to apply a properly military category to the war machine (that of "military democracy") and a properly sedentary category to nomadism (that of "feudalism"). But these two hypotheses presuppose a territorial principle: either that an imperial State appropriates the war machine, distributing land to warriors as a benefit of their position (*cleroi* and false fiefs), or that property, once it has become private, in itself posits relations of dependence among the property owners constituting the army (true fiefs and vassalage).[73] In both cases, the number is subordinated to an "immobile" fiscal organization, in order to establish which land can be or has been ceded, as well as to set the taxes owed by the beneficiaries themselves. There is no doubt that nomad organization and the war machine deal with these same problems, both the level of land and of taxation (in which the nomadic warriors were great innovators, despite what is said to the contrary). But they invent a territoriality and a "movable" fiscal organization that testify to the autonomy of a numerical principle: there can be a confusion or combination of the systems, but the specificity of the nomadic system remains the subordination of land to numbers that are displaced and deployed, and of taxation to relations internal to those numbers (already with Moses, for example, taxation played a role in the relation between the numerical bodies and the special body of the number). In short, military democracy and feudalism, far from explaining the numerical composition of the nomads, instead testify to what may survive of them in sedentary regimes.

PROPOSITION VII. *Nomad existence has for "affects" the weapons of a war machine.*

A distinction can always be made between weapons and tools on the basis of their usage (destroying people or producing goods). But although this extrinsic distinction explains certain secondary adaptations of a technical object, it does not preclude a general convertibility between the two groups, to the extent that it seems very difficult to propose an intrinsic difference between weapons and tools. The types of percussion, as defined by André Leroi-Gourhan, are found on both sides. "For ages on end agricultural implements and weapons of war must have remained identical."[74] Some have spoken of an "ecosystem," not only situated at the origin, in which work tools and weapons of war exchange their determinations: it seems that the same *machinic phylum* traverses both. And yet we have the feeling that there are many internal differences, even if they are not intrinsic, in other words, logical or conceptual, and even if they remain approximate. As a first approximation, weapons have a privileged relation with projection. Anything that throws or is thrown is fundamentally a weapon, and propulsion is its essential moment. The weapon is ballistic; the very notion of the "problem" is related to the war machine. The more mechanisms of projection a tool has, the more it behaves like a weapon, potentially or simply metaphorically. In addition, tools are constantly compensating for the projective mechanisms they possess, or else they adapt them to other ends. It is true that missile weapons, in the strict sense, whether projected or projecting, are only one kind among others; but even handheld weapons require a usage of the hand and arm different from that required by tools, a projective usage exemplified in the martial arts. The tool, on the other hand, is much more introceptive, introjective: it prepares a matter from a distance, in order to bring it to a state of equilibrium or to appropriate it for a form of interiority. Action at a distance exists in both cases, but in one case it is centrifugal and in the other, centripetal. One could also say that the tool encounters resistances, to be conquered or put to use, while the weapon has to do with counterattack, to be avoided or invented (the counterattack is in fact the precipitating and inventive factor in the war machine, to the extent that it is not simply reducible to a quantitative rivalry or defensive parade).

Second, weapons and tools do not "tendentially" (approximately) have the same relation to movement, to speed. It is yet another essential contribution of Paul Virilio to have stressed this weapon-speed complementarity: the weapon invents speed, or the discovery of speed invents the weapon (the projective character of weapons is the result). The war machine releases a vector of speed so specific to it that it needs a special name; it is not only the power of destruction, but "dromocracy" (= *nomos*). Among other advantages, this idea articulates a new mode of distinction between the hunt and war. For it is certain not only that war does not derive from the hunt but also that the hunt does not promote weapons: either war evolved in the sphere of indistinction and convertibility between weapons and tools, or it used to its own advantage weapons already distinguished, already constituted. As Virilio says, war in no way appears when man applies to man the relation of the *hunter* to the animal, but on the contrary when he captures the force of the *hunted* animal and enters an entirely new relation to man, that of war (enemy, no longer prey). It is therefore not surprising that the war machine was the invention of the animal-raising nomads: animal breeding and training are not to be confused either with the primitive hunt or with sedentary domestication, but are in fact the discovery of a projecting and projectile system. Rather than operating by blow-by-blow violence, or constituting a violence "once and for all," the war machine, with breeding and training, institutes an entire economy of violence, in other words, a way of making violence durable, even unlimited. "Bloodletting, immediate killing, run contrary to the unlimited usage of violence, that is, to its economy. . . . *The economy of violence is not that of the hunter in the animal raiser, but that of the hunted animal.* In horseback riding, one conserves the kinetic energy, the speed of the horse, and no longer its proteins (the motor, and no longer the flesh). . . . Whereas in the hunt the hunter's aim was to arrest the movement of wild animality through systematic slaughter, the animal breeder [sets about] conserving it, and, by means of training, the rider joins with this movement, orienting it and provoking its acceleration." The technological motor would develop this tendency further, but "horseback riding was the first projector of the warrior, his first system of arms."[75] Whence becoming-animal in the war machine. Does this mean that the war machine did not exist before horseback riding and the cavalry? That is not the issue. The issue is that the war machine implies the release of a Speed vector that becomes a free or independent variable; this does not occur in the hunt, where speed is associated primarily with the hunted animal. It is possible for this race vector to be released in an infantry, without recourse to horseback riding; it is possible, moreover, for there to be horseback riding, but as a means of transportation or even of portage having nothing to do with the free vector. In any event, what the warrior borrows from the animal is more the idea of the motor than the model of the prey. He does not generalize the idea of the prey by applying it to the enemy; he abstracts the idea of the motor, applying it to himself.

Two objections immediately arise. According to the first, the war machine possesses as much weight and gravity as it does speed (the distinction between the heavy and the light, the dissymmetry between defense and attack, the opposition between rest and tension). But it would be easy to demonstrate that phenomena of "temporization," and even of immobility and catatonia, so important in wars, relate in certain cases to a component of pure speed. And the rest of the time, they relate to the conditions under which State apparatuses appropriate the war machine, notably by arranging a striated space where opposing forces can come to an equilibrium. It can happen that speed is abstracted as the property of a projectile, a bullet or artillery shell, which condemns the weapon itself, and the soldier, to immobility (for example, immobility in the First World War). But an equilibrium of forces is a phenomenon of resistance, whereas the counterattack implies a rush or change of speed that breaks the equilibrium: it was the tank that regrouped all of the operations in the speed vector and recreated a smooth space for movement by uprooting men and arms.[76]

The opposite objection is more complex: it is that speed does indeed seem to be as much a part of the tool as of the weapon, and is no way specific to the war machine. The history of the motor is not only military. But perhaps there is too much of a tendency to think in terms of quantities of movement, instead of seeking qualitative models. The two ideal models of the motor are those of work and *free action*. Work is a motor cause that meets resistances, operates upon the exterior, is consumed and spent in its effect, and must be renewed from one moment to the next. Free action is also a motor cause, but one that has no resistance to overcome, operates only upon the mobile body itself, is not consumed in its effect, and continues from one moment to the next. Whatever its measure or degree, speed is relative in the first case, absolute in the second (the idea of a *perpetuum mobile*). In work, what counts is the point of application of a resultant force exerted by the weight of a body considered as "one" (gravity), and the relative displacement of this point of application. In free action, what counts is the way in which the elements of the body escape gravitation to occupy absolutely a nonpunctuated space. Weapons and weapon handling seem to be linked to a free-action model, and tools to a work model. Linear displacement, from one point to another, constitutes the relative movement of the tool, but it is the vortical occupation of a space that constitutes the absolute movement of the weapon. It is as though the weapon were moving, self-propelling, while the tool is moved. This link between tools and work remains obscured unless work receives the motor, or real, definition we have just given it. The tool does not define work; just the opposite. The tool presupposes work. It must be added that weapons, also, obviously imply a renewal of the cause, an expending or even disappearance in the effect, the encountering of external resistances, a displacement of force, etc. It would be futile to credit weapons with a magical power in contrast to the constraints of tools: weapons and tools are subject to the same laws, which define, precisely, their common sphere. But the principle behind all technology is to demonstrate that a technical element remains abstract, entirely undetermined, as long as one does not relate it to an *assemblage* it presupposes. It is the machine that is primary in relation to the technical element: not the technical machine, itself a collection of elements, but the social or collective machine, the machinic assemblage that determines what is a technical element at a given moment, what is its usage, extension, comprehension, etc.

It is through the intermediary of assemblages that the *phylum* selects, qualifies, and even invents the technical elements. Thus one cannot speak of weapons or tools before defining the constituent assemblages they presuppose and enter into. This is what we meant when we said that weapons and tools are not merely distinguished from one another in an extrinsic manner, and yet they have no distinctive intrinsic characteristics. They have internal (and not intrinsic) characteristics relating to the respective assemblages with which they are associated. What effectuates a free-action model is not the weapons in themselves and in their physical aspect but the "war machine" assemblage as formal cause of the weapons. And what effectuates the work model is not the tools but the "work machine" assemblage as formal cause of the tools. When we say that the weapon is inseparable from a speed vector, while the tool remains tied to conditions of gravity, we are claiming only to signal a difference between two types of assemblage, a distinction that holds even if in the assemblage proper to it the tool is abstractly "faster," and the weapon abstractly "weightier." The tool is essentially tied to a genesis, a displacement, and an expenditure of force whose laws reside in work, while the weapon concerns only the exercise or manifestation of force in space and time, in conformity with free action. The weapon does not fall from the sky, and obviously assumes production, displacement, expenditure, and resistance. But this aspect relates to the common sphere of the weapon and the tool, and does not yet concern the specificity of the weapon, which appears only when force is considered in itself, when it is no longer tied to anything but the number, movement, space, or time, or *when speed is added to displacement*.[77] Concretely, a weapon as such relates not to the Work model but to the Free-Action model, with the assumption that the conditions of work are fulfilled elsewhere. In short, from the point of view of force, the tool is tied to a gravity-displacement, weight-height system, and the weapon to a speed-*perpetuum mobile* system (it is in this sense that it can be said that speed in itself is a "weapons system").

The very general primacy of the collective and machinic assemblage over the technical element applies generally, for tools as for weapons. Weapons and tools are consequences, nothing but consequences. It has often been remarked that a weapon is nothing outside of the combat organization it is bound up with. For example, "hoplite" weapons existed only by virtue of the phalanx as a mutation of the war machine: the only new weapon at the time, the two-handled shield, was created by this assemblage; the other weapons were preexistent, but in other combinations where they had a different function, a different nature.[78] It is always the assemblage that constitutes the weapons system. The lance and the sword came into bring in the Bronze Age only by virtue of the man-horse assemblage, which caused a lengthening of the dagger and pike, and made the first infantry weapons, the morning star and the battle-ax, obsolete. The stirrup, in turn, occasioned a new figure of the man-horse assemblage, entailing a new type of lance and new weapons; and this man-horse-stirrup constellation is itself variable, and has different effects depending on whether it is bound up with the general conditions of nomadism, or later readapted to the sedentary conditions of feudalism. The situation is exactly the same for the tool: once again, everything depends on an organization of work, and variable assemblages of human, animal, and thing. Thus the heavy plow exists as a specific tool only in a constellation where "long open fields" predominate, where the horse tends to replace the ox as draft animal, where the land begins to undergo triennial rotation, and where the economy becomes communal. Beforehand, the heavy plow may well have existed, but on the margins of other assemblages that did not bring out its specificity, that left unexploited its differential character with the scratch plow.[79]

Assemblages are passional, they are compositions of desire. Desire has nothing to do with a natural or spontaneous determination; there is no desire but assembling, assembled, desire. The rationality, the efficiency, of an assemblage does not exist without the passions the assemblage brings into play, without the desires that constitute it as much as it constitutes them. Detienne has shown that the Greek phalanx was inseparable from a whole reversal of values, and from a passional mutation that drastically changed the relations between desire and the war machine. It is a case of man dismounting from the horse, and of the man-animal relation being replaced by a relation between men in an infantry assemblage that paves the way for the advent of the peasant-soldier, the citizen-soldier: the entire Eros of war changes, a group homosexual Eros tends to replace the zoosexual Eros of the horseman. Undoubtedly, whenever a State appropriates the war machine, it tends to assimilate the education of the citizen to the training of the worker to the apprenticeship of the soldier. But if it is true that all assemblages are assemblages of desire, the question is whether the assemblages of war and work, considered in themselves, do not fundamentally mobilize passions of different orders. Passions are effectuations of desire that differ according to the assemblage: it is not the same justice or the same cruelty, the same pity, etc. The work regime is inseparable from an organization and a development of Form, corresponding to which is the formation of the subject. This is the passional regime of feeling as "the form of the worker." Feeling implies an evaluation of matter and its resistances, a direction (*sens*, also "meaning") to form and its developments, an economy of force and its displacements, an entire gravity. But the regime of the war machine is on the contrary that of *affects*, which relate only to the moving body in itself, to speeds and compositions of speed among elements. Affect is the active discharge of emotion, the counterattack, whereas feeling is an always displaced, retarded, resisting emotion. Affects are projectiles just like weapons; feelings are introceptive like tools. There is a relation between the affect and the weapon, as witnessed not only in mythology but also in the *chanson de geste*, and the chivalric novel or novel of courtly love. Weapons are affects and affects weapons. From this standpoint, the most absolute immobility, pure catatonia, is a part of the speed vector, is carried by this vector, which links the petrification of the act to the precipitation of movement. The knight sleeps on his mount, then departs like an arrow. Kleist is the author who best integrated these sudden catatonic fits, swoons, suspenses, with the utmost speeds of a war machine. He presents us with a becoming-weapon of the technical element simultaneous to a becoming-affect of the passional element (the Penthesilea equation). The martial arts have always subordinated weapons to speed, and above all to mental (absolute) speed; for this reason, they are also the arts of suspense and immobility. The affect passes through both extremes. Thus the martial arts do not adhere to a *code*, as an affair of the State, but follow *ways*, which are so many paths of the affect; upon these ways, one learns to "unuse" weapons as much as one learns to use them, as if the power and cultivation of the affect were the true goal of the assemblage, the weapon being only a provisory means. Learning to undo things, and to undo oneself, is proper to the war machine: the "not-doing" of the warrior, the undoing of the subject. A movement of decoding runs through the war machine, while overcoding solders the tool to an organization of work and of the State (the tool is never unlearned; one can only compensate for its absence). It is true that the martial arts continually invoke the center of gravity and the rules for its displacement. That is because these ways are not the ultimate ones. However far they go, they are still in the domain of Being, and only translate absolute movements of another nature into the common space—those effectuated in the Void, not in nothingness, but in the smooth of the void where there is no longer any goal: attacks, counterattacks, and headlong plunges.[80]

Still from the standpoint of the assemblage, there is an essential relation between tools and signs. That is because the work model that defines the tool belongs to the State apparatus. It has often been said that people in primitive societies do not, strictly speaking, work, even if their activities are very constrained and regulated; and the man of war, in his capacity as a man of war, does not work either (the "labors" of Hercules assume submission to a king). The technical element becomes a tool when it is abstracted from the territory and is applied to the earth as an object; but at the same time, the sign ceases to be inscribed upon the body and is written upon an immobile, objective matter. For there to be work, there must be a capture of activity by the State apparatus, and a semiotization of activity by writing. Hence the affinity between the assemblages signs-tools, and signs of writing-organization of work. Entirely different is the case of the weapon, which is in an essential relation with jewelry. Jewelry has undergone so many secondary adaptations that we no longer have a clear understanding of what it is. But something lights up in our mind when we are told that metalworking was the "barbarian," or nomad, art par excellence, and when we see these masterpieces of minor art. These fibulas, these gold or silver plaques, these pieces of jewelry, are attached to small movable objects; they are not only easy to transport, but pertain to the object only as object in motion. These plaques constitute traits of expression of pure speed, carried on objects that are themselves mobile and moving. The relation between them is not that of form-matter but of motif-support, where the earth is no longer anything more than ground (*sol*), where there is no longer even any ground at all because the support is as mobile as the motif. They lend colors the speed of light, turning gold to red and silver to white light. They are attached to the horse's harness, the sheath of the sword, the warrior's garments, the handle of the weapon; they even decorate things used only once, such as arrowheads. Regardless of the effort or toil they imply, they are of the order of free action, related to pure mobility, and not of the order of work with its conditions of gravity, resistance, and expenditure. The ambulant smith links metalworking to the weapon, and vice versa. Gold and silver have taken on many other functions but cannot be understood apart from this nomadic contribution made by the war machine, in which they are not matters but traits of expression appropriate to weapons (the whole mythology of war not only subsists in money but is the active factor in it). Jewels are the affects corresponding to weapons, that are swept up by the same speed vector.

Metalworking, jewelry making, ornamentation, even decoration, do not form a writing, even though they have a power of abstraction that is in every way equal to that of writing. But this power is assembled differently. In the case of writing, the nomads had no need to create their own system; they borrowed that of their sedentary imperial neighbors, who even furnished them with a phonetic transcription of their languages.[81] "The goldsmith's and silversmith's is the barbarian art par excellence; filigree and gold and silver plating. . . . Scythian art, tied as it was to a nomadic and warlike economy that both used and repudiated a commerce reserved for foreigners, now moved toward this luxurious and decorative type of work. The barbarians . . . did not need to possess or create a precise code, such as for instance an elementary picto-ideographic one—still less a syllabic writing of their own, which would indeed have had to compete with the ones in use among their more advanced neighbors. Toward the fourth and third centuries B.C. the Scythian art of the Black Sea region thus tends naturally toward a graphic schematization of its forms, which makes them more of a linear ornamentation than a proto-writing."[82] Of course, one may write on jewelry, metal plaques, or even weapons, but only in the sense that one applies a preexisting writing system to these matters. The case of *runic writing* is more troubling because its origins seem exclusively tied to jewelry, fibulas, elements of metalworking, small movable objects. The point is that in its early period runic writing had only a weak communication value and a very restricted public function. Its secret character has led many to interpret it as magical writing. Rather, it is an affective semiotic, comprising in particular: (1) signatures, as marks of possession or fabrication, and (2) short war or love messages. It constitutes a text that is "ornamental" rather than scriptural, "an invention with little utility, half-aborted," a substitute writing. It only takes on the value of writing during a second period, when monumental inscriptions appear, with the Danish reform of the ninth century A.D., in connection with the State and work.[83]

It may be objected that tools, weapons, signs, and jewelry in fact occur everywhere, in a common sphere. But that is not the problem, any more than it is to seek an origin in each case. It is a question of assigning assemblages, in other words, of determining the *differential traits* according to which an element formally belongs to one assemblage rather than to another. It could also be said that architecture and cooking have an apparent affinity with the State, whereas music and drugs have differential traits that place them on the side of the nomadic war machine.[84] *It is therefore a differential method that establishes the distinction between weapons and tools*, from at least five points of view: the direction (*sens*) (projection-introception), the vector (speed-gravity), the model (free action-work), the expression (jewelry-signs), and the passional or desiring tonality (affect-feeling). Doubtless the State apparatus tends to bring uniformity to the regimes, by disciplining its armies, by making work a fundamental unit, in other words, by imposing its own traits. But it is not impossible for weapons and tools, if they are taken up by new assemblages of metamorphosis, to enter other relations of alliance. The man of war may at times form peasant or worker alliances, but it is more frequent for a worker, industrial or agricultural, to reinvent a war machine. Peasants made an important contribution to the history of artillery during the Hussite wars, when Žižka armed mobile fortresses made from oxcarts with portable cannons. A worker-soldier, weapon-tool, sentiment-affect affinity marks the right time, however fleeting, for revolutions and popular wars. There is a schizophrenic taste for the tool that moves it away from work and toward free action, a schizophrenic taste for the weapon that turns it into a means for peace, for obtaining peace. A counterattack and a resistance simultaneously. Everything is ambiguous. But we do not believe that Ernst Junger's analyses are disqualified by this ambiguity when he portrays the "Rebel" as a transhistorical figure drawing the Worker, on the one hand, and the Soldier, on the other, down a shared line of flight where one says simultaneously "I seek a weapon" and "I am looking for a tool": Draw the line, or what amounts to the same thing, cross the line, pass over the line, for the line is only drawn by surpassing the line of separation.[85] Undoubtedly, nothing is more outmoded than the man of war: he has long since been transformed into an entirely different character, the military man. And the worker himself has undergone so many misadventures . . . And yet men of war reappear, with many ambiguities: they are all those who know the uselessness of violence but who are adjacent to a war machine to be recreated, one of active, revolutionary counterattacks. Workers also reappear who do not believe in work but who are adjacent to a work machine to be recreated, one of active resistance and technological liberation. They do not resuscitate old myths or archaic figures; they are the new figures of a transhistorical assemblage (neither historical nor eternal, but untimely): the nomad warrior and the ambulant worker. A somber caricature already precedes them, the mercenary or mobile military adviser, and the technocrat or transhumant analyst, CIA and IBM. But transhistorical figures must defend themselves as much against old myths as against preestablished, anticipatory disfigurations. "One does not go back to reconquer the myth, one encounters it anew, when time quakes at its foundations under the empire of extreme danger." Martial arts and state-of-the-art technologies have value only because they create the possibility of bringing together worker and warrior masses of a new type. The shared line of flight of the weapon and the tool: a pure possibility, a mutation. There arise subterranean, aerial, submarine technicians who belong more or less to the world order, but who involuntarily invent and amass virtual charges of knowledge and action that are usable by others, minute but easily acquired for new assemblages. The borrowings between warfare and the military apparatus, work and free action, always run in both directions, for a struggle that is all the more varied.

PROBLEM III. *How do the nomads invent or find their weapons?*

PROPOSITION VIII. *Metallurgy in itself constitutes a flow necessarily confluent with nomadism.*

The political, economic, and social regime of the peoples of the steppe are less well known than their innovations in war, in the areas of offensive and defensive weapons, composition or strategy, and technological elements (the saddle, stirrup, horseshoe, harness, etc.). History contests each innovation but cannot succeed in effacing the nomad traces. What the nomads invented was the man-animal-weapon, man-horse-bow assemblage. Through this assemblage of speed, the ages of metal are marked by innovation. The socketed bronze battle-ax of the Hyksos and the iron sword of the Hittites have been compared to miniature atomic bombs. It has been possible to establish a rather precise periodization of the weapons of the steppe, showing the alternation between heavy and light armament (the Scythian type and the Sarmatian type), and their mixed forms. The cast steel saber, often short and curved, a weapon for side attack with the edge of the blade, envelops a different dynamic space than the forged iron sword used for frontal attack with the point: it was the Scythians who brought it to India and Persia, where the Arabs would later acquire it. It is commonly agreed that the nomads lost their role as innovators with the advent of firearms, in particular the cannon ("gunpowder overtook them"). But it was not necessarily because they did not know how to use them. Not only did armies like the Turkish army, whose nomadic traditions remained strong, develop extensive firepower, a new space, but additionally, and even more characteristically, light artillery was thoroughly integrated into mobile formations of wagons, pirate ships, etc. If the cannon marks a limit for the nomads, it is on the contrary because it implies an economic investment that only a State apparatus can make (even commercial cities do not suffice). The fact remains that for weapons other than firearms, and even for the cannon, there is always a nomad on the horizon of a given *technological lineage*.[86]

Obviously, each case is controversial, as demonstrated by the debates on the stirrup.[87] The problem is that it is generally difficult to distinguish between what comes from the nomads as such, and what they receive from the empire they communicate with, conquer, or integrate with. There are so many gray areas, intermediaries, and combinations between an imperial army and a nomad war machine that it is often the case that things originate in the empire. The example of the saber is typical, and unlike the stirrup, there is no longer any doubt. Although it is true that the Scythians were the propagators of the saber, introducing it to the Hindus, Persians, and Arabs, they were also its first victims, they started off on the receiving end; it was invented by the Chinese empire of the Ch'in and Han dynasties, the exclusive master of steel casting or crucible steel.[88] This is a good example to illustrate the difficulties facing modern archaeologists and historians. Even archaeologists are not immune from a certain hatred or contempt for the nomads. In the case of the saber, where the facts already speak sufficiently in favor of an imperial origin, the best of the commentators finds it fitting to add that the Scythians could not have invented it at any rate—poor nomads that they were—and that crucible steel necessarily came from a sedentary milieu. But why follow the very old, official Chinese version according to which deserters from the imperial army revealed the secrets to the Scythians? And what can "revealing the secret" mean if the Scythians were incapable of putting it to use, and understood nothing of all that? Blame the deserters, why don't you. You don't make an atomic bomb with a secret, any more than you make a saber if you are incapable of reproducing it, and of integrating it under different conditions, of transferring it to other assemblages. Propagation and diffusion are fully a part of the line of innovation; they mark a bend in it. On top of that, why say that crucible steel is necessarily the property of sedentaries or imperial subjects, when it is first of all the invention of metallurgists? It is assumed that these metallurgists were necessarily controlled by a State apparatus; but they also had to enjoy a certain technological autonomy, and social clandestinity, so that, even controlled, they did not belong to the State any more than they were themselves nomads. There were no deserters who betrayed the secret, but rather metallurgists who communicated it and made its adaptation and propagation possible: an entirely different kind of "betrayal." In the last analysis, what makes the discussions so difficult (both in the controversial case of the stirrup and in the definite case of the saber) are not only the prejudices about the nomads but also the absence of a sufficiently elaborated concept of the technological lineage (what defines a *technological line or continuum*, and its variable extension, from a given standpoint?).

It would be useless to say that metallurgy is a science because it discovers constant laws, for example, the melting point of a metal at all times and in all places. For metallurgy is inseparable from several lines of variation: variation between meteorites and indigenous metals; variation between ores and proportions of metal; variation between alloys, natural and artificial; variation between the operations performed upon a metal; variation between the qualities that make a given operation possible, or that result from a given operation (for example, twelve varieties of copper identified and inventoried at Sumer by place of origin and degree of refinement).[89] All of these variables can be grouped under two overall rubrics: *singularities or spatiotemporal haecceities* of different orders, and the operations associated with them as processes of deformation or transformation; *affective qualities or traits of expression* of different levels, corresponding to these singularities and operations (hardness, weight, color, etc.). Let us return to the example of the saber, or rather of crucible steel. It implies the actualization of a first singularity, namely, the melting of the iron at high temperature; then a second singularity, the successive decarbonations; corresponding to these singularities are traits of expression—not only the hardness, sharpness, and finish, but also the undulations or designs traced by the crystallization and resulting from the internal structure of the cast steel. The iron sword is associated with entirely different singularities because it is forged and not cast or molded, quenched and not air cooled, produced by the piece and not in number; its traits of expression are necessarily very different because it pierces rather than hews, attacks from the front rather than from the side; even the expressive designs are obtained in an entirely different way, by inlay.[90] We may speak of a *machinic phylum*, or technological lineage, wherever we find *a constellation of singularities, prolongable by certain operations, which converge, and make the operations converge, upon one or several assignable traits of expression*. If the singularities or operations diverge, in different materials or in the same material, we must distinguish two different phyla: this is precisely the case for the iron sword, descended from the dagger, and the steel saber, descended from the knife. Each phylum has its own singularities and operations, its own qualities and traits, which determine the relation of desire to the technical element (the affects the saber "has" are not the same as those of the sword).

But it is always possible to situate the analysis on the level of singularities that are prolongable from one phylum to another, and to tie the two phyla together. At the limit, there is a single phylogenetic lineage, a single machinic phylum, ideally continuous: the flow of matter-movement, the flow of matter in continuous variation, conveying singularities and traits of expression. This operative and expressive flow is as much artificial as natural: it is like the unity of human beings and Nature. But at the same time, it is not realized in the here and now without dividing, differentiating. We will call an *assemblage* every constellation of singularities and traits deducted from the flow—selected, organized, stratified—in such a way as to converge (consistency) artificially and naturally; an assemblage, in this sense, is a veritable invention. Assemblages may group themselves into extremely vast constellations constituting "cultures," or even "ages"; within these constellations, the assemblages still differentiate the phyla or the flow, dividing it into so many different phylas, of a given order, on a given level, and introducing selective discontinuities in the ideal continuity of matter-movement. The assemblages cut the phylum up into distinct, differentiated lineages, at the same time as the machinic phylum cuts across them all, taking leave of one to pick up again in another, or making them coexist. A certain singularity embedded in the flanks of the phylum, for example, the chemistry of carbon, will be brought up to the surface by a given assemblage that selects, organizes, invents it, and through which all or part of the phylum passes, at a given place at a given time. We may distinguish in every case a number of very different lines. Some of them, phylogenetic lines, travel long distances between assemblages of various ages and cultures (from the blowgun to the cannon? from the prayer wheel to the propeller? from the pot to the motor?); others, ontogenetic lines, are internal to one assemblage and link up its various elements, or else cause one element to pass, often after a delay, into another assemblage of a different nature but of the same culture or age (for example, the horseshoe, which spread through agricultural assemblages). It is thus necessary to take into account the selective action of the assemblages upon the phylum, and the evolutionary reaction of the phylum as the subterranean thread that passes from one assemblage to another, or quits an assemblage, draws it forward and opens it up. *Vital impulse*? Leroi-Gourhan has gone the farthest toward a technological vitalism taking biological evolution in general as the model for technical evolution: a *Universal Tendency*, laden with all of the singularities and traits of expression, traverses technical and interior milieus that refract or differentiate it in accordance with the singularities and traits each of them retains, selects, draws together, causes to converge, invents.[91] There is indeed a machinic phylum in variation that creates the technical assemblages, whereas the assemblages invent the various phyla. A technological lineage changes significantly according to whether one draws it upon the phylum or inscribes it in the assemblages; but the two are inseparable.

So how are we to define this matter-movement, this matter-energy, this matter-flow, this matter in variation that enters assemblages and leaves them? It is a destratified, deterritorialized matter. It seems to us that Husserl brought thought a decisive step forward when he discovered a region of *vague and material* essences (in other words, essences that are vagabond, anexact and yet rigorous), distinguishing them from fixed, metric and formal, essences. We have seen that these vague essences are as distinct from formed things as they are from formal essences. They constitute fuzzy aggregates. They relate to a *corporeality* (materiality) that is not to be confused either with an intelligible, formal essentiality or a sensible, formed and perceived, thinghood. This corporeality has two characteristics: on the one hand, it is inseparable from passages to the limit as changes of state, from processes of deformation or transformation operate in a space-time itself anexact and that act in the manner of events (ablation, adjunction, projection . . .); on the other hand, it is inseparable from expressive or intensive qualities, which can be higher or lower in degree, and are produced in the manner of variable affects (resistance, hardness, weight, color . . .). There is thus an ambulant coupling, *events-affects*, which constitutes the vague corporeal essence and is distinct from the sedentary linkage, "fixed essence-properties of the thing deriving from the essence." Doubtless Husserl had a tendency to make the vague essence a kind of intermediary between the essence and the sensible, between the thing and the concept, a little like the Kantian schema. Is not roundness a schematic or vague essence, intermediary between rounded sensible things and the conceptual essence of the circle? In effect, roundness exists only as a threshold-affect (neither flat nor pointed) and as a limit-process (becoming rounded), through sensible things and technical agents, millstone, lathe, wheel, spinning wheel, socket, etc. But it is only "intermediary" to the extent that what is intermediary is autonomous, initially stretching *itself* between things, and between thoughts, to establish a whole new relation between thoughts and things, a *vague* identity between the two.

Certain distinctions proposed by Simondon can be compared to those of Husserl. For Simondon exposes the technological insufficiency of the matter-form model, in that it assumes a fixed form and a matter deemed homogeneous. It is the idea of the law that assures the model's coherence, since laws are what submit matter to this or that form, and, conversely, realize in matter a given property deduced from the form. But Simondon demonstrates that the *hylomorphic* model leaves many things, active and affective, by the wayside. On the one hand, to the formed or formable matter we must add an entire energetic materiality in movement, carrying *singularities or haecceities* that are already like implicit forms that are topological, rather than geometrical, and that combine with processes of deformation: for example, the variable undulations and torsions of the fibers guiding the operation of splitting wood. On the other hand, to the essential properties of the matter deriving from the formal essence we must add *variable intensive affects*, now resulting from the operation, now on the contrary making it possible: for example, wood that is more or less porous, more or less elastic and resistant. At any rate, it is a question of surrendering to the wood, then following where it leads by connecting operations to a materiality, instead of imposing a form upon a matter: what one addresses is less a matter submitted to laws than a materiality possessing a *nomos*. One addresses less a form capable of imposing properties upon a matter than material traits of expression constituting affects. Of course, it is always possible to "translate" into a model that which escapes the model; thus, one may link the materiality's power of variation to laws adapting a fixed form and a constant matter to one another. But this cannot be done without a distortion that consists in uprooting variables from their state of continuous variation, in order to extract from them fixed points and constant relations. Thus one throws the variables off, even changing the nature of the equations, which cease to be immanent to matter-movement (inequations, adequations). The question is not whether such a translation is conceptually legitimate—it is—but what intuition gets lost in it. In short, what Simondon criticizes the hylomorphic model for is taking form and matter to be two terms defined separately, like the ends of two half-chains whose connection can no longer be seen, like a simple relation of molding behind which there is a perpetually variable, continuous modulation that it is no longer possible to grasp.[92] The critique of the hylomorphic schema is based on "the existence, between form and matter, of a zone of medium and intermediary dimension," of energetic, molecular dimension—a space unto itself that deploys its materiality through matter, a number unto itself that propels its traits through form.

We always get back to this definition: the *machinic phylum* is materiality, natural or artificial, and both simultaneously; it is matter in movement, in flux, in variation, matter as a conveyor of singularities and traits of expression. This has obvious consequences: namely, this matter-flow can only be *followed.* Doubtless, the operation that consists in following can be carried out in one place: an artisan who planes follows the wood, the fibers of the wood, without changing location. But this way of following is only one particular sequence in a more general process. For artisans are obliged to follow in another way as well, in other words, to go find the wood where it lies, and to find the wood with the right kind of fibers. Otherwise, they must have it brought to them: it is only because merchants take care of one segment of the journey in reverse that the artisans can avoid making the trip themselves. But artisans are complete only if they are also prospectors; and the organization that separates prospectors, merchants, and artisans already mutilates artisans in order to make "workers" of them. We will therefore define the artisan as one who is determined in such a way as to follow a flow of matter, a *machinic phylum.* The artisan is *the itinerant, the ambulant.* To follow the flow of matter is to itinerate, to ambulate. It is intuition in action. Of course, there are second-order itinerancies where it is no longer a flow of matter that one prospects and follows, but, for example, a market. Nevertheless, it is always a flow that is followed, even if the flow is not always that of matter. And, above all, there are secondary itinerancies, which derive from another "condition," even if they are necessarily entailed by it. For example, a *transhumant,* whether a farmer or an animal raiser, changes land after it is worn out, or else seasonally; but transhumants only secondarily follow a land flow, because they undertake a rotation meant from the start to return them to the point from which they left, after the forest has regenerated, the land has rested, the weather has changed. Transhumants do not follow a flow, they draw a circuit; they only follow the part of the flow that enters into the circuit, even an ever-widening one. Transhumants are therefore itinerant only consequentially, or become itinerant only when their circuit of land or pasture has been exhausted, or when the rotation has become so wide that the flows escape the circuit. Even the merchant is a transhumant, to the extent that mercantile flows are subordinated to the rotation between a point of departure and a point of arrival (go get-bring back, import-export, buy-sell). Whatever the reciprocal implications, there are considerable differences between a flow and a circuit. The *migrant*, we have seen, is something else again. And the *nomad* is not primarily defined as an *itinerant* or as a *transhumant*, nor as a *migrant*, even though nomads become these consequentially. The primary determination of nomads is to occupy and hold a smooth space: it is this aspect that determines them as nomad (essence). On their own account, they will be transhumants, or itinerants, only by virtue of the imperatives imposed by the smooth spaces. In short, whatever the de facto mixes between nomadism, itinerancy, and transhumance, the primary concept is different in the three cases (smooth space, matter-flow, rotation). It is only on the basis of the distinct concept that we can make a judgment on the mix—on when it is produced, on the form in which it is produced, and on the order in which it is produced.

But in the course of the preceding discussion, we have wandered from the question: Why is the *machinic phylum*, the flow of matter, essentially metallic or metallurgical? Here again, it is only the distinct concept that can give us an answer, in that it shows that there is a special, primary relation between itinerance and metallurgy (deterritorialization). However, the examples we took from Husserl and Simondon concerned wood and clay as well as metals. Besides, are there not flows of grass, water, herds, which form so many phyla or matters in movement? It is easier for us to answer these questions now. For it is as if metal and metallurgy imposed upon and raised to consciousness something that is only hidden or buried in the other matters and operations. The difference is that elsewhere the operations occur between two thresholds, one of which constitutes the matter prepared for the operation, and the other the form to be incarnated (for example, the clay and the mold). The hylomorphic model derives its general value from this, since the incarnated form that marks the end of an operation can serve as the matter for a new operation, but in a fixed order marking a succession of thresholds. In metallurgy, on the other hand, the operations are always astride the thresholds, so that an energetic materiality overspills the prepared matter, and a qualitative deformation or transformation overspills the form.[93] For example, quenching follows forging and takes place after the form has been fixed. Or, to take another example, in molding, the metallurgist in a sense works inside the mold. Or again, steel that is melted and molded later undergoes a series of successive decarbonations. Finally, metallurgy has the option of melting down and reusing a matter to which it gives an *ingot-form*: the history of metal is inseparable from this very particular form, which is not to be confused with either a stock or a commodity; monetary value derives from it. More generally, the metallurgical idea of the "reducer" expresses this double liberation of a materiality in relation to a prepared matter, and of a transformation in relation to the form to be incarnated. Matter and form have never seemed more rigid than in metallurgy; yet the succession of forms tends to be replaced by the form of a continuous development, and the variability of matters tends to be replaced by the matter of a continuous variation. If metallurgy has an essential relation with music, it is by virtue not only of the sounds of the forge but also of the tendency within both arts to bring into its own, beyond separate forms, a continuous development of form, and beyond variable matters, a continuous variation of matter: a widened chromaticism sustains both music and metallurgy; the musical smith was the first "transformer."[94] In short, what metal and metallurgy bring to light is a life proper to matter, a vital state of matter as such, a material vitalism that doubtless exists everywhere but is ordinarily hidden or covered, rendered unrecognizable, dissociated by the hylomorphic model. Metallurgy is the consciousness or thought of the matter-flow, and metal the correlate of this consciousness. As expressed in panmetallism, metal is coextensive to the whole of matter, and the whole of matter to metallurgy. Even the waters, the grasses and varieties of wood, the animals are populated by salts or mineral elements. Not everything is metal, but metal is everywhere. Metal is the conductor of all matter. The machinic phylum is metallurgical, or at least has a metallic head, as its itinerant probe-head or guidance device. And thought is born more from metal than from stone: metallurgy is minor science in person, "vague" science or the phenomenology of matter. The prodigious idea of *Nonorganic Life*—the very same idea Worringer considered the barbarian idea par excellence[95]—was the invention, the intuition of metallurgy. Metal is neither a thing nor an organism, but a *body* without organs. The "Northern, or Gothic, line" is above all a mining or metallic line delimiting this body. The relation between metallurgy and alchemy reposes not, as Jung believed, on the symbolic value of metal and its correspondence with an organic soul but on the immanent power of corporeality in all matter, and on the esprit de corps accompanying it.

The first and primary itinerant is the artisan. But artisans are neither hunters, farmers, nor animal raisers. Neither are they winnowers or potters, who only secondarily take up craft activity. Rather, artisans are those who follow the matter-flow as pure productivity: therefore in mineral form, and not in vegetable or animal form. They are not of the land, or of the soil, but of the subsoil. Because metal is the pure productivity of matter, those who follow metal are producers of objects par excellence. As demonstrated by V. Gordon Childe, the metallurgist is the first specialized artisan, and in this respect forms a collective *body* (secret societies, guilds, journeymen's associations). Artisans-metallurgists are itinerants because they follow the matter-flow of the subsoil. Of course metallurgists have relations with "the others," those of the soil, land, and sky. They have relations with the farmers of the sedentary communities, and with the celestial functionaries of the empire who overcode those communities; in fact, they need them to survive, they depend on an imperial agricultural stockpile for their very sustenance.[96] But in their work, they have relations with the forest dwellers, and partially depend on them: they must establish their workshops near the forest in order to obtain the necessary charcoal. In their space, they have relations with the nomads, since the subsoil unites the ground (*sol*) of smooth space and the land of striated space: there are no mines in the alluvial valleys of the empire-dominated farmers; it is necessary to cross deserts, approach the mountains; and the question of control over the mines always involves nomadic peoples. *Every mine is a line of flight* that is in communication with smooth spaces—there are parallels today in the problems with oil.

Archaeology and history remain strangely silent on this question of the control over the mines. There have been empires with a strong metallurgical organization that had no mines; the Near East lacked tin, so necessary for the fabrication of bronze. Large quantities of metal arrived in ingot form, and from very far away (for instance, tin from Spain or even from Cornwall). So complex a situation implies not only a strong imperial bureaucracy and elaborate long-distance commercial circuits; it also implies a shifting politics, in which States confront an outside, in which very different peoples confront one another, or else reach some accommodation on particular aspects of the control of mines (extraction, charcoal, workshops, transportation). It is not enough to say that there are wars and mining expeditions; or to invoke "a Eurasian synthesis of the nomadic workshops from the approaches of China to the tip of Britanny," and remark that "the nomadic populations had been in contact with the principal metallurgical centers of the ancient world since prehistoric times."[97] What is needed is a better knowledge of the nomads' relations with these centers, with the smiths they themselves employed or frequented, with properly metallurgical peoples or groups who were their neighbors. What was the situation in the Caucasus and in the Altai? In Spain and North Africa? Mines are a source of flow, mixture, and escape with few equivalents in history. Even when they are well controlled by an empire that owns them (as in the Chinese and Roman empires), there is a major movement of clandestine exploitation, and of miners' alliances either with nomad and barbarian incursions or peasant revolts. The study of myths, and even ethnographic considerations on the status of smiths, divert us from these political questions. Mythology and ethnology do not have the right method in this regard. It is too often asked how *the others* "react" to the smith, and as a result, one succumbs to the usual platitudes about the ambivalence of *feelings;* it is said that the smith is simultaneously honored, feared, and scorned—more or less scorned among the nomads, more or less honored among the sedentaries.[98] But this loses sight of the reasons for this situation, of the specificity of the smiths themselves, of the nonsymmetrical relation they entertain with the nomads and the sedentaries, the type of *affects* they invent (metallic affect). Before looking at the feelings of others toward smiths, it is necessary to evaluate the smiths themselves as Other; as such, they have different affective relations with the sedentaries and the nomads.

There are no nomadic or sedentary smiths. Smiths are ambulant, itinerant. Particularly important in this respect is the way in which smiths live: their space is neither the striated space of the sedentary nor the smooth space of the nomad. Smiths may have a tent, they may have a house; they inhabit them in the manner of an "ore bed" (gîte, shelter, home, mineral deposit), like metal itself, in the manner of a cave or a hole, a hut half or all underground. They are cave dwellers not by nature but by artistry and need.[99] A splendid text by Elie Faure evokes the infernal progress of the itinerant peoples of India as they bore holes in space and create the fantastic forms corresponding to these breakthroughs, the vital forms of nonorganic life: "There at the shore of the sea, at the base of a mountain, they encountered a great wall of granite. Then they all entered the granite; in its shadows they lived, loved, worked, died, were born, and, three or four centuries afterward, they came out again, leagues away, having traversed the mountain. Behind them they left the emptied rock, its galleries hollowed out in every direction, its sculptured, chiseled walls, its natural or artificial pillars turned into a deep lacework with ten thousand horrible or charming figures. . . . Here man confesses unresistingly his strength and his nothingness. He does not exact the affirmation of a determined ideal from form. . . . He extracts it rough from formlessness, according to the dictates of the formless. He utilizes the indentations and accidents of the rock."[100] Metallurgical India. Transpierce the mountains instead of scaling them, excavate the land instead of striating it, bore holes in space instead of keeping it smooth, turn the earth into swiss cheese. An image from the film *Strike* [by Eisenstein] presents a holey space where a disturbing group of

Holey Space

people are rising, each emerging from his or her hole as if from a field mined in all directions. The sign of Cain is the corporeal and affective sign of the subsoil, passing through both the striated land of sedentary space and the nomadic ground (*sol*) of smooth space without stopping at either one, the vagabond sign of itinerancy, the double theft and double betrayal of the metallurgist, who shuns agriculture at the same time as animal raising. Must we reserve the name Cainite for these metallurgical peoples who haunt the depths of History? Prehistoric Europe was crisscrossed by the *battle-ax people*, who came in off the steppes like a detached metallic branch of the nomads, and the people known for their bell-shaped pottery, the *beaker people*, originating in Andalusia, a detached branch of megalithic agriculture.[101] Strange peoples, dolicocephalics and brachycephalics who mix and spread across all of Europe. Are they the ones who kept up the mines, boring holes in European space from every direction, constituting our European space?

Smiths are not nomadic among the nomads and sedentary among the sedentaries, nor half-nomadic among the nomads, half-sedentary among sedentaries. Their relation to others results from their internal itinerancy, from their vague essence, and not the reverse. It is in their specificity, it is by virtue of their itinerancy, by virtue of their inventing a holey space, that they necessarily communicate with the sedentaries *and* with the nomads (and with others besides, with the transhumant forest dwellers). They are in themselves double: a hybrid, an alloy, a twin formation. As Griaule says, Dogon smiths are not "impure" but "mixed," and it is because they are mixed that they are *endogamous*, that they do not intermarry with the pure, who have a simplified progeny while they reconstitute a twin progeny.[102] Childe demonstrates that metallurgists are necessarily doubled, that they exist two times, once as captured by and maintained within the apparatus of the oriental empire, again in the Aegean world, where they were much more mobile and much freer. *But the two segments cannot be separated*, simply by relating each of them to their particular context. The metallurgist belonging to an empire, the worker, presupposes a metallurgist-prospector, however far away; and the prospector ties in with a merchant, who brings the metal to the first metallurgist. In addition, the metal is worked on by each segment, and the ingot-form is common to them all: we must imagine less separate segments than a chain of mobile workshops constituting, from hole to hole, a line of variation, a gallery. Thus the metallurgists' relation to the nomads and the sedentaries also passes through the relations they have with other metallurgists.[103] This hybrid metallurgist, a weapon- and toolmaker, communicates with the sedentaries *and* with the nomads at the same time. Holey space itself communicates with smooth space and striated space. In effect, the machinic phylum or the metallic line passes through all of the assemblages: nothing is more deterritorialized than matter-movement. But it is not at all in the same way, and the two communications are not symmetrical. Worringer, in the domain of aesthetics, said that the abstract line took on two quite different expressions, one in barbarian Gothic art, the other in the organic classical art. Here, we would say that the phylum simultaneously has two different modes of liaison: it is always *connected* to nomad space, whereas it *conjugates* with sedentary space. On the side of the nomadic assemblages and war machines, it is a kind of rhizome, with its gaps, detours, subterranean passages, stems, openings, traits, holes, etc. On the other side, the sedentary assemblages and State apparatuses effect a capture of the phylum, put the traits of expression into a form or a code, make the holes resonate together, plug the lines of flight, subordinate the technological operation to the work model, impose upon the connections a whole regime of arborescent conjunctions.

AXIOM III. *The nomad war machine is the form of expression, of which itinerant metallurgy is the correlative form of content.*

	Content	Expression
Substance	Holey space (machinic phylum or matter-flow)	Smooth space
Form	Itinerant metallurgy	Nomad war machine

PROPOSITION IX. *War does not necessarily have the battle as its object, and more important, the war machine does not necessarily have war as its object, although war and the battle may be its necessary result (under certain conditions).*

We now come to three successive problems. First, is the battle the "object" of war? But also, is war the "object" of the war machine? And finally, to what extent is the war machine the "object" of the State apparatus? The ambiguity of the first two problems is certainly due to the term "object," but implies their dependency on the third. We must nevertheless approach these problems gradually, even if we are reduced to multiplying examples. The first question, that of the battle, requires an immediate distinction to be made between two cases: when a battle is sought, and when it is essentially avoided by the war machine. These two cases in no way coincide with the offensive and the defensive. But war in the strict sense (according to a conception of it that culminated in Foch) does seem to have the battle as its object, whereas guerrilla warfare explicitly aims for the *nonbattle*. However, the development of war into the war of movement, and into total war, also places the notion of the battle in question, as much from the offensive as the defensive points of view: the concept of the nonbattle seems capable of expressing the speed of a flash attack, and the counterspeed of an immediate response.[104] Conversely, the development of guerilla warfare implies a moment when, and forms under which, a battle must be effectively sought, in connection with exterior and interior "support points." And it is true that guerrilla warfare and war proper are constantly borrowing each other's methods and that the borrowings run equally in both directions (for example, stress has often been laid on the inspirations land-based guerrilla warfare received from maritime war). All we can say is that the battle and the nonbattle are the double object of war, according to a criterion that does not coincide with the offensive and the defensive, or even with war proper and guerrilla warfare.

That is why we push the question further back, asking if war itself is the object of the war machine. It is not at all obvious. To the extent that war (with or without the battle) aims for the annihilation or capitulation of enemy forces, the war machine does not necessarily have war as its object (for example, the *raid* can be seen as another object, rather than as a particular form of war). But more generally, we have seen that the war machine was the invention of the nomad, because it is in its essence the constitutive element of smooth space, the occupation of this space, displacement within this space, and the corresponding composition of people: this is its sole and veritable positive object (*nomos*). Make the desert, the steppe, grow; do not depopulate it, quite the contrary. If war necessarily results, it is because the war machine collides with States and cities, as forces (of striation) opposing its positive object: from then on, the war machine has as its enemy the State, the city, the state and urban phenomenon, and adopts as its objective their annihilation. It is at this point that the war machine becomes war: annihilate the forces of the State, destroy the State-form. The Attila, or Genghis Khan, adventure clearly illustrates this progression from the positive object to the negative object. Speaking like Aristotle, we would say that war is neither the condition nor the object of the war machine, but necessarily accompanies or completes it; speaking like Derrida, we would say that war is the "supplement" of the war machine. It may even happen that this supplementarity is comprehended through a progressive, anxiety-ridden revelation. Such, for example, was the adventure of Moses: leaving the Egyptian State behind, launching into the desert, he begins by forming a war machine, on the inspiration of the old past of the nomadic Hebrews and on the advice of his father-in-law, who came from the nomads. This is the machine of the Just, already a war machine, but one that does not yet have war as its object. Moses realizes, little by little, in stages, that war is the necessary supplement of that machine, because it encounters or must cross cities and States, because it must send ahead spies (*armed observation*), then perhaps take things to extremes (*war of annihilation*). Then the Jewish people experience doubt, and fear that they are not strong enough; but Moses also doubts, he shrinks before the revelation of this supplement. And it will be Joshua, not Moses, who is charged with waging war. Finally, speaking like Kant, we would say that the relation between war and the war machine is necessary but "synthetic" (Yahweh is necessary for the synthesis).

The question of war, in turn, is pushed further back and is subordinated to the relations between the war machine and the State apparatus. States were not the first to make war: war, of course, is not a phenomenon one finds in the universality of Nature, as nonspecific violence. But war is not the object of States, quite the contrary. The most archaic States do not even seem to have had a war machine, and their domination, as we will see, was based on other agencies (comprising, rather, the police and prisons). It is safe to assume that the intervention of an extrinsic or nomad war machine that counterattacked and destroyed the archaic but powerful States was one of the mysterious reasons for their sudden annihilation. But the State learns fast. One of the biggest questions from the point of view of universal history is: How will the State *appropriate* the war machine, that is, constitute one for itself, in conformity with its size, its domination, and its aims? And with what risks? (What we call a military institution, or army, is not at all the war machine in itself, but the form under which it is appropriated by the State.) In order to grasp the paradoxical character of such an undertaking, we must recapitulate the hypothesis in its entirety. (1) The war machine is that nomad invention that in fact has war not as its primary object but as its second-order, supplementary or synthetic objective, in the sense that it is determined in such a way as to destroy the State-form and city-form with which it collides. (2) When the State appropriates the war machine, the latter obviously changes in nature and function, since it is afterward directed against the nomad and all State destroyers, or else expresses relations between States, to the extent that a State undertakes exclusively to destroy another State or impose its aims upon it. (3) It is precisely after the war machine has been appropriated by the State in this way that it tends to take war for its direct and primary object, for its "analytic" object (and that war tends to take the battle for its object). In short, it is at one and the same time that the State apparatus appropriates a war machine, that the war machine takes war as its object, and that war becomes subordinated to the aims of the State.

This question of appropriation is so varied historically that it is necessary to distinguish between several kinds of problems. The first concerns the possibility of the operation: it is precisely because war is only the supplementary or synthetic object of the nomad war machine that it experiences the hesitation that proves fatal to it, and that the State apparatus for its part is able to lay hold of war and thus turn the war machine back against the nomads. The hesitation of the nomad is legendary: What is to be done with the lands conquered and crossed? Return them to the desert, to the steppe, to open pastureland? Or let a State apparatus survive that is capable of exploiting them directly, at the risk of becoming, sooner or later, simply a new dynasty of that apparatus: sooner or later because Genghis Khan and his followers were able to hold out for a long time by partially integrating themselves into the conquered empires, while at the same time maintaining a smooth space on the steppes to which the imperial centers were subordinated. That was their genius, the *Pax Mongolica*. It remains the case that the integration of the nomads into the conquered empires was one of the most powerful factors of appropriation of the war machine by the

State apparatus: the inevitable danger to which the nomads succumbed. But there is another danger as well, the one threatening the State when it appropriates the war machine (all States have felt the weight of this danger, as well as the risks this appropriation represents for them). Tamerlane is the extreme example. He was not Genghis Khan's successor but his exact opposite: it was Tamerlane who constructed a fantastic war machine turned back against the nomads, but who, by that very fact, was obliged to erect a State apparatus all the heavier and more unproductive since it existed only as the empty form of appropriation of that machine.[105] Turning the war machine back against the nomads may constitute for the State a danger as great as that presented by nomads directing the war machine against States.

A second type of problem concerns the concrete forms the appropriation of the war machine takes: Mercenary or territorial? A professional army or a conscripted army? A special body or national recruiting? Not only are these formulas not equivalent, but there are all the possible mixes between them. Perhaps the most relevant distinction to make, or the most general one, would be: Is there merely "encastment" of the war machine, or "appropriation" proper? The capture of the war machine by the State apparatus took place following two paths, by encasting a society of warriors (who arrived from without or arose from within), or on the contrary by constituting it in accordance with rules corresponding to civil society as a whole. Once again, there is passage and transition from one formula to another. Last, the third type of problem concerns the means of appropriation. We must consider from this standpoint the various data pertaining to the fundamental aspects of the State apparatus: *territoriality, work or public works, taxation*. The constitution of a military institution or an army necessarily implies a territorialization of the war machine, in other words, the granting of land ("colonial" or domestic), which can take very diverse forms. But at the same time, fiscal regimes determine both the nature of the services and taxes owed by the beneficiary warriors, and especially the kind of civil tax to which all or part of society is subject for the maintenance of the army. And the State enterprise of public works must be reorganized along the lines of a "laying out of the territory" in which the army plays a determining role, not only in the case of fortresses and fortified cities, but also in strategic communication, the logistical structure, the industrial infrastructure, etc. (the role and function of the Engineer in this form of appropriation).[106]

Let us compare this hypothesis as a whole with Clausewitz's formula: "War is the continuation of politics by other means." As we know, this formula is itself extracted from a theoretical and practical, historic and transhistoric, aggregate whose parts are interconnected. (1) There is a pure concept of war as absolute, unconditioned war, an Idea not given in experience (bring down or "upset" the enemy, who is assumed to have no other determination, with no political, economic, or social considerations entering in). (2) What is given are real wars as submitted to State aims; States are better or worse "conductors" in relation to absolute war, and in any case condition its realization in experience. (3) Real wars swing between two poles, both subject to State politics: the war of annihilation, which can escalate to total war (depending on the objectives of the annihilation) and tends to approach the unconditioned concept via an ascent to extremes; and limited war, which is no "less" a war, but one that effects a descent toward limiting conditions, and can de-escalate to mere "armed observation."[107]

In the first place, the distinction between absolute war as Idea and real wars seems to us to be of great importance, but only if a different criterion than that of Clausewitz is applied. The pure Idea is not that of the abstract elimination of the adversary but that of a war machine *that does not have war as its object* and that only entertains a potential or supplementary synthetic relation with war. Thus the nomad war machine does not appear to us to be one case of real war among others, as in Clausewitz, but on the contrary the content adequate to the Idea, the invention of the Idea, with its own objects, space, and composition of the *nomos*. Nevertheless it is still an Idea, and it is necessary to retain the concept of the pure Idea, even though this war machine was realized by the nomads. It is the nomads, rather, who remain an abstraction, an Idea, something real and nonactual, and for several reasons: first, because the elements of nomadism, as we have seen, enter into de facto mixes with elements of migration, itinerancy, and transhumance; this does not affect the purity of the concept, but introduces always mixed objects, or combinations of space and composition, which react back upon the war machine from the beginning. Second, even in the purity of its concept, the nomad war machine necessarily effectuates its synthetic relation with war as supplement, uncovered and developed in opposition to the State-form, the destruction of which is at issue. But that is exactly it; it does not effectuate this supplementary object or this synthetic relation without the State, for its part, finding the opportunity to appropriate the war machine, and the means of making war the direct object of this turned-around machine (thus the integration of the nomad into the State is a vector traversing nomadism from the very beginning, from the first act of war against the State).

The question is therefore less the realization of war than the appropriation of the war machine. It is at the same time that the State apparatus *appropriates* the war machine, subordinates it to its "political" *aims*, and gives it war as its direct *object*. And it is one and the same historical tendency that causes State to evolve from a triple point of view: going from figures of encastment to forms of appropriation proper, going from limited war to so-called total war, and transforming the relation between aim and object. The factors that make State war total war are closely connected to capitalism: it has to do with the investment of constant capital in equipment, industry, and the war economy, and the investment of variable capital in the population in its physical and mental aspects (both as warmaker and as victim of war).[108] Total war is not only a war of annihilation but arises when annihilation takes as its "center" not only the enemy army, or the enemy State, but the entire population and its economy. The fact that this double investment can be made only under prior conditions of limited war illustrates the irresistible character of the capitalist tendency to develop total war.[109] It is therefore true that total war remains subordinated to State political aims and merely realizes the *maximal conditions* of the appropriation of the war machine by the State apparatus. But it is also true that when total war becomes the object of the appropriated war machine, then at this level in the set of all possible conditions, the object and the aim enter into new relations that can reach the point of contradiction. This explains Clausewitz's vacillation when he asserts at one point that total war remains a war conditioned by the political aim of States, and at another that it tends to effectuate the Idea of unconditioned war. In effect, the aim remains essentially political and determined as such by the State, but the object itself has become unlimited. We could say that the appropriation has changed direction, or rather that States tend to unleash, reconstitute, an immense war machine of which they are no longer anything more than the opposable or apposed parts. This worldwide war machine, which in a way "reissues" from the States, displays two successive figures: first, that of fascism, which makes war an unlimited movement with no other aim than itself; but fascism is only a rough sketch, and the second, postfascist, figure is that of a war machine that takes peace as its object directly, as the peace of Terror or Survival. The war machine reforms a smooth space that now claims to control, to surround the entire earth. Total war itself is surpassed, toward a form of peace more terrifying still. The war machine has taken charge of the aim, worldwide order, and the States are now no more than objects or means adapted to that machine. This is the point at which Clausewitz's formula is effectively reversed; to be entitled to say that politics is the continuation of war by other means, it is not enough to invert the order of the words as if they could be spoken in either direction; it is necessary to follow the real movement at the conclusion of which the States, having appropriated a war machine, and having adapted it to their aims, reimpart a war machine that takes charge of the aim, appropriates the States, and assumes increasingly wider political functions.[110]

Doubtless, the present situation is highly discouraging. We have watched the war machine grow stronger and stronger, as in a science fiction story; we have seen it assign as its objective a peace still more terrifying than fascist death; we have seen it maintain or instigate the most terrible of local wars as parts of itself; we have seen it set its sights on a new type of enemy, no longer another State, or even another regime, but the "unspecified enemy"; we have seen it put its counterguerrilla elements into place, so that it can be caught by surprise once, but not twice. Yet the very conditions that make the State or World war machine possible, in other words, constant capital (resources and equipment) and human variable capital, continually recreate unexpected possibilities for counterattack, unforeseen initiatives determining revolutionary, popular, minority, mutant machines. The definition of the Unspecified Enemy testifies to this: "multiform, maneuvering and omnipresent . . . of the moral, political, subversive or economic order, etc.," the unassignable material Saboteur or human Deserter assuming the most diverse forms.[111] The first theoretical element of importance is the fact that the war machine has many varied meanings, and this is *precisely because the war machine has an extremely variable relation to war itself.* The war machine is not uniformly defined, and comprises something other than increasing quantities of force. We have tried to define two poles of the war machine: *at one pole*, it takes war for its object and forms a line of destruction prolongable to the limits of the universe. But in all of the shapes it assumes here—limited war, total war, worldwide organization—war represents not at all the supposed essence of the war machine but only, whatever the machine's power, either the set of conditions under which the States appropriate the machine, even going so far as to project it as the horizon of the world, or the dominant order of which the States themselves are now only parts. *The other pole* seemed to be the essence; it is when the war machine, with infinitely lower "quantities," has as its object not war but the drawing of a creative line of flight, the composition of a smooth space and of the movement of people in that space. At this other pole, the machine does indeed encounter war, but as its supplementary or synthetic object, now directed against the State and against the worldwide axiomatic expressed by States.

We thought it possible to assign the invention of the war machine to the nomads. This was done only in the historical interest of demonstrating that the war machine as such was invented, even if it displayed from the beginning all of the ambiguity that caused it to enter into composition with the other pole, and swing toward it from the start. However, in conformity with the essence, the nomads do not hold the secret: an "ideological," scientific, or artistic movement can be a potential war machine, to the precise extent to which it draws, in relation to a *phylum*, a plane of consistency, a creative line of flight, a smooth space of displacement. It is not the nomad who defines this constellation of characteristics; it is this constellation that defines the nomad, and at the same time the essence of the war machine. If guerrilla warfare, minority warfare, revolutionary and popular war are in conformity with the essence, it is because they take war as an object all the more necessary for being merely "supplementary": *they can make war only on the condition that they simultaneously create something else*, if only new nonorganic social relations. The difference between the two poles is great, even, and especially, from the point of view of death: the line of flight that creates, *or* turns into a line of destruction; the plane of consistency that constitutes itself, even piece by piece, *or* turns into a plan(e) of organization and domination. We are constantly reminded that there is communication between these two lines or planes, that each takes nourishment from the other, borrows from the other: the worst of the world war machines reconstitutes a smooth space to surround and enclose the earth. But the earth asserts its own powers of deterritorialization, its lines of flight, its smooth spaces that live and blaze their way for a new earth. The question is not one of quantities but of the incommensurable character of the quantities that confront one another in the two kinds of war machine, according to the two poles. War machines take shape against the apparatuses that appropriate the machine and make war their affair and their object: they bring connections to bear against the great conjunction of the apparatuses of capture or domination.

13. 7000 B.C.: Apparatus of Capture

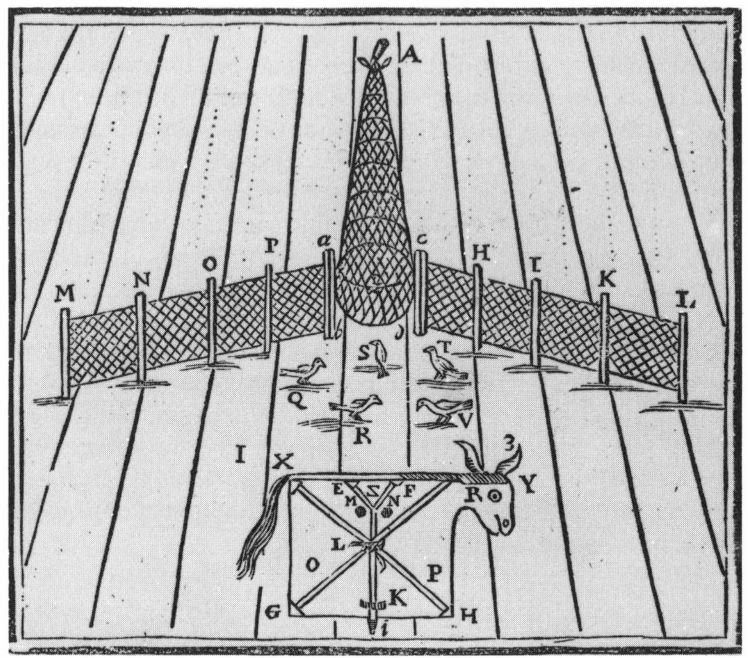

PROPOSITION X. *The State and its poles.*

Let us return to Dumézil's theses: (1) Political sovereignty has two poles, the fearsome magician-emperor, operating by capture, bonds, knots, and nets, and the jurist-priest-king, proceeding by treaties, pacts, contracts (the couples Varuna-Mitra, Odin-Tyr, Wotan-Tiwaz, Uranus-Zeus, Romulus-Numa . . .); (2) the war function is exterior to political sovereignty and is equally distinct from both its poles (Indra or Thor or Tullus Hostilius . . .).[1]

1. The State apparatus is thus animated by a curious rhythm, which is first of all a great mystery: that of the Binder-Gods or magic emperors, *One-Eyed* men emitting from their single eye signs that capture, tie knots at a distance. The jurist-kings, on the other hand, are *One-Armed* men who raise their single arm as an element of right and technology, the law and the tool. In the succession of men of State, look always for the One-Eyed and the One-Armed, Horatius Cocles and Mucius Scaevola (de Gaulle and

Pompidou?). This is not to say that one has exclusive right to signs, the other to tools. The fearsome emperor is already the master of large-scale works; the wise king takes up and transforms the entire regime of signs. What it means is that the combination, signs-tools, constitutes the differential trait of political sovereignty, or the complementarity of the State.[2]

2. Of course, the two men of State are always getting mixed up in affairs of war. But either the magic emperor sends to battle warriors who are not his own, whom he takes into his service by capture; or, more important, when he makes his appearance on the battlefield, he suspends the use of weapons, he throws his net over the warriors, his single eye throws them into petrified catatonia, "he binds without combat," he *encasts* the war machine (this State capture is not to be confused with the captures of war: conquests, prisoners, spoils).[3] As for the other pole, the jurist-king is a great organizer of war; but he gives it laws, lays out a field for it, makes it principled, imposes a discipline upon it, subordinates it to political ends. He turns the war machine into a military institution, he *appropriates* the war machine for the State apparatus.[4] We should not be too hasty in speaking of a softening, a humanization: on the contrary, this is perhaps when the war machine has only one remaining object, that of war itself. Violence is found everywhere, but under different regimes and economies. The violence of the magic emperor: his knot, his net, his way of "making his moves once and for all" . . . The violence of the jurist-king: his way of beginning over again every move, always with attention to ends, alliances, and laws . . . All things considered, the violence of the war machine might appear softer and more supple than that of the State apparatus because it does not yet have war as its "object," because it eludes both poles of the State. That is why the man of war, in his exteriority, is always protesting the alliances and pacts of the jurist-king, as well as severing the bonds of the magic emperor. He is equally an unbinder and a betrayer: twice the traitor.[5] He has another economy, another cruelty, but also another justice, another pity. To the signs and tools of the State, the man of war opposes his weapons and jewelry. Once again, who could say which is better and which is worse? It is true that war kills, and hideously mutilates. But it is especially true after the State has appropriated the war machine. Above all, the State apparatus makes the mutilation, and even death, come first. It needs them preaccomplished, for people to be born that way, crippled and zombielike. The myth of the zombie, of the living dead, is a work myth and not a war myth. Mutilation is a consequence of war, but it is a necessary condition, a presupposition of the State apparatus and the organization of work (hence the native infirmity not only of the worker but also of the man of State himself, whether of the One-Eyed or the One-Armed type): "The brutal exhibition of severed flesh shocked me. . . . Wasn't it an integral part of technical per-

fection and the intoxication of it . . . ? Mankind has waged wars since the world began, but I can't remember one single example in the *Iliad* where the loss of an arm or a leg is reported. Mythology reserved mutilation for monsters, for human beasts of the race of Tantalus or Procrustes. . . . It is an optical illusion to attribute these mutilations to accidents. Actually, accidents are the result of mutilations that took place long ago in the embryo of our world; and the increase in amputations is one of the symptoms bearing witness to the triumph of the morality of the scalpel. The loss occurred long before it was visibly taken into account."[6] The State apparatus needs, at its summit as at its base, predisabled people, preexisting amputees, the stillborn, the congenitally infirm, the one-eyed and one-armed.

Thus there is a tempting three-part hypothesis: the war machine is "between" the two poles of political sovereignty and assures the passage from one pole to the other. It is indeed in that order, 1-2-3, that things seem to present themselves in myth and history. Take two versions of the One-Eyed and the One-Armed gods analyzed by Dumézil: (1) the god Odin, who has a single eye, ties up the wolf of war and holds him in his magic bond; (2) but the wolf is wary and has at its disposal all its power of exteriority; (3) the god Tyr gives the wolf a legal security by leaving one of his hands in the wolf's mouth so the wolf can bite it off if it does not succeed in extricating itself from the bond. (1) Horatius Cocles, the One-Eyed, using only his face, his grimace and magic power, prevents the Etruscan commander from attacking Rome; (2) the war commander then decides to lay siege; (3) Mucius Scaevola takes a political tack, offering his hand as a security in order to persuade the warrior that it would be best to abandon the siege and conclude a pact.

In an entirely different, historical, context, Marcel Detienne suggests an analogous schema in three moments for ancient Greece: (1) The magic sovereign, the "Master of Truth," has at his disposal a war machine that doubtless does not originate with him, and which enjoys a relative autonomy within his empire; (2) this class of warriors has its own rules, defined by "isonomy," an isotropic space, and a "milieu" (war spoils are in the middle [*au milieu*], he who speaks places himself in the middle of the assembly); this is another space, the rules are different from those of the sovereign, who captures and speaks from on high; (3) the hoplite reform, the groundwork for which was laid in the warrior class, spread throughout the social body, promoting the formation of an army of citizen-soldiers; at the same time, the last vestiges of the imperial pole of sovereignty were replaced by the juridical pole of the city-state (with isonomy as its law, and isotropy as its space).[7] Thus in every case, the war machine seems to intervene "between" the two poles of the State apparatus, assuring and necessitating the passage from one to the other.

We cannot, however, assign this schema a causal meaning (the authors cited do not do so). In the first place, the war machine explains nothing; for it is either exterior to the State, and directed against it; or else it already belongs to the State, encasted and appropriated, and presupposes it. If the war machine has a part in the evolution of the State, it is therefore necessarily in conjunction with other internal factors. And this is the second point: if there is an evolution of the State, the second pole, the evolved pole, must be in resonance with the first, it must continually recharge it in some way, and the State must have only one milieu of interiority; in other words, it must have a *unity of composition*, in spite of all the differences in organization and development among States. It is even necessary for each State to have both poles, as the essential moments of its existence, even though the organization of the two varies. Third, if we call this interior essence or this unity of the State "capture," we must say that the words "magic capture" describe the situation well because it always appears as preaccomplished and self-presupposing; but how is this capture to be explained then, if it leads back to no *distinct* assignable cause? That is why theses on the origin of the State are always tautological. At times, exogenous factors, tied to war and the war machine, are invoked; at times endogenous factors, thought to engender private property, money, etc.; and at times specific factors, thought to determine the formation of "public functions." All three of these theses are found in Engels, in relation to a conception of the diversity of the roads to Domination. But they beg the question. War produces the State only if at least one of the two parts is a preexistent State; and the organization of war is a State factor only if that organization is a part of the State. Either the State has no war machine (and has policemen and jailers before having soldiers), or else it has one, but in the form of a military institution or public function.[8] Similarly, private property presupposes State public property, it slips through its net; and money presupposes taxation. It is even more difficult to see how public functions could have existed before the State they imply. We are always brought back to the idea of a State that comes into the world fully formed and rises up in a single stroke, the unconditioned *Urstaat*.

PROPOSITION XI. *Which comes first?*

We shall call the first pole of capture imperial or despotic. It corresponds to Marx's Asiatic formation. Archaeology discovers it everywhere, often lost in oblivion, at the horizon of all systems or States—not only in Asia, but also in Africa, America, Greece, Rome. Immemorial *Urstaat*, dating as far back as Neolithic times, and perhaps farther still. Following the Marxist description: a State apparatus is erected upon the primitive agricultural communities, which already have lineal-territorial codes; *but it overcodes them*, submitting them to the power of a despotic emperor, the sole and transcendent public-property owner, the master of the surplus or the stock, the organizer of large-scale works (surplus labor), the source of public functions and bureaucracy. This is the *paradigm* of the bond, the knot. Such is the regime of signs of the State: overcoding, or the Signifier. It is a system of *machinic enslavement*: the first "megamachine" in the strict sense, to use Mumford's term. A prodigious success in a single stroke; other States will be mere runts measured against this model. The emperor-despot is not a king or a tyrant; these will come into existence only as a function of private property once it has arisen.[9] In the imperial regime, everything is public: ownership of land is communal, each individual is an owner only insofar as he or she is a member of the community; the eminent property of the despot is that of the supposed Unity of the communities; and the functionaries themselves have land only if it comes with their position (although the position may be hereditary). Money may exist, notably in the form of the tax that the functionaries owe the emperor, but it is not used for buying-selling, since land does not exist as an alienable commodity. This is the regime of the *nexum*, the bond: something is lent or even given without a transfer of ownership, without private appropriation, and the compensation for it does not come in the form of interest or profit for the donor but rather as a "rent" that accrues to him, accompanying the lending of something for another's use or the granting of revenue.[10]

Marx, the historian, and Childe, the archaeologist, are in agreement on the following point: the archaic imperial State, which steps in to overcode agricultural communities, presupposes at least a certain level of development of these communities' productive forces since there must be a potential surplus capable of constituting a State stock, of supporting a specialized handicrafts class (metallurgy), and of progressively giving rise to public functions. That is why Marx links the archaic State to a certain "mode of production." However, the origin of these Neolithic States is still being pushed back in time. What is at issue when the existence of near-Paleolithic empires is conjectured is not simply the quantity of time; the qualitative problem changes. Çatal Hüyük, in Anatolia, makes possible a singularly reinforced imperial paradigm: it is a stock of uncultivated seeds and relatively tame animals from different territories that performs, and makes it possible to perform, at first by chance, hybridizations and selections *from which agriculture and small-scale animal raising arise*.[11] It is easy to see the significance of this change in the givens of the problem. It is no longer the stock that presupposes a potential surplus, but the other way around. It is no longer the State that presupposes advanced agricultural communities and developed forces of production. On the contrary, the State is established directly in a milieu of hunter-gatherers having no prior agriculture or metallurgy, and it is the State that creates agriculture, animal raising, and metallurgy; it does so first on its own soil, then imposes them upon the surrounding world. It is not the country that progressively creates the town but the town that creates the country. It is not the State that presupposes a mode of production; quite the opposite, it is the State that makes production a "mode." The last reasons for presuming a progressive development are invalidated. Like seeds in a sack: It all begins with a chance intermixing. The "state and urban revolution" may be Paleolithic, not Neolithic as Childe believed.

Evolutionism has been challenged in many different ways (zigzag movements, stages skipped here or there, irreducible overall breaks). We have seen in particular how Pierre Clastres tried to shatter the evolutionist framework by means of the following two theses: (1) societies termed primitive are not societies without a State, in the sense that they failed to reach a certain stage, but are counter-State societies organizing mechanisms that ward off the State-form, which make its crystallization impossible; (2) when the State arises, it is in the form of an irreducible break, since it is not the result of a progressive development of the forces of production (even the "Neolithic revolution" cannot be defined in terms of an economic infrastructure).[12] However, one does not depart from evolutionism by establishing a clean break. In the final state of his work, Clastres maintained the preexistence and autarky of counter-State societies, and attributed their workings to an overmysterious presentiment of what they warded off and did not yet exist. More generally, one marvels at the bizarre indifference that ethnology manifests for archaeology. It seems as though ethnologists, fenced off in their respective territories, are willing to compare their territories in an abstract, or structural, way, if it comes to that, but refuse to set them against archaeological territories that would compromise their autarky. They take snapshots of their primitives but rule out in advance the coexistence and superposition of the two maps, the ethnographical and the archaeological. Çatal Hüyük, however, would have had a zone of influence extending two thousand miles; how can the ever-recurring problem of the relation of coexistence between primitive societies and empires, even those of Paleolithic times, be left unattended to? As long as archaeology is passed over, the question of the relation between ethnology and history is reduced to an idealist confrontation, and fails to wrest itself from the absurd theme of society without history, or society against history. *Everything is not of the State precisely because there have been States always and everywhere.* Not only does writing presuppose the State, but so do speech and language. The self-sufficiency, autarky, independence, preexistence of primitive communities, is an ethnological dream: not that these communities necessarily depend on States, but they coexist with them in a complex network. It is plausible that "from the beginning" primitive societies have maintained distant ties to one another, not just short-range ones, and that these ties were channeled through States, even if States effected only a partial and local capture of them. Speech communities and languages, independently of writing, do not define closed groups of people who understand one another but primarily determine relations between groups who do not understand one another: if there is language, it is fundamentally between those who do not speak the same tongue. Language is made for that, for translation, not for communication. And in primitive societies there are as many tendencies that "seek" the State, as many vectors working in the direction of the State, as there are movements within the State or outside it that tend to stray from it or guard themselves against it, or else to stimulate its evolution, or else already to abolish it: everything coexists, in perpetual interaction.

Economic evolutionism is an impossibility; even a ramified evolution, "gatherers—hunters—animal breeders—farmers-industrialists," is hardly believable. An evolutionary ethnology is no better: "nomads—seminomads—sedentaries." Nor an ecological evolutionism: "dispersed autarky of local groups—villages and small towns—cities—States." All we need to do is combine these abstract evolutions to make all of evolutionism crumble; for example, it is the city that creates agriculture, without going through small towns. To take another example, the nomads do not precede the sedentaries; rather, nomadism is a movement, a becoming that affects sedentaries, just as sedentarization is a stoppage that settles the nomads. Griaznov has shown in this connection that the most ancient nomadism can be accurately attributed only to populations that abandoned their semiurban sedentarity, or their primitive itineration, to set off nomadizing.[13] It is under these conditions that the nomads invented the war machine, as that which occupies or fills nomad space and opposes towns and States, which its tendency is to abolish. Primitive peoples already had mechanisms of war that converged to prevent the State formation; but these mechanisms change when they gain autonomy in the form of a specific nomadism machine that strikes back against the States. We cannot, however, infer from this even a zigzag evolution that would go from primitive peoples to States, from States to nomad war machines; or at least the zigzagging is not successive but passes through the loci of a topology that defines primitive societies here, States there, and elsewhere war machines. And even when the State appropriates the war machine, once again changing its nature, it is a phenomenon of transport, of transfer, and not one of evolution. The nomad exists only in becoming, and in interaction; the same goes for the primitive. All history does is to translate a coexistence of becomings into a succession. And collectivities can be transhumant, semisedentary, sedentary, or nomadic, without by the same token being preparatory stages for the State, which is already there, elsewhere or beside.

Can it at least be said that the hunter-gatherers are the "true" primitives and remain in spite of it all the basis or minimal presupposition of the State formation, however far back in time we place it? This point of view can be maintained only at the price of a very inadequate conception of causality. And it is true that the human sciences, with their materialist, evolutionary, and even dialectical schemas, lag behind the richness and complexity of causal relations in physics, or even in biology. Physics and biology present us with reverse causalities that are *without finality* but testify nonetheless to an action of the future on the present, or of the present on the past, for example, the convergent wave and the anticipated potential, which imply an inversion of time. More than breaks or zigzags, it is these reverse causalities that shatter evolution. Similarly, in the present context, it is not adequate to say that the Neolithic or even Paleolithic State, once it appeared, reacted back on the surrounding world of the hunter-gatherers; it was already acting before it appeared, as the actual limit these primitive societies warded off, or as the point toward which they converged but could not reach without self-destructing. These societies simultaneously have vectors moving in the direction of the State, mechanisms warding it off, and a point of convergence that is repelled, set outside, as fast as it is approached. To ward off is also to anticipate. Of course, it is not at all in the same way that the State appears in existence, and that it preexists in the capacity of a warded-off limit; hence its irreducible contingency. But in order to give a positive meaning to the idea of a "presentiment" of what does not yet exist, it is necessary to demonstrate that what does not yet exist is already in action, in a different form than that of its existence. Once it has appeared, the State reacts back on the hunter-gatherers, imposing upon them agriculture, animal raising, an extensive division of labor, etc.; it acts, therefore, in the form of a centrifugal or divergent wave. But before appearing, the State already acts in the form of the convergent or centripetal wave of the hunter-gatherers, *a wave that cancels itself out precisely at the point of convergence marking the inversion of signs or the appearance of the State* (hence the functional and intrinsic instability of these primitive societies).[14] It is necessary from this standpoint to conceptualize the contemporaneousness or coexistence of the two inverse movements, of the two directions of time—of the primitive peoples "before" the State, and of the State "after" the primitive peoples—as if the two waves that seem to us to exclude or succeed each other unfolded simultaneously in an "archaeological," micropolitical, micrological, molecular field.

There exist collective mechanisms that simultaneously ward off and anticipate the formation of a central power. The appearance of a central power is thus a function of *a threshold or degree* beyond which what is anticipated takes on consistency or fails to, and what is conjured away ceases to be so and arrives. This threshold of consistency, or of constraint, is not evolutionary but rather coexists with what has yet to cross it. Moreover, a distinction must be made between different thresholds of consistency: the town and the State, however complementary, are not the same thing. The "urban revolution" and the "state revolution" may coincide but do not meld. In both cases, there is a central power, but it does not assume the same figure. Certain authors have made a distinction between the palatial or imperial system (temple-palace), and the urban, town system. In both cases there is a town, but in one case the town is an outgrowth of the palace or temple, and in the other case the palace, the temple, is a concretion of the town. In one case, the town par excellence is the capital, and in the other it is the metropolis. Sumer already attests to a town solution, as opposed to the imperial solution of Egypt. But to an even greater extent, it was the Mediterranean world, with the Pelasgians, Phoenicians, Greeks, Carthaginians, that created an urban fabric distinct from the imperial organisms of the Orient.[15] Once again, the question is one not of evolution but of two thresholds of consistency that are themselves coexistent. They differ in several respects.

The town is the correlate of the road. The town exists only as a function of circulation, and of circuits; it is a remarkable point on the circuits that create it, and which it creates. It is defined by entries and exits; something must enter it and exit from it. It imposes a frequency. It effects a polarization of matter, inert, living or human; it causes the *phylum*, the flow, to pass through specific places, along horizontal lines. It is a phenomenon of *transconsistency*, a *network*, because it is fundamentally in contact with other towns. It represents a threshold of deterritorialization, because whatever the material involved, it must be deterritorialized enough to enter the network, to submit to the polarization, to follow the circuit of urban and road recoding. The maximum deterritorialization appears in the tendency of maritime and commercial towns to separate off from the backcountry, from the countryside (Athens, Carthage, Venice). The commercial character of the town has often been emphasized, but the commerce in question is also spiritual, as in a network of monasteries or temple-cities. Towns are circuit-points of every kind, which enter into counterpoint along horizontal lines; they effect a complete but local, town-by-town, integration. Each one constitutes a central power, but it is a power of polarization or of the middle (*milieu*), of forced coordination. That is why this kind of power has egalitarian pretensions, regardless of the form it takes: tyrannical, democratic, oligarchic, aristocratic. Town power invents the idea of the *magis-*

trature, which is very different from the State *civil-service sector* (*fonctionnariat*).[16] Who can say where the greatest civil violence resides?

The State indeed proceeds otherwise: it is a phenomenon of *intraconsistency*. It makes points *resonate* together, points that are not necessarily already town-poles but very diverse points of order, geographic, ethnic, linguistic, moral, economic, technological particularities. It makes the town resonate with the countryside. It operates by stratification; in other words, it forms a vertical, hierarchized aggregate that spans the horizontal lines in a dimension of depth. In retaining given elements, it necessarily cuts off their relations with other elements, which become exterior, it inhibits, slows down, or controls those relations; if the State has a circuit of its own, it is an internal circuit dependent primarily upon resonance, it is a zone of recurrence that isolates itself from the remainder of the network, even if in order to do so it must exert even stricter controls over its relations with that remainder. The question is not to find out whether what is retained is natural or artificial (boundaries), because in any event there is deterritorialization. But in this case deterritorialization is a result of the territory itself being taken as an object, as a material to stratify, to make resonate. Thus the central power of the State is hierarchical, and constitutes a civil-service sector; the center is not in the middle (*au milieu*), but on top, because the only way it can recombine what it isolates is through subordination. Of course, there is a multiplicity of States no less than of towns, but it is not the same type of multiplicity: there are as many States as there are vertical cross sections in a dimension of depth, each separated from the others, whereas the town is inseparable from the horizontal network of towns. Each State is a global (not local) integration, a redundancy of resonance (not of frequency), an operation of the stratification of the territory (not of the polarization of the milieu).

It is possible to reconstruct how primitive societies warded off both thresholds while at the same time anticipating them. Lévi-Strauss has shown that the same villages are susceptible to two presentations, one segmentary and egalitarian, the other encompassing and hierarchized. These are like *two potentials*, one anticipating a central point common to two horizontal segments, the other anticipating a central point external to a straight line.[17] Primitive societies do not lack formations of power; they even have many of them. But what prevents the potential central points from crystallizing, from taking on consistency, are precisely those mechanisms that keep the formations of power both from resonating together in a higher point and from becoming polarized at a common point: the circles are not concentric, and the two segments require a third segment through which to communicate.[18] This is the sense in which primitive societies have crossed neither the town-threshold nor the State-threshold.

If we now turn our attention to the two thresholds of consistency, it is clear that they imply a deterritorialization in relation to the primitive territorial codes. It is futile to ask which came first, the city or the State, the urban or state revolution, because the two are in reciprocal presupposition. Both the melodic lines of the towns and the harmonic cross sections of the States are necessary to effect the striation of space. The only question that arises is the possibility that there may be an inverse relation at the heart of this reciprocity. For although the archaic imperial State necessarily included towns of considerable size, they remained more or less strictly subordinated to the State, depending on how complete the State's monopoly over foreign trade was. On the other hand, the town tended to break free when the State's *overcoding* itself provoked *decoded* flows. A decoding was coupled with the deterritorialization, and amplified it; the necessary recoding was then achieved through a certain autonomy of the towns, or else directly through corporative and commercial towns freed from the State-form. Thus towns arose that no longer had a connection to their own land, because they assured the trade between empires, or better, constituted on their own a free commercial network with other towns. There is therefore an adventure specific to towns in the zones where the most intense decoding occurs, for example, the ancient Aegean world or the Western world of the Middle Ages and the Renaissance. Could it not be said that capitalism is the fruit of the towns, and arises when an urban recoding tends to replace State overcoding? This, however, was not the case. The towns did not create capitalism. The banking and commercial towns, being unproductive and indifferent to the backcountry, did not perform a recoding without also inhibiting the general conjunction of decoded flows. If it is true that they anticipated capitalism, they in turn did not anticipate it without also warding it off. They do not cross this new threshold. Thus it is necessary to expand the hypothesis of mechanisms both anticipatory and inhibiting: these mechanisms are at play not only in primitive societies but also in the conflict of towns "against" the State *and* "against" capitalism. Finally, it was through the State-form and not the town-form that capitalism triumphed; this occurred when the Western States became models of realization for an axiomatic of decoded flows, and in that way resubjugated the towns. As Braudel says, there were "*always two runners*, the state and the town"—two forms and two speeds of deterritorialization—and "the state usually won. . . . everywhere in Europe, it disciplined the towns with instinctive relentlessness, whether or not it used violence. . . . [The states] caught up with the forward gallop of the towns."[19] But the relation is a reciprocal one: if it is the modern State that gives capitalism its models of realization, what is thus realized is an independent, worldwide axiomatic that is like a single City, megalopolis, or "megamachine" of which the States are parts, or neighborhoods.

We define social formations by *machinic processes* and not by modes of production (these on the contrary depend on the processes). Thus primitive societies are defined by mechanisms of prevention-anticipation; State societies are defined by apparatuses of capture; urban societies, by instruments of polarization; nomadic societies, by war machines; and finally international, or rather ecumenical, organizations are defined by the encompassment of heterogeneous social formations. But precisely because these processes are variables of coexistence that are the object of a social topology, the various corresponding formations are coexistent. And they coexist in two fashions, extrinsically and intrinsically. Primitive societies cannot ward off the formation of an empire or State without anticipating it, and they cannot anticipate it without its already being there, forming part of their horizon. And States cannot effect a capture unless what is captured coexists, resists in primitive societies, or escapes under new forms, as towns or war machines . . . The numerical composition of the war machine is superposed upon the primitive lineal organization and simultaneously opposes the geometric organization of the State and the physical organization of the town. It is this extrinsic coexistence—interaction—that is brought to its own expression in international aggregates. For these obviously did not wait for capitalism before forming: as early as Neolithic times, even Paleolithic, we find traces of ecumenical organizations that testify to the existence of long-distance trade, and simultaneously cut across the most varied of social formations (as we have seen in the case of metallurgy). The problem of diffusion, or of diffusionism, is badly formulated if one assumes a center at which the diffusion would begin. Diffusion occurs only through the placing in communication of potentials of very different orders: all diffusion happens in the in-between, goes between, like everything that "grows" of the rhizome type. An international ecumenical organization does not proceed from an imperial center that imposes itself upon and homogenizes an exterior milieu; neither is it reducible to relations between formations of the same order, between States, for example (the League of Nations, the United Nations). On the contrary, it constitutes an intermediate milieu between the different coexistent orders. Therefore it is not exclusively commercial or economic, but is also religious, artistic, etc. From this standpoint, we shall call an international organization anything that has the capacity to move through diverse social formations simultaneously: States, towns, deserts, war machines, primitive societies. The great commercial formations in history do not simply have city-poles, but also primitive, imperial, and nomadic segments through which they pass, perhaps issuing out again in another form. Samir Amin is totally correct in saying that there can be no economic theory of international relations, even economic ones, because they sit astride heterogeneous formations.[20] The point of departure for ecumenical organization is not a State, even an imperial one; the imperial State is only one part of it, and it constitutes a part of it in its own mode, according to its own order, which consists in capturing everything it can. It does not proceed by progressive homogenization, or by totalization, but by the taking on of consistency or the consolidation of the diverse as such. For example, monotheistic religion is distinguished from territorial worship by its pretension to universality. But this pretension is not homogenizing, it makes itself felt only by spreading everywhere; this was the case with Christianity, which became imperial and urban, but not without giving rise to bands, deserts, war machines of its own.[21] Similarly, there is no artistic movement that does not have its towns and empires, but also its nomads, bands, and primitives.

It might be objected that, at least in the case of capitalism, international economic relations, and at the limit all international relations, tend toward the homogenization of social formations. One could cite not only the cold and concerted destruction of primitive societies but also the fall of the last despotic formations, for example, the Ottoman Empire, which met capitalist demands with too much resistance and inertia. This objection, however, is only partially accurate. To the extent that capitalism constitutes an axiomatic (production for the market), all States and all social formations tend to become *isomorphic* in their capacity as models of realization: there is but one centered world market, the capitalist one, in which even the so-called socialist countries participate. Worldwide organization thus ceases to pass "between" heterogeneous formations since it assures the isomorphy of those formations. But it would be wrong to confuse isomorphy with homogeneity. For one thing, isomorphy allows, and even incites, a great heterogeneity among States (democratic, totalitarian, and, especially, "socialist" States are not facades). For another thing, the international capitalist axiomatic effectively assures the isomorphy of the diverse formations only where the domestic market is developing and expanding, in other words, in "the center." But it tolerates, in fact it requires, a certain peripheral polymorphy, to the extent that it is not saturated, to the extent that it actively repels its own limits;[22] this explains the existence, at the periphery, of heteromorphic social formations, *which certainly do not constitute vestiges or transitional forms* since they realize an ultramodern capitalist production (oil, mines, plantations, industrial equipment, steel, chemistry), but which are nonetheless precapitalist, or extracapitalist, owing to other aspects of their production and to the forced inadequacy of their domestic market in relation to the world market.[23] When international organization becomes the capitalist axiomatic, it continues to imply a heterogeneity of social formations, it gives rise to and organizes its "Third World."

There is not only an external coexistence of formations but also an intrinsic coexistence of machinic processes. Each process can also function at a "power" other than its own; it can be taken up by a power corresponding to another process. The State as apparatus of capture has a *power of appropriation*; but this power does not consist solely in capturing all that it can, all that is possible, of a matter defined as *phylum*. The apparatus of capture also appropriates the war machine, the instruments of polarization, and the anticipation-prevention mechanisms. This is to say, conversely, that anticipation-prevention mechanisms have a high *power of transference:* they are at work not only in primitive societies, but move into the towns that ward off the State-form, into the States that ward off capitalism, into capitalism itself, insofar as it wards off and repels its own limits. And they are not satisfied to switch over to other powers but form new focal points of resistance and contagion, as we have seen in the case of "band" phenomena, which have their own towns, their own brand of internationalism, etc. Similarly, war machines have a *power of metamorphosis*, which of course allows them to be captured by States, but also to resist that capture and rise up again in other forms, with other "objects" besides war (revolution?). Each power is a force of deterritorialization that can go along with the others or go against them (even primitive societies have their vectors of deterritorialization). Each process can switch over to other powers, but also subordinate other processes to its own power.

PROPOSITION XII. *Capture.*

Is it possible to conceive of an "exchange" between separate primitive groups, independent of any reference to such notions as stock, labor, and commodity? It seems that a modified marginalism provides a basis for a hypothesis. For the interest of marginalism resides not in its economic theory, which is extremely weak, but in a logical power that makes Jevons, for example, a kind of Lewis Carroll of economics. Take two abstract groups, one of which (A) gives seeds and receives axes, while the other (B) does the opposite. What is the collective evaluation of the objects based on? It is based on the *idea* of the last objects received, or rather receivable, on each side. By "last" or "marginal" we must understand not the most recent, nor the final, but rather the penultimate, the next to the last, in other words, the last one *before* the apparent exchange loses its appeal for the exchangers, or forces them to modify their respective assemblages, to enter another assemblage. We will consider that the farmer-gatherer group A, which receives axes, has an "idea" of the number of axes that would force it to change assemblage; and the manufacturing group B, of the quantity of seeds that would force it to change assemblage. We may say, then, that the seed-ax relation is determined by the last quantity of seeds (for group B) corresponding to the last ax (for group A). The last as the object of a collective evaluation determines the value of the entire series. It marks the exact point at which the assemblage must reproduce itself, begin a new operation period or a new cycle, lodge itself on another territory, and beyond which the assemblage could not continue as such. This is indeed a next-to-the-last, a penultimate, since it comes before the ultimate. The ultimate is when the assemblage must change its nature: B would have to plant the excess seeds. A would have to increase the rhythm of its own plantings and remain on the same land.

We can now posit a conceptual difference between the "limit" and the "threshold": the limit designates the penultimate marking a necessary rebeginning, and the threshold the ultimate marking an inevitable change. It is an economic given of every enterprise to include an evaluation of the limit beyond which the enterprise would have to modify its structure. Marginalism claims to demonstrate the frequency of this penultimate mechanism: it applies not only to the last exchangeable objects but also to the last producible object, or the last producer him- or herself, the marginal or limit-producer before the assemblage changes.[24] This is an economics of everyday life. For example, what does an alcoholic call the *last glass?* The alcoholic makes a subjective evaluation of how much he or she can tolerate. What can be tolerated is precisely the limit at which, as the alcoholic sees it, he or she will be able to start over again (after a rest, a pause . . .). But beyond that limit there lies a threshold that would cause the alcoholic to change assemblage: it would change either the nature of the drinks or the customary places and hours of the drinking. Or worse yet, the alcoholic would enter a suicidal assemblage, or a medical, hospital assemblage, etc. It is of little importance that the alcoholic may be fooling him- or herself, or makes a very ambiguous use of the theme "I'm going to stop," the theme of the last one. What counts is the existence of a spontaneous marginal criterion and marginalist evaluation determining the value of the entire series of "glasses." The same goes for having *the last word* in a domestic-squabble assemblage. Both partners evaluate from the start the volume or density of the last word that would give them the advantage and conclude the discussion, marking the end of an operation period or cycle of the assemblage, allowing it to start all over again. Both calculate their words in accordance with their evaluation of this last word, and the vaguely agreed time for it to come. And beyond the last (penultimate) word there lie still other words, this time final words that would cause them to enter another assemblage, divorce, for example, because they would have overstepped "bounds." The same could be said for the *last love.* Proust has shown how a love can be oriented toward its own limit, its own margin: it repeats its own ending. A new love follows, so that each love is serial, so that there is a series of loves. But once again, "beyond" lies the ultimate, at the point where the assemblage changes, where the assemblage of love is superseded by an artistic assemblage—the Work to be written, which is the problem Proust tackles . . .

Exchange is only an appearance: each partner or group assesses the value of the last receivable object (limit-object), and the apparent equivalence derives from that. The equalization results from the two heterogeneous series, the exchange or communication results from two monologues (*palabre*). There is neither exchange value nor use value but rather an evaluation of the last by both parties (a calculation of the risk involved in crossing the limit), an anticipation-evaluation that takes into account the ritual character as well as the utilitarian, the serial character as well as the exchangist. The evaluation of the limit is there from the start in both groups, and already governs the first "exchange" between them. Of course there is groping in the dark; the evaluation is inseparable from a collective feeling out. But it does not bear on the quantity of social labor but on the idea of the last on both sides; the speed with which it is accomplished varies, but it is always done faster than the time necessary effectively to arrive at the last object, or even to pass from one operation to another.[25] This is the sense in which the evaluation is essentially anticipatory, that it is already present in the first terms of the series. It can be seen that marginal utility (pertaining to the last objects receivable on both sides) is relative not to an abstractly posited stock but to the respective assemblages of the two groups. Pareto was moving in this direction when he spoke of "ophelimity" rather than of marginal utility.[26] The issue is one of *desirability* as an assemblage component: every group desires according to the value of the last receivable object beyond which it would be obliged to change assemblage. And every assemblage has two sides, the machining of bodies or objects, and group enunciation. The evaluation of the last is the collective enunciation to which the *entire series* of objects corresponds; in other words, it is an assemblage cycle or operation period. Exchangist primitive groups thus appear to be serial groups. Theirs is a special regime, even with respect to violence. For even violence can be submitted to a marginal ritual treatment, that is, to an evaluation of the "last violence" insofar as it impregnates the entire series of blows (beyond which another regime of violence would begin). We previously defined primitive societies by the existence of *anticipation-prevention* mechanisms. Now we can see more clearly how these mechanisms are constituted and distributed: it is the evaluation of the last as limit that constitutes an anticipation and simultaneously wards off the last as threshold or ultimate (a new assemblage).

The threshold comes "after" the limit, "after" the last receivable objects: it marks the moment when the apparent exchange is no longer of interest. We believe that it is precisely at this moment that stockpiling begins; beforehand, there may be exchange granaries, granaries specifically for exchange purposes, but there is no stock in the strict sense. Exchange does not assume a preexistent stock, it assumes only a certain "elasticity." Stockpiling begins only once exchange has lost its interest, its desirability for both parties. Additionally, conditions must exist giving stockpiling an interest in its own right, a desirability of its own (otherwise, the objects would be destroyed or depleted rather than stockpiled: depletion is the means by which primitive groups ward off the stock and maintain their assemblage). The stock depends on a new type of assemblage. The expressions "after," "new," "to be superseded" are doubtless very ambiguous. The threshold is in fact already there, but outside the limit, which is satisfied to place the threshold at a distance, keep it at a distance. The problem is to know what this other assemblage is that gives the stock an actual interest, a desirability. The stock seems to us to have a necessary correlate: *either the coexistence of simultaneously exploited territories, or a succession of exploitations on one and the same territory.* It is at this point that the territories form a Land, are superseded by a Land. This is the assemblage that necessarily includes stockpiling, and which constitutes in the first case an extensive system of cultivation, in the second case an intensive system of cultivation (following Jane Jacobs's paradigm). The way in which the stock-threshold differs from the exchange-limit is now clear: primitive assemblages of hunter-gatherers have an operation period defined by the exploitation of a territory; the law is one of temporal succession because the assemblage perseveres only by switching territories at the conclusion of each operation period (itinerancy, itineration); and within each operation period there is a repetition or temporal series that tends toward the last object as an "index," as the marginal or limit-object of the territory (this iteration will govern the apparent exchange). On the other hand, in the other assemblage, in the stock assemblage, the law is one of spatial coexistence and concerns the simultaneous exploitation of different territories; or, when the exploitation is successive, the succession of operation periods bears on one and the same territory; and in the framework of each operation period or exploitation the force of serial iteration is superseded by a power of symmetry, reflection, and global comparison. In solely descriptive terms, we therefore distinguish between serial, itinerant, or territorial assemblages (which operate by codes) and sedentary, global, or Land assemblages (which operate by overcoding).

Ground rent, in its abstract model, appears precisely when a comparison is drawn between different simultaneously exploited territories, or between the successive exploitations of the same territory. The worst land (or the poorest exploitation) bears no rent, but it makes it so that the other soils do bear rent, "produce" it in a comparative way.[27] A stock is what permits the yields to be compared (the same planting on different soils, or various successive plantings on the same soil). The category of the *last* confirms once again its economic importance, but it has totally changed meaning: it no longer designates the end point of a self-fulfilling movement but the center of symmetry for two movements, one of which is descending and the other ascending; it no longer designates the limit of an ordinal series but the lowest element in a cardinal set, that set's threshold—the least fertile land in the set of simultaneously exploited lands.[28] Ground rent homogenizes, equalizes different conditions of productivity by linking the excess of the highest conditions of productivity over the lowest to a *landowner:* since the price (profit included) is established on the basis of the least productive land, rent taps the surplus profit accruing to the best lands; it taps "the difference between the product of two equal amounts of capital and labor."[29] This is the very model of an apparatus of capture, inseparable from a process of relative deterritorialization. The land as the object of agriculture in fact implies a deterritorialization, because instead of people being distributed in an itinerant territory, pieces of land are distributed among people according to a common quantitative criterion (the fertility of plots of equal surface area). That is why the earth, unlike other elements, forms the basis of a striation, proceeding by geometry, symmetry, and comparison. The other elements, water, air, wind, and subsoil, cannot be striated and for that very reason bear rent only by virtue of their emplacement, in other words, as a function of the land.[30] The land has two potentialities of deterritorialization: (1) its differences in quality are *comparable* to one another, from the standpoint of a quantity establishing a correspondence between them and exploitable pieces of land; (2) the set of exploited lands is *appropriable*, as opposed to exterior unclaimed land, from the standpoint of a monopoly that fixes the landowner or -owners.[31] The second potentiality is the necessary condition for the first. Both were warded off by the territory's territorialization of the earth but are now effectuated in the agricultural assemblage thanks to stockpiling, by means of a deterritorialization of the territory. Land as compared and appropriated extracts from the territories a center of convergence located outside them; the land is an idea of the town.

Rent is not the only apparatus of capture. The stock has as its correlate not only the land, from the double point of view of the comparison of lands and the monopolistic appropriation of land; it has work as another correlate, from the double point of view of the comparison of activities and the monopolistic appropriation of labor (surplus labor). Once again, it is by virtue of the stock that activities of the "free action" type come to be compared, linked, and subordinated to a common and homogeneous quantity called labor. Not only does labor concern the stock—either its constitution, conservation, reconstitution, or utilization—but labor itself is stockpiled activity, just as the worker is a stockpiled "actant." Moreover, even when labor is clearly separated from surplus labor, they cannot be held to be independent: there is no so-called necessary labor, and beyond that surplus labor. Labor and surplus labor are strictly the same thing; the first term is applied to the quantitative comparison of activities, the second to the monopolistic appropriation of labor by the entrepreneur (and no longer the landowner). As we have seen, even when they are distinct and separate, there is no labor that is not predicated on surplus labor. Surplus labor is not that which exceeds labor; on the contrary, labor is that which is subtracted from surplus labor and presupposes it. It is only in this context that one may speak of labor value, and of an evaluation bearing on the quantity of social labor, whereas primitive groups were under a regime of free action or activity in continuous variation. Since it depends on surplus labor and surplus value, entrepreneurial profit is just as much an apparatus of capture as proprietary rent: not only does surplus labor capture labor, and landownership the earth, but labor and surplus labor are the apparatus of capture of activity, just as the comparison of lands and the appropriation of land are the apparatus of capture of the territory.[32]

Finally, there is a third apparatus of capture in addition to rent and profit: taxation. To understand this third form, and its creative range, we must first determine the internal relation upon which the commodity depends. Edouard Will has shown, in relation to the Greek city and in particular the Corinthian tyranny, that money derived not from exchange, the commodity, or the demands of commerce, but from taxation, which first introduces the possibility of an equivalence money = goods or services and which makes money a general equivalent. In effect, money is a correlate of the stock; it is a subset of the stock in that it can be constituted by any object that can be preserved over the long term. In the case of Corinth, metal money was first distributed to the "poor" (in their capacity as producers), who used it to buy land rights; it thus passed into the hands of the "rich," on the condition that it not stop there, that everyone, rich and poor, pay a tax, the poor in goods or services, the rich in money, such that an equivalence money-goods and services was established.[33] We will return to the significance of this reference to rich and poor in the already late case of Corinth. But beyond the context and particularities of this example, money is always distributed by an apparatus of power under conditions of conservation, circulation, and turnover, so that an equivalence goods-services-money is be established. We therefore do not believe in a succession, according to which labor rent would come first, followed by rent in kind, followed by money rent.[34] It is directly in taxation that the equivalence and simultaneity of the three develop. As a general rule, it is taxation that monetarizes the economy; it is taxation that creates money, and it necessarily creates it in motion, in circulation, with turnover, and also in a correspondence with services and goods in the current of that circulation. The State finds in taxation the means for foreign trade, insofar as it appropriates that trade. Yet it is not from trade but from taxation that the money-form derives.[35] And the money-form thus derived from taxation makes possible a monopolistic appropriation of outside exchange by the State (monetarized trade). Everything is different in the regime of exchanges. We are no longer in the "primitive" situation where exchange is carried out indirectly, subjectively, through the respective equalization of the last receivable objects (the law of demand). Of course, exchange remains what it is in essence, that is to say, unequal, productive of an equalization resulting from inequality: but this time there is direct comparison, objective pricing, and monetary equalization (the law of supply). It is through taxation that goods and services come to be like commodities, and the commodity comes to be measured and equalized by money. That is why, even today, the meaning and impact of taxation appear in what is called indirect taxation, in other words, a tax that is included in the price and influences the value of the commodity, independent of and outside the market.[36] However, the indirect tax is not simply an additional element that is tacked onto prices and inflates them. It is only the index or expression of a deeper movement, in which the tax constitutes the first layer of an "objective" price, the monetary magnet to which the other elements—price, rent, and profit—add on and adhere, converging in the same apparatus of capture. It was a great moment in capitalism when the capitalists realized that taxation could be productive, that it could be particularly favorable to profits and even to rents. But as with indirect taxation, this is a favorable case; it should not obscure an even deeper and more archaic accord, a convergence and essential identity between three aspects of a single apparatus. A three-headed apparatus of capture, a "trinity formula" derived from that of Marx (although it distributes things differently):[37]

LAND
(as opposed to territory)

a) Direct comparison of lands, differential rent; b) Monopolistic appropriation of land, absolute rent.	Rent The Landowner

WORK
(as opposed to activity)

Stock	a) Direct comparison of activities, labor;	Profit The Entrepreneur
	b) Monopolistic appropriation of labor, surplus labor.	

MONEY
(as opposed to exchange)

	a) Direct comparison of the objects exchanged, the commodity;	Taxation The Banker
	b) Monopolistic appropriation of the means of comparison, the issuance of currency.	

1. The stock has three simultaneous aspects: land and seeds, tools, money. Land is stockpiled territory, the tool is stockpiled activity, and money is stockpiled exchange. But the stock does not *come* from either territories, activities, or exchanges. It marks another assemblage; it comes from that other assemblage.

2. That assemblage is the "megamachine," or the apparatus of capture, the archaic empire. It functions in three modes, which correspond to the three aspects of the stock: rent, profit, taxation. And the three modes converge and coincide in it, in an agency of overcoding (or signifiance): the despot, at once the eminent landowner, entrepreneur of large-scale projects, and master of taxes and prices. This is like three capitalizations of power, or three articulations of "capital."

3. What forms the apparatus of capture are two operations always found in the convergent modes: direct comparison and monopolistic appropriation. And the comparison always presupposes the appropriation: labor presupposes surplus labor; differential rent presupposes absolute rent; commercial money presupposes taxation. The apparatus of capture constitutes a general space of comparison and a mobile center of appropriation. This is a white wall/black hole system of the kind that, as we have seen, constitutes the *face* of the despot. A point of resonance circulates in a space of comparison and constitutes that space as it circulates. That is what distinguishes the State apparatus from primitive mechanisms, with their noncoexistent territories and nonresonating centers. What begins with the State or the apparatus of capture is a general semiology that overcodes the primitive semiotic systems. Instead of traits of expression that follow a machinic *phylum* and wed it in a distribution of

singularities, the State constitutes a form of expression that subjugates the phylum: the phylum or matter is no longer anything more than an equalized, homogenized, compared content, while expression becomes a form of resonance or appropriation. Apparatus of capture—the semiological operation par excellence . . . (In this sense, the associationist philosophers were not wrong in explaining political power by operations of the mind dependent upon the association of ideas.)

Bernard Schmitt has proposed a model of the apparatus of capture that takes into account the operations of comparison and appropriation. This model admittedly revolves around money as a capitalist economics. But it seems to be based on abstract principles that transcend these limits.[38]

A. The point of departure is an undivided flow that has yet to be appropriated or compared, a "pure availability," "nonpossession and nonwealth": this is precisely what occurs when banks create money, but taken more generally it is the establishment of the stock, which is the creation of an undivided flow.

B. The undivided flow becomes divided to the extent it is allocated to the "factors," distributed to the "factors." There is only one kind of factor, the immediate producers. We could call them the "poor" and say that the flow is distributed among the poor. But this would be inaccurate because there are no preexistent "rich." What counts, the important thing, is that the producers do not yet acquire possession of what is distributed to them, and that what is distributed to them is not yet wealth: *remuneration* assumes neither comparison and appropriation, nor buying-selling; it is much more an operation of the *nexum* type. There is only equality between set B and set A, between the distributed set and the undivided set. The distributed set could be called *nominal wage;* nominal wages are the form of expression of the entire undivided set ("the entire nominal expression," or as it is often put, "the expression of total national income"). This is the point at which the apparatus of capture becomes semiological.

C. Thus it cannot even be said that wages, conceived as distribution, remuneration, constitute a purchase; on the contrary, purchasing power derives from wages: "The remuneration of the producers is not a purchase, it is the operation by which purchasing becomes possible in a second moment, when money begins to exercise its new power." It is after it has been distributed that set B becomes wealth, or acquires a comparative power, in relation to something else entirely. This something else is the determinate set of the goods that have been produced and are thus purchasable. At first heterogeneous to goods and products, money later becomes a good homogeneous to the products it can buy; it acquires a purchasing power that is extinguished with the real purchase. Or more generally, between the two sets, the distributed set B and the set of real goods C, there is established a *correspondence*, a *comparison* ("the power of acquisition is created in direct conjunction with the set of real productions").

D. This is where the mystery or the magic resides, in a kind of disjunction. For if we call B′ the comparative set, in other words, the set placed in correspondence with the real goods, we see that it is necessarily smaller than the distributed set. B′ is necessarily smaller than B: even if we assume that purchasing power has available to it all of the objects produced during a given period, the distributed set is always greater than the set that is used or compared, meaning that the immediate producers are able to convert only a portion of the distributed set. *Real wages* are only a portion of nominal wages; similarly, "useful" labor is only a portion of labor, and "utilized" land is only a portion of the land that has been distributed. We shall call Capture this difference or excess constitutive of profit, surplus labor, or the surplus product: "Nominal wages include everything, but the wage-earners retain only the income *they succeed in converting into goods;* they lose the income siphoned off by the enterprises." It can be said that the whole was in fact distributed to the "poor"; the poor, however, find themselves extorted of everything they do not succeed in converting in the course of this strange race: the capture effects an inversion of the wave or of the divisible flow. It is precisely capture that is the object of monopolistic appropriation. And this appropriation (by the "rich") does not come after: it is included in nominal wages, while eluding real wages. It is between the two, it inserts itself between the distribution without possession and the conversion by correspondence or comparison; it expresses the difference in power between the two sets, between B′ and B. In the end, there is no mystery at all: *the mechanism of capture contributes from the outset to the constitution of the aggregate upon which the capture is effectuated.*

This schema, according to its author, is very difficult to understand, and yet it is operative. It consists in bringing into relief an abstract machine of capture or of extortion by presenting a very specific "order of reasons." For example, remuneration is not itself a purchase since purchasing power derives from it. As Schmitt says, there is neither thief nor victim, for the producer only loses what he does not have and has no chance of acquiring: as in seventeenth-century philosophy, there are negations but not privation . . . And everything coexists in this logical apparatus of capture. Any succession is purely logical: the capture in itself appears between B and C, but exists as well between A and B, between C and A; it impregnates the entire apparatus, it acts as a nonlocalizable liaison for the system. The same goes for surplus labor: How could one specify its location since labor presupposes it? Now the State—the archaic imperial State in any case—is this very apparatus. It is always a mistake to appeal to a supplementary explanation for the State: this pushes the State back behind the State, ad infinitum. It is better to leave it where it is from the start, for it exists punctually, beyond the limit of the primitive series. It is enough for this point of comparison and appropriation to be effectively occupied in order for the apparatus of capture to function, an apparatus that overcodes the primitive codes, substitutes sets for the series, or reverses the direction of the signs. This point is necessarily occupied, effectuated, because it already exists in the convergent wave that moves through the primitive series and draws them toward a threshold at which, after passing their limits, the wave itself changes direction. Primitive peoples have always existed only as vestiges, already plied by the reversible wave that carries them off (vector of deterritorialization). What is contingent upon external circumstances is only the place where the apparatus is effectuated—the place where the agricultural "mode of production" was able to arise: the Orient. It is in this sense that the apparatus is abstract. But in itself, it marks not simply an abstract possibility of reversibility but the real existence of a point of inversion as an autonomous, irreducible phenomenon.

Hence the very particular character of State violence: it is very difficult to pinpoint this violence because it always presents itself as preaccomplished. It is not even adequate to say that the violence rests with the mode of production. Marx made the observation in the case of capitalism: there is a violence *that necessarily operates through the State*, precedes the capitalist mode of production, constitutes the "primitive accumulation," and makes possible the capitalist mode of production itself. From a standpoint within the capitalist mode of production, it is very difficult to say who is the thief and who the victim, or even where the violence resides. That is because the worker is born entirely naked and the capitalist objectively "clothed," an independent owner. That which gave the worker and the capitalist this form eludes us because it operated in other modes of production. It is a violence that posits itself as preaccomplished, even though it is reactivated every day.[39] This is the place to say it, if ever there was one: *the mutilation is prior, preestablished.* However, these analyses of Marx should be enlarged upon. For the fact remains that there is a primitive accumulation that, far from deriving from the agricultural mode of production, precedes it: as a general rule, there is primitive accumulation whenever an apparatus of capture is mounted, with that very particular kind of violence that creates or contributes to the creation of that which it is directed against, and thus presupposes itself.[40] The problem then becomes one of distinguishing between regimes of violence. We can draw a distinction between struggle, war, crime and policing as so many regimes of violence. *Struggle* would be like the regime of primitive violence (including primitive "wars"); it is a blow-by-blow violence, which is not without its code, since the value of the blows is fixed according to the law of the series, as a function of the value of the last exchangeable blow, or of the last woman to conquer, etc. Thus there is a certain ritualization of violence. *War*, at least when linked to the war machine, is another regime, because it implies the mobilization and autonomization of a violence directed first and essentially against the State apparatus (the war machine is in this sense the invention of a primary nomadic organization that turns against the State). *Crime* is something else, because it is a violence of illegality that consists in taking possession of something to which one has no "right," in capturing something one does not have a "right" to capture. But *State policing or lawful violence* is something else again, because it consists in capturing while simultaneously constituting a right to capture. It is an incorporated, structural violence distinct from every kind of direct violence. The State has often been defined by a "monopoly of violence," but this definition leads back to another definition that describes the State as a "state of Law" (*Rechtsstaat*). State overcoding is precisely this structural violence that defines the law, "police" violence and not the violence of war. There is lawful violence wherever violence contributes to the creation of that which it is used against, or as Marx says, wherever capture contributes to the creation of that which it captures. This is very different from criminal violence. It is also why, *in contradistinction to* primitive violence, State or lawful violence always seems to presuppose itself, for it preexists its own use: the State can in this way say that violence is "primal," that it is simply a natural phenomenon the responsibility for which does not lie with the State, which uses violence only against the violent, against "criminals"—against primitives, against nomads—in order that peace may reign.

PROPOSITION XIII. *The State and its forms.*

We start with the archaic imperial State: overcoding, apparatus of capture, machine of enslavement. It comprises a particular kind of property, money, public works—a formula complete in a single stroke but one that presupposes nothing "private" and does not even assume a preexistent mode of production since it is what gives rise to the mode of production. The point of departure that the preceding analyses give us is well established by archaeology. The question now becomes: Once the State has appeared, formed in a single stroke, how will it evolve? What are its factors of evolution or mutation, and what is the relation between evolved States and the archaic imperial State?

The principle of evolution is internal, whatever the external factors that contribute to it. *The archaic State does not overcode without also freeing a large quantity of decoded flows that escape from it.* Let us recall that "decoding" does not signify the state of a flow whose code is understood (*compris*) (deciphered, translatable, assimilable), but, in a more radical sense, the state of a flow that is no longer contained in (*compris dans*) its own code, that escapes its own code. On the one hand, when the primitive codes cease to be self-regulating and are subordinated to the higher agency, codes that had been coded in a relative way by the primitive communities find the opportunity to escape. But on the other hand, *the overcoding of the archaic State itself makes possible and gives rise to new flows that escape from it*. The State does not create large-scale works without a flow of independent labor escaping its bureaucracy (notably in the mines and in metallurgy). It does not create the monetary form of the tax without flows of money escaping, and nourishing or bringing into being other powers (notably in commerce and banking). And above all, it does not create a system of public property without a flow of private appropriation growing up *beside* it, then beginning to pass beyond its grasp; this private property does not itself issue from the archaic system but is constituted on the margins, all the more necessarily and inevitably, slipping through the net of overcoding. It is undoubtedly Tökei who has formulated the problem of an origin of private property in the most serious way, in the context of a system that seems to exclude it from every angle. For private property can arise neither on the side of the emperor-despot nor on the side of the peasants, whose autonomy is tied to communal possession, nor on the side of the functionaries whose existence and income are based on that public communal form ("the aristocrats can under these conditions become petty despots but not private landowners"). Even the slaves belong to the community or the public function. The question then becomes, Are there people who are constituted in the overcoding empire, but constituted as necessarily excluded and decoded? Tökei's answer is the *freed slaves*. It is they who have no place. It is their lamentations that are heard the length and breadth of the Chinese Empire: the plaint (elegy) has always been a political factor. But it is also they who form the first seeds of private property, who develop trade, and with metallurgy invent a kind of private slavery in which they will be the new master.[41] We saw previously the role played by freed slaves in the war machine, in the formation of the special body. It is in a different form, and following entirely different principles, that they play an important role in the State apparatus and in the evolution of that apparatus, this time in the formation of a private body. The two aspects can combine, but they belong to two different lines.

What counts is not the particular case of the freed slave. What counts is the collective figure of the Outsider. What counts is that in one way or another the apparatus of overcoding gives rise to flows that are themselves decoded—flows of money, labor, property. . . These flows are the correlate of the apparatus. And the correlation is not only social, internal to the archaic empire, it is also geographical. This would be the place to bring up the confrontation between the East and the West. According to V. Gordon Childe's great archaeological thesis, the archaic imperial State implies a stockpiled agricultural surplus, which makes possible the maintenance of a specialized body of mercantile and metallurgical artisans. Indeed, the surplus as the content proper to overcoding must be not only stockpiled but absorbed, consumed, realized. Doubtless, this economic requirement that the surplus be absorbed is one of the principal aspects of the appropriation of the war machine by the imperial State: The military institution is from the start one of the most effective means of absorbing surplus. If, however, we assume that the bureaucratic and military institutions are not enough, the way is cleared for this specialized body of nonagricultural artisans, whose labor will reinforce the sedentarization of agriculture. It was in Afro-Asia and the Orient that all of these conditions were fulfilled and that the State apparatus was invented: in the Middle East, Egypt, and Mesopotamia, but also in the valley of the Indus (and in the Far East). That was where agricultural stock and its bureaucratic, military, but also metallurgical and commercial concomitants came into being. But this oriental or imperial "solution" is threatened by an impasse: State overcoding keeps the metallurgists, both craft and mercantile, within strict bounds, under powerful bureaucratic control, with monopolistic appropriation of foreign trade in the service of a ruling class, so that the peasants themselves benefit little from the State innovations. So it is indeed true that the State-form spreads and that archaeology discovers it everywhere on the horizon of Western history in the Aegean world. But not under the same conditions. Minos and Mycenae are more a caricature of an empire, Agamemnon of Mycenae is not the Chinese emperor or Egyptian pharaoh; the Egyptian can say to the Greeks: "You will always be like children. . ." That is because the Aegean peoples were both too far away to fall into the oriental sphere and too poor to stockpile a surplus themselves, but neither far enough away nor impoverished enough to ignore the markets of the Orient. Moreover, oriental overcoding itself assigned its merchants a long-distance role. Thus the Aegean peoples found themselves in a situation where they could take advantage of the oriental agricultural stock *without having to constitute one for themselves:* they plundered it when they could, and on a more regular basis procured a share of it in exchange for raw materials (notably wood and metals), coming from as far away as Central and Western Europe. Of course, the Orient continually had to reproduce its stocks; but formally, it had made a move "once and for all," from which the West benefited without having to reproduce it. It follows that the metallurgical artisans and the merchants assumed an entirely different status in the West, since their existence did not directly depend on a surplus accumulated by a local State apparatus: even if the peasant suffered an exploitation as bad as or worse than that of the Orient, the artisan and the merchant enjoyed a freer status and a more diversified market, prefiguring a middle class. Many metallurgists and merchants from the Orient moved to the Aegean world, where they were to find freer, more varied and more stable conditions. In short, *the same flows that are overcoded in the Orient tend to become decoded in Europe*, in a new situation that is like the flipside or correlate of the other. Surplus value is no longer surplus value of code (overcoding) but becomes surplus value of flow. It is as if two solutions were found for the same problem, the Oriental solution and then the Western one, which grafts itself upon the first and brings it out of the impasse while continuing to presuppose it. The European metallurgist and merchant faced a much less thoroughly coded international market, one not limited to an imperial house or class. And as Childe said, the Western and Aegean States were immersed in a supranational economic system from the start; they bathed in it, instead of containing it within the limits of their own net.[42]

It is indeed another pole of the State that arises, one that could be defined in summary fashion as follows. The *public sphere* no longer characterizes the objective nature of property but is instead the shared means for a now private appropriation; this yields the public-private mixes constitutive of the modern world. *The bond becomes personal*; personal relations of dependence, both between owners (contracts) and between owned and owners (conventions), parallel or replace community relations or relations based on one's public function. Even slavery changes; it no longer defines the public availability of the communal worker but rather private property as applied to individual workers.[43] The *law* in its entirety undergoes a mutation, becoming subjective, conjunctive, "topical" law: this is because the State apparatus is faced with a new task, which consists less in overcoding already coded flows than in *organizing conjunctions of decoded flows as such*. Thus the regime of signs has changed: in all of these respects, the operation of the imperial "signifier" has been superseded by *processes of subjectification*; machinic enslavement tends to be replaced by a regime of *social subjection*. And unlike the relatively uniform imperial pole, this second pole presents the most diverse of forms. But as varied as relations of personal dependence are, they always mark qualified and topical conjunctions. It was the evolved empires, of the East and of the West, that first developed this new public sphere *of* the private, through institutions such as the *consilium* and the *fiscus* in the Roman Empire (it was through these institutions that freed slaves acquired a political power paralleling that of the functionaries).[44] But it was also the autonomous cities, the feudal systems. . . The question as to whether these last-mentioned formations still answer to the concept of the State can be formulated only after certain correlations have been taken into account. Every bit as much as the evolved empires, the autonomous cities, and feudal systems presuppose an archaic empire that served as their foundation; they were themselves in contact with evolved empires that reacted back upon them; they actively prepared the way for new forms of the State (for example, absolute monarchy as the culmination of a certain kind of subjective law and a feudal process).[45] In effect, in the rich domain of personal relations, what counts is not the capriciousness or variability of the individuals but the consistency of the relations, and the adequation between a subjectivity that can reach the point of delirium and qualified acts that are sources of rights and obligations. In a beautiful passage, Edgar Quinet underlines this coincidence between "the delirium of the twelve Cesars and the golden age of Roman law."[46]

The subjectifications, conjunctions, and appropriations do not prevent the decoded flows from continuing to flow, and from ceaselessly engendering new flows that escape (we saw this, for example, at the level of a micropolitics of the Middle Ages). This is where there is an ambiguity in these apparatuses: they can only function with decoded flows, and yet they do not let them stream together; they perform topical conjunctions that stand as so many knots or recodings. This accounts for the historians' impression that capitalism "could have" developed beginning at a certain moment, in China, in Rome, in Byzantium, in the Middle Ages, that the conditions for it existed but were not effectuated or even capable of being effectuated. The situation is that the pressure of the flows draws capitalism in negative outline, but for it to be realized there must be a whole *integral of decoded flows*, a whole *generalized conjunction* that overspills and overturns the preceding apparatuses. And in fact when Marx sets about defining capitalism, he begins by invoking the advent of a single unqualified and global Subjectivity, which capitalizes all of the processes of subjectification, "all activities without distinction": "productive activity in general," "the sole subjective essence of wealth . . ." And this single Subject now expresses itself in an Object in general, no longer in this or that qualitative state: "Along with the abstract universality of wealth-creating activity we have now the universality of the object defined as wealth, viz. the product in general, or labor in general, but as past, materialized labor."[47] Circulation constitutes capital as a subjectivity commensurate with society in its entirety. But this new social subjectivity can form only to the extent that the decoded flows overspill their conjunctions and attain a level of decoding that the State apparatuses are no longer able to reclaim: *on the one hand*, the flow of labor must no longer be determined as slavery or serfdom but must become naked and free labor; and *on the other hand*, wealth must no longer be determined as money dealing, merchant's or landed wealth, but must become pure homogeneous and independent capital. And doubtless, these two becomings at least (for other flows also converge) introduce many contingencies and many different factors on each of the lines. But it is their abstract conjunction in a single stroke that constitutes capitalism, providing a universal subject and an object in general for one another. Capitalism forms when the flow of unqualified wealth encounters the flow of unqualified labor and conjugates with it.[48] This is what the preceding conjunctions, which were still topical or qualitative, had always inhibited (the two principal inhibitors were the feudal organization of the countryside and the corporative organization of the towns). This amounts to saying that capitalism forms with *a general axiomatic of decoded flows*. "Capital is a right, or, to be more precise, a relation of production that is manifested as a right, and as such it is independent of the concrete form that it cloaks at each moment of its productive function."[49] Private property no longer expresses the bond of personal dependence but the independence of a Subject that now constitutes the sole bond. This makes for an important difference in the evolution of private property: private property in itself relates to rights, instead of the law relating it to the land, things, or people (this raises in particular the famous question of the elimination of ground rent in capitalism). *A new threshold of deterritorialization.* And when capital becomes an active right in this way, the entire historical figure of the law changes. The law ceases to be the overcoding of customs, as it was in the archaic empire; it is no longer a set of topics, as it was in the evolved States, the autonomous cities, and the feudal systems; it increasingly assumes the direct form and immediate characteristics of an axiomatic, as evidenced in our civil "code."[50]

When the flows reach this capitalist threshold of decoding and deterritorialization (naked labor, independent capital), it seems that there is no longer a need for a State, for distinct juridical and political domination, in order to ensure appropriation, which has become directly economic. The economy constitutes a worldwide axiomatic, a "universal cosmopolitan energy which overflows every restriction and bond,"[51] a mobile and convertible substance "such as the total value of annual production." Today we can depict an enormous, so-called stateless, monetary mass that circulates through foreign exchange and across borders, eluding control by the States, forming a multinational ecumenical organization, constituting a de facto supranational power untouched by governmental decisions.[52] But whatever dimensions or quantities this may have assumed today, capitalism has from the beginning mobilized a force of deterritorialization infinitely surpassing the deterritorialization proper to the State. For since Paleolithic and Neolithic times, the State has been deterritorializing to the extent that it makes the earth an *object* of its higher unity, a forced aggregate of coexistence, instead of the free play of territories among themselves and with the lineages. But this is precisely the sense in which the State is termed "territorial." Capitalism, on the other hand, is not at all territorial, even in its beginnings: its power of deterritorialization consists in taking as its object, not the earth, but "materialized labor," the commodity. And private property is no longer ownership of the land or the soil, nor even of the means of production as such, but of convertible abstract rights.[53] That is why capitalism marks a mutation in worldwide or ecumenical organizations, which now take on a consistency of their own: the worldwide axiomatic, instead of resulting from heterogeneous social formations and their relations, for the most part distributes these formations, determines their relations, while organizing an international division of labor. From all these standpoints, it could be said that capitalism develops an economic order that could do without the State. And in fact capitalism is not short on war cries against the State, not only in the name of the market, but by virtue of its superior deterritorialization.

This, however, is only one very partial aspect of capital. If it is true that we are not using the word axiomatic as a simple metaphor, we must review what distinguishes an axiomatic from all manner of codes, overcodings, and recodings: the axiomatic deals directly with purely functional elements and relations whose nature is not specified, and which are immediately realized in highly varied domains simultaneously; codes, on the other hand, are relative to those domains and express specific relations between qualified elements that cannot be subsumed by a higher formal unity (overcoding) except by transcendence and in an indirect fashion. The *immanent axiomatic* finds in the domains it moves through so many models, termed *models of realization*. It could similarly be said that capital as right, as a "qualitatively homogeneous and quantitatively commensurable element," is realized in sectors and means of production (or that "unified capital" is realized in "differentiated capital"). However, the different sectors are not alone in serving as models of realization—*the States* do too. Each of them groups together and combines several sectors, according to its resources, population, wealth, industrial capacity, etc. Thus the States, in capitalism, are not canceled out but change form and take on a new meaning: models of realization for a worldwide axiomatic that exceeds them. But to exceed is not at all the same thing as doing without. We have already seen that capitalism proceeds by way of the State-form rather than the town-form; the basis for the fundamental mechanisms described by Marx (the colonial regime, the public debt, the modern tax system and indirect taxation, industrial protectionism, trade wars) may be laid in the towns, but the towns function as mechanisms of accumulation, acceleration, and concentration only to the extent that they are appropriated by States. Recent events tend to confirm this principle from another angle.

For example, NASA appeared ready to mobilize considerable capital for interplanetary exploration, as though capitalism were riding a vector taking it to the moon; but following the USSR, which conceived of extraterrestrial space as a belt that should circle the earth taken as the "object," the American government cut off funds for exploration and returned capital in this case to a more centered model. It is thus proper to State deterritorialization to moderate the superior deterritorialization of capital and to provide the latter with compensatory reterritorializations. More generally, this extreme example aside, we must take into account a "materialist" determination of the modern State or nation-state: a group of producers in which labor and capital circulate freely, in other words, in which the homogeneity and competition of capital is effectuated, in principle without external obstacles. In order to be effectuated, capitalism has always required there to be a new force and a new law of States, on the level of the flow of labor as on the level of the flow of independent capital.

So States are not at all transcendent paradigms of an overcoding but immanent models of realization for an axiomatic of decoded flows. Once again, our use of the word "axiomatic" is far from a metaphor; we find literally the same theoretical problems that are posed by the models in an axiomatic repeated in relation to the State. For models of realization, though varied, are supposed to be *isomorphic* with regard to the axiomatic they effectuate; however, this isomorphy, concrete variations considered, accommodates itself to the greatest of formal differences. Moreover, a single axiomatic seems capable of encompassing polymorphic models, not only when it is not yet "saturated," but with those models as integral elements of its saturation.[54] These "problems" become singularly political when we think of modern States.

1. Are not all modern States isomorphic in relation to the capitalist axiomatic, to the point that the difference between democratic, totalitarian, liberal, and tyrannical States depends only on concrete variables, and on the worldwide distribution of those variables, which always undergo eventual readjustments? Even the so-called socialist States are isomorphic, to the extent that there is *only one world market*, the capitalist one.

2. Conversely, does not the world capitalist axiomatic tolerate a real polymorphy, or even a heteromorphy, of models, and for two reasons? On the one hand, capital as a general relation of production can very easily integrate concrete sectors or modes of production that are noncapitalist. But on the other hand, and this is the main point, the bureaucratic socialist States can themselves develop different modes of production that only conjugate with capitalism to form a set whose "power" exceeds that of the axiomatic itself (it will be necessary to try to determine the nature of this

power, why we so often think of it in apocalyptic terms, what conflicts it spawns, what slim chances it leaves us . . .).

3. A typology of modern States is thus coupled with a metaeconomics: it would be inaccurate to treat all States as "interchangeable" (even isomorphy does not have that consequence), but it would be no less inaccurate to privilege a certain form of the State (forgetting that polymorphy establishes strict complementarities between the Western democracies and the colonial or neocolonial tyrannies that they install or support in other regions) or to equate the bureaucratic socialist States with the totalitarian capitalist States (neglecting the fact that the axiomatic can encompass a real heteromorphy from which the higher power of the aggregate derives, even if it is for the worse).

What is called a nation-state, in the most diverse forms, is precisely the State as a model of realization. And the birth of nations implies many artifices: Not only are they constituted in an active struggle against the imperial or evolved systems, the feudal systems, and the autonomous cities, but they crush their own "minorities," in other words, minoritarian phenomena that could be termed "nationalitarian," which work from within and if need be turn to the old codes to find a greater degree of freedom. The constituents of the nation are a land and a people: the "natal," which is not necessarily innate, and the "popular," which is not necessarily pregiven. The problem of the nation is aggravated in the two extreme cases of a land without a people and a people without a land. How can a people and a land be made, in other words, a nation—a refrain? The coldest and bloodiest means vie with upsurges of romanticism. The axiomatic is complex, and is not without passions. The natal or the land, as we have seen elsewhere, implies a certain deterritorialization of the territories (community land, imperial provinces, seigneurial domains, etc.), and the people, a decoding of the population. The nation is constituted on the basis of these flows and is inseparable from the modern State that gives consistency to the corresponding land and people. It is the flow of naked labor that makes the people, just as it is the flow of Capital that makes the land and its industrial base. In short, the nation is the very operation of a collective subjectification, to which the modern State corresponds as a process of subjection. It is in the form of the nation-state, with all its possible variations, that the State becomes the model of realization for the capitalist axiomatic. This is not at all to say that nations are appearances or ideological phenomena; on the contrary, they are the passional and living forms in which the qualitative homogeneity and the quantitative competition of abstract capital are first realized.

We distinguish *machinic enslavement* and *social subjection* as two separate concepts. There is enslavement when human beings themselves are constituent pieces of a machine that they compose among themselves and with other things (animals, tools), under the control and direction of a higher unity. But there is subjection when the higher unity constitutes the human being as a subject linked to a now exterior object, which can be an animal, a tool, or even a machine. The human being is no longer a component of the machine but a worker, a user. He or she is subjected *to* the machine and no longer enslaved *by* the machine. This is not to say that the second regime is more human. But the first regime does seem to have a special relation to the archaic imperial formation: human beings are not subjects but pieces of a machine that overcodes the aggregate (this has been called "generalized slavery," as opposed to the private slavery of antiquity, or feudal serfdom). We believe that Lewis Mumford is right in designating the archaic empires megamachines, and in pointing out that, once again, it is not a question of a metaphor: "If a machine can be defined more or less in accord with the classic definition of Reuleaux, as a combination of resistant parts, each specialized in function, operating under human control to transmit motion and to perform work, then the *human machine* was a real machine."[55] Of course, it was the modern State and capitalism that brought the triumph of machines, in particular of motorized machines (whereas the archaic State had simple machines at best); but what we are referring to now are *technical machines*, which are definable extrinsically. One is not enslaved by the technical machine but rather subjected to it. It would appear, then, that the modern State, through technological development, has substituted an increasingly powerful social subjection for machinic enslavement. Ancient slavery and feudal serfdom were already procedures of subjection. But the naked or "free" worker of capitalism takes subjection to its most radical expression, since the processes of subjectification no longer even enter into partial conjunctions that interrupt the flow. In effect, capital acts as the point of subjectification that constitutes all human beings as subjects; but some, the "capitalists," are subjects of enunciation that form the private subjectivity of capital, while the others, the "proletarians," are subjects of the statement, subjected to the technical machines in which constant capital is effectuated. The wage regime can therefore take the subjection of human beings to an unprecedented point, and exhibit a singular cruelty, yet still be justified in its humanist cry: No, human beings are not machines, we don't treat them like machines, we certainly don't confuse variable capital and constant capital . . .

Capitalism arises as a worldwide enterprise of subjectification by constituting an axiomatic of decoded flows. Social subjection, as the correlate of subjectification, appears much more in the axiomatic's models of realization than in the axiomatic itself. It is within the framework of the nation-State, or of national subjectivities, that processes of subjectification and the corresponding subjections are manifested. The axiomatic itself, of which the States are models of realization, restores or reinvents, in new and now technical forms, an entire system of machinic enslavement. This in no way represents a return to the imperial machine since we are now in the immanence of an axiomatic, and not under the transcendence of a formal Unity. But it is the reinvention of a machine of which human beings are constituent parts, instead of subjected workers or users. If motorized machines constituted the second age of the technical machine, cybernetic and informational machines form a third age that reconstructs a generalized regime of subjection: recurrent and reversible "humans-machines systems" replace the old nonrecurrent and nonreversible relations of subjection between the two elements; the relation between human and machine is based on internal, mutual communication, and no longer on usage or action.[56] In the organic composition of capital, variable capital defines a regime of subjection of the worker (human surplus value), the principal framework of which is the business or factory. But with automation comes a progressive increase in the proportion of constant capital; we then see a new kind of enslavement: at the same time the work regime changes, surplus value becomes machinic, and the framework expands to all of society. It could also be said that a small amount of subjectification took us away from machinic enslavement, but a large amount brings us back to it. Attention has recently been focused on the fact that modern power is not at all reducible to the classical alternative "repression or ideology" but implies processes of normalization, modulation, modeling, and information that bear on language, perception, desire, movement, etc., and which proceed by way of microassemblages. This aggregate includes both subjection and enslavement taken to extremes, as two simultaneous parts that constantly reinforce and nourish each other. For example, one is subjected to TV insofar as one uses and consumes it, in the very particular situation of a subject of the statement that more or less mistakes itself for a subject of enunciation ("you, dear television viewers, who make TV what it is . . ."); the technical machine is the medium between two subjects. But one is enslaved by TV as a human machine insofar as the television viewers are no longer consumers or users, nor even subjects who supposedly "make" it, but intrinsic component pieces, "input" and "output," feedback or recurrences that are no longer connected to the machine in such a way as to produce or use it. In machinic enslavement, there is nothing but transformations and exchanges of information, some of which are mechanical, others human.[57] The term "subjection," of course, should not be confined to the national aspect, with enslavement seen as international or worldwide. For information technology is also the property of the States that set themselves up as humans-machines systems. But this is so precisely to the extent that the two aspects, the axiomatic and the models of realization, constantly cross over into each other and are themselves in communication. Social subjection proportions itself to the model of realization, just as machinic enslavement expands to meet the dimensions of the axiomatic that is effectuated in the model. We have the privilege of undergoing the two operations simultaneously, in relation to the same things and the same events. Rather than stages, subjection and enslavement constitute two coexistent poles.

We may return to the different forms of the State, from the standpoint of a universal history. We distinguish three major forms: (1) imperial archaic States, which are paradigms and constitute a machine of enslavement by overcoding already-coded flows (these States have little diversity, due to a certain formal immutability that applies to all of them); (2) extremely diverse States—evolved empires, autonomous cities, feudal systems, monarchies—which proceed instead by subjectification and subjection, and constitute qualified or topical conjunctions of decoded flows; 3) the modern nation-States, which take decoding even further and are models of realization for an axiomatic or a general conjugation of flows (these States combine social subjection and the new machinic enslavement, and their very diversity is a function of isomorphy, of the eventual heteromorphy or polymorphy of the models in relation to the axiomatic).

There are, of course, all kinds of external circumstances that mark profound breaks between these types of States, and above all submit the archaic empires to utter oblivion, a shrouding lifted only by archaeology. The empires disappeared suddenly, as though in an instantaneous catastrophe. As in the Dorian invasion, a war machine looms up and bears down from without, killing memory. Yet things proceed quite differently on the inside, where all the States resonate together, appropriate armies for themselves, and exhibit a unity of composition in spite of their differences in organization and development. It is evident that all decoded flows, of whatever kind, are prone to forming a war machine directed against the State. But everything changes depending on whether these flows connect up with a war machine or, on the contrary, enter into conjunctions or a general conjugation that appropriates them for the State. From this standpoint, the modern States have a kind of transspatiotemporal unity with the archaic State. The internal correlation between 1 and 2 appears most clearly in the fact that the fragmented forms of the Aegean world presuppose the great imperial form of the Orient and find in it a stock or agricultural surplus, which they consequently have no need to produce or accumulate for themselves. And to the extent that the States of the second age are nevertheless obliged to reconstitute a stock, if only because of external circumstances—what State can do without one?—in so doing they always reactivate an evolved imperial form. We find the revival of this form in the Greek, Roman, and feudal worlds: there is always an empire on the horizon, which for the subjective States plays the role of signifier and encompassing element. And the correlation between 2 and 3 is no less pronounced, for industrial revolutions are not wanting, and the difference between topical conjunctions and the great conjugation of decoded flows is so thin that one is left with the impression that capitalism was continually being born, disappearing and reviving at every crossroads of history. And the correlation between 3 and 1 is also a necessary one: the modern States of the third age do indeed restore the most absolute of empires, a new "megamachine," whatever the novelty or timeliness of its now immanent form; they do this by realizing an axiomatic that functions as much by machinic enslavement as by social subjection. Capitalism has reawakened the *Urstaat*, and given it new strength.[58]

Not only, as Hegel said, does every State imply "the essential moments of its existence as a State," but there is a unique moment, in the sense of a coupling of forces, and this moment of the State is capture, bond, knot, *nexum*, magical capture. Must we speak of a second pole, which would operate instead by pact and contract? Is this not instead that other force, with capture as the unique moment of coupling? For the two forces are the overcoding of coded flows, and the treatment of decoded flows. The contract is a juridical expression of the second aspect: it appears as the proceeding of subjectification, the outcome of which is subjection. And the contract must be pushed to the extreme; in other words, it is no longer concluded between two people but between self and self, within the same person—*Ich = Ich*—as subjected and sovereign. The extreme perversion of the contract, reinstating the purest of knots. The knot, bond, capture, thus travel a long history: first, the objective, imperial collective bond; then all of the forms of subjective personal bonds; finally, the Subject that binds itself, and in so doing renews the most magical operation, "a cosmopolitan, universal energy which overflows every restriction and bond so as to establish itself instead as the sole bond."[59] Even subjection is only a relay for the fundamental moment of the State, namely, civil capture or machinic enslavement. The State is assuredly not the locus of liberty, nor the agent of a forced servitude or war capture. Should we then speak of "voluntary servitude"? This is like the expression "magical capture": its only merit is to underline the apparent mystery. There is a machinic enslavement, about which it could be said in each case that it presupposes itself, that it appears as preaccomplished; this machinic enslavement is no more "voluntary" than it is "forced."

PROPOSITION XIV. *Axiomatics and the presentday situation.*

Politics is by no means an apodictic science. It proceeds by experimentation, groping in the dark, injection, withdrawal, advances, retreats. The factors of decision and prediction are limited. It is an absurdity to postulate a world supergovernment that makes the final decisions. No one is even capable of predicting the growth in the money supply. Similarly, the States are affected by all kinds of coefficients of uncertainty and unpredictability. John Kenneth Galbraith and François Châtelet have formulated the concept of constant and decisive errors, which make the glory of men of State no less than their rare successful evaluations. But that is just one more reason to make a connection between politics and axiomatics. For in science an axiomatic is not at all a transcendent, autonomous, and decision-making power opposed to experimentation and intuition. On the one hand, it has its own gropings in the dark, experimentations, modes of intuition. Axioms being independent of each other, can they be added, and up to what point (a saturated system)? Can they be withdrawn (a "weakened" system)? On the other hand, it is of the nature of axiomatics to come up against *so-called undecidable propositions*, to confront *necessarily higher powers* that it cannot master.[60] Finally, axiomatics does not constitute the cutting edge of science; it is much more a stopping point, a reordering that prevents decoded semiotic flows in physics and mathematics from escaping in all directions. The great axiomaticians are the men of State of science, who seal off the lines of flight that are so frequent in mathematics, who would impose a new *nexum*, if only a temporary one, and who lay down the official policies of science. They are the heirs of the theorematic conception of geometry. When intuitionism opposed axiomatics, it was not only in the name of intuition, of construction and creation, but also in the name of a calculus of problems, a problematic conception of science that was not less abstract but implied an entirely different abstract machine, one working in the undecidable and the fugitive.[61] It is the real characteristics of axiomatics that lead us to say that capitalism and present-day politics are an axiomatic in the literal sense. But it is precisely for this reason that nothing is played out in advance. From this standpoint, we may present a summary sketch of the "givens."

1. *Addition, subtraction.* The axioms of capitalism are obviously not theoretical propositions, or ideological formulas, but operative statements that constitute the semiological form of Capital and that enter as component parts into assemblages of production, circulation, and consumption. The axioms are primary statements, which do not derive from or depend upon another statement. In this sense, a flow can be the object of one or several axioms (with the set of all axioms constituting the conjugation of the flows); but it can also lack any axioms of its own, its treatment being

only a consequence of other axioms; finally, it can remain out of bounds, evolve without limits, be left in the state of an "untamed" variation in the system. There is a tendency within capitalism continually to add more axioms. After the end of World War I, the joint influence of the world depression and the Russian Revolution forced capitalism to multiply its axioms, to invent new ones dealing with the working class, employment, union organization, social institutions, the role of the State, the foreign and domestic markets. Keynesian economics and the New Deal were axiom laboratories. Examples of the creation of new axioms after the Second World War: the Marshall Plan, forms of assistance and lending, transformations in the monetary system. It is not only in periods of expansion or recovery that axioms multiply. What makes the axiomatic vary, in relation to the States, is the distinction and relation between the foreign and domestic markets. There is a multiplication of axioms most notably when an integrated domestic market is being organized to meet the requirements of the foreign market. Axioms for the young, for the old, for women, etc. A very general pole of the State, "social democracy," can be defined by this tendency to add, invent axioms in relation to spheres of investment and sources of profit: the question is not that of freedom and constraint, nor of centralism and decentralization, but of the manner in which one masters the flows. In this case, they are mastered by the multiplication of directing axioms. The opposite tendency is no less a part of capitalism: the tendency to withdraw, subtract axioms. One falls back on a very small number of axioms regulating the dominant flows, while the other flows are given a derivative, consequential status (defined by the "theorems" ensuing from the axioms), or are left in an untamed state that does not preclude the brutal intervention of State power, quite the contrary. The "totalitarianism" pole of the State incarnates this tendency to restrict the number of axioms, and operates by the exclusive promotion of the foreign sector: the appeal to foreign sources of capital, the rise of industries aimed at the exportation of foodstuffs or raw materials, the collapse of the domestic market. The totalitarian State is not a maximum State but rather, following Virilio's formulation, the *minimum State* of anarcho-capitalism (cf. Chile). At the limit, the only axioms that are retained concern the equilibrium of the foreign sector, reserve levels and the inflation rate; "the population is no longer a given, it has become a consequence." As for untamed evolutions, they appear among other places in the variations in the employment level, in the phenomena of exodus from the countryside, shantytown-urbanization, etc.

The case of fascism ("national socialism") is distinct from totalitarianism. It coincides with the totalitarian pole in the collapse of the domestic market and the reduction in the number of axioms. However, the promotion of the foreign sector does not at all take place through an appeal to foreign sources of capital and through export industries, but through a war economy, which entails an expansionism foreign to totalitarianism and an autonomous fabrication of capital. As for the domestic market, it is effectuated in a specific production of the *Ersatz*. This means that fascism, too, brings a proliferation of axioms, which explains why it has often been compared to a Keynesian economy. Fascism, however, is a tautological or fictitious proliferation, a multiplication by subtraction; this makes it a very special case.[62]

2. *Saturation*. Can we express the distribution of the two opposite tendencies by saying that the saturation of the system marks the point of inversion? No, for the saturation is itself relative. If Marx demonstrated the functioning of capitalism as an axiomatic, it was above all in the famous chapter on the tendency of the rate of profit to fall. Capitalism is indeed an axiomatic, because it has no laws but immanent ones. It would like for us to believe that it confronts the limits of the Universe, the extreme limit of resources and energy. But all it confronts are its own limits (the periodic depreciation of existing capital); all it repels or displaces are its own limits (the formation of new capital, in new industries with a high profit rate). This is the history of oil and nuclear power. And it does both at once: capitalism confronts its own limits and simultaneously displaces them, setting them down again farther along. It could be said that the totalitarian tendency to restrict the number of axioms corresponds to the confrontation with the limits, whereas the social democratic tendency corresponds to the displacement of the limits. But one does not come without the other, either in two different but coexistent places or in two successive but closely linked moments; they always have a hold on each other, or are even contained in each other, constituting the same axiomatic. A typical example would be present-day Brazil, with its ambiguous alternative "totalitarianism-social democracy." As a general rule, the limits are all the more mobile if axioms are subtracted in one place but added elsewhere.

It would be an error to take a disinterested stance toward struggle on the level of the axioms. It is sometimes thought that every axiom, in capitalism or in one of its States, constitutes a "recuperation." But this disenchanted concept is not a good one. The constant readjustments of the capitalist axiomatic, in other words, the additions (the enunciation of new axioms) and the withdrawals (the creation of exclusive axioms), are the object of struggles in no way confined to the technocracy. Everywhere, the workers' struggles overspill the framework of the capitalist enterprises, which imply for the most part derivative propositions. The struggles bear directly upon the axioms that preside over the State's public spending, or that even concern a specific international organization (for example, a multinational corporation can at will plan the liquidation of a factory inside a country). The resulting danger of a worldwide labor bureaucracy or technocracy taking charge of these problems can be warded off only to the extent that local struggles directly target national and international axioms, at the precise point of their insertion in the field of immanence (the potential of the rural world in this respect). There is always a fundamental difference between living flows and the axioms that subordinate them to centers of control and decision making, that make a given segment correspond to them, which measure their quanta. But the pressure of the living flows, and of the problems they pose and impose, must be exerted inside the axiomatic, as much in order to fight the totalitarian reductions as to anticipate and precipitate the additions, to orient them and prevent their technocratic perversion.

3. *Models, isomorphy.* In principle, all States are isomorphic; in other words, they are domains of realization of capital as a function of a sole external world market. But the first question is whether isomorphy implies a homogeneity or even a homogenization of States. The answer is yes, as can be seen in present-day Europe with respect to justice and the police, the highway code, the circulation of commodities, production costs, etc. But this is true only insofar as there is a tendency toward a single integrated domestic market. Otherwise, isomorphy in no way implies homogeneity: there is isomorphy, but heterogeneity, between totalitarian and social democratic States wherever the mode of production is the same. The general rules regarding this are as follows: the consistency, *the totality* (*l'ensemble*), *or unity of the axiomatic* are defined by capital as a "right" or relation of production (for the market); *the respective independence of the axioms* in no way contradicts this totality but derives from the divisions or sectors of the capitalist mode of production; *the isomorphy of the models*, with the two poles of addition and subtraction, depends on how the domestic and foreign markets are distributed in each case.

But this is only a first bipolarity, applying to the States that are located at the center and are under the capitalist mode of production. A second, West-East, bipolarity has been imposed on the States of the center, that of the capitalist States and the bureaucratic socialist States. Although this new distinction may share certain traits of the first (the so-called socialist States being assimilable to the totalitarian States), the problem lies elsewhere. The numerous "convergence" theories that attempt to demonstrate a certain homogenization of the States of the East and West are not very convincing. Even isomorphism is not applicable: there is a real heteromorphy, not only because the mode of production is not capitalist, but also because the relation of production is not Capital (rather, it is the Plan). If the socialist States are nevertheless still models of realization for the capitalist axiomatic, it is due to the existence of a single external world market, which remains the deciding factor here, even above and beyond the relations of production from which it results. It can even happen that the *socialist bureaucratic plan(e)* takes on a parasitic function in relation to the *plan(e) of capital*, which manifests a greater creativity, of the "virus" type.

Finally, the third fundamental bipolarity is the center and the periphery (North-South). In view of the respective independence of the axioms, we can join Samir Amin in saying that the axioms of the periphery differ from those of the center.[63] And here again, the difference and independence of the axioms in no way compromise the consistency of the overall axiomatic. On the contrary, central capitalism needs the periphery constituted by the Third World, where it locates a large part of its most modern industries; it does not just invest capital in these industries, but is also furnished with capital by them. The issue of the dependence of the Third World States is of course an obvious one, but not the most important one (it was bequeathed by the old colonialism). It is obvious that having independent axioms has never guaranteed the independence of States; rather it ensures an international division of labor. The important question, once again, is that of isomorphy in relation to the worldwide axiomatic. To a large extent, there is isomorphy between the United States and the bloodiest of the South American tyrannies (or between France, England, and West Germany and certain African States). The center-periphery bipolarity, States of the center and States of the Third World, may well exhibit some of the distinguishing traits of the two preceding bipolarities, but it also evades them, raising other problems. Throughout a vast portion of the Third World, the general relation of production is capital—even throughout the entire Third World, in the sense that the socialized sector may utilize that relation, adopting it in this case. But the mode of production is not necessarily capitalist, either in the so-called archaic or transitional forms, or in the most productive, highly industrialized sectors. This indeed represents a third case, included in the worldwide axiomatic: when capital acts as the relation of production but in noncapitalist modes of production. We may therefore speak of a polymorphy of the Third World States in relation to the States of the center. And this dimension of the axiomatic is no less necessary than the others; it is even much more necessary, for the heteromorphy of the so-called socialist States was imposed upon capitalism, which digested it as best it could, whereas the polymorphy of the Third World States is partially organized by the center, as an axiom providing a substitute for colonization.

We are always brought back to the literal question of the models of realization of a worldwide axiomatic: there is in principle an *isomorphy* of the States of the center, a *heteromorphy* imposed by the bureaucratic socialist

State, and a *polymorphy* organized by the Third World States. Once again, it would be absurd to think that the insertion of popular movements is condemned in advance throughout this field of immanence, and to assume that there are either "good" States that are democratic, social democratic or at the other extreme socialist, or that on the contrary all States are equivalent and homogeneous.

4. *Power* (*puissance*). Let us suppose that the axiomatic necessarily marshals a power higher than the one it treats, in other words, than that of the aggregates serving as its models. This is like a power of the continuum, tied to the axiomatic but exceeding it. We immediately recognize this power as a power of destruction, of war, a power incarnated in financial, industrial, and military technological complexes that are in continuity with one another. On the one hand, war clearly follows the same movement as capitalism: In the same way as the proportion of constant capital keeps growing, war becomes increasingly a "war of matériel" in which the human being no longer even represents a variable capital of subjection, but is instead a pure element of machinic enslavement. On the other hand, and this is the main point, the growing importance of constant capital in the axiomatic means that the depreciation of existing capital and the formation of new capital assume a rhythm and scale that necessarily take the route of a war machine now incarnated in the complexes: the complexes actively contribute to the redistributions of the world necessary for the exploitation of maritime and planetary resources. There is a continuous "threshold" of power that accompanies in every instance the shifting of the axiomatic's limits; it is as though the power of war always supersaturated the system's saturation, and was its necessary condition.

The classical conflicts among the States of the center (as well as peripheral colonization) have been joined, or rather replaced, by two great conflictual lines, between West and East and North and South; these lines intersect and together cover everything. But the overarmament of the West and East not only leaves the reality of local wars entirely intact and gives them a new force and new stakes; it not only founds the "apocalyptic" possibility of a direct confrontation along the two great axes; it also seems that the war machine takes on a specific supplementary meaning: industrial, political, judicial, etc. It is indeed true that the States, throughout their history, have repeatedly appropriated the war machine; and it was after the war machine was appropriated that war, its preparation and effectuation, became the exclusive object of the machine, but as a more or less "limited" war. As for the aim, it remained the political aim of the States. The various factors that tended to make war a "total war," most notably the fascist factor, marked the beginning of an inversion of the movement: as though the

States, through the war they waged against one another, had after a long period of appropriation reconstituted an autonomous war machine. But this unchained or liberated war machine continued to have as its object war in action, a now total, unlimited kind of war. The entire fascist economy became a war economy, but the war economy still needed total war as its object. For this reason, fascist war still fell under Clausewitz's formula, "the continuation of politics by other means," even though those other means had become exclusive, in other words, the political aim had entered into contradiction with the object (hence Virilio's idea that the fascist State was a "suicidal" State more than a totalitarian one). It was only after World War II that the automatization, then automation of the war machine had their true effect. The war machine, the new antagonisms traversing it considered, no longer had war as its exclusive object but took in charge and as its object peace, politics, the world order, in short, the aim. This is where the inversion of Clausewitz's formula comes in: it is politics that becomes the continuation of war; *it is peace that technologically frees the unlimited material process of total war.* War ceases to be the materialization of the war machine; *the war machine itself becomes materialized war.* In this sense, there was no longer a need for fascism. The Fascists were only child precursors, and the absolute peace of survival succeeded where total war had failed. The Third World War was already upon us. The war machine reigned over the entire axiomatic like the power of the continuum that surrounded the "world-economy," and it put all the parts of the universe in contact. The world became a smooth space again (sea, air, atmosphere), over which reigned a single war machine, even when it opposed its own parts. Wars had become a part of peace. More than that, the States no longer appropriated the war machine; they reconstituted a war machine of which they themselves were only the parts.

Of all the authors who have developed an apocalyptic or millenarian sense, it is to Paul Virilio's credit to have emphasized these five rigorous points: that the war machine finds its new object in the absolute peace of terror or deterrence; that it performs a technoscientific "capitalization"; that this war machine is terrifying not as a function of a possible war that it promises us, as by blackmail, but, on the contrary, as a function of the real, very special kind of peace it promotes and has already installed; that this war machine no longer needs a qualified enemy but, in conformity with the requirements of an axiomatic, operates against the "unspecified enemy," domestic or foreign (an individual, group, class, people, event, world); that there arose from this a new conception of security as materialized war, as organized insecurity or molecularized, distributed, programmed catastrophe.[64]

5. *The included middle.* No one has demonstrated more convincingly than Braudel that the capitalist axiomatic requires a center and that this center was constituted in the North, at the outcome of a long historical process: "There can only be a world-economy when the mesh of the network is sufficiently fine, and when exchange is regular and voluminous enough to give rise to a central zone."[65] Many authors believe on this account that the North-South, center-periphery axis is more important today than the West-East axis, and even principally determines it. This is expressed in a common thesis, taken up and developed by Valéry Giscard d'Estaing: the more equilibrated things become at the center between the West and the East, beginning with the equilibrium of overarmament, the more they become disequilibrated or "destabilized" from North to South and destabilize the central equilibrium. It is clear that in these formulas the South is an abstract term designating the Third World or the periphery; and even that there are Souths or Third Worlds inside the center. It is also clear that this destabilization is not accidental but is a (theorematic) consequence of the axioms of capitalism, principally of the axiom called *unequal exchange*, which is indispensable to capitalism's functioning. This formula is therefore the modern version of the oldest formula, which already obtained in the archaic empires under different conditions. The more the archaic empire overcoded the flows, the more it stimulated decoded flows that turned back against it and forced it to change. The more the decoded flows enter into a central axiomatic, the more they tend to escape to the periphery, to present problems that the axiomatic is incapable of resolving or controlling (even by adding special axioms for the periphery).

The four principal flows that torment the representatives of the world economy, or of the axiomatic, are the flow of matter-energy, the flow of population, the flow of food, and the urban flow. The situation seems inextricable because the axiomatic never ceases to create all of these problems, while at the same time its axioms, even multiplied, deny it the means of resolving them (for example, the circulation and distribution that would make it possible to feed the world). Even a social democracy adapted to the Third World surely does not undertake to integrate the whole poverty-stricken population into the domestic market; what it does, rather, is to effect the class rupture that will select the integratable elements. And the States of the center deal not only with the Third World, each of them has not only an external Third World, but there are internal Third Worlds that rise up within them and work them from the inside. It could even be said in certain respects that the periphery and the center exchange determinations: a deterritorialization of the center, a decoding of the center in relation to national and territorial aggregates, cause the peripheral formations to become true centers of investment, while the central formations peripheralize. This simultaneously strengthens and relativizes Samir Amin's theses. The more the worldwide axiomatic installs high industry and highly industrialized agriculture at the periphery, provisionally reserving for the center so-called postindustrial activities (automation, electronics, information technologies, the conquest of space, overarmament, etc.), the more it installs peripheral zones of underdevelopment inside the center, internal Third Worlds, internal Souths. "Masses" of the population are abandoned to erratic work (subcontracting, temporary work, or work in the underground economy), and their official subsistence is assured only by State allocations and wages subject to interruption. It is to the credit of thinkers like Antonio Negri to have formulated, on the basis of the exemplary case of Italy, the theory of this internal margin, which tends increasingly to merge the students with the *emarginati*.[66] These phenomena confirm the difference between the new machinic enslavement and classical subjection. For subjection remained centered on labor and involved a bipolar organization, property-labor, bourgeoisie-proletariat. In enslavement and the central dominance of constant capital, on the other hand, labor seems to have splintered in two directions: intensive surplus labor that no longer even takes the route of labor, and extensive labor that has become erratic and floating. The totalitarian tendency to abandon axioms of employment and the social democratic tendency to multiply statutes can combine here, but always in order to effect class ruptures. The opposition between the axiomatic and the flows it does not succeed in mastering becomes all the more accentuated.

6. *Minorities*. Ours is becoming the age of minorities. We have seen several times that minorities are not necessarily defined by the smallness of their numbers but rather by becoming or a line of fluctuation, in other words, by the gap that separates them from this or that axiom constituting a redundant majority ("Ulysses, or today's average, urban European"; or as Yann Moulier says, "the national Worker, qualified, male and over thirty-five"). A minority can be small in number; but it can also be the largest in number, constitute an absolute, indefinite majority. That is the situation when authors, even those supposedly on the Left, repeat the great capitalist warning cry: in twenty years, "whites" will form only 12 percent of the world population. . . Thus they are not content to say that the majority will change, or has already changed, but say that it is impinged upon by a nondenumerable and proliferating minority that threatens to destroy the very concept of majority, in other words, the majority as an axiom. And the curious concept of nonwhite does not in fact constitute a denumerable set. What defines a minority, then, is not the number but the relations internal to the number. A minority can be numerous, or even infinite; so can a

majority. What distinguishes them is that in the case of a majority the relation internal to the number constitutes a set that may be finite or infinite, but is always denumerable, whereas the minority is defined as a nondenumerable set, however many elements it may have. What characterizes the nondenumerable is neither the set nor its elements; rather, it is the *connection*, the "and" produced between elements, between sets, and which belongs to neither, which eludes them and constitutes a line of flight. The axiomatic manipulates only denumerable sets, even infinite ones, whereas the minorities constitute "fuzzy," nondenumerable, nonaxiomizable sets, in short, "masses," multiplicities of escape and flux.

Whether it be the infinite set of the nonwhites of the periphery, or the restricted set of the Basques, Corsicans, etc., everywhere we look we see the conditions for a worldwide movement: the minorities recreate "nationalitarian" phenomena that the nation-states had been charged with controlling and quashing. The bureaucratic socialist sector is certainly not spared by these movements, and as Amalrik said, the dissidents are nothing, or serve only as pawns in international politics, if they are abstracted from the minorities working the USSR. It matters little that the minorities are incapable of constituting viable States from the point of view of the axiomatic and the market, since in the long run they promote compositions that do not pass by way of the capitalist economy any more than they do the State-form. The response of the States, or of the axiomatic, may obviously be to accord the minorities regional or federal or statutory autonomy, in short, to add axioms. But this is not the problem: this operation consists only in translating the minorities into denumerable sets or subsets, which would enter as elements into the majority, which could be counted among the majority. The same applies for a status accorded to women, young people, erratic workers, etc. One could even imagine, in blood and crisis, a more radical reversal that would make the white world the periphery of a yellow world; there would doubtless be an entirely different axiomatic. But what we are talking about is something else, something even that would not resolve: women, nonmen, as a minority, as a nondenumerable flow or set, would receive no adequate expression by becoming elements of the majority, in other words, by becoming a denumerable finite set. Nonwhites would receive no adequate expression by becoming a new yellow or black majority, an infinite denumerable set. What is proper to the minority is to assert a power of the nondenumerable, even if that minority is composed of a single member. That is the formula for multiplicities. Minority as a universal figure, or becoming-everybody/everything (*devenir tout le monde*). Woman: we all have to become that, whether we are male or female. Nonwhite: we all have to become that, whether we are white, yellow, or black.

Once again, this is not to say that the struggle on the level of the axioms is without importance; on the contrary, it is determining (at the most diverse levels: women's struggle for the vote, for abortion, for jobs; the struggle of the regions for autonomy; the struggle of the Third World; the struggle of the oppressed masses and minorities in the East or West . . .). But there is also always a sign to indicate that these struggles are the index of another, coexistent combat. However modest the demand, it always constitutes a point that the axiomatic cannot tolerate: when people demand to formulate their problems themselves, and to determine at least the particular conditions under which they can receive a more general solution (hold to the *Particular* as an innovative form). It is always astounding to see the same story repeated: the modesty of the minorities' initial demands, coupled with the impotence of the axiomatic to resolve the slightest corresponding problem. In short, the struggle around axioms is most important when it manifests, itself opens, the gap between two types of propositions, propositions of flow and propositions of axioms. The power of the minorities is not measured by their capacity to enter and make themselves felt within the majority system, nor even to reverse the necessarily tautological criterion of the majority, but to bring to bear the force of the nondenumerable sets, however small they may be, against the denumerable sets, even if they are infinite, reversed, or changed, even they if imply new axioms or, beyond that, a new axiomatic. The issue is not at all anarchy versus organization, nor even centralism versus decentralization, but a calculus or conception of the problems of nondenumerable sets, against the axiomatic of denumerable sets. Such a calculus may have its own compositions, organizations, even centralizations; nevertheless, it proceeds not via the States or the axiomatic process but via a pure becoming of minorities.

7. *Undecidable propositions*. It will be objected that the axiomatic itself marshals the power of a nondenumerable infinite set: precisely that of the war machine. It seems difficult, however, to use the war machine in the general "treatment" of minorities without triggering the absolute war it is supposed to ward off. We have seen the war machine institute quantitative and qualitative processes, miniaturizations, and adaptations that enable it to graduate its attacks or counterattacks, each time as a function of the nature of the "unspecified enemy" (individuals, groups, peoples. . .). But under these conditions, the capitalist axiomatic continually produces and reproduces what the war machine tries to exterminate. Even the organization of famine multiplies the starving as much as it kills them. Even the organization of *camps*, an area where the socialist sector has dreadfully distinguished itself, does not assure the radical solution of which power dreams. The extermination of a minority engenders a minority of that minority.

However relentless the killing, it is relatively difficult to liquidate a people or a group, even in the Third World, once it has enough connections with elements of the axiomatic. In still other respects, it can be predicted that the impending problems of the economy, which will consist in reforming capital in relation to new resources (undersea oil, metallic nodules, foodstuffs), will require not only a redistribution of the world that will mobilize the worldwide war machine and train its parts on the new objectives; we will also probably see the formation or re-formation of minoritarian aggregates, in relation to the affected regions.

Generally speaking, minorities do not receive a better solution of their problem by integration, even with axioms, statutes, autonomies, independences. Their tactics necessarily go that route. But if they are revolutionary, it is because they carry within them a deeper movement that challenges the worldwide axiomatic. The power of minority, of particularity, finds its figure or its universal consciousness in the proletariat. But as long as the working class defines itself by an acquired status, or even by a theoretically conquered State, it appears only as "capital," a part of capital (variable capital), and does not leave the *plan(e) of capital*. At best, the plan(e) becomes bureaucratic. On the other hand, it is by leaving the plan(e) of capital, and never ceasing to leave it, that a mass becomes increasingly revolutionary and destroys the dominant equilibrium of the denumerable sets.[67] It is hard to see what an Amazon-State would be, a women's State, or a State of erratic workers, a State of the "refusal" of work. If minorities do not constitute viable States culturally, politically, economically, it is because the State-form is not appropriate to them, nor the axiomatic of capital, nor the corresponding culture. We have often seen capitalism maintain and organize inviable States, according to its needs, and for the precise purpose of crushing minorities. The minorities issue is instead that of smashing capitalism, of redefining socialism, of constituting a war machine capable of countering the world war machine by other means.

If the two solutions of extermination and integration hardly seem possible, it is due to the deepest law of capitalism: it continually sets and then repels its own limits, but in so doing gives rise to numerous flows in all directions that escape its axiomatic. *At the same time as capitalism is effectuated in the denumerable sets serving as its models, it necessarily constitutes nondenumerable sets that cut across and disrupt those models.* It does not effect the "conjugation" of the deterritorialized and decoded flows without those flows forging farther ahead; without their escaping both the axiomatic that conjugates them and the models that reterritorialize them; without their tending to enter into "connections" that delineate a new Land; without their constituting a war machine whose aim is neither the war of extermination nor the peace of generalized terror, but revolutionary movement (the connection of flows, the composition of nondenumerable aggregates, the becoming-minoritarian of everybody/everything). This is not a dispersion or a fragmentation: we are instead back at *the opposition between, on the one hand, a plane of consistency and, on the other, the plane of organization and development of capital and the bureaucratic socialist plane.* There is in each case a constructivism, a "diagrammatism," operating by the determination of the conditions of the problem and by transversal links between problems: it opposes both the automation of the capitalist axioms and bureaucratic programming. From this standpoint, when we talk about "undecidable propositions," we are not referring to the uncertainty of the results, which is necessarily a part of every system. We are referring, on the contrary, to the coexistence and inseparability of that which the system conjugates, and that which never ceases to escape it following lines of flight that are themselves connectable. The undecidable is the germ and locus par excellence of revolutionary decisions. Some people invoke the high technology of the world system of enslavement; but even, and especially, this machinic enslavement abounds in undecidable propositions and movements that, far from belonging to a domain of knowledge reserved for sworn specialists, provides so many weapons for the becoming of everybody/everything, becoming-radio, becoming-electronic, becoming-molecular . . .[68] Every struggle is a function of all of these undecidable propositions and constructs *revolutionary connections* in opposition to the *conjugations of the axiomatic.*

14. 1440: The Smooth and the Striated

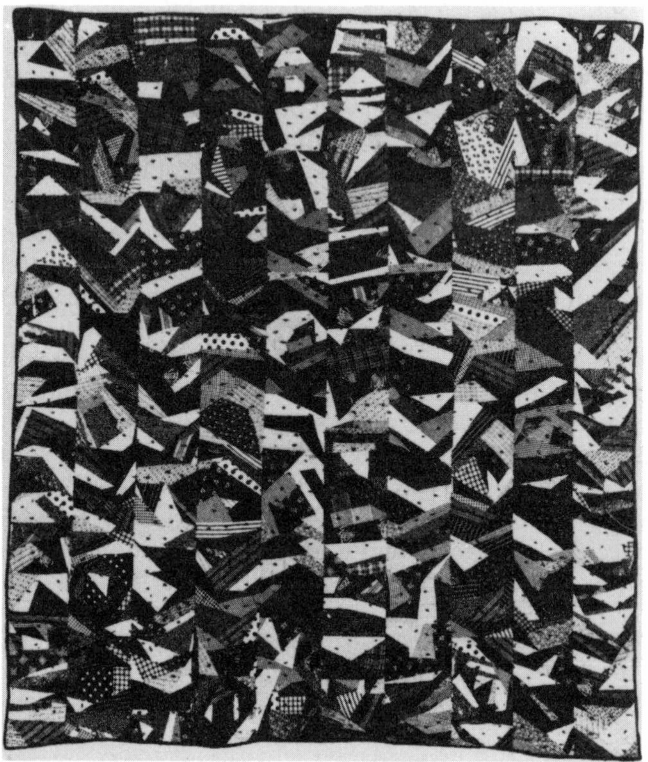

Quilt

Smooth space and striated space—nomad space and sedentary space—the space in which the war machine develops and the space instituted by the State apparatus—are not of the same nature. No sooner do we note a simple opposition between the two kinds of space than we must indicate a much more complex difference by virtue of which the successive terms of the oppositions fail to coincide entirely. And no sooner have we done that than we must remind ourselves that the two spaces in fact exist only in mixture: smooth space is constantly being translated, transversed into a striated space; striated space is constantly being reversed, returned to a smooth space. In the first case, one organizes even the desert; in the second, the desert gains and grows; and the two can happen simultaneously. But the de facto mixes do not preclude a de jure, or abstract, distinction between the two spaces. That there is such a distinction is what accounts for the fact that the two spaces do not communicate with each other in the same way: it is the de jure distinction that determines the forms assumed by a given de facto mix and the direction or meaning of the mix (is a smooth space captured, enveloped by a striated space, or does a striated space dissolve into a smooth space, allow a smooth space to develop?). This raises a number of simultaneous questions: the simple oppositions between the two spaces; the complex differences; the de facto mixes, and the passages from one to another; the principles of the mixture, which are not at all symmetrical, sometimes causing a passage from the smooth to the striated, sometimes from the striated to the smooth, according to entirely different movements. We must therefore envision a certain number of models, which would be like various aspects of the two spaces and the relations between them.

The Technological Model. A fabric presents in principle a certain number of characteristics that permit us to define it as a striated space. First, it is constituted by two kinds of parallel elements; in the simplest case, there are vertical and horizontal elements, and the two intertwine, intersect perpendicularly. Second, the two kinds of elements have different functions; one is fixed, the other mobile, passing above and beneath the fixed. Leroi-Gourhan has analyzed this particular figure of "supple solids" in basketry and weaving: stake and thread, warp and woof.[1] Third, a striated space of this kind is necessarily delimited, closed on at least one side: the fabric can be infinite in length but not in width, which is determined by the frame of the warp; the necessity of a back and forth motion implies a closed space (circular or cylindrical figures are themselves closed). Finally, a space of this kind seems necessarily to have a top and a bottom; even when the warp yarn and woof yarn are exactly the same in nature, number, and density, weaving reconstitutes a bottom by placing the knots on one side. Was it not these characteristics that enabled Plato to use the model of weaving as the paradigm for "royal science," in other words, the art of governing people or operating the State apparatus?

Felt is a supple solid product that proceeds altogether differently, as an anti-fabric. It implies no separation of threads, no intertwining, only an entanglement of fibers obtained by fulling (for example, by rolling the block of fibers back and forth). What becomes entangled are the microscales of the fibers. An aggregate of intrication of this kind is in no way *homogeneous:* it is nevertheless smooth, and contrasts point by point with the space of fabric (it is in principle infinite, open, and unlimited in every direction; it has neither top nor bottom nor center; it does not assign fixed and mobile elements but rather distributes a continuous variation). Even the technologists who express grave doubts about the nomads' powers of innovation at least give them credit for felt: a splendid insulator, an ingenious invention, the raw material for tents, clothes, and armor among the Turco-Mongols. Of course, the nomads of Africa and the Maghreb instead treat wool as a fabric. Although it might entail displacing the opposition, do we not detect two very different conceptions or even practices of weaving, the distinction between which would be something like the distinction between fabric as a whole and felt? For among sedentaries, clothes-fabric and tapestry-fabric tend to annex the body and exterior space, respectively, to the immobile house: fabric integrates the body and the outside into a closed space. On the other hand, the weaving of the nomad indexes clothing and the house itself to the space of the outside, to the open smooth space in which the body moves.

There are many interlacings, mixes between felt and fabric. Can we not displace the opposition yet again? In knitting, for example, the needles produce a striated space; one of them plays the role of the warp, the other of the woof, but by turns. Crochet, on the other hand, draws an open space in all directions, a space that is prolongable in all directions—but still has a center. A more significant distinction would be between embroidery, with its central theme or motif, and patchwork, with its piece-by-piece construction, its infinite, successive additions of fabric. Of course, embroidery's variables and constants, fixed and mobile elements, may be of extraordinary complexity. Patchwork, for its part, may display equivalents to themes, symmetries, and resonance that approximate it to embroidery. But the fact remains that its space is not at all constituted in the same way: there is no center; its basic motif ("block") is composed of a single element; the recurrence of this element frees uniquely rhythmic values distinct from the harmonies of embroidery (in particular, in "crazy" patchwork, which fits together pieces of varying size, shape, and color, and plays on the *texture* of the fabrics). "She had been working on it for fifteen years, carrying about with her a shapeless bag of dingy, threadbare brocade containing odds and ends of colored fabric in all possible shapes. She could never bring herself to trim them to any pattern; so she shifted and fitted and mused and fitted and shifted them like pieces of a patient puzzle-picture, trying to fit them to a pattern or create a pattern out of them without using her scissors, smoothing her colored scraps with flaccid, putty-colored fingers."[2] An amorphous collection of juxtaposed pieces that can be joined together in an infinite number of ways: we see that patchwork is literally a Riemannian space, or vice versa. That is why very special work groups were formed for patchwork fabrication (the importance of the quilting bee in America, and its role from the standpoint of a women's collectivity). The smooth space of patchwork is adequate to demonstrate that "smooth" does not mean homogeneous, quite the contrary: it is an *amorphous*, nonformal space prefiguring op art.

The story of the quilt is particularly interesting in this connection. A quilt comprises two layers of fabric stitched together, often with a filler in between. Thus it is possible for there to be no top or bottom. If we follow the history of the quilt over a short migration sequence (the settlers who left Europe for the New World), we see that there is a shift from a formula dominated by embroidery (so-called "plain" quilts) to a patchwork formula ("appliqué quilts," and above all "pieced quilts"). The first settlers of the seventeenth century brought with them plain quilts, embroidered and striated spaces of extreme beauty. But toward the end of the century patchwork technique was developed more and more, at first due to the scarcity of textiles (leftover fabric, pieces salvaged from used clothes, remnants taken from the "scrap bag"), and later due to the popularity of Indian chintz. It is as though a smooth space emanated, sprang from a striated space, but not without a correlation between the two, a recapitulation of one in the other, a furtherance of one through the other. Yet the complex difference persists. Patchwork, in conformity with migration, whose degree of affinity with nomadism it shares, is not only named after trajectories, but "represents" trajectories, becomes inseparable from speed or movement in an open space.[3]

The Musical Model. Pierre Boulez was the first to develop a set of simple oppositions and complex differences, as well as reciprocal nonsymmetrical correlations, between smooth and striated space. He created these concepts and words in the field of music, defining them on several levels precisely in order to account for the abstract distinction at the same time as the concrete mixes. In the simplest terms, Boulez says that in a smooth space-time one occupies without counting, whereas in a striated space-time one counts in order to occupy. He makes palpable or perceptible the difference between nonmetric and metric multiplicities, directional and dimensional spaces. He renders them sonorous or musical. Undoubtedly, his personal work is composed of these relations, created or recreated musically.[4]

At a second level, it can be said that space is susceptible to two kinds of breaks: one is defined by a standard, whereas the other is irregular and undetermined, and can be made wherever one wishes to place it. At yet another level, it can be said that frequencies can be distributed either in the intervals between breaks, or statistically without breaks. In the first case, the principle behind the distribution of breaks and intervals is called a "module"; it may be constant and fixed (a *straight* striated space), or regularly or irregularly variable (*curved* striated spaces, termed focalized if the variation of the module is regular, nonfocalized if it is irregular). When there is no module, the distribution of frequencies is without break: it is "statistical," however small the segment of space may be; it still has two aspects, however, depending on whether the distribution is equal (nondirected smooth space), or more or less rare or dense (directed smooth space). Can we say that in the kind of smooth space that is without break or module there is no interval? Or, on the contrary, has everything become interval, intermezzo? The smooth is a nomos, whereas the striated always has a logos, the octave, for example. Boulez is concerned with the communication between the two kinds of space, their alternations and superpositions: how "a strongly directed smooth space tends to meld with a striated space," how "a striated space in which the statistical distribution of the pitches used is *in fact* equal tends to meld with a smooth space";[5] how the octave can be replaced by "non-octave-forming scales" that reproduce themselves through a principle of spiraling; how "texture" can be crafted in such a way as to lose fixed and homogeneous values, becoming a support for slips in tempo, displacements of intervals, and *son art* transformations comparable to the transformations of *op art*.

Returning to the simple opposition, the striated is that which intertwines fixed and variable elements, produces an order and succession of distinct forms, and organizes horizontal melodic lines and vertical harmonic planes. The smooth is the continuous variation, continuous development of form; it is the fusion of harmony and melody in favor of the production of properly rythmic values, the pure act of the drawing of a diagonal across the vertical and the horizontal.

The Maritime Model. Of course, there are points, lines, and surfaces in striated space as well as in smooth space (there are also volumes, but we will leave this question aside for the time being). In striated space, lines or trajectories tend to be subordinated to points: one goes from one point to another. In the smooth, it is the opposite: the points are subordinated to the trajectory. This was already the case among the nomads for the clothes-tent-space vector of the outside. The dwelling is subordinated to the journey; inside space conforms to outside space: tent, igloo, boat. There are stops and trajectories in both the smooth and the striated. But in smooth space, the stop follows from the trajectory; once again, the interval takes all, the interval is substance (forming the basis for rhythmic values).[6]

In smooth space, the line is therefore a vector, a direction and not a dimension or metric determination. It is a space constructed by local operations involving changes in direction. These changes in direction may be due to the nature of the journey itself, as with the nomads of the archipelagoes (a case of "directed" smooth space); but it is more likely to be due to the variability of the goal or point to be attained, as with the nomads of the desert who head toward local, temporary vegetation (a "nondirected" smooth space). Directed or not, and especially in the latter case, smooth space is directional rather than dimensional or metric. Smooth space is filled by events or haecceities, far more than by formed and perceived things. It is a space of affects, more than one of properties. It is *haptic* rather than optical perception. Whereas in the striated forms organize a matter, in the smooth materials signal forces and serve as symptoms for them. It is an intensive rather than extensive space, one of distances, not of measures and properties. Intense *Spatium* instead of *Extensio*. A Body without Organs instead of an organism and organization. Perception in it is based on symptoms and evaluations rather than measures and properties. That is why smooth space is occupied by intensities, wind and noise, forces, and sonorous and tactile qualities, as in the desert, steppe, or ice.[7] The creaking of ice and the song of the sands. Striated space, on the contrary, is canopied by the sky as measure and by the measurable visual qualities deriving from it.

This is where the very special problem of the sea enters in. For the sea is a smooth space par excellence, and yet was the first to encounter the demands of increasingly strict striation. The problem did not arise in proximity to land. On the contrary, the striation of the sea was a result of navigation on the open water. Maritime space was striated as a function of two astronomical and geographical gains: *bearings*, obtained by a set of calculations based on exact observation of the stars and the sun; and *the map*, which intertwines meridians and parallels, longitudes and latitudes, plotting regions known and unknown onto a grid (like a Mendeleyev table). Must we accept the Portuguese argument and assign 1440 as the turning point that marked the first decisive striation, and set the stage for the great discoveries? Rather, we will follow Pierre Chaunu when he speaks of an extended confrontation at sea between the smooth and the striated during the course of which the striated progressively took hold.[8] For before longitude lines had been plotted, a very late development, there existed a complex and empirical nomadic system of navigation based on the wind and noise, the colors and sounds of the seas; then came a directional, preastronomical or already astronomical, system of navigation employing only latitude, in which there was no possibility of "taking one's bearings," and which had only portolanos lacking "translatable generalization" instead of true maps; finally, improvements upon this primitive astronomical navigation were made under the very special conditions of the latitudes of the Indian Ocean, then of the elliptical circuits of the Atlantic (straight and curved spaces).[9] It is as if the sea were not only the archetype of all smooth spaces but the first to undergo a gradual striation gridding it in one place, then another, on this side and that. The commercial cities participated in this striation, and were often innovators; but only the States were capable of carrying it to completion, of raising it to the global level of a "politics of science."[10] A *dimensionality* that subordinated *directionality*, or superimposed itself upon it, became increasingly entrenched.

This is undoubtedly why the sea, the archetype of smooth space, was also the archetype of all striations of smooth space: the striation of the desert, the air, the stratosphere (prompting Virilio to speak of a "vertical coastline," as a change in direction). It was at sea that smooth space was first subjugated and a model found for the laying-out and imposition of striated space, a model later put to use elsewhere. This does not contradict Virilio's other hypothesis: in the aftermath of striation, the sea reimparts a kind of smooth space, occupied first by the "fleet in being," then by the perpetual motion of the strategic submarine, which outflanks all gridding and invents a neonomadism in the service of a war machine still more disturbing than the States, which reconstitute it at the limit of their striations. The sea, then the air and the stratosphere, become smooth spaces again, but, in the strangest of reversals, it is for the purpose of controlling striated space more completely.[11] The smooth always possesses a greater power of deterritorialization than the striated. When examining the new professions, or new classes even, how can one fail to mention the military technicians who stare into screens night and day and live for long stretches in strategic submarines (in the future it will be on satellites), and the apocalyptic eyes and ears they have fashioned for themselves, which can barely distinguish any more between a natural phenomenon, a swarm of locusts, and an "enemy" attack originating at any given point? All of this serves as a reminder that the smooth itself can be drawn and occupied by diabolical powers of *organization*; value judgments aside, this demonstrates above all that there exist two nonsymmetrical movements, one of which striates the smooth, and one of which reimparts smooth space on the basis of the striated. (Do not new smooth spaces, or holey spaces, arise as parries even in relation to the smooth space of a worldwide organization? Virilio invokes the beginnings of subterranean habitation in the "mineral layer," which can take on very diverse values.)

Let us return to the simple opposition between the smooth and the striated since we are not yet at the point where we can consider the dissymmetrical and concrete mixes. The smooth and the striated are distinguished first of all by an inverse relation between the point and the line (in the case of the striated, the line is between two points, while in the smooth, the point is between two lines); and second, by the nature of the line (smooth-directional, open intervals; dimensional-striated, closed intervals). Finally, there is a third difference, concerning the surface or space. In striated space, one closes off a surface and "allocates" it according to determinate intervals, assigned breaks; in the smooth, one "distributes" oneself in an open space, according to frequencies and in the course of one's crossings (*logos* and *nomos*).[12] As simple as this opposition is, it is not easy to place it. We cannot content ourselves with establishing an immediate opposition between the smooth ground of the nomadic animal raiser and the striated land of the sedentary cultivator. It is evident that the peasant, even the sedentary peasant, participates fully in the space of the wind, the space of tactile and sonorous qualities. When the ancient Greeks speak of the open space of the *nomos*—nondelimited, unpartitioned; the preurban countryside; mountainside, plateau, steppe—they oppose it not to cultivation, which may actually be part of it, but to the *polis*, the city, the town. When Ibn Khaldūn speaks of *badiya*, bedouinism, the term covers cultivators as well as nomadic animal raisers: he contrasts it to *hadara*, or "city life." This clarification is certainly important, but it does not change much. For from the most ancient of times, from Neolithic and even Paleolithic times, *it is the town that invents agriculture:* it is through the actions of the town that the farmers and their striated space are superposed upon the cultivators operating in a still smooth space (the transhumant cultivator, half-sedentary or already completely sedentary). So on this level we reencounter the simple opposition we began by challenging, between farmers and nomads, striated land and smooth ground: but only after a detour through the town as a force of striation. Now not only the sea, desert, steppe, and air are the sites of a contest between the smooth and the striated, but the earth itself, depending on whether there is cultivation in nomos-space or agriculture in city-space. Must we not say the same of the city itself? In contrast to the sea, the city is the striated space par excellence; the sea is a smooth space fundamentally open to striation, and the city is the force of striation that reimparts smooth space, puts it back into operation everywhere, on earth and in the other elements, outside but also inside itself. The smooth spaces arising from the city are not only those of worldwide organization, but also of a counterattack combining the smooth and the holey and turning back against the town: sprawling, temporary, shifting shantytowns of nomads and cave dwellers, scrap metal and fabric, patchwork, to which the striations of money, work, or housing are no longer even relevant. An explosive misery secreted by the city, and corresponding to Thom's mathematical formula: "retroactive smoothing."[13] Condensed force, the potential for counterattack?

In each instance, then, the simple opposition "smooth-striated" gives rise to far more difficult complications, alternations, and superpositions. But these complications basically confirm the distinction, precisely because they bring dissymmetrical movements into play. For now, it suffices to say that there are two kinds of voyage, distinguished by the respective role of the point, line, and space. Goethe travel and Kleist travel? French travel and English (or American) travel? Tree travel and rhizome travel? But nothing completely coincides, and everything intermingles, or crosses over. This is because the differences are not objective: it is possible to live striated on the deserts, steppes, or seas; it is possible to live smooth even in the cities, to be an urban nomad (for example, a stroll taken by Henry Miller in Clichy or Brooklyn is a nomadic transit in smooth space; he makes the city disgorge a patchwork, differentials of speed, delays and accelerations, changes in orientation, continuous variations . . . The beatniks owe much to Miller, but they changed direction again, they put the space outside the cities to new use). Fitzgerald said it long ago: it is not a question of taking off for the South Seas, that is not what determines a voyage. There are not only strange voyages in the city but voyages in place: we are not thinking of drug users, whose experience is too ambiguous, but of true nomads. We can say of the nomads, following Toynbee's suggestion: *they do not move*. They are nomads by dint of not moving, not migrating, of holding a smooth space that they refuse to leave, that they leave only in order to conquer and die. Voyage in place: that is the name of all intensities, even if they also develop in extension. To think is to voyage; earlier we tried to establish a theo-noological model of smooth and striated spaces. In short, what distinguishes the two kinds of voyages is neither a measurable quantity of movement, nor something that would be only in the mind, but the mode of spatialization, the manner of being in space, of being for space. Voyage smoothly or in striation, and think the same way . . . But there are always passages from one to the other, transformations of one within the other, reversals. In his film, *Kings of the Road*, Wenders intersects and superposes the paths of two characters; one of them takes a still educational, memorial, cultural, Goethean journey that is thoroughly striated, whereas the other has already conquered smooth space, and only experiments, induces amnesia in the German "desert." But oddly enough, it is the former who opens space for himself and performs a kind of retroactive smoothing, whereas striae reform around the latter, closing his space again. Voyaging smoothly is a becoming, and a difficult, uncertain becoming at that. It is not a question of returning to preastronomical navigation, nor to the ancient nomads. The confrontation between the smooth and the striated, the passages, alternations and superpositions, are under way today, running in the most varied directions.

The Mathematical Model. It was a decisive event when the mathematician Riemann uprooted the multiple from its predicate state and made it a noun, "multiplicity." It marked the end of dialectics and the beginning of a typology and topology of multiplicities. Each multiplicity was defined by *n* determinations; sometimes the determinations were independent of the situation, and sometimes they depended upon it. For example, the magnitude of a vertical line between two points can be compared to the magnitude of a horizontal line between two other points: it is clear that the multiplicity in this case is metric, that it allows itself to be striated, and that its determinations are magnitudes. On the other hand, two sounds of equal pitch and different intensity cannot be compared to two sounds of equal intensity and different pitch; in this case, two determinations can be compared only "if one is a part of the other and if we restrict ourselves to the judgment that the latter is smaller than the former, without being able to say by how much."[14] Multiplicities of this second kind are not metric and allow themselves to be striated and measured only by indirect means, which they always resist. They are anexact yet rigorous. Meinong and Russell opposed the notion of *distance* to that of *magnitude*.[15] Distances are not, strictly speaking, indivisible: they can be divided precisely in cases where the situation of one determination makes it part of another. But unlike magnitudes, *they cannot divide without changing in nature each time*. An intensity, for example, is not composed of addable and displaceable magnitudes: a temperature is not the sum of two smaller temperatures, a speed is not the sum of two smaller speeds. Since each intensity is itself a difference, it divides according to an order in which each term of the division differs in nature from the others. Distance is therefore a set of ordered differences, in other words, differences that are enveloped in one another in such a way that it is possible to judge which is larger or smaller, but not their exact magnitudes. For example, one can divide movement into the gallop, trot, and walk, but in such a way that what is divided changes in nature at each moment of the division, without any one of these moments entering into the composition of any other. Therefore these multiplicities of "distance" are inseparable from a process of continuous variation, whereas multiplicities of "magnitude" distribute constants and variables.

That is why we consider Bergson to be of major importance (much more so than Husserl, or even Meinong or Russell) in the development of the theory of multiplicities. Beginning in *Time and Free Will*, he presents duration as a type of multiplicity opposed to metric multiplicity or the multiplicity of magnitude. Duration is in no way indivisible, but is that which cannot be divided without changing in nature at each division (Achilles' running is not divided into steps, his steps do not compose it in the manner of magnitudes).[16] On the other hand, in a multiplicity such as homogeneous extension, the division can be carried as far as one likes without changing anything in the constant object; or the magnitudes can vary with no other result than an increase or a decrease in the amount of space they striate. Bergson thus brought to light "two very different kinds of multiplicity," one qualitative and fusional, continuous, the other numerical and homogeneous, discrete. It will be noted that *matter* goes back and forth between the two; sometimes it is already enveloped in qualitative multiplicity, sometimes already developed in a metric "schema" that draws it outside of itself. The confrontation between Bergson and Einstein on the topic of Relativity is incomprehensible if one fails to place it in the context of the basic theory of Riemannian multiplicities, as modified by Bergson.

We have on numerous occasions encountered all kinds of differences between two types of multiplicities: metric and nonmetric; extensive and qualitative; centered and acentered; arborescent and rhizomatic; numerical and flat; dimensional and directional; of masses and of packs; of magnitude and of distance; of breaks and of frequency; *striated and smooth*. Not only is that which peoples a smooth space a multiplicity that changes in nature when it divides—such as tribes in the desert: constantly modified distances, packs that are always undergoing metamorphosis—but smooth space itself, desert, steppe, sea, or ice, is a multiplicity of this type, nonmetric, acentered, directional, etc. Now it might be thought that the Number would belong exclusively to the *other multiplicities*, that it would accord them the scientific status nonmetric multiplicities lack. But this is only partially true. It is true that the number is the correlate of the metric: magnitudes can striate space only by reference to numbers, and conversely, numbers are used to express increasingly complex relations between magnitudes, thus giving rise to ideal spaces reinforcing the striation and making it coextensive with all of matter. There is therefore a correlation within metric multiplicities between geometry and arithmetic, geometry and algebra, which is constitutive of major science (the most profound authors in this respect are those who have seen that the number, even in its simplest forms, is exclusively cardinal in character, and the unit exclusively divisible).[17] It could be said on the other hand that nonmetric multiplicities or the multiplicities of smooth space pertain only to a minor geometry that is purely operative and qualitative, in which calculation is necessarily very limited, and the local operations of which are not even capable of general translatability or a homogeneous system of location. Yet this "inferiority" is only apparent; for the independence of this nearly illiterate, ametric geometry is what makes possible the independence of the number, the subsequent function of which is to measure magnitudes in striated space (or to striate). The number distributes itself in smooth space; it does not divide without changing nature each time, without changing units, each of which represents a distance and not a magnitude. The ordinal, directional, nomadic, articulated number, the numbering number, pertains to smooth space, just as the numbered number pertains to striated space. So we may say of every multiplicity that it is already a number, and still a unit. But the number and the unit, and even the way in which the unit divides, are different in each case. Minor science is continually enriching major science, communicating its intuitions to it, its way of proceeding, its itinerancy, its sense of and taste for matter, singularity, variation, intuitionist geometry and the numbering number.

But so far we have only considered the first aspect of smooth and nonmetric multiplicities, as opposed to metric multiplicities: how the situation of one determination can make it part of another without our being able either to assign that situation an exact magnitude or common unit, or to discount it. This is the enveloping or enveloped character of smooth space. But there is a second, more important, aspect: when the situation of the two determinations precludes their comparison. As we know, this is the case for Riemannian spaces, or rather, Riemannian patches of space: "Riemann spaces are devoid of any kind of homogeneity. Each is characterized by the form of the expression that defines the square of the distance between two infinitely proximate points. . . . It follows that two neighboring observers in a Riemann space can locate the points in their immediate vicinity but cannot locate their spaces in relation to each other without a new convention. Each vicinity is therefore like a shred of Euclidean space, *but the linkage between one vicinity and the next is not defined and can be effected in an infinite number of ways. Riemann space at its most general thus presents itself as an amorphous collection of pieces that are juxtaposed but not attached to each other.*" It is possible to define this multiplicity without any reference to a metrical system, in terms of the conditions of frequency, or rather *accumulation*, of a set of vicinities; these conditions are entirely different from those determining metric spaces and their breaks (even though a relation between the two kinds of space necessarily results).[18] In short, if we follow Lautman's fine description, Riemannian space is pure patchwork. It has connections, or tactile relations. It has rhythmic values not found elsewhere, even though they can be translated into a metric space. Heterogeneous, in continuous variation, it is a smooth space, insofar as smooth space is amorphous and not homogeneous. We can thus define two positive characteristics of smooth space in general: when there are determinations that are part of one another and pertain to enveloped distances or ordered differences, independent of magnitude; when, independent of metrics, determinations arise that cannot be part of one another but are connected by processes of frequency or accumulation. These are the two aspects of the *nomos* of smooth space.

We are always, however, brought back to a dissymmetrical necessity to cross from the smooth to the striated, and from the striated to the smooth. If it is true that itinerant geometry and the nomadic number of smooth spaces are a constant inspiration to royal science and striated space, conversely, the metrics of striated spaces (*metron*) is indispensable for the translation of the strange data of a smooth multiplicity. Translating is not a simple act: it is not enough to substitute the space traversed for the movement; a series of rich and complex operations is necessary (Bergson was the first to make this point). Neither is translating a secondary act. It is an operation that undoubtedly consists in subjugating, overcoding, *metricizing* smooth space, in neutralizing it, but also in giving it a milieu of propagation, extension, refraction, renewal, and impulse without which it would perhaps die of its own accord: like a mask without which it could neither breathe nor find a general form of expression. Major science has a perpetual need for the inspiration of the minor; but the minor would be nothing if it did not confront and conform to the highest scientific requirements. Let us take just two examples of the richness and necessity of translations, which include as many opportunities for openings as risks of closure or stoppage: first, the complexity of the means by which one translates intensities into extensive quantities, or more generally, multiplicities of distance into systems of magnitudes that measure and striate them (the role of logarithms in this connection); second, and more important, the delicacy and complexity of the means by which Riemannian patches of smooth space receive a Euclidean conjunction (the role of the parallelism of vectors in striating the infinitesimal).[19] The mode of connection proper to patches of Riemannian space ("accumulation") is not to be confused with the Euclidean conjunction of Riemann space ("parallelism"). Yet the two are linked and give each other impetus. Nothing is ever done with: smooth space allows itself to be striated, and striated space reimparts a smooth space, with potentially very different values, scope, and signs. Perhaps we must say that all progress is made by and in striated space, but all becoming occurs in smooth space.

Is it possible to give a very general mathematical definition of smooth spaces? Benoit Mandelbrot's "fractals" seem to be on that path. Fractals are aggregates whose number of dimensions is fractional rather than whole, or else whole but with continuous variation in direction. An example would be a line segment whose central third is replaced by the angle of an equilateral triangle; the operation is repeated for the four resulting segments, and so on ad infinitum, following a relation of similarity—such a segment would constitute an infinite line or curve with a dimension greater than one, but less than a surface (= 2). Similar results can be

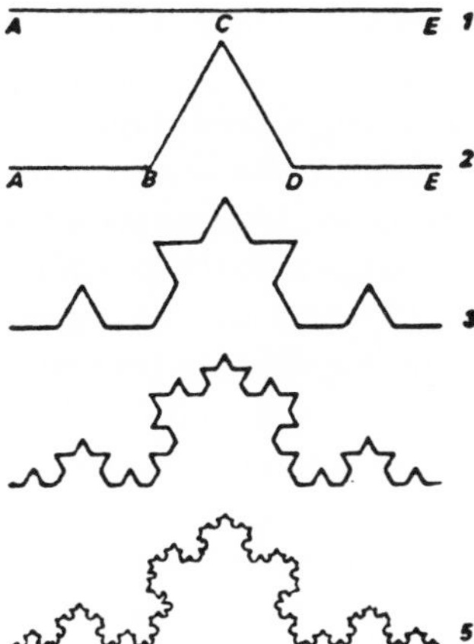

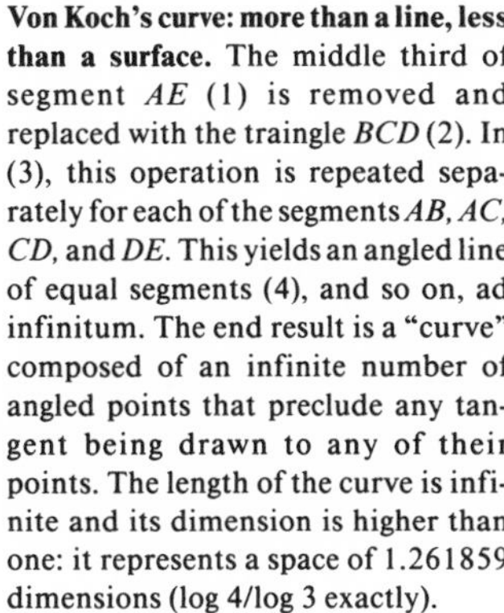

Von Koch's curve: more than a line, less than a surface. The middle third of segment *AE* (1) is removed and replaced with the traingle *BCD* (2). In (3), this operation is repeated separately for each of the segments *AB, AC, CD,* and *DE.* This yields an angled line of equal segments (4), and so on, ad infinitum. The end result is a "curve" composed of an infinite number of angled points that preclude any tangent being drawn to any of their points. The length of the curve is infinite and its dimension is higher than one: it represents a space of 1.261859 dimensions (log 4/log 3 exactly).

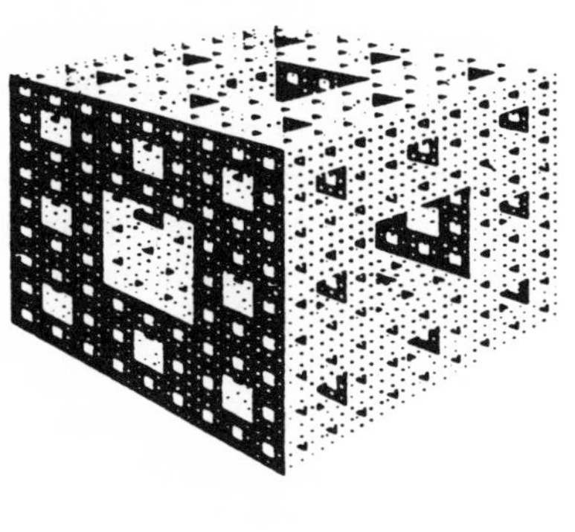

Sierpensky's sponge: more than a surface, less than a volume. The law according to which this cube was hollowed can be understood intuitively at a glance. Each square hole is surrounded by eight holes a third its size. These holes are in turn surrounded by eight holes, also a third their size. And so on, endlessly. The illustrator could not represent the infinity of holes of decreasing size beyond the fourth degree, but it is plain to see that this cube is in the end infinitely hollow. Its total volume approaches zero, while the total lateral surface of the hollowings infinitely grows. This space has a dimension of 2.7268. It therefore lies between a surface (with a dimension of 2) and a volume (with a dimension of 3). "Sierpinsky's rug" is one face of this cube; the hollowings are then squares and the dimension of the "surface" is 1.2618. From *Studies in Geometry* by Leonard M. Blumenthal and Karl Menger. Copyright © 1970 W. H. Freeman and Company. Reprinted with permission.

Concerning Benoit Mandelbrot's "Fractals"

obtained by making holes, by cutting "windows" into a circle, instead of adding "points" to a triangle; likewise, a cube into which holes are drilled according to the principle of similarity becomes less than a volume but more than a surface (this is the mathematical presentation of the affinity between a free space and a holey space). In still other forms, Brownian motion, turbulence, and the sky are "fractals" of this kind.[20] Perhaps this provides us with another way of defining *fuzzy aggregates.* But the main thing is that it provides a general determination for smooth space that takes into account its differences from and relations to striated space: (1) we shall call striated or metric any aggregate with a whole number of dimensions, and for which it is possible to assign constant directions; (2) nonmetric smooth space is constituted by the construction of a line with a fractional number of dimensions greater than one, or of a surface with a fractional number of dimensions greater than two; (3) a fractional number of dimensions is the index of a properly directional space (with continuous variation in direction, and without tangent); (4) what defines smooth space, then, is that it does not have a dimension higher than that which moves through it or is inscribed in it; in this sense it is a flat multiplicity, for example, a line that fills a plane without ceasing to be a line; (5) space and that which occupies space tend to become identified, to have the same power, in the anexact yet rigorous form of the numbering or nonwhole number (occupy without counting); (6) a smooth, amorphous space of this kind is constituted by an accumulation of proximities, and each accumulation defines a *zone of indiscernibility* proper to "becoming" (more than a line and less than a surface; less than a volume and more than a surface).

The Physical Model. The various models confirm a certain idea of striation: two series of parallels that intersect perpendicularly, some of which, the verticals, are more in the role of fixed elements or constants, whereas the others, the horizontals, are more in the role of variables. This is roughly the case for the warp and the woof, harmony and melody, longitude and latitude. The more regular the intersection, the tighter the striation, the more homogeneous the space tends to become; it is for this reason that from the beginning homogeneity did not seem to us to be a characteristic of smooth space, but on the contrary, the extreme result of striation, or the limit-form of a space striated everywhere and in all directions. If the smooth and the homogeneous seem to communicate, it is only because when the striated attains its ideal of perfect homogeneity, it is apt to reimpart smooth space, by a movement that superposes itself upon that of the homogeneous but remains entirely different from it. In each model, the smooth actually seemed to pertain to a fundamental heterogeneity: felt or patchwork rather than weaving, rhythmic values rather than harmony-melody, Riemannian space rather than Euclidean space—a continuous variation that exceeds any distribution of constants and variables, the freeing of a line that does not pass between two points, the formation of a plane that does not proceed by parallel and perpendicular lines.

The link between the homogeneous and the striated can be expressed in terms of an imaginary, elementary physics. (1) You begin by striating space with parallel *gravitational* verticals. (2) The resultant of these parallels or forces is applied to a point inside the body occupying the space (*center of gravity*). (3) The position of this point does not change when the direction of the parallel forces is changed, when they become *perpendicular* to their original direction. (4) You discover that gravity is a particular case of a universal *attraction* following straight lines or biunivocal relations between two bodies. (5) You define a general notion of *work* as a force-displacement relation in a certain direction. (6) You then have the physical basis for an increasingly perfect striated space, running not only vertically and horizontally, but in every direction subordinated to points.

It is not even necessary to invoke this Newtonian pseudophysics. The Greeks already went from a space striated vertically, top to bottom, to a centered space with reversible and symmetrical relations in all directions, in other words, striated in every direction in such a way as to constitute a homogeneity. There is no question that these are like two models of the State apparatus, the vertical apparatus of the empire and the isotropic apparatus of the city-state.[21] Geometry lies at the crossroads of a physics problem and an affair of the State.

It is obvious that the striation thus constituted has its limits: they are reached not only when the infinite (either infinitely large or small) is brought in, but also when more than two bodies are considered ("the three-body problem"). Let us try to understand in the simplest terms how space escapes the limits of its striation. At one pole, it escapes them by *declination*, in other words, by the smallest deviation, by the infinitely small deviation between a gravitational vertical and the arc of a circle to which the vertical is tangent. At the other pole, it escapes them by the *spiral or vortex*, in other words, a figure in which all the points of space are simultaneously occupied according to laws of frequency or of accumulation, distribution; these laws are distinct from the so-called laminar distribution corresponding to the striation of parallels. From the smallest deviation to the vortex there is a valid and necessary relation of consequence: what stretches between them is precisely a smooth space whose element is declination and which is peopled by a spiral. Smooth space is constituted by the minimum angle, which deviates from the vertical, and by the vortex, which overspills striation. The strength of Michel Serres's book is that it demonstrates this link between the *clinamen* as a generative differential element, and the formation of vortices and turbulences insofar as they occupy an engendered smooth space; in fact, the atom of the ancients, from Democritus to Lucretius, was always inseparable from a hydraulics, or a generalized theory of swells and flows. The ancient atom is entirely misunderstood if it is overlooked that its essence is to course and flow. The theory of atomism is the basis for a strict correlation between Archimedean geometry (very different from the striated and homogeneous space of Euclid) and Democritean physics (very different from solid or lamellar matter).[22] The same coincidence means that this aggregate is no longer tied in any way to a State apparatus, but rather to a war machine: a physics of packs, turbulences, "catastrophes," and epidemics corresponding to a geometry of war, of the art of war and its machines. Serres states what he considers to be Lucretius's deepest goal: to go from Mars to Venus, to place the war machine in the service of peace.[23] But this operation is not accomplished through the State apparatus; it expresses, on the contrary, an ultimate metamorphosis of the war machine, and occurs in smooth space.

Earlier we encountered a distinction between "free action" in smooth space and "work" in striated space. During the nineteenth century a twofold elaboration was undertaken: of a physicoscientific concept of Work (weight-height, force-displacement), and of a socioeconomic concept of labor-power or abstract labor (a homogeneous abstract quantity applicable to all work, and susceptible to multiplication and division). There was a profound link between physics and sociology: society furnished an economic standard of measure for work, and physics a "mechanical currency" for it. The wage regime had as its correlate a mechanics of force. Physics had never been more social, for in both cases it was a question of defining the constant mean value of a force of lift and pull exerted in the most uniform way possible by a standard-man. Impose the Work-model upon every activity, translate every act into possible or virtual work, discipline free action, or else (which amounts to the same thing) relegate it to "leisure," which exists only by reference to work. We now understand why the Work-model, in both its physical and social aspects, is a fundamental part of the State apparatus. Standard-man began as the man of *public works*.[24] It was not in relation to pin manufacturing that the problems of abstract labor, the multiplication of its results, and the division of its operations were first formulated; it was in public construction and in the organization of armies (not only the disciplining of men, but also the industrial production of weapons). Nothing more normal. The war machine in itself did not imply this normalization. But the State apparatus, in the eighteenth and nineteenth centuries, found a new way of appropriating the war machine: by subjugating it before all else to the Work-model of the construction site and factory, which were in the process of developing elsewhere, but more slowly. The war machine was perhaps the first thing to be striated, to produce an abstract labor-time whose results could be multiplied and operations divided. That is where free action in smooth space must have been conquered. The physicosocial model of Work pertains to the State apparatus, it is one of its inventions, and for two reasons. First, because labor appears only with the constitution of a *surplus*, there is no labor that is not devoted to *stockpiling;* in fact, labor (in the strict sense) begins only with what is called *surplus labor*. Second, labor performs a generalized operation of striation of space-time, a subjection of free action, a nullification of smooth spaces, the origin and means of which is in the essential enterprise of the State, namely, its conquest of the war machine.

Counterdemonstration: where there is no State and no surplus labor, there is no Work-model either. Instead, there is the continuous variation of free action, passing from speech to action, from a given action to another, from action to song, from song to speech, from speech to enterprise, all in a strange chromaticism with intense but rare peak moments or moments of effort that the outside observer can only "translate" in terms of work. It is true that it has been said of blacks through the ages that "they don't work, they don't know what work is." It is true that they were forced to work, and to work more than anyone else, in terms of abstract quantity. It also seems to be true that the Indians had no understanding of, and were unsuited for, any organization of work, even slavery: the Americans apparently imported so many blacks only because they could not use the Indians, who would rather die. Certain outstanding ethnologists have raised an essential question. They have turned the problem around: so-called primitive societies are not societies of shortage or subsistence due to an absence of work, but on the contrary are societies of free action and smooth space that have no use for a work-factor, anymore than they constitute a stock.[25] They are not societies of sloth, even though their differences with work may be expressed in the form of a "right to laziness." They are not without laws, even though their differences with the law may be expressed in the guise of "anarchy." What they have instead is a law of the nomos regulating a continuous variation of activity with a rigor and cruelty all its own (get rid of whatever cannot be transported, the old, children . . .).

If work constitutes a striated space-time corresponding to the State apparatus, is this not especially true of its archaic or ancient forms? For it is there that surplus labor is isolated, distinguished, in the form of tribute or corvée. Consequently, it is there that the concept of labor appears at its clearest, for example, in the large-scale works of the empires, the urban, agricultural, or hydraulic works by which a "laminar" flow in supposedly parallel layers (striation) is imposed upon the waters. It seems on the contrary that in the capitalist regime, surplus labor becomes less and less distinguishable from labor "strictly speaking," and totally impregnates it. Modern public works have a different status from that of large-scale imperial works. How could one possibly distinguish between the time necessary for reproduction and "extorted" time, when they are no longer separated in time? This remark certainly does not contradict the Marxist theory of surplus value, for Marx shows precisely that surplus value *ceases to be localizable* in the capitalist regime. That is even his fundamental contribution. It gave him a sense that machines would themselves become productive of surplus value and that the circulation of capital would challenge the distinction between variable and constant capital. In these new conditions, it remains true that all labor involves surplus labor; but surplus labor no longer requires labor. Surplus labor, capitalist organization in its entirety, operates less and less by the striation of space-time corresponding to the physicosocial concept of work. Rather, it is as though human alienation through surplus labor were replaced by a generalized "machinic enslavement," such that one may furnish surplus-value without doing any work (children, the retired, the unemployed, television viewers, etc.). Not only does the user as such tend to become an employee, but capitalism operates less on a quantity of labor than by a complex qualitative process bringing into play modes of transportation, urban models, the media, the entertainment industries, ways of perceiving and feeling—every semiotic system. It is as though, at the outcome of the striation that capitalism was able to carry to an unequaled point of perfection, circulating capital necessarily recreated, reconstituted, a sort of smooth space in which the destiny of human beings is recast. Striation, of course, survives in the most perfect and severest of forms (it is not only vertical but operates in all directions); however, it relates primarily to the state pole of capitalism, in other words, to the role of the modern State apparatuses in the organization of capital. On the other hand, at the complementary and dominant level of *integrated (or rather integrating) world capitalism*, a new smooth space is produced in which capital reaches its "absolute" speed, based on machinic components rather than the human component of labor. The multinationals fabricate a kind of deterritorialized smooth space in which points of occupation as well as poles of exchange become quite independent of the classical paths to striation. What is really new are always the new forms of turnover. The present-day accelerated forms of the circulation of capital are making the distinctions between constant and variable capital, and even fixed and circulating capital, increasingly relative; the essential thing is instead the distinction between *striated capital* and *smooth capital*, and the way in which the former gives rise to the latter through complexes that cut across territories and States, and even the different types of States.

The Aesthetic Model: Nomad Art. Several notions, both practical and theoretical, are suitable for defining nomad art and its successors (barbarian, Gothic, and modern). First, "close-range" vision, as distinguished from long-distance vision; second, "tactile," or rather "haptic" space, as distinguished from optical space. "Haptic" is a better word than "tactile" since it does not establish an opposition between two sense organs but rather invites the assumption that the eye itself may fulfill this nonoptical function. It was Aloïs Riegl who, in some marvelous pages, gave fundamental aesthetic status to the couple, *close vision-haptic space*. But for the moment we should set aside the criteria proposed by Riegl (then by Wilhelm Worringer, and more recently by Henri Maldiney), and take some risks ourselves, making free use of these notions.[26] It seems to us that the Smooth is both the object of a close vision par excellence and the element of a haptic space (which may be as much visual or auditory as tactile). The Striated, on the contrary, relates to a more distant vision, and a more optical space—although the eye in turn is not the only organ to have this capacity. Once again, as always, this analysis must be corrected by a coefficient of transformation according to which passages between the striated and the smooth are at once necessary and uncertain, and all the more disruptive. The law of the painting is that it be done at close range, even if it is viewed from relatively far away. One can back away from a thing, but it is a bad painter who backs away from the painting he or she is working on. Or from the "thing" for that matter: Cézanne spoke of the need to *no longer see* the wheat field, to be too close to it, to lose oneself without landmarks in smooth space. Afterward, striation can emerge: drawing, strata, the earth, "stubborn geometry," the "measure of the world," "geological foundations," "everything falls straight down" . . . The striated itself may in turn disappear in a "catastrophe," opening the way for a new smooth space, and another striated space . . .

A painting is done at close range, even if it is seen from a distance. Similarly, it is said that composers do not hear: they have close-range hearing, whereas listeners hear from a distance. Even writers write with short-term memory, whereas readers are assumed to be endowed with long-term memory. The first aspect of the haptic, smooth space of close vision is that its orientations, landmarks, and linkages are in continuous variation; it operates step by step. Examples are the desert, steppe, ice, and sea, local spaces of pure connection. Contrary to what is sometimes said, one never sees from a distance in a space of this kind, nor does one see it from a distance; one is never "in front of," any more than one is "in" (one is "on" . . .). Orientations are not constant but change according to temporary vegetation, occupations, and precipitation. There is no visual model for points of reference that would make them interchangeable and unite them in an inertial class assignable to an immobile outside observer. On the contrary, they are tied to any number of observers, who may be qualified as "monads" but are instead *nomads* entertaining tactile relations among themselves. The interlinkages do not imply an ambient space in which the multiplicity would be immersed and which would make distances invariant; rather, they are constituted according to ordered differences that give rise to intrinsic variations in the division of a single distance.[27] These questions of orientation, location, and linkage enter into play in the most famous works of nomad art: the twisted animals have no land beneath them; the ground constantly changes direction, as in aerial acrobatics; the paws point in the opposite direction from the head, the hind part of the body is turned upside down; the "monadological" points of view can be interlinked only on a nomad space; the whole and the parts give the eye that beholds them a function that is haptic rather than optical. This is an animality that can be seen only by touching it with one's mind, but without the mind becoming a finger, not even by way of the eye. (In a much cruder fashion, the kaleidoscope has exactly the same function: to give the eye a digital function.) Striated space, on the contrary, is defined by the requirements of long-distance vision: constancy of orientation, invariance of distance through an interchange of inertial points of reference, interlinkage by immersion in an ambient milieu, constitution of a central perspective. It is less easy to evaluate the creative potentialities of striated space, and how it can simultaneously emerge from the smooth and give everything a whole new impetus.

The opposition between the striated and the smooth is not simply that of the global and the local. For in one case, the global is still relative, whereas in the other the local is already absolute. Where there is close vision, space is not visual, or rather the eye itself has a haptic, nonoptical function: no line separates earth from sky, which are of the same substance; there is neither horizon nor background nor perspective nor limit nor outline or form nor center; there is no intermediary distance, or all distance is intermediary. Like Eskimo space.[28] In a totally different way, in a totally different context, Arab architecture constitutes a space that begins very near and low, placing the light and the airy below and the solid and heavy above. This reversal of the laws of gravity turns *lack of direction* and negation of volume into constructive forces. There exists a nomadic absolute, as a local integration moving from part to part and constituting smooth space in an infinite succession of linkages and changes in direction. It is an absolute that is one with becoming itself, with process. It is the absolute of passage, which in nomad art merges with its manifestation. Here the absolute is local, precisely because place is not delimited. If we now turn to the striated and optical space of long-distance vision, we see that the relative global that characterizes that space also requires the absolute, but in an entirely different way. The absolute is now the horizon or background, in other words, the Encompassing Element without which nothing would be global or englobed. It is against this background that the relative outline or form appears. The absolute itself can appear in the Encompassed, but only in a privileged place well delimited as a center, which then functions to repel beyond the limits anything that menaces the global integration. We can see clearly here how smooth space subsists, but only to give rise to the striated.

The desert, sky, or sea, the Ocean, the Unlimited, first plays the role of an encompassing element, and tends to become a horizon: the earth is thus surrounded, globalized, "grounded" by this element, which holds it in immobile equilibrium and makes Form possible. Then to the extent that the encompassing element itself appears at the center of the earth, it assumes a second role, that of casting into the loathesome deep, the abode of the dead, anything smooth or nonmeasured that may have remained.[29] The striation of the earth implies as its necessary condition this double treatment of the smooth: on the one hand, it is carried or reduced to the absolute state of an encompassing horizon, and on the other it is expelled from the relative encompassed element. Thus the great imperial religions need a smooth space like the desert, but only in order to give it a law that is opposed to the *nomos* in every way, and converts the absolute.

This perhaps explains for us the ambiguity of the excellent analyses by Riegl, Worringer, and Maldiney. They approach haptic space under the imperial conditions of Egyptian art. They define it as the presence of a horizon-background; the reduction of space to the plane (vertical and horizontal, height and width); and the rectilinear outline enclosing individuality and withdrawing it from change. Like the pyramid-form, every side a plane surface, against the background of the immobile desert. On the other hand, they show how in Greek art (then in Byzantine art, and up to the Renaissance), an optical space was differentiated from haptic space, one merging background with form, setting up an interference between the planes, conquering depth, working with cubic or voluminous extension, organizing perspective, and playing on relief and shadow, light and color. Thus at the very beginning they encounter the haptic at a point of mutation, in conditions under which it already serves to striate space. The optical makes that striation tighter and more perfect, or rather tight and perfect in a different way (it is not associated with the same "artistic will"). Everything occurs in a striated space that goes from empires to city-states, or evolved empires. It is not by chance that Riegl tends to eliminate the specific factors of nomad or even barbarian art; or that Worringer, when he introduces the idea of Gothic art in the broadest sense, relates it on the one hand to the Germanic and Celtic migrations of the North, and on the other to the empires of the East. But between the two were the nomads, who are reducible neither to empires they confronted nor the migrations they triggered. The Goths themselves were nomads of the steppe, and with the Sarmatians and Huns were an essential vector of communication between the East and the North, a factor irreducible to either of these two dimensions.[30] On one side, Egypt had its Hyksos, Asia Minor its Hittites, China its Turco-Mongols; and on the other, the Hebrews had their Habiru, the Germans, Celts, and Romans their Goths, the Arabs their Bedouins. The nomads have a specificity that is too hastily reduced to its consequences, by including them in the empires or counting them among the migrants, assimilating them to one or the other, denying them their own "will" to art. Again, there is a refusal to accept that the intermediary between the East and the North had its own absolute specificity, that the intermediary, the interval, played exactly this substantial role. Moreover, it does not have that role in the guise of a "will"; it only has a becoming, it invents a "becoming-artist."

When we invoke a primordial duality between the smooth and the striated, it is in order to subordinate the differences between "haptic" and "optic," "close vision" and "distant vision" to this distinction. Hence we will not define the haptic by the immobile background, by the plane and the contour, because these have to do with an already mixed state in which the haptic serves to striate, and uses its smooth components only in order to convert them to another kind of space. The haptic function and close vision presuppose the smooth, which has no background, plane, or contour, but rather changes in direction and local linkages between parts. Conversely, the developed optical function is not content to take striation to a new level of perfection, endowing it with an imaginary universal value and scope; it is also capable of reinstating the smooth, liberating light and modulating color, restoring a kind of aerial haptic space that constitutes the unlimited site of intersection of the planes.[31] In short, the smooth and the striated must be defined in themselves before the relative distinctions between haptic and optical, near and distant, can be derived.

This is where a third couple enters in: "abstract line-concrete line" (in addition to "haptic-optical," "close-distant"). It is Worringer who accorded fundamental importance to the abstract line, seeing it as the very beginning of art or the first expression of an artistic will. Art as abstract machine. Once again, it will doubtless be our inclination to voice in advance the same objections: for Worringer, the abstract line seems to make its first appearance in the crystalline or geometrical imperial Egyptian form, the most rectilinear of forms possible. It is only afterward that it assumes a particular avatar, constituting the "Gothic or Northern line" understood very broadly.[32] For us, on the other hand, the abstract line is fundamentally "Gothic," or rather, nomadic, not rectilinear. Consequently, we do not understand the aesthetic motivation for the abstract line in the same way, or its identity with the beginning of art. Whereas the rectilinear (or "regularly" rounded) Egyptian line is negatively motivated by anxiety in the face of all that passes, flows, or varies, and erects the constancy and eternity of an In-Itself, the nomad line is abstract in an entirely different sense, precisely because it has a multiple orientation and passes *between* points, figures, and contours: it is positively motivated by the smooth space it draws, not by any striation it might perform to ward off anxiety and subordinate the smooth. The abstract line is the affect of smooth spaces, not a feeling of anxiety that calls forth striation. Furthermore, although it is true that art begins only with the abstract line, the reason is not, as Worringer says, that the rectilinear is the first means of breaking with the nonaesthetic imitation of nature upon which the prehistoric, savage, and childish supposedly depend, lacking, as he thinks they do, a "will to art." On the contrary, if prehistoric art is fully art it is precisely because it manipulates the abstract, though nonrectilinear, line: "Primitive art begins with the abstract, and even the prefigurative. . . . Art is abstract from the outset, and at its origin could not have been otherwise."[33] In effect, the line is all the more abstract when writing is absent, either because it has yet to develop or only exists outside or alongside. When writing takes charge of abstraction, as it does in empires, the line, already downgraded, necessarily tends to become concrete, even figurative. Children forget how to draw. But in the absence of writing, or when peoples have no need for a writing system of their own because theirs is borrowed from more or less nearby empires (as was the case for the nomads), the line is necessarily abstract; it is necessarily invested with all the power of abstraction, which finds no other outlet. That is why we believe that the different major types of imperial lines—the Egyptian rectilinear line, the Assyrian (or Greek) organic line, the supraphenomenal, encompassing Chinese line—convert the abstract line, rend it from its smooth space, and accord it concrete values. Still, it can be argued that these imperial lines are contemporaneous with the abstract line; the abstract line is no less at the "beginning," inasmuch as it is a pole always presupposed by any line capable of constituting another pole. The abstract line is at the beginning as much because of its historical abstraction as its prehistoric dating. It is therefore a part of the originality or irreducibility of nomad art, even when there is reciprocal interaction, influence, and confrontation with the imperial lines of sedentary art.

The abstract is not directly opposed to the figurative. The figurative as such is not inherent to any "will to art." In fact, we may oppose a figurative line in art to one that is not. The figurative, or imitation and representation, is a consequence, a result of certain characteristics of the line when it assumes a given form. We must therefore define those characteristics first. Take a system in which transversals are subordinated to diagonals, diagonals to horizontals and verticals, and horizontals and verticals to points (even when there are virtual). A system of this kind, which is rectilinear or unilinear regardless of the number of lines, expresses the formal conditions under which a space is striated and the line describes a contour. Such a line is inherently, formally, representative in itself, even if it does not represent anything. On the other hand, *a line that delimits nothing, that describes no contour*, that no longer goes from one point to another but instead passes between points, that is always declining from the horizontal and the vertical and deviating from the diagonal, that is constantly changing direction, a mutant line of this kind that is without outside or inside, form or background, beginning or end and that is as alive as a continuous variation—such a line is truly an abstract line, and describes a smooth space. It is not inexpressive. Yet is true that it does not constitute a stable and symmetrical *form of expression* grounded in a resonance of points and a conjunction of lines. It is nevertheless accompanied by *material traits of expression*, the effects of which multiply step by step. This is what Worringer means when he says that the Gothic line (for us, the nomadic line invested with abstraction) has the power of expression and not of form, that it has repetition as a power, not symmetry as form. Indeed, it is through symmetry that rectilinear systems limit repetition, preventing infinite progression and maintaining the *organic* domination of a central point with radiating lines, as in reflected or star-shaped figures. It is free action, however, which by its essence unleashes the power of repetition as a *machinic* force that multiplies its effect and pursues an infinite movement. Free action proceeds by disjunction and decentering, or at least by peripheral movement: disjointed polythetism instead of symmetrical antithetism.[34] Traits of expression describing a smooth space and connecting with a matter-flow thus should not be confused with striae that convert space and make it a form of expression that grids and organizes matter.

Worringer's finest pages are those in which he contrasts the abstract with the organic. The organic does not designate something represented, but above all the form of representation, and even the feeling that unites representation with a subject (*Einfühlung*, "empathy"). "Formal processes occur within the work of art which correspond to the natural organic tendencies in man."[35] But the rectilinear, the geometrical, cannot be opposed to the organic in this sense. The Greek organic line, which subordinates volume and spatiality, takes over from the Egyptian geometrical line, which reduced them to the plane. The organic, with its symmetry and contours inside and outside, still refers to the rectilinear coordinates of a striated space. The organic body is prolonged by straight lines that attach it to what lies in the distance. Hence the primacy of human beings, or of the face: We are this form of expression itself, simultaneously the supreme organism and the relation of all organisms to metric space in general. The abstract, on the contrary, begins only with what Worringer presents as the "Gothic" avatar. It is this nomadic line that he says is mechanical, but in free action and swirling; it is inorganic, yet alive, and all the more alive for being inorganic. It is distinguished both from the geometrical and the organic. It raises "mechanical" relations to the level of *intuition*. Heads (even a human being's when it is not a face) unravel and coil into ribbons in a continuous process; mouths curl in spirals. Hair, clothes . . . This streaming, spiraling, zigzagging, snaking, feverish line of variation liberates a power of life that human beings had rectified and organisms had confined, and which matter now expresses as the trait, flow, or impulse traversing it. If everything is alive, it is not because everything is organic or organized but, on the contrary, because the organism is a diversion of life. In short, the life in question is inorganic, germinal, and intensive, a powerful life without organs, a Body that is all the more alive for having no organs, everything that passes *between* organisms ("once the natural barriers of organic movement have been overthrown, there are no more limits").[36] Many authors have wished to establish a kind of duality in nomad art between the ornamental abstract line and animal motifs, or more subtly, between the speed with which the line integrates and carries expressive traits, and the slowness or fixity of the animal matter traversed, between a line of flight without beginning or end and an almost immobile swirling. But in the end everyone agrees that it is a question of a single will, or a single becoming.[37] This is not because the abstract engenders organic motifs, by chance or by association. Rather, it is precisely because pure animality is experienced as inorganic, or supraorganic, that it can combine so well with abstraction, and even combine the slowness or heaviness of a matter with the extreme speed of a line that has become entirely spiritual. The slowness belongs to the same world as the extreme speed: relations of speed and slowness between elements, which surpass in every way the movement of an organic form and the determination of organs. The line escapes geometry by a fugitive mobility at the same time as life tears itself free from the organic by a permutating, stationary whirlwind. This vital force specific to the Abstraction is what draws smooth space. The abstract line is the affect of smooth space, just as organic representation was the feeling presiding over striated space. The haptic-optical, near-distant distinctions must be subordinated to the distinction between the abstract line and the organic line; they must find their principle in a general confrontation of spaces. The abstract line cannot be defined as geometrical and rectilinear. What then should be termed *abstract* in modern art? A line of variable direction that describes no contour and delimits no form . . .[38]

Do not multiply models. We are well aware that there are many others: a ludic model, which would compare games according to their type of space and found game theory on different principles (for example, the smooth space of Go versus the striated space of chess); and a noological model concerned not with thought contents (ideology) but with the form, manner or mode, and function of thought, according to the mental space it draws and from the point of view of a general theory of thought, a thinking of thought. And so on. Moreover, there are still other kinds of space that should be taken into account, for example, holey space and the way it communicates with the smooth and the striated in different ways. What interests us in operations of striation and smoothing are precisely the passages or combinations: how the forces at work within space continually striate it, and how in the course of its striation it develops other forces and emits new smooth spaces. Even the most striated city gives rise to smooth spaces: to live in the city as a nomad, or as a cave dweller. Movements, speed and slowness, are sometimes enough to reconstruct a smooth space. Of course, smooth spaces are not in themselves liberatory. But the struggle is changed or displaced in them, and life reconstitutes its stakes, confronts new obstacles, invents new paces, switches adversaries. Never believe that a smooth space will suffice to save us.

15. Conclusion: Concrete Rules and Abstract Machines

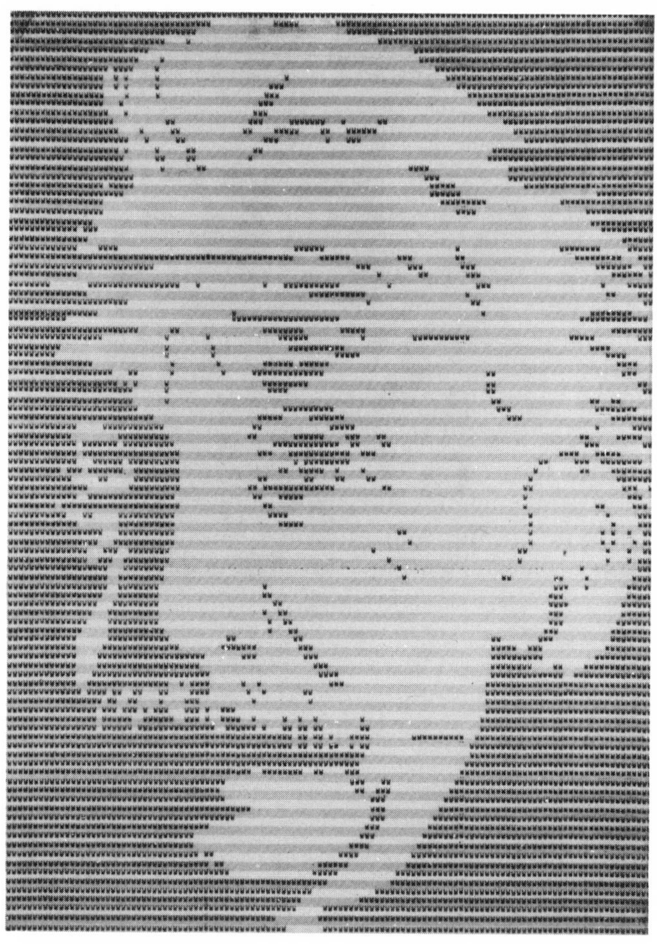

Computer Einstein

S

Strata, stratification

The strata are phenomena of thickening on the Body of the earth,
3 simultaneously molecular and molar: accumulations, coagulations, sedimentations, foldings. They are Belts, Pincers, or Articulations. Summarily and traditionally, we distinguish three major strata: physicochemical, organic, and anthropomorphic (or "alloplastic"). Each stratum, or articulation, consists of coded milieus and formed substances. *Forms and substances, codes and milieus* are not really distinct. They are the abstract components of every articulation.

A stratum obviously presents very diverse forms and substances, a variety of codes and milieus. It thus possesses both different formal Types of organization and different substantial Modes of development, which divide it into *parastrata and epistrata,* for example, the divisions of the organic stratum. The epistrata and parastrata subdividing a stratum can be considered strata themselves (so that the list is never exhaustive). A given stratum retains a unity of composition in spite of the diversity in its organization and development. The unity of composition relates to formal traits common to all of the forms or codes of a stratum, and to substantial elements, materials common to all of the stratum's substances or milieus.

The strata are extremely mobile. One stratum is always capable of serving as the *substratum* of another, or of colliding with another, independently of any evolutionary order. Above all, beween two strata or between two stratic divisions, there are *interstratic* phenomena: transcodings and passages between milieus, intermixings. Rhythms pertain to these interstratic movements, which are also acts of stratification. Stratification is like the creation of the world from chaos, a continual, renewed creation. And the strata constitute the Judgment of God. Classical artists are like God, they make the world by organizing forms and substances, codes and milieus, and rhythms.

Articulation, which is constitutive of a stratum, is always a double articulation (double pincer). What is articulated is *a content and an expression.* Whereas form and substance are not really distinct, content and expression are. Hjelmslev's net is applicable to the strata: articulation of content and articulation of expression, with content and expression each possessing its own form and substance. Between them, between content and expression, there is neither a correspondence nor a cause-effect relation nor a signified-signifier relation:

there is real distinction, reciprocal presupposition, and only isomorphy. But content and expression are not distinguished from each other in the same fashion on each stratum: the distribution of content and expression is not the same on the three major strata (there is, for example, a "linearization" of expression on the organic stratum, and a "superlinearity" of the anthropomorphic strata). That is why the molar and the molecular have very different combinations depending on the stratum considered.

3 What movement, what impulse, sweeps us outside the strata
and (*metastrata*)? Of course, there is no reason to think that all matter is
4 confined to the physicochemical strata: there exists a submolecular,
unformed Matter. Similarly, not all Life is confined to the organic
strata: rather, the organism is that which life sets against itself in order
to limit itself, and there is a life all the more intense, all the more pow-
erful for being anorganic. There are also nonhuman Becomings of
human beings that overspill the anthropomorphic strata in all direc-
tions. But how can we reach this "plane," or rather how can we con-
struct it, and how can we draw the "line" leading us there? For outside
the strata or in the absence of strata we no longer have forms or sub-
stances, organization or development, content or expression. We are
disarticulated; we no longer even seem to be sustained by rhythms.
How could unformed matter, anorganic life, nonhuman becoming be
anything but chaos pure and simple? Every undertaking of
destratification (for example, going beyond the organism, plunging
into a becoming) must therefore observe concrete rules of extreme
6 caution: a too-sudden destratification may be suicidal, or turn can-
cerous. In other words, it will sometimes end in chaos, the void and
destruction, and sometimes lock us back into the strata, which
become more rigid still, losing their degrees of diversity, differentia-
tion, and mobility.

A

Assemblages

Assemblages are already different from strata. They are produced in
11 the strata, but operate in zones where milieus become decoded: they
begin by extracting a *territory* from the milieus. Every assemblage is
basically territorial. The first concrete rule for assemblages is to discover what territoriality they envelop, for there always is one: in their trash can or on their bench, Beckett's characters stake out a territory. Discover the territorial assemblages of someone, human or animal:

"home." The territory is made of decoded fragments of all kinds, which are borrowed from the milieus but then assume the value of "properties": even rhythms take on a new meaning (refrains). The territory makes the assemblage. The territory is more than the organism and the milieu, and the relation between the two; that is why the assemblage goes beyond mere "behavior" (hence the importance of the relative distinction between territorial animals and milieu animals).

Inasmuch as they are territorial, assemblages still belong to the strata. At least they pertain to them in one of their aspects, and it is under this aspect that we distinguish in every assemblage content
4 from expression. It is necessary to ascertain the content and the expression of each assemblage, to evaluate their real distinction, their reciprocal presupposition, their piecemeal insertions. The reason that the assemblage is not confined to the strata is that expression in it becomes a *semiotic system*, a regime of signs, and content becomes a *pragmatic system*, actions and passions. This is the double articulation face-hand, gesture-word, and the reciprocal presupposition between the two. This is the first division of every assemblage: it is simultaneously and inseparably a machinic assemblage and an assemblage of enunciation. In each case, it is necessary to ascertain both what is said and what is done. There is a new relation between content and expression that was not yet present in the strata: the statements or expressions express *incorporeal transformations* that are "attributed" as such (properties) to bodies or contents. In the strata, expressions do not form signs, nor contents *pragmata*, so this autonomous zone of incorporeal transformations expressed by the former and attributed to the latter does not appear. Of course, regimes of signs develop only in the alloplastic or anthropomorphic strata (including territorialized animals). But this does not mean that they do not permeate all of the strata, and overspill each of them. Assemblages belong to the strata to the extent that the distinction between content and expression still holds for them. We may also think of regimes of signs and pragmatic systems as strata in their own right, in the broad sense previously mentioned. But because the content-expression distinction assumes a new figure, we are already in a different element than that of the strata in the narrow sense.

The assemblage is also divided along another axis. Its territoriality (content and expression included) is only a first aspect; the other aspect is constituted by *lines of deterritorialization* that cut across it and carry it away. These lines are very diverse: some open the territorial assemblage onto other assemblages (for example, the territorial

refrain of the animal becomes a courtship or group refrain). Others
operate directly upon the territoriality of the assemblage, and open it
onto a land that is eccentric, immemorial, or yet to come (for exam-
ple, the game of territory and the earth in the lied, or in the romantic
11 artist in general). Still others open assemblages onto abstract and cos-
and mic machines that they effectuate. The territoriality of the assem-
4 blage originates in a certain decoding of milieus, and is just as
necessarily extended by lines of deterritorialization. The territory is
just as inseparable from deterritorialization as the code from decod-
ing. Following these lines, the assemblage no longer presents an
expression distinct from content, only unformed matters, destrati-
fied forces, and functions. The concrete rules of assemblage thus
operate along these two axes: On the one hand, what is the territorial-
ity of the assemblage, what is the regime of signs and the pragmatic
system? On the other hand, what are the cutting edges of deterritori-
alization, and what abstract machines do they effectuate? The assem-
blage is tetravalent: (1) content and expression; (2) territoriality and
deterritorialization. That is why there were four aspects in the privi-
leged example of Kafka's assemblages.

R

Rhizome

10 Not only strata, assemblages are complexes of lines. We can identify a
first state of the line, or a first kind of line: the line is subordinated to
the point; the diagonal is subordinated to the horizontal and vertical;
the line forms a contour, whether figurative or not; the space it consti-
tutes is one of striation; the countable multiplicity it constitutes
remains subordinated to the One in an always superior or supplemen-
tary dimension. Lines of this type are molar, and form a segmentary,
9 circular, binary, arborescent system.

and The second kind is very different, molecular and of the "rhizome"
1 type. The diagonal frees itself, breaks or twists. The line no longer
forms a contour, and instead passes *between* things, *between* points. It
belongs to a smooth space. It draws a plane that has no more dimen-
sions than that which crosses it; therefore the multiplicity it consti-
tutes is no longer subordinated to the One, but takes on a consistency
2 of its own. These are multiplicities of masses or packs, not of classes;
10 anomalous and nomadic multiplicities, not normal or legal ones;
12 multiplicities of becoming, or transformational multiplicities, not
and 14 countable elements and ordered relations; fuzzy, not exact aggre-

gates, etc. At the level of *pathos*, these multiplicities are expressed by psychosis and especially schizophrenia. At the level of pragmatics, they are utilized by sorcery. At the level of theory, the status of multiplicities is correlative to that of spaces, and vice versa: smooth spaces of the type desert, steppe, or sea are not without people; they are not depopulated but rather are populated by multiplicities of this second kind (mathematics and music have gone quite far in the elaboration of this theory of multiplicities).

It is not enough, however, to replace the opposition between the One and the multiple with a distinction between types of multiplici-
9 ties. For the distinction between the two types does not preclude their immanence to each other, each "issuing" from the other after its fashion. It is not so much that some multiplicities are arborescent and others not, but that there is an arborification of multiplicities. That is what happens when the black holes scattered along a rhizome begin to resonate together, or when the stems form segments that striate space in all directions, rendering it comparable, divisible, homoge-
12 neous (as we saw in particular in the case of the Face). That is also what happens when "mass" movements or molecular flows conjugate at points of accumulation or stoppage that segment and rectify them. But conversely, and without symmetry, the stems of the rhizome are always taking leave of the trees, the masses and flows are constantly escaping, inventing connections that jump from tree to tree and uproot them: a whole smoothing of space, which in turn reacts back upon striated space. Even, and especially, territories are perturbed by these deep movements. Or language: the trees of language are shaken by buddings and rhizomes. So that rhizome lines oscillate between
8 tree lines that segment and even stratify them, and lines of flight or
and rupture that carry them away.

9 We are therefore made of three lines, but each kind of line has its dangers. Not only the segmented lines that cleave us, and impose upon us the striations of a homogeneous space, but also the molecular lines, already ferrying their micro-black holes, and finally the lines of flight themselves, which always risk abandoning their creative potentialities and turning into a line of death, being turned into a line of destruction pure and simple (fascism).

C

Plane of Consistency, Body without Organs

The plane of consistency or of composition (planomenon) is opposed

10 to the plane of organization and development. Organization and development concern form and substance: at once the development of form and the formation of substance or a subject. But the plane of consistency knows nothing of substance and form: haecceities, which are inscribed on this plane, are precisely modes of individuation proceeding neither by form nor by the subject. The plane consists abstractly, but really, in relations of speed and slowness between unformed elements, and in compositions of corresponding intensive affects (the "longitude" and "latitude" of the plane). In another sense, consistency concretely ties together heterogeneous, disparate ele-
11 ments as such: it assures the consolidation of fuzzy aggregates, in other words, multiplicities of the rhizome type. In effect, consistency, proceeding by consolidation, acts necessarily in the middle, by the middle, and stands opposed to all planes of principle or finality. Spinoza, Hölderlin, Kleist, Nietzsche are the surveyors of such a plane of consistency. Never unifications, never totalizations, but rather consistencies or consolidations.

10 Inscribed on the plane of consistency are *haecceities*, events, incorporeal transformations that are apprehended in themselves; *nomadic essences*, vague yet rigorous; *continuums of intensities* or continuous
4, 6 variations, which go beyond constants and variables; *becomings*,
7, 9 which have neither culmination nor subject, but draw one another into zones of proximity or undecidability; *smooth spaces*, composed from within striated space. We will say that a body without organs, or
6 bodies without organs (plateaus) comes into play in individuation by
and haecceity, in the production of intensities beginning at a degree zero,
10 in the matter of variation, in the medium of becoming or transformation, and in the smoothing of space. A powerful nonorganic life that
14 escapes the strata, cuts across assemblages, and draws an abstract line without contour, a line of nomad art and itinerant metallurgy.

Does the plane of consistency constitute the body without organs, or does the body without organs compose the plane? Are the Body without Organs and the Plane the same thing? In any event, composer and composed have the same power: the line does not have a dimension superior to that of the point, nor the surface to that of the line,
10 nor the volume to that of the surface, but always an anexact, frac-
and tional number of dimensions that constantly increase or decrease
14 with the number of its parts. The plane sections multiplicities of variable dimensions. The question is, therefore, the mode of connection between the different parts of the plane: To what extent do the bodies without organs interconnect? How are the continuums of intensity extended? What is the order of the transformational series? What are

these alogical linkages always effected in the middle, through which the plane is constructed piece by piece in ascending or descending fractional order? The plane is like a row of doors. And the concrete rules for the construction of the plane obtain to the extent that they exercise a selective role. It is the plane, in other words, the mode of connection, that provides the means of eliminating the empty and cancerous bodies that rival the body without organs, of rejecting the homogeneous surfaces that overlay smooth space, and neutralizing the lines of death and destruction that divert the line of flight. What is retained and preserved, therefore created, what consists, is only *that which increases the number of connections* at each level of division or composition, thus in descending as well as ascending order (that which is cannot be divided without changing in nature, or enter into a larger composition without requiring a new criterion of comparison . . .).

D

Deterritorialization

The function of deterritorialization: D is the movement by which
5 "one" leaves the territory. It is the operation of the line of flight. There are very different cases. D may be overlaid by a compensatory reterritorialization obstructing the line of flight: D is then said to be *negative*. Anything can serve as a reterritorialization, in other words, "stand for" the lost territory; one can reterritorialize on a being, an object, a book, an apparatus or system . . . For example, it is inaccurate to say that the State apparatus is territorial: it in fact performs a D, but one immediately overlaid by reterritorializations on property, work, and money (clearly, that landownership, public or private, is not territorial but reterritorializing). Among regimes of signs, the *signifying regime* certainly attains a high level of D; but because it simultaneously sets up a whole system of reterritorializations on the signified, and on the signifier itself, it blocks the line of flight, allowing only a negative D to persist. Another case is when D becomes positive—in other words, when it prevails over the reterritorializations, which play only a secondary role—but nevertheless remains *relative* because the line of flight it draws is segmented, is divided into successive "proceedings," sinks into black holes, or even ends up in a generalized black hole (catastrophe). This is the case of the *regime of subjective signs*, with its passional and consciousness-related D, which is positive but only in

a relative sense. It will be noted immediately that these two major forms of D are not in a simple evolutionary relation to each other: the second may break away from the first, or it may lead into it (notably when the segmentations of converging lines of flight bring an overall reterritorialization or one benefiting a particular segment, thus arresting the movement of escape). There are all kinds of mixed figures, assuming highly varied forms of D.

Is there *absolute* D, and what does "absolute" mean? We must
first have a better understanding of the relations between D, the
territory, reterritorialization, and the earth. To begin with, the terri-
tory itself is inseparable from vectors of deterritorialization work-
9 ing it from within: either because the territoriality is supple and
and "marginal," in other words, itinerant, or because the territorial
13 assemblage itself opens onto and is carried off by other types of
11 assemblages. Second, D is in turn inseparable from correlative
reterritorializations. D is never simple, but always multiple and
composite: not only because it participates in various forms at the
same time, but also because it converges distinct speeds and move-
ments on the basis of which one may assign at a given moment a
"deterritorialized element" and a "deterritorializing element."
Now, reterritorialization as an original operation does not express a
return to the territory, but rather these differential relations inter-
7 nal to D itself, this multiplicity internal to the line of flight (cf. "The-
and orems of D"). Finally, the earth is not at all the opposite of D: This
10 can already be seen in the mystery of the "natal," in which the earth
as ardent, eccentric, or intense focal point is outside the territory
11 and exists only in the movement of D. More than that, the earth, the
glacial, is Deterritorialization par excellence: that is why it belongs
3 to the Cosmos, and presents itself as the material through which
human beings tap cosmic forces. We could say that the earth, as
deterritorialized, is itself the strict correlate of D. To the point that
D can be called the creator of the earth—of a new land, a universe,
not just a reterritorialization.

This is the meaning of "absolute." The absolute expresses nothing
transcendent or undifferentiated. It does not even express a quantity
that would exceed all given (relative) quantities. It expresses only a
type of movement qualitatively different from relative movement. A
movement is absolute when, whatever its quantity and speed, it
7 relates "a" body considered as multiple to a smooth space that it
and occupies in the manner of a vortex. A movement is relative, whatever
14 its quantity and speed, when it relates a body considered as *One* to a
striated space through which it moves, and which it measures with

straight lines, if only virtual. D is negative or relative (yet already effective) when it conforms to the second case and operates either by principal reterritorializations that obstruct the lines of flight, or by secondary reterritorializations that segment and work to curtail them. D is absolute when it conforms to the first case and brings about the creation of a new earth, in other words, when it connects lines of flight, raises them to the power of an abstract vital line, or draws a plane of consistency. Now what complicates everything is that this absolute D necessarily proceeds by way of relative D, precisely because it is not transcendent. Conversely, relative or negative D itself requires an absolute for its operation: it makes the absolute something "encompassing," something totalizing that overcodes the earth and then conjugates lines of flight in order to stop them, destroy them—rather than connecting them in order to create (it is in this sense that we have opposed *conjunction* to *connection*, although we have often treated them as synonyms from a very general point of view). Thus there is a limitative absolute already at work in properly
9 negative, or even relative, D's. Above all, at this turning point the
and lines of flight are not only obstructed or segmented but turn into lines
14 of destruction or death. For the stakes here are indeed the negative
and the positive in the absolute: the earth girded, encompassed,
11 overcoded, conjugated as the object of a mortuary and suicidal
organization surrounding it on all sides, *or* the earth consolidated, connected with the Cosmos, brought into the Cosmos following lines of creation that cut across it as so many becomings (Nietzsche's expression: Let the earth become lightness . . .). There are thus at least four forms of D that confront and combine, and must be distinguished from one another following concrete rules.

M

Abstract Machines (Diagram and Phylum)

There is no abstract machine, or machines, in the sense of a Platonic Idea, transcendent, universal, eternal. Abstract machines operate within concrete assemblages: They are defined by the fourth aspect of assemblages, in other words, the cutting edges of decoding and
11 deterritorialization. They draw these cutting edges. Therefore they
make the territorial assemblage open onto something else, assemblages of another type, the molecular, the cosmic; they constitute becomings. Thus they are always singular and immanent. Contrary to the strata, and the assemblages considered under their other aspects,

abstract machines know nothing of forms and substances. This is what makes them abstract, and also defines the concept of the machine in the strict sense. They surpass any kind of mechanics. They are opposed to the abstract in the ordinary sense. Abstract machines consist of *unformed matters and nonformal functions.* Every abstract machine is a consolidated aggregate of matters-
5 functions (*phylum* and *diagram*). This is evident on a technological "plane": such a plane is not made up simply of formed substances (aluminum, plastic, electric wire, etc.) or organizing forms (program, prototypes, etc.), but of a composite of unformed matters exhibiting only degrees of intensity (resistance, conductivity, heating, stretching, speed or delay, induction, transduction . . .) and diagrammatic functions exhibiting only differential equations or, more generally, "tensors." Of course, within the dimensions of the assemblage, the abstract machine, or machines, is effectuated in forms and substances, in varying states of freedom. But the abstract machine must first have composed itself, and have simultaneously composed a plane of consistency. Abstract, singular, and creative, here and now, real yet nonconcrete, actual yet noneffectuated—that is why abstract machines are dated and named (the Einstein abstract machine, the Webern abstract machine, but also the Galileo, the Bach, or the Beethoven, etc.). Not that they refer to people or to effectuating moments; on the contrary, it is the names and dates that refer to the singularities of the machines, and to what they effectuate.

But if abstract machines know nothing of form and substance, what happens to the other determination of strata, or even of assemblages—content and expression? In a certain sense, it could be said that this distinction is also irrelevant to the abstract machine,
3 precisely because it no longer has the forms and substances the distinction requires. The plane of consistency is a plane of continuous variation; each abstract machine can be considered a "plateau" of variation that places variables of content and expression in continuity. Content and expression thus attain their highest level of relativity, becoming "functives of one and the same function" or materials of a single matter [see 4, "November 20, 1923: Postulates of Linguistics," note 21—Trans.]. But in another sense, it could be said that the
4 distinction subsists, and is even recreated, on the level of *traits:* there
and are traits of content (unformed matters or intensities) and traits of
5 expression (nonformal functions or tensors). Here, the distinction has become entirely displaced, or even a different distinction, since it now concerns cutting edges of deterritorialization. Absolute deterritorialization implies a "deterritorializing element" and a "deterri-

torialized element," one of which in each case is allocated to expres-
sion, the other to content, *or vice versa*, but always in such a way as to
convey a relative distinction between the two. Thus both content and
expression are necessarily affected by continuous variation, but it
still assigns them two dissymmetrical roles as elements of a single
becoming, or as quanta of a single flow. That is why it is impossible to
define a continuous variation that would not take in both the content
and the expression, rendering them indiscernible, while simultane-
ously proceeding by one *or* the other, determining the two mobile and
relative poles of that which has become indiscernible. For this reason,
one must define both traits or intensities of content and traits or ten-
1, 2 sors of expression (*indefinite article, proper name, infinitive, and*
4, 10 *date*), which take turns leading one another across the plane of con-
sistency. Unformed matter, the phylum, is not dead, brute, homo-
12 geneous matter, but a matter-movement bearing singularities or
haecceities, qualities, and even operations (itinerant technological
lineages); and the nonformal function, the diagram, is not an in-
expressive metalanguage lacking a syntax, but an expressivity-
movement always bearing a foreign tongue within each language and
4 nonlinguistic categories within language as a whole (nomad poetic
lineages). One writes, then, on the same level as the real of an
unformed matter, at the same time as that matter traverses and
extends all of nonformal language: a becoming-animal like Kafka's
10 mouse [p. 243], Hofmannsthal's rats [p. 240], Moritz's calves [p.
240]? A revolutionary machine, all the more abstract for being real. A
regime that no longer operates by the signifier or the subjective.

That covers singular and immanent abstract machines. What we
have said does not preclude the possibility of "the" abstract machine
serving as a transcendent model, under very particular conditions.
This time the concrete assemblages are related to an abstract idea of
the Machine and, depending on how they effectuate it, are assigned
coefficients taking into account their potentialities, their creativity.
The coefficients that "quantify" assemblages bear on the varying
assemblage components (territory, deterritorialization, reterritori-
alization, earth, Cosmos), the various entangled lines constituting
the "map" of an assemblage (molar lines, molecular lines, lines of
flight), and the different relations between the assemblage and the
plane of consistency (phylum and diagram). For example, the "grass
stem" component may have different coefficients in assemblages of
11 animal species that are nevertheless closely related [p. 324-25]. As a
general rule, an assemblage is all the closer to the abstract machine
the more lines without contour passing between things it has, and the

4 more it enjoys a power of metamorphosis (transformation and trans-
and substantiation) corresponding to the matter-function: cf. *The Waves*
10 machine [p. 252].

We have considered in particular two great alloplastic and anthropomorphic assemblages, *the war machine and the State apparatus.* These two assemblages not only differ in nature but are quantifiable in relation to "the" abstract machine in different ways. They do not have the same relation to the phylum, the diagram; they do not have the same lines, or the same components. This analysis of the two
12 assemblages and their coefficients demonstrates *that the war ma-*
and *chine does not in itself have war for its object*, but necessarily adopts it
13 as its object when it allows itself to be appropriated by the State apparatus. At this very precise point, the line of flight and the abstract vital line it effectuates turn into a line of death and destruction. Hence the name war "machine," which is much closer to the abstract machine than is the State apparatus, which divests the war machine of its power of metamorphosis. Writing and music can be war machines. The more an assemblage opens and multiplies connections and draws a plane of consistency with its quantifiers of intensities and of consol-
1, 4 idation, the closer it is to the living abstract machine. But it strays
5, 9 from it to the extent that it replaces creative connections with con-
12 junctions causing blockages (*axiomatics*), organizations forming
and strata (*stratometers*), reterritorializations forming black holes
14 (*segmentometers*), and conversions into lines of death (*deleometers*). Thus there is a whole process of selection of assemblages according to their ability to draw a plane of consistency with an increasing number of connections. Schizoanalysis is not only a qualitative analysis of abstract machines in relation to the assemblages, but also a quantitative analysis of the assemblages in relation to a presumably pure abstract machine.

There is one last point of view, that of typological analysis. For there exist general types of abstract machines. The abstract machine or machines of the plane of consistency do not exhaust or dominate the entirety of the operations that constitute the strata and even the assemblages. The strata "take" on the plane of consistency itself, forming areas of thickening, coagulations, and belts organized and developing along the axes of another plane (substance-form, content-
3 expression). This means that each stratum has a unity of consistency or of composition relating above all to substantial elements and formal traits, and testifying to the existence of a properly stratic abstract machine presiding over this other plane. And there is a third type: on the alloplastic strata, which are particularly propitious for the assem-

blages, there arise abstract machines that compensate for deterritori-
9 alizations with reterritorializations, and especially for decodings
with overcodings or overcoding equivalents. We have seen in particu-
lar that if abstract machines open assemblages they also close them.
4, 7 An order-word machine overcodes language, a faciality machine
and overcodes the body and even the head, a machine of enslavement
8 overcodes or axiomatizes the earth: these are in no way illusions, but
real machinic effects. We can no longer place the assemblages on a
quantitative scale measuring how close or far they are from the plane
of consistency. There are different types of abstract machines that
overlap in their operations and qualify the assemblages: *abstract
machines of consistency*, singular and mutant, with multiplied con-
nections; *abstract machines of stratification* that surround the plane
5 of consistency with another plane; and *axiomatic or overcoding
and abstract machines* that perform totalizations, homogenizations, con-
13 junctions of closure. Every abstract machine is linked to other
abstract machines, not only because they are inseparably political,
economic, scientific, artistic, ecological, cosmic—perceptive, affec-
tive, active, thinking, physical, and semiotic—but because their vari-
ous types are as intertwined as their operations are convergent.
Mechanosphere.

Notes

Notes

Translator's Foreword

1. Gilles Deleuze, in Deleuze and Claire Parnet, *Dialogues* (Paris: Flammarion, 1977; forthcoming from University of Minnesota Press), p. 10.

2. Gilles Deleuze, interview with Catherine Clément, *L'Arc*, no. 49 (revised ed., 1980), p. 99.

3. Gilles Deleuze, "Nomad Thought," in *The New Nietzsche*, ed. Donald B. Allison (Cambridge, Mass.: MIT Press, 1985), p. 148. *Semiotext(e), Nietzsche's Return* 3, 1 (1978), p. 20.

4. Deleuze and Parnet, *Dialogues*, p. 20. On the relationship between philosophy and the State, see also pp. 351–473 of the present work. Deleuze develops an extended critique of rationalist philosophy in *Différence et répétition* (Paris: PUF, 1968); see especially, "L'Image de la pensée," pp. 169-217.

5. Deleuze, "I Have Nothing to Admit," trans. Janis Forman, *Semiotext(e), Anti-Oedipus* 2, 3 (1977), p. 12 (translation modified).

6. "What I detested more than anything else was Hegelianism and the Dialectic" (ibid).

7. Ibid.

8. See Deleuze's discussion with Michel Foucault, "Intellectuals and Power," in Foucault, *Language, Counter-Memory, Practice*, ed. Donald Bouchard (Ithaca, N.Y.: Cornell University Press, 1977), pp. 205-217.

9. Deleuze, "I Have Nothing to Admit," p. 113.

10. Félix Guattari, "Sur les rapports infirmiers-médecins" (1955), in *Psychanalyse et transversalité* (Paris: Maspero, 1972), p. 11.

11. Guattari, *Psychanalyse et transversalité*, pp. 40, 173n, 288-289. The journal *Recherches*, of which Guattari was an editor, was the mouthpiece of the institutional analysis movement.

12. Uneasy because Guattari believed that Laing's communitarian solution reconstituted an extended Oedipal family (*La Révolution moléculaire*, [Paris: Editions Recherches,

1977], p. 121), and because he was critical of Basaglia's assimilation of mental illness and social alienation and his rejection of any kind of institutions for the insane (*Psychanalyse et transversalité*, p. 264).

13. In 1973, Guattari was tried and fined for committing an "outrage to public decency" by publishing an issue of *Recherches* on homosexuality. All copies were ordered destroyed (*La Révolution moléculaire*, p. 110n).

14. *Anti-Oedipus*, trans. Robert Hurley, Mark Seem, and Helen R. Lane (Minneapolis: University of Minnesota Press, 1983).

15. *La Révolution moléculaire*, p. 144. The disintegration of the Left into dogmatic "groupuscules" and the amoeba-like proliferation of Lacanian schools based on personality cults confirmed the charge of bureaucratism but belied the potency of the mix. Guattari himself began his political life in the early 1950s with stormy attempts at membership in two Trotskyist splinter parties (*Psychanalyse et transversalité*, pp. 268-271).

16. *Différence et répétition*, pp. 49-55, 337-349.

17. Jean-François Lyotard, *The Postmodern Condition: A Report on Knowledge*, trans. Geoff Bennington and Brian Massumi (Minneapolis: University of Minnesota Press, 1984), pp. 32-33.

18. Jürgen Habermas's notion of "consensus" is the updated, late-modern version.

19. Interview with Gilles Deleuze, *Libération*, October 23, 1980, p. 16.

20. See Foucault's essay on Blanchot, often quoted by Deleuze: "The Thought from Outside," in *Foucault/Blanchot,* trans. Brian Massumi, Maurice Blanchot, and Michel Foucault (New York: Zone Books, 1987).

21. Deleuze's books on cinema (*Cinema I: The Movement-Image* [Minneapolis: University of Minnesota Press, 1986], and *Cinema II: The Time-Image* [forthcoming from University of Minnesota Press]) and on painting (*Francis Bacon: Logique de la sensation* [Paris: Ed. de la Différence, 1981]) are not meant as exercises in philosophical expansionism. Their project is not to bring these arts to philosophy, but to bring out the philosophy already in them.

22. The terms "smooth space" and "striated space" were in fact coined by Pierre Boulez. See p. 361-62 of the present work and note 20.

23. Interview with Gilles Deleuze, *Libération*, October 23, 1980, p. 17.

24. See page 158 of the present work and note.

25. On style in literature, see Deleuze, *Proust and Signs*, trans. Richard Howard (New York: Braziller, 1972), pp. 142-150.

26. Deleuze and Foucault, "Intellectuals and Power," p. 208.

1. Introduction: Rhizome

1. [TRANS: U. Weinreich, W. Labov, and M. Herzog, "Empirical Foundations for a Theory of Language," in W. Lehmann and Y. Malkeiel, eds., *Directions for Historical Linguistics* (1968), p. 125; cited by Françoise Robert, "Aspects sociaux du changement dans une grammaire générative," *Langages*, no. 32 (December 1973), p. 90.]

2. Bertil Malmberg, *New Trends in Linguistics*, trans. Edward Carners (Stockholm: Lund, 1964), pp. 65-67 (the example of the Castilian dialect).

3. Ernst Jünger, *Approches; drogues et ivresse* (Paris: Table Ronde, 1974), p. 304, sec. 218.

4. Rémy Chauvin in *Entretiens sur la sexualité*, ed. Max Aron, Robert Courrier, and Etienne Wolff (Paris: Plon, 1969), p. 205.

5. On the work of R. E. Benveniste and G. J. Todaro, see Yves Christen, "Le role des virus dans l'évolution," *La Recherche*, no. 54 (March 1975): "After integration-extraction in a cell, viruses may, due to an error in excision, carry off fragments of their host's DNA and

transmit them to new cells: this in fact is the basis for what we call 'genetic engineering.' As a result, the genetic information of one organism may be transferred to another by means of viruses. We could even imagine an extreme case where this transfer of information would go from a more highly evolved species to one that is less evolved or was the progenitor of the more evolved species. This mechanism, then, would run in the opposite direction to evolution in the classical sense. If it turns out that this kind of transferral of information has played a major role, we would in certain cases have to *substitute reticular schemas (with communications between branches after they have become differentiated) for the bush or tree schemas currently used to represent evolution*" (p. 271).

6. François Jacob, *The Logic of Life*, trans. Betty E. Spillmann (New York: Pantheon, 1973), pp. 291-292, 311 (quote).

7. Carlos Castaneda, *The Teachings of Don Juan* (Berkeley: University of California Press, 1971), p. 88.

8. Pierre Boulez, *Conversations with Célestin Deliège* (London: Eulenberg Books, 1976): "a seed which you plant in compost, and suddenly it begins to proliferate like a weed" (p. 15); and on musical proliferation: "a music that floats, and in which the writing itself makes it impossible for the performer to keep in with a pulsed time" (p. 69 [translation modified]).

9. See Melanie Klein, *Narrative of a Child Analysis* (London: Hogarth Press, 1961): the role of war maps in Richard's activities. [TRANS: Deleuze and Guattari, with Claire Parnet and André Scala, analyze Klein's Richard and Freud's Little Hans in "The Interpretation of Utterances," in *Language, Sexuality and Subversion*, trans. Paul Foss and Meaghan Morris (Sydney: Feral Publications, 1978), pp. 141-157.]

10. Fernand Deligny, *Cahiers de l'immuable*, vol. 1, *Voix et voir, Recherches*, no. 8 (April 1975).

11. See Dieter Wunderlich, "Pragmatique, situation d'énonciation et Deixis," in *Langages*, no. 26 (June 1972), pp. 50ff.: MacCawley, Sadock, and Wunderlich's attempts to integrate "pragmatic properties" into Chomskian trees.

12. Steven Rose, *The Conscious Brain* (New York: Knopf, 1975), p. 76; on memory, see pp. 185-219.

13. See Julien Pacotte, *Le réseau arborescent, schème primordial de la pensée* (Paris: Hermann, 1936). This book analyzes and develops various schemas of the arborescent form, which is presented not as a mere formalism but as the "real foundation of formal thought." It follows classical thought through to the end. It presents all of the forms of the "One-Two," the theory of the dipole. The set, trunk-roots-branches, yields the following schema:

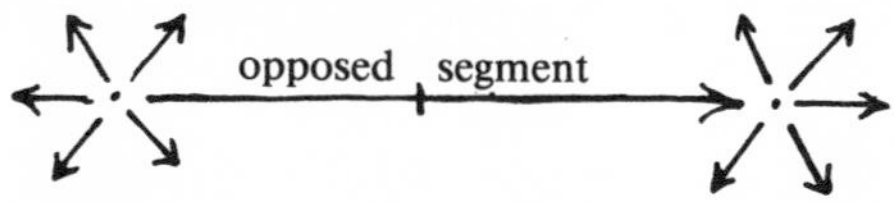

opposed segment

More recently, Michel Serres has analyzed varieties and sequences of trees in the most diverse scientific domains: how a tree is formed on the basis of a "network." *La traduction* (Paris: Minuit, 1974), pp. 27ff.; *Feux et signaux de brume* (Paris: Grasset, 1975), pp. 35ff.

14. Pierre Rosenstiehl and Jean Petitot, "Automate asocial et systèmes acentrés," *Communications*, no. 22 (1974), pp. 45-62. On the friendship theorem, see Herbert S. Wilf, *The Friendship Theorem in Combinatorial Mathematics* (Welsh Academic Press); and on a similar kind of theorem, called the theorem of group indecision, see Kenneth J. Arrow, *Social Choice and Individual Values* (New York: Wiley, 1963).

15. Rosenstiehl and Petitot, "Automate asocial." The principal characteristic of the acentered system is that local initiatives are coordinated independently of a central power,

with the calculations made throughout the network (multiplicity). "That is why the only place files on people can be kept is right in each person's home, since they alone are capable of filling in the description and keeping it up to date: society itself is the only possible data bank on people. A naturally acentered society rejects the centralizing automaton as an asocial intrusion" (p. 62). On the "Firing Squad Theorem," see pp. 51-57. It even happens that generals, dreaming of appropriating the formal techniques of guerrilla warfare, appeal to *multiplicities* "of synchronous modules . . . based on numerous but independent lightweight cells" having in theory only a minimum of central power and "hierarchical relaying"; see Guy Brossollet, *Essai sur la non-bataille* (Paris: Belin, 1975).

16. On Western agriculture of grain plants and Eastern horticulture of tubers, the opposition between sowing of seeds and replanting of offshoots, and the contrast to animal raising, see André Haudricourt, "Domestication des animaux, culture des plantes et traitement d'autrui," *L'Homme*, vol. 2, no. 1 (January-April 1962), pp. 40-50, and "Nature et culture dans la civilisation de l'igname: l'origine des clones et des clans," *L'Homme*, vol. 4, no. 1 (January-April 1964), pp. 93-104. Maize and rice are no exception: they are cereals "adopted at a late date by tuber cultivators" and were treated in a similar fashion; it is probable that rice "first appeared as a weed in taro ditches."

17. Henry Miller, in Henry Miller and Michael Fraenkel, *Hamlet* (New York: Carrefour, 1939), pp. 105-106.

18. See Leslie Fiedler, *The Return of the Vanishing American* (New York: Stein and Day, 1968). This book contains a fine analysis of geography and its role in American mythology and literature, and of the reversal of directions. In the East, there was the search for a specifically American code and for a recoding with Europe (Henry James, Eliot, Pound, etc.); in the South, there was the overcoding of the slave system, with its ruin and the ruin of the plantations during the Civil War (Faulkner, Caldwell); from the North came capitalist decoding (Dos Passos, Dreiser); the West, however, played the role of a line of flight combining travel, hallucination, madness, the Indians, perceptive and mental experimentation, the shifting of frontiers, the rhizome (Ken Kesey and his "fog machine," the beat generation, etc.). Every great American author creates a cartography, even in his or her style; in contrast to what is done in Europe, each makes a map that is directly connected to the real social movements crossing America. An example is the indexing of geographical directions throughout the work of Fitzgerald.

19. [TRANS: Karl Wittfogel, *Oriental Despotism* (New Haven, Conn.: Yale University Press, 1957).]

20. Gregory Bateson, *Steps to an Ecology of Mind* (New York: Ballantine Books, 1972), p. 113. It will be noted that the word "plateau" is used in classical studies of bulbs, tubers, and rhizomes; see the entry for "Bulb" in M. H. Baillon, *Dictionnaire de botanique* (Paris: Hachette, 1876-1892).

21. For example, Joëlle de La Casinière, *Absolument nécessaire. The Emergency Book* (Paris: Minuit, 1973), a truly nomadic book. In the same vein, see the research in progress at the Montfaucon Research Center.

22. *The Diaries of Franz Kafka*, ed. Max Brod, trans. Joseph Kresh (New York: Schocken, 1948), p. 12.

23. Marcel Schwob, *The Children's Crusade*, trans. Henry Copley (Boston: Small, Maynard, 1898); Jersy Andrzejewski, *Les portes du paradis* (Paris: Gallimard, 1959); Armand Farrachi, *La dislocation* (Paris: Stock, 1974). It was in the context of Schwob's book that Paul Alphandéry remarked that literature, in certain cases, could revitalize history and impose upon it "genuine research directions"; *La chrétienté et l'idée de croisade* (Paris: Albin Michel, 1959), vol. 2, p. 116.

24. See Paul Virilio, "Véhiculaire," in *Nomades et vagabonds*, ed. Jacques Bergue (Paris:

Union Générale d'Editions, 1975), p. 43, on the appearance of linearity and the disruption of perception by speed.

25. See Jean-Cristophe Bailly's description of movement in German Romanticism, in his introduction to *La légende dispersée. Anthologie du romantisme allemand* (Paris: Union Générale d'Editions, 1976), pp. 18ff.

2. 1914: One or Several Wolves?

1. Sigmund Freud, *Papers on Metapsychology*, vol. 14, *Standard Edition*, trans. James Strachey (London: Hogarth Press, 1957), p. 200.

2. [TRANS: Virginia Woolf, *Mrs. Dalloway* (New York: Harcourt, Brace and World, 1925), p. 11).]

3. E. A. Bennet, *What Jung Really Said* (New York: Schocken, 1967), p. 74.

4. Ruth Mack Brunswick, "A Supplement to Freud's History of an Infantile Neurosis," in *The Wolf-Man*, ed. Muriel Gardiner (New York: Basic Books, 1971), p. 268.

5. Elias Canetti, *Crowds and Power*, trans. Carol Stewart (New York: Viking Press, 1963), pp. 29-30, 93ff. Some of the distinctions mentioned here are noted by Canetti.

6. [TRANS: Ibid., p. 93.]

7. Letter cited by Roland Jaccard, *L'homme aux loups* (Paris: Ed. Universitaires, 1973), p. 113.

3. 10,000 B.C.: The Geology of Morals

1. Roland Omnès, *L'univers et ses métamorphoses* (Paris: Hermann, 1973), p. 164: "A star that has collapsed so far that its radius has fallen below the critical point becomes what is called a black hole (an occluded star). This expression means that nothing sent in the direction of such an object will ever come back. It is therefore perfectly black since it does not emit or reflect any light."

2. Marcel Griaule, *Dieu d'eau* (Paris: Fayard, 1975), pp. 38-41.

3. For a general treatment of the two aspects of morphogenesis, see Raymod Ruyer, *La genèse de formes vivantes* (Paris: Flammarion, 1958), pp. 54ff., and Pierre Vendryès, *Vie et probabilité* (Paris: Albin Michel, 1945). Vendryès analyzes the role of the articulatory relation and articulated systems. On the two structural aspects of protein, see Jacques Monod, *Chance and Necessity*, trans. Austryn Wainhouse (New York: Vintage, 1972), pp. 90-95.

4. François Jacob, *The Logic of Life*, trans. Betty E. Spillman (New York: Pantheon, 1973), pp. 269-270 [translation modified].

5. François Jacob, "Le modèle linguistique en biologie," *Critique*, no. 322 (March 1974), p. 202: "Genetic material has two roles: it must be reproduced in order to be transmitted to the following generation, and it must be expressed in order for it to determine the organism's structures and functions."

6. Louis Hjelmslev, *Prolegomena to a Theory of Language*, trans. Francis J. Whitfield (Madison: University of Wisconsin Press, 1969), p. 60.

7. See Geoffroy Saint-Hilaire, *Principes de philosophie zoologique* (Paris: Picton et Didier, 1830), which quotes extracts from the debate with Cuvier; and *Notions synthétiques, historiques et physiologiques de philosophie naturelle* (Paris: Denain, 1838), in which Geoffroy sets forth his molecular conception of combustion, electrification, and attraction. Karl Ernest von Baer, *Über Entwicklungsgeschichte der Thiere* (Königsberg: Beiden Gehrüdern Bornträger, 1828-88), and "Biographie de Cuvier," in *Annales des sciences naturelles* (1908). Vialleton, *Membres et ceintures des vertébrés tétrapodes* (Paris: Doin, 1924).

8. Edmond Perrier deserves a place, although not a decisive one, in this long history. He returned to the problem of unity of composition, updating the work of Geoffroy with the aid of Darwin, and especially Lamarck. Perrier's entire work is organized around two themes: animal colonies or multiplicities, and the speeds necessary to account for heterodox degrees and foldings ("tachygenesis"). For example, the brain of a vertebrate may come to occupy the position of the mouth of an annelid, in the "fight between the mouth and the brain." See *Les colonies animales et la formation des organismes* (Paris: G. Masson, 1881), and "L'origine des embranchements du règne animal," *Scienta* (May-June 1918). Perrier wrote a history entitled *Philosophie zoologique avant Darwin* (Paris: Alcan, 1884), which includes excellent chapters on Geoffroy and Cuvier.

9. Georges Canguilhem et al., "Du développement à l'évolution au XIXe siècle," *Thalès* (1960), p. 34.

10. George Gaylord Simpson, *The Meaning of Evolution* (New Haven, Conn.: Yale University Press, 1950).

11. Gilbert Simondon, *L'individu et sa genèse physico-biologique* (Paris: PUF, 1964). On the interior and exterior in the crystal and the organism, and on the role of the limit or membrane, see pp. 107-114 and 259-264.

12. J. H. Rush, *The Dawn of Life* (Garden City, N.Y.: Hanover House, 1957), p. 165: "Primitive organisms lived, in some sense, in a state of suffocation. Life had been born, but it had not yet begun to breathe."

13. Jakob Johann von Uexküll, *Mondes animaux et monde humain* (Paris: Gonthier, 1965).

14. See Pia Laviosa-Zambotti, *Origini e diffusione della civilità* (Milan: C. Marzorati, 1947): her use of the notions of strata, substratum, and parastratum (although she does not define the last.)

15. Jacob, *The Logic of Life*, pp. 290-292, 310-312, and what Rémy Chauvin calls "aparallel evolution."

16. See Laviosa-Zambotti, *Origini:* her conception of waves and flows from center to periphery, and of nomadism and migrations (nomadic flows).

17. On phenomena of resonance between different orders of magnitude, see Simondon, *L'individu*, pp. 16-20, 124-131, and passim.

18. Claude Popelin, *Le taureau et son combat* (Paris: Julliard, 1981): see chapter 4 on the problem of human and bull territories inside the arena.

19. See Simondon, *L'individu*, on orders of magnitude and the establishment of resonance between them; actions of the "mold," "modulation," and "modeling" types; and exterior forces and intermediate states.

20. Obviously there is a multiplicity of sequences or lines. But that does not preclude the "order of order" being unilinear (see Jacob, *The Logic of Life*, p. 286, and "Le modèle linguistique en biologie," pp. 199-203).

21. On the respective independence of proteins and nucleic acids, and their reciprocal presupposition, see Jacob, *The Logic of Life*, pp. 304-306, and Jacques Monod, *Chance and Necessity*, pp. 96-98, 107-109, 114-115, and 142-144.

22. On the notion of transduction, see Simondon, *L'individu*, pp. 18-21 (however, he takes the word in its most general sense and uses it to refer to the entire system). On the membrane, see pp. 259ff.

23. André Leroi-Gourhan, *Le geste et la parole*, vol. 1, of *Technique et langage* (Paris: Albin Michel, 1964), p. 161.

24. On all of these problems (the free hand, the supple larynx, the lips, and the role of the steppe as factors of deterritorialization), see Emile Devaux's fine book, *Trois problèmes: l'espèce, l'instinct, l'homme* (Paris: Le François, 1933), part 3 (chapter 7: "The anthropoid, severed from the forest, retarded in its development, infantilized, had to acquire free hands

and a supple larynx"; and chapter 9: "The forest made the monkey, the cave and the steppe made the human").

25. Jacob, *The Logic of Life*, pp. 278, 289-290, 298. Jacob and Monod sometimes use the word "translation" for the genetic code, but only for reasons of convenience. As Monod points out, "The code can be translated only by products of translation."

26. Leroi-Gourhan, *Le geste et la parole*, pp. 269-275.

27. [TRANS: A reference to the work of Julia Kristeva. On the *chora*, see Kristeva, *Revolution in Poetic Language*, trans. Margaret Waller (New York: Columbia University Press, 1984), pp. 25-30.]

28. That is why we consider Hjelmslev, despite his own reservations and vacillations, to be the only linguist to have actually broken with the signifier and the signified. Many other linguists seem to make this break deliberately and without reservations, but retain the implicit presuppositions of the signifier.

29. Michel Foucault, *Discipline and Punish*, trans. A. M. Sheridan Smith (New York: Vintage, 1975). Already in *The Archaeology of Knowledge*, trans. A. M. Sheridan Smith (New York: Pantheon, 1982), Foucault outlines his theory of the two kinds of multiplicities, multiplicities of expression or statements and multiplicities of contents or objects. He shows that they are irreducible to the signifier-signified couple. He also explains why the title of one of his earlier books, *Les mots et les choses* [Words and Things, translated as *The Order of Things* (New York: Vintage, 1970)], must be understood negatively (pp. 48-49).

30. [TRANS: Foucault, *The Order of Things*, p. 9.]

31. Simondon, *L'individu*, pp. 139-141.

32. H. P. Lovecraft, "Through the Gates of the Silver Key," in *The Dream-Quest of Unknown Kadath* (New York: Ballantine Books, 1970), pp. 168, 217-218.

4. November 20, 1923: Postulates of Linguistics

1. [TRANS: *Mot d'ordre:* in standard French, "slogan," (military) "password." Deleuze and Guattari are also using the term literally: "word of order," in the double sense of a word or phrase constituting a command and a word or phrase creative of order.]

2. Georges Darien, *L'épaulette* (Paris: 10/18, 1973), p. 435. Or Zola, *La Bête Humaine*, trans. Leonard Tancock (New York: Penguin, 1977), p. 148: "She was saying this not to convince him, but solely to warn him that she had to be innocent in the eyes of the world at large." This type of phrase seems to us to be much more characteristic of the novel in general than the informational phrase, "the marquess went out at five o'clock."

3. Oswald Spengler, *Man and Technics*, trans. Charles Francis Atkinson (New York: Knopf, 1932), p. 54 [translation modified].

4. Brice Parain, *Sur la dialectique* (Paris: Gallimard, 1953). Parain develops a theory of "supposition" or the presupposed in language in relation to the orders given to life; but he sees this less as a power in the political sense than a duty in the moral sense.

5. Two authors in particular have brought out the importance of indirect discourse, especially in its so-called free form, from the viewpoint of a theory of enunciation that goes beyond the traditional categories of linguistics: V. N. Vološinov (for Russian, German, and French), *Marxism and the Philosophy of Language* [attributed to Mikhail Bakhtin in the French edition cited by the authors—TRANS], trans. Ladislav Matejka and I. R. Titunik. (Cambridge, Mass.: Harvard University Press, 1986), Part 3, "Toward a History of Forms and Utterance in Language Constructions," pp. 109-200; Pier Paolo Pasolini (for Italian), *L'expérience hérétique* (Paris: Payot, 1976), part 1. We have also referred to an unpublished study by J.-P. Bamberger, "Les formes du discours indirect dans le cinéma, muet et parlant."

6. Emile Benveniste, *Problems in General Linguistics*, trans. Mary Elizabeth Meek

(Coral Gables, Fla.: University of Miami Press, 1971), p. 53: "There is no indication, for example, that a bee goes off to another hive with the message it has received in its own hive. This would constitute a kind of transmission or relay."

7. William Labov has clearly shown the contradiction, or at least paradox, created by the distinction between language and speech: language is defined as the "social part" of language, and speech is consigned to individual variations; but since the social part is self-enclosed, it necessarily follows that a single individual would be enough to illustrate the principles of language, without reference to any outside data, whereas speech could only be studied in a social context. The same paradox recurs from Saussure to Chomsky: "The social aspect of language is studied by observing any one individual, but the individual aspect only by observing language in its social context"; Labov, *Sociolinguistic Patterns* (Philadelphia: University of Pennsylvania Press, 1972), p. 186.

8. Benveniste, *Problems in General Linguistics*, part 4 ("Man and Language"); on the elimination of the illocutionary, see pp. 237-238.

9. Oswald Ducrot, *Dire et ne pas dire* (Paris: Hermann, 1972), pp. 70-80, and "De Saussure à la philosophie du langage," preface to the French translation of S. R. Searle's *Speech Acts*, *Actes de langage* (Paris: Hermann, 1972). Ducrot challenges the notions of linguistic information and code, and communication and subjectivity. He develops a theory of "linguistic presupposition" or nondiscursive implicitness, as opposed to concluded and discursive implicitness still referring to a code. He constructs a pragmatics covering all of linguistics and moves toward a study of assemblages of enunciation, considered from a "juridical," "polemical," or "political" point of view.

10. Bakhtin and Labov have stressed the social character of enunciation, in different ways. They are consequently in opposition not only to subjectivism but also to structuralism, to the extent that the latter ties the system of language to the understanding of an ideal individual, and social factors to actual individuals as speakers.

11. Ducrot, *Dire et ne pas dire*, p. 77: "To qualify an action as criminal (theft, fraud, blackmail, etc.) is not, in our sense of the term, to present it as an *act* since the legal situation of guilt, which defines a crime, is supposed to derive from other given consequences of the activity described: the activity is considered punishable because it is harmful to another person, to order, to society, etc. The judge's statement of a sentence can, on the other hand, be considered a juridical act because there is no intervening effect between the speech of the judge and the transformation of the accused into a convict."

12. John Kenneth Galbraith, *Money* (Boston: Houghton Mifflin, 1975), chapter 12, "The Ultimate Inflation": "On November 20, 1923, the curtain was rolled down. As in Austria a year earlier, the end came suddenly. As with the milder French inflation, *the end came* with astonishing ease. Perhaps it ended simply because it could not go on. On November 20, the old reichsmark *was declared* to be no longer money. A new currency, the rentenmark, was introduced . . . . The new rentenmark *was declared* to be backed by a first mortgage on all the land and other physical assets of the Reich. This idea had its ancestry in the assignats; it was, however, appreciably *more fraudulent* [Galbraith means to say 'deterritorialized'—Au.]. In France in 1789, there was extant, visible land freshly taken from the church for which currency initially could be exchanged; any German seeking to exercise rights of foreclosure on German property with his rentenmarks would have been thought mentally unstable. Nevertheless, it worked. Circumstances helped. . . . If, after 1923, the previous claims on the German budget had continued—the reparations claims and the cost of passive resistance—nothing would have saved the mark and [the head of the Reichsbank's] reputation"; pp. 159, 161.

13. Vološinov [Bakhtin], *Marxism and the Philosophy of Language*, p. 110. And on "symbolic relations of force" as variables internal to enunciation, see Pierre Bourdieu,

"L'économie des échanges linguistiques," in *Linguistique et sociolinguistique, Langue Française*, May 1977, pp. 18-21.

14. The very notion of the proletarian class hinges on the question, Does the proletariat already exist at a given moment, and if so as a body? (Or, does it still exist?) It is evident that Marxists use it in an anticipatory sense, as, for example, when they speak of an "embryonic proletariat."

15. [TRANS: V. I. Lenin, "On Slogans," *Selected Works* (Moscow: Progress Publishers, 1975), vol. 3, p. 148.]

16. Quoted by David Cooper, *The Language of Madness* (London: Allen Lane, 1978), p. 34. Cooper comments that "the language of 'hearing voices' . . . means that one becomes aware of something that exceeds the consciousness of normal [i.e., direct] discourse and which therefore must be experienced as 'other'" (p. 34).

17. Elias Canetti is one of the rare authors who has dealt with the psychological mode of action of the order-word, or "command": *Crowds and Power*, trans. Carol Stewart (New York: Viking Press, 1963), pp. 303-333. He hypothesizes that an order inflicts a kind of sting on the soul, which forms a cyst, a hardening that never goes away. When this happens, the only way to find relief is to pass it on to others as quickly as possible, to "massify," even though the mass may turn back against the emitter of the order-word. In addition, the fact that the order-word is like a foreign body within the body, an indirect discourse within speech, explains the extraordinary forgetting that occurs: "The person who carries out a command . . . does not accuse himself, but the sting: this is the true culprit, whom he carries with him everywhere. . . . It is his permanent witness that it was not he himself who perpetrated a given wrong. He sees himself as its victim and thus has no feeling left for the real victim. It is true, therefore, that people who have acted on orders can feel entirely guiltless," making it all the easier for them to move on to other order-words (p. 332). This provides a profound explanation for the Nazis' feeling of innocence, or for the capacity of forgetfulness displayed by old Stalinists, whose amnesia worsens the more they invoke their memory and past in order to claim the right to follow new and even more insidious order-words—"sting mania." In this respect, Canetti's analysis seems essential. However, it presupposes the existence of a very particular psychic faculty in the absence of which the order-word would not have this mode of action. The whole classical rationalist theory—of "common sense," of universally shared good sense based on information and communication—is a way to cover up or hide, and to justify in advance, a much more disturbing faculty, that of order-words. This singularly irrational faculty is best safeguarded by gracing it with the name of pure reason, by saying that it is nothing but pure reason . . .

18. See Emile Bréhier's classic study, *La théorie des incorporels dans l'ancien stoïcisme* (Paris: Vrin, 1970). On "the knife cuts the flesh" and "the tree turns green," see pp. 12 and 20.

19. [TRANS: Kafka, *The Castle*, trans. Willa and Edwin Muir (New York: Knopf, 1976), p. 12.]

20. [TRANS: Kafka, "The Stoker," chapter 1 of *Amerika*, trans. Edwin Muir (Norfolk, Conn.: New Directions, 1940.]

21. Stalin, in his famous text on linguistics [*Marxism and Linguistics* (New York: International Publishers, 1951)—Trans.], claims to identify two neutral forms serving all of society, all classes, and all regimes equally: instruments and machines as pure means of production of goods, and language as a pure means of information and communication. Even Bakhtin defines language as the form of ideology, but he specifies that the form of ideology is not itself ideological.

22. On these problems, see J. M. Sadock, "Hypersentences" (Diss. University of Illinois, 1968); Dieter Wunderlich, "Pragmatique, situation d'énonciation et Deixis," *Langages*, no. 36 (June 1972), pp. 34-58; and especially S. K. Saumjan, "Aspects algébriques de la gram-

maire applicative," *Langages*, no. 33 (March 1974), pp. 95-122. Saumjan proposes a model of abstract objects based on the operation of application called AGM (applicative generative model). He cites Hjelmslev as an influence; Hjelmslev's strength is to have conceived of the form of expression and the form of content as two entirely relative variables on one and the same plane, as "functives of one and the same function," Hjelmslev, *Prolegomena to a Theory of Language*, trans. Francis J. Whitfield (Madison: University of Wisconsin Press, 1969). This advance toward a diagrammatic conception of the abstract machine is, however, counteracted by the fact that Hjelmslev still conceives the distinction between expression and content in the signifier-signified mode and therefore retains the subordination of the abstract machine to linguistics.

23. See Herbert Brekle, *Sémantique* (Paris: A. Colin, 1974), pp. 94-104, on the idea of a universal pragmatics and of "universals of dialogue."

24. On this budding and various representations of it, see Wunderlich, "Pragmatique, situation d'énonciation et Deixis."

25. Noam Chomsky, *Language and Responsibility. Based on Conversations with Mitsou Ronat*, trans. John Viertel (New York: Pantheon, 1979), pp. 53-55.

26. William Labov, *Sociolinguistic Patterns*, especially pp. 187-190. It will be noted that Labov at times limits himself to statements that have approximately the same meaning and at other times disregards this condition in order to follow a sequence of complementary but heterogeneous statements.

27. [TRANS: This is a phrase from Proust's *Time Regained* in *Remembrance of Things Past*, trans. C. K. Scott Moncrieff, Terence Kilmartin, and Andreas Mayor (New York: Random House, 1981), vol. 3, p. 905 (vol. 3, p. 872, in the French "Pléiade" edition). See Deleuze, *Proust and Signs*, trans. Richard Howard (New York: Braziller, 1972), pp. 59-60.]

28. This is indeed how Labov tends to define his notion of "optional or variable rules," as opposed to constant rules: not simply an observed frequency, but a specific quantity expressing the probability of the frequency or the application of the rule. See *Language in the Inner City* (Philadelphia: University of Pennsylvania Press, 1972), pp. 94ff.

29. See Gilbert Rouget's article, "Un chromatisme africain," in *L'Homme*, vol. 1, no. 3 (September-December 1961), pp. 32-46 (this issue comes with a recording of ritual chants of Dahomey).

30. Ghérasim Luca, *Le chant de la carpe* (Paris: Soleil Noir, 1973), and the recording put out by Givaudan, on which Luca recites the poem "Passionnément."

31. [TRANS: See Carmelo Bene and Gilles Deleuze, *Superpositions* (Paris: Minuit, 1979). Forthcoming in English translation from *Semiotext(e)*.]

32. "And" has an especially important role in English literature, as a function not only of the Old Testament but also of the "minorities" at work on the language: one case in point is J. M. Synge (see François Regnault's remarks on coordination in Anglo-Irish in the French translation of *Playboy of the Western World, Baladin du monde occidental* [Paris: Bibliothèque du Graphe]). It should not be thought adequate to analyze the "and" as a conjunction; rather, "and" is a special form of every possible conjunction and brings into play a logic of language. Jean Wahl's works contain profound reflections on this sense of "and," on the way it challenges the primacy of the verb "to be."

33. Hjelmslev, *Language: An Introduction*, trans. Francis J. Whitfield (Madison: University of Wisconsin Press, 1970), pp. 39ff.

34. Nicolas Ruwet, "Parallélisme et déviations en poésie," in *Langue, discours, société. Pour Emile Benveniste*, ed. Julia Kristeva, Nicolas Ruwet, and Jean-Claude Milner (Paris: Seuil, 1975). Ruwet analyzes Poem 29 in Cummings's *Fifty Poems* (New York: Duell, Sloan and Pearce, 1940); he gives a restricted and structuralist interpretation of this phenomenon of variation, invoking the notion of parallelism; in other texts, he minimizes the importance of

these variations, treating them as marginal exercises irrelevant to true changes in language; still, his comments seem to us to transcend all of these interpretive restrictions.

35. See Vidal Sephiha, "Introduction à l'étude de l'intensif," *Langages*, no. 29 (March 1973). This is one of the first studies of the atypical tensions and variations of language, particularly as they appear in so-called minor languages.

36. On the expansion and diffusion of states of language, in the "patch of oil" mode or the "paratrooper" mode, see Bertil Malmberg, *New Trends in Linguistics*, trans. Edward Carners (Stockholm: Lund, 1964), chapter 3 (which uses N. Lindqvist's important studies on dialect). What are needed now are comparative studies of how homogenizations and centralizations of given major languages take place. In this respect, the linguistic history of French is not at all the same as that of English; neither is their relation to writing as a form of homogenization the same. For French, the centralized language par excellence, one may refer to the analysis of Michel de Certeau, Dominique Julia, and Jacques Revel, *Une politique de la langue* (Paris: Gallimard, 1975). The analysis covers a very brief period at the end of the eighteenth century, focusing on Abbot Gregory, and notes two distinct periods: one in which the central language opposed the rural dialects, just as the town opposed the countryside, and the capital the provinces; and another in which it opposed "feudal idioms," as well as the language of the émigrés, just as the Nation opposes everything that is foreign to it, an enemy of it (pp. 160ff.: "It is also obvious that the rejection of the dialects resulted from a technical inability to grasp stable laws in regional speech patterns").

37. See Michel Lalonde, *Change*, no. 30 (March 1977), pp. 100-122, where the poem, "Speak White," quoted in text, appears, along with a manifesto on the Québecois language ("La deffense et illustration de la langue québecqoyse").

38. On the complex situation of Afrikaans, see Breyten Breytenbach's fine book, *Feu Froid* (Paris: Bourgois, 1976); G. M. Lory's study (pp. 101-107) elucidates Breytenbach's project, the violence of his poetic treatment of the language, and his will to be a "bastard, with a bastard language."

39. On the double aspect of minor language, poverty-ellipsis, and overload-variation, one may refer to a certain number of exemplary studies: Klauss Wagenbach's study of the German of Prague at the beginning of the twentieth century (*Franz Kafka. Eine Biographie seiner Jugend* [Bern: Francke, 1958]); Pasolini's study demonstrating that Italian was not constructed on the basis of a new standard or mean, but exploded in two simultaneous directions, "upward and downward," in other words, toward simplified material and expressive exaggeration (*L'expérience hérétique*, pp. 46-47); J. L. Dillard's study bringing out the double tendency of Black English on the one hand to omit, lose, disencumber, and on the other to overload, to develop "fancy talk" (*Black English* [New York: Random House, 1972]). As Dillard notes, there is no inferiority to the standard language; instead there is a correlation between two movements that necessarily escape from the standard level of language. Still on the topic of Black English, LeRoi Jones shows the extent to which the two conjoined directions approximate language to music (*Blues People* [New York: William Morrow, 1963], pp. 30-31 and all of chapter 3). On a more general level, one will recall Pierre Boulez's analysis of a double movement in music, dissolution of form, and dynamic overload or proliferation: *Conversations with Célestin Deliège*, (London: Eulenberg Books, 1976), pp. 20-22.

40. Yann Moulier, preface to Mario Tronti, *Ouvriers et Capital* (Paris: Bourgois, 1977), p. 6.

41. Pasolini, *L'expérience hérétique*, p. 62

42. See the "Strategy Collective" manifesto on the Québecois language in *Change*, no. 30 (March 1977): it denounces the "myth of subversive language," which implies that simply being in a minority is enough to make one a revolutionary ("this mechanist equation derives from a populist conception of language. . . . Speaking the language of the working class is not

what links an individual to the positions of that class. . . . The argument that Joual has a subversive, countercultural force is entirely idealistic"; p. 188).

43. Elias Canetti, *Crowds and Power* (see the two essential chapters corresponding to the two aspects of the order-word, "The Command" and "Transformation"; especially pp. 313-314, describing the pilgrimage to Mecca and its two coded aspects, mortifying petrification and panicked flight).

44. [TRANS: Translated as "prohibitions of transformation" in the English version of *Crowds and Power. Enantio-* is from the Greek, "to oppose."]

45. [TRANS: Canetti, *Crowds and Power*, pp. 378, 380.]

46. As we have seen, Hjelmslev imposes a restrictive condition, that of assimilating the plane of content to a kind of "signified." Certain authors are therefore correct in objecting that the analysis of content he proposes has less to do with linguistics than other disciplines, such as zoology (for example, André Martinet, with the collaboration of Jeanne Martinet and Henriette Walter, *La linguistique. Guide alphabétique* [Paris: Danoël, 1969], p. 353). It seems to us, however, that this objection applies only to Hjelmslev's restrictive condition.

47. [TRANS: See 12, "1227: Treatise on Nomadology," pp. 351-423.]

48. See the details of the text of Hugo von Hofmannsthal, *Lettres du voyageur à son retour*, trans. Jean-Claude Schneider (Paris: Mercure de France, 1969), letter of May 9, 1901.

5. 587 B.C.-A.D. 70: On Several Regimes of Signs

1. Claude Lévi-Strauss, "Introduction à l'oeuvre de Marcel Mauss," in Marcel Mauss, *Sociologie et anthropologie* (Paris: PUF, 1973), pp. 48-49 (later in this text Lévi-Strauss brings out another aspect of the signified). On this first aspect of the atmospheric continuum, see the Binswanger's and Arieti's psychiatric descriptions.

2. See Lévi-Strauss, *The Savage Mind* (Chicago: University of Chicago Press, 1966), pp. 209ff. (an analysis of the two cases).

3. Lévi-Strauss, preface to Don C. Talayesva, *Soleil Hopi* (Paris: Plon, 1968), p. vi [translation of *Sun Chief*, ed. Leo W. Simmons (New Haven, Conn.: Yale University Press, 1942)].

4. For example, in Bantu myth the first founder of the State shows his face and eats and drinks in public, whereas the hunter, subsequently the warrior, invents the art of secrecy. See Luc de Heusch, *Le roi ivre ou l'origine de l'Etat* (Paris: Gallimard, 1972), pp. 20-25. Heusch sees the second moment as proof of a more "refined" civilization; to us, on the other hand, it is a different semiotic system, that of war rather than public works.

5. Michel Foucault, *Discipline and Punish*, trans. A. M. Sheridan Smith (New York: Vintage, 1975), p. 29 [translation modified].

6. See A. J. Greimas, "Pratiques et langages gestuels," in *Conditions d'une sémiotique du monde naturel, Langages*, no. 10 (June 1968), pp. 3-35. Greimas, however, relates this semiotic to categories such as "the subject of the statement" and the "subject of enunciation," which seem to us to belong to other regimes of signs.

7. On cannibalism as a way of protecting against the souls or names of the dead, and on its semiotic function as "calendar," see Pierre Clastres, *Chronique des Indiens Guayaki* (Paris: Plon, 1972), pp. 332-340.

8. The foregoing expressions concerning the number are borrowed from Julia Kristeva. Kristeva, however, uses them in an analysis of literary texts based on the hypothesis of the "signifier": *Semiotikè. Recherches pour une sémanalyse* (Paris: Seuil, 1969), pp. 294ff., 317.

9. See Paul Sérieux and Joseph Capgras, *Les folies raisonnantes* (Paris: Alcan, 1909), and Gatian Clérambault, *Oeuvre psychiatrique*, rpt. (Paris: PUF, 1942). Capgras believes in an essentially mixed or polymorphous semiotic; Clérambault abstractly analyzes two pure semiotics, although he does recognize that they form de facto mixes. The principal texts on

the origin of the distinction between two groups of delusions are Jean Esquirol, *Des maladies mentales* (Brussels: J. B. Tircher, 1838) (to what extent is "monomania" distinguishable from mania?); and Emil Kraepelin, *Psychiatrie. Ein Lehrbuch für Studierende und Ärtze*, 8th ed. (Leipzig: J. A. Barth, 1920) [English translation, *Lectures on Clinical Psychiatry*, rpt., ed. Thomas Johnstone (New York: Hafner, 1968)] (to what extent is "querulous delusion" distinguishable from paranoia?). The question of the second group of delusions, or the passional delusions, was broached and analyzed historically by Jacques Lacan, *De la psychose paranoïaque* (Paris: Seuil, 1975), and by Daniel Lagache, *La jalousie amoureuse* (Paris: PUF, 1947).

10. See Sérieux and Capgras, *Les folies raisonnantes*, pp. 340ff., and Clérambault, *Oeuvre psychiatrique*, pp. 369ff.: people with passional delusion are overlooked, even in the asylum, because they are calm and cunning, "suffering from a limited enough delusion that they know how we judge them." This makes it all the more necessary to keep them confined; "such patients must not be questioned, but rather maneuvered, and the only way to maneuver them is to move them emotionally."

11. Esquirol suggests that monomania is a "disease of civilization" and has a social evolution: it begins religious but tends to become more and more political, tracked by the police (*Des maladies mentales*, vol. 1, p. 400). See also the remarks of Emmanuel Regis, *Les régicides dans l'histoire et dans le présent* (Lyons: A. Storck, 1890).

12. Deuteronomy 1:12. In the "Pléiade" edition of the Bible (Paris: Gallimard, 1959), vol. 1, p. 510, editor Edouard Dhorme specifies: "Your grievance, literally your proceeding."

13. D. H. Lawrence, *Apocalypse* (New York: Viking, 1932), pp. 93-94.

14. See Edouard Dhorme, *La religion des Hébreux nomades* (Brussels: Nouvelle Société d'Editions, 1937), and Zecharia Mayani, *Les Hyksos et le monde de la Bible* (Paris: Payot, 1956). The author emphasizes the connections between the Hebrews and the Habiru (nomadic warriors) and Kenites (nomadic metal workers); what is specific to Moses is not the principle of numerical organization, which was borrowed from the nomads, but the idea of an always revocable convention-proceeding, contract-proceeding. This idea, according to Mayani, derives neither from the rooted farmers nor from the nomadic warriors, nor even from the migrants, but from a tribe on the march that thinks of itself in terms of subjective destiny.

15. See Franz Kafka, *The Trial*, trans. Willa and Edwin Muir (New York: Schocken, 1968). The painter Titorelli originates the theory of indefinite postponement. Aside from definite acquittal, which does not exist, Titorelli differentiates the two juridical regimes of "ostensible acquittal" and "indefinite postponement"; the first is circular and linked to a semiotic of the signifier, whereas the second is linear and segmentary, linked to the passional semiotic (pp. 152-162).

16. [TRANS: The King James Bible reads "to flee . . . from the presence of the Lord." Jonah 1:3.]

17. Jérôme Lindon was the first to analyze the relation between Jewish prophetism and betrayal, in the exemplary case of Jonah. *Jonas* (Paris: Minuit, 1955).

18. Friedrich Hölderlin, *Remarques sur Oedipe* (Paris: Union Générale d'Edition, 1965). Hölderlin already puts limits on the character of this "slow and difficult" death; see Jean Beaufret's fine discussion of the nature of this death and its relation to betrayal: "Man must match the categorical turning away of the god, now no more than Time, by himself turning away as a traitor."

19. Friedrich Nietzsche, *The Birth of Tragedy*, trans. Walter Kaufmann (New York: Vintage, 1967), sec. 9.

20. [TRANS: See 10, "1730: Becoming-Intense . . . ," note 10.]

21. [TRANS: "Buggers," from the Middle French for "Bulgarians," originally referred to a

sect of heretics from Bulgaria suspected of 'unnatural' practices, and later became a general term for heretics before taking on its modern meaning.]

22. On the nature of the epic "library" (its imperial character, the role of priests, the circulation between sanctuaries and cities), see Charles Autran, *Homère et les origines sacerdotales de l'épopée grecque*, 3 vols. (Paris: Denoël, 1938-1944).

23. See the techniques for the interpretation of books in the Middle Ages, and the extreme attempt by Joachim de Flore, who, on the basis of similarities between the two Testaments, induces from within a third state or proceeding. *L'Evangile éternel* (Paris: Rieder, 1928).

24. For example, Exodus 19:2: "For *they* were departed from Rephidim, and were come to the desert of Sinai, and had pitched in the wilderness, and there *Israel* camped before the mount."

25. Henry Miller, *Sexus* (New York: Grove Press, 1965), p. 250.

26. Louis Althusser, "Idéologie et appareils idéologiques d'Etat," *La pensée*, no. 151 (May-June 1970), pp. 29-35.

27. In *Problems of General Linguistics*, trans Mary Elizabeth Meek (Coral Gables, Fla.: University of Florida Press, 1971), pp. 217-222, Emile Benveniste speaks of a proceeding, or process (*procès*).

28. One aspect of Strindberg's genius was to elevate the couple, and the domestic squabble, to an intense semiotic level, and to make it a creative factor in the regime of signs. This was not the case with Jouhandeau. Klossowski, on the other hand, was able to invent new sources and conflicts for the passional cogito for two, from the standpoint of a general theory of signs; *Les lois de l'hospitalité* (Paris: Gallimard, 1965).

29. See also Dostoyevsky's *The Double*.

30. On these two forms of redundancy, see the entry on "Redondance" in André Martinet, *La linguistique. Guide alphabétique* (Paris: Danoël, 1969), pp. 331-333.

31. Henry Miller, *Sexus*, p. 229. The theme of the idiot is itself quite diverse. It is an explicit part of the cogito according to Descartes, and feeling according to Rousseau. Russian literature, however, takes it down other paths, beyond consciousness or passion.

32. Ghérasim Luca, *Le chant de la carpe* (Paris: Soleil Noir, 1973), pp. 87-94.

33. For example, when the whites introduced money to the Siane of New Guinea, the latter started off by translating the bills and coins into two categories of nonconvertible goods. See Maurice Godelier, "Economie politique et anthropologie économique," *L'Homme*, vol. 14, no. 3 (September-December 1964), p. 123.

34. On these translations-transformations, see LeRoi Jones, *Blues People* (New York: Morrow, 1963), chapters 3-7.

35. Miller, *Sexus*, pp. 479-480.

36. Mary Barnes and Joseph Berke, *Mary Barnes: Two Accounts of a Journey through Madness* (New York: Harcourt Brace Jovanovich, 1971), p. 233. The failure of the antipsychiatry experiment of Kingsley Hall apparently was due as much to these internal factors as to external circumstances.

37. Carlos Castaneda, *Journey to Ixtlan* (New York: Simon and Schuster, 1973), p. 14.

38. "Generative" and "transformational" are Chomsky's terms. For him, the transformational is precisely the best and most profound way of realizing the generative; we, however, are using the terms in a different sense.

39. Michel Foucault has developed, in successive levels, a theory of statements addressing all of these problems. (1) In *The Archaeology of Knowledge*, trans. A. M. Sheridan Smith (New York: Pantheon, 1982), Foucault distinguishes two kinds of "multiplicities," of content and of expression, which are not reducible to relations of correspondence or causality, but are in reciprocal presupposition. (2) In *Discipline and Punish*, trans. A. M. Sheridan Smith (New York: Vintage, 1975), he looks for an agency capable of accounting for the two imbricated,

heterogeneous forms, and finds it in assemblages of power, or micropowers. (3) But these collective assemblages (school, army, factory, hospital, prison, etc.) are only degrees or singularities in an abstract "diagram," which for its part has only matter and function (the unspecified multiplicity of human beings to be controlled). (4) *The History of Sexuality. Vol. 1, An Introduction*, trans. Robert Hurley (New York: Pantheon, 1978), takes yet another direction since assemblages are no longer related to and contrasted with a diagram, but rather to a "biopolitics of population" as an abstract machine. Our only points of disagreement with Foucault are the following: (1) to us the assemblages seem fundamentally to be assemblages not of power but of desire (desire is always assembled), and power seems to be a stratified dimension of the assemblage; (2) the diagram and abstract machine have lines of flight that are primary, which are not phenomena of resistance or counterattack in an assemblage, but cutting edges of creation and deterritorialization.

40. Louis Hjelmslev proposed a very important conception of "matter" or "purport" (*sens*) as unformed, amorphous, or formless: *Prolegomena to a Theory of Language*, trans. Francis J. Whitfield (Madison: University of Wisconsin Press, 1969), sec. 13, pp. 47-60, and *Essais linguistiques* (Paris: Minuit, 1971), pp. 58ff. (see also the preface by François Rastier, p. 9).

41. The distinction between indexes, icons, and symbols comes from C. S. Peirce, *Collected Papers*, ed. Charles Hartshorne and Paul Weiss (Cambridge, Mass.: Harvard University Press, 1931-1958). But his distinctions are based on signifier-signified relations (contiguity for the index, similitude for the icon, conventional rule for the symbol); this leads him to make the "diagram" a special case of the icon (the icon of relation). Peirce is the true inventor of semiotics. That is why we can borrow his terms, even while changing their connotations. First, indexes, icons, and symbols seem to us to be distinguished by territoriality-deterritorialization relations, not signifier-signified relations. Second, the diagram as a result seems to have a distinct role, irreducible to either the icon or the symbol. On Peirce's fundamental distinctions and the complex status of the diagram, one may refer to Jakobson's analysis, "A la recherche de l'essence du langage," in *Problèmes du langage*, ed. Emile Benveniste (Paris: Gallimard, 1966).

6. November 28, 1947: How to Make Yourself a Body without Organs

1. [TRANS: Antonin Artaud, "To Have Done With the Judgement of God," *Selected Writings*, ed. Susan Sontag (New York: Farrar, Straus and Giroux, 1976), p. 571.]

2. [TRANS: Jules Cotard, *Etard sur les maladies cérébrales et mentales* (Paris: Braillière, 1891).]

3. [TRANS: Dr. Schreber's *Memoirs*, quoted by Sigmund Freud, *Notes on a Case of Paranoia*, vol. 12, *Standard Edition*, trans. James Strachey (London: Hogarth Press, 1957), p. 17.]

4. William Burroughs, *Naked Lunch* (New York: Grove Press, 1966), p. 131.

5. The opposition program-phantasy appears clearly in the work of Michel de M'uzan, in relation to a case of masochism. See M'uzan in *La sexualité perverse*, ed. Isle and Robert Barande et al. (Paris: Payot, 1972), p. 36. Although he does not specifically discuss this opposition, M'uzan uses the notion of the program to question the themes of Oedipus, anxiety, and castration.

6. See Kurt Lewin's description of the flow of meat in the American family, "Psychological Ecology," *Field Theory in Social Science*, ed. Dorwin Cartwright (New York: Harper and Brothers, 1951), pp. 170-187.

7. Albert Dalcq, *L'oeuf et son dynamisme organisateur* (Paris: Albin Michel, 1941), p. 95: "Forms are contingent upon kinematic dynamism. It is secondary whether or not an orifice forms in the germ. All that counts is the process of immigration itself; what yields an ori-

fice fissure or primitive line is not invagination, but pure chronological and quantitative variations."

8. Burroughs, *Naked Lunch*, p. 8.

9. Ibid., pp. xlv-xlvi.

10. [TRANS: *Jouissance:* "pleasure, enjoyment, orgasm." In Lacanian psychoanalysis, the object of desire is irrevocably lost and the subject eternally split. *Jouissance* is doubly impossible: life is a *manque-à-jouir*, read as "lack of enjoyment," because the true object of desire is unattainable; and it is a *manque-à-jouir*, read as "a lack to be enjoyed," because *jouissance* as the orgasmic plenitude of union with a substitute object means the annulment of the constitutionally split subject. One of the necessary terms, the subject or the object, is always missing.]

11. Roger Dupouy, "Du masochisme," *Annales médico-psychologiques*, series 12, vol. 2 (1929), p. 405.

12. Ibid.

13. On courtly love, and its radical immanence rejecting both religious transcendence and hedonist exteriority, see René Nelli, *L'érotique des troubadours* (Paris: Union Générale d'Editions, 1974), in particular, vol. 1, pp. 267, 316, 358, and 370, and vol. 2, pp. 47, 53, and 75. (Also vol. 1, p. 128: one of the major differences between chivalric love and courtly love is that for "knights the valor by which one merits love is always *external* to love," whereas in the system of courtly love, the test is essentially *internal* to love; war valor is replaced by "sentimental heroism." This is a mutation in the war machine.)

14. Robert Van Gulik, *Sexual Life in Ancient China* (Leiden: Brill, 1961); and Jean-François Lyotard's discussion of it, *Economie libidinale* (Paris: Minuit, 1974), pp. 241-251.

15. Gregory Bateson, *Steps to an Ecology of Mind* (New York: Ballantine Books, 1972), p. 113.

16. Artaud, *Héliogabale*, in *Oeuvres Complètes* (Paris: Gallimard), pp. 50-51. It is true that Artaud still presents the identity of the One and the Multiple as a dialectical unity, one that reduces the multiple by gathering it into the One. He makes Heliogabalus a kind of Hegelian. But that is a manner of speaking, for from the beginning multiplicity surpasses all opposition and does away with dialectical movement.

17. [TRANS: Artaud, "The Body Is the Body," trans. Roger McKeon, *Semiotext(e), Anti-Oedipus*, vol. 2, no. 3 (1977), p. 59.]

18. Artaud, *The Peyote Dance* (translation of *Les Tarahumaras*), trans. Helen Weaver (New York: Farrar, Straus and Giroux, 1976), pp. 38-39 [translation modified].

19. [TRANS: Carlos Castaneda, *Tales of Power* (New York: Simon and Schuster, 1974), p. 125.]

20. [TRANS: Ibid., p. 183.]

21. [TRANS: Ibid., p. 161.]

22. See *Cause commune*, no. 3 (October 1972).

7. Year Zero: Faciality

1. Josef von Sternberg, *Fun in a Chinese Laundry* (New York: MacMillan, 1965), p. 324. [TRANS: The English version of this phrase reads "merciful darkness."]

2. [TRANS: "Blumfeld. An Elderly Gentleman." *The Complete Stories of Franz Kafka*, ed. Nahum N. Glazer (New York: Schocken, 1983), pp. 183-205.]

3. On this ballet, see Jean Barraqué's *Debussy* (Paris: Seuil, 1977), which cites the text of the argument, pp. 166-171.

4. See Otto Isakower, "Contribution à la psychopathologie des phénomènes associés à l'endormissement," *Nouvelle revue de psychanalyse*, no. 5 (Spring 1972), pp. 197-210; Bertram D. Lewin, "Le sommeil, la bouche et l'écran du rêve," ibid., pp. 211-224; and René

Spitz, with the collaboration of W. Godfrey Cobliner, *The First Year of Life* (New York: International Publishers, 1965), pp. 75-82.

5. Henry Miller, *Tropic of Capricorn* (New York: Grove Press, 1961), pp. 121-123.

6. Klaatsch, "L'évolution du genre humain," in Kreomer, *L'Univers et l'humanité*, vol. 2: "In vain, we tried to find a trace of red edging around the lips of live, young chimpanzees, which resemble man so closely in all other respects. . . . How would the face of the most gracious young woman look if her mouth was a stripe between two white borders? . . . In addition, the pectoral region of the anthropoid possesses the two nipples of the mammary glands, but folds of fat comparable to the breasts never form." And Emile Devaux's formula in *Trois problèmes: l'espèce, l'instinct, l'homme* (Paris: Le François, 1933), p. 264: "The child made the woman's breast, and the mother the child's lips."

7. Face exercises play an essential role in the pedagogical principles of J.-B. de la Salle. Even Ignacio de Loyola integrated his teaching landscape exercises or "compositions of place" relative to the life of Christ, hell, the world, etc. As Barthes points out, this involves skeletal images subordinated to a language, but also active schemas to be completed, colored in, like those found in catechisms and devotional handbooks [*Sade, Fourier, Loyola*, trans. Richard Miller (New York: Hill and Wang, 1976)—Trans.]

8. Chrétien de Troyes, *The Story of the Grail*, trans. Robert White Linker (Chapel Hill: University of North Carolina Press, 1952), pp. 88-89. A similar scene, dominated by the "machinery" of the boat, is found in Malcolm Lowry's novel *Ultramarine* (Philadelphia: Lippincott, 1962), pp. 159-172: a pigeon drowns in waters infested by sharks, "as if a red leaf should fall on a white torrent" (p. 170), and this inevitably evokes the image of a bloody face. Lowry's scene is imbedded in such different elements and is so particularly organized that there can be no question of influence by Chrétien de Troyes's scene, only confluence with it. This makes it an even better confirmation of the existence of a veritable black hole or red mark-white wall abstract machine (snow or water).

9. [TRANS: Continued in 10, "1730: Becoming-Intense . . . ," pp. 232-309]

10. Sergei Eisenstein, *Film Form and Film Sense*, trans. Jay Leyda (New York: Meridian Books, 1957), p. 195-199: "'The kettle began it . . .' Thus Dickens opens his *Cricket on the Hearth*. . . . What could be further from films! . . . But, strange as it may seem, movies also were boiling in that kettle. . . . As soon as we recognize this kettle as a typical close-up, we exclaim: '. . . of course this is the purest Griffith.' . . . Certainly, this kettle is a typical Griffith-esque close-up. A close-up saturated, we now become aware, with typically Dickens-esque 'atmosphere,' with which Griffith, with equal mastery, can envelop the severe face of life in *Way Down East*, and the icy cold moral face of his characters, who push the guilty Anna onto the shifting surface of a swirling ice-break" (the white wall again).

11. Jacques Lizot, *Le cercle des feux* (Paris: Seuil, 1976), pp. 34ff.

12. On the stranger grasped as Other, see André Haudricourt, "Nature et culture dans la civilisation de l'igname: l'origine des clones et des clans," *L'Homme* vol. 4, no. 1 (January-April 1964), pp. 98-102. And Robert Jaulin, *Gens de soi, gens de l'autre* (Paris: Union Générale d'Editions, 1973), preface, p. 20.

13. Maurice Ronai demonstrates that the landscape, the reality as well as the notion, is tied to a very particular semiotic system and very particular apparatuses of power: this is one of the sources of geography, as well as a principle behind its political subordination (the landscape as "the face of the fatherland or nation"). See "Paysages," in *Hérodote*, no. 1 (January-March 1976), pp. 125-159.

14. See Jacques Mercier, *Ethiopian Magic Scrolls*, trans. Richard Pevear (New York: Braziller, 1979). And "Les peintures des rouleaux protecteurs éthiopiens," *Journal of Ethiopian Studies*, vol. 14, fasc. 2 (Summer 1974), pp. 89-106 ("The eye stands for the face which stands for the body. . . . The pupils are drawn in the inner spaces. . . . That is why we must

speak of directions of magic meaning based on eyes and faces, with the use of traditional decorative motifs such as cross-hatching, check patterns, four-pointed stars, etc."). The power of Negus, with his ancestry going back to Solomon and his court of magicians, was based on his ember-eyes, operating like a black hole, angelic or demonic. Mercier's analyses in their entirety constitute an essential contribution to the analysis of facial functions.

15. For Eisenstein's own distinction between his conception of the close-up and Griffith's, see *Film Form and Film Sense.*

16. This is a recurring theme in horror novels and science fiction: the eyes are in the black hole, not the opposite ("I see a luminous disk emerging from the black hole, resembling eyes"). Comic books, *Circus* No. 2, for example, depict black holes populated by faces and eyes, and the traversing of that black hole. On the relation of eyes to holes and walls, see the texts and drawing of Jean-Luc Parant, in particular, *Les yeux MMDVI* (Paris: Bourgois, 1976).

17. See Jean Paris's analyses, *L'espace et le regard* (Paris: Seuil, 1965), vol. 1, chapter 1 (also, the evolution of the Virgin and the variation in the relations between her face and that of the infant Jesus: vol. 2, chapter 2).

18. D. H. Lawrence, "Melville's 'Typee' and 'Omoo,'" *Studies in Classic American Literature* (New York: Thomas Seltzer, 1923), p. 197. Lawrence's essay begins with a lovely distinction between terrestrial and maritime eyes.

19. Miller, *Tropic of Capricorn*, p. 239.

20. Ibid., p. 63.

21. Ibid., pp. 63-64.

22. Wilhelm Reich's *Character-Analysis*, trans. Theodore P. Wolfe (New York: Farrar, Straus and Giroux, 1970), considers the face and faciality traits to be among the first pieces of character "armor" and the first ego resistances (the "occular ring," followed by the "oral ring"). The organization of these rings occurs on planes perpendicular to the "orgonotic streaming" and oppose the free movement of this streaming throughout the body. Hence the importance of eliminating the armor and "dissolving the rings." See pp. 370ff.

23. Lawrence, *Studies in Classic American Literature*, p. 200.

24. D. H. Lawrence, *Kangaroo* (London: William Heinemann, 1964), p. 339.

8. 1874: Three Novellas, or "What Happened?"

1. See Jules Amédée Barbey d'Aurevilly, *The Diaboliques*, trans. Ernest Boyd (New York: Knopf, 1925). Of course, the work of Maupassant is not limited to tales; he also wrote novellas, or novels containing elements of the novellas. For example, the episode of Lison in chapter 4 of *Une vie:* "It was at the time of Aunt Lison's sudden impulse. . . . It was never spoken of again, and remained as though enveloped in fog. One evening, Lise, then twenty, threw herself into the water without anyone having an inkling why. Nothing in her life or manners, could have allowed one to predict this act of madness."

2. Vladimir Propp, *Morphology of the Folktale*, 2nd ed., trans. Laurence Scott (Austin: University of Texas Press, 1968).

3. Marcel Arland, *Le Promeneur* (Paris: Pavois, 1944).

4. [TRANS: "In the Cage," *The Novels and Tales of Henry James* (Fairfield, N.J.: Augustus M. Kelley, 1979), vol. 11, p. 469.]

5. Nathalie Sarraute, in "Conversation and Sub-conversation," *The Age of Suspicion*, trans. Maria Jolas (New York: Braziller, 1963), shows how Proust analyzes the smallest movements, glances, or intonations. However, he apprehends them through memory, he assigns them a "position," he thinks of them as a sequence of causes and effects; "he rarely . . . tried to relive them and make them relive for the reader in the present, while they were forming and

developing, like so many tiny dramas, each one of which has its adventures, its mystery and its unforeseeable ending" (p. 92).

6. [TRANS: The French translation consulted by the authors reversed the meaning of this passage. The original reads: "She knew at last so much that she had quite lost her earlier sense of merely guessing. There were no different shades of distinctions—it all bounced out." *In the Cage, The Novels and Tales of Henry James*, vol. 11, p. 472.]

7. Søren Kierkegaard, *Fear and Trembling*, trans. Walter Lowrie (Princeton, N.J.: Princeton University Press, 1954), pp. 49ff.

8. [TRANS: Scott Fitzgerald, "The Crack-up," in *The Crack-up. With Other Uncollected Pieces*, ed. Edmund Wilson (New York: New Directions, 1956), p. 69.]

9. [TRANS: Ibid., pp. 82, 84.]

10. Pierrette Fleutiaux, *Histoire du gouffre et de la lunette et autres nouvelles* (Paris: Julliard, 1976), pp. 9-50.

11. In another novella in the same collection, "Le dernier angle de transparence" (The last angle of transparency), Fleutiaux distinguishes three lines of perception, but without applying a preestablished schema. The hero has *molar perception*, which takes in overall aggregates and clear-cut elements, well-distributed areas of fullness and emptiness (this perception is coded, inherited, and overcoded by the walls: Don't miss your chair, etc.). But he is also caught up in a *molecular perception* composed of fine and shifting segmentations and autonomous traits, where holes appear in what is full and microforms in emptiness, between two things, where everything "teems and stirs" with a thousand cracks. The hero's problem is that he cannot make up his mind between the two lines and constantly jumps from one to the other. Will he be saved by a third line of perception, the *perception of escape*, a "hypothetical direction barely hinted at" by the angle of the two others, the "angle of transparency" opening a new space?

12. Fernand Deligny, *Cahiers de l'immuable*, vol. 1, *Voix et voir, Recherches*, no. 8 (April 1975).

13. Henri Laborit wrote a book "in praise of flight," *Eloge de la fuite* (Paris: Laffont, 1976). In it, he demonstrates the biological importance of lines of flight among animals, but his approach is too formalistic; among human beings, he thinks flight is associated with values of the imaginary functioning to increase one's "information" about the world.

14. [TRANS: See p. 186.]

15. Leon Shestov, *Chekhov and Other Essays* (Ann Arbor: University of Michigan Press, 1966), pp. 8-9 [translation modified to agree with the French edition cited by the authors—Trans].

9. 1933: Micropolitics and Segmentarity

1. Jacques Lizot, *Le cercle des feux* (Paris: Seuil, 1976), p. 118.

2. Claude Lévi-Strauss, *Structural Anthropology*, trans. Claire Jacobson and Brooke Grundfest Schoeft (New York: Basic Books, 1963): "Do Dual Organizations Exist?" pp. 132-163.

3. See two exemplary studies in *African Political Systems*, ed. Meyer Fortes and E. E. Evans-Pritchard (New York: Oxford University Press, 1978): Fortes, "The Political System of the Tellensi of the Northern Territories of the Gold Coast," pp. 239-271, and Evans-Pritchard, "The Nuer of the Southern Sudan," pp. 272-296.

4. Georges Balandier analyzes the ways in which ethnologists and sociologists define this opposition: *Political Anthropology*, trans. A. M. Sheridan Smith (New York: Pantheon, 1970), pp. 137-143.

5. On the initiation of a shaman and the role of the tree among the Yanomami Indians, see Jacques Lizot, *Le cercle des feux*, pp. 127-135: "Between his legs a hole is hastily dug in

which they place the base of the pole they erect there. Turaewë draws imaginary lines on the ground radiating in all directions. He says, 'These are the roots.' "

6. The State, therefore, is not defined solely by the type of public powers it has, but also as a resonance chamber for private as well as public powers. It is for this reason that Althusser says: "The distinction between public and private is a distinction internal to bourgeois law, and valid in the subordinate domains where bourgeois law exercises its powers. The domain of the State eludes it because it is beyond Law. . . . It is on the contrary the foundation for any distinction between the public and the private." "Idéologie et appareils idéologiques d'Etat," *La Pensée*, no. 151 (June 1970), pp. 29-35.

7. Jean-Pierre Vernant, *Mythe et pensée chez les Grecs* (Paris: Maspero, 1971-1974), vol. 1, part 3 ("When it becomes communal, when it is erected in the public and open space of the agora and no longer inside private residences . . . the hearth [*foyer:* also, focus, focal point—Trans.] expresses the center as common denominator of all of the houses constituting the *polis*"; p. 210).

8. Paul Virilio, *L'insécurité du territoire* (Paris: Stock, 1975), pp. 120, 174-175. On "castrametation": "Geometry is the necessary foundation for a calculated expansion of State power in space and time; conversely, this supplies the State with an ideal, sufficient figure, provided that the figure is ideally geometrical. . . . But Fénélon, voicing his opposition to the State policies of Louis XIV, exclaimed: 'Beware the bewitchments and diabolical attributes of geometry!'"

9. Meyer Fortes analyzes the difference among the Tellensi between "guardians of the earth" and chiefs. This distinction between powers is fairly widespread among primitive societies; but the important thing is that it is organized in such a way as to prevent the powers from resonating. For example, according to Louis Berthe's analysis of the Baduj of Java, the power of the guardian of the earth, on the one hand, is considered to be passive and feminine but, on the other hand, is assigned to the eldest son: this is not an "intrusion of kinship into the political order" but on the contrary "a requirement of a political order translated in kinship terms" in order to prevent the establishment of a resonance leading to private property. See Berthe, "Aînés et cadets, l'alliance et la hiérarchie chez les Baduj," *L'Homme*, vol. 5, nos. 3/4 (July-December 65), pp. 189-223.

10. Franz Kafka, *The Castle*, trans. Willa and Edwin Muir (New York: Knopf, 1976), especially chapter 15 (Barnabas's statements [the phrase quoted is on p. 228—Trans]). The parable of the two offices—molar and molecular—does not just have a physical interpretation, as in Eddington, but a properly bureaucratic one as well.

11. The strength of Jean-Pierre Faye's book, *Langages totalitaires* (Paris: Hermann, 1972), is that it illustrates the multiplicity of these focuses, both practical and semiotic, on the basis of which Nazism was constituted. That is why Faye is the first both to do a rigorous analysis of the concept of the totalitarian State (in its Italian and German origins) and to refuse to define Italian fascism and German Nazism by that concept (which operates on a different plane than the "subjacent process"). Faye goes into all of these points in *La critique du langage et son économie* (Paris: Galilée, 1973).

12. On the complementarity between the "macropolitics of security" and the "micropolitics," see Virilio, *L'insécurité du territoire*, pp. 96, 130, 228-235. The microorganization of permanent stress in large modern cities has frequently been noted.

13. Valéry Giscard d'Estaing, speech of June 1, 1976, before the Institut des Hautes Etudes de Défense Nationale (complete text in *Le Monde*, June 4, 1976).

14. On the "flow with mutant power" and the distinction between the two kinds of money, see Bernard Schmitt, *Monnaie, salaires et profits* (Paris: Castella, 1980), pp. 236, 275-277.

15. Michel Lelart, *Le dollar. Monnaie internationale* (Paris: Albatros, 1975), p. 57.

16. Take Foucault's analysis, in *Discipline and Punish*, trans. A. M. Sheridan Smith (New

York: Vintage, 1975), of what he calls the "microphysics of power." First, it is indeed a question of miniaturized mechanisms, or molecular focuses operating in detail or in the infinitely small and forming any number of "disciplines" in the school, army, factory, prison, etc. (see pp. 138ff.). But second, these segments themselves, and the focuses operating within them at the molecular level, present themselves as the singularities of an "abstract" diagram coextensive with the entire social field, or as quanta deducted from a flow of a nonspecific nature—the nonspecific flow being defined by "a multiplicity of individuals" to be controlled (see pp. 205ff. [translation modified]).

17. On "quantitative sinfulness," quanta, and the qualitative leap, one may refer to the microtheology constructed by Søren Kierkegaard in *The Concept of Dread*, trans. Walter Lowrie (Princeton, N.J.: Princeton University Press, 1957).

18. According to Tarde, psychology is quantitative, but only insofar as it studies the desire and belief components of sensation. And logic is quantitative when it does not restrict itself to forms of representation, but extends to degrees of belief and desire, and their combinations; see *La logique sociale* (Paris: Alcan, 1893).

19. On all of these points, see especially Maurice Dobb, *Studies in the Development of Capitalism*, rev. ed. (New York: International Publishers, 1964), and Georges Duby, *The Early Growth of the European Economy: Warriors and Peasants from the Seventh to Twelfth Century*, trans. Howard E. Clarke (London: Weidenfeld & Nicolson, 1974).

20. Rosa Luxemburg, in "Social Reform or Revolution," and "Mass Strike, Party and Trade Unions," in *Selected Political Writings*, ed. Dick Howard (New York: Monthly Review, 1971), formulated the problem of the differences and relations between masses and classes, but from a still-subjective point of view: masses as the "instinctual basis of class consciousness" (see Nicolas Boulte and Jacques Moiroux, "Masse et Parti," *Partisans*, no. 45, *Rose Luxemburg vivante* [December-January 1969], pp. 29-38. Alain Badiou and François Balmès advance a more objective hypothesis: masses are "invariants" that oppose the State-form in general and exploitation, whereas classes are the historical variables that determine the concrete State, and, in the case of the proletariat, the possibility of its effective dissolution; *De l'idéologie* [Paris: Maspero, 1976]). But it is difficult to see, first of all, why masses are not themselves historical variables, and second, why the word is applied only to the exploited (the "peasant-plebeian" mass), when it is also suitable for seigneurial, bourgeois masses—or even monetary masses.

21. Jules Michelet, *Histoire de France au seizième siècle* in *Oeuvres Complètes*, vol. 7, ed. Paul Viallaneix (Paris: Flammarion, 1971-).

22. Henri Pirenne, *Mohammed and Charlemagne*, trans. Bernard Miall (New York: Norton, 1939), p. 22.

23. See Emile Félix Gautier, *Genséric, roi des Vandales* (Paris: Payot, 1932). ("Precisely because they were the weakest, eternally being pushed from behind, they were forced to go the farthest.")

24. Totalitarianism is not defined by the size of the public sector because in many cases there is still a liberal economy. What defines it is the artificial constitution of "closed vessels," particularly monetary and industrial. It is primarily in this sense that Italian fascism and German Nazism were totalitarian States, as demonstrated by Daniel Guérin in *Fascism and Big Business*, trans. Frances and Mason Merrill (New York: Pioneer Publishers, 1939), chapter 9.

25. Foucault, *Discipline and Punish*, p. 27: "These relations go right down into the depths of society, they are not localized in the relations between the state and its citizens or on the frontier between classes and they do not merely reproduce. . . the general form of the law or government. . . . They define innumerable points of confrontation, focuses of instability, each of which has its own risks of conflict, of struggle, and of an at least temporary inversion of the power relation."

26. [TRANS: Kafka, *The Castle*, pp. 233, 238.]

27. On these aspects of banking power, see Suzanne de Brunhoff, *L'offre de monnaie. Critique d'un concept* (Paris: Maspero, 1971), especially pp. 102-131.

28. Carlos Castaneda, *The Teachings of Don Juan* (Berkeley: University of California Press, 1971), pp. 57-60.

29. Maurice Blanchot, *L'amitié* (Paris: Gallimard, 1971), p. 232.

30. F. Scott Fitzgerald, "The Crack-up," in *The Crack-up. With Other Uncollected Pieces*, ed. Edmund Wilson (New York: New Directions, 1956), pp. 77-78, 81.

31. [TRANS: See 12, "1227: Treatise on Nomadology," Proposition IX, pp. 416-423.]

32. Klaus Mann, *Mephisto*, trans. Robin Smith (New York: Random House, 1977), pp. 202-204. This kind of declaration abounds, at the very moment when the Nazis were succeeding. See Goebbels's famous formulations: "In the world of absolute fatality in which Hitler moves, nothing has meaning any longer, neither good nor bad, time nor space, *and what other people call success cannot be used as a criterion*. . . . Hitler will probably end in catastrophe"; *Hitler parle à ses généraux* (Paris: Albin Michel, 1964). This catastrophism can be reconciled with considerable satisfaction, good conscience and comfortable tranquillity. There is a whole bureaucracy of catastrophe. On Italian fascism, one may consult, in particular, the analysis of Maria-Antonietta Macciochi, "Sexualité féminine dans l'idéologie fasciste," *Tel Quel*, no. 66 (Summer 1976), pp. 26-42: the women's death squad, the public display of widows and mothers in mourning, the slogan (*mots d'ordre*) "Coffins and Cradles."

33. Paul Virilio, *L'insécurité du territoire*, chapter 1. Although Hannah Arendt identifies Nazism and totalitarianism, she expressed this principle of Nazi domination: "Their idea of domination was something that no state and no mere apparatus of violence can ever achieve, but only a movement that is constantly kept in motion"; *The Origins of Totalitarianism* (New York: Harcourt, Brace and World, 1966), p. 326; even the war, and the danger of losing the war, acted as accelerators (pp. 325-326, 394ff., 410ff., 462ff.).

10. 1730: Becoming-Intense, Becoming-Animal, Becoming-Imperceptible

1. On the complementarity between series and structure, and how it differs from evolutionism, see Henri Daudin, *Cuvier et Lamarck. Les classes zoologiques et l'idée de série animale*, vol. 2 of *Etudes d'histoire des sciences naturelles* (Paris: Alcan, 1926); and Michel Foucault, *The Order of Things* (New York: Vintage, 1970).

2. See Carl Jung, *Symbols of Transformation*, trans. R. F. C. Hull (New York: Harper, 1962), and Gaston Bachelard, *Lautréamont* (Paris: Librairie José Corti, 1939).

3. Claude Lévi-Strauss, *Totemism*, trans. Rodney Needham (Boston: Beacon Press, 1963), p. 78.

4. Jean-Pierre Vernant in *Problèmes de la guerre en Grèce ancienne* (*Civilisations et sociétés*, no. 11), ed. Jean-Pierre Vernant (The Hague: Mouton, 1968), pp. 15-16.

5. On the opposition between sacrificial series and totemic structure, see Lévi-Strauss, *The Savage Mind* (Chicago: University of Chicago Press, 1966), pp. 223-228. Despite all of his severity toward the series, Lévi-Strauss recognizes the compromise between the two themes: structure itself implies a very concrete feeling for affinities (pp. 37-38) and is based on two series between which it organizes homologies of relations. In particular, "becoming-historical" can bring complications or degradations that replace these homologies with resemblances and identifications between terms (see pp. 115ff., and what Lévi-Strauss calls the "flipside of totemism").

6. Jean Duvignaud, *L'anomie. Hérésie et Subversion* (Paris: Ed. Anthropos, 1973).

7. [TRANS: H. P. Lovecraft, "Through the Gates of the Silver Key," in *The Dream-Quest of Unknown Kadath* (New York: Ballantine Books, 1970), pp. 191-192.]

8. Hugo von Hofmannsthal, *Lettres du voyageur à son retour*, trans. Jean-Claude Schneider (Paris: Mercure de France, 1969), letter of May 9, 1901.

9. *Anton Reiser* (extracts) in *La légende dispersée. Anthologie du romantisme allemand* (Paris: Union Générale d'Editions, 1976), pp. 36-43.

10. [TRANS: *A Universal History of Infamy*, trans. Norman Thomas di Giovanni (New York: Dutton, 1972); Jorge Luis Borges and Margarita Guerrero, *Manual de zoología fantástica* (Mexico City: Fondo de Cultura Económica, 1957), p. 9. The *lobizón* is a fantastic creature of Uruguayan folklore to which many shapes are attributed.]

11. On the man of war, his extrinsic position in relation to the State, the family, and religion, and on the becomings-animal, becomings-wild animal he enters into, see Dumézil, in particular, *Mythes et dieux des Germains* (Paris: E. Leroux, 1939); *Horace et les Curiaces* (Paris: Gallimard, 1942); *The Destiny of the Warrior*, trans. Alf Hiltebeital (Chicago: University of Chicago Press, 1970); *Mythe et épopée* (Paris: Gallimard, 1968-1973), vol. 2. One may also refer to the studies on leopard-man societies, etc., in Black Africa; it is probable that these societies derive from brotherhoods of warriors. But after the colonial State prohibited tribal wars, they turned into crime associations, while still retaining their territorial and political importance. One of the best studies on this subject is Paul Ernest Joset, *Les sociétés secrètes des hommes-léopards en Afrique noire* (Paris: Payot, 1955). The becomings-animal proper to these groups seem to us to be very different from the symbolic relations between human and animal as they appear in State apparatuses, but also in pre-State institutions of the totemism type. Lévi-Strauss clearly demonstrates that totemism already implies a kind of embryonic State, to the extent that it exceeds tribal boundaries (*The Savage Mind*, pp. 157ff.).

12. [TRANS: Kafka, "Josephine the Singer, or the Mouse Folk," in *The Complete Stories of Franz Kafka*, ed. Nahum N. Glazer (New York: Schocken, 1983).]

13. Georges Canguilhem, *On the Normal and the Pathological*, trans. Carolyn R. Fawcett, intro. Michel Foucault (Boston: Reidel, 1978), pp. 73-74.

14. D. H. Lawrence: "I am tired of being told there is no such animal. . . . If I am a giraffe, and the ordinary Englishmen who write about me and say they know me are nice well-behaved dogs, there it is, the animals are different. . . . You don't love me. The animal that I am you instinctively dislike"; *The Collected Letters of D. H. Lawrence*, vol. 2, ed. Harry T. Moore (New York: Viking, 1962), letter to J. M. Murry, May 20, 1929, p. 1154.

15. [TRANS: Herman Melville, *Moby Dick*, chapter 36, "The Quarter-Deck."]

16. René Thom, *Structural Stability and Morphogenesis*, trans. D. H. Fowler (Reading, Mass.: Benjamin Fowler/Cummings, 1975), p. 319.

17. Edward Leach, *Rethinking Anthropology* (New York: Humanities Press, 1971), pp. 18-25.

18. [TRANS: Emile Erckmann and Alexandre Chatrian, *Hugues-le-loup* (Paris: J. Bonaventure, n.d.).]

19. [TRANS: Leach, *Rethinking Anthropology*, p. 18.]

20. See Jacques Lacarrière, *Les hommes ivres de dieu* (Paris: Fayard, 1975).

21. Pierre Gordon, in *Sex and Religion*, trans. Renée and Hilda Spodheim (New York: Social Science Publishers, 1949), studied the role of animal-men in rites of "sacred defloration." These animal-men impose a ritual alliance upon filiative groups, themselves belong to brotherhoods that are on the outside or on the fringes, and are masters of contagion and epidemic. Gordon analyzes the reaction of the villages and cities when they begin to fight the animal-men in order to win the right to perform their own initiations and order their alliances according to their respective filiations (for example, the fight against the dragon). We find the same theme, for example, in Geneviève Calame-Griaule and Z. Ligers, "L'homme-

hyène dans la tradition soudanaise," *L'Homme*, 1, 2 (May-August 1961), pp. 89-118: the hyena-man lives on the fringes of the village, or between two villages, and can keep a lookout in both directions. A hero, or even two heroes with a fiancée in each other's village, triumphs over the man-animal. It is as though it were necessary to distinguish two very different states of alliance: a demonic alliance that imposes itself from without, and imposes its law upon all of the filiations (a forced alliance with the monster, with the man-animal), and a consensual alliance, which is on the contrary in conformity with the law of filiations and is established after the men of the villages have defeated the monster and have organized their own relations. This sheds new light on the question of incest. For it is not enough to say that the prohibition against incest results from the positive requirements of alliance in general. There is instead a kind of alliance that is so foreign and hostile to filiation that it necessarily takes the position of incest (the man-animal always has a relation to incest). The second kind of alliance prohibits incest because it can subordinate itself to the rights of filiation only by lodging itself, precisely, between two distinct filiations. Incest appears twice, once as a monstrous power of alliance when alliance overturns filiation, and again as a prohibited power of filiation when filiation subordinates alliance and must distribute it among distinct lineages.

22. [TRANS: See Fitzgerald, "The Crack-up," in *The Crack-up. With Other Uncollected Pieces*, ed. Edmund Wilson (New York: New Directions, 1956). The allusion to Faust is to Goethe, *Faust*, Part I, lines 1323-1324.]

23. Richard Matheson and Isaac Asimov are of particular importance in this evolution (Asimov extensively develops the theme of symbiosis).

24. Carlos Castaneda, *Tales of Power* (New York: Simon and Schuster, 1974), p. 159.

25. [TRANS: Lovecraft, "Through the Gates of the Silver Key," p. 197.]

26. See D. H. Lawrence, the first and second poems of *Tortoises* (New York: T. Selzer, 1921).

27. [TRANS: Virginia Woolf, *The Waves* (New York: Harcourt Brace Jovanovich, 1931), p. 139.]

28. See the Inquisition manual, *Le marteau des sorciers* (1486), ed. H. Institoris and J. Sprengler (Paris: Plon, 1973), vol. 1, p. 10, and vol. 2, p. 8. The first and simplest case is that of Ulysses' companions, who believed themselves, and were believed to have been, transformed into pigs (or again, King Nebuchadnezzar, transformed into an ox). The second case is more complicated: Diomedes' companions do not believe they have been changed into birds, since they are dead, but demons take over birds' bodies and pass them off as those of Diomedes' companions. The need to distinguish this more complex case is explained by phenomena of transfer of affects; for example, a lord on a hunting excursion cuts off the paw of a wolf and returns home to find his wife, who had not left the house, with a hand cut off; or a man strikes cats, and the exact wounds he inflicts turn up on women.

29. On the problem of intensities in the Middle Ages, the proliferation of theses on this topic, the constitution of kinetics and dynamics, and the particularly important role of Nicholas Oresme, see Pierre Duhem's classic work, *Le système du monde* (Paris: A. Hermann & Fils, 1913-1959), vols. 7-9 (*La physique parisienne au XIVe siècle*).

30. Etienne Geoffroy Saint-Hilaire, *Principes de philosophie zoologique* (Paris: Picton et Didier, 1930). And on particles and their movements, *Notions synthétiques, historiques et physiologiques de philosophie naturelle* (Paris: Denain, 1838).

31. Vladimir Slepian, "Fils de chien," *Minuit*, no. 7 (January 1974). We have given a very simplified presentation of this text.

32. See Roger Dupouy, "Du masochisme," *Annales Médico-psychologiques*, series 12, vol. 2 (1929), p. 405.

33. This is sometimes written "ecceity," deriving the word from *ecce*, "here is." This is an error, since Duns Scotus created the word and the concept from *haec*, "this thing." But it is a

fruitful error because it suggests a mode of individuation that is distinct from that of a thing or a subject.

34. Michel Tournier, *Les météores* (Paris: Gallimard, 1975), chapter 23, "L'âme déployée."

35. [TRANS: On *Aeon* versus *chronos*, see Deleuze, *Logique du sens* (Paris: Minuit, 1969), especially series 23, pp. 190-197.]

36. Pierre Boulez, *Conversations with Célestin Deliège* (London: Eulenberg Books, 1976), pp. 68-71 ("It is not possible to introduce phenomena of tempo into music that has been calculated only electronically, in . . . lengths expressed in seconds or microseconds"; p. 70).

37. Ray Bradbury, *The Machineries of Joy* (New York: Simon and Schuster, 1964), p. 53.

38. [TRANS: Virginia Woolf, *Mrs. Dalloway* (New York: Harcourt Brace and World, 1925), p. 11.]

39. Gustave Guillaume has proposed a very interesting conception of the verb. He distinguishes between an interior time, enveloped in the "process," and an exterior time pertaining to the distinction between epochs (*Epoques et niveaux temporels dans le système de la conjugaison française, Cahiers de linguistique structurale* [Université de Laval, Quebec], no. 4 [1955]). It seems to us that these two poles correspond respectively to the infinitive-becoming, Aeon, and the present-being, Chronos. Each verb leans more or less in the direction of one pole or the other, not only according to its nature, but also according to the nuances of its modes and tenses, with the exception of "becoming" and "being," which correspond to both poles. Proust, in his study of Flaubert's style, shows how the imperfect tense in Flaubert takes on the value of an infinitive-becoming: *Chroniques* (Paris: Gallimard, 1927), pp. 197-199.]

40. On the problem of proper names (in what sense is the proper name outside the limits of classification and of another nature, and in what sense is it at the limit and still a part of classification?), see Alan Henderson Gardiner, *The Theory of Proper Names*, 2nd ed. (New York: Oxford University Press, 1957), and Lévi-Strauss, *The Savage Mind*, chapter 7 ("Time Regained"), pp. 217-244.

41. We have already encountered this problem of the indifference of psychoanalysis to the use of the indefinite article or pronoun among children: as early as Freud, but more especially in Melanie Klein (the children she analyzes, in particular, Little Richard, speak in terms of "a," "one," "people," but Klein exerts incredible pressure to turn them into personal and possessive family locutions). It seems to us that Laplanche and Pontalis are the only ones in psychoanalysis to have had any inkling that indefinites play a specific role; they protested against any overrapid interpretive reduction: "Fantasme originaire," *Les temps modernes*, no. 215 (April 1964), pp. 1861, 1868.

42. See the subjectivist or personalist conception of language in Emile Benveniste, *Problems in General Linguistics*, trans. Mary Elizabeth Meek (Coral Gables, Fla.: University of Miami Press, 1971), chapters 20 ("Subjectivity in Language," pp. 223-230) and 21 ("Analytical Philosophy and Language," pp. 231-238), especially pp. 220-221 and 225-226.

43. The essential texts of Maurice Blanchot serve to refute the theory of the "shifter" and of personology in linguistics. See *L'entretien infini* (Paris: Gallimard, 1969), pp. 556-567. And on the difference between the two propositions, "I am unfortunate" and "he is unfortunate," or between "I die" and "one dies," see *La part du feu* (Paris: Gallimard, 1949), pp. 29-30, and *The Space of Literature*, trans. Ann Smock (Lincoln: University of Nebraska Press, 1982), pp. 90, 122, 126. Blanchot demonstrates that in all of these cases the indefinite has nothing to do with "the banality of daily life," which on the contrary would be on the side of the personal pronoun.

44. [TRANS: These quotes, the first from Nietzsche, the second from Kafka, are quoted more fully in 12, "1227: Treatise on Nomadology," p. 353.]

45. For example, François Cheng, *Chinese Poetic Writing*, trans. Donald A. Riggs and Jerome P. Seaton (Bloomington: Indiana University Press, 1982), his analysis of what he calls "the passive procedures," pp. 23-42.

46. See the statements of the "repetitive" American musicians, particularly Steve Reich and Philip Glass.

47. Nathalie Sarraute, in *The Age of Suspicion*, trans. Marie Jolas (New York: Braziller, 1963), shows how Proust, for example, is torn between the two planes, in that he extracts from his characters "the infinitesimal particles of an impalpable matter," but also glues all of the particles back into a coherent form, slips them into the envelope of this or that character. See pp. 50, 94-95.

48. See the distinction between the two Planes in Artaud. One of them is denounced as the source of all illusions: *The Peyote Dance* (translation of *Les Tarahumaras*), trans. Helen Weaver (New York: Farrar, Straus and Giroux, 1976), pp. 12-13.

49. Robert Rovini, introduction to Friedrich Hölderlin, *Hypérion* (Paris: 10/18, 1968).

50. We have referred to an unpublished study of Kleist by Mathieu Carrière.

51. "Where did the title of your second book, *A Year From Monday*, come from?" "From a plan a group of friends and I made to meet each other again in Mexico 'a year from next Monday.' We were together on a Saturday. And we were never able to fulfil that plan. It's a form of silence. . . . The very fact that our plan failed, the fact we were unable to meet does not mean that everything failed. The plan wasn't a failure"; John Cage and Daniel Charles, *For the Birds* (Boston: Marion Boyers, 1981), pp. 116-117.

52. That is why we were able to take Goethe as an example of a transcendental plane. Goethe, however, passes for a Spinozist; his botanical and zoological studies uncover an immanent plane of composition, which allies him to Geoffroy Saint-Hilaire (this resemblance has often been pointed out). Nonetheless, Goethe retains the twofold idea of a development of form and a formation-education of the Subject; for this reason, his plane of immanence has already crossed over to the other side, to the other pole.

53. On all of these points (proliferations-dissolutions, accumulations, indications of speed, the affective and dynamic role), see Pierre Boulez, *Conversations with Célestin Deliège*, pp. 21-22, 68-71. In another text, Boulez stresses a little-known aspect of Wagner: not only are the leitmotifs freed from their subordination to the scenic characters, but the speeds of development are freed from the hold of a "formal code" or a tempo ("Le temps re-cherché," in *Das Rheingold Programmheft*, vol. I [Bayreuth, 1976], pp. 3-11). Boulez pays homage to Proust for being one of the first to understand this floating and transformable role of Wagnerian motifs.

54. The themes of speed and slowness are most extensively developed in *The Captive:* "To understand the emotions which they arouse, and which others even better-looking do not, we must realise that they are not immobile, but in motion, and add to their person a sign corresponding to that which in physics denotes speed . . . to such beings, such fugitive beings, their own nature and our anxiety fasten wings"; vol. 3 of *Remembrance of Things Past*, trans. C. K. Moncrieff, Terence Kilmartin, and Andreas Mayor (New York: Random House, 1981), pp. 86-87, 88.

55. [TRANS: The word translated as "proximity" is *voisinage*, which Deleuze and Guattari draw from set theory. The corresponding mathematical term in English is "neighborhood."]

56. Louis Wolfson, *Le schizo et les langues*, preface by Gilles Deleuze (Paris: Gallimard, 1970).

57. René Schérer and Guy Hocquenghem, *Co-ire*, *Recherche*, no. 22 (1976), pp. 76-82: see their critique of Bettelheim's thesis, which considers the becomings-animal of the child merely an autistic symbolism that expresses the anxiety of the parents more than any reality of the child. See Bruno Bettelheim, *The Empty Fortress* (New York: Free Press, 1967).

58. Philippe Gavi, "Les philosophes du fantastique," *Libération*, March 31, 1977. For the preceding cases, what we must arrive at is an understanding of certain so-called neurotic behaviors as a function of becomings-animal, instead of relegating becomings-animal to a psychoanalytic interpretation of behaviors. We saw this in relation to masochism (and Lolito explains that the origin of his feats lies in certain masochistic experiences; a fine text by Christian Maurel conjugates a becoming-monkey and a becoming-horse in a masochistic pairing). Anorexia would also have to be understood from the point of view of becoming-animal.

59. See *Newsweek*, May 16, 1977, p. 57.

60. See Trost, *Visible et invisible* (Paris: Arcanes) and *Librement mécanique* (Paris: Minotaure): "She was simultaneously, in her sensible reality and in the ideal prolongation of her lines, like the projection of a human group yet to come."

61. See the examples of structural explanation proposed by Jean-Pierre Vernant, in *Problèmes de la guerre en Grèce ancienne*, pp. 15-16.

62. On transvestism in primitive societies, see Bruno Bettelheim (who offers an identificatory psychological interpretation), *Symbolic Wounds* (Glencoe, Ill.: Free Press, 1954), and especially Gregory Bateson (who proposes an original structural interpretation), *Naven: A Survey of the Problems Suggested by a Composite Picture of the Culture of a New Guinea Tribe Drawn from Three Points of Views*, 2nd ed. (Stanford, Calif.: Stanford University Press, 1958).

63. François Cheng, *Chinese Poetic Writing*, p. 13.

64. *The Diary of Virginia Woolf*, ed. Anne Olivier Bell (London: Hogarth Press, 1980), vol. 3, p. 209: "The idea has come to me that what I want now to do is to saturate every atom." On all of these points, we make use of an unpublished study on Virginia Woolf by Fanny Zavin.

65. [TRANS: Søren Kierkegaard, *Fear and Trembling*, trans. Walter Lowrie (Princeton, N.J.: Princeton University Press, 1954), p. 104.]

66. Ibid., p. 49. *Fear and Trembling* seems to us to be Kierkegaard's greatest book because of the way it formulates the problem of movement and speed, not only in its content, but also in its style and composition.

67. [TRANS: *Fear and Trembling*, p. 61.]

68. Carlos Castaneda, *Journey to Ixtlan* (New York: Simon and Schuster, 1973), pp. 297ff.

69. Leslie Fiedler, *The Return of the Vanishing American* (New York: Stein and Day, 1968). Fiedler explains the secret alliance of the white American with the black or the Indian by a desire to escape the molar form and ascendancy of the American woman.

70. Henri Michaux, *Miserable Miracle: Mescaline*, trans. Louise Varèse (San Francisco: City Lights, 1963), p. 87: "The horror of it was that I was nothing but a line. In normal life one is a sphere, a sphere that surveys panoramas. . . . Now only a line . . . the accelerated line I had become." See Michaux's line drawings. In the first eighty pages of *The Major Ordeals of the Mind, and the Countless Minor Ones*, trans. Richard Howard (New York: Harcourt Brace Jovanovich, 1974), Michaux further develops the analysis of speeds, molecular perceptions, and "microphenomena" or "microoperations."

71. [TRANS: A rewriting of Freud's famous phrase, "Where id was, there ego shall be" (*New Introductory Lectures*, *Standard Edition*, vol. 22, p. 80), and Lacan's earlier rewriting of it in "The Freudian Thing," *Ecrits*, trans. Alan Sheridan (New York: Norton, 1977), pp. 128-129, 136.]

72. Artaud, *The Peyote Dance*, pp. 12-14.

73. Michaux, *Miserable Miracle* ("Remaining Master of One's Speeds," pp. 87-88).

74. On the possibilities of silicon, and its relation to carbon from the point of view of organic chemistry, see the article, "Silicium," in the *Encyclopedia Universalis*.

75. Luc de Heusch shows that it is the man of war who brings the secret: he thinks, eats,

loves, judges, arrives in secret, while the man of the State proceeds publicly. See *Le roi ivre ou l'origine de l'Etat* (Paris: Gallimard, 1972). The idea of the State secret is a late one and assumes that the war machine has been appropriated by the State apparatus.

76. In particular, Georg Simmel. See *The Sociology of Georg Simmel*, trans. Kurt H. Wolff (Glencoe, Ill.: Free Press, 1950), chapter 3.

77. Paul Ernest Joset clearly notes these two aspects of the secret initiatory society, the Mambela of the Congo: on the one hand, its relation of influence over the traditional political leaders, which gets to the point of a transfer of social powers; and on the other hand, its de facto relation with the Anioto, as a secret hindsociety of crime or leopard-men (even if the Anioto are of another origin than the Mambela). See *Les sociétés secrètes des hommes-léopards en Afrique noire*, chapter 5.

78. On the psychoanalytic conceptions of the secret, see *Du secret, Nouvelle revue de psychanalyse*, no. 14 (Fall 1976); and for the evolution of Freud on this subject, the article by Claude Girard, "Le secret aux origines," pp. 55-83.

79. Bernard Pingaud shows, on the basis of the exemplary text of Henry James, "The Figure in the Carpet" [*The Novels and Tales of Henry James* (New York: C. Scribner's Sons, 1907-1917), vol. 15—Trans.], how the secret jumps from content to form, and escapes both: *Du secret*, pp. 247-249. This text has been frequently commented upon from the viewpoint of psychoanalysis; above all, J.-B. Pontalis, *Après Freud* (Paris: Gallimard, 1968). But psychoanalysis remains prisoner to a necessarily disguised content and a necessarily symbolic form (structure, absent cause . . .), at a level that defines both the unconscious and language. That is why, in its aesthetic or literary applications, it misses the secret *in* an author, as well as the secret *of* an author. The same goes for the secret of Oedipus: they concern themselves with the first two kinds of secret but not with the second, which is nevertheless the most important.

80. On the fogginess of the idea of majority, see Kenneth Arrow's two famous themes, "the Condorcet effect" and the "theorem of collective decision."

81. See William Faulkner, *Intruder in the Dust* (New York: Vintage, 1948), p. 216. Speaking of Southern whites after the Civil War (not only the poor but also the old monied families), Faulkner writes, "We are in the position of the German after 1933 who had no other alternative but to be a Nazi or a Jew."

82. The subordination of the line to the point is clearly evident in the arborescent schemas: see Julien Pacotte, *Le réseau arborescent, schème primordial de la pensée* (Paris: Hermann, 1936), and the status of centered or hierarchical systems according to Pierre Rosenthiehl and Jean Petitot, "Automate asocial et systèmes acentrés," *Communications*, no. 22 (1974), pp. 45-62. The arborescent schema of majority could be presented as follows:

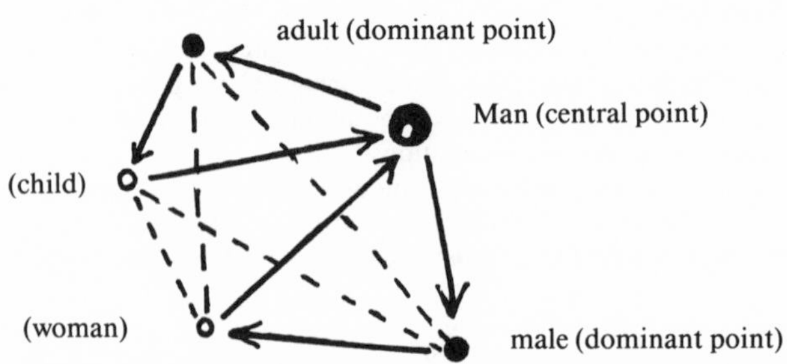

83. A line of becoming, in relation to the localizable connection of A and B (distance), or in relation to their contiguity:

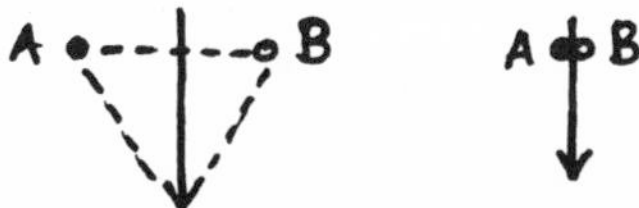

84. *The Diary of Virginia Woolf*, vol. 3, p. 236 (Wednesday, November 28, 1928). The same thing applies to the works of Kafka, in which childhood blocks function as the opposite of childhood memories. Proust's case is more complicated because he performs a mixture of the two. The situation of the psychoanalyst is to grasp memories or phantasies, but never childhood blocks.

85. For example, in the system of memory, the formation of a memory implies a diagonal that turns present A into representation A' in relation to the new present B, and into A" in relation to C, etc.:

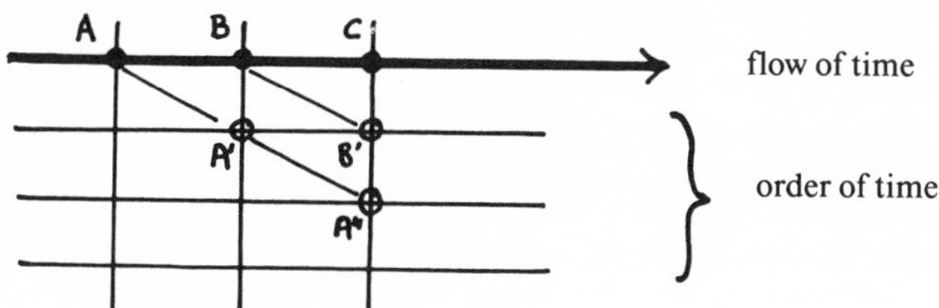

See Edmund Husserl, *The Phenomenology of Internal Time-Consciousness*, ed. Martin Heidegger, trans. James S. Churchill, intro. Calvin O. Schrag (Bloomington: Indiana University Press, 1964), pp. 48-50.

86. Friedrich Nietzsche, *Untimely Meditations*, trans. R. J. Hollingdale (New York: Cambridge University Press, 1983), "On the Uses and Disadvantages of History for Life," sec. 1, pp. 63-64.

87. On all of these themes, see Pierre Boulez. (1) On how transversals always tend to escape horizontal and vertical coordinates of music, sometimes even drawing "virtual lines," see *Notes of an Apprenticeship*, ed. Paule Thévenin, trans. Robert Weinstock (New York: Knopf, 1968), pp. 231-232, 295-301, 382-383. (2) On the idea of the sound block or "block of duration," in relation to this transversal, see *Boulez on Music Today*, trans. Susan Bradshaw and Richard Bennett (Cambridge, Mass.: Harvard University Press, 1971), pp. 55-59. (3) On the distinction between points and blocks, "punctual sets," and "aggregative sets" with varying individuality, see "Sonate que me veux-tu?", *Médiations*, no. 7 (1964). The hatred of memory appears frequently in Boulez; see "Eloge de l'amnésie," *Musique en jeu*, no. 4 (1971), pp. 5-14, and "J'ai horreur du souvenir," in *Roger Desormière et son temps*, ed. Denise Mayer and Pierre Souvtchinsky (Monaco: Ed. du Rocher, 1966). Confining ourselves to contemporary examples, one finds analogous declarations in Stravinsky, Cage, Berio. Of course, there is a musical memory that is tied to coordinates and is exercised in social settings (getting up, going to bed, beating a retreat). But the perception of a musical "phrase" appeals less to memory, even of the reminiscence type, than to an extension or contraction of perception of the encounter type. It should be studied how each musician sets in motion veritable *blocks of forgetting:* for example, what Jean Barraqué calls "slices of forgetting" and "absent developments" in the work of Debussy; *Debussy* (Paris: Seuil, 1977), pp. 169-171. One can refer to a general study by Daniel Charles, "La musique et l'oubli," *Traverses*, no. 4 (1977), pp. 14-23.

88. Roland Barthes, "Rasch," in *The Responsibility of Forms*, trans. Richard Howard (New York: Hill and Wang, 1985), pp. 300-302, 308-309.

89. There are many differences among painters, in all respects, but also a common

movement: see Wassily Kandinsky, *Point and Line to Plane* in vol. 2 of *Complete Writings on Art*, ed. Kenneth C. Lindsay and Peter Vergo (Boston: G. K. Hall, 1982), pp. 524-700; and Paul Klee, *On Modern Art*, trans. Paul Findlay, intro. Herbert Reed (London: Faber, 1966). The aim of statements like those of Mondrian on the exclusive value of the vertical and the horizontal is to show the conditions under which the vertical and horizontal are sufficient to create a transversal, which does not even have to be drawn; for example, coordinates of unequal thickness intersect inside the frame and extend outside the frame, opening a "dynamic axis" running transversally (see Michel Butor's comments in *Répertoire* [Paris: Minuit, 1960-], vol. 3, "Le carré et son habitant"). One can also consult Michel Fried's article on Pollock's line, *Three American Painters* (Cambridge, Mass.: Fogg Art Museum, 1965), and Henry Miller's discussion of Nash's line, *On Turning Eighty* (London: Village Press, 1973).

90. "There was something tense, exasperated to the point of intolerable anger, in his good-humored breast, as he played the finely-spun peace-music. The more exquisite the music, the more perfectly he produced it, in sheer bliss; and at the same time, the more intense was the maddened exasperation within him"; D. H. Lawrence, *Aaron's Rod* (New York: Thomas Seltzer, 1922), p. 16.

91. Although Luciano Berio indicates otherwise, it seems to us that his work, *Visage*, is composed according to the three states of faciality: first, a multiplicity of sound bodies and silhouettes, then a short symphonic and dominant organization of the face, and finally a launching of probe-heads in all directions. However, there is no question here of music "imitating" the face and its avatars, or of the voice constituting a metaphor. Instead, the sounds accelerate the deterritorialization of the face, giving it a properly acoustical power, and the face reacts musically by in turn inducing a deterritorialization of the voice. This is a molecular face, produced by electronic music. The voice precedes the face, itself forms the face for an instant, and outlives it, increasing in speed—on the condition that it is unarticulated, asignifying, asubjective.

92. Will Grohman, *Paul Klee* (New York: Harry N. Abrams, n.d.): "Somewhat paradoxically he remarked that perhaps it had been his good fortune to develop painting, at least on the formal plane, to the stage reached in music by Mozart" (p. 71).

93. Dominique Fernandez, *La rose des Tudors* (Paris: Julliard, 1976) (and the novel *Porporino* [Paris: Grasset, 1974]). Fernandez cites pop music as a timid return to great English vocal music. It would be necessary to take into consideration techniques of circular breathing, in which one sings breathing in as well as out, or of sound filtering using zones of resonance (nose, forehead, cheekbones—a properly musical use of the face).

94. Marcel Moré, *Le dieu Mozart et le monde des oiseaux* (Paris: Gallimard, 1971).

95. As we have seen, imitation can be conceived either as a resemblance of terms culminating in an archetype (series), or as a correspondence of relations constituting a symbolic order (structure); but becoming is not reducible to either of these. The concept of mimesis is not only inadequate, it is radically false.

96. François Truffaut, *Hitchcock* (New York: Simon and Schuster, 1967): "I took the dramatic licence of not having the birds scream at all" (p. 224).

97. See Ernesto de Martino, *La terre du remords* (Paris: Gallimard, 1966), pp. 142-170. Martino, however, retains an interpretation based on the archetype, imitation, and identification.

98. Jean Claude Larouche, *Alexis le trotteur* (Montreal: Ed. du Jour, 1971). They quote this account: "He didn't play music with his mouth like one of us; he had a huge harmonica we couldn't even play. . . . When he played with us, he would decide all of a sudden to double us. In other words, he doubled the beat; in the time we played one beat, he played two, which required extraordinary wind" (p. 95).

99. [TRANS: See Kafka, *The Castle*, trans. Willa and Edwin Muir (New York: Knopf, 1976).]

100. [TRANS: See 7, "Year Zero: Faciality," pp. 167-191.]

101. André Tétry, *Les outils chez les êtres vivants* (Paris: Gallimard, 1948), the chapter on "musical instruments," with bibliography. An animal's movement or labor may make noise, but we speak of a musical instrument whenever animals use apparatuses whose sole function is to produce various sounds (the musical character, to the extent that it is determinable, is quite variable, as is the case with the vocal apparatus of birds; there are veritable virtuosos among insects). From this standpoint, we distinguish: (1) stridulatory apparatuses, of the stringed instrument type: the rubbing of a rigid surface against another surface (insects, crustaceans, spiders, scorpions, pedipalps); (2) percussive apparatuses, of the drum, cymbal, or xylophone type: direct application of muscles to a vibratory membrane (crickets and certain fish). Not only is there an infinite variety of apparatuses and sounds, but the same animal varies its rhythm, tonality, intensity according to still more mysterious urgencies. "It then becomes a song of anger, anxiety, fear, triumph, love. When there is keen excitation, the rhythm of the stridulation varies: in *Crioceris lilii*, the frequency of the rubbing goes from 228 strokes per minute to 550 or more."

102. Gisèle Brelet, "Musique contemporaine en France," in *Histoire de la musique*, ed. Roland Manuel, "Pléiade" (Paris: Gallimard, 1977), vol. 2, pp. 1166.

103. A text by Henry Miller for Varèse, *The Air-Conditioned Nightmare* (New York: New Directions, 1945), pp. 176-177.

11. 1837: Of the Refrain

1. Fernand Deligny, *Voix et Voir, Recherches*, no. 8 (April 1975), on the way in which, among autistic children, a "line of drift" deviates from the customary path and begins to "vibrate," "toss about," "yaw."

2. Paul Klee, *On Modern Art*, trans. Paul Findlay, intro. Herbert Reed (London: Faber, 1966), p. 43 [translation modified to agree with the French version cited by the authors]. See Henri Maldiney's comments in *Regard, parole, espace* (Lausanne: L'Age d'homme, 1973), pp. 149-151.

3. On the musical nome, the ethos, and the ground or land, notably in polyphony, see Joseph Samson in *Histoire de la musique*, ed. Roland Manuel (Paris: Gallimard, 1977), vol. 2, pp. 1168-1172. One may also refer to the role in Arab music of the "maqām," which is both a modal type and a melodic formula: Simon Jargy, *La musique arabe* (Paris: PUF, 1971), pp. 55ff.

4. Gaston Bachelard, *La dialectique de la durée* (Paris: Bovin, 1936), pp. 128-129. Emphasis added.

5. Jakob Johann von Uexküll, *Mondes animaux et monde humain* (Paris: Gonthier, 1965).

6. "Their glorious dress is constant. . . . The coloring of coral fish is distributed in large, sharply contrasting areas of the body. This is quite different from the color patterns not only of most fresh-water fish but of nearly all less aggressive and less territorial fish. . . . Like the colors of the coral fish, the song of the nightingale signals from a distance to all members of its species that a territory has found an owner." Konrad Lorenz, *On Aggression*, trans. Marjorie Kerr Wilson (New York: Harcourt, Brace and World, 1966), pp. 19-20.

7. Irenäus Eibl-Eibesfeldt, *Ethology*, trans. Erich Klinghammer (New York: Holt, Rinehart and Winston, 1975): on monkeys, p. 487; on rabbits, p. 346; on birds, p. 171: "Zebra finches with colorful plumage maintain a certain distance from one another, while all-white birds of the same species perch much closer together."

8. W. H. Thorpe, *Learning and Instinct in Animals* (London: Methuen, 1956), p. 364 (Fig. 2).

9. Lorenz has a constant tendency to present territoriality as an effect of intraspecific aggression; see *On Agression*, pp. 38-39, 42-43, 53-54, 161-162.

10. On the aesthetic and vital primacy of "having," see Gabriel Tarde, *L'opposition universelle* (Paris: Alcan, 1897).

11. Details on Messiaen's conceptions of bird song, his evaluation of its aesthetic qualities, and his methods for both reproducing it and using it as a material are to be found in Claude Samuel, *Conversations with Olivier Messiaen*, trans. Felix Aprahamian (London: Stainer and Bell, 1976), and in Antoine Goléa, *Rencontres avec Olivier Messiaen* (Paris: Julliard, 1961). In particular, on why Messiaen does not use a tape recorder or sonograph as ornithologists usually do, see Samuel, pp. 61-63.

12. [TRANS: Lorenz, *On Aggression*, p. 87.]

13. On all of these points, see Claude Samuel, *Conversations*, chapter 4. On the "rhythmic character," see pp. 36-39.

14. Pierre Boulez, "Le temps re-cherché," in *Das Rheingold Programmheft*, vol. 1 (Bayreuth, 1976), pp. 5-15.

15. [TRANS: Proust, *The Captive*, vol. 3 of *Remembrance of Things Past*, trans. C. K. Scott Moncrief, Terence Kilmartin, and Andreas Mayor (New York: Random House, 1981), p. 156. Translation modified.]

16. On mannerism and chaos, baroque dances, and the relation of schizophrenia to mannerism and dance, see Evelyne Sznycer, "Droit de suite baroque," in *Schizophrénie et art*, ed. Leo Navratil (Paris: Ed. Complexe, 1978).

17. Lorenz, *On Aggression*, pp. 39-40. On the three rhythmic personages defined respectively as active, passive, and witness, see Messiaen and Goléa, *Rencontres*, pp. 90-91.

18. [TRANS: Mircea Eliade, *Patterns in Comparative Religion*, trans. Rosemary Sheed (New York: World, 1963), pp. 242-243.]

19. [TRANS: This "close embrace" of energies recalls Proust's description of Vinteuil's little phrase; *The Captive*, p. 262.]

20. On "the primary intuition of the earth as a religious form" (p. 242), see Eliade, *Patterns in Comparative Religion*, pp. 245ff.; on the center of the territory, see pp. 374ff. Eliade makes it clear that the center is simultaneously outside the territory, very difficult to attain, and inside the territory, within our immediate reach.

21. Biologists have often made a distinction between two factors of transformation: those of the mutation type, and processes of isolation or separation, which may be genetic, geographical, or even psychical. Territoriality would be a factor of the second type. See Lucien Cuénot, *L'espèce* (Paris: G. Doin, 1936).

22. Paul Géroudet, *Les passereaux*, 3 vols. (Paris: Delachaux et Niestlé, 1951-1957), vol. 2, pp. 88-94.

23. In *On Aggression*, Lorenz makes a clear distinction between "anonymous flocks" such as schools of fish, which form milieu blocks; "local groups," where recognition occurs only inside the territory and, at its strongest, between "neighbors"; and finally, societies founded on an autonomous "bond."

24. K. Immelmann, *Beiträge zu einer vergleichenden Biologie australischer Prachtfinken, Zoologische Jahrbücher; Abteilung für Systematik, Ökologie und Geographie de Tiere*, 90 (1962).

25. Eibl-Eibesfeldt, *Ethology*, p. 225: "Carrying nesting material for nest building evolved into the male courtship actions using grass stems. This was again secondarily reduced in some species and became rudimentary, while at the same time the song, which originally served the function of staking out a territory, also underwent a change in function. These animals are gre-

garious and are not really territorial. Instead of courting with grass stems, these males sing softly while sitting next to the females." Eibl-Eibesfeldt, however, interprets the grass-stem behavior as a vestige.

26. See *L'Odyssée sous-marine de l'équipe Cousteau*, film no. 36, *La marche des langoustes* (L. R. A.), commentary by Cousteau-Diolé: spiny lobsters along the northern coast of the Yucatan Peninsula sometimes leave their territories. They assemble, at first in small groups, before the first winter storm, and before any sign detectable by human instruments. When the storm comes, they form long march processions, in single file, with a leader that is periodically relieved and a rearguard (the speed of the march is five-eighths of a mile per hour, for sixty miles or more). This migration does not seem to be associated with egg laying, which does not take place until six months later. Hernnkind, a lobster specialist, hypothesizes that this is a "vestige" from the last ice age (more than 10,000 years ago). Cousteau leans toward a more current interpretation, even mentioning the possibility that it is a premonition of a new ice age. The factual issue is that in this exceptional case the lobsters' territorial assemblage opens onto a social assemblage, and that this social assemblage is connected to cosmic forces, or, as Cous[illegible] "pulsations of the earth." But "the enigma remains entirely unsolved," all the more so because this lobster procession occasions a slaughter by fishermen, and also because lobsters cannot be tagged since they shed their shells.

27. The best book of nursery rhymes, and on nursery rhymes, seems to be *Les comptines de langue française*, with the commentary by editors Jean Beaucomot, Franck Guibat, et al. (Paris: Seghers, 1970). The territorial character of nursery rhymes appears in such privileged examples as "Pimpanicaille," two distinct versions of which exist in Gruyères on "the two sides of the street" (pp. 27-28); but it is a nursery rhyme in the strict sense only when there is a distribution of specialized roles in a game, and the formation of an autonomous game assemblage that reorganizes the territory.

28. Nikolaas Tinbergen, *The Study of Instinct* (Oxford: The Clarendon Press, 1969).

29. On the one hand, the experiments of W. R. Hess have shown that there is not a cerebral center but instead points that are concentrated in one zone and disseminated in another, and are capable of inciting the same effect; conversely, the effect may change according to the duration and intensity of the excitation of a point. On the other hand, E. von Holst's experiments on "deafferented" fish demonstrate the importance of central nervous coordination in fin rhythms; Tinbergen's schema takes these interactions into account only secondarily. The hypothesis of a "population of oscillators" or a "pack of oscillating molecules" forming systems of articulation from the inside, independent of any common measure, is most compelling in view of the problem of circadian rhythms. See A. Reinberg, "La chronobiologie," *Sciences*, vol. 1 (1970); and T. van den Dreissche and A. Reinberg, "Rythmes biologiques," in *Encyclopedia Universalis*, vol. 14, p. 572: "It does not seem possible to reduce the mechanism of circadian rhythmicity to a simple sequence of elementary processes."

30. Jacques Monod, *Chance and Necessity*, trans. Austryn Wainhouse (New York: Vintage, 1972): on indirect interactions and their nonlinear character, pp. 69-71 and 76-77; on corresponding molecules that are least two-headed, pp. 68-69; on the inhibiting or releasing character of these interactions, pp. 63-67. Circadian rhythms also depend on these characteristics (see the chart in the *Encyclopedia Universalis* under "Rhythmes biologiques").

31. Eugène Dupréel elaborated a set of original notions, "consistency" (in relation to "precariousness"), "consolidation," "interval," "intercalation." See *Théorie de la consolidation: La cause et l'intervalle* (Brussels: M. Lamertin, 1933); *La consistance et la probabilité objective* (Brussels: Académie Royale de Belgique, 1961); *Esquisse d'une philosophie des valeurs* (Paris: Alcan, 1939); Bachelard, in *La dialectique de la durée*, draws on Dupréel.

32. [TRANS: *The Diary of Virginia Woolf*, ed. Anne Olivier Bell (London: Hogarth Press, 1980), vol. 3, p. 209.]

33. On the song of the chaffinch, and the distinction between the "subsong" and "full song," see Thorpe, *Learning and Instinct*, pp. 420-426.

34. Alexander James Marshall, *Bower-Birds* (Oxford: The Clarendon Press, 1954).

35. Thorpe, *Learning and Instinct*, p. 426. In this respect, songs present an entirely different problem than calls, which are often not very differentiated, and quite similar from species to species.

36. Raymond Ruyer, *La genèse des formes vivantes* (Paris: Flammarion, 1958), chapter 7.

37. In particular, on widow birds (*Viduinae*), parasitic birds whose territorial song is species-specific and whose courtship song is learned from their adoptive host, see J. Nicolai, *Der Brutparasitismus der Viduinae, Z. Tierps.*, vol. 21 (1964).

38. The participation of a black hole in an assemblage appears in numerous examples of inhibition, or fascination-ecstasy, notably in the peacock: "The male peacock spreads his tail feathers. . . . Then he bends the spread-out tail forward and points downward with his beak, while his head is still upright. As a result, the female runs in front of him and pecks in a searching manner on the ground in the focal point of the concave mirrorlike shape of the fanned tail. The male peacock points, so to speak, with his fanned-out tail toward imaginary food," Eibl-Eibesfeldt, *Ethology*, p. 116. But the peacock's focal point is no more imaginary than the finch's grass stem is a vestige or symbol; it is an assemblage converter, the passage to a courtship assemblage, in this instance, effected by a black hole.

39. Ruyer, *La genèse des formes vivantes*, pp. 54ff.

40. François *Meyer, Problématique de l'évolution* (Paris: PUF, 1954).

41. Monod, *Chance and Necessity.*

42. Female birds, which do not normally sing, start singing when they are administered male sex hormones, "and they will sing the song of the species on which they have become imprinted." Eibl-Eibesfeldt, *Ethology*, p. 265.

43. [TRANS: Klee, *On Modern Art*, p. 43. Translation modified to agree with the French translation cited by the authors.]

44. Klee, *On Modern Art*, p. 55 [translation modified—Trans.].

45. See *Renaissance, maniérisme, baroque, Actes du XIe stage international de Tours* (Paris: Vrin, 1972), part 1, "Periodizations."

46. Proust, *Swann's Way*, in vol. 1 of *Remembrance of Things Past*, p. 382 [translation modified—Trans.].

47. See the ambiguous role of the friend at the end of *Das Lied von der Erde*. Or Eichendorff's poem in Schumann's lied, *Zwielicht* (in Opus 39): "If you have a friend in this world, do not trust him at this hour, for even if he is kind in eye and mouth, he dreams of war in deceitful peace." (On the problem of the One-Alone, or "solitary Being," in German romanticism, see Hölderlin, "Le cours et la destination de l'homme en général," trans. Emmanuel Marineau, *Poésie*, no. 4 [1978], pp. 6-22.)

48. "The people in Mussorgsky's *Boris* do not form a true crowd; at times one group sings, then another, and then a third, each in turn, and most often in unison. As for the people in *Maîtres chanteurs*, it is not a crowd but an army that is powerfully organized in the German manner and marches in rows. What I would like is something sparser, more divided, more relaxed, more impalpable, something in appearance inorganic and yet at bottom ordered." Quoted by Jean Barraqué, *Debussy* (Paris: Seuil, 1977), p. 159. This problem—how to do a crowd—obviously recurs in other arts also, painting, cinema, etc. One may refer in particular to the films of Eisenstein, which proceed by this type of very special group individuation.

49. On the relations between the cry, the voice, the instrument, and music as "theater," see Berio's statements introducing his records. One will recall the eminently musical Nietzschean theme of *a* multiple cry of all superior men, at the end of *Thus Spoke Zarathustra.*

50. On Bartók's chromaticism, see Gisèle Brelet's study in *Histoire de la musique*, vol. 2, pp. 1036-1072.

51. In his book on Debussy, Barraqué analyzes the "dialogue of the wind and the sea" in terms of forces instead of themes: pp. 153-154. See Messiaen's statements on his own works: sounds are no longer anything more "than vulgar means of expression intended to make durations measurable."

52. Odile Vivier describes Varèse's procedures for treating sound matter, in *Varèse* (Paris: Seuil, 1973): the use of pure sounds acting as a prism (p. 36); mechanisms of projection onto a plane (pp. 45 and 50); non-octave-forming scales (p. 75); the "ionization" procedure (pp. 98ff.); the theme of sound *molecules*, the transformations of which are determined by forces or energies (*passim*).

53. See the interview with Stockhausen on the role of synthesizers and the effectively "cosmic" dimension of music, in *Le Monde*, July 21, 1977: "Work with very limited materials and integrate the universe into them through a continuous variation." Richard Pinhas has written an excellent analysis of the possibilities of synthesizers in this regard, in relation to pop music: "Input, Output," in *Atem*, no. 10 (1977).

54. The definition of fuzzy aggregates brings up all kinds of problems because one cannot appeal to a local determination: "The set of all objects on this table" is obviously not a fuzzy set. Mathematicians concerned with the question speak only of "fuzzy subsets" because the reference set must always be an ordinary set. See Arnold Kaufmann, *Introduction to the Theory of Fuzzy Subsets*, foreword L. A. Zadeh, trans. D. L. Swanson (New York: Academic Press, 1975), and Hourya Sinacoeur, "Logique et mathématique du flou," *Critique*, no. 372 (May 1978), pp. 512-525. In considering fuzziness as the characteristic of certain sets, our point of departure was a functional, as opposed to a local, definition: sets of heterogeneous elements that have a territorial, or rather territorializing, function. But this is a nominal definitiion that does not take "what happened" into account. The real definition can come only at the level of processes affecting the fuzzy set; a set is fuzzy if its elements belong to it only by virtue of specific operations of consistency and consolidation, which themselves follow a special logic.

55. Paul Klee, *On Modern Art*, p. 53: "The legend of the childishness of my drawing must have originated from those linear compositions of mine in which I tried to combine a concrete image, say that of a man, with the pure representation of the linear element. Had I wished to present man 'as he is,' then I should have had to use such a bewildering confusion of lines that pure elementary representation would have been out of the question. The result would have been vagueness beyond recognition."

56. Paul Virilio, *L'insécurité du territoire* (Paris: Stock, 1975), p. 49. Henry Miller develops this theme in *The Time of the Assassins. A Study of Rimbaud* (Norfolk, Conn.: J. Laughlin, 1956), and in the text he wrote for Varèse, "Lost! Saved!" (*The Air-Conditioned Nightmare* [New York: New Directions, 1945]). It is undoubtedly Miller who has taken the modern figure of the writer as cosmic artisan the farthest, particularly in *Sexus*.

57. On the relation of colors to sound, see Messiaen and Samuel, *Conversations*, pp. 15-17. Messiaen faults drug users for oversimplifying the relation, which they make into a relation between a noise and a color, instead of isolating complexes of sounds-durations and complexes of colors.

58. On the crystal, or the crystalline type, added and subtracted values, retrograde motion, see also Messiaen's texts in Samuel, *Conversations*, and those of Paul Klee in his diary, *The Diaries of Paul Klee, 1898-1918*, ed. and intro. Felix Klee (Berkeley: University of California Press, 1964).

59. See Roland-Manuel's article, "L'évolution de l'harmonie en France et le renouveau de 1880" (pp. 867-879), and the article by Delage on Chabrier (pp. 831-840), in *Histoire de la musique*, vol. 2. And especially, Brelet's article on Bartók: "Are not the difficulties learned

music experiences in utilizing popular music due to this antinomy between melody and theme? Popular music is melody, in its fullest sense, melody persuading us that it is self-sufficient and is in fact synonymous with music itself. How could it not refuse to bend to the learned development of a musical work pursuing its own ends? Many symphonies inspired by folklore are only symphonies *about* a popular theme, to which the learned development remains alien and exterior. The popular melody could never constitute a true theme; and that is why, in popular music, the melody is the entire work, and why once it is over it has no other resource than to repeat itself. But can't the melody transform itself into a theme? Bartók solves this problem, which was thought insoluble" (p. 1056).

60. Marcel Moré, *Le dieu Mozart et le monde des oiseaux* (Paris: Gallimard, 1971), p. 168. And, on the crystal, pp. 83-89.

61. See Alban Berg's famous analysis of "Rêverie" in *Ecrits* (Paris: Ed. du Rocher, 1957), pp. 44-64.

12. 1227: Treatise on Nomadology—the War Machine

1. Georges Dumézil, *Mitra-Varuna* (Paris: Gallimard, 1948 [forthcoming in English translation from Zone Books]). On *nexum* and *mutuum*, the bond and the contract, see pp. 118-124.

2. "The first pole of the State (Varuna, Uranus, Romulus) operates by magic bond, seizure, or immediate capture: it does not wage battles, and has no war machine, it binds, and that is all." Its other pole (Mitra, Zeus, Numa) appropriates an army but imposes upon it juridical and institutional rules that become nothing more than a piece in the State apparatus: thus Mars-Tiwaz is not a warrior god, but a god who is a "jurist of war." See Dumézil, *Mitra-Varuna*, pp. 113ff., 148ff., 202ff.

3. Dumézil, *The Destiny of the Warrior*, trans. Alf Hiltebeital (Chicago: University of Chicaga Press, 1970).

4. For the role of the warrior as one who "unties" and opposes both the magic bond and the juridical contract, see Dumézil, *Mitra-Varuna*, pp. 124-132. See also the analysis of *furor* in the works of Dumézil.

5. [TRANS: The first quote is from Friedrich Nietzsche, *The Genealogy of Morals*, second essay, sect. 17, trans. Walter Kaufmann and R. J. Hollingdale (New York: Vintage, 1967), p. 86; the second is from Franz Kafka, "An Old Manuscript," *The Complete Stories*, ed. Nahum N. Glazer (New York: Schocken, 1983), p. 416.]

6. Luc de Heusch emphasizes the public nature of Nkongolo's actions, in contrast to the secrecy of the actions of Mbidi and his son; in particular, the former eats in public, whereas the others hide during their meals. Later, we will see the essential relation of the war machine with the secret, which is as much a matter of principle as a result: espionage, strategy, diplomacy. Commentators have often underlined this link. *Le roi ivre ou l'origine de l'État* (Paris: Gallimard, 1972).

7. For an analysis of the three sins in the cases of the Indian god Indra, the Scandinavian hero Starcatherus, and the Greek god Hercules, see Dumézil, *Mythe et épopée*, vol. 2, pp. 17-19 (Paris: Gallimard, 1971). See also Dumézil, *The Destiny of the Warrior.*

8. Dumézil, *Mitra-Varuna*, p. 135. Dumézil analyzes the dangers and causes of the confusion, which could be due to economic variables. See pp. 153, 159.

9. [TRANS: *Richard III*, act I, scene i, line 158.]

10. On Ajax and the tragedy of Sophocles, see the analysis of Jean Starobinski, *Trois Fureurs* (Paris: Gallimard, 1974). Starobinski explicitly raises the question of war and the State.

11. These themes are analyzed by Mathieu Carrière in an as yet unpublished study of Kleist.

12. Pierre Clastres, *Society against the State*, trans. Robert Hurley (New York: Urizen, 1977), and "Archéologie de la violence: la guerre dans les sociétés primitives" and "Malheur du guerrier sauvage" in *Recherches d'anthropologie politique* (Paris: Seuil, 1980), pp. 171-208, 209-248. In the last text, Clastres depicts the destiny of the warrior in primitive society and analyzes the mechanism that prevents the concentration of power (in the same way that Mauss demonstrated that the potlatch was a mechanism preventing the concentration of wealth).

13. Jacques Meunier, *Les gamins de Bogotâ* (Paris: Lattès, 1977), p. 159 ("blackmail for dispersion") and p. 177: if necessary, "it is the other street children who, by means of a complicated interplay of humiliations and silence, get the idea across that he must leave the gang." Meunier emphasizes the degree to which the fate of the ex-gang member is jeopardized: not only for health reasons, but because he finds it hard to integrate himself into the criminal underworld, a society too hierarchical, too centralized, too centered on organs of power for him to fit into (p. 178). On child gangs, see also the novel by Jorge Amado, *Capitães de areia* (Sáo Paolo: Livraria Martins, 1944).

14. See I. S. Bernstein, "La dominance sociale chez les primates" in *La Recherche*, no. 91 (July 1978).

15. Clastres, *Society against the State*, p. 169: "The emergence of the State brought about the great typological division between Savage and Civilized man; it created the unbridgeable gulf whereby everything was changed, for, on the other side, Time became History." In order to account for this emergence, Clastres cites first a demographic factor ("but there is no question of replacing an economic determinism with a demographic determinism"; p. 180), then the possibility of a warring machine (?) running amok; he also cites, more unexpectedly, the indirect role of a certain mode of *prophetic speech*, which, directed first against the "chiefs," produces a formidable new kind of power. But one obviously cannot prejudge more elaborated solutions Clastres might have found for this problem. On the possible role of prophetic speech, refer to Hélène Clastres, *La terre sans mal, le prophétisme tupi-guarani* (Paris: Editions du Seuil, 1975).

16. Michel Serres, *La naissance de la physique dans le texte de Lucrèce. Fleuves et turbulences* (Paris: Minuit, 1977). Serres was the first to make the first three points given in the text; the fourth seems to follow from them.

17. [TRANS: According to Serres, the *clinamen*, or declination of the atom, is the "minimal angle leading to the formation of a vortex, and appears by chance in a laminar flow" (*La naissance de la physique*, p. 14). The *clinamen* is the angle between a curve and its tangent, or "the smallest [angle] one can make, preventing anything from coming between the two lines which form it. . . . In other words, the angle appears at the same time as curvature" (p. 18). "The *clinamen* is a differential" (p. 11).]

18. [TRANS: A flow is laminar when, "no matter how small we make the layers (or lamellae) into which we divide the flow, they remain strictly parallel to one another in their movements"; Serres, ibid., p. 12.]

19. [TRANS: *Turba* "designates a multitude, a large population, confusion and tumult." *Turbo* "is a round form in movement . . . a revolving cone or vortical spiral." "The origin of things and the beginning of order consists simply in the subtle passage from *turba* to *turbo*"; Serres, ibid., pp. 38-39.]

20. This is the distinction Pierre Boulez makes between two kinds of space-time in music: in striated space, the measure can be irregular or regular, but it is always assignable; in smooth space, the partition, or break, "can be effected at will." *Boulez on Music Today*, trans.

Susan Bradshaw and Richard Bennett (Cambridge, Mass.: Harvard University Press, 1971), p. 85.

21. Greek geometry is thoroughly marked by the opposition between these two poles, the theorematic and problematic, and by the relative triumph of the former: in his *Commentary of the First Book of Euclid's Elements*, trans. and intro. Glenn R. Murrow (Princeton, N.J.: Princeton University Press, 1970), Proclus analyzes the difference between the poles, taking the Speusippus-Menaechmus opposition as an example. Mathematics has always been marked by this tension also; for example, the axiomatic element has confronted a problematic, "intuitionist," or "constructivist" current emphasizing a calculus of problems very different from axiomatics, or any theorematic approach. See Georges Bouligand, *Le déclin des absolus mathématico-logiques* (Paris: Ed. d'Enseignement Supérieur, 1949).

22. Paul Virilio, *L'insécurité du territoire* (Paris: Stock, 1975), p. 120: "We know that the youth of geometry, geometry as free, creative investigation, came to an end with Archimedes. . . . The sword of a Roman soldier cut the thread, tradition says. In killing geometrical creation, the Roman State lay the foundation for the geometrical imperialism of the West."

23. With Monge, and especially Poncelet, the limits of sensible, or even spatial, representation (striated space) are indeed surpassed, but less in the direction of a symbolic power (*puissance*) of abstraction than toward a transspatial imagination, or a transintuition (continuity). See Léon Brunschvicg's commentary on Poncelet, *Les étapes de la philosophie mathématique* (Paris: PUF, 1947).

24. Michel Serres (*La naissance de la physique*, pp. 105-107) analyzes the opposition d'Alembert-Bernoulli from this point of view. More generally, what is at issue is the difference between two models of space: "In the Mediterranean basin there is a shortage of water, and he who harnesses water rules. Hence that world of physics in which the conduit is essential, and the *clinamen* seems like freedom because it is precisely a turbulence that rejects forced flow. Incomprehensible to scientific theory, incomprehensible to the master of the waters. . . . Hence the great figure of Archimedes: the master of floating bodies and military machines" (p. 106).

25. See Benveniste, "The Notion of Rhythm in Its Linguistic Expression" in *Problems in General Linguistics*, trans. Mary Elizabeth Meek (Coral Gables, Fla.: University of Miami Press, 1971), pp. 281-288. This text, often considered decisive, seems ambiguous to us because it invokes Democritus and atomism without dealing with the hydraulic question, and because it treats rhythm as a "secondary specialization" of the form of the body (p. 286).

26. Anne Querrien, *Devenir fonctionnaire ou le travail de l'Etat* (Paris: Cerfi). We have drawn from this book, as well as from unpublished studies by Anne Querrien.

27. See Raoul Vergez, *Les illuminés de l'art royal. Huit siècles de compagnonnages* (Paris: Julliard, 1976), p. 54. [TRANS: In the present context, *trait* refers to the cutting line followed by the artisan and to the working sketch of the construction under way. Vergez gives the following definition: "The Trait is a kind of graphic poem derived from geometry, which indicates the building plan in sketches drawn with precision on the ground, showing sections, elevations and all other projections, the three dimensions of a volume"; p. 86.]

28. Gérard Desargues, *Oeuvres* (Paris: Leiber, 1864). See also the text by Michel Chasles [*Aperçu historique sur l'origine et le développement de méthodes en géométrie* . . . (Brussels: M. Hayez, 1837)—Trans.], which establishes a continuity between Desargues, Monge, and Poncelet as the "founders of a modern geometry."

29. Anne Querrien, *Devenir fonctionnaire*, pp. 26-27: "Is the State founded upon the collapse of experimentation? . . . The State is not under construction, its construction sites must be short-lived. An installation is made to function, not to be socially constructed: from this

point of view, the State involves in the construction only those who are paid to implement or command, and who are obliged to follow the model of a preestablished experimentation."

30. On the question of the "Colbert lobby," see Daniel Dessert and Jean-Louis Journet, "Le Lobby Colbert. Un royaume, ou une affaire de famille?" *Annales*, 30, no. 6 (November-December 1975), pp. 1303-1336.

31. See Ibn Khaldūn, *The Muqaddimah: An Introduction to History*, trans. Franz Rosenthal (Princeton, N.J.: Princeton University Press, 1967). One of the essential themes of this masterpiece is the sociological problem of the esprit de corps, and its ambiguity. Ibn Khaldūn contrasts bedouinism (the bedouin life-style, not the ethnic group) with sedentarity or city living. The first aspect of this opposition is the inverted relation between the public and the secret: not only is there a secrecy of the bedouin war machine, as opposed to the publicity of the State city dweller, but in the first case "eminence" is based on a secret solidarity, while in the second case the secret is subordinated to the demands of social eminence. Second, bedouinism brings into play both a great purity and a great mobility of the lineages and their genealogy, whereas city life makes for lineages that are very impure, and at the same time rigid and fixed: Solidarity has a different meaning at either pole. Third, and this is the main point, bedouin lineages mobilize an esprit de corps and integrate into it, as a new dimension: this is *asabîyah*, or *ikhtilât*, from which the Arabic word for socialism is derived (Ibn Khaldūn stresses the absence of any "power" residing in the tribal chief, who has no State constraints at his disposal). On the other hand, in city living the esprit de corps becomes a dimension of power and is adapted for "autocracy."

32. The principal texts of Husserl are *Ideas*, trans. W. R. Gibson (New York: Humanities Press, 1976), part 1, sec. 74, and *Edmund Husserl's Origin of Geometry: An Introduction*, trans. John P. Leavey, Jr., ed. David B. Allison (Stoney Brook, N.Y.: N. Hayes, 1978) (with Derrida's very important commentary, pp. 118-132). On the issue of a vague yet rigorous science, we may refer to the formula of Michel Serres, in his commentary on the geometrical figure called the *salinon*: "It is rigorous, anexact. And not precise, exact or inexact. Only a metrics is exact" (*Naissance de la physique*, p. 29). Gaston Bachelard's book *Essai sur la connaissance approchée* (Paris: Vrin, 1927) remains the best study of the steps and procedures constituting a rigor of the anexact, and of their creative role in science.

33. Gilbert Simondon has contributed much to the analysis and critique of the hylomorphic schema and of its social presuppositions ("form corresponds to what the man in command has thought to himself, and must express in a positive manner when he gives his orders: form is thus of the order of the expressible"). To the form-matter schema, Simondon opposes a dynamic schema, that of matter endowed with singularities-forces, or the energetic conditions at the basis of a system. The result is an entirely different conception of the relations between science and technology. See *L'individu et sa genèse physico-biologique* (Paris: PUF, 1964).

34. In *Timaeus*, 28-29, Plato entertains for an instant the thought that Becoming is not simply the inevitable characteristic of copies or reproductions, but could itself be a model rivaling the Identical and the Uniform. He states this hypothesis only in order to reject it; for it is true that if becoming is a model, not only must the duality of the model and the copy, of the model and reproduction, disappear, but the very notions of model and reproduction tend to lose all meaning. [TRANS: Deleuze develops this point in "Plato and the Simulacrum," trans. Rosalind Krauss, *October*, 27 (Winter 1983), pp. 45-56. See especially p. 53.]

35. [TRANS: Friedrich Nietzsche, *The Will to Power*, trans. Walter Kaufmann (New York: Vintage, 1968), sec. 630 (1885), p. 336.]

36. The situation is in fact more complex than that, and gravity is not the only feature of the dominant model: there is heat in addition to gravity (already in chemistry, combustion is coupled with weight). Even so, the problem was to know to what extent the "thermal field"

deviated from gravitational space, or on the contrary was integrated with it. Monge is a typical example; he began by grouping heat, light, and electricity as "variable affections of bodies," the concern of "specific physics," while general physics would deal with extension, gravity, and movement. It was only later that Monge unified all of the fields under general physics (Anne Querrien).

37. Serres, *La naissance de la physique*, p. 65.

38. Carlos Castaneda, *The Teachings of Don Juan* (Berkeley: University of California Press, 1971), p. 88.

39. Albert Lautman has shown quite clearly how Riemann spaces, for example, admit a Euclidean conjunction making it possible at all times to define the parallelism of two neighboring vectors; this being the case, instead of exploring a multiplicity by legwork, the multiplicity is treated as though "immersed in a Euclidean space with a sufficient number of dimensions." See *Les schêmas de structure* (Paris: Hermann, 1938), pp. 23-24, 43-47.

40. In Bergson, the relations between intuition and intelligence are very complex, and they are in perpetual interaction. Bouligand's theme is also relevant here: the dualism of the two mathematical elements, the "problem" and the "global synthesis," is developed only when they enter a field of interaction in which the global synthesis defines the "categories" without which the problem would have no general solution. See *Le déclin des absolus mathématico-logiques*.

41. Marcel Detienne, in *Les maîtres de vérité dans la Grèce archaïque* (Paris: Maspero, 1973), clearly articulates these two poles of thought, which correspond to the two aspects of sovereignty according to Dumézil: the magico-religious speech of the despot or of the "old man of the sea," and the dialogue-speech of the city. Not only are the principal character types of Greek thought (the Poet, the Physicist, the Philosopher, the Sophist, etc.) situated in relation to these poles, but Detienne interposes between the two poles a distinct group, the Warriors, which brings about transition or evolution.

42. There exists a Hegelianism of the right that lives on in official political philosophy and weds the destiny of thought to the State. Alexandre Kojève ("Tyranny and Wisdom," in Leo Strauss, *On Tyranny* [New York: Free Press of Glencoe, 1963]) and Eric Weil (*Hegel et l'Etat. Philosophie politique* [Paris: Vrin, 1974]) are its recent representatives. From Hegel to Max Weber there developed a whole line of reflection on the relation of the modern State to Reason, both as rational-technical and as reasonable-human. If it is objected that this rationality, already present in the archaic imperial State, is the *optimum* of the governors themselves, the Hegelians respond that the rational-reasonable cannot exist without a minimum of participation by everybody. The question, rather, is whether the very form of the rational-reasonable is not extracted from the State, in a way that necessarily makes it right, gives it "reason" (*lui donner nécessairement "raison"*).

43. On the role of the ancient poet as a "functionary of sovereignty," see Dumézil, *Servius et la Fortune* (Paris: Gallimard, 1943), pp. 64ff., and Detienne, *Les maîtres de vérité*, pp. 17ff.

44. See Michel Foucault's analysis of Maurice Blanchot and the form of exteriority of thought: "La pensée du dehors," *Critique*, no. 229 (June 1966), pp. 523-548.

45. Nietzsche, *Schopenhauer as Educator*, in *Untimely Meditations*, trans. R. J. Hollingdale (Cambridge: Cambridge University Press, 1983), pp. 177-178.

46. A curious text of Karl Jaspers, entitled *Descartes und die Philosophie* (Berlin: W. de Gruyter, 1956), develops this point of view and accepts its implications.

47. Kenneth White, *Intellectual Nomadism*. The title of the second volume of this unpublished work is *Poetry and Tribe*.

48. [TRANS: Arthur Rimbaud, *A Season in Hell*, trans. Louise Varèse (Norfolk, Conn.: New Directions, 1952), pp. 9, 13, 17, 39.]

49. Anny Milovanoff, "La seconde peau du nomade," *Nouvelles littéraires*, no. 2646 (July 27, 1978), p. 18: "The Larbaâ nomads, on the border of the Algerian Sahara, use the word *trigâ*, which generally means road or way, to designate the woven straps serving to reinforce the cords holding the tent to the stakes. . . . In nomad thought, the dwelling is tied not to a territory but rather to an itinerary. Refusing to take possession of the land they cross, the nomads construct an environment out of wool and goat hair, one that leaves no mark at the temporary site it occupies. . . . Thus wool, a soft material, gives nomad life its unity. . . . Nomads pause at the representation of their journeys, not at a figuration of the space they cross. They leave space to space. . . . Woolly polymorphism."

50. See W. Montgomery Watt, *Mohammed at Medina* (London: Oxford University Press, 1956), pp. 85-86, 242.

51. Emmanuel Laroche, *Histoire de la racine "Nem" en grec ancien* (Paris: Klincksieck, 1949). The root "Nem" indicates distribution, not allocation, even when the two are linked. In the pastoral sense, the distribution of animals is effected in a nonlimited space and implies no parceling out of land: "The occupation of shepherd, in the Homeric age, had nothing to do with a parceling of land; when the agrarian question came to the foreground, in the time of Solon, it was expressed in an entirely different vocabulary." *To take to pasture* (nemô) refers not to a parceling out but to a scattering, to a repartition of animals. It was only after Solon that Nomos came to designate the principle at the basis of the laws and of right (Thesmoï and Dikè), and then came to be identified with the laws themselves. Prior to that, there was instead an alternative between the city, or polis, ruled by laws, and the outskirts as the place of the nomos. A similar alternative is found in the work of Ibn Khaldūn: between *hadara* as city living, and *badiya* as nomos (not the town, but the preurban countryside, the plateau, steppe, mountain, or desert).

52. Arnold Toynbee, *A Study of History* (New York: Oxford University Press, 1947), abridged by D. C. Somerwell, vol. 1, pp. 164-186: "They flung themselves upon the Steppe, not to escape beyond its bounds but to make themselves at home on it" (p. 168).

53. See Pierre Hubac, *Les nomades* (Paris: La Renaissance du Livre, 1948), pp. 26-29 (although Hubac tends to confuse nomads and migrants).

54. On the nomads of the sea, or of the archipelago, José Emperaire writes: "They do not grasp an itinerary as a whole, but in a fragmentary manner, by juxtaposing in order its various successive stages, from campsite to campsite in the course of the journey. For each of these stages, they estimate the length of the crossing and the successive changes in direction marking it." *Les nomades de la mer* (Paris: Gallimard, 1954), p. 225.

55. Wilfred Thesiger, *Arabian Sands* (London: Longmans, Green, 1959), pp. 112-113, 125, 165-166.

56. See the two admirable descriptions, of the sand desert by Wilfred Thesiger and of the ice desert by Edmund Carpenter, in *Eskimo* (Toronto: University of Toronto Press, 1964): the winds, and tactile and sound qualities; the secondary character of visual data, particularly the indifference of the nomads to astronomy as a royal science; and yet the presence of a whole minor science of qualitative variables and traces.

57. Emile Félix Gautier, *Le passé de l'Afrique du Nord* (Paris: Payot, 1952), pp. 267-316.

58. From this perspective, Clastres's analysis of Indian prophetism can be generalized: "On one side, the chiefs, on the other, and standing against them, the prophets. . . . And the prophetic machine worked perfectly well since the *karai* were able to sweep astonishing masses of Indians along behind them. . . . the insurrectional act of the prophets against the chiefs conferred on the former, through a strange reversal of things, infinitely more power than was held by the latter." *Society against the State*, pp. 184-185.

59. One of the most interesting themes of the classic work by Paul Alphandéry (*La chrétienté et l'idée de croisade* [Paris: Albin Michel, 1959] is his demonstration that the

changes in course, the pauses, the detours were an integral part of the Crusade: "this army of crusaders that we envision as a modern army, like those of Louis XIV or Napoleon, marching with absolute passivity, obeying the will of a diplomatic officer and staff. Such an army knows where it is going, and when it makes a mistake, it is not for lack of reflection. A history more attentive to differences accepts a more realistic image of the army of the Crusade. The army of the Crusade was freely, sometimes anarchically alive. . . . This army was motivated from within, as a function of a complex coherence by virtue of which nothing happened by chance. It is certain that the conquest of Constantinople had its reason, necessity and a religious character, like the other deeds of the Crusades" (vol. 2, p. 7). Alphandéry shows in particular that the idea of a battle against the Infidel, *at any point*, appeared early on, along with the idea of liberating the Holy Land (vol. 1, p. 219).

60. Modern historians have been inspired to fine analyses by this confrontation between the East and the West, which began in the Middle Ages (and is tied to the question, Why did capitalism develop in the West and not elsewhere?). See especially Fernand Braudel, *Capitalism and Material Life, 1400-1800*, trans. Miriam Kochan (New York: Harper and Row, 1967), pp. 97-108; Pierre Chaunu, *L'expansion européenne du XIIIe au XVe siècle* (Paris: PUF, 1969), pp. 334-339 ("Why Europe? Why not China?"); Maurice Lombard, *Espaces et réseaux du haut Moyen Age* (The Hague: Mouton, 1971), chapter 8 (and p. 219: "What is called deforestation in the East is named clearing in the West. The first deep cause of the shift of the dominant centers from the East to the West is therefore a geographical reason: forest-clearing proved to have more potential than desert-oasis").

61. Marx's observations on the despotic formations of Asia have been confirmed by the African analyses of Max Gluckman, *Custom and Conflict in Africa* (Glencoe, Ill.: Free Press, 1959): at the same time immutability of form and constant rebellion. The idea of a "transformation" of the State indeed seems to be a Western one. And that other idea, the "destruction" of the State, belongs much more to the East and to the conditions of a nomad war machine. Attempts have been made to present the two ideas as successive phases of revolution, but there are too many differences between them and they are difficult to reconcile; they reflect the opposition between the socialist and anarchist currents of the nineteenth century. The Western proletariat itself is perceived from two points of view: as having to seize power and transform the State apparatus (the point of view of labor power), and as willing or wishing for the destruction of the State (this time, the point of view of nomadization power). Even Marx defines the proletariat not only as alienated (labor) but as deterritorialized. The proletariat, in this second perspective, appears as the heir to the nomad in the Western world. Not only did many anarchists invoke nomadic themes originating in the East, but the bourgeoisie above all were quick to equate proletarians and nomads, comparing Paris to a city haunted by nomads (see Louis Chevalier, *Laboring Classes and Dangerous Classes in Paris during the First Half of the Nineteenth Century*, trans. Frank Jellenck [New York: H. Fertig, 1973], pp. 362-366).

62. See Lucien Musset, *Les invasions. Le second assaut* (Paris: PUF, 1965), for example, the analysis of the Danes' three "phases," pp. 135-137.

63. Paul Virilio, *Speed and Politics*, trans. Mark Polizzotti (New York: Semiotext[e], 1986), pp. 12-13 and *passim*. Not only is the "town" unthinkable apart from the exterior flows with which it is in contact, and the circulation of which it regulates, but specific architectural aggregates, the fortress, for example, are veritable transformers, by virtue of their interior spaces, which allow an analysis, prolongation, or restitution of movement. Virilio concludes that the issue is less confinement than the management of the public ways, or the control of movement. Foucault was already moving in this direction with his analysis of the *naval hospital* as operator and filter; see *Discipline and Punish*, trans. A. M. Sheridan Smith (New York: Vintage, 1975), pp. 143-146.

64. On Chinese, and Arab, navigation, the reasons behind their failure, and the impor-

tance of this question in the East-West "dossier," see Braudel, *Capitalism and Material Life*, pp. 300-309, and Chaunu, *L'expansion européenne*, pp. 145-147.

65. Virilio gives a very good definition of the fleet in being and its historical consequences: "The fleet in being . . . is the permanent presence in the sea of an invisible fleet able to strike no matter where and no matter when . . . it is a new idea of violence that no longer comes from direct confrontation . . . but rather from the unequal properties of bodies, evaluation of the number of movements allowed them in a chosen element, permanent verification of their dynamic efficiency. . . . Henceforth it is no longer a question of crossing a continent or an ocean from one city to the next, one shore to the next. The fleet in being creates . . . the notion of displacement without destination in space and time. . . . The strategic submarine has no need to go anywhere in particular; it is content, while controlling the sea, to remain invisible . . . the realization of the absolute, uninterrupted, circular voyage, since it involves neither departure nor arrival. . . . If, as Lenin claimed, 'strategy means choosing which points we apply force to,' we must admit that these 'points', today, are no longer geostrategic strongpoints, since from any given spot we can now reach any other, no matter where it might be . . . *geographic localization* seems to have definitively lost its strategic value, and, inversely, that this same value is attributed to the *delocalization of the vector,* of a vector in permanent movement"; *Speed and Politics,* pp. 38, 40-41, 134-135. Virilio's texts are of great importance and originality in every respect. The only point that presents a difficulty for us is his assimilation of three groups of speed that seem very different to us: (1) speeds of nomadic, or revolutionary, tendency (riot, guerrilla warfare); (2) speeds that are regulated, converted, appropriated by the State apparatus (management of the public ways); (3) speeds that are reinstated by a worldwide organization of total war, or planetary overarmament (from the fleet in being to nuclear strategy). Virilio tends to equate these groups on account of their interactions and makes a general case for the "fascist" character of speed. It is, nevertheless, his own analyses that make these distinctions possible.

66. Jean-Pierre Vernant in particular has analyzed the connection between the Greek city-state and a homogeneous geometrical extension, *Mythe et pensée chez les Grecs* (Paris: Maspero, 1971-1974), vol. 1, part 3. The problem is necessarily more complicated in relation to the archaic empires, or in relation to formations subsequent to the classical city-state. That is because the space in question is very different. But it is still the case that the number is subordinated to space, as Vernant suggests with regard to Plato's ideal state. The Pythagorean or Neoplatonic conceptions of number envelop imperial astronomical spaces of a type other than homogeneous extension, but they maintain the subordination of the number; that is why Numbers become *ideal,* but not strictly speaking "numbering."

67. Dumézil stresses the role played by the arithmetic element in the earliest forms of political sovereignty. He even tends to make it a third pole of sovereignty. See *Servius et la Fortune* and *Le troisième souverain* (Paris: Maisonneuve, 1949). But the role of this arithmetic element is, rather, to organize a matter; in so doing it submits that matter to one or the other of the two principal poles.

68. Karl von Clausewitz stresses the secondary role of geometry, in tactics and in strategy: *On War,* trans. Michael Howard, Peter Paret, and Bernard Brodie (Princeton, N. J.: Princeton University Press, 1976), pp. 214-216 ("The Geometrical Factor").

69. See one of the most profound ancient texts relating the number and direction to the war machine, Ssu-ma Ch'ien, *The Records of the Grand Historian,* trans. Burton Watson (New York: Columbia University Press, 1961), vol. 2, pp. 155-193 ("The Account of the Hsiung-nu").

70. Frank Herbert, *Children of Dune* (New York: Berkley Books, 1977), p. 212. One may refer to the characteristics proposed by Julia Kristeva to define the numbering number:

"arrangement," "plural and contingent distribution," "infini-point," "rigorous approximation," etc. *Semeiotikè. Recherches pour une sémanalyse* (Paris: Seuil, 1969), pp. 293-297.

71. Boris Iakovlevich Vladimirtsov, *Le régime social des Mongols*, trans. Michel Carsow (Paris: Maisonneuve, 1948). The term used by Vladimirtsov, "antrustions," is borrowed from the Saxon regime, in which the king's *company*, or "trust," was composed of Franks.

72. A particularly interesting case is that of a special body of smiths among the Tuareg, called the *Enaden* (the "Others"); the Enaden are thought to have been originally Sudanese slaves, Jewish settlers in the Sahara, or descendants of the knights of Saint Louis. See René Pottier, "Les artisans sahariens du métal chez les Touareg," in *Techniques et civilisations*, vol. 1 (*Métaux et civilisations*), no. 2 (1945), pp. 31-40.

73. Feudalism is no less a military system than so-called military democracy; but both systems assume an army integrated into some kind of State apparatus (for feudalism, it was the Carolingian land reform). It is Vladimirtsov who developed a feudal interpretation of the nomads of the steppe, whereas Mikhail Griaznov, *The Ancient Civilization of Southern Siberia*, trans. James Hogarth (New York: Cowles, 1969), leans toward military democracy. But one of Vladimirtsov's main arguments is that the organization of the nomads becomes feudal precisely to the extent that it is in disintegration, or is integrated into the empires it conquers. He himself remarks that in the beginning the Mongols did not organize the sedentary land they took over into fiefs, true or false.

74. J. F. C. Fuller, *Armament and History* (New York: Charles Scribner's Sons, 1945), p. 5.

75. Paul Virilio, "Métempsychose du passager," *Traverses*, no. 8 (May 1977), pp. 11-19. Virilio, however, asserts that there was an indirect transition from hunting to war: when women served as "portage or pack" animals, which already enabled the hunters to enter into a relation of "homosexual duel" transcending the hunt. But it seems that Virilio himself invites us to make a distinction between *speed*, as projector and projectile, and *displacement*, as transport and portage. The war machine is defined from the first point of view, while the second relates to the public sphere. The horse, for example, is not a part of the war machine if it serves only to transport men who dismount to do battle. The war machine is defined by action, not transport, even if the transport reacts upon the action.

76. J. F. C. Fuller, *Armaments and History*, pp. 137ff., shows that the First World War was first conceived as an offensive war of movement based on artillery. But artillery was turned against artillery, forcing immobility. It was not possible to reinstate mobility in the war through "ever-increasing shell fire" (p. 138) since the craters made the terrain all the harder to negotiate. The solution, to which the English, and General Fuller in particular, made decisive contributions, came in the form of the tank: the tank, a "landship" (p. 139), reconstituted a kind of maritime or smooth space on land, and "superimposed naval tactics on land warfare" (p. 140). As a general rule, military response is never in kind: the tank was the response to artillery, the helicopter to the tank, etc. This makes for an innovation factor in the war machine that is very different from innovation in the work machine.

77. On this general distinction between the two models, "work-free action," "consuming force/conserving force," "real effect/formal effect," etc., see Martial Guéroult's exposition, *Dynamique et métaphysique leibniziennes* (Paris: Les Belles Lettres, 1934), pp. 55, 119 ff., 222-224.

78. Marcel Detienne, "La phalange, problèmes et controverses," in *Problèmes de la guerre en Grèce ancienne* (*Civilisations et sociétés*, no. 11), ed. Jean-Pierre Vernant (The Hague: Mouton, 1968), pp. 119-143: "Technology is in a way internal to the social and the mental," (p. 134).

79. On the stirrup and the plow, see Lynn Townsend White, Jr., *Medieval Technology and Social Change* (New York: Oxford University Press, 1962), chapters 1 and 2. Similarly, it has

been shown in the case of dry rice cultivation in Asia that the digging stick, the hoe, and the plow depend upon collective assemblages that vary according to population density and the fallow period. This enables Braudel to conclude: "The tool, according to this theory, is the result and no longer the cause"; *Capitalism and Material Life*, p. 116.

80. Treatises on martial arts remind us that the Ways, which are still subject to the laws of gravity, must be transcended in the void. Kleist's *About Marionettes*, trans. Michael Lebeck (Mindelheim: Three Kings Press, 1970), without question one of the most spontaneously oriental texts in Western literature, presents a similar movement: the linear displacement of the center of gravity is still "mechanical" and relates to something more "mysterious" that concerns the soul and knows nothing of weight.

81. See Paul Pelliot, "Les systèmes d'écriture en usage chez les anciens Mongols," *Asia Major* 2 (1925), pp. 284-289: The Mongols used the Uighur script, with the Syriac alphabet (it was the Tibetans who produced a phonetic theory of Uighur writing); the two versions of the *Secret History of the Mongols* that have been passed down to us are a Chinese translation and a phonetic transcription in Chinese characters.

82. Georges Charrière, *Scythian Art* (New York: Alpine Fine Arts Collection, 1979), p. 185 [translation modified].

83. See Lucien Musset, *Introduction à la runologie* (Paris: Aubier-Montaigne, 1965).

84. There are, of course, forms of cooking and architecture that are part of the nomad war machine, but they fall under a different "trait," one distinguishing them from their sedentary form. Nomad architecture, for example, the Eskimo igloo or the Hunnish wooden palace, is a derivative of the tent: its influence on sedentary art came by way of domes and half-domes, and above all of *space starting very low*, as in a tent. As for nomad cooking, it consists literally of break-fast (the paschal tradition is nomadic). And it is under this trait that it can be part of a war machine: for example, the Janissaries used a cooking pot as their rallying point; there were different ranks of cooks, and their hat had a wooden spoon through it.

85. It is in the *Traité du rebelle* (Paris: Bourgois, 1981) that Jünger takes his clearest stand against national socialism and develops certain points contained in *Der Arbeiter:* a conception of the "line" as an active escape passing between the two figures of the old Soldier and the modern Worker, carrying both toward another destiny in another assembly (nothing of this remains in Heidegger's notion of the Line, although it is dedicated to Jünger).

86. Lynn White, Jr., who is actually not inclined to ascribe much power of innovation to the nomads, sometimes establishes extensive technological lineages with surprising origins: he traces hot-air and turbine technologies to Malaya (*Medieval Technology and Social Change*, p. 95 and note): "Thus a chain of technological stimuli may be traced back from some of the major figures of early modern science and technology through the later Middle Ages to the jungles of Malaya. A second, and related, Malay invention, the fire piston, may have had significant influence upon the European understanding of air pressure and its applications."

87. On the particularly thorny question of the stirrup, see Lynn White, Jr., *Medieval Technology and Social Change*, chapter 1.

88. See the fine article by A. Mazaheri, "Le sabre contre l'épée," *Annales* 13, no. 4 (October-December 1958), pp. 669-686.

89. Henri Limet, *Le travail du métal au pays de Sumer au temps de la IIIe dynastie d'Ur* (Paris: Les Belles Lettres, 1960), pp. 33-40.

90. Along these lines, Mazaheri effectively demonstrates that the saber and sword belong to two distinct technological lineages. In particular, *damasking* (*damassage*), which does not come from Damascus at all, but rather from the Greek or Persian word for diamond, designates the treatment of cast steel that makes it as hard as a diamond and the designs in this steel resulting from the crystallization of the cement ("true damask was made in the centers

that had never experienced Roman domination"). But on the other hand, *damascening* (*damasquinage*), which did come from Damascus, designates only inlay in metal (or in fabric), intentional designs imitating damasking using entirely different means.

91. André Leroi-Gourhan, *Milieu et techniques* (Paris: Albin Michel, 1945), pp. 356ff. Gilbert Simondon, discussing short series, takes up the question of the "absolute origins of a technological lineage," or of the creation of a "technical essence": *Du mode d'existence des objects techniques* (Paris: Aubier, 1969), pp. 41-49.

92. On the mold-modulation relation, and the way in which molding hides or contracts an operation of modulation that is essential to matter-movement, see Simondon, *Du mode d'existence*, pp. 28-50 ("modulation is molding in a continuous and perpetually variable manner"; p. 42). Simondon clearly shows that the hylomorphic schema owes its power not to the technological operation but to the social model of *work* subsuming that operation (pp. 47-49).

93. Simondon feels no special attraction for the problems of metallurgy. His analysis is not, in fact, historical and prefers to deal with examples drawn from electronics. But, historically, there is no electronics without metallurgy. Thus Simondon pays homage to metallurgy: "Metallurgy does not entirely accommodate itself to an analysis using the hylomorphic schema. The fixing of the form is not accomplished visibly in a single stroke, but in several successive operations; the forging and quenching of steel are anterior and posterior, respectively, to the fixing of the form in the strict sense; forging and quenching are, nevertheless, operations that constitute objects" (*L'individu*, p. 59).

94. Not only must myths be taken into account, but also positive history, for example, the role of "the brass" in the evolution of musical form; or again, the constitution of a "metallic synthesis" in electronic music (Richard Pinhas).

95. Wilhelm Worringer defines Gothic art in terms of a geometrical line that is "primitive" but has taken on life. But this vitality is not organic, as it will be in the classical world: this line "embodies no organic expression . . . it is nevertheless of the utmost vitality. . . . Since this line is lacking in all organic timbre, its expression of life must, as an expression, be divorced from organic life. . . . The pathos of movement which lies in this vitalized geometry—a prelude to the vitalized mathematics of Gothic architecture—forces our sensibility to an effort unnatural to it." *Form in Gothic* (London: Putnam's and Sons, 1927), pp. 41-42.

96. This is one of the essential points of V. Gordon Childe's argument in *The Prehistory of European Civilization* (London: Cassell, 1962): the metallurgist is the first specialized artisan, whose sustenance is made possible by the formation of an agricultural surplus. The relation of the smith to agriculture has to do not only with the tools smiths manufacture but also with the food they take or receive. The Dogon myth, as analyzed in its variants by Griaule, can be seen as marking this relation, in which the smith receives or steals grains, and hides them in his mallet.

97. Maurice Lombard, *Les métaux dans l'ancien monde du Ve au XIe siècle* (The Hague: Mouton, 1974), pp. 75, 255.

98. The social position of the smith has been the object of detailed studies; for Africa in particular see the classic study by W. B. Cline, "Mining and Metallurgy in Negro Africa," *General Series in Anthropology*, no. 5 (1937); and Pierre Clément, "Le forgeron en Afrique noire," *Revue de géographie humaine et d'ethnologie*, no. 2 (April-June 1948), pp. 35-58. But these studies are hardly conclusive; the better defined the principles invoked—"reaction of contempt," "of approbation," "of apprehension"—the hazier and more overlapping the results, as seen in Clément's tables.

99. See Jules Bloch, *Les Tziganes*, Que sais-je?, no. 580 (Paris: PUF, 1969). Bloch demonstrates precisely that the distinction between sedentaries and nomads becomes secondary in connection with cave dwelling.

100. Elie Faure, *Medieval Art*, vol. 2 of *History of Art*, trans. Walter Pach (Garden City, N.Y.: Garden City Publishing, 1937), pp. 12-14.

101. On these peoples and their mysteries, see the analyses of V. Gordon Childe, *The Prehistory of European Society*, chapter 7 ("Missionaries, Traders and Warriors of Temperate Europe"), and *The Dawn of European Civilization* (New York: Knopf, 1958).

102. Maurice Griaule and Germaine Dieterlen, *Le renard pâle*, vol. 1 (Paris: Institut d'ethnologie, 1965), p. 376.

103. The book by Robert James Forbes, *Metallurgy in Antiquity* (Leiden: Brill, 1950), analyzes the different ages of metallurgy, as well as the types of metallurgists that existed in the "ore stage": the "miner," who did the prospecting and mining; the "smelter" [who produced the crude metal or alloy]; the "blacksmith" [who manufactured mass products from crude metals]; and the "metalworker" [who produced smaller objects; includes gold- and silver-smiths] (pp. 74-76). The specialization system becomes more complicated in the Iron Age, with attendant variations in the nomad-itinerant-sedentary distribution.

104. The texts of T. E. Lawrence, *Seven Pillars of Wisdom* (New York: Doubleday, Doran, 1935) and "The Science of Guerrilla War," in *Encyclopedia Britannica*, 14th ed. (1929), vol. 10, pp. 950-953, remain among the most significant works on guerrilla warfare; they present themselves as an "anti-Foch" theory and elaborate the notion of the nonbattle. But the nonbattle has a history that is not entirely dependent on guerrilla warfare: (1) the traditional distinction between the "battle" and the "maneuver" in war; see Raymon Aron, *Penser la guerre. Clausewitz* (Paris: Gallimard, 1976), vol. 1, pp. 122-131; (2) the way in which the war of movement places the role and importance of the battle in question (as early as Marshal de Saxe, and the controversial question of the battle during the Napoleonic Wars); (3) finally, more recently, the critique of the battle in the name of nuclear arms, which play a deterrent role, with conventional forces now having a role only in "testing" or "maneuver"; see the Gaullist conception of the nonbattle, and Guy Brossollet, *Essai sur la non-bataille* (Paris: Belin, 1975). The recent return to the notion of the battle cannot be explained simply by technological factors such as the development of tactical nuclear arms, but implies political considerations—it is upon these that the role assigned to the battle (or nonbattle) in war depends.

105. On the fundamental differences between Tamerlane and Genghis Khan, see René Grousset, *The Empire of the Steppes*, trans. Naomi Walford (New Brunswick, N.J.: Rutgers University Press, 1970), pp. 417-419.

106. See *Armées et fiscalité dans le monde antique*, ed. A. Chastagnol, C. Nicolet, and H. van Effenterre (Paris: CNRS, 1977); this colloquium best covers the fiscal aspect but deals with the other two as well. The question of the distribution of land to soldiers and the families of soldiers comes up in every State and plays an essential role. In one particular form, it lay the foundation for fiefs and feudalism. But it already lay at the basis of "false fiefs" around the world, most notably of the *cleros* and cleruchy in Greek civilization. Claire Préaux, *L'économie royale des Lagides* (Brussels: Ed. de la Fondation Egyptologique Reine Elisabeth, 1939), pp. 463ff.

107. Clausewitz, *On War*, especially book 8, and the commentary on these three theses by Raymond Aron, *Penser la guerre*, vol. 1 (particularly pp. 139 ff., "Pourquoi les guerres de la deuxième espèce?").

108. Erich Ludendorff, *Der totale Krieg* (Munich: Ludendorff Verlag, 1935), notes that the evolution has been toward attributing more and more importance to the "people" and "domestic policies" in war, whereas Clausewitz still puts the emphasis on armies and foreign policy. This criticism is true overall, despite certain texts of Clausewitz. The same criticism is also made by Lenin and the Marxists (although they obviously have a totally different conception of the people and domestic policy than Ludendorff). Certain authors have convincingly

demonstrated that the proletariat is as much of military origin, naval in particular, as of industrial origin; see, for example, Virilio, *Speed and Politics,* pp. 38, 40-41, 134-35.

109. As John Ulric Nef shows, it was during the great period of "limited war" (1640-1740) that the phenomena of concentration, accumulation, and investment emerged—the same phenomena that were later to determine "total war." See *War and Human Progress* (New York: Norton, 1968). The Napoleonic code of war represents a turning point that brought together the elements of total war: mobilization, transport, investment, information, etc.

110. On this "transcending" of fascism, and of total war, and on the new point of inversion of Clausewitz's formula, see Virilio's entire analysis in *L'insécurité du territoire*, especially chapter 1.

111. Guy Brossollet, *Essai sur la non-bataille,* pp. 15-16. The axiomatic notion of the "unspecified enemy" is already well developed in official and unofficial texts on national defense, on international law, and in the judicial or police spheres.

13. 7000 B.C.: Apparatus of Capture

1. The principal book in this respect is *Mitra-Varuna* (Paris: Gallimard, 1948) (it also contains the analysis of the "One-Eyed" and the "One-Armed" gods).

2. The theme of the Binder-God and the magic knot has been the object of general studies in mythology, notably Mircea Eliade, *Images and Symbols,* trans. Philip Mairet (Kansas City: Sheed, Andrews, and McMeel, 1961), chapter 3. But these studies are ambiguous because they use a syncretic and archetypal method. Dumézil's method, on the other hand, is differential: the theme of capture or of the bond only groups various data together under a differential trait, which is constituted precisely by political sovereignty. On the opposition between these two methods, one can refer to Edmond Ortigues, *Le discours et le symbole* (Paris: Aubier, 1962).

3. Dumézil, *Mitra-Varuna,* pp. 113-114, 151, 202-203.

4. Ibid., p. 150: "There are many ways of being a god of war, and Tiwaz defines one that is very badly expressed by the labels warrior god, god of combat. . . . Tiwaz is something else: the jurist of war, and at the same time a kind of diplomat" (the same applies for Mars).

5. Ibid., pp. 124-132.

6. Ernst Jünger, *The Glass Bees,* trans. Louise Bogan and Elizabeth Mayer (New York: Noonday Press, 1960), p. 112 [translation modified to agree with the French translation cited by the authors].

7. Marcel Detienne, *Les maîtres de vérité dans la Grèce archaïque* (Paris: Maspero, 1973), and "Le phalange, problèmes et controverses," in *Problèmes de la guerre en Grèce ancienne* (Civilisations et sociétés, no. 11), ed. Jean-Pierre Vernant (The Hague: Mouton, 1968). See also Jean-Pierre Vernant, *The Origins of Greek Thought* (Ithaca, N.Y.: Cornell University Press, 1982).

8. Jacques Harmand cites an "enterprise using extensive manpower exceptionally directed by a functionary, Ouni, under the Pharaoh Pepi I toward 1400 B.C."; *La guerre antique* (Paris: PUF, 1973), p. 28. Even the military democracy Morgan described does not explain, but presupposes, an archaic State of the imperial type (the work of Detienne and Vernant establishes this). This imperial State itself functions first with jailers and police, and not warriors: see Dumézil, *Mitra-Varuna,* pp. 200-204.

9. The idea itself of an Asiatic despotic formation appeared in the eighteenth century, notably in Montesquieu, but was used to describe an evolved state of the empires and corresponded to absolute monarchy. Entirely different is the viewpoint of Marx, who recreates the notion in order to define the archaic empires. The principal texts in this regard are Marx,

Grundrisse, trans. Martin Nicolaus (New York: Vintage, 1973), pp. 471-514; Karl Wittfogel, *Oriental Despotism* (New Haven, Conn.: Yale University Press, 1957); and Pierre Vidal-Naquet's preface to the first French edition, *Le despotisme oriental* (Paris: Minuit, 1964), which was surpressed in the second edition at Wittfogel's request; Ferenc Tökei, *Essays on the Asiatic Mode of Production* (Budapest: Akademiai Kiado, 1979); and the studies in CERM, *Sur le mode de production asiatique* (Paris: Ed. Sociales, 1969).

10. Varron made a famous pun on *nexum* and *nec suum fit* (= the thing does not become the property of he who receives it). In effect, the *nexum* is a fundamental form of archaic Roman law, according to which it is not an accord between contracting parties that creates an obligation, but the borrower's or donor's word, in a magico-religious mode. This is not a contract (*mancipatio*), and it involves no buying-selling, even deferred, and no interest, although it seems to us that it may involve a kind of rent. See in particular Pierre Noailles, *Fas et Jus* (Paris: Les Belles Lettres, 1948); and Dumézil, who stresses the connection between the *nexum* and the magic bond, *Mitra-Varuna*, pp. 118-124.

11. See the excavations and studies of James Mellaart, *Earliest Civilizations in the Near East* (New York: McGraw-Hill, 1965) and *Çatal Hüyük* (New York: McGraw-Hill, 1967). The urbanist Jane Jacobs has drawn on this work in proposing an imperial model she calls "New Obsidian" (after the name of the lava used to make tools), which may go back to the beginning of Neolithic times, or even much further into the past. She stresses the "urban" origin of agriculture and the role of hybridizations occurring in the urban grain stocks: It is agriculture that presupposes the stock, and not the reverse. In an as yet unpublished study, Jean Robert analyzes Mellaart's theses and Jacobs's hypothesis, applying them to new perspectives (*Décoloniser l'espace*).

12. Clastres, *Society against the State*, trans. Robert Hurley (New York: Urizen, 1977). We have seen that, according to Clastres, primitive war is one of the principal mechanisms warding off the State in that it maintains the opposition and dispersion of small segmentary groups. But also, from this viewpoint, primitive war remains subordinated to these preventive mechanisms and does not become autonomous as a machine, even when it comprises a specialized body.

13. According to Griaznov, it was the sedentary farmers who went out on the steppe and became nomadic, during the Bronze Age: This is a case of a zigzag movement in evolution. See *The Ancient Civilization of Southern Siberia*, trans. James Hogarth (New York: Cowles, 1969), pp. 97-98, 131-133.

14. Jean Robert develops this notion of an "inversion of signs and messages": "In a first phase, information circulates principally from the periphery toward the center, but at a certain critical point, the town begins to emit, in the direction of the rural world, increasingly imperative messages"; the town becomes an exporter (*Décoloniser l'espace*).

15. On Chinese towns and their subordination to the imperial principle, see Etienne Balazs, *Chinese Civilization and Bureaucracy*, trans. H. M. Wright (New Haven, Conn.: Yale University Press, 1964), p. 410: "The social structures in both India and China automatically rejected the town and offered, as it were, refractory, substandard material to it. It was because society was well and truly frozen in a sort of irreducible system, a previous crystallization."

16. From all of these standpoints, François Châtelet questions the classical notion of the city-state and doubts that the Athenian city can be equated with any variety of State: "La Grèce classique, la Raison, l'Etat," in Alberto Asor Rosa et al., *En marge. L'Occident et ses "autres"*, (Paris: Aubier Montaigne, 1978). Islam was to confront analogous problems, as would Italy, Germany, and Flanders beginning in the eleventh century; in these cases, political power does not imply the State-form. An example is the community of Hanseatic towns, which lacked functionaries, an army , and even legal status. The town is always inside a network of towns, but, precisely, "the network of towns" does not coincide with "mosaic of

States." On all of these points, see the analyses of François Fourquet and Lion Murard, *Les équipements de pouvoir: ville, territoires et équipements collectifs* (Paris: 10/18, 1976), pp. 79-106.

17. Claude Lévi-Strauss, *Structural Anthropology*, trans Claire Jacobson and Brooke Grundfest Schoeft (New York: Basic Books, 1963), pp. 150-151.

18. Louis Berthe analyzes a specific example of the need for a "third village" to prevent the directional circuit from closing: "Aînés et cadets, l'alliance et la hiérarchie chez les Baduj," *L'Homme*, vol. 5, no. 3/4 (July-December 1965), pp. 214-215.

19. Fernand Braudel, *Capitalism and Material Life, 1400-1800*, trans. Miriam Kochan (New York: Harper and Row, 1967), 60), pp. 398, 405, 411. Emphasis added. (On town-State relations in the West, see pp. 396-406.) And as Braudel notes, one of the reasons for the victory of the States over the towns from the beginning of the fifteenth century was that the State alone had the ability fully to appropriate the war machine: by means of the territorial recruitment of men, material investment, the industrialization of war (it was more in the arms factories than in the pin factories that mass production and mechanical division appeared). The commercial towns, on the other hand, required wars of short duration, resorted to mercenaries, and were only able to encast the war machine.

20. This theme is frequently developed by Samir Amin: "Since the theory of relations between different social formations cannot be an economistic one, international relations, which belong precisely to this context, cannot give rise to an economic theory." *Unequal Development*, trans. Brian Pearce (New York: Monthly Review Press, 1976), p. 146.

21. See Jacques Lacarrière, *Les hommes ivres de Dieu* (Paris: Fayard, 1975).

22. [TRANS: On capitalism repelling its limits, see Deleuze and Guattari, *Anti-Oedipus*, trans. Robert Hurley, Mark Seem, and Helen R. Lane (Minneapolis: University of Minnesota Press, 1983), pp. 230-232.]

23. Samir Amin analyzes this particularity of the "peripheral formations" of the Third World and distinguishes two principal types, the oriental and African, and the American: "The Americas, Asia and the Arab world, and Black Africa were not transformed in the same way because they were not integrated at the same stage of capitalist development at the center and therefore did not fulfill the same function in development." *Unequal Development*, p. 295. See also *Accumulation on a World Scale*, vol. 2, trans. Brian Pearce (New York: Monthly Review Press, 1974), pp. 390-394. We shall see, however, that under certain conditions the center and the periphery are determined in such a way as to exchange their characteristics.

24. Gaëtan Pirou, *Economie libérale et économie dirigée*, vol. 1 (Paris: Ed. Sedes, 1946-1947), p. 117: "The productivity of the marginal worker determines not only that worker's wage but that of all the others, in the same way that, when it was a question of commodities, the utility of the last bucket of water or last sack of wheat governed the value not only of that bucket or that sack but of all the other buckets and all the other sacks." (Marginalism seeks to quantify the assemblage, when in fact all kinds of qualitative factors are at work in the evaluation of the "last.")

25. On the importance of the theory of evaluation and feeling out for marginalism, see Jacques Fradin's critical discussion, *Les fondements logiques de la théorie néoclassique de l'échange* (Grenoble: Presses Universitaires de Grenoble, 1976). For Marxists, there is also a groping evaluation, but one that can bear only on the quantity of socially necessary labor; Engels speaks of this precisely in the context of precapitalist societies. He invokes "a process of zig-zag approximation, often groping back and forth in the dark," which is governed more or less by the "need for each person to have a rough idea of his costs" (one may wonder if this last part of the phrase does not reinstate a sort of marginalist criterion). Engels, "Supplement to Volume Three of Capital," in Marx, *Capital*, vol. 3, trans. David Fernbach (New York: Vintage, 1981), p. 1036.

26. [TRANS: "Ophelimity" (from the Greek for "useful," "serviceable") was introduced by Vilfredo Pareto in his *Cours d'économie politique* (1896), ed. G.-H. Bousquet and G. Busino (Geneva: Librairie Droz, 1964), pp. 2-16. The first portion of this discussion is translated in Vilfredo Pareto, *Sociological Writings*, ed. and intro. S. E. Fine, trans. Derick Mirtin (New York: Praeger, 1966), pp. 97-102.]

27. David Ricardo, *On the Principles of Political Economy*, in *The Works and Correspondence of David Ricardo*, vol. 1, ed. Piero Sraffa (London: Cambridge University Press, 1962), chapter 2. See also Marx's analysis of the two forms of "differential rent," *Capital*, vol. 3, part 6.

28. Of course, the least fertile land is also in theory the most recent or the last in a series (which allows many commentators to say that Ricardo prefigured marginalism in his theory of rent). But this is not even a rule, and Marx shows that an "increasing sequence" is just as possible as a "decreasing sequence" and that a better soil can "take the lowest place instead of that which was formerly the worst." *Capital*, vol. 3, p. 798.

29. [TRANS: *Capital*, vol. 3, p. 788.]

30. Ricardo, *On the Principles of Political Economy*, p. 75: "If air, water, the elasticity of steam, and the pressure of the atmosphere, were of different qualities; if they could be appropriated, and each quality existed only in moderate abundance, they, as well as the land, would afford a rent, as the successive qualities were brought into use."

31. The two forms of *differential rent* are based on comparison. But Marx maintains the existence of another form, unknown to the theorists (Ricardo), but with which the practitioners, he says, are quite familiar: *absolute rent*, based on the special character of landed property as monopoly. In effect, land is not a commodity like the others because it is not reproducible at the level of a determinable aggregate. There is therefore monopoly, which is not the same as "monopoly price" (monopoly price, and the eventual corresponding rent, are totally different questions). In the simplest terms, differential rent and absolute rent can be distinguished in the following manner: since the price of the product is calculated on the basis of the worst soil, the entrepreneur with the best soil would have a surplus profit if the latter were not transformed into differential rent accruing to the landowner; but on the other hand, since agricultural surplus value is proportionally greater than industrial surplus value (?), the agricultural entrepreneur in general would have a surplus profit if the latter were not transformed into absolute rent accruing to the landowner. Rent is thus a necessary element in the equalization and adjustment of profit: whether it be the equalization of the agricultural profit rate (differential rent), or the equalization of this rate and the rate of industrial profit (absolute rent). Certain Marxist economists have proposed an entirely different schema of absolute rent, but one that maintains Marx's necessary distinction. [TRANS: On absolute rent, see Marx, *Capital*, vol. 3, part 6, chapter 45, pp. 895-899.]

32. Bernard Schmitt, *Monnaie, salaires et profit* (Paris: Castella, 1980), pp. 289-290, distinguishes between two forms of capture or "harnessing," which correspond moreover to the two principal figures of the hunt, *waiting* and *pursuit*. Rent would be a residual or waiting kind of capture because it depends on external forces and operates by transfer; profit would be a capture of pursuit or conquest because it derives from a specific action and requires a force of its own or a "creation." This holds true, however, only in relation to differential rent; as Marx noted, absolute rent represents the "creative" aspect of landed property (*Capital*, vol. 3, p. 889).

33. Edouard Will, *Korinthiaka* (Paris: Ed. De Boccard, 1955), pp. 470ff., analyzes a late, but exemplary, case, that of the tyrant Cypselos's reform in Corinth: (1) a portion of the land belonging to the hereditary aristocracy was confiscated and distributed to the poor peasants; (2) but at the same time a metallic stock was constituted, through seizure of the property of proscribed persons; (3) this money itself was distributed to the poor, but in order for them to

give it to the old owners as an indemnity; (4) the old owners from then on paid their taxes in money, so as to ensure a circulation or turnover of the currency, and an equivalence between money, goods, and services. We already find analogous figures directly inscribed in the archaic empires, independently of the problems of private property. For example, land is distributed to the functionaries in their capacity as functionaries, and they exploit or lease it. But if the functionary thereby receives a rent in labor or in kind from it, he owes the emperor a tax payable in money. Hence the necessity of "banks," which, under complex conditions, ensure the equivalence, conversion, and circulation of goods-money throughout the economy; see Guillaume Cardascia, "Armée et fiscalité dans la Babylone achéménide," in *Armées et fiscalité dans le monde antique* (Paris: CNRS, 1977).

34. [TRANS: On these three forms of rent, see Marx, *Capital*, vol. 3, part 6, chapter 47, pp. 925-938.]

35. Authors like Will and Gabriel Ardant have demonstrated that the commercial function does not account for the origin of money, tied to ideas of "payment," "settlement," "taxation." Will proves this in particular for the Greek and Western worlds; but even in the oriental empires, we think that the monopoly over monetarized trade assumes monetary taxation. See Edouard Will, "Réflexions et hypothèses sur les origines du monnayage," *Revue numismatique*, vol. 17 (1955), pp. 3-24; Gabriel Ardant, *Histoire financière de l'antiquité à nos jours* (Paris: Gallimard, 1976), pp. 28ff.: "The milieus that gave rise to taxation also gave rise to money."

36. On this aspect of indirect taxation, see Arghiri Emmanuel, *Unequal Exchange*, trans. Brian Pearce (New York: Monthly Review Press, 1972), pp. 1-2, 228-236 (in relation to foreign trade). Concerning the relations taxation-trade, a particularly interesting case is that of mercantilism, analyzed by Eric Alliez (*Capital et pouvoir*, unpublished manuscript).

37. [TRANS: Marx presents his trinity formula (capital-profit, land-ground rent, labor-wages) in *Capital*, vol. 3, chapter 48.]

38. Bernard Schmitt, *Monnaie, salaires et profits*.

39. Marx often emphasizes the following points, particularly in his analysis of primitive accumulation: (1) Primitive accumulation precedes the mode of production and makes it possible. (2) It therefore implies specific action by the State and the law, which are not opposed to violence but, on the contrary, promote it ("These methods depend in part on brute force. . . . But they all employ the power of the state, the concentrated and organized force of society." *Capital*, vol. 1, trans. Ben Fowkes [New York: Vintage, 1977], chapter 31, p. 915). (3) This lawful violence appears first in its raw form but ceases to be conscious to the degree that the mode of production becomes established; it seems to be a fact of nature pure and simple ("direct extra-economic force is still of course used, but only in exceptional cases"; ibid., p. 899). (4) A movement such as this is explained by the particular character of this violence, which is in no case reducible to theft, crime, or illegality (see *Notes sur Adolph Wagner* in *Oeuvres de Karl Marx*, "Pléiade" edition, vol. 2, ed. Maximilien Rubel [Paris: Gallimard, 1968]): what is taken away from the worker is not something surface level; the capitalist "does not limit himself to taking away or stealing, but extorts the production of a surplus value, *in other words*, he first contributes to the creation of that from which he takes away. . . . A part of the value created without the labor of the capitalist can be appropriated legally by the capitalist, in other words, without violating the corresponding right to the exchange of commodities."

40. Jean Robert thoroughly demonstrates, in this context, that primitive accumulation implies the violent construction of a homogenized, "colonized" space ("Décoloniser l'espace," unpublished manuscript).

41. Ferenc Tökei, "Les conditions de la propriété foncière dans la Chine de l'époque Tcheou," *Acta Antiqua*, vol. 6 (1958), pp. 245-300. Marx and Engels already noted that the Roman plebs (partially composed of freedmen) alone had the right to the "transfer of property

out of the *ager publicus*" (Marx, *Grundrisse*, p. 477): the plebeians became private owners of landed property, and also of commercial and industrial wealth, precisely insofar as they were "excluded from all public rights" (Engels, *The Origin of the Family, Private Property and the State* [New York: International Publishers, 1972], p. 190).

42. See the two great books by V. Gordon Childe, *The Most Ancient East* (London: K. Paul, Trench, Trübner, 1928) and especially *The Prehistory of European Civilization* (London: Cassell, 1962). In particular, archaeological analysis permits Childe to conclude that nowhere in the Aegean world were there accumulations of wealth or food comparable to those of the Orient (*The Prehistory of European Civilization*, pp. 106-110).

43. On the differences between "generalized slavery" in the archaic empire, and private slavery, feudal corvée, etc., see Charles Parain, "Protohistoire méditerranéenne et mode de production asiatique," in CERM, *Sur le mode de production asiatique*, pp. 170-173.

44. Gérard Boulvert, *Domestique et fonctionnaire sous le haut-empire romain* (Paris: Les Belles Lettres, 1974). More generally, Paul Veyne has analyzed the formation of "subjective law" in the Roman Empire, the corresponding institutions, and the new meaning of the public and private. He demonstrates that Roman law is a "law without concepts" that proceeds by "topics," and in this sense differs from the modern, "axiomatic" conception of the law. See Veyne, *Le pain et le cirque* (Paris: Seuil, 1976), chapters 3 and 4, and p. 744.

45. See François Hincker, "La monarchie absolue française," in CERM, *Sur le féodalisme* (Paris: Ed. Sociales, 1971).

46. Edgar Quinet, *La gênie des religions*, vol. 1 of *Oeuvres Complètes* (Paris: Hachette, ca. 1899).

47. Marx, "Introduction to the Critique of Political Economy," in *A Contribution to the Critique of Political Economy*, trans. N. I. Stone (Chicago: Charles H. Kerr, 1904), p. 298 [translation modified].

48. On the historical independence of the two series, and their "encounter," see Etienne Balibar in Althusser and Balibar, *Lire le Capital*, vol. 2 (Paris: Maspero, 1968), pp. 286-289.

49. Arghiri Emmanuel, *Unequal Exchange*, pp. 13-14, and the following passage he cites from Paul Sweezy, *The Theory of Capitalist Development* (New York: Monthly Review Press, 1942), p. 338: "'Capital' is not simply another name for means of production; it is means of production reduced to a qualitatively homogeneous and quantitatively measurable fund of value" (whence the equalization of profit). In his analysis of the primitive accumulation of capital, Maurice Dobb (*Studies in the Development of Capitalism*, rev. ed. [New York: International Publishers, 1964], pp. 177-186) effectively demonstrates that primitive accumulation bears not on the means of production but on "rights or titles to wealth" (p. 177; modified to agree with the French translation cited by the authors), which, depending on the circumstances, are convertible into means of production.

50. See the distinction certain jurists make between Roman, "topical," law, and modern, "axiomatic," law of the civil-code type. We may define certain fundamental ways in which the French Civil Code is closer to an axiomatic than to a code: (1) the predominance of the enunciative form over the imperative and over affective formulas (damnation, exhortation, admonishment, etc.); (2) the code's pretension that it forms a complete and saturated rational system; (3) but at the same time the relative independence of the propositions, which permit axioms to be added. On these aspects, see Jean Ray, *Essai sur la structure logique du code civil français* (Paris: Alcan, 1926). It has been established that the systematization of Roman law took place very late, in the sixteenth and seventeenth centuries.

51. [TRANS: Marx, *Economic and Philosophic Manuscripts of 1844*, ed. and intro. Dirk J. Struik, trans. Martin Mulligan (New York: International Publishers, 1964), p. 129.]

52. See Jean Saint-Geours, *Pouvoir et finance* (Paris: Fayard, 1979). Saint-Geours is one

of the best analysts of the monetary system, as well as of "private-public" mixes in the modern economy.

53. On the tendency toward the elimination of ground rent in capitalism, see Samir Amin and Kostas Vergopoulos, *La question paysanne et le capitalisme* (Paris: Ed. Anthropos, 1974). Amin analyzes the reasons why ground rent and rent of mines keep or assume a present-day meaning in the peripheral regions, although in different ways; *The Law of Value and Historical Materialism*, trans. Brian Pearce (New York: Monthly Review Press, 1978), chapters 4 and 6.

54. Introductory books on the axiomatic method emphasize a certain number of problems. For example, Robert Blanché's fine book, *L'axiomatique* (Paris: PUF, 1959) [abridged and translated by G. B. Keene as *Axiomatics* (New York: Free Press of Glencoe, 1962)]. There is first of all the question of the respective independence of the axioms, and whether or not the system is saturated, or "strongly complete" (sec. 14 and 15). Second, there is the question of "models of realization," their heterogeneity, but also their isomorphy in relation to the axiomatic system (sec. 12). Then there is the possibility of a polymorphy of models, not only in a nonsaturated system, but even in a saturated axiomatic (sec. 12, 15, and 26). Then, once again, there is the question of the "undecidable propositions" an axiomatic confronts (sec. 20). Finally, there is the question of "power," by which nondemonstrable infinite sets exceed the axiomatic (sec. 26 and "the power of the continuum"). The comparison of politics to an axiomatic is based on all of these aspects.

55. Lewis Mumford, "The First Megamachine," *Diogenes*, no. 55 (July-September 1966), p. 3. [translation modified to agree with the French translation cited by the authors].

56. Ergonomics distinguishes between "human-machine" systems (or work posts) and "human*s*-machine*s*" systems (communicational aggregates composed of human and nonhuman elements). But this is not only a difference of degree; the second point of view is not a generalization of the first: "The notion of information loses its anthropocentric aspect," and the problems are not of adaptation but of the choice of a human or nonhuman element depending on the case. See Maurice de Montmollin, *Les systèmes hommes-machines* (Paris: PUF, 1967). The issue is no longer to adapt, even under violence, but to localize: Where is your place? Even handicaps can be made useful, instead of being corrected or compensated for. A deaf-mute can be an essential part of a "humans-machines" communicational system.

57. One of the basic themes of science fiction is to show how machinic enslavement combines with processes of subjection, but exceeds and differs from them, performing a qualitative leap. Take Ray Bradbury: television not as an instrument located at the center of the house, but as forming the walls of the house.

58. See Lewis Mumford, *The Pentagon of Power*, vol. 2 of *The Myth of the Machine* (New York: Harcourt Brace Jovanovich, 1970), pp. 236-360 (a comparison of the "old megamachine" and the modern one; despite writing, the old megamachine notably suffered from difficulties in "communication").

59. Marx, *Manuscripts of 1844*, p. 129.

60. Historically, these have been the major problems in axiomatics: "undecidable" propositions (contradictory statements are also nondemonstrable); the powers of infinite sets, which by nature elude axiomatic treatment ("the continuum, for example, cannot be conceived axiomatically in its structural specificity since every axiomatization one can give it will rely on a denumerable model"). See Blanché, *L'axiomatique*, p. 80.

61. The "intuitionist" school (Brouwer, Heytig, Griss, Bouligand, etc.) is of great importance in mathematics, not because it asserted the irreducible rights of intuition, or even because it elaborated a very novel constructivism, but because it developed a conception of *problems*, and of a *calculus of problems* that intrinsically rivals axiomatics and proceeds by other rules (notably with regard to the excluded middle).

62. In our opinion, one of the best analyses of the Nazi economy is Jean-Pierre Faye's

Langages totalitaires (Paris: Hermann, 1972), pp. 664-676. Faye shows that Nazism is indeed a totalitarianism, precisely because of its minimal State, its refusal of any statification of the economy, its reduction of wages, its hostility toward large-scale public works. But at the same time, he shows that Nazism carries out the creation of domestic capital, strategic construction, and the building of an arms industry, which makes it rival or sometimes even meld with an economy of socialist leaning ("something that seems to resemble the Swedish loans praised by Myrdal with a view to large-scale projects, but which is in fact and immediately its opposite, the writing of an arms economy and a war economy," and the corresponding difference between "the public works entrepreneur" and the "army supplier"; pp. 668, 674).

63. See the critical list of the axioms of the periphery presented by Samir Amin, *Accumulation on a World Scale*, pp. 390-394.

64. Paul Virilio, *L'insécurité du territoire* (Paris: Stock, 1975); *Speed and Politics,* trans. Mark Polizzotti (New York: Semiotext[e], 1986); *Défense populaire et luttes écologiques* (Paris: Galilée, 1978), forthcoming in English translation from Semiotext(e) as *Popular Defense and Ecological Struggles:* it is precisely beyond fascism and total war that the war machine finds its complete object, in the menacing peace of nuclear deterrence. It is there that the reversal of Clausewitz's formula takes on a concrete meaning, at the same time as State politics tends to wither and the war machine takes over a maximum of civil functions ("place the whole of civil society under the regime of military security," "disqualify the whole of the planet's habitat by stripping the peoples of their quality of inhabitant," "erase the distinction between wartime and peacetime"; see the role of the media in this respect). Certain European police forces could be taken as an example, when they claim the right to "shoot on sight": they cease to be a cogwheel in the State apparatus and become pieces in a war machine.

65. Braudel shows how this center of gravity formed in northern Europe, but at the outcome of movements that, starting in the ninth and tenth centuries, put the European spaces of the North and the South in competition or rivalry with one another (this problem is not to be confused with that of the town-form and State-form, but does intersect with it). See "Naissance d'une économie-monde," *Urbi*, no. 1 (September 1979), pp. 3-20.

66. A movement in Marxist research formed on the basis of the work of Mario Tronti (*Operai e capitale* [Turin: G. Einaudi, 1971]; French translation, *Ouvriers et capital* [Paris: Bourgois, 1977]), then that of Italian autonomy and Antonio Negri, whose aim was to analyze the new forms of work and the struggle against work. It was a question of showing simultaneously: (1) that the struggle against work is not an accidental or "marginal" phenomenon in capitalism, but one essential to the composition of capital (the growth in the proportion of constant capital), and, (2) that this phenomenon engenders a new type of worldwide struggle—workers' struggles, popular struggles, ethnic struggles—in every domain. See Antonio Negri, especially *Marx Beyond Marx: Lessons on the Grundrisse*, ed. Jim Fleming, trans. Harry Cleaver, Michael Ryan, and Maurizion Viano (South Hadley, Mass.: Bergin and Garvey, 1984); Karl Heinz Roth, *Die "andere" Arbeiterbewegung* (Munich: Trikont, 1974); and the current work in France of Yann Moulier, Alain and Danièle Guillerm, Benjamin Coriat, etc. [TRANS: The best sources on the autonomy movement in English are *Italy: Autonomia. Post-Political Politics, Semiotext(e),* vol. 3, no. 3 (1980) and *Autonomy and the Crisis. Italian Marxist Texts of the Theory and Praxis of a Class Movement: 1964-1979* (London: Red Notes and CSE Books, 1979). *Marx Beyond Marx* includes a lengthy epilogue by Michael Ryan summarizing Negri's major works and a bibliography of writings on the Italian movement available in English.]

67. This is one of the essential theses of Tronti, who defined the new conceptions of the "mass-worker" and of the relation to work: "To struggle against capital, the working class must fight against itself insofar as it is capital; this is the maximal stage of contradiction, not for the workers, but for the capitalists. . . . The plan of capital begins to run backward, not as a *social*

development, but as a *revolutionary process*." See *Ouvriers et capital*, p. 322; this is what Negri has called the "crisis of the planning state" (*Crisi dello Stato-plano* [Milan: Feltrinelli, 1974]).

68. This is another aspect of the present-day situation: in addition to the new struggles tied to work and the evolution in work, there is the entire domain of what are called "alternative practices" and the construction of such practices (pirate radio stations would be the simplest example; other examples are urban community networks, the alternative to psychiatry, etc.). On all these points, and the link between the two aspects, see Franco Berardi Bifo, *Finalemente il cielo e caduto sulla terra* (Milan: Squilibri, 1978); and *Les Untorelli*, *Recherches*, no. 30 (1977) (special issue on autonomia).

14. 1440: The Smooth and the Striated

1. André Leroi-Gourhan, *L'homme et la matière* (Paris: Albin Michel, 1971), pp. 244ff. (and the opposition between fabric and felt).

2. William Faulkner, *Sartoris* (New York: Random House, 1956), p. 151.

3. On the history of the quilt and patchwork in American immigration, see Jonathan Holstein, *American Pieced Quilts* (New York: Viking, 1973) (with reproductions and bibliography). Holstein does not claim that the quilt is the principal source of American art, but he does note the extent to which the "white on white" of plain quilts and patchwork compositions inspired or gave impetus to certain tendencies in American painting: "We can see in many [quilts] such phenomena as 'op' effects, serial images, use of 'color fields,' deep understanding of negative space, mannerisms of formal abstraction and the like," (p. 13).

4. Pierre Boulez, *Boulez on Music Today*, trans. Susan Bradshaw and Richard Bennett (Cambridge, Mass.: Harvard University Press, 1971), pp. 83ff. We provide a summary of Boulez's analysis in the following paragraph.

5. [TRANS: Boulez, *Boulez on Music Today*, p. 87. Translation modified.]

6. On this indexing of the inside and the outside among the nomads of the desert, see Annie Milovanoff, "La seconde peau du nomade," *Nouvelles littéraires*, no. 2646 (July 27, 1978), p. 18. And on the relations between the igloo and the outside among the nomads of the ice, see Edmund Carpenter, *Eskimo* (Toronto: Toronto University Press, 1964).

7. See the two convergent descriptions of the space of ice and the space of sand: Edmund Carpenter, *Eskimo*, and Wilfred Thesiger, *Arabian Sands* (London: Longmans, Green, 1959). (In both cases, there is an indifference to astronomy.)

8. See Pierre Chaunu's study, *L'expansion européenne du XIIIe au XVe siècle* (Paris: PUF, 1969), pp. 288-305.

9. See in particular Paul Adam, "Navigation primitive et navigation astronomique," in *Les aspects internationaux de la découverte océanique aux XVe et XVIe siècles. Ve Colloque international d'histoire maritime*, ed. Michel Mollat and Paul Adam (Paris: SEVPEN, 1960), pp. 91-112. (See the operative geometry of the pole star.)

10. Guy Beaujouan, "Science livresque et nautique au XVe siècle," *Les aspects internationaux de la découverte océanique*, pp. 61-90.

11. See Paul Virilio, *L'insécurité du territoire* (Paris: Stock, 1975), on how the sea reconstitutes a smooth space with the "fleet in being," etc.; and how a vertical smooth space of aerial and stratospheric domination springs up (especially chapter 4, "Le littoral vertical," pp. 93-109).

12. Emmanuel Laroche, *Histoire de la racine "Nem" en grec ancien* (Paris: Klincksieck, 1949), clearly notes the difference between the ideas of distribution and allocation, between the two linguistic groups concerned, between the two kinds of space, between the "province" pole and the "city" pole.

13. This expression is found in René Thom, who applies it to a continuous variation in

which the variable reacts upon its antecedents: *Modèles mathématiques de la morphogenèse* (Paris: 10/18, 1974), pp. 218-219.

14. On Riemann's and Helmholtz's presentations of multiplicity, see Jules Vuillemin, *Philosophie de l'algèbre* (Paris: PUF, 1962), pp. 409ff.

15. See Bertrand Russell, *The Principles of Mathematics* (New York: Norton, 1964), chapter 31. The following discussion does not conform to Russell's theory. An excellent analysis of the notions of distance and magnitude according to Meinong and Russell may be found in Albert Spaier, *La pensée et la quantité* (Paris: Alcan, 1927).

16. Beginning in chapter 2 of *Time and Free Will: An Essay on the Immediate Data of Consciousness*, trans. F. L. Pogson (New York: Macmillan, 1958), Bergson repeatedly uses the noun "multiplicity," under conditions that should attract the attention of commentators; that there is an implicit reference to Riemann seems beyond doubt. Later, in *Matter and Memory*, trans. Nancy Margaret Paul and W. Scott Palmer (New York: Humanities Press, 1978), he explains that Achilles' stride can be divided perfectly into "submultiples" that differ in nature, however, from that which they divide; the same goes for the tortoise's stride; and the submultiples, "in both cases," themselves differ in nature.

17. See Bergson, *Time and Free Will*, p. 82: if a multiplicity "implies the possibility of treating any number whatever as a provisional unit which can be added to itself, inversely the units in their turn are true numbers which are as big as we like, but are regarded as provisionally indivisible for the purpose of compounding them with one another."

18. Albert Lautman, *Les schémas de structure* (Paris: Hermann, 1938), pp. 23, 34-35.

19. On this properly Euclidean conjunction (which is very different from the process of accumulation), see Lautman, ibid., pp. 45-48.

20. Benoit Mandelbrot, *Fractals: Form, Chance, and Dimension* (San Francisco: W. H. Freeman, 1977).

21. On these two kinds of space, see Jean-Pierre Vernant, *Mythe et pensée chez les Grecs*, vol. 1 (Paris: Maspero, 1971-1974), pp. 174-175.

22. Michel Serres, *La naissance de la physique dans le texte de Lucrèce. Fleuves et turbulences* (Paris: Minuit, 1977): "Physics is based much more on a vectorial space than on a metric space" (p. 79). On the hydraulic problem, see pp. 104-107.

23. Serres, *La naissance de la physique*, pp. 35, 135ff.

24. Anne Querrien has clearly demonstrated the importance of the Ecole des Ponts et Chaussées (School of Bridges and Roadways) in this elaboration of the concept of work. For example, Navier, an engineer and professor of mechanics, wrote in 1819: "We must establish a mechanical currency with which to estimate the quantities of work used to accomplish every kind of fabrication."

25. It is a commonplace of missionaries' narratives that there is nothing corresponding to the category of work, even in transhumant agriculture, with its laborious ground-clearing activities. Marshall Sahlins is not content to remark the briefness of the time devoted to the labor necessary for maintenance and reproduction, but goes on to stress qualitative factors: the continuous variation that regulates activity, and the mobility or freeness of movement, which excludes stockpiling and is measured in terms of the "convenience of transporting the object." "La première société d'abondance," *Les temps modernes*, no. 268 (October 1968), pp. 654-656, 662-663, 672-673.

26. The principal texts are Aloïs Riegl, *Die Spätrömische Kunstindustrie* (Vienna: Staatdruckerei, 1927); Wilhelm Worringer, *Abstraction and Empathy; A Contribution to the Psychology of Style*, trans. Michael Bullock (New York: International Universities Press, 1963); Henri Maldiney, *Regard, parole, espace* (Lausanne: L'Age d'homme, 1973), especially "L'art et le pouvoir du fond," and Maldiney's discussion of Cézanne.

27. All of these points already relate to Riemannian space, with its essential relation to

"monads" (as opposed to the unitary Subject of Euclidean space): see Gilles Chatelet, "Sur une petite phrase de Riemann," *Analytiques*, no. 3 (May 1979). Although the "monads" are no longer thought to be closed upon themselves, and are postulated to entertain direct, step-by-step local relations, the purely monadological point of view proves inadequate and should be superseded by a "nomadology" (the ideality of striated space versus the realism of smooth space).

28. See Edmund Carpenter's description in *Eskimo* of ice space, and of the igloo: "There is no middle distance, no perpective, no outline, nothing the eye can cling to except thousands of smokey plumes of snow . . . a land without bottom or edge . . . a labyrinth alive with the movements of crowded people. No flat static walls arrest the ear or eye . . . and the eye can glance through here, past there" (no pagination).

29. These two aspects, the Encompassing Element and the Center, figure in Jean-Pierre Vernant's analysis of space in Anaximander; *Mythe et penséee chez les Grecs* (Paris: Maspero, 1971-1974), vol. 1, part 3. From another perspective, the entire history of the desert concerns the possibility of its becoming the encompassing element, and also of being repelled, rejected by the center, as though in an inversion of movement. In a phenomenology of religion like that of Van der Leeuw, the *nomos* itself does indeed appear as the encompassing-limit or ground, and also as that which is repelled, excluded, in a centrifugal movement.

30. Whatever interactions there may be, the "art of the steppes" had a specificity that was communicated to the migrating Germans; in spite of his many reservations about nomad culture, René Grousset makes this point in *The Empire of the Steppes*, trans. Naomi Walford (New Brunswick, N.J.: Rutgers University Press, 1970). pp. 11-25. He notes the irreducibility of Scythian art to Assyrian art, Sarmatian art to Persian art, and Hunnic art to Chinese art. He even points out that the art of the steppes influenced more than it borrowed (see in particular the question of Ordos art and its relations to China).

31. On this question of light and color, in particular in Byzantine art, see Henri Maldiney, *Regard, parole, espace*, pp. 203ff., 239ff.

32. The correlation, "haptic-close-abstract," was already suggested by Riegl. But it was Worringer who developed the theme of the abstract line. Although he conceives of it essentially in its Egyptian form, he describes a second form in which the abstract assumes an intense life and an expressionist value, all the while remaining inorganic: *Abstraction and Empathy*, chapter 5, and especially *Form in Gothic* (London: Putnam's and Sons, 1927), pp. 38-55.

33. André Leroi-Gourhan, *Le geste et la parole* (Paris: Albin Michel, 1964-1965), vol. 1, *Technique et langage*, pp. 263ff.; vol. 2, *La mémoire et les rythmes*, pp. 219ff. ("Rhythmic marks are anterior to explicit figures.") Worringer's position is very ambiguous; thinking that prehistoric art is fundamentally figurative, he excludes it from Art, on the same grounds as he excludes the "scribblings of a child" (*Abstraction and Empathy*, pp. 51-55). Then he advances the hypothesis that the cave dwellers were the "ultimate result" of a series he says began with the abstract (p. 130). But would not such a hypothesis force Worringer to revise his conception of the abstract, and to cease identifying it with Egyptian geometricism?

34. Worringer establishes an opposition between the power of repetition, which is mechanical, multiplying, and without fixed orientation, and the force of symmetry, which is organic, additive, oriented, and centered. He sees this as the fundamental difference between Gothic ornamentation and Greek or classical ornamentation: *Form in Gothic*, pp. 53-55 ("The Ceaseless Melody of the Northern Line"). In a fine book, *Esthétiques d'Orient et d'Occident* (Paris: E. Leroux, 1937), Laura Morgenstern develops a particular example, distinguishing the "symmetrical antithetism" of Sassanid Persian art from the "disjointed antithetism" of the art of the proto-Iranian nomads (Sarmatians). Many authors, however, have stressed the centered and symmetrical motifs in barbarian or nomad art. Worringer

anticipated this objection: "Instead of the regular and invariably geometrical star or rosette or similar restful forms, in the North we find the revolving wheel, the turbine or the so-called sun wheel, all designs which express violent movement. Moreover, the movement is peripheral and not radial" (*Form in Gothic*, p. 54). The history of technology confirms the importance of the turbine in the life of the nomads. In another, bio-aesthetic, context, Gabriel Tarde opposes repetition as indefinite potential (*puissance*) to symmetry as limitation. With symmetry, life constituted an organism for itself, taking a star-shaped or reflected, infolded form (the radiata and mollusks). It is true that in doing so it unleashed another type of repetition, external reproduction; see *L'opposition universelle* (Paris: Alcan, 1897).

35. [TRANS: Worringer, *Abstraction and Empathy*, p. 33]

36. [TRANS: Worringer, *Abstraction and Empathy*, p. 42]

37. On all of these points, see Georges Charrière's very intuitive book, *Scythian Art* (New York: Alpine Fine Arts Collection, 1979), which includes a great number of reproductions. It is doubtless René Grousset who has most effectively emphasized "slowness" as a dramatic pole of nomad art: *The Empire of the Steppes*, pp. 13-14.

38. Dora Vallier, in her preface to the French translation of *Abstraction and Empathy* (*Abstraction et Einfühlung* [Paris: Klincksieck, 1978]), is right to note Worringer and Kandinsky's independence from one another, and the differences between the problems they were addressing. However, she maintains that there is still convergence and resonance between them. In a sense, all art is abstract, with the figurative springing from certain types of abstraction. But in another sense, since there are very different types of lines (Egyptian-geometrical, Greek-organic, Gothic-vital, etc.), the question then becomes one of determining which line remains abstract, or realizes abstraction as such. It is doubtful that it is the geometrical line, since it still draws a figure, even though an abstract and nonrepresentative one. Rather, the abstract line is that defined by Michael Fried in relation to certain works by Pollock: multidirectional, with neither inside nor outside, form nor background, delimiting nothing, describing no contour, passing between spots or points, filling a smooth space, stirring up a close-lying haptic visual matter that "both invites the act of seeing on the part of the spectator yet gives his eye nowhere to rest once and for all," (*Three American Painters* [Cambridge, Mass.: Fogg Art Museum, 1965], p. 14). In Kandinsky himself, abstraction is realized not so much by geometrical structures as by lines of march or transit that seem to recall Mongolian nomadic motifs.

Bibliography

Bibliography

(compiled by Brian Massumi)

I before an entry indicates an interview.
P before an entry indicates a preface, postface, introduction, or afterword.

by Gilles Deleuze and Félix Guattari

English

Anti-Oedipus: Capitalism and Schizophrenia. Preface by Michel Foucault. Trans. Robert Hurley, Mark Seem, and Helen R. Lane. New York: Viking, 1977; rpt. Minneapolis: University of Minnesota Press, 1983. Translation of *l'Anti-Oedipe.*

Kafka: Toward a Minor Literature. Trans. Dana Polan. Minneapolis: University of Minnesota Press, 1986. Translation of *Kafka: Pour une littérature mineure.*

Nomadology: The War Machine. Trans. Brian Massumi. New York: Semiotext(e), 1986. Translation of Chapter 12 of *Mille Plateaux.*

On the Line. Trans. John Johnston. New York: Semiotext(e), 1983. Translation of "Rhizome" (the final version published in *Mille plateaux*) and "Politics" (Chapter 6 of *Dialogues*).

A Thousand Plateaus: Capitalism and Schizophrenia. Trans. Brian Massumi. Minneapolis: University of Minnesota Press, 1987. Translation of *Mille Plateaux.*

"Balance Sheet-Program for Desiring-Machines." Trans. Robert Hurley. *Semiotext(e), Anti-Oedipus,* vol. 2, no. 5 (1977), pp. 117-135. Translation of "Bilan-programme pour machines désirantes."

"Becoming-Woman." Trans. Brian Massumi. *Subjects/Objects,* no. 3 (Spring 1985), pp. 24-32. Extracts from Chapter 10 of *Mille Plateaux.*

"A Bloated Oedipus." Trans. Rachel McComas. *Semiotext(e), Polysexuality,* vol. 4, no. 1

(1981), pp. 97-101. Abridged translation of Chapter 2 of *Kafka: Pour une littérature mineure.*

"City-State." Trans. Brian Massumi. *Zone*, no. 1/2 (1985), pp. 195-199. Extract from Chapter 13 of *Mille Plateaux.*

"Concrete Rules and Abstract Machines." Trans. Charles Stivale. *Sub/Stance*, vol. 13, nos. 3/4 (1984), pp. 7-19. Translation of Chapter 15 of *Mille Plateaux.*

"How to Make Yourself a Body without Organs." Trans. Suzanne Guerlac. *Semiotext(e), Polysexuality*, vol. 4, no. 1 (1981), pp. 265-270. Abridged translation of "Comment se faire un corps sans organes," first version.

"The Interpretation of Utterances." With Claire Parnet and A. Scala. Trans. and ed. Paul Foss and Meaghan Morris. In *Language, Sexuality and Subversion.* Ed. Paul Foss and Meaghan Morris. Sydney: Feral Publications, 1978, pp. 141-157. Papers delivered at the Milan conference on Psychoanalysis and Politics (May 1973); published in Deleuze and Guattari, *Politique et psychanalyse.*

"One or Several Wolves?" Trans. Mark Seem. *Semiotext(e), Anti-Oedipus*, vol. 2, no. 3 (1977), pp. 137-147. Translation of "Un seul ou plusieurs loups?", first version.

"Nomad Art." Trans. Brian Massumi. *Art and Text*, no. 19 (Oct.-Dec. 1985), pp. 16-24. Extracts from Chapter 14 of *Mille Plateaux.*

"Rhizome." Trans. Paul Foss and Paul Patton. In *Ideology and Consciousness*, no. 8 (Spring 1981), pp. 49-71. Translation of *Rhizome* (the first version, published as a separate book).

"What Is a Minor Literature?" Trans. Robert Brinkley. *Mississippi Review*, vol. 2, no. 3 (Winter/Spring 1983), pp. 13-33. Translation of Chapter 3 of *Kafka.*

French

l'Anti-Oedipe. Vol. 1 of *Capitalisme et schizophrénie.* Paris: Minuit, 1972; 2nd ed., 1973, with added appendix, "Bilan-Programme pour machines désirantes."

Kafka: Pour une littérature mineure. Paris: Minuit, 1975.

Mille Plateaux. Vol. 2 of *Capitalisme et schizophrénie.* Paris: Minuit, 1980.

Politique et psychanalyse. Alençon: Bibliothèque des Mots Perdues, 1977. Texts from the Milan conference on Psychoanalysis and Politics (May 1973). Contains: "La place du signifiant dans l'institution," Guattari (revised version reprinted in *La révolution moléculaire*, and included in the English edition); "Psychanalyse et politique," Guattari; "Quatre propositions sur la psychanalyse," Deleuze; and "L'interprétation des énoncés," Deleuze, Guattari, Claire Parnet, and André Scala.

Rhizome. Paris: Minuit, 1976. Modified and reprinted as the introduction to *Mille Plateaux.*

"Bilan-Programme pour machines désirantes." *Minuit*, no. 2 (January 1973), pp. 1-25. Reprinted as appendix to second edition of *l'Anti-Oedipe.*

Discussions, in François Fourquet and Lion Murard, *Les équipements de pouvoir* (Paris: 10/18, 1976), pp. 39-47, 161-195, 212-227. Revised version of *Recherches*, no. 13 [December 1973], *Les équipements collectifs.*

"Le nouvel arpenteur. Intensités et blocs d'enfance dans 'le Château.'" *Critique*, vol. 29, no. 318 (November 1973), pp. 1046-1054.

"La synthèse disjonctive." *L'Arc, Klossowski*, no. 43 (1970), pp. 54-62. Modified and reprinted as Chapter 2, part 4 of *l'Anti-Oedipe.*

"Un seul ou plusieurs loups?" *Minuit*, no. 5 (Sept. 1973), pp. 2-16. Modified and reprinted as Chapter 2 of *Mille Plateaux.*

by Gilles Deleuze

English

Cinema 1: The Movement-Image. Trans. Hugh Tomlinson and Barbara Habberjam. Minneapolis: University of Minnesota Press, 1986. Translation of *Cinéma I: L'image-mouvement.*

Kant's Critical Philosophy. Trans. Hugh Tomlinson and Barbara Habberjam. Minneapolis: University of Minnesota Press, 1984. With preface to the English edition. Translation of *La philosophie critique de Kant.*

Masochism: An Interpretation of Coldness and Cruelty. Trans Jean McNeil. New York: Braziller, 1971. With the text of *Venus in Furs*, Leopold von Sacher-Masoch. Translation of *Présentation de Sacher-Masoch.*

Nietzsche and Philosophy. Trans. Hugh Tomlinson. New York: Columbia University Press, 1983. Translation of *Nietzsche et la philosophie.*

Proust and Signs. Trans. Richard Howard. New York: Braziller, 1972. Translation of *Proust et les signes*, 2nd ed.

"Active and Reactive." Trans. Richard Cohen. In *The New Nietzsche*, ed. David B. Allison. Cambridge, Mass.: MIT Press, 1985, pp. 80-106. Translation of Chapter 2 of *Nietzsche et la philosophie.*

"Four Propositions on Psychoanalysis." Trans. Meaghan Morris. In *Language, Sexuality and Subversion.* Ed. Paul Foss and Meaghan Morris. Sidney: Feral Publications, 1978, pp. 134-140. Translation of "Quatre propositions sur la psychanalyse" in Deleuze and Guattari, *Politique et psychanalyse.*

"I Have Nothing to Admit." Trans. Janis Forman. *Semiotext(e), Anti-Oedipus*, vol. 2, no. 3 (1977), pp. 111-116. Translation of "Lettre à Michel Cressole."

"Intellectuals and Power." Discussion with Michel Foucault in Foucault, *Language, Counter-Memory, Practice.* Ed. and trans. Donald Bouchard. Ithaca, N.Y.: Cornell University Press, 1977, pp. 205-217. Also trans. Mark Seem, *Telos* 16 (Summer 1973), pp. 103-109. Translation of "Les intellectuels et le pouvoir."

"On Four Poetic Formulas Which Might Summarize the Kantian Philosophy." Preface to Deleuze, *Kant's Critical Philosophy.*

"Open Letter to Negri's Judges." Trans. Committee April 7, London. *Semiotext(e), Italy: Autonomia*, vol. 3, no. 3 (1980), pp. 182-184. From *La Repubblica.*

"Nomad Thought." Trans. Jacqueline Wallace. *Semiotext(e), Nietzsche's Return*, vol. 3, no. 1 (1978), pp. 12-20. Translation of "Pensée nomade." Also trans. David B. Allison in *The New Nietzsche*, ed. David B. Allison (Cambridge, Mass.: MIT Press, 1985), pp. 142-149.

"Plato and the Simulacrum." Trans. Rosalind Krauss. *October*, no. 16 (Winter 1983), pp. 45-56. Translation of "Platon et le simulacre." "The Rise of the Social." Foreword to Jacques Donzelot, *The Policing of Families.* Trans. Robert Hurley. New York: Pantheon, 1979, pp. ix-xvii. Translation of "L'ascension du social."

"The Schizophrenic and Language: Surface and Depth in Lewis Carroll and Antonin Artaud." In *Textual Strategies.* Ed. and trans. Josué Harari. Ithaca, N.Y.: Cornell University Press, 1979, pp. 277-295. Translation of "Le schizophrène et le mot." Reprinted in *Literature and Psychoanalysis.* Ed. Edith Kurzweil and William Phillips. New York: Columbia University Press, 1983.

"Three Group Problems." Trans. Mark Seem. *Semiotext(e), Anti-Oedipus*, vol. 2, no. 3 (1977), pp. 99-109. Translation of "Trois problèmes de groupe."

French

Le Bergsonisme. Paris: PUF, 1966.

Bergson. Mémoire et vie. Paris: PUF, 1957. Extracts from Bergson selected by Deleuze.

Cinéma I: L'image-mouvement. Paris: Minuit, 1983.

Cinéma II: L'image-temps. Paris: Minuit, 1985.

David Hume, la vie, son oeuvre. Paris: PUF, 1952. Extracts from Hume with an introduction by Deleuze and André Cresson.

Dialogues. With Claire Parnet. Paris: Flammarion, 1977.

Différence et Répétition. Paris: PUF, 1968.

Empirisme et subjectivité. Paris: PUF, 1953. 3rd ed., 1980.

Foucault. Paris: Minuit, 1986.

Francis Bacon. Logique de la Sensation. 2 vols. Paris: Ed. de la Différence, 1981.

Instincts et Institutions. Paris: Hachette, 1953. Texts selected by Deleuze.

Logique du sens. Paris: Minuit, 1969.

Nietzsche. Paris: PUF, 1965. Extracts from Nietzsche with an introduction by Deleuze.

Nietzsche et la philosophie. Paris: PUF, 1962. 4th ed., 1973.

Un nouvel archiviste. Illustrations by d'Ipoustiguy. Montpellier: Fata Morgana, 1972. Reprint of "Un nouvel archiviste."

La philosophie critique de Kant. Paris: PUF, 1963.

Présentation de Sacher-Masoch. Paris: Minuit, 1967. Rpt. Paris: 10/18, 1971. Lengthy introduction by Deleuze with the text of Leopold von Sacher-Masoch's *La Vénus à la fourrure.*

Proust et les signes. Paris: PUF, 1964. Augmented 2nd ed., 1970.

Spinoza et le problème de l'expression. Paris: Minuit, 1968.

Spinoza. Philosophie pratique. Paris: PUF, 1970. Augmented 2nd ed. Paris: Minuit, 1981.

Superpositions. With Carmelo Bene. Paris: Minuit, 1979. The play, *Richard III*, by Bene with an essay on Bene by Deleuze entitled "Un manifeste de moins."

I "A propos des nouveaux philosophes et d'un problème plus général." *Le Monde*, June 19-20, 1977, p. 16. Reprinted *Recherches, Les Untorelli*, no. 30 (November 1977), pp. 179-184. Interview from June 5, 1977.

P "L'ascension du social." Postface to Jacques Donzelot, *La police des familles.* Paris: Minuit, 1977, pp. 220.

"Capitalisme et schizophrénie." *L'Arc, Deleuze*, no. 49 (1972; 2nd ed., 1980), pp. 47-55. Interview with Catherine Bakis-Clément from March 2, 1972.

"La conception de la différence chez Bergson." *Etudes bergsoniennes*, vol. 4 (1956), pp. 79-112.

"Deux régimes de fous." In *Psychanalyse et Sémiotique. Actes du Colloque de Milan, 1974.* Ed. Armando Verdiglione. Paris: 10/18, 1975, pp. 165-186. Presentation by Deleuze with discussion.

"Ecrivain non: un nouveau cartographe." *Critique*, no. 343 (December 1975), pp. 1207-1227. Review of Michel Foucault, *Surveiller et Punir* (*Discipline and Punish*). Modified and reprinted as "Un nouveau cartographe" in *Foucault*, pp. 31-51.

"En quoi la philosophie peut servir à des mathématiciens ou même à des musiciens, même et surtout quand elle ne parle pas de musique ou de mathématiques," in *Vincennes, ou le désir d'apprendre.* Ed. Pierre Merlin. Paris: Alain, Moreau, 1979, pp. 120-121.

"Faille et feux locaux. Kostas Axelos." *Critique* no. 275 (April 1970), pp. 344-351.

"Grandeur de Yasser Arafat." *Revue d'Etudes Palestiniennes*, no. 10 (Winter 1984), pp. 41-43.

"L'Homme: une existence douteuse." *Le Nouvel Observateur*, no. 81 (June 1-7, 1966), pp. 32-34. Review of Michel Foucault, *Les mots et les choses* (*The Order of Things*).

I "Huit ans après." *L'Arc, Deleuze*, no. 49 (1972; 2nd ed., 1980), pp. 99-102. Interview with Catherine Clément from 1980.

"Hume." In *La philosophie*, ed. François Châtelet. Paris: Hachette, 1979. Vol. 2, pp. 226-239.

I "Les intellectuels et le pouvoir." *L'Arc, Deleuze*, no. 49 (1972; 2nd ed., 1980), pp. 3-10. Discussion with Michel Foucault.

I Interview. *Libération*. October 23, 1980, pp. 16-17.

I Interview. *Libération*. October 3, 1983, pp. 30-31.

I Interview. *Le Monde*. October 6, 1983, pp. 1, 17.

I Interview. *L'autre journal*, no. 8 (October 1985), pp. 12-22.

I Interview. *Libération*. September 2, 1986, pp. 27-28 and September 3, 1986, p. 38.

P "Introduction à 'La Bête humaine' de Balzac." In *Oeuvres Complètes d'Emile Zola*. Paris: Cercle du Livre Précieux, 1967. Vol. 6, pp. 13-21. Modified and reprinted under the title "Zola et la fêlure" as an appendix to *Logique du sens*.

P Introduction to Friedrich Nietzsche, *Le gai savoir. Les fragments posthumes (1881-82)*. Trans. Pierre Klossowski. Vol. 5 of *Oeuvres philosophiques complètes*. Paris: Gallimard, 1967, pp. i-iv. With Michel Foucault.

P Introduction to Johann Malfatti von Monteregio, *Etudes sur la mathèse, ou anarchie et hierarchie de la science*. Paris: Ed. du Griffon d'Or, 1946, pp. ix-xxiv.

"Klossowski et le corps-langage." *Critique*, no. 214 (March 1965), pp. 199-219. Modified and reprinted as an appendix to *Logique du sens*.

"Lettre à Michel Cressole," in Michel Cressole, *Deleuze*. Paris: Editions Universitaires, 1973, pp. 107-118. Translated as "I Have Nothing to Admit."

"Lucrèce et le naturalisme." *Etudes philosophiques*, series 16, no. 1 (Jan.-March 1961), pp. 19-29. Modified and reprinted under the title "Lucrèce et le simulacre" as an appendix to *Logique du sens*.

"Lucrèce et le simulacre." See "Lucrèce et le naturalisme."

"Méthode de dramatisation." *Bulletin de la Société Française de Philosophie*, vol. 61, no. 3 (July-September 1967), pp. 89-118. Presentation followed by discussion.

"Michel Tournier et le monde sans autrui." See "Une théorie d'Autrui."

"Mystère d'Ariane." *Etudes nietzschéennes* (1963).

"Nous croyons au caractère constructiviste de certaines agitations de gauche." *Recherches, Les Untorelli*, no. 30 (November 1977), pp. 149-150. Statement on repression in Italy written by Deleuze and signed by a number of French Intellectuals, September 20, 1977.

"Un nouvel archiviste." *Critique*, no. 274 (March 1970), pp. 195-209. Review of Michel Foucault, *L'archéologie du savoir*. Modified and reprinted in *Foucault*, pp. 11-30.

"Pensée nomade." In *Nietzsche aujourd'hui?* Vol. 1. Paris: 10/18, 1973, pp. 159-190. Presentation by Deleuze to the Colloque de Cérisy (1972), with discussion.

"Philosophie et minorité." *Critique*, no. 369 (February 1978), pp. 154-155.

"La photographie est déjà tirée dans les choses," *Cahiers du Cinéma*, no. 352 (October 1983), pp. 35-40. Interview with Pascal Bonitzer and Jean Narboni.

"Platon et le simulacre." See "Renverser le platonisme."

P Preface to Antonio Negri, *L'anomalie sauvage. Puissance et pouvoir chez Spinoza*. Paris: PUF, 1981, pp. 9-12.

P Preface to Guy Hocquenghem. *L'après-mai des faunes*. Paris: Grasset, 1974, pp. 7-17.

P "Qu'est-ce que c'est, tes 'machines désirantes' à toi?" *Les Temps Modernes*, no. 316 (November 1972), pp. 854-856. Introduction to Pierre Bénichou, "Saint Jackie, Comedienne et Bourreau."

"A quoi reconnaît-on le structuralisme?" In *La philosophie*. Ed. François Châtelet. Paris: Hachette, 1979. Vol. 4, pp. 293-339. (Abridged version of *Histoire de la philosophie*. 8 volumes. Paris: Hachette, 1972-1973.)

"Renverser le platonisme (les simulacres)," *Revue de Métaphysique et de Morale*, vol. 71, no. 4

(October-December 1967), pp. 426-438. Modified and reprinted under the title "Platon et le simulacre" as an appendix to *Logique du sens.*

"De Sacher Masoch au masochisme." *Arguments*, vol. 5, no. 21 (Jan.-April 1961), pp. 40-46.

P "Schizologie." Preface to Louis Wolfson, *Le schizo et les langues.* Paris: Gallimard, 1970, pp. 5-23.

"Le schizophrène et le mot." *Critique*, no. 255/256 (August-September 1968), pp. 731-746. Modified and reprinted in *Logique du sens*, series 2 and 13.

"Schizophrénie et société" in *Encyclopaedia Universalis* (1985), vol. 16, pp. 524-527.

"Sens et valeurs." *Arguments*, vol. 3, no. 15 (Sept.-Dec. 1959), pp. 20-28. Modified and reprinted in Chapter 1 of *Nietzsche et la philosophie.*

"Spinoza et la méthode générale de M. Gueroult." *Revue de Métaphysique et de Morale*, vol. 74, no. 2 (April-June 1970), pp. 426-437.

"Spinoza et nous." *Revue de Synthèse*, 3rd series, nos. 89-91 (January-September 1978). Reprinted as Chapter 6 of *Spinoza. Philosophie pratique*, 2nd ed.

"Une théorie d'Autrui. Michel Tournier." *Critique*, no. 241 (June 1967), pp. 503-525. Modified and reprinted under the title "Michel Tournier et le monde sans autrui" as an appendix to *Logique du sens.* Reprinted as the postface to Tournier, *Vendredi, ou les limbes du Pacifique.* Paris: Gallimard, 1972.

P "Trois problèmes de groupe." Preface to Félix Guattari, *Psychanalyse et transversalité.* Paris: Maspero, 1972, pp. i-xi.

"Unité de 'A la Recherche du Temps Perdu.'" *Revue de Métaphysique et de Morale*, vol. 68, no. 4 (Oct.-Dec. 1963), pp. 427-442.

"Sur la volonté de puissance et l'éternel retour." In *Nietzsche. Cahiers de Royaumont.* Paris: Minuit, 1967, pp. 275-287.

"Zola et la fêlure." See "Introduction à 'la Bête humaine' de Balzac."

by Félix Guattari

English

Molecular Revolution: Psychiatry and Politics. Trans. Rosemary Sheed. New York: Penguin, 1984. A selection of essays from *Psychanalyse et transversalité* and the two versions of *La révolution moléculaire*, with a previously unpublished essay, "Capitalistic Systems, Structures and Processes" (with Eric Alliez), later published in French in Guattari, *Les années d'hiver.*

"Becoming-Woman." Trans. Rachel McComas and Stamos Metzidakis. *Semiotext(e), Polysexuality*, vol. 4, no. 1 (1981), pp. 86-88. Also translated as "Becoming a Woman" by Rosemary Sheed in Guattari, *Molecular Revolution*, pp. 233-235. Translation of "Devenir femme," *La révolution moléculaire* (both editions).

"Everybody Wants to Be a Fascist." Trans. Suzanne Fletcher. *Semiotext(e), Anti-Oedipus*, vol. 2, no. 3 (1977), pp. 87-98.

"Freudo-Marxism." *Semiotext(e), Anti-Oedipus*, vol. 2, no. 3 (1977), pp. 73-75. Intended for *Le Nouvel Observateur* but never published in French.

"Genet Regained." Trans. Brian Massumi. *LAICA Journal*, vol. 5, no. 47 (Spring 1987).

I Interview with Félix Guattari by Mark Seem. *Diacritics*, vol. 4, no. 3 (Fall 1974), pp. 38-41.

"Like an Echo of a Collective Melancholy." Trans. Mark Polizzotti. *Semiotext(e), The German Issue*, vol. 4, no. 2 (1982), pp. 102-110. Translation of "Comme un écho de la mélancholie collective," in *La révolution moléculaire* (10/18 edition).

I "The New Alliance." Interview with Sylvère Lotringer. *Impulse*, vol. 10, no. 2 (Winter 1982), pp. 41-44.

"The Proliferation of Margins." Trans. Richard Gardner and Sybil Walker. *Semiotext(e), Italy: Autonomia*, vol. 3, no. 3 (1980), pp. 108-111.

"Psychoanalysis and Politics." Trans. Paul Foss. *Language, Sexuality and Subversion*. Ed. Paul Foss and Meaghan Morris. Sydney: Feral Publications, 1978, pp. 125-133. Translation of "Psychanalyse et politique," first published in *Politique et psychanalyse*. Revised and published in *La révolution moléculaire* under the title "Les luttes du désir et la psychanalyse"; translated in *The Molecular Revolution* as "Psychoanalysis and the Struggles of Desire."

"Psycho-Analysis and Schizo-Analysis." Trans. Janis Forman. *Semiotext(e), Anti-Oedipus*, vol. 2, no. 3 (1977), pp. 77-85. Extracts from an interview about *Anti-Oedipus* with Arno Munster originally published in the *Frankfurter Rundschau* (January 17, 1973). Other portions of this interview were published as "La fin de fétichismes," *La révolution moléculaire*.

Response to questionnaire on the city. Trans. Bruce Benderson. *Zone*, no. 1/2 (1985), p. 460.

I "Why Italy?" Trans. John Johnston. *Semiotext(e), Italy: Autonomia*, vol. 3, no. 3 (1980), pp. 234-237. Interview, unpublished in French.

French

Les années d'hiver. Paris: Barrault, 1986. Collected essays 1980-1985.

L'inconscient moléculaire. Essais de Schizo-analyse. Paris: Recherches, 1979.

Les nouveaux espaces de liberté. With Toni Negri. Followed by Guattari, "Des libertés en Europe," and Negri, "Lutte archéoligique." Paris: Dominique Bedou, 1985.

Psychanalyse et transversalité. Preface by Gilles Deleuze ("Trois problèmes de groupe"). Paris: Maspero, 1972. Collected essays 1965-1970.

La révolution moléculaire. Fontenay-sous-Bois: Recherches, 1977. Essays 1971-1977. *La révolution moléculaire*. Paris: Union Générale d'Editions (10/18), 1980. Essays 1972-1979.

NOTE: The two collections entitled *La révolution moléculaire* are substantially different. The Recherches edition includes a section on cinema and extensive selections on semiotics that do not appear in the 10/18 version; the 10/18 version deals extensively with the Italian Autonomia movement.

I Interview. *L'Autre Journal*, no. 5 (May 1985), pp. 6-22.

"Masses et minorités à la recherche d'une nouvelle stratégie." *Recherches, Les Untorelli*, no. 30 (November 1977), pp. 113-122.

"Sémiologies signifiantes et sémiologies asignifiantes," in *Psychanalyse et sémiotique. Actes du Colloque de Milan, 1974*. Ed. Armando Verdiglione. Paris: 10/18, 1975, pp. 151-163.

Index

Index

Compiled by Hassan Melehy

Illustrations

Gilles Deleuze is a professor of philosophy at the University of Paris at Vincennes. English translations of Deleuze's work include *Kant's Critical Philosophy: The Doctrine of the Faculties, Cinema 1: Image/ Movement* (both published by Minnesota) and *Nietzsche and Philosophy.* **Félix Guattari**, a practicing psychoanalyst and lifelong political activist, has worked since the mid-1950s at La Borde, an experimental psychiatric clinic. He is an active participant in the European Network for Alternatives to Psychiatry. Together, Deleuze and Guattari have written *Anti-Oedipus* and *Kafka: Toward a Minor Literature*, also available in translation from Minnesota.

Brian Massumi received his Ph.D. in French at Yale University, and is currently a Mellon Postdoctoral Fellow at Stanford University. Massumi translated Jacques Attali's *Noise*, Michel de Certeau's *Heterologies*, and (with Geoff Bennington) Jean-Francois Lyotard's *Postmodern Condition*—all published by Minnesota.